GW00599798

# 1996 LECTURES
## and
# MEMOIRS

PROCEEDINGS OF THE BRITISH ACADEMY · 94

# 1996 LECTURES
# and
# MEMOIRS

*Published for* THE BRITISH ACADEMY
*by* OXFORD UNIVERSITY PRESS

*Oxford University Press, Great Clarendon Street, Oxford* OX2 6DP

*Oxford New York*
*Athens Auckland Bangkok Bogota Bombay*
*Buenos Aires Calcutta Cape Town Dar es Salaam*
*Delhi Florence Hong Kong Istanbul Karachi*
*Kuala Lumpur Madras Madrid Melbourne*
*Mexico City Nairobi Paris Singapore*
*Taipei Tokyo Toronto Warsaw*

*and associated companies in*
*Berlin Ibadan*

*Published in the United States by*
*Oxford University Press Inc., New York*

© *The British Academy, 1997*

*All rights reserved. No part of this publication may be reproduced,*
*stored in a retrieval system, or transmitted, in any form or by any means,*
*without the prior permission in writing of the British Academy*

*British Library Cataloguing in Publication Data*
*Data available*

*ISBN 0–19–726180–9*
*ISSN 0068–1202*

*Typeset by J&L Composition Ltd, Filey, North Yorkshire*
*Printed in Great Britain*
*on acid-free paper*
*at the Alden Press*
*Oxford*

*All the papers in this volume have been refereed*

*The Academy is grateful to Dr Marjorie Chibnall, FBA*
*for her editorial work on this volume*

# Contents

# Memoirs

*Proceedings of the British Academy,* **94**, 1–43

ALBERT RECKITT ARCHAEOLOGICAL LECTURE

# Early and Medieval Merv: A Tale of Three Cities

## GEORGINA HERRMANN
*University College London*

## Introduction

'NOWHERE ELSE IN ALL CENTRAL ASIA are ruins so abundant or so vast', wrote the American archaeologist R. Pumpelly in the early years of this century when describing the historic urban centre of the Merv oasis. This series of adjacent walled city-sites occupies more than a thousand hectares and, in Pumpelly's time, 'In preservation . . . reach from Bairam Ali's state of brick-robbed walls and still-standing battlements, with gates and inner streets that may yet be ridden through (Figure 23) to the round-worn mounds of far more ancient cities' (Figures 3 and 4; 1908: 333). The earliest of the city-sites was founded in the sixth century BC, and the largest became the capital of the empire of the Great Seljuks, an empire which stretched from Central Asia to the Mediterranean. The much smaller post-medieval foundation demonstrated Merv's relative decline by the fifteenth century.

The reason for Merv's long and distinguished history can be accounted for by its strategic position in a large and fertile oasis in the Kara Kum desert in present-day Turkmenistan (Figures 1 and 2). Today the oasis supports a population in excess of a million. Before modern transport it was the last major centre before caravans embarked on the long stage 'across the sorriest waste that ever met the human eye' to Amul (modern Chardzjou or 'Four Canals'), some 180 km distant.

Read at the Academy 21 May 1996. © The British Academy 1997.

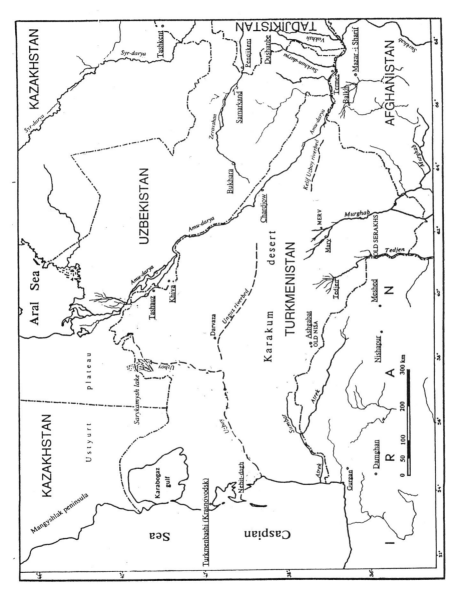

**Figure 1.** Map of western Central Asia, north-eastern Iran and western Afghanistan. (From Bader, A. N. and Usupov, Kh. 1995, 'Gold Earrings from NW Turkmenistan' in Invernizzi, A. (ed.), *In the Land of the Gryphons, Papers on Central Asian Archaeology in Antiquity* (Turin), 29.)

Amul is built at a crossing point of the Amu Darya, the Greek River Oxus, or in the flowing prose of Curzon 'the broad bosom of the mighty river that from the glaciers of the Pamir rolls its 1,500 miles of current down to the Aral Sea' (Curzon 1889: 140, 143). From Amul it is an easy stage to Bukhara and points east on the so-called 'Silk Road', or downstream to Termez. In Achaemenid times Amul was on the way to the satrapies of Bactria and Sogdia. The importance of Merv's location, widely appreciated during the years of the 'Great Game' (Hopkirk: 1990, 408–17), was demonstrated as recently as the 1980s, when the oasis formed one of the bases for the Soviet invasion of Afghanistan.

The Merv oasis is formed of alluvial silts deposited by the River Murghab. This rises in the Afghan mountains, crosses the desert and enters the oasis at its southern end, where it is dammed—today there are no less than six dams, although previously there was probably only the Sultanband dam[1]—eventually drying up in the desert to the north. A little-known Chinese source written by Du Huan, in 765 after his return from ten years in captivity at Merv described 'a big river which flows into its territory, where it divides into several hundred canals irrigating the whole area'.[2] Agriculture in the Merv oasis is totally dependent on irrigation, as is evident today, in medieval sources and earlier.

Since 1954 the oasis has also been watered by the Kara Kum canal, which enters the oasis on the east, traversing it before crossing the desert to form a large reservoir on the edge of the Tedzhen oasis and continuing westwards (Figure 2). The arrival of the canal has greatly increased the potential for irrigation in both oases. As a result, the Merv oasis is probably at its maximum extent, measuring on a map of 1991 in the region of 85 × 74 km. This area has since been enlarged, for areas in the north, unused since the Bronze Age, are being irrigated. Interestingly, the 1991 oasis is similar in size to that measured by Du Huan, 'the area of this kingdom from east to west is 140 li [70 km] and from north to south 180 li [90 km]'.[3]

Archaeologically, the oasis is one of the most intensively studied regions in Central Asia. In the 1950s, M. E. Masson of Tashkent

---

[1] For a vivid description of the dam in 1880 see O'Donovan 1882: 184–5.

[2] Du Huan wrote a book about his experiences on his return to China. Unfortunately, this has been lost: what survives is a synopsis written by an uncle. We are grateful to Professor Liu Ying Shen of Nanking University for drawing our attention to this source. Dr Oliver Moore of the British Museum is currently studying the text, and we thank him for this preliminary translation.

[3] See above, n. 2.

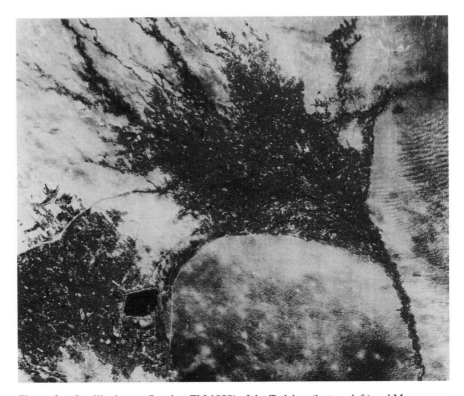

**Figure 2.** Satellite image (Landsat TM 1988) of the Tedzhen (bottom left) and Merv oases. The courses of the Murghab river and Karakum canal are recognisable, as is the reservoir on the edge of the Tedzhen oasis. The historic urban centre of the Merv oasis is visible as a white dot on the central eastern edge: the modern centre, Mary, is on the western side.

University set up the YuTAKE, the South Turkmenistan Multi-Disciplinary Archaeological Expedition of the Academy of Sciences of Turkmenistan, which from that time has undertaken campaigns throughout southern Turkmenistan, including many both in historic Merv and in the oasis.[4] The oasis is also the focus of a series of major survey and mapping programmes. These include:

**1** A long-running programme, mapping the pre-Timurid sites of the Merv oasis and excavating a Partho-Sasanian fort at Gobekli, initiated in 1980 by Professor G. Koshelenko of the Moscow Institute

---

[4] The YuTAKE published their work in *Trudy Instituta istorii, arxeologii i etnografii AN Turkmenskoj SSR*, usually abbreviated to *Trudy YuTAKE*, the last volume of which, 19, was published in 1989. Shortage of funds is currently preventing further publications.

of Archaeology (Academy of Sciences of the USSR), with the collaboration of the Moscow State University and the Turkmen State University (Gubaev *et al.* 1990; Koshelenko *et al.* 1991; Bader *et al.* 1992).

**2** A survey of sites of the Bronze and Early Iron Ages on the edge
of the Central Kara Kum, in progress since 1989, by Professor V.
Sarianidi (Moscow Institute of Archaeology, Academy of Sciences of
the USSR) and I. Massimov (Institute of History, Academy of Sciences
of Turkmenistan). Their programme includes excavations at the extensive Bronze Age centres of Togoluk and Gonur (Hiebert and Lamberg-
Karlovsky 1992; Sarianidi 1993; Hiebert 1994: 15–38).

**3** Surveys of early sites in the north by a team from Instituto
Italiano per il Medio ed Estremo Oriente Rome (IsMEO), directed by
Professor Maurizio Tosi, with Professor A. Gubaev of the Turkmen
State University, begun in 1989.

Work by these teams continues to refine our understanding of the
ancient settlement patterns in the Merv oasis. The surviving Bronze
Age settlements were located in the north, where the Murghab fanned
out into a delta. It was not until the development of more sophisticated
irrigation techniques that occupation developed further to the south and
east. This shift occurred in the Late Bronze and Early Iron Ages or Yaz
Depe I–III periods (Gubaev *et al.* 1990; Koshelenko *et al.* 1991; Bader
*et al.* 1992). It was during Yaz II–III that the first of the historic urban
centres of Merv, a polygonal walled city known today as Erk Kala, was
founded in the sixth century.

## The International Merv Project

The International Merv Project (IMP) is a collaboration between the
Institute of Archaeology, University College London, and YuTAKE, the
Academy of Sciences of Turkmenistan (1992–7): for the first three years
the Institute for the History of Material Culture, St Petersburg, also
formed part of the collaboration, which was established with the assistance of Professor V. M. Masson, Director of that Institute. The reasons
why we chose to work at Merv were varied. One was the opportunity to
work as an international team in an area of major significance to Iranian
studies at a time when Iran itself was and remains largely closed to
foreign archaeologists. Another was Merv's location as a 'gateway' to
Central Asia: control of Merv is an indicator of the relative power of

states to east and west. For instance, Merv was an important administrative and military centre in the north-east quarter of the Achaemenian,
Seleucid, Parthian and Sasanian empires (Frye 1984: 112, 173, 295,
298), although control may have been lost for a while to the Greco-
Bactrian kings (Frye 1984: 180), in late Parthian times when the kings of
Merv minted their own coins (Frye 1984: 202; Loginov and Nikitin
1993a), and again by the Sasanian king Peroz to the Hephthalite Huns
in the fifth century (Frye 1984: 322; Loginov and Nikitin 1993b). The
last Sasanian king, Yazdigird III (633–51), fled to the oasis where he
was murdered, prior to Merv's conquest by the Arabs (Le Strange 1905:
400). With Nishapur, Herat and Balkh, Merv was one of the principal
cities of Khurasan, the 'Eastern land' of the early Islamic empires (Le
Strange 1905: 382) and was a capital city of the Abbasids. Arab domination was followed by Turkic, and it was under the Seljuk Sultans that
Merv achieved its high-point in the eleventh and twelfth centuries.

Equally decisive in our choice of Merv was its unusual pattern of
urban development. A consecutive series of city-sites gradually developed on adjacent virgin sites, protected from recent development by the
Soviet and Turkmen authorities. These extensive remains offered a
unique opportunity to record the varying plans of the cities, since their
walls define their size and general layout, and it is usually possible to
identify gateways, principal roads, some buildings, and the courses of
some canals. From an archaeological point of view a number of periods
can be examined near surface. Merv presented, therefore, the possibility
of surveying urban development through time, up to the present day if
the modern Soviet-style city, Bairam Ali, is included.

Obvious problems in working at Merv include both the sheer scale of
the site and the degradation of the immediate suburban hinterland caused
by nearly half a century of Soviet-style agriculture and collectivisation.
The landscape has been brutalised to achieve large fields for the intensive
monoculture of cotton: entire tell sites, together with many ancient buildings, have been swept away. This environmental degradation must have
transformed the ecology of much of the oasis, which was regularly praised
for its fertility in medieval sources. The Chinese Du Huan wrote that
'villages and fences touch each other and everywhere there are trees
[growing close together]'.[5] Islamic scholars commented on the produc-
tiveness and variety of the crops of the oasis: the tenth century Ibn Hawkal
claimed that the fruits of Merv were finer than those of any other place

---

[5] See above, n. 2.

(Curzon 1889: 113), while Mustawfi reported that seed-corn gave a hundredfold the first year (Le Strange 1905: 402–3). Earlier, Strabo noted the size to which the vine grew (XI.10.2). Just how different the oasis may have been is indicated by Ibn Hawkal who claimed that in no other city are to be seen such palaces and groves, gardens and streams (Curzon 1889: 113). An idea of what these were like was suggested by our visits to the Bairam Ali sanatorium, built early in the twentieth century as a palace for Tsar Nicholas II. The numerous trees and running water in the gardens created a different world, cool and pleasant.

Another problem affecting our work is the high water-table caused by irrigation using the resources of the Kara Kum canal. This has changed the arid conditions which once preserved the cities and their associated standing monuments: in YuTAKE reports of the 1950s the surface of the cities was bare, while today large areas are obscured by dense scrub. The surfaces of low-lying mounds and depressions within the sites are heavily salted, and the uppermost deposits have deteriorated into a soft dust below a puffy crust. In the late 1950s when the canal was opened, these low areas were flooded. The situation was improved, although not solved, by cutting drainage channels.

When starting work at Merv, we had to decide whether to focus on a single problem or city or to undertake a more broad-brush approach. Since Western awareness of the site is limited and long-term access can never be taken for granted, we chose a broader approach aiming at obtaining an overview of the occupational history of these important centres. As much information as possible about all the cities is therefore being collected and prepared for publication. The cities consist of ancient Gyaur Kala with its citadel Erk Kala, medieval Sultan Kala, and post-medieval Abdullah Khan Kala with an eighteenth-century extension, Bairam Ali Khan Kala (Figure 3). Another 'city' of Merv was a square walled area of some 110 ha, 1 km south-east of Gyaur Kala, known today as Shaim Kala and now almost totally destroyed (Herrmann et al. 1995: 57–9).[6] The cities are being mapped, a number of surveys and selective excavations undertaken and a gazetteer of the standing monuments in and around the cities and in the oasis prepared.

---

[6] Although initially considered to date from the Seljuk period, Shaim Kala may have been an eighth-century Arab military camp.

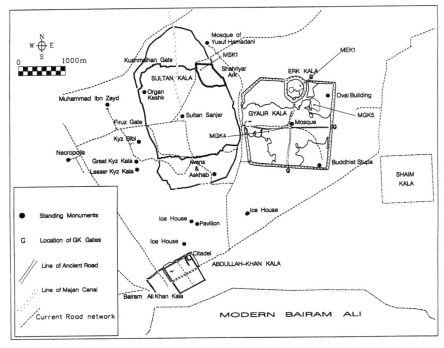

**Figure 3.** Site plan of the ancient city-sites of Merv, the monuments and IMP excavation trenches: map drawn from geo-rectified satellite images and air photographs (G. Barratt in Herrmann *et al.* 1997: 3).

## The Early City, Erk Kala and Gyaur Kala

The longest-lived of the cities of Merv was Gyaur Kala and its citadel, Erk Kala (Figures 3 and 4). Erk Kala, the first 'city', was founded in the sixth century BC at a time which may have coincided with the arrival of the Achaemenian Persians, or possibly their predecessors, the Medes.[7]

---

[7] Only the western boundary of the Median empire is known with any certainty. However, two factors suggest extensive Median possessions to the east: first, their access to fine horses and lapis lazuli (Kuhrt 1995: 480). The Central Asian republics are known for their horses, while the principal ancient source of lapis lazuli was the mine at Sar-i Sang in Badakhshan, north-east Afghanistan. The Medes gave both horses and lapis lazuli as tribute to the Assyrian kings—specific references to Median gifts of lapis lazuli occur in the reigns of Tiglath Pileser III, 300 talents (Luckenbill 1926: I, 768); and Esarhaddon (Wiseman 1958: 1), although there are also references to 'heavy tribute' without further definition in the reigns of Sargon and Sennacherib. Secondly, the fact that Cyrus II, having conquered more of the ancient world than any other king, with his control of the Median, Neo-Babylonian and Lydian empires, undertook campaigns in Trans-Oxiana may have been because he was reclaiming former Median territory, which was attempting to regain its independence.

**Figure 4.** Aerial view of the early city, Gyaur Kala, and its citadel Erk Kala (c.500 BC–1100 AD) from the east (1992): in the distance the walls of the medieval city, Sultan Kala. The mound of the Buddhist stupa can be seen in the bottom left, south-east corner of Gyaur Kala: the Oval Building near the wall in the north-east quarter. The old east-west road dividing the city is also evident.

Achaemenian control of the oasis, known as Margiana, was established by Cyrus II the Great (559–530 BC) (Dandamaev 1989: 33; Kuhrt 1995: 660). The first historical reference occurs in the trilingual inscription of Darius the Great at Bisitun near Kermanshah in Iran (Kent 1953: 131), where he recorded the defeat of the Margian rebel Frada (Dandamaev 1989: 125–6). At this time Margiana formed part of the satrapy of Baktra (Frye 1984: 112), continuing earlier close cultural links between the two areas in the Bronze Age (Hiebert 1994: 174–8).

Erk Kala's massive mud-brick walls still stand some 30 m in height and enclose an area of some 20 ha. The highest point on the walls and in the area is the look-out tower in the south-east, which originally guarded the probable entrance to the citadel. This may have been via a ramp over the moat, leading to a gate set high in its walls, as can be seen in the citadel at Bukhara today. The southern half of the citadel consists of occupation build-up, including a platform to the west, once crowned with an administrative building of the early Arab period. This was excavated in the 1930s and removed in the 1980s prior to planning. To the north is one of the low areas, a feature of Central Asian cities.

According to the Arab geographers Istakhri, Ibn Hawkal and Muqaddasi, Erk Kala was still in use in the tenth century, when it was described as ' "high-built and itself of the size of a town", surrounded by the inner city with its four gates [Gyaur Kala], beyond which again were extensive suburbs stretching along the banks of the great canals' (Le Strange 1905: 398–9). By this time, however, occupation in the old city of Erk and Gyaur Kala was in decline, with an extensive medieval city developing over the canal to the west. The latest levels revealed by IMP's first excavation on the occupation platform adjacent to the east wall have been dated by the coins and ceramics to the sixth/seventh centuries. This multi-phase house was probably constructed during the reign of the successful king Khusrau I (531–79) (Herrmann *et al.* 1993: 50–5; 1994: 66–70; 1995: 34–7). A number of modifications and refurbishments were made in the following years, the house finally being abandoned after the conquest of Merv by the Arabs in the mid-seventh century.

The metropolis of Antiochia Margiana was founded by Antiochus I (281–261) (Wiesehöfer 1996: 108). In this new foundation, Erk Kala became the citadel of the Hellenistic city, modern Gyaur Kala. This walled city was essentially square, except for the west wall and the north-west corner which followed the course of the pre-existing Razik canal, and the curve of the citadel in the north wall. It measured approximately 2 km across. The walls still survive to a height of some 20 m, with regular hummocks representing towers: the defences were reinforced by an outer moat. The gates were located in the centre of the walls, except for the north gate which was set to the east of Erk Kala, and were connected by roads which quartered the city. Occupation was essentially cruciform, concentrating on these major arteries and leaving the corners relatively empty. Since Gyaur Kala was a Hellenistic city, the occupied areas would probably have been laid out in a grid plan with regular blocks of housing and a series of public buildings, temples, an agora, theatre, gymnasia, bath houses, etc.

Since Gyaur Kala was occupied for more than a thousand years, through the Parthian and Sasanian periods and into the Islamic period, the Seleucid city-plan would obviously not have survived intact but would have changed organically. However, it may not have changed fundamentally, for traces of regular *insulae* can be seen from the air in the north-west of the site (Figure 5). This regularity is confirmed by Du Huan's description of Merv, which provides some fascinating details: 'Within the city [wall] there is a saline [or salines]. There are also two Buddhist temples. The [city] walls and houses are very thick and high. The urban quarters are very regular.'[8] Numerous low white saltpans or 'salines' still exist in the city today, one close to our Middle Sasanian excavation (Figure 6). Geoarchaeological borings were undertaken here in an attempt to determine the method of formation of this area, whether it was excavated for mud bricks or whether this was an unoccupied garden or pond (Barham and Mellalieu in Herrmann *et al.* 1994: 56–8).

One of the 'Buddhist temples' referred to by Du Huan was sited in a corner in the south-east of the city, close to the walls (Figure 4). The stupa and associated monastery/*sangharama*, excavated by M. E. Masson in the 1950s, has been variously dated to the first century BC, the first/second centuries AD, and recently, after reanalysis of the coins, to a much later date in the fourth century, a time of close contacts between Sasanian Merv and Bactria (Pugachenkova and Usmanova 1995). The stupa was reconstructed a number of times, and the *sangharama* considerably enlarged: the latest coin identified in the bricks of the staircase was one of Khusrau I (531–79). The remains of one or two more stupas outside the eastern wall of Gyaur Kala and dated to the sixth/seventh centuries were recorded in YuTAKE excavations of 1963 but have subsequently been demolished (Pugachenkova and Usmanova 1995: 76–7).

Another isolated structure was an unusual building in the north-east quarter of Gyaur Kala (Figure 6). The monumental 'Oval Building' was

[8] See above, n. 2.

**Figure 5.** The western half of Gyaur Kala from the north (1992). Traces of regular *insulae* can be seen on the surface of the occupation mound near the western wall. The trench cut through the walls of Erk Kala by YuTAKE is visible near the bottom left, as are Soviet excavations of the 1980s and early 1990s on the bulldozed flat top of the inner citadel.

**Figure 6.** The north-east quarter of Gyaur Kala from the west (1992). The Oval Building near the east wall, Soviet excavations next to the north gate and the low mound, Gyaur Kala Area 5, with Middle Sasanian settlement, currently being excavated by IMP, can all be seen: see Figure 3. The IMP excavations in Erk Kala can also be made out on the mound adjacent to the east wall. Note the white 'salines' in the vicinity of Area 5.

constructed on a platform, accessed by a ramp, and consisted of rooms
built round a courtyard. M. E. Masson originally suggested that it was a
Christian monastery, but this idea has been dismissed, both because of a
lack of archaeological evidence and because most Nestorian monasteries
are built some distance away from cities: Simpson considers a more
probable use would have been as a storehouse (Simpson, forthcoming).

Even if the Oval Building was secular, literary sources provide
evidence for a flourishing Christian community in Merv (Koshelenko
1995): bishops of Merv attended a number of Ecumenical Councils of
the Eastern and after 485 the Nestorian Church (Asmussen 1983: 932;
Fiey 1973). The position of the Christian community in Merv was
sufficiently established to ensure that the local bronze coins of Yazdigird I carried the sign of the cross on their reverses (Loginov and
Nikitin 1993*b*: 272, fig. 11, nos 10–29). A cross was employed on a
jar handle reused as a mould for casting small pendants and found in the
Erk Kala excavations (Figure 7), rare archaeological evidence of a
Christian presence (Simpson 1996).

Cosmopolitan Merv also hosted a Jewish community, as has been
shown by Jewish headstones. The variety of religions in the city, which
would of course have included Zoroastrianism and Manichaeism, is

**Figure 7.**   A jar handle reused as a mould for pendants found in the Late Sasanian house in
Erk Kala: the cross is rare archaeological evidence for the presence of Christians at Merv.

reaffirmed by the range of burial practices discovered at an extramural necropolis, located 3 km to the west of Gyaur Kala. This consisted of the remains of seven built structures excavated in the 1950s with burials in ossuaries, built graves, ceramic coffins or jars, and bodies either on the floor or in mass burials (Grenet 1984: 187–97, pl. 18). The structures continued in use for some time.

A large low mound in the north-east quarter, not far from the Oval Building (Figure 6), was the location of our second excavation. This was chosen because of the absence of an Islamic overburden, a predicted date of the Middle Sasanian period, thus complementing work in Erk Kala, and the presence of near-surface buildings visible from the air and confirmed by a geophysical prospection (Figure 8; Strange and Falkner in Herrmann *et al.* 1994: 58–9). By the end of our fifth season in 1996 a programme of shovel-scraping had revealed a number of private houses separated by irregular, narrow alleys, a plan more typical of a medieval Islamic city than the Hellenistic grid suggested for the

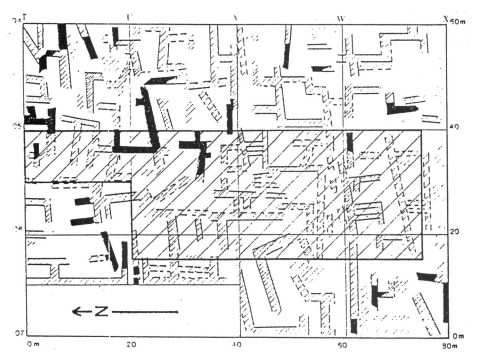

**Figure 8.** Gyaur Kala Area 5: resistivity plan after interpretation. The hatched area represents the excavations (P. Strange in Herrmann *et al.* 1995: 38–9).

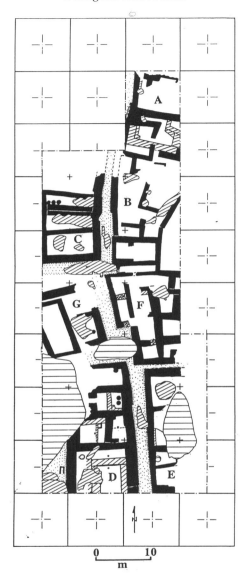

**Figure 9.**   Gyaur Kala Area 5: plan of a Sasanian residential quarter following scraping and
partial excavation (Herrmann *et al*. 1997: 5).

main city (Figure 9; Herrmann *et al*. 1994: 69–70; 1995: 37–42; 1996:
4–8; 1997: 4–6). However, Area 5 is located outside the planned city in
one of the 'empty corners', like the Buddhist stupa and 'Oval Building'.
Du Huan's description of the houses of Merv—'The wooden parts of

the [buildings] are elaborately carved and the mud parts are painted with pictures'[9]—may suggest their original appearance, with balconies overhanging the alleys as in old areas of Damascus.

Analysis of the tens of thousands of potsherds from these two excavations by St J. Simpson and Gabriele Puschnigg will provide the first reliable coin-dated corpus of Sasanian ceramics from the fifth to seventh centuries from this region and from Western Asia. The vessels were made locally and range from open lamps to tall elegant jars with long handles and curious rippled decoration on the shoulders, possibly inspired by fluted metalwork. Many sherds from the Erk Kala excavations belong to jars with knobbed handles, the most famous example of which is the 'Merv Vase' (Figure 10; Koshelenko 1966), found concealed near the Buddhist stupa (Pugachenkova and Usmanova 1995: 71–2). The similar form of the 'Merv Vase' to our Erk Kala jars reinforces the dating of the final phase of the stupa to the Late Sasanian period, a date otherwise based on numismatic evidence.

Moulded and handmade figurines are a relatively common find in Erk and Gyaur Kala, both on the surface and in excavation. One well-known type features a lady with a mirror, the so-called 'Great Margiana Goddess': the example illustrated in Figure 11 was found in Structure C of the area of Middle Sasanian housing. While ceramic is abundant at Merv, and glass in the later periods, glass is relatively rare in Middle Sasanian levels. This tiny figurine of a naked woman in the birthing position (Figure 12) is a unique find from Gyaur Kala Area 5, although it is a well-known type in India.

Our third excavation was in an industrial area on the main platform of Gyaur Kala. This area was identified by the Surface Artefact Team in 1992 because of the presence of numerous highly vitrified, crucible fragments (Tucker and Stoll Tucker in Herrmann et al. 1994: 59–61). It was the discovery of steel droplets in the glassy slags remaining inside the crucibles, found during analyses undertaken by Merkel, Griffiths and Feuerbach in the Wolfson Archaeological Science Laboratories of the Institute of Archaeology (Merkel 1989; Merkel et al. 1995: 12–14), that led to the excavation of this area. This resulted in the discovery, first, of two furnaces, the rims of which were just visible on the surface, and then to the excavation of the surrounding workshop and the recovery of a total of four furnaces (Figure 13; Herrmann et al. 1994: 70–1; 1995: 42–5; 1996: 15–16; 1997: 10–13).

[9] See above, n. 2.

**Figure 10.**   The 'Merv Vase', found in the Buddhist stupa in the south-east corner of Gyaur
Kala in the 1950s (Ashgabat Historical Museum).

The metallurgical remains are of particular interest because analyses
showed that the crucibles were used for the production of steel by the
co-fusion method, where wrought iron and cast iron are heated to some
1,200 degrees centigrade. This process is distinctly different from the

**Figure 11.** A moulded figurine, a 'mirrored lady', from Structure C in Gyaur Kala Area 5 (Mary Museum) (height 9.0 cm).

**Figure 12.**   Glass was relatively rare in Middle Sasanian levels. This tiny female figurine in the birthing position was found in Gyaur Kala Area 5. Similar examples can be found in India (Mary Museum) (height 2.0 cm).

'wootz' method known from India and Sri Lanka, where wrought iron is packed with carbon to produce steel (Bronson 1986). According to Arab writers such as the twelfth century al-Biruni, the co-fusion method produces excellent steel with attractive 'Damascus' or watered patterning, and he refers to its production at another major city, nearby Herat (Allan 1979: 65–76). The furnaces at Merv have been dated to the ninth to tenth centuries AD by ceramic and numismatic evidence and are the first metallurgical remains to document the co-fusion process. Many questions remain to be resolved about this type of steel production, for our furnaces represent an accomplished, not a developing, technology. According to Professor James Allan, there are no known examples of cast iron objects from Early Islamic times (personal communication). However, cast iron was extensively used in China as early as the third century BC, and a Chinese text of the sixth century has described the co-fusion process (Wagner 1993: 335).

It is also noteworthy that steel production at Merv occurred in a city lacking all the relevant resources. There are no metal deposits in the oasis. The kaolin for the crucibles probably came from the only known source in Turkmenistan near Kara Bogaz Gol on the east of the Caspian Sea; while the wood for firing the furnaces has been identified by Rowena Gale as pistachio and juniper, used in twig form (Herrmann *et al.* 1996: 20). This too must have been imported, presumably from the Kopet Dagh or Badghiz, despite supplies of excellent timber such as saxaul in the oasis and surrounding desert. It may have been the presence of the relevant specialists at Merv that led to production in this great centre, where the technology may have been a closely guarded secret. Interestingly, the magnetometer survey undertaken in 1996 of areas adjacent to the workshop failed to identify further steel furnaces. It may be that only a few workshops at Merv produced such high-technology steel.

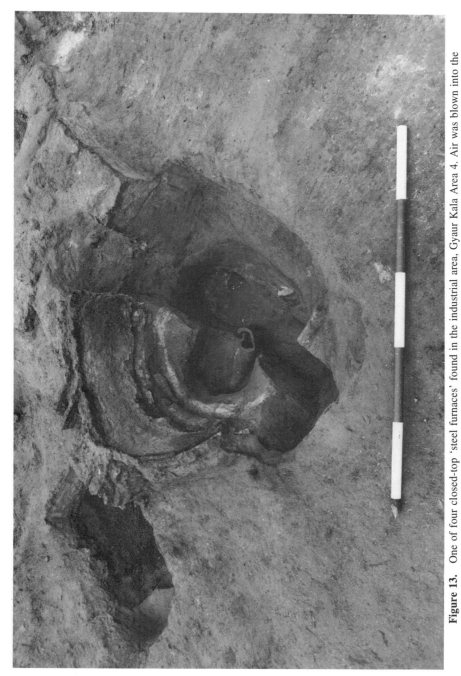

**Figure 13.** One of four closed-top 'steel furnaces' found in the industrial area, Gyaur Kala Area 4. Air was blown into the furnace via the *tuyère* at the bottom and vented through an exit flue near ground level.

## The Medieval City, Sultan Kala

In the eighth century a new suburb grew up to the west of Gyaur Kala along the banks of the Majan canal, and this gradually developed into the next 'city' of Merv, replacing the old town (Figure 3). The consequent decline of Gyaur Kala has been documented by an initial analysis of their results by the Surface Artefact Survey (Figure 14; Herrmann *et al.* 1993: 59–61), with occupation of the old city being heavily reduced and the centre being turned over to industry, such as the production of steel.

The new suburb developed into the Seljuk metropolis, known as Marv-ash-Shahijan or 'Royal Merv' (Le Strange 1905: 398), which became the capital of the Seljuk state and one of the most important cultural centres of the eastern Muslim world. This was the time of Merv's greatest glory, only terminated by the arrival of the Mongols in 1221. It was in Merv that the Seljuk sultans Toghril (1040–63), Alp-Arslan (1063–72), Malik-shah (1072–92) and, of course, Sultan Sanjar (1118–57) himself were buried. Of their mausolea, it is only that of Sanjar that survives above ground today. Merv was also the home of a number of outstanding medieval scholars, astronomers, philosophers, historians and poets, including the astronomer and poet Omar Khayyam (eleventh century) and the geographer Yaqut al-Khamavi (thirteenth century), who were attracted by its famous libraries and observatory (Le Strange 1905: 402).

The main city was much the same size as Gyaur Kala, *c.*400 ha, although its walls were less regular, reflecting its organic pattern of growth. By the tenth century the 'great Majan suburb . . . lay round the Maydan, or public square, on which stood the New Mosque, the Government-house, and the prison; all these having been built by Abu Muslim, the great partizan of the Abbasids' (Le Strange 1905: 399). Like many early Islamic cities, it was not walled until the eleventh century, when Sultan Malik-shah is credited with building the 'great wall round the city 12,300 paces in circuit' (Bosworth, 1968: 85; Le Strange 1905: 402). With the extensive suburban areas to north and south enclosed by Sultan Sanjar, the city occupied some 630 ha and was one of the largest of the medieval world. Sultan Sanjar was also probably responsible for walling an irregular area in the north-east corner of the city, the Shahriyar Ark or 'Royal Citadel' (Figures 15 and 16). The city's defences are impressive with massive, multi-phase

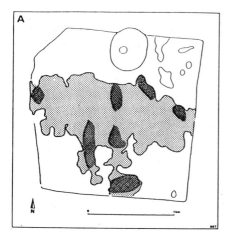
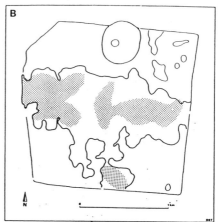
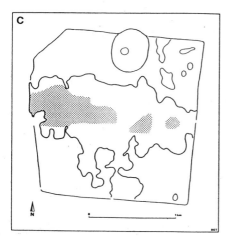
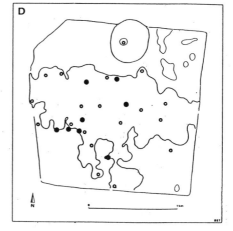

**Figure 14.** Preliminary surface survey distribution maps for Late Sasanian-Islamic periods
of occupation in Gyaur Kala.
A. Late Sasanian ceramic distribution, *c*.6th–7th century.
B. Early Islamic ceramic distribution, *c*.9th–10 century.
C. Islamic ceramic distribution, *c*.11th–12th century.
D. Early Islamic copper coin distribution, 8th–9th century. Open circle one coin; solid circle
two or more coins (Tucker and Stoll Tucker in Herrmann *et al.* 1994: 60).

**Figure 15.** The northern half of Sultan Kala from the east, showing in the left foreground the Royal Citadel or Shahriyar Ark; part of the main city with the mausoleum of Sultan Sanjar at the extreme left centre; and the northern suburb to the right (1992).

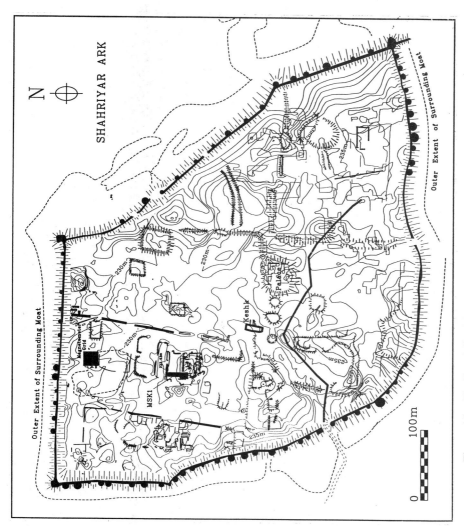

**Figure 16.** The Royal Citadel or Shahriyar Ark, from remotely sensed images, verified by ground survey (G. Barratt in Herrmann *et al.* 1997: 19).

*Georgina Herrmann*

**Figure 17.**   The eastern wall of Sultan Kala at its junction with the wall of Shahriyar Ark (1995).

walls, reinforced by towers and deep moats (Figure 17). In 1996 we began a study of the military architecture, starting with the walls of Shahriyar Ark (Brun and Annaev in Herrmann *et al*. 1997: 20–2): this survey should be completed in 1997.[10]

According to medieval accounts, the creation of the citadel caused major changes to the plan of the city centre. The royal residences, administrative buildings and the mint were moved to the citadel, while the centre was turned over to religious buildings, including the great Friday Mosque and the mausolea of the Seljuk sultans. Turkmen excavations beside the mausoleum of Sultan Sanjar have revealed buildings of the earlier, pre-Sanjar phase. To the left is a small house with elegant arched shelved niches and to the right a fine bathhouse (Figure 18). Information on these excavations, together with much other previously unpublished work, has been assembled and will form part of the IMP volume on the medieval city.

Divorced from the structures of which it once formed a part, the mausoleum externally looks rather like a sore thumb, although from the air, the outlines of the courtyard of the Friday mosque of which it once formed a part are clearly visible (Figure 18), as they are from the windows of the mausoleum. The mausoleum still remains a landmark today, while Yaqut commented that its high dome, originally covered with gleaming turquoise tiles, could be seen three days' march away (Le Strange 1905: 401). This outer dome has not survived although the magnificent inner dome of this spectacular and important early Seljuk building can still be appreciated. The dome is carried on four giant squinches, alternating with blind arches, both pierced with windows. The transition from the octagon to the circular base of the drum is made by eight stalactite pendentives, from which rise four radiating ribs forming an interlacing pattern making an eight-pointed star. Traces of painting remain on the ribs and walls. The mausoleum was built by the Serrakhs architect, Muhammad ibn Atsys, whose modest signature in a panel in the dome was hidden by plaster: it was only revealed in the 1950s (Masson 1969: 194–205).[11] Work was begun in 1140 and must have been finished before the invasion by the Ghuzz in 1153.

The Mausoleum of Sultan Sanjar is one of eighty standing monuments being recorded by Andrew Petersen as part of the IMP's

[10] A study of the less well preserved fortifications of Erk Kala and Gyaur Kala is being undertaken by V. Zavyalov.

[11] Ibn Atsys may have built a smaller unsigned version at Serrakhs.

**Figure 18.** The mausoleum of Sultan Sanjar (1993). The outlines of the courtyard of the Friday Mosque are visible, as are the excavations of the earlier bath-house between the mausoleum and the range of rooms to the right.

programme. This task is an urgent one. At Merv the contradictory pressures of tourism on the one hand and increasing religious fervour on the other are causing particular problems. Mausolea are being actively conserved and equipped with facilities for pilgrims. With the help of the officers of the Archaeological Park 'Ancient Merv', A. Annaev and R. Dzhapar, we are assembling old plans and preparing new, recording the current state of conservation and building up an archive of photographs.

Although the mausolea of the other Seljuk Sultans once built in the centre of the city have not survived, a fine example outside the walls is preserved and has been sympathetically conserved. This mausoleum was commissioned by Sharaf al-Din Abu-Tahir, Sanjar's vizier, and was constructed in 1112–13 in commemoration of the fifth descendant of Ali, Muhammad ibn Zayd, murdered in Merv in the eighth century. It forms the heart of a delightful complex within a sacred grove of saxaul trees, equipped with cistern, kitchen and guardian's house (all relatively late in date). Although the exterior is much restored, the unusual shell-shaped *mihrab* still preserves traces of painting and a superb inscription in cut brick-work written in floriate Kufic runs round all four walls (Figure 19).

The most distinctive buildings in the Merv oasis are the corrugated castles or *keshks*, referred to in the anonymous geographical work, the *Hudud al Alam*, compiled in 982/3:'there are numerous castles (*kushk*)' (Minorsky 1937: 105). These fortified buildings were built on platforms with sloping sides: the walls were formed of large corrugations, probably crenellated at the top. They are of varying sizes, fulfilled different functions and continued to be built over a considerable period. *Keshks* can be found both in and around the walls of the Seljuk city and elsewhere in the oasis. One of the largest and certainly the best known is the Great Kiz Kala (Figure 20). Nearby is a second, smaller, corrugated building, unfortunately in a more ruined state. Both of these contained a central courtyard, surrounded by vaulted and domed rooms on the first floor.

According to written sources (Ibn al-Asir, Dzhuveini and Khafiz i Abru), Merv was laid waste by three successive invasions of Mongol forces in 1221–2, the population was slaughtered or driven out, the wealth and treasures of the city plundered, and the dam on the Murghab river destroyed. Ibn al-Asir refers to the invasion as a 'great disaster, the like of which neither day nor night had brought forth before', while Dzhuveini wrote that 'the city which had been embellished by great men of the world became the haunt of hyenas and beasts of prey'. More than a hundred years later, in the early fourteenth century when

*Georgina Herrmann*

**Figure 19.** Part of the floriated Kufic inscription running round the walls of the shrine of Muhammad ibn Zayd.

**Figure 20.** The Great Kiz Kala, one of the early Islamic corrugated buildings or *keshks* found in and around Sultan Kala and in the oasis (Chronos archive, State Hermitage Museum, St Petersburg).

**Figure 21.**   A wall plaque found in the Mongol Buddhist Temple located in the southern
suburb of Sultan Kala (Ashgabat Historical Museum).

Mustawfi and Ibn Battuta passed through Merv, it was still 'one great
ruin' (Le Strange 1905: 402–3). Such accounts have led to the impression that Merv died as a result of the Mongol invasions. Certainly there
is evidence for widespread burning in many areas of the city. However,
Turkmen excavations have provided evidence for considerable post-
Seljuk occupation, both inside and outside the city walls. A post-Seljuk
building excavated by Professor Terkesh Khodjaniasov was located in
the southern suburb of Sultan Kala. A small Buddhist temple was built
on a platform and measured 11 m on each side. It consisted of two
rooms, decorated with ceramic wall plaques, one of which is illustrated
in Figure 21. Unusually, it was roofed with ridge tiles which show
strong Chinese influence. Professor Khodjaniasov dates the temple's
destruction to Ghazan's degree of 1295, ordering the destruction of all

non-Islamic religious buildings (Boyle 1968: 379–80). There is also over a metre of post-Seljuk occupation in excavations near the mausoleum of Kiz Bibi (Herrmann *et al.* 1996: 19).

## The Royal Citadel or Shahriyar Ark

The citadel is located in the north-east corner of Sultan Kala and is roughly triangular in form (Figure 15): it was mapped in 1996 from remotely sensed images, verified by ground survey. Surviving within it are the remains of a number of structures (Figure 16), the best preserved of which are all located on low mounds. They include an unusual and small version of a *keshk*, consisting of a single, long, vaulted room divided into three, with the remains of niches on surviving internal sections of the walls. This may have been the *kepter khana* or pigeon house—ready access to an independent communications system would obviously have been essential for any ruler. Parts of a surprisingly small four-iwan palace no larger than domestic structures elsewhere in the citadel have been identified as that of the Seljuk Sultans. The combination of its size and height above present ground level, as well as the presence of *balkhi* vaults, had already suggested that the date proposed could be too early, a hypothesis we hope will be confirmed by our excavations.

It was with this problem in mind—the date of the final phase of occupation in the citadel that excavation was begun in a corner of a relatively destroyed courtyard house (Herrmann *et al.* 1996: 17–19; 1997: 22–6). Most of the house was sub-surface, although some walls survive at the eastern end. In its final phase the house (35 × 25 m) probably consisted of two parts, a principal courtyard with four iwans, visible as shallow depressions, at the better preserved eastern end, and a secondary courtyard to the west surrounded by further ranges of rooms. Excavations in the poorly preserved north-west corner and the adjacent courtyard (*c.*45 × 35 m) have so far distinguished three phases. The latest, a squatter occupation, was characterised by small hearths cut into fallen mud-brick. The second phase, probably dating to the Timurid period, had plastered gypsum floors cut with a number of features, the most impressive of which was a large circular oven lined with fired bricks. This phase is some 2 m below surface. Only a little of the third phase has been revealed so far, but it is also post-Seljuk. This suggests that the standing walls in the 'Seljuk' citadel may all be post-Seljuk. The excavation is planned to continue in 1997.

Evidence both from our own work and from Turkmen excavations in the city, its suburbs and outside its walls all indicate post-Seljuk occupation. Certainly, parts of the medieval city were abandoned, or turned over to industrial processes; however, some reappraisal of the currently accepted post-1221 history of Merv should be considered.

Environmental studies of the medieval period have not been undertaken previously in Iran or Central Asia. An important question on which our archaeobotanical record may shed light is that of the degree of damage inflicted by the Mongols on Merv's vital irrigation systems (Le Strange 1905: 402). However, just as reports of the 'death' of the city may have been exaggerated, so may reports of the level of destruction of the complex water-management system. A programme of full environmental recovery based on large-scale water flotation has been underway since the outset and is now beginning to shed light on the irrigation history of the oasis (Nesbitt in Herrmann *et al.* 1993: 56–8; 1994: 71–3; and Boardman in Herrmann *et al.* 1995: 49–52; 1996: 19–20; 1997: 29–31). In addition to material from IMP excavations, archaeobotanical work has been carried out on Late Bronze to Early Iron Age samples from Tahirbaj, excavated by the IsMEO team, on Parthian (first century AD) samples from Gobekli Depe, excavated by G. Koshelenko, and on Seljuk, Timurid and later samples from Annaev's 1995 excavations at the Kiz Bibi complex to the west of Sultan Kala (Herrmann *et al.* 1995: 19). Also included are published results from Bronze Age Gonur Depe. Archaeobotanical analyses are therefore able to suggest trends in plant use in snapshot form for over 1,500 years.

Most striking is the consistency in the major species present, regardless of the number of samples collected per site/period. Free threshing wheat, hulled barley, broomcorn millet and grape have been recovered from samples from the Bronze Age to the eighteenth century. Barley is the most frequent crop at almost all sites. However, the presence of wheat throughout suggests that well-publicised problems associated with long-term irrigation agriculture, notably salinisation, were overcome at Merv. Regarding other crop plants, several species present at Gonur Depe, such as emmer wheat, chickpea and plum, have not yet been recovered elsewhere. In 1993 when records were only available for Erk Kala and Gonur Depe, Nesbitt noted that millet, while present throughout, was surprisingly sparse in the plant records for the oasis (in Herrmann *et al.* 1994: 73), an observation borne out by further work and reinforced by a seventh-century Chinese reference to the absence of millet and rice among the Persians (Miller 1959: 15).

From an economic point of view the most significant discovery has been that cotton, still the principal crop of the oasis, was a major summer crop at Merv by the mid-Sasanian period—the date of its introduction awaits definition through continued excavation. Since no cotton seeds have been recovered in samples from Achaemenian through Parthian levels (Gobekli and Tahirbaj Depe), this may be at some point in the early Sasanian period and may have been made possible by the introduction of the intensive irrigation agriculture practiced in the Sasanian empire (Adams 1962, 1965, 1981; Wenke 1975/76, 1987). Merv was, of course, famous in medieval sources for its textiles, both cotton and silk.[12]

Although our own and Turkmen excavations suggest the continued occupation of parts of Sultan Kala and its citadel into the Timurid period, it was said to be in 1409 that the Timurid ruler Shah Rukh (1408–47) built a new city, some 3 km to the south of Sanjar's Mausoleum (Figures 3, 22 and 23). This moated and walled city, known today as Abdullah Khan Kala, is considerably smaller than the earlier cities, occupying only a square kilometre. The reduced size of Timurid Merv thus illustrates the relative decline of the oasis at this time, reflecting both its loss of status to centres such as Samarkand and Herat and the effects on overland trade of the increased use of maritime routes. Interestingly, unlike the organic Seljuk city, Timurid Merv was regularly planned and square in form. Like Gyaur Kala it was quartered by the principal arteries, which ran to the four gates. The streets were laid out on a grid pattern; there was a mosque and madrassah in the north of the city, and a citadel with palace and caravanserai in the north-east corner. The plan was fairly typical for a fifteenth-century town of Khurasan.

The post-Timurid history of Merv is one of further decline and frequent conquest, finally by the Russians, who annexed the Merv oasis, together with the other Central Asian khanates in the 1880s (Hopkirk 1990). The Timurid city, already at least partially abandoned, was plundered for bricks for building the Tsar's Murghab estate and the Russian Orthodox Church. Apart from the city walls, little now survives. Fortunately the Russian scholar V. A. Zhukovsky (1894) recorded the remains at a time when much was still standing, as did G. Pugachenkova in the 1950s (1958).

---

[12] 'Marv produces good cotton, . . . textiles of raw silk (qazzin) and of mulham silk', *Hudud al-'Alam* (Minorsky 1937: 105).

**Figure 22.** The Timurid city, Abdullah Khan Kala, from the north-east (1992). The walls of the citadel in the north-east corner still survive, although little remains of the buildings still standing at the turn of the century (Figure 23).

**Figure 23.** The buildings in the citadel of the Timurid city (Figure 22) at the turn of the century (Chronos archive, State Hermitage Museum, St Petersburg).

## The Mapping Programme

Working in a new area presents special problems. Initially, we were unable to obtain any maps or even coordinates. To unify the various aspects of our work, some of which have been mentioned above, we decided to undertake a cartographic programme to record the cities of Merv and the locations of the monuments in their environs. Fortunately, the virtual revolution in survey technology and portable computing power in recent years made it possible to create a digital map base for the cities based on earlier Soviet mapping (obtained in our second season), corrected satellite imagery and aerial photography (Figures 3 and 16: Barratt in Herrmann *et al.* 1993: 44–8; 1994: 55–6; 1996: 20–2; Barratt and Doyle in Herrmann *et al.* 1997: 19–20; Herrmann and Barratt 1995, 1996).

The use of satellite technology is well established in environmental and landscape studies, and with steadily improving resolution—it is already down to two metres[13]—such data seems certain to become a standard tool for city planning. Although such fine imagery was not available to the IMP, SPOT XS images, with a pixel resolution of 20 m, and hard copy of Landsat images of the oasis were obtained (Figure 2). Derrold Holcomb of ERDAS, USA, arranged to have Merv targeted by the NASA Shuttle in 1994 and subsequently interrogated the data. There was a possibility that the side scan radar of the Shuttle imaging platform might have provided useful sub-surface information. However, while this technique is one of proven value elsewhere, it was not particularly useful at Merv because of the alluvial mud of which the city is formed.

To combine information from satellite images and aerial photographs for mapping purposes it is necessary to geo-rectify them to a known or arbitrary coordinate system, and a series of ground control points were fixed by Total Station electronic theodolites and a Leica System 200/300 Differential Global Positioning System (GPS). The GPS was also used to carry out mobile mapping in kinematic mode, which allows continuous position fixing at pre-set time intervals, either from a car or on foot. Figure 3 shows the resultant field plot of the modern road system, created from GPS data in Leica Ski software. This application of GPS is comparatively new to survey and offers the ability

[13] Currently limited to military users. Soviet Soyuz images to 5 m resolution are, however, available for civilian use.

to record to a high resolution the ground surface of an archaeological site. Terrain models created by this method are arguably more objective and detailed than models created by more traditional levelling techniques. Work carried out at Merv using a combination of survey GPS and Total Station has allowed some conclusions to be drawn on their relative strengths in relation to the collection of archaeological survey data. Neither technology has all the answers desired by the field archaeologist, but in combination they provide a comprehensive data collection facility.

Much has been accomplished during our first five years at Merv: much remains to be done. In addition to the basic recording of cities and monuments and the collection of unpublished data, major contributions have been made in a number of areas. Considerably more is known of the final phases of occupation of Erk and Gyaur Kala, while our work in Shahriyar Ark may suggest a fundamental redating of the late occupation history of that area, with a consequent re-evaluation of historical 'facts' concerning the Mongols. We are assembling for the first time a coin-dated sequence of ceramics and other material culture from the Middle and Late Sasanian periods through the Early Islamic period. The archaeobotanic record, although sketchy in parts, is providing evidence of successful irrigation agriculture through time, while archaeometallurgical studies are illustrating advanced technology at an unexpectedly early date. We hope to continue work at Merv until 2000.

*Note.*   We are deeply grateful for all the support received from our sponsors. The British Academy, the British Museum, and the British Institute of Persian Studies have supported us from the outset. We wish to thank the National Geographic Society, the Max van Berchem Foundation, and the Wenner Gren Foundation for generous grants. We are grateful to the Ancient India and Iran Trust, the Lukonin Foundation, Oxford University (Craven Committee), the Royal Society, the Stein-Arnold Exploration Fund, the Society of Antiquaries of London, the Samuel H. Kress Foundation, and the University of London (Central Research Fund), for their help. Finally, I wish to thank my own institution, University College London, for help of many kinds, financial and logistic, including the use of the Wolfson Archaeological Science Laboratories of the Institute of Archaeology, and support from the Department of Photogrammetry and Surveying, and the Centre for Applied Spatial Analysis. UCL has also helped with travel costs (Dean's Fund, Graduate School).

I was honoured to be selected as a 1996 Laureate by the Rolex Awards for Enterprise on behalf of the International Merv Project. In addition to a valuable cash prize, this has resulted in world-wide publicity and numerous popular articles.

Our work is only made possible by generous loans of advanced survey equipment by Leica UK, who provided equipment in three of our five seasons, by the Department of Photogrammetry and Surveying, UCL, the University of East

London, Optimal Solutions, and Bartington Instruments. Photographic and survey equipment is lent by the Institute of Archaeology. All printing is undertaken by the Photographic Department of the Institute of Archaeology (S. Laidlaw, M. Halliwell, and K. Walton).

The Kung Peh Shan Foundation provided funds to enable the Institute to rent a computer and suite of Intergraph software, dedicated to the analysis of Merv survey and satellite data. Satellite data has been provided free of charge by Professor P. Gentelle of CNRS, Derrold Holcomb of ERDAS, and Professor Toshibumi Sakata of Tokai University Research and Information Centre, to all of whom we are grateful. We also wish to thank the UNESCO Space Archaeology Project, of which Merv forms a part, for arranging stimulating seminars (Herrmann and Barratt 1995).

Magnificent logistical support in 1996 was provided by Bridas Energy. Funds to publish the Visitor's Guide were donated by H. B. M. Ambassador to Turkmenistan, Mr Neil Hook MVO: funds to help with publication expenses by A. J. Laing and the Boeing Corporation.

Funds and equipment are only part of the story: team personnel are a major factor in any expedition's success and the IMP has been extremely fortunate in the dedication and hard work of its members. Direction of the project is shared by Georgina Herrmann and Murad Kurbansakhatov. The Islamic aspects of the project benefit from the advice of Professor J. M. Rogers FBA (1993). The excavation programme is directed by St John Simpson (1992–6, British Museum), who shares the overall direction of the project. The cartographic programme is directed by Glynn Barratt (1992–3, 1995–6). The Gazetteer is undertaken by Andrew Petersen (1994–6). Our skilled liaison officer is Kathy Judelson (1992–6). Many members participate in more than one aspect of the programme—names are only given once. Professor T. Khodjaniasov is an invaluable source on his excavations in Sultan Kala. S. Khamrakuliev (1994–6) represents the Ministry of Culture.

*Topographic programme*: C. Barratt Phillips (1992–3), P. Boyer (1992), S. Campbell (1995), S. Doyle (1996), M. Herrmann (1993), F. Litovchenko (1996, BRIDAS), D. Mackie (1992), E. Moth (1993), I. Peet (1993), D. Holcomb (1995, ERDAS, Atlanta, satellite imagery).

*Archaeologists*: T. Adams (1994–5), A. Berdiev (1992–6, YuTAKE), K. Bonner (1995), I. Cheyne (1995), R. Hobbs (1993), D. Jennings (1992, 1994–5), J. MacGinnis (1994), P. Murray (1995–6), A. Powell (1996), N. Redvers-Higgins (1996), A. Roy (1996), N. Savonidi (1992–3), K. Spandl (1994–5), J. Stedman (1995–6), J. Wright (1996), V. Zavyalov (1992–6, Institute for the History of Material Culture, St Petersburg).

*Numismatics programme*: A. B. Nikitin (1992–5, State Hermitage Museum, St Petersburg), N. Smirnova (1992–6, Pushkin Museum, Moscow), S. D. Loginov (1992–5, YuTAKE), L. Treadwell (1994, Ashmolean Museum, Oxford), R. Hobbs (1993), M. Kotchoubeev (1993).

*Environmental programme*: M. Nesbitt (1993), S. Boardman (1994–6), I. Smith (1996).

*Survey programme*: D. Tucker and B. Stoll-Tucker (1992–4, surface artefact); A. J. Barham and S. Mellalieu (1992–3, geoarchaeological); P. Strange and R. Falkner (1993, geophysical); S. Bullas (1996, magnetometer survey).

*Archaeometallurgical programme*: J. Merkel (1993), A. Feuerbach (1994, 1996).

*House teams*:

*Illustrators*: K. Morton (1992), O. Smirnova (1992), A. Fisher (1993), J. Read (1993), D. Connolly (1994–5), J. Goddard (1996), F. Pewtress (1996).

*Ceramics*: A. D. Grey (1994), G. Puschnigg (1995–6), C. Davies (1996), D. Gilbert (1996).

*Gazetteer and survey of walls*: K. Agajanov (1992, 1996), A. Annaev (1992–6, Merv Archaeological Park), Pierre Brun (1996), F. B. Flood (1992).

*Architects*: R. Dzhapar (1992–6, Merv Archaeological Park), A. Kononenko (1993), H. Mahdi (1992).

# References

Adams, R. McC. (1962), 'Agriculture and Urban Life in Early South-western Iran', *Science* 136, no. 3511, 109–22.

— (1965), *Land behind Baghdad. A History of Settlement on the Diyala Plains* (Chicago).

— (1981), *Heartland of Cities. Surveys of Ancient Settlement and Land Use on the Central Floodplain of the Euphrates* (Chicago).

Allan, J. W. (1979), *Persian Metal Technology, 700–1300 AD* (London).

Asmussen, J. P. (1983), 'Christians in Iran', *Cambridge History of Iran* 3(2), ed. E. Yarshater (Cambridge), 924–48.

Bader, A., Gaibov, V., and Koshelenko, G. (1992), 'Materials for an Archaeological Map of the Merv Oasis: Köne Kishman', *Mesopotamia* 27, 225–50.

Bosworth, C. E. (1968), 'The Political and Dynastic History of the Iranian World (AD 1000–1217)', *Cambridge History of Iran* 5, ed. J. A. Boyle (Cambridge).

Boyle, J. A. (1968), 'Dynastic and Political History of the Il-Khans', *Cambridge History of Iran* 5 (Cambridge).

Bronson, B. (1986), 'The Making and Selling of Wootz, a Crucible steel of India', *Archaeomaterials* 1, 13–51.

Curzon, G. N. (1889: new impression 1967), *Russia in Central Asia in 1889 and the Anglo-Russian Question* (London).

Dandamaev, M. A. (1989), *A Political History of the Achaemenid Empire* (Leiden).

Fiey, J. M. (1973), 'Chrétientés syriaques du Horasan et du Segestan', *Le Muséon* 86, (Louvain), 75–104.

Frye, R. N. (1984), *The History of Ancient Iran* (Munich).

Grenet, F. (1984), *Les Pratiques Funéraires dans l'Asie Centrale sédentaire*, (Paris).

Gubaev, A., Koshelenko, G., and Novikov, S. (1990), 'Archaeological Exploration of the Merv Oasis', *Mesopotamia* 25, 51–60.

Herrmann, G. (1996), 'Merv, "Queen of the World", Uncovering a City on the "Great Silk Road"', *Minerva* 7/6, November/December, 15–22.

— et al. (1993), 'The International Merv Project, Preliminary Report on the First Season (1992)', *Iran* 31, 39–62.

— — (1994), 'The International Merv Project, Preliminary Report on the Second Season (1993)', *Iran* 32, 53–75.

— — (1995), 'The International Merv Project, Preliminary Report on the Third Season (1994)', *Iran* 33, 31–60.

— — (1996), 'The International Merv Project, Preliminary Report on the Fourth Season (1995)', *Iran* 34, 1–22.

— — (1997), 'The International Merv Project, Preliminary Report on the Fifth Season (1996)', *Iran* 35, 1–33.

— — and Barratt, G. (1995), 'The "Silk Road" Cities of Merv and "Space Archaeology"', *Bulletin of the Research Center for Silk Roadology, Silk Roadology I: Space Archaeology* (Nara), 71–84

— — (1966), 'Space Archaeology and the Cities of Merv', *Space Archaeology*, Vol. 1, no. 1, 8–9.

Hiebert, F. T. (1994), *Origins of the Bronze Age Oasis Civilization in Central Asia*, (Cambridge, MA).

— and Lamberg-Karlovsky, C. C. (1992), 'Central Asia and the Indo-Iranian Borderlands', *Iran* 30, 1–15.

Hopkirk, P. (1990), *The Great Game: On Secret Service in High Asia* (Oxford).

Kent, R. G. (1953), *Old Persian* (New Haven).

Koshelenko, G. A. (1966), 'Unikal'naja vaza iz Merva', *Vestnik Drevnii Istorii*, 92–105.

— (1995), 'The Beginnings of Christianity in Merv', *Iranica Antiqua* 30/2, 56–70.

— Bader, A. and Gaibov, V. (1991), 'Materials for an Archaeological Map of Margiana: The Changly Region', *Mesopotamia* 26, 165–86.

Kuhrt, A. (1995), *The Ancient Near East c.3000–330 BC* (London and New York).

Le Strange, Guy (1905), *The Lands of the Eastern Caliphate* (London).

Loginov, S. D. and Nikitin, A. B. (1993a), 'Sasanian coins of the third century from Merv', *Mesopotamia* 28, 225–41.

— — (1993b), 'Sasanian coins of the late 4th–7th centuries from Merv', *Mesopotamia* 28, 271–96.

Luckenbill, D. D. (1926), *Ancient Records of Assyria and Babylonia, I. Historical Records of Assyria from the Earliest Times to Sargon* (Chicago).

Masson, M. E. (1969), *Trudy Instituta istorii, arxeologii I etnografii AN Turkmenskoj SSR* 4, Ashgabat.

Merkel, J. (1989), 'Experience with Refractories in Reconstruction Copper Smelting Experiments Based upon Archaeo-metallurgical Evidence from Timna', *Cross-Craft and Cross-Cultural Interactions in Ceramics, Advances in Ceramics and Civilization* - I, ed. P.E. McGovern (Westerville, OH), 217–34.

— Feuerbach, A. and Griffiths, D. (1995), 'Analytical Investigation of Crucible Steel Production at Merv, Turkmenistan', *IAMS* (Institute for Archaeometallurgical Studies) 19, 12–14.

Miller, R. A. (1959), *Accounts of the Western Nations in the History of the Northern Chou Dynasty* (Berkeley & Los Angeles).

Minorsky, V. (1937), *Hudud al 'Alam: ' The Regions of the World': A Persian Geography 372 AH–982 AD*, trans. and with a preface by V.V. Barthold (London).

O'Donovan, E. (1882), *The Merv Oasis, Travels and Adventures East of the Caspian During the Years 1879–80–81, Including Five Months' Residence Among the Tekkés of Merv* (London).

Pugachenkova, G. (1958), *The Ways of Development of the Architecture of South Turkmenistan in the Ages of Slavery and Feudalism* (Moscow).

— and Usmanova, Z.I. (1995), 'Buddhist monuments in Merv' in Invernizzi, A. (ed.), *In the Land of the Gryphons, Papers on Central Asian Archaeology in Antiquity* (Florence), 51–81.

Pumpelly, R. (1908), *Explorations in Turkestan. Expedition of 1904* 2 (Washington).

Sarianidi, V. (1993), 'Excavations at Southern Gonur', *Iran* 31 (25–37).

Simpson, St J. (1996), 'Digging on Iran's Backdoor', *British Museum Magazine* 24, Spring, 30–2.

— (forthcoming), 'Sasanian Merv' in Invernizzi, A. (ed.), *In the Land of the Gryphons, Papers on Central Asian Archaeology in Antiquity* 2 (Turin).

Usmanova, Z. I. (1992), 'New Material on Ancient Merv', *Iran* 30, 55–63.

Wagner, D. (1993), *Iron and Steel in Ancient China* (Leiden).

Wenke, R. J. (1975/76), 'Imperial Investments and Agricultural Developments in Parthian and Sasanian Khuzestan: 150 BC to AD 640', *Mesopotamia* 10/11, 31–221, figs 3–13.

— (1987), 'Western Iran in the Partho-Sasanian Period: The Imperial Transformation' in Hole, F. (ed.), *The Archaeology of Western Iran, Settlement and Society from Prehistory to the Islamic Conquest* (Washington D.C.), 251–81.

Wiesehöfer, J. (1996), *Ancient Persia* (London).

Willcox, G. H. (1992), 'List of Trees and Shrubs of Economic Importance in Iraq', *Bulletin of Sumerian Agriculture* VI, 101–4.

Wiseman, D. J. (1958), 'The Vassal Treaties of Esarhaddon', *Iraq* 20, 1–100.

Zhukovsky, V. A. (1894), *Antiquities of the Trans-Caspian Region, The Ruins of Old Merv* (St Petersburg).

*Proceedings of the British Academy*, **94**, 45–62

SIR ISRAEL GOLLANCZ MEMORIAL LECTURE

# *Beowulf* in the Twentieth Century

### FRED C. ROBINSON
*Yale University*
*Fellow of the Academy*

WHEN I FIRST CONCEIVED my title '*Beowulf* in the Twentieth Century', my hybristic intention was to touch on all major aspects of the scholarly study of *Beowulf* over the past ninety-six years and to attempt a summary statement of where matters stand today and of where study of the poem needs to go in the next century. The unfeasibility of such a project soon became apparent, however, as did its superfluity in view of Eric Gerald Stanley's recent and wide-ranging assessment of the field in his book *In the Foreground: Beowulf*.[1] I therefore reconceived the word *Beowulf* in my title as referring exclusively to the text of *Beowulf* and thought to review how that text has fared at the hands of editors and textual scholars in the twentieth century; but growing awareness of the dimensions of even this more modest endeavour soon led me to focus my attention on the one edition of the poem that has emerged as our century's standard edition—Friedrich Klaeber's *Beowulf and the Fight at Finnsburg*[2] as it was progressively revised throughout the first half of this century and then widely received as virtually canonical in most of the second half.

Before I take up this subject, however, allow me to return for a moment to that more grandiose prospect of *Beowulf* scholarship that

---

Read at the Academy 27 November 1996. © The British Academy 1997.

[1] Cambridge, 1994.

[2] Boston, 1922; London 1923; 2nd edn., 1928; 3rd edn., 1936, reissued with supplements in 1941 and 1950. My ensuing quotations from *Beowulf* are from this edition unless otherwise indicated. Quotations from other Old English poetry are from G. P. Krapp and E. V. K. Dobbie (eds.), *The Anglo-Saxon Poetic Records*, 6 vols. (New York, 1931–53).

had tempted me when I was first honoured with the invitation to deliver this Sir Israel Gollancz Memorial Lecture. Any mention of the British Academy's distinguished series of Gollancz Lectures will inevitably bring to mind that turning-point in *Beowulf* studies in the twentieth century, the delivery just sixty years ago this week of J. R. R. Tolkien's Gollancz Lecture of 1936, a performance which I daresay will never be equalled, certainly not this afternoon. Thanks in no small part to '*Beowulf*: the Monsters and the Critics'[3] the poem has attained in our century the status it deserves in English literary studies the world over. Approbation will never be universal, of course; superficial acquaintance with the text has left some readers with the impression that *Beowulf* says little more than that

> Terribly unimportant kings
> Grimly gave each other rings.[4]

But informed and thoughtful readers of the poem have, with Tolkien's firm guidance, seen very much more in the poem than that. Although bedeviled at times by curiously dualistic approaches to the poem—oral or written, early or late, pagan or Christian, allegorical or literal—scholarship and criticism in the twentieth century have, on the whole, increased vastly our sense of an established text and of the poem's place within its culture as that culture has been revealed through studies of its archaeological remains and its literature, religion, and art. Crucially important pieces of information like *Beowulf*'s date and place of origin and the identity of its author remain, it is true, elusive, and the resulting frustration has provoked some to form desperate hypotheses founded tenuously on overinterpretation of the small residue of evidence available to us, while others, lapsing from the true way of rationality and patient endeavour altogether, have turned to voodoo numerology for quick answers. Few are the scholars who have turned down these paths, however, and, happily, fewer yet are those who follow them.

Nowhere has twentieth-century *Beowulf* scholarship shown itself more hot for certainties than in the quest for an established text of the poem, and this brings me to my topic today. Our century has seen many editions of the poem, and there are still more in preparation. But few will deny that one edition has dominated and continues to dominate our century—Friedrich Klaeber's *Beowulf and the Fight at Finnsburg*,

---

[3] *The Proceedings of the British Academy*, 22 (1936), pp. 245–95.

[4] John Hollander, 'The Four Ages', 1–2, in *Harp Lake* (New York, 1988), p. 14. The couplet is in the context of a fifty-seven-line poem and should not be taken to represent this learned poet's actual assessment of the contents of *Beowulf*.

which first appeared in 1922 and was steadily revised until the third edition with supplements appeared in 1950, four years before Klaeber's death in Berlin at the age of ninety-one. One American scholar has characterised the almost unquestioned supremacy of this edition as 'the Klaeber consensus'[5]—a tacit understanding among Old English scholars that the main problems presented by the text of *Beowulf* have been solved by Klaeber and the general shape of the poem determined once and for all by his edition, the long shadow of which even falls chillingly on subsequent editions of the poem. Even E. V. K. Dobbie's painstaking edition prepared as part of the standard published corpus of Old English poetry[6] made little progress toward dethroning Klaeber, in part, no doubt, because Klaeber's edition managed to serve as a popular classroom edition while simultaneously providing a summative account of the textual scholarship that preceded it.[7] In any case, it is Klaeber, by and large, that scholars continue to teach in their classrooms (especially in the United States) and to cite in their publications.

One might well ask, however, 'What's wrong with a "Klaeber consensus"?' His edition is the result of half a century's planning, execution, and thoughtful revision by a scholar of great learning and sound judgment. Shouldn't we acknowledge that with this edition we have arrived at a satisfactory text of the poem and turn our attention to other problems? It will occasion little surprise that my answer is 'no'. In what follows I should like to review with you some of the ways in which Klaeber's text has, I think, tended to fix and limit our thinking about the poem's text, sometimes without our being fully aware of it. And occasionally I shall propose alternatives to some of his decisions. My conclusion will be that we need to look beyond the Klaeber consensus.

In his introduction to 'The Text' (p. [cxc]) and in his appendix on 'Textual Criticism' (pp. 274–8) Klaeber spells out many of his editorial

---

[5] Raymond P. Tripp Jr, 'Recent Books on *Beowulf*', *Proceedings of the Illinois Medieval Association,* 2 (1985), 1–26.

[6] E. V. K. Dobbie (ed.), *Beowulf and Judith,* Anglo-Saxon Poetic Records, vol. 4 (New York, 1953).

[7] I am not suggesting, of course, that textual scholarship on the poem ceased with Klaeber's edition. Continuing challenge and debate on problem passages are registered dramatically in, for example, Robert J. Hasenfratz, *Beowulf Scholarship: An Annotated Bibliography, 1979– 1990* (New York and London, 1993), pp. 403–7 and Birte Kelly, 'The Formative Stages of *Beowulf* Textual Scholarship: Part II,' *Anglo-Saxon England,* 12 (1983), 239–75. But new textual studies usually begin by citing Klaeber's reading, and when later scholars quote passages from *Beowulf,* they usually quote from Klaeber's text with his original readings intact despite all the subsequent challenges that may have been made to them.

procedures, but some important matters are left vague or not even
mentioned. He speaks briefly and generally, for example, about what
he calls 'the somewhat uncertain matter of punctuating' (p. [cxc]), and
yet his punctuation has guided generations through the poem, influen-
cing at every turn their assessment of style and meaning. Let me cite
one illustration of how great the difference between editorial punctua-
tors can be. In A. J. Wyatt's 1898 edition of *Beowulf*[8] there are a total
of eleven exclamation points, while R. W. Chambers's edition of 1914[9]
has only ten. Klaeber's edition has fifty-five. Whether Klaeber's hyper-
exclamatory *Beowulf* results from the editor's having been German or
his having been a punctuational hysteric we cannot say with certainty;
but we may be sure that the insertion into the poem of all this stylistic
emphasis has profoundly affected our reading of *Beowulf*, and it has
also influenced later editions.

   In yet another way his edition silently predetermines our perception
of the narrative structure of the poem. Spaced throughout his edition,
signalling (presumably) what he takes to be different stages of the
narrative, are indentations. These typographic devices and their principle of application are nowhere discussed in Klaeber's edition; they
simply appear like some kind of textual *donnée*. Most earlier editions
of the poem—Kemble's, Schaldemose's, Thorpe's, Grundtvig's, Hey-
ne's, and Grein's[10]—did not presume to depart from or add to the
structural divisions supplied in the manuscript itself—the fitt divisions.[11]
It was Ettmüller's edition of 1875—an edition which takes many

---

[8] *Beowulf* (Cambridge, 1898).

[9] *Beowulf with the Finnsburg Fragment* (Cambridge, 1914).

[10] These editions were published, respectively, in 1833, 1847, 1855, 1861, 1863, and 1867.
For bibliographical details see Stanley B. Greenfield and Fred C. Robinson, *A Bibliography
of Publications on Old English Literature to the End of 1972* (Toronto and Buffalo, 1980),
items 1633–8.

[11] Following a fifty-two-line unnumbered section, the poem is segmented into fitts marked
with a capital letter at their beginnings and numbered one through forty-three—with two
anomalies: fitt thirty-nine has no number (but everyone agrees that it begins at line 2821,
where the scribe has a small capital letter at the outset), and between fitts number twenty-
eight and thirty-one there is a long, 181-verse stretch of text, but no fitts are marked.
Klaeber, like those before him, handles this second anomaly in an arbitrary and unconvincing
way. He confidently assigns fitt-number twenty-nine to the beginning of line 2034, where
there is a capital *O* and then declares that the scribe simply lost count or forgot about fitt
thirty. But approximately midway between fitt twenty-eight and the presumed fitt twenty-
nine there is another capital letter—at the beginning of verse 1999. Surely the logical
procedure would be to supply number twenty-nine at the first capital (line 1999) and number
thirty at the second capital (line 2034). The presumed fitt twenty-nine (at line 1999) comes at
the beginning of a *maEelode* formula. Since nine of the other fitt-numbers come at the
beginning of a *maEelode* formula, there is good reason for assuming that this is where fitt
twenty-nine began.

liberties with the text (such as excising 286 long-lines not to the editor's taste) which introduced editorial indentations, fully 156 of them, along with an arbitrary breakdown of the poem into two major sections, Part I and Part II.[12] Thereafter Holder, Harrison, Holthausen, Sedgefield,[13] and others use editorial indentations, and Klaeber adapts them to his purposes in his edition, which has 106 of them. Once introduced, the indentations seem to take on a life of their own. Dobbie in his edition submissively retains eighty-two of Klaeber's 106 indentations, while the two most recent editions of *Beowulf*, appearing in 1994 and 1995,[14] both preserve ninety-two of them. These structural markers, which have no authority whatever from the poet or the manuscript, seem now to have attained virtually canonical status—and without any editorial comment or explanation of their use. They have the effect of artificially recasting the poem into a series of verse groups of varying length somewhat like the *laisse* divisions of the *chansons de geste* and *The Cid*. But *Beowulf* is not *The Cid* and not a *chanson de geste*.

While we are thinking of the way in which scholarship can sometimes build unauthorised interpretation into the text of a poem, let us reflect for a moment on the poem's title, which is of course a modern invention pure and simple, Old English poems being almost always untitled in the surviving manuscripts. The French poet Mallarmé thought that poems should not have titles because titles are too overwhelming.[15] By this he seems to mean that titles anticipate the poem with too much interpretation before we experience the text. However, scholars have never shared such scruples, as the history of poem-naming shows. Epic poems, for example, have been named either for a hero (*The Odyssey, The Aeneid, The Song of Roland*) or for a people or a place (*The Iliad, The Nibelungenlied, The Kalevala*). The earliest titles assigned to *Beowulf* were of the latter type. In 1790 John

---

[12] Ludwig Ettmüller (ed.), *Carmen de Beóvvulfi* (Zurich, 1875). Ettmüller ignores the fitt numbers altogether

[13] See Greenfield and Robinson, *A Bibliography of Publications*, items 1641, 1642, 1648, 1649, for bibliographical details.

[14] George Jack (ed.), *Beowulf: A Student Edition* (Oxford, 1994) and Michael Alexander (ed.), *Beowulf* (Harmondsworth, 1995).

[15] Stéphane Mallarmé, *Réponse à des enquêtes sur l'évolution littéraire* (1891) in Henri Mondor and G. Jean-Aubry (eds.), *Oeuvres complètes* (Paris, 1945), p. 869: '*Nommer* un objet, c'est supprimer les trois-quarts de la jouissance du poëme qui est faite de deviner peu à peu: le suggérer, voilà le rêve.'

Pinkerton calls the poem 'a romance on the wars between Denmark and Sweden',[16] and Thorkelin entitles the *editio princeps De Danorum rebus gestis*, a title which is not altogether inappropriate if we ascribe to the proper noun *Dani* the generalised sense 'Scandinavian' which it can have in Old English and Anglo-Latin.[17] With Sharon Turner, Grundtvig, and Conybeare, however, references to the poem emphasise the role of the hero,[18] and when Kemble gives his 1833 edition the title *Beowulf*, he settles the issue once and for all.[19] I think, however, that we should reflect from time to time on the difference it makes in the way each generation of students approaches the poem that it is told that the poem's name is *Beowulf* rather than, say, *Some Deeds of the Northmen* or *Men and Monsters in Early Times*.

Returning specifically to Klaeber's edition, his glossary has, of course, committed users of his edition to one arbitrary interpretation of the poem, a glossary being nothing more than one person's translation of a text distributed alphabetically through the last one hundred pages of an edition. For a teaching text a glossary is clearly essential. No novice reader of *Beowulf* would want to sift through all forty-six possible translations of the word *ār*, for example, each time that word occurs in the poem. I would also trust the judgment of Klaeber as much as any scholar's in making the decisions of selection and exclusion which constitute glossary-making; yet a recent article has argued rather persuasively that several of Klaeber's definitions appear to have been unduly influenced by late nineteenth-century German preconceptions about the role of women in society.[20] One wonders what other hitherto unsuspected preconceptions may have been at work in his glossary-making and whether these should continue to direct and constrain readers' understanding of the text of *Beowulf* into the twenty-first century.

[16] John Barbour, *The Bruce; or, the History of Robert I, King of Scotland*, ed. John Pinkerton, vol. 1 (London, 1790), p. xii.

[17] Grímur Jónsson Thorkelin (ed.), *De Danorum rebus gestis secul. III et IV. Poëma Danicum dialecto Anglosaxonica* (Copenhagen, 1815). In his preface Thorkelin speaks of three Northern peoples (including the English!) 'qvi vocati uno nomine Dani, omnes ore eodem dialectice solummodo differente loqvebantur'; but elsewhere in the preface he uses *Dani* in the narrow sense, equivalent to *Scyldingas*. See also p. 259, *s.v. Dani*.

[18] Greenfield and Robinson, *A Bibliography of Publications*, items 534, 1636, 278. Turner refers to the text specifically as 'The Poem on Beowulf'.

[19] John Mitchell Kemble (ed.), *The Anglo-Saxon Poems of Beowulf, The Travellers Song, and The Battle of Finnes–burh* (London, 1833).

[20] Josephine Bloomfield, 'Diminished by Kindness: Frederick Klaeber's Rewriting of Wealhtheow,' *JEGP*, 93 (1994), 183–203.

One example of a problematic glossary entry is *āglǣca*, which occurs nineteen times in the poem referring to Grendel or the dragon and three times referring to the heroes Beowulf and Sigemund. (One of the three—in line 1512—is grammatically ambiguous and hence ambiguous in its reference.) Klaeber defines the word primarily as meaning 'wretch, monster, demon, fiend' with ad hoc glosses 'warrior, hero' to accommodate the references to Beowulf and Sigemund. This has led to extensive and (to my mind) misguided theorising by scholars and critics over the deep implications of the poet's using a word with the primary meaning 'monster' to refer to the hero Beowulf. But Klaeber's definition of *āglǣca* is probably overdetermined. Since we do not know the etymology of the word, we are hampered in assessing its meaning.[21] But we do have the noun *āglǣc* of which *āglǣca* seems to be an agent form. *Āglǣc* means 'trouble, vexation', and so *āglǣca* would appear to mean 'troubler, vexer'. That is, it looks like a neutral term meaning one who troubles or vexes another—as a hero might do as easily as a monster. Perhaps 'assailant', 'fierce combatant', or 'antagonist' would be appropriate translations, or we might accept the *Dictionary of Old English* definition: 'awesome opponent, ferocious fighter'[22]—words which are equally applicable to hero and monstrous adversary. *Āglǣca* is very likely a word like *fēond* 'enemy, foe', which is also used of both monsters and heroes. Just as it would be a mistake to gloss *fēond* 'foe' as 'monster' when it refers to Grendel and 'hero' when it refers to Beowulf, so is it mistaken to gloss *āglǣca* as Klaeber has, a mistake which has led to all the tiresome discussion of monstrous heroes and heroic monsters.[23]

Again, Klaeber's glossary-rendering of *fāh* as 'blood-stained' in seven of the word's occurrences conceals the grim figuration in the usage 'adorned (with blood)' and repeatedly leads students to the unfortunate translation 'blood-stained with blood'. He also mischaracterises Ongentheow's wife as elderly by translating *gēomēowle* 'woman of old, woman of a former day' as 'old woman'. A grammatical

---

[21] Sherman M. Kuhn's proposed etymology in 'Old English *āglǣca*—Middle Irish *oclach*,' in Irmengard Rausch and Gerald F. Carr (eds.), *Linguistic Method: Essays in Honor of Herbert Penzl* (The Hague, 1979), pp. 213–30, is well argued and attractive but has not received general acceptance.

[22] Antonette diPaolo Healey *et al.*, *Dictionary of Old English: A* (Toronto, 1994), s.v. *āglǣca*.

[23] I have dealt with this word in more detail in T. Nevalainen and L. Kahlas-Tarkka (eds.), *To explain the Present: Studies . . . in Honour of Matti Rissanen* (Helsinki, 1997).

misconstrual (as I take it to be) has actually misled him into an unnecessary emendation. The poet says of Thryth in lines 1954–6:

> hīold hēahlufan    wið hæleþa brego,
> ealles moncynnes    mīne gefrǣge
> þone [ms. þæs] sēlestan    bī sǣm twēonum . . .

Following his predecessors, Klaeber glosses *brego* in line 1954 as accusative singular. That is, he decides that of the three possible cases that *wið* can govern—accusative, genitive, and dative—*brego* here is accusative. The decision is arbitrary since *brego* is indeclinable in form,[24] and this arbitrary decision then forces Klaeber (following Thorpe's lead) to emend *þæs sēlestan* to *þone sēlestan* in line 1956. It would seem more logical to assume that the indeclinable *brego* is here functioning as a genitive object of *wið* and is in agreement with its appositive *þæs sēlestan* in line 1956. The long-standing emendation of *þæs* to *þone* is unnecessary.

In line 2940 appears the verb *gētan* in the passage reporting Ongentheow's threat to deal severely (once day comes) with the Geatas whom he has cornered in the Battle of Ravenswood. Klaeber, following the dictionaries, glosses *gētan* 'destroy, kill' and then, since the meaning makes poor sense in context, he suggests in a note on p. 223 that a scribe has bungled and text has probably been lost. But *gētan*, a causative weak verb formed on the strong verb *gēotan* 'pour, flow, [bleed]' means 'to cause to bleed, let blood', and the passage in the manuscript makes sense: '[Ongentheow] said that in the morning he would with the swords' blades let the blood of some of them on the gallows tree.' He is vowing to sacrifice his vanquished enemies to the war god. Reports of Germanic people sacrificing soldiers they have captured are found in Strabo (who describes the neighbouring Cimbri hanging their war prisoners and then piercing them and collecting the blood in a bowl), Jordanes, Tacitus, Procopius, and Orosius, while some of the surviving Scandinavian artefacts seem to attest to the practice in that area.[25] Ongentheow's threat would seem to be one of those

---

[24] Both nominative and accusative singular forms occur as *brego, -u, -a*, and in *Resignation*, l. 79 *brego* is clearly dative:

> Gode ic hæbbe
> abolgen, brego moncynnes . . .

Like the similarly indeclinable *fela*, *brego* was originally a *u*-stem, and it is the phonetic instability (virtual interchangeability) of the *u*-stem singular endings *-a, -o, -u* that led to these words becoming indeclinables.

[25] H. R. Ellis Davidson, *Gods and Myths of Northern Europe* (Harmondsworth, 1964), pp. 54–6 lists the relevant sources.

moments in the poem when the poet allows himself to characterise his heathen subjects as frankly heathen—as in his accounts of cremations, ship-burials, and of pagan Danes worshipping idols. These deft allusions to characters' behaviour in the dark, pre-Christian past are an important element in the poet's representation of his subject and should not be obscured by misleading commentary and glossing.

Another crux in *Beowulf* where Klaeber (amongst others) has suspected loss of text unnecessarily is the beginning of the so-called digression on Thryth and Offa, lines 1931–2. The full context (lines 1925–32) according to Klaeber's edition is as follows:

> Bold wæs bētlīc,    bregorōf cyning
> hēa[h on] healle,    Hygd swīðe geong,
> wīs welþungen,    þēah ðe wintra lȳt
> under burhlocan    gebiden hæbbe,
> Hæreþes dohtor;    næs hīo hnāh swā þēah,
> nē tō gnēað gifa    Gēata lēodum,
> māþmgestrēona.    Mōdþrȳðo wæg,
> fremu folces cwēn,    firen' ondrysne . . .

A literal translation of Klaeber's text will reveal the difficulty:

> The building [i.e. Hygelac's hall] was grand, the famous
> king [was] exalted in his hall. Hygd, the daughter of
> Hæreth, [was] very young, wise, and accomplished,
> although she had lived but few years in the castle. Yet
> she was not illiberal or too sparing of gifts, of treasures,
> to the people of the Geatas. Modthryth, an excellent
> queen of her people, carried on terrible crime . . .

and we are told of the awful things that Modthryth did early in her reign before her husband took her in hand. The problems are twofold: first, the impossibly abrupt transition from Hygd to Modthryth, or rather the total absence of any transition, this being the reason editors have assumed loss of text here; secondly, there is the absurdity of introducing the unspeakably vicious Modthryth as *fremu folces cwēn* 'excellent queen of her people'. Besides this there is the uncertainty over Modthryth's name: the analogues give us as much reason to assume that her name is Thryth as Modthryth, and if we take the name as Thryth, then we are left with *mōd* as the common noun meaning 'pride, boldness, arrogance', and we must decide what to do with it.

A quite satisfactory solution to this crux was proposed—or rather implied—in 1941 by Kemp Malone. In an article focused primarily on other matters Malone edits and translates the passage as follows:

Bold wæs betlic, bregorof cyning,
hēa, healle, Hygd swīðe geong,
wis, welþungen. Þēah ðe wintra lȳt
under burhlocan gebiden hæbbe,
Hæreþes dohtor, næs hio hnah swa þeah,
ne to gneað gifa Geata leodum,
maþmgestreona: mod Þryðo wæg,
fremu folces cwen, firen ondrysne.

The building was grand, the king renowned, high, the
hall even so, Hygd very young, wise, virtuous. Though
she may have spent only a few years at court, the
daughter of Hæreth, nevertheless she was not
ungenerous, nor too sparing of gifts and treasure to the
men of the Geatas: the good folk-queen had weighed
the arrogance and terrible wickedness of Thryth.'[26]

By taking *wæg* (line 1931) 'weighed' in the common figurative sense
'considered, weighed the merits of', Malone provides a logical circumstance for the introduction of Thryth: Hygd was well-behaved because
she had given thought to the unbecoming conduct (*mod*) of Thryth and
evidently resolved not to follow her example. By taking *fremu folces
cwen* as referring to Hygd rather than Thryth Malone effectively dis-
poses of the problem Klaeber created in assigning the phrase to Thryth.

In a comment in the final supplement to his edition[27] Klaeber takes
note of Malone's translation, but only to dismiss it. Acknowledging that
Malone's rendering successfully removes 'the harshness of transition
from Hygd to Thryth', Klaeber nonetheless doubts that Old English
*wegan* 'weigh, measure, bear' could be used metaphorically to mean
'consider, weigh the merits of', and Klaeber adds that 'the whole idea'
of a queen considering the negative example of a precursor in fashioning her own behaviour 'strikes one as altogether too modern'.

But the metaphor by which a word meaning 'weigh' comes to mean
'consider, think about, weigh the merits of' is something approaching a
linguistic universal. Latin *ponderare* and *pensare* both meant 'weigh'
originally but come to mean 'think, ponder' as well. The Old English
borrowing from Latin *pensare, pinsian,* shows the same duality, with
the verb (*ā*)*pinsian* usually meaning 'to weigh in the mind, consider'
while the noun form *āpinsung* retains the original, literal sense 'weighing scales, balance'. *Deliberare*, formed on the root *libra* 'scales'

---

[26] 'Hygd', *Modern Language Notes*, 56 (1941), 356–8 at 356.
[27] p. 468.

similarly comes to mean 'deliberate, weigh the pros and cons'. German *wägen* (a direct cognate of Old English *wegan*) and *erwägen* can mean 'ponder, consider', and Old High German *wegan* already evinces such a metaphorical sense,[28] as does Old Norse *vega*.[29] For an example outside of Indo-European we might consider Finnish *punnita*, which is used to mean 'weigh' (as in weighing vegetables, meat, or people) but which also means 'consider, ponder' as in *Tätä täytyy punnita tarkasti* 'we must give careful consideration to this'.[30] And so, acknowledging the prior likelihood of a metaphorical sense in *wæg*, and noting the evidence for it in other early Germanic languages and beyond, we might well accept Malone's suggested reading and substitute it for the troubled, unsatisfactory presentation of the passage in Klaeber's text. Klaeber's objection that Malone's interpretation is 'altogether too modern' is odd. In *Beowulf* lines 898–915 and 1709–24 Hrothgar urges Beowulf to heed and avoid the negative example of Heremod in fashioning his own conduct. What could be more in keeping with the poem's mores than having Hygd heed and avoid the negative example of Thryth in shaping her own conduct? The often noted onomastic play by which Hygd, whose name means 'thought, reflection' rejects the behaviour of Thryth, whose name means 'force, physical power' underscores nicely the contrast the poet is pointing here.

In one surprising instance Klaeber, his precursors, and editors after them have perpetrated and perpetuated a faulty verse by ignoring evidence in the very manuscript itself. Lines 746–8 describe Grendel's attack on Beowulf as follows:

> nam þā mid handa   higeþīhtigne
> rinc on ræste,   ræhte ongēan
> fēond mid folme . . .

---

[28] Rudolf Schützeichel, *Althochdeutsches Wörterbuch* (Tubingen, 3rd edn., 1981), s.v. *wegan* cites in addition to the literal senses *wiegen* and *wägen* the extended senses *abwägen, einschätzen, bestimmen, festsetzen*.

[29] See the metaphorical senses illustrated in Richard Cleasby and Gudbrand Vigfusson, *An Icelandic-English Dictionary*, with a supplement by Sir William Craigie (Oxford, 2nd edn., 1957), s.v. *vega* III. I should mention that long before Klaeber rejected the reading I am recommending here, L. L. Schücking (ed.), *Beowulf* (Paderborn, 1910), who emended l. 1931b to 'mōd þrȳðe ne-wæg', took *cwēn* in line 1932 as a nominative referring to Hygd and interpreted *wæg* as having something like the sense I am suggesting for it here.

[30] Professor Merja Kytö of Uppsala University kindly supplied me with this example. Japanese friends, moreover, tell me that the Japanese word *hakaru* 'weigh, measure' is also used in the extended sense 'judge, consider'.

The failure of sense will be apparent from my transation: 'He [Grendel] seized with his hand the stout-hearted warrior in his resting-place; the opponent with his hand reached towards . . . '. Towards what or whom? The preposition *ongēan* has no object. Instead of *ræhte ongēan* we would expect the half-line to be *him ræhte ongēan* 'he reached towards him'. Compare *him gangað ongean* in the *Paris Psalter* 84, 9:1 and *þē him foran ongēan* in *Beowulf* 2364. A second problem with the half-line *ræhte ongēan* is that, lacking an unaccented syllable before *ræhte*, it is metrically short. For some years before Klaeber's edition, editors tried to remedy the metrical deficiency by emending *ongēan* to *tōgēanes*, but this leaves the problem of the missing object unaddressed, and so Klaeber returned to the manuscript reading *ræhte ongēan*, deciding, apparently, to leave bad enough alone.

But is *ræhte ongēan* the manuscript reading? When we look at the manuscript page, we find that there, just before the word *ræhte* is a space with the remnants of several erased or partially erased letters. The first of these letters is pretty clearly *h*, the very letter we are looking for if we want to read the half-line as *him ræhte ongēan*. Since the actual manuscript reading is *h . . . ræhte ongēan,* I suggest that an editor should supply for his text the metrically perfect line *him ræhte ongēan*, explaining that the *-im* of *him* is a conjecture based on illegible letters in the manuscript.

After I reached this conclusion, I discovered that John C. Pope in *The Rhythm of Beowulf* had anticipated me in calling attention to the remnant of letters before *ræhte*, proposing the reconstruction *him swā ræhte ongēan*.[31] But in the revised edition of his book Pope says, 'Klaeber (Second Supplement, p. 466) objected that *him swā ræhte ongēan* "hardly makes acceptable sense," and of course if this is so, the suggestion must be abandoned'.[32]

What makes Pope's reading problematic is the awkward *swā* in *him swā ræhte ongēan*. Apparently Pope thought it was necessary to have *him swā* because in the manuscript the erasure has room for five or six letters, not just three, and Pope assumed that any reconstruction must fill up the amount of space in the manuscript. But this assumption is fallacious. Whatever the scribe was removing when he erased the letters was presumably wrong. Otherwise, why would he have erased it? Therefore a reconstruction of the intended word need not fill the space

[31] *The Rhythm of Beowulf* (New Haven, 1942), p. 237.
[32] Pope, *Rhythm* (New Haven, rev. edn., 1966), p. xxxi.

left by the erased incorrect letters. Conjecturally, we may reconstruct the process of error. The erasure consists of a partially erased *h* followed by a letter which Zupitza thought had probably been an *a* before it was erased.[33] Now above and to the right of the erasure in the preceding line of the manuscript are the letters *han*, the first syllable of *handa,* which is completed in the next line. Apparently, when the scribe went to write *him,* his eye was caught by the neighbouring word *handa* in his exemplar, and he copied that. Then noticing his mistake, he erased *handa,* all except for the initial *h,* which he intended to complete as *him.* But he neglected to complete the correction. We can with considerable confidence complete his correction for him, being guided by syntax, sense, metre, and by the vestigial evidence in the manuscript. But the first step in making the correction is to free ourselves from the seeming authority of Klaeber both when he initially edited the passage without considering the manuscript evidence and when he summarily rejects Pope's attempt to improve on his reading.[34]

In other places as well Klaeber has given authority and longevity to readings which do not agree with the evidence of the manuscript. His reading *ābrocene* at line 2064 provides a minor example. All that is left intact in the manuscript today is *ocene,* but Thorkelin A and B agree on *orocene.* The word began originally with *b-,* as the alliterative pattern confirms, and evidently the ascender was missing when the transcripts were made and so the bowl of the *b* was mistaken for *o.* There was originally space before the *b-* in the manuscript, and Klaeber, following Kemble, inserts the prefix *ā-,* but this will not fill the space that was there. Better is *gebrocene,* a verb and a past participle which is attested elsewhere in *Beowulf,* as *ābrocen* is not.

A remarkable indifference to the evidence of the manuscript may be seen in Klaeber's emendation *lǣndaga* in line 2341:

> . . . lind wið līge.   Sceolde *lǣn*daga
> æþeling ǣrgōd   ende gebīdan,
> worulde līfes . . .

---

[33] Julius Zupitza (ed.), *Beowulf Reproduced in Facsimile,* Early English Text Society os 245 (Oxford, 2nd edn. 1959), p. 36.

[34] The reading *him rǣhte ongēan* is so completely suitable that, not suprisingly, it has been proposed before as an outright emendation (Moritz Trautmann (ed.), *Das Beowulflied* (Bonn, 1904)) and as a restoration (Michael Swanton (ed.), *Beowulf* (Manchester, 1978)). Neither of these editors discusses the manuscript evidence.

*Sceolde* appears now at the charred edge of the vellum leaf, and the text format indicates that there was room for two or three letters after *sceolde*, and the first of these letters would have to have been *l-* in order to make the alliteration with *lind* and *līge* in the on-verse. The syllable *þend* at the beginning of the next line of text looks like *þ* followed by a present participal ending, and then *daga*. Klaeber ignores all this evidence and, following his precursors, simply substitutes *læn* for *þend* without even trying to suggest how such an error might have come about. Malone,[35] again, had a much better suggestion. He leaves the clear reading *þend* intact and suggests that *lī* is the syllable which originally followed *Sceolde*. This would make a compound *līþenddaga*, and a half-line that is type b alliterating properly with the preceding half-line. Malone's *līþenddaga* has the same morphological make-up as the documented compound *swǣsenddagas* and could mean either 'fleeting days' or 'seafaring days'. Adopting Malone's suggestion, I would translate the resulting passage: 'The atheling good of old must experience the end of his fleeting days, of life in this world'.[36] This seems to me to make good sense, and unlike Klaeber's text, does not defy the evidence of the manuscript.

A final example of Klaeber's doing his editing at too far a remove from the manuscript is his emendation *lǣded* in the passage near the end of the poem which says that it is proper for retainers to praise their king 'when he must be led forth from his body' (lines 3174–5):

> þonne hē forð scile
> of līchaman    (lǣded) weorðan.

Klaeber's word *lǣded* 'led' (supplied where the manuscript is illegible) makes excellent sense, and it has the support of two documentations of the words *of līchaman lǣded wǣre* in the poem *Soul and Body*.[37] The problem is that there is not space in the manuscript for *lǣded*. Probably what the scribe wrote was the contracted form of the past participle *lǣd*, for which there is ample space. We need to recall that this passage

[35] Kemp Malone (ed.), *The Nowell Codex*, Early English Manuscripts in Facsimile, vol. 12 (Copenhagen, 1963), p. 89.

[36] Malone takes *līþend* in the sense 'seafarer', which he describes as 'a good epithet for Beowulf'. I suppose *līþenddaga* could be translated as 'days as a seafarer', but I think 'transient days', 'fleeting days' gives better sense.

[37] At l. 21 both Vercelli and Exeter versions of the poem record the phrase. See also *sawla lædan* in *Christ and Satan* 398 and *gregorius . . . to þam ecan setle þæs heofonlican rices læded wæs* in Thomas Miller (ed.), *The Old English Version of Bede's Ecclesiastical History*, Early English Text Society os 95 (London, 1890), p. 94.

occurs in the closing lines of the manuscript where the scribe was abbreviating extensively so that he could finish the poem without running over onto a new leaf. He would naturally have chosen the brief form of the past participle, even though the poet no doubt intended the full form *lǣded*, which is needed for the metre. Which form to put in the text is a nice question for the editor, but whichever one chooses, some paleographical commentary is necessary.

There are many more places where long-accepted textual decisions by Klaeber need to be rethought, but I forbear to continue with a form of textual criticism which makes tedious listening if pursued excessively. I turn instead for the remainder of my remarks to two brief points about Klaeber's commentary by way of suggesting that here too there is room for fresh consideration of matters long left as they stand in Klaeber.

Early in his career Klaeber published a four-part article called 'Die christlichen Elemente im *Beowulf*'[38] in which he itemised every passage in the poem for which he could recall a biblical analogue. A commendable reaction against the *Deutschtümelei* of many German scholars before him, his article did much to right the balance between Christian and pagan emphases in the reading of *Beowulf* and helped students of the poem to see it as a whole rather than a patchwork.[39] When in later years his edition appeared, the commentary in the edition seems to have become a repository for all the biblical parallels which Klaeber had conceived in his article, and the resulting plethora of biblical analogues has had the effect in some quarters of encouraging scholars to assert an exclusively Christian *Beowulf* (often accompanied by strenuous allegorising) and to deny altogether the secular, pre-Christian element in the poem. Let one example serve for many. After Beowulf's triumph over Grendel, King Hrothgar extols the hero in the following terms (lines 942–6):

> Hwæt, þæt secgan mæg
> efne swā hwylc mægþa swā ðone magan cende
> æfter gumcynnum, gyf hēo gȳt lyfað,
> þæt hyre Ealdmetod ēste wǣre
> bearngebyrdo.

---

[38] *Anglia*, 35 (1911–12), 111–36, 249–70, 453–82; 36 (1912), 169–99.
[39] The context in which Klaeber's article appeared is clarified by Eric Gerald Stanley in *The Search for Anglo-Saxon Paganism* (Cambridge, 1975), pp. 48–50.

Saying that the mother who gave birth to this hero was blessed would seem to be a commonplace of heroic literature, and indeed a variant of it appears later when Hrothgar again praises Beowulf in lines 1700–3. Bugge, moreover, long ago called attention to Scandinavian ballads in which a similar compliment is paid to heroes after they have accomplished daring deeds.[40] But according to the note in Klaeber's edition (which is based on his earlier article), the first of the two passages in *Beowulf* is a biblical reference, an allusion to Luke 11:27, where a woman in a crowd which had been listening to Jesus respond to some accusing critics cries out, 'Blessed is the womb which bore thee and the breasts that nursed thee!' And so with this note Beowulf becomes a Christ figure and Hrothgar a quoter of Scripture.

A compliment of this kind would seem to be so commonplace[41] that it would seem inadvisable for an editor to declare it a 'biblical reminiscence' (while dismissing any other occurrences of the motif in literature as 'of no importance'). Where loose parallels with Scripture do occur in speeches of the pre-Christian characters in the poem, they are, as I have argued elsewhere, probably to be taken not as explicit allusions or reminiscences but as subtle suggestions by the poet that there is 'a kind of natural, universal wisdom that any noble heathen might share with a Christian'[42] and that the poet's introduction of these points of convergence would lend dignity to his heroic heathen characters without denying their heathen status.

My example of this dubious scriptural allusion is by way of suggesting that Klaeber's notes would at times be better if they supplied less. The opposite is also the case. One instance where more information would be helpful is at lines 1855–8, where Hrothgar says to Beowulf:

> Hafast þū gefēred,   þæt þām folcum sceal,
> Gēata lēodum   ond Gār-Denum
> sib gemǣne,   ond sacu restan,
> inwitnīþas,   þē hīe ǣr drugon . . .

---

[40] Cited by Klaeber, p. xvii, n. 3, but dismissed by him as a 'coincidence' which 'need not be considered of importance'.

[41] Many years ago when I was in the American Army, stationed near the Mexican border, I used to visit towns such as Juarez from time to time. There I would see young Mexican men lounging on the street corners who would occasionally whistle at a pretty girl passing by and shout at her, '¡Dichosa la madre que té parió!', that is: 'Lucky the mother who gave birth to you!'. Only years later when I was reading Klaeber's edition of *Beowulf* did I realise that those young men were alluding to Luke 11:27.

[42] Fred C. Robinson, *Beowulf and the Appositive Style* (Knoxville, 1985), p. 33.

> You have brought it about that peace shall prevail
> between the nations of the Geatas and the Danes,
> and the strife and hostilities
> that they formerly experienced shall cease . . .

So far as I am aware no one has explained—or even asked—what the former hostilities between Geatas and Danes were. But in Saxo Grammaticus we are told that the son of the Danish King Skjoldus—the Scyld Scefing of *Beowulf*—waged wars against the folk in Geatland (*Gothia*), killing their leader Suarinus and his brothers.[43] This would seem to be worth mentioning in a note since it may suggest that there was lore about earlier hostilities between Danes and Geatas, and this lore would complete the sense of Hrothgar's otherwise puzzling reference. That a specific altercation between Danes and Geatas may have been in the poet's mind here might also lead us to reconsider Klaeber's emendation in the ensuing line 1862, where he changes *ofer heaþu* 'after the war' to *ofer heafu* 'across the ocean'.[44] Once again, Klaeber's text as well as his commentary seems in need of fresh scrutiny.

It is no disparagement of Friedrich Klaeber's monumental achievement to suggest that now it may be time to move on from the long hegemony of his edition. In the half-century since his last supplement appeared, Old English scholars have placed at our disposal much that would be of inestimable value to an editor of a new and comprehensive edition of *Beowulf*, and the next few years are going to see yet more. Nearly fifty years of sustained textual criticism of the poem have suggested many options which could not have occurred to Klaeber when he was meditating over the poem's textual puzzles. *The Dictionary of Old English* project in Toronto will soon provide (already indeed, provides in part) an informed analysis of the vocabulary of Old English which would have been a godsend to Klaeber, as would the exhaustive

---

[43] C. Knabe, P. Herrmann, J. Olrik, and H. Raeder (eds.), *Saxonis Gesta Danorum*, vol. 1 (Copenhagen, 1931), p. 18: 'Occiso Suetiæ rege Sigtrugo, Gram quæsitum armis imperium possessione firmare cupiens Suarinum Gothiæ præfectum ob affectati regni suspicionem in pugnæ certamen devocatum oppressit fratresque eius septem matrimonio, novem pelice procreatos impari dimicationis genere fraternæ necis ultionem petentes absumpsit'. The name Gram for Scyld's son is probably the common epithet for 'prince' misunderstood or substituted deliberately for the son's actual name. See Paul Hermann, *Die Heldensagen des Saxo Grammaticus: Erläuterungen zu den ersten neuen Büchern der dänischen Geschichte des Saxo Grammaticus,* 2. Teil (Leipzig, 1922), p. 78.

[44] It is true that *heaþu* elsewhere occurs only as a compound element, not as a simplex. But the fact that *heoru* 'sword' occurs only as a compound element everywhere except at l. 1285, where it is a simplex, does not prevent Klaeber and other editors from acknowledging the simplex in l. 1285 and printing it in the text.

microfiche concordance on which the Toronto dictionary is founded. Jane Roberts and Christian Kay's *Thesaurus of Old English*[45] would give a modern editor an enormous advantage over Klaeber. The manuscript (study of which seems to have been a weak point in Klaeber's editorial methodology) has been analysed closely with technology not even envisioned in Klaeber's day, and British Museum Publications together with the University of Michigan Press will make available in summer 1997 Kevin Kiernan's compact disk version of the *Beowulf* manuscript which will make it possible to read text behind the paper frames of the charred pages with the benefit of digitised images read over fibre-optic light. This should provide the clearest possible view of all that survives in the manuscript, while James R. Hall's exhaustive analysis and collation of the early transcripts and early collations of the manuscript by scholars like Thorkelin, Conybeare, Grundtvig, Kemble, Madden, and Thorpe will assure that we shall not lose one jot of the surviving testimony to the manuscript's contents before it reached its present state of arrested decay. Bruce Mitchell's magisterial *Old English Syntax*[46] will be as valuable to a new editor of *Beowulf* as it is to other Old English scholars, and his particular guidance on the punctuation of Old English poetry will provide a remedy for one aspect of Klaeber's edition which has always been a source of dissatisfaction. I am even optimistic enough to think that out of the welter of uneven literary criticism of *Beowulf* since 1950 we have acquired some wisdom in judging matters of fact and interpretation which Klaeber did not have. It is in the light of these end-of-the-century realities that I have offered my points today suggesting that Klaeber's text is in need of supersession and that insofar as there is a 'Klaeber consensus' constraining our study and textual criticism of the poem, this is a matter for some concern.

*Beowulf* in the twentieth century has indeed been Klaeber's *Beowulf,* and his text has served our century well. My purpose in these remarks has been to suggest that Klaeber should *not* be *Beowulf* in the twenty-first century as well.

---

[45] King's College London Medieval Studies 9 (London, 1995), 2 vols.
[46] Oxford, 1985, 2 vols.

Proceedings of the British Academy, **94**, 63–84

ITALIAN LECTURE

# Michelangelo and his First Biographers

## MICHAEL HIRST
*Courtauld Institute of Art*
*Fellow of the Academy*

## I

I HAVE CHOSEN for my lecture this afternoon the two lives of Michelangelo which appeared in his lifetime, that of Giorgio Vasari which concluded his *Vite* of 1550, and that which appeared three years later by Ascanio Condivi. Despite the very different circumstances of their origins, the two lives are inseparably related. For without the appearance of Vasari's *Life*, the only one of a living and still active artist included in his book, there would have been no *Life* by Condivi. Only Michelangelo's own dissatisfaction with Vasari's account could have overcome his inveterate reticence and prompted him to promote a corrective.

There are reasons for suggesting that Michelangelo had not been very well informed of Vasari's plans prior to publication, but he soon received his copy of the *Vite*, for he was one of twelve men honoured with complimentary copies. His own seems to have arrived in Rome at a

*For Nicolai Rubinstein.*
Read at the Academy 13 December 1995. © The British Academy 1997.
[The following abbreviations will be used: *Carteggio* = *Il Carteggio di Michelangelo*, eds. P. Barocchi and R. Ristori, vols i–v (Florence, 1965–1983); Frey i = G. Vasari, *Der literarische Nachlass*, ed. K. Frey, i (Munich, 1923); Vasari, *Vite* = G. Vasari, *Le Vite de' più eccellenti pittori scultori e architettori nelle redazioni del 1550 e 1568*, eds. R. Bettarini and P. Barocchi, 6 vols. (Florence 1966–87); *La Vita* 1962 = G. Vasari, *La Vita di Michelangelo nelle redazioni del 1550 e del 1568*, ed. P. Barocchi, 5 vols. (Milan and Naples, 1962); Condivi, *Vita* = Ascanio Condivi, *Vita di Michelagnolo Buonarroti Roma 1553 con postille contemporanee*, ed. G. Nencioni, with preface by M. Hirst and note by C. Elam (Florence, forthcoming).]

moment in the spring of 1550 close to his seventy-fifth birthday. He responded with a sonnet which Vasari would proudly publish in his second edition of 1568; there was probably a brief accompanying note but this has not survived.[1] A few months later, in August, he wrote to Vasari about the plans of the recently elected Pope Julius III for a Del Monte family chapel in Rome. He expresses no specific opinion on the extraordinary achievement of the *Lives*, referring to the book only in a play of words that his biographer was a reviver of the dead and a prolonger of the lives of the living. The tone is one of scarcely concealed irony.[2]

If we are to believe Vasari, his close relations with the man whom he, like others, calls divine, began a number of years earlier, on an important stay of Vasari's in Rome from 1542 to 1543. He states this in his autobiographical *coda* to the 1568 second edition. At that time, he tells us, Michelangelo showed him great friendship and encouraged Vasari to concentrate on his career as an architect.[3] But everything we learn about the intimacy of the two artists from the *Vite* of 1568, published four years after Michelangelo had died, comes from Vasari himself. At the time in question, Vasari had not carried out any architecture. And everything that Vasari writes in his later account about his relations with Michelangelo should be treated with great caution, although, regrettably, this caution is still all too rarely exercised about Vasari even now.[4] It is my conviction that the episodes we read about in the second edition are, for the most part, dated earlier than

---

[1] For the text of the sonnet, see Michelangiolo Buonarroti, *Rime*, ed. E. N. Girardi (Bari, 1960), p. 132.

[2] See *Carteggio*, iv, pp. 346–7, and for an assessment of the context Frey i, pp. 290–4. Vasari included a part of the letter in his 1568 *Life* of the artist. Michelangelo's reference to his biographer as 'risuscitatore d'uomini morti' could be read as a covert allusion to Vasari's description of him as a raiser of the dead in successfully rehabilitating the block for the marble *David* in the 1550 text: 'E certo fu miracolo quello di Michele Angelo, far risuscitare uno ch'era tenuto per morto': Vasari, *Vite*, vi, p. 20.

[3] 'Nel medesimo tempo, facendo io gran servitù a Michelangnolo Buonarroti e pigliando da lui parere in tutte le cose mie, egli mi pose per sua bontà molto più affezione: e fu cagione il suo consigliarmi a ciò, per avere veduto alcuni disegni miei, che io mi diedi di nuovo e con miglior modo allo studio delle cose d'architettura . . .': Vasari, *Vite*, vi, p. 383. Vasari's first building project of any consequence was for the future Pope Julius III in 1548; see Frey i, p. 229.

[4] Vasari's account was accepted at face value by W. Kallab, *Vasaristudien* (Vienna, 1908), p. 72, and is endorsed in P. Rubin, *Giorgio Vasari, Art and History* (New Haven and London, 1995), p. 11, despite an appropriate note of caution struck by Karl Frey: Frey i, p. 123. That Michelangelo could have offered this advice in Rome around 1550 is far more plausible.

they should be. It is, for example, telling that there is no surviving exchange of letters between the two in the 1540s.

Vasari's first securely established meeting with Michelangelo took place early in 1547, just three years before the appearance of his book. The circumstances of the encounter were not auspicious. Vasari had been asked by Benedetto Varchi—many years later the author of Michelangelo's funeral oration—to sound out the great man on the issue of the *paragone*, the rival claims of painting and sculpture. The outcome was not encouraging. Vasari reported back to Varchi that Michelangelo had little to say to him on this still fashionable topic; he had remarked that painting and sculpture shared a common end and that both were very difficult: 'dificilmente operato da uno et dall'altro'. Vasari writes that he could not get another word out of him: 'né altro potrei tra'ne da esso'. The wording of this letter does not suggest a long-established intimacy with Michelangelo.[5]

The two men met frequently from 1550; from, that is, the period after the appearance of the book, for Michelangelo was consultant on the projects which Vasari would now undertake for Pope Julius III. And it is to this time that Vasari assigns (in 1568) his conversations with Michelangelo on artistic issues planned for a never-published dialogue.

This dialogue raises a number of problems best left on one side today. Vasari's dependability on the issue has been much impugned. It is, however, worth pointing out that Vasari, in stating that the conversations took place as the two men rode round the Seven Churches in Rome in the Holy Year of 1550, was employing a literary *topos* already used several years earlier for the circumstances of discussions on art by a man who had taught Vasari for a period in his youth.[6]

---

[5] For the different texts and an extensive commentary, see Frey i, pp. 185–93.

[6] Vasari writes in the second edition *Life of Michelangelo*: 'Era in quel tempo (1550) ogni giorno il Vasari con Michelagnolo; dove una mattina il Papa (Julius III) dispensò per amorevolezza ambidue, che facendo le sette chiese a cavallo, ch'era l'anno santo, ricevissino il perdono a doppio; dove nel farle ebbono fra l'una e l'altra chiesa molti utili e begli ragionamenti dell'arte et industriosi, che'l Vasari ne distese un dialogo, che a migliore occasioni si manderà fuori con altre cose attenente all'arte': Vasari, *Vite*, vi, p. 83. Opinion has been divided over the implications of this passage; there is a useful overview in *La Vita* 1962, iv, p. 1567. Some scholars have accepted the reality of Vasari's intention (no trace of any text has been found), whilst others have argued for a different conclusion, based on a letter of Vasari to Duke Cosimo of April 1560: Frey i, pp. 559–60. In this letter, Vasari writes of his repeated recent meetings with Michelangelo and of their exchanges over the design of the projected new bridge (the 'ponte Santa Trinita') in Florence, and then refers to 'molti ragionamenti fatti delle cose dell'arte per poter finire quel Dialogo che gia Vi lessi, ragionando lui et io insieme.' Frey, followed by others, believed that this was not a 'dialogo

In the early 1550s, Vasari may well have seized the chance to deepen his knowledge of Michelangelo's life. But the situation was never an easy one, for he would become deeply implicated in Duke Cosimo's efforts to entice Michelangelo to return to his native Florence, perhaps the most eagerly sought objective of his artistic programme. The attempt did not succeed but the issues involved cast a shadow over Vasari's relations with the old man and the biographer's mortification emerges in the 1568 *Lives* (when Michelangelo was dead), above all in those laments over Michelangelo's failure to exchange, in Paola Barocchi's words, the purgatory of the Fabbrica of St Peter's for the Medicean paradise which awaited him.[7] Vasari was also not alone in encountering problems in his attempts to discover how the artist's abandoned Florentine projects should be completed. The San Lorenzo library still lacked its staircase. One or two of Michelangelo's own surviving letters about these issues survive and are at best evasive, at worst obfuscatory.[8]

Put briefly, I think we may conclude that, although Vasari's 1550 *Life of Michelangelo* is the only one of an active artist included in his book, the fact did not play an important part in its composition. Although his subject had been, so to speak, a live target, Vasari had not been in range. There remained further problems for the biographer

---

michelangiolesco' but the text of one of Vasari's *Ragionamenti*. But this is not very credible. Could the old artist and Vasari have had long discussions about the latter's paintings in Palazzo Vecchio which Michelangelo had never seen? Against Vasari's dependability about a dialogue, one can cite the point I have raised in my text: his adoption of the *topos* of discussions about art whilst engaged in a 'cavalcata'. Pierio Valeriano had only recently employed the same device in his introduction to Book XXVII of his *Hieroglylphica*; here too, the interlocutors visit the Seven Churches on horseback: '. . . A questi giorni santi ultimamente passati . . . essendo venuto per il perdono con esso voi a visitare le sette chiese . . .'. The group proceed to discuss the study of sculpture. See Pierio Valeriano, *I ieroglifici overo Comentarii delle occulte significationi de gl'Egittij e altre nazioni* (Venice, 1625), pp. 58–9; first Latin edition Basle, 1556. Without further evidence, the problem of the alleged dialogue cannot be resolved and Paola Barocchi was justified in leaving the issue open. The fact remains that Vasari does not tell us that the projected dialogue with Michelangelo concerned his own work; if it had, his reticence is uncharacteristic.

[7] See *La Vita* 1962, p. xxx, where a letter of Michelangelo's is cited referring to Rome as the 'avara Babillonia', echoing Petrarch.

[8] Vasari eventually took on the task, earlier assumed by Niccolò Tribolo, following the latter's death in 1550. For Michelangelo's vagueness, see his letter to his nephew Leonardo of 28 September 1555, or that of the same moment to Vasari in which he writes: 'Mi ritorna bene nella mente come un sognio una certa iscala, ma non credo che sia a punto quella che io pensai allora, perché mi torna cosa ghoffa . . .': *Carteggio*, v, pp. 45–8.

engendered by Michelangelo's very longevity. Some of the benefits which might have been expected to accrue from dealing with a living man were absent because, for the artist's distant youth, those familiar with events were long since dead. For example, only one of Vasari's close Florentine friends involved in the preparation of the *Lives* was even alive when Michelangelo began the marble *David* in 1501.[9] It is to this aspect of Vasari's situation, lack of personal knowledge, that Condivi most damagingly refers in his subsequent account (although Vasari is never specifically named). And it was this charge of Condivi's which led, in turn, to the introduction of autobiographical accretions in the revised Vasari *Life* of 1568, a number of which are complete fictions.[10] Indeed, it may have been the very nature of Condivi's book, devoted exclusively to Michelangelo, that led Vasari to take the remarkable step of issuing his enormously expanded 1568 *Vita* as a separate publication, with the same pagination but with its own dedication, something which has been claimed as the first offprint in the history of printing.[11]

Vasari seems to have completed the manuscript of the Michelangelo *Vita* in the middle of 1547. He succeeded in reporting the artist's appointment as head of the Fabbrica of St Peter's but missed the correct

[9] This was Pierfrancesco Giambullari, who was born in 1495. Another significant collaborator, Cosimo Bartoli, was born as late as 1503. However, it is worth noting that his father, Matteo Bartoli, had known Michelangelo and in 1518 had sought to find him a *cantiere* where he could construct a workshop. See the artist's letter to Cardinal Giulio de' Medici, undated but of the autumn: *Carteggio* ii, p. 109. This working space is for 'questa opera, cioè le fighure di marmo e di bronzo . . .'. E. H. Ramsden, in *The Letters of Michelangelo* (London, 1963), i, pp. 278–9, redated the letter to 1521 and identified the project with the New Sacristy at San Lorenzo. But no bronze statues were envisaged for the chapel, whereas they were explicitly planned in the 1518 contract for the church façade; see G. Milanesi, *Le Lettere di Michelangelo Buonarroti . . .* (Florence, 1875), p. 671. Given Matteo Bartoli's known competence as a bronze founder, Michelangelo could well have seen him as a future collaborator.

[10] Vasari's most transparent attempt to rebut Condivi's strictures is his claim in the 1568 *Vita* that much of his 1550 information had come from Michelangelo himself: '. . . dove molti ricordi di cose aveva avuto dalla voce sua il Vasari . . .': Vasari, *Vite*, vi, p. 83. The autobiography is, of course, even more self-assertive. But Kallab, *Vasaristudien*, pp. 24–5, whilst discrediting Vasari's claim to have studied with the master, did not appreciate how large a part Condivi's book had played in the adjustments of 1568.

[11] I owe this suggestion to an unidentified participant in a seminar held at the Villa Spellman, Florence, in April 1995. For the offprint, see U. Procacci, in *Giorgio Vasari. Principi, letterati e artisti nelle carte di Giorgio Vasari . . . , Pittura vasariana dal 1532 al 1554 . . .* , exhibition Arezzo 1981 (Florence, 1981), pp. 284–5. For the claim that it is the first of its kind, see B. H. Breslauer in *The Book Collector*, vi (1957), p. 403.

subject of Michelangelo's second mural in the Pauline Chapel (preparations for which were already under way in 1546). As is well known, both Paolo Giovio and Annibale Caro were reading parts of the manuscript of the *Vite* before the end of 1547. Whilst encouraging, neither could help very substantially with information about Michelangelo, least of all about his early years. Giovio had written a very brief account of the artist many years earlier, a manuscript not published until the eighteenth century. It comprised only thirty printed lines and, despite the friendship, it is clear that Vasari had not read it.[12] Caro, about whom I will have more to say later, a man of exceptional literary culture, was not an historian. From his letter to Vasari he seems to have been chiefly concerned with style; he exhorts Vasari (without total success) to write simply.[13]

Vasari's errors and omissions in his *Life of Michelangelo* of 1550 are very conspicuous. And while one school of modern art history would consider censure of them anachronistic, that cannot have been the view of the subject himself. Indeed, both the existence of Condivi's book and the contents of its text demonstrate that Michelangelo read his birthday present (or at least that part pertaining to himself) rather carefully. The mistakes are, not surprisingly, especially grave over the early years. Vasari states that Michelangelo had been born in Florence. More seriously, he was completely unaware of the young man's stay in Bologna in 1494–5 after the expulsion of the Medici. It is an episode to which, surely at the artist's instance, Condivi devotes special attention in his own book.[14] Vasari seems to have had little chance to study the very early sculpture in Florence; nowhere

---

[12] For the most accessible text, see *Scritti d'Arte del Cinquecento*, i, ed. P. Barocchi (Milan and Naples, 1971), pp. 10–12. Both Karl Frey and W. Kallab noted that Giovio's text was unknown to Vasari. It is, for example, telling that whilst Giovio refers to Cardinal Riario's part in the episode of the sleeping *Cupid*, Vasari makes no reference to him in his 1550 text.

[13] For this much-discussed letter of 15 December 1547, see Frey i, pp. 209–10 and Frey's own comments, pp. 210–13. Caro's most familiar remark is that the written word should conform to the spoken one: 'In un'opera simile vorrei la scrittura apunto come il parlare.'

[14] Vasari's ignorance of Michelangelo's statues on the Arca of San Domenico is noteworthy, the more so as he elsewhere states that, prior to starting work in San Michele in Bosco in mid-summer 1539, he was shown all the most famous paintings in Bologna; see Vasari, *Vite*, vi, p. 378. The *lacuna* could be construed as evidence that Vasari was as yet not collecting material for a future book, although the energy he devoted to familiarising himself with paintings in Bolognese private houses might point to a contrary conclusion. Vasari himself refers to the Arca in 1550, but limits himself to noting the small narrative reliefs of Alfonso Lombardo; there is no word about the sculpture of Niccolò dell'Arca either.

mentioned is so conspicuous an example of Michelangelo's early skills as *The Battle of the Centaurs*, which may have been accessible.[15] But the text contains misunderstanding of a much more serious kind. Michelangelo's notorious flight from the court of Pope Julius II in 1506, the prelude to the tragedy of the papal tomb, is placed by Vasari midway through work on the Sistine Chapel ceiling, a consequence of a quarrel between patron and artist over a visit of the pope to the chapel. Thus, its part in the story of the Della Rovere monument is altogether obscured. We find an extraordinary and vivid recital of the episode, culminating in the artist's flight to Poggibonsi, in Condivi's book of three years later.[16] But deficiencies extend to many periods of the *Life*: witness the statement that Michelangelo had returned to Florence only after the siege of the city had ended in 1530—a confusion which might have been construed as sparing the artist a highly embarrassing episode but which Condivi's subsequent account would, in a fashion, amend. Almost every omission and error would be made good in the amplified *Life* of 1568 in a feat of astonishingly massive revision.[17]

We should, however, note that Vasari did not wish, or did not have the time, to change the most lengthy passages of what we may call stylistic appreciation between his two editions, even in a rather sensitive context like his long evaluation of the *Last Judgement*, a work which had acquired an ever greater notoriety in the intervening period. Some of the most familiar passages, like that on Michelangelo's

---

[15] Vasari correctly assigns Michelangelo's work on the never-completed *St Matthew* to the early Florentine years of the sixteenth century: Vasari, *Vite*, vi, pp. 21–2. His misunderstanding revealed elsewhere about the Florentine Cathedral *Apostles* commission suggests that the information in the Michelangelo *Vita* came from someone else and was never reconciled with the misinformation we are given in the *Life* of Andrea Ferrucci: *Vite*, iv, p. 257. Here he dates the *Apostles* commission to the end of the second decade of the sixteenth century (after Cardinal Giulio de' Medici had assumed power in Florence) and states that Benedetto da Maiano (d. 1497), the young Jacopo Sansovino, Michelangelo, Baccio Bandinelli, and Ferrucci were each assigned an *Apostle* at the same time, a confusion made worse in the second edition.

[16] For Vasari's confusion, see *Vite*, vi, pp. 35–6. He corrected himself, in the light of Condivi, in the 1568 Michelangelo *Vita*. But he had recounted a similar story in the 1550 *Life of Raphael* and this he completely failed to change in the second edition. I have relegated to a brief appendix observations on Vasari's statement that Pope Julius II had also wanted the artist to paint the walls of the Sistine Chapel.

[17] Although it is repeatedly stressed, reasonably enough, that Vasari's decision to end his 1550 *Vite* with Michelangelo's *Life* emphasises its unique and privileged place in his history, it is worth noting that, in terms of length, the *Vita* is not much longer than that of Raphael.

architectural licence in the New Sacristy, could scarcely have been
altered for the better, but here we confront the problem of how far a
passage such as this is, in effect, the work of a collaborator.[18] Such
extended and ambitious evocations of Michelangelo's achievements
were not Condivi's chief concern; they were not, to put it differently,
the issues foremost in Michelangelo's mind when he promoted the
publication of a very different book in 1553.


## II


Whilst we know a great deal about Vasari, about Condivi we are very
poorly informed. Had he not written the book that here concerns us, he
would—at best—have warranted a footnote as a frequenter of Michelangelo's circle and workshop and as the recipient of an exceptional
present from the master, a cartoon which Condivi endeavoured to
translate into a painting on panel. Both cartoon and painting survive,
the former in the British Museum, the latter in the Casa Buonarroti.[19]
Probably born in 1524 or 1525, Ascanio Condivi came from Ripatransone in the Marches. The circumstances in which he moved to Rome are
still frustratingly obscure, but it is probable that he was there by 1546 at
the latest. Ripatransone was in the papal states and Condivi's later
career shows that he occasionally visited the city on business relating
to his birthplace.[20] In his book, he states that Cardinal Niccolò Ridolfi
was his Roman patron and it was almost certainly in the circle of Ridolfi
that he met the subject of the future book. Prominent in the household
was Donato Giannotti, both confidant of the cardinal and a good friend
of Michelangelo's. Michelangelo's familiarity with Giannotti may have
extended back to 1520 in Florence and was almost certainly renewed in

[18] The vocabulary employed, the actual word order (for example the sequence 'misura,
ordine e regola'), and the conceptual framework, suggest that this canonical piece was
written not by Vasari himself but by Cosimo Bartoli; but the proposal cannot be elaborated
on here.

[19] For the cartoon, see J. Wilde, *Italian Drawings in the Department of Prints and Drawings
in the British Museum, Michelangelo and his Studio* (London, 1953), pp. 114–6. Condivi's
painting, now in bad condition and heavily repainted, is reproduced in C. de Tolnay,
*Michelangelo, The Final Period* (Princeton, 1960), pl. 333. It came late into the Casa
Buonarroti collection and its early history remains completely obscure.

[20] The most useful biographical study of Condivi remains C. Grigioni, *Ascanio Condivi, la
vita e le opere* (Ascoli Piceno, 1908). Much of the material in a more recent book, G.
Settimo's *Ascanio Condivi, biografo di Michelangelo* (Ascoli Piceno, 1975), derives from
the earlier work.

the brief period of the last Florentine republic.[21] Giannotti played a role in the drawing up of the final contract for the tomb of Julius II in 1542. More significantly, he was the author of two dialogues concerning Dante's journey through Hell, in both of which Michelangelo is cast as one of the interlocutors.[22] Unlike the artist, but like his protector Ridolfi, Giannotti was a declared rebel, one of that group of Florentine *fuorusciti* who enjoyed the passive protection of Pope Paul III and the friendship of Michelangelo.[23]

Condivi's stay in Rome did not long outlast the appearance of the *Life* in the late summer of 1553; two years later he was back in the Marches.[24] Nevertheless, he could be described as upwardly mobile; in 1555 he married no less than the niece of the celebrated Annibale Caro, who had offered stylistic advice to Giorgio Vasari in 1547. The re-emergence of Caro's name here is significant. For, once one has held in one's hand the surviving letters of Condivi, the conclusion is inescapable that he was incapable of writing the text of the 1553 *Life* as we now read it in print. The contrast between his epistolary skills and the book

---

[21] A biography of Giannotti does not exist. For a useful profile, see R. von Albertini, *Firenze dalla repubblica al principato* (Turin, 1970), pp. 145–166 (1st ed., *Das florentinische Staatsbewusstsein im Übergang von der Republik zum Prinzipat* (Bern, 1955)). There are several important contributions by R. Ridolfi; most useful here is his 'Sommario della vita di Donato Giannotti' in *Opuscoli di storia letteraria e di erudizione* (Florence, 1942), pp. 55–164. There is further important material in R. Starn, *Donato Giannotti and his Epistolae* (Geneva, 1968).

[22] The best available edition of the dialogues (first published only in 1859) is *Dialogi di Donato Giannotti*, ed. Redig de Campos (Florence, 1939).

[23] For the group, still awaiting a detailed study, see Ridolfi's *Opuscoli*, pp. 132 *et seq.* Giannotti had served as secretary to the Dieci in the last republic, was subsequently exiled and moved to Rome and Ridolfi's circle in 1539. Absent from Rome from 1543 to 1545, he remained close to Michelangelo. It is likely that he and Luigi del Riccio planned an edition of the artist's poetry which fell through after the latter's death in 1546. It was Luigi who wrote the letter to Roberto Strozzi in July 1544, reporting the artist's offer to make at his own expense an equestrian bronze statue of Francis I for the Piazza della Signoria if the French king would liberate Florence from Medicean rule: *Carteggio*, iv, pp. 183–4).

[24] It has been claimed that Condivi was elected to the Accademia Fiorentina in September 1565; D. Summers, *Michelangelo and the Language of Art* (Princeton, 1981), pp. 24 and 465, n. 48. The new member was called 'M. Aschanio da Ripa' (Florence, Biblioteca Marucelliana, Codice B III 54, 15[r]). However, this same Aschanio played a very active role as member in 1566 and 1567 (see 16[v], 22[v], 23[r]) when, as shown by Grigioni, pp. 24 *et seq.* and 123 *et seq.*, Condivi was busy as property purchaser, painter, and local administrator in Ripatransone. It would seem that the identification must be abandoned.

was already clear to Gaetano Milanesi in the nineteenth century.[25] More recently, Johannes Wilde adduced a number of reasons why Caro is likely to have acted as reviser—or even 'ghost writer'. Indeed, in a neglected aside, he went so far as to call Condivi 'the ostensible author of the book'.[26] He listed a number of points indicating Caro's involvement. Caro is described as having recently become a friend of the artist, although no independent record of this friendship exists. His name is included alongside those of Bembo, Sannazaro, and Vittoria Colonna as one of the best poets to have taken Petrarch as a model. Condivi would marry Caro's niece two years after the appearance of the book. The simplicity of the style of the *Vita* also conforms closely to Caro's own literary prescription given to Vasari in 1547, referred to above. Further, a letter of Caro's of August 1553, to which I will return, shows his familiarity with Condivi's text.[27] Other points could be added. It is important to recall that both Caro and Condivi came from the same area of Italy, the Marche.[28] And the inclusion of the name of Giovanni Guidiccioni among the poets who follow Petrarch, which seems to have puzzled Wilde, goes even further to strengthen the case, for Guidiccioni had been one of Caro's most esteemed early patrons.[29]

A close comparison of the text of the *Vita* with comparable texts of Caro has not yet been undertaken, although the appearance of a critical edition of Condivi's book now allows a detailed philological analysis.[30]

[25] G. Milanesi, 'Alcune lettere di Ascanio Condivi e di altri a messer Lorenzo Ridolfi', *Il Buonarroti*, 2nd ser., III (1868), pp. 206–13. They were reprinted on pp. 73–5 of Grigioni's book (see above n. 20). All four were written in the summer and early autumn of 1551. One is now missing, but another, not mentioned by Milanesi, of 4 July 1551, exists: the group is in the Archivio di Stato, Florence, Acquisti e Doni, 67, Insert 1). Milanesi, on the evidence of their 'grande rozzezza di stile', concluded that the Michelangelo *Vita* had been worked over by a collaborator, and although he did not name Caro, subsequent editors of the *Life* assumed that this was in his mind. A letter of Condivi's to Michelangelo from the Marche, similarly ill-written, also survives (*Carteggio*, v, p. 61; there dated May 1556 with a query).

[26] J. Wilde, *Michelangelo, Six Lectures* (Oxford, 1978), p. 8.

[27] This letter of Caro's, of 20 August 1553, for which see A. Caro, *Lettere Familiari*, ed. A. Greco, ii (Florence, 1959), pp. 147–8, explains that he has delayed writing because he was awaiting the appearance of the *Vita*. Wilde inferred from the letter that Caro knew its contents prior to publication, but a doubt must remain, for Condivi's *Life* appeared in two slightly different issues, the later one incorporating significant additions. Both issues have the same title-page with the date 16 July 1553.

[28] Condivi's marriage to Porzia Caro actually took place in the Marche, at Civitanova, from where the Caro family originated.

[29] Caro had been briefly in Guidiccioni's service from 1539 to 1540; for his grief at his death, see *Lettere Familiari*, i (1957), pp. 240–247. Caro had actually served as 'revisore' of his patron's *Canzoniere* at the author's wish.

[30] See Condivi, *Vita*.

In fact, only one prose text can usefully serve, Caro's translation of Longo Sofista's *Amori pastorali di Dafni e di Cloe*, a narrative where the parallels of construction and vocabulary are very striking. However, it is worth adding here that one highly idiosyncratic usage in the book, the adoption of 'corna delle lunette' in the long description of the Sistine ceiling, finds a remarkable parallel in Caro's well-known letter to Taddeo Zuccaro of 1562 concerning the projected murals at Caprarola. When he turns to the lunettes, Caro uses 'corni' and 'corno' repeatedly.[31]

That it was Condivi who accumulated the material for the *Vita* is not in doubt; that it was Annibale Caro who fashioned or refashioned its presentation to the reading public is, if not proven, extremely probable. We can note that Condivi, in the title of the book, '*Vita . . . raccolta per Ascanio Condivi*', is described as the collector or assembler, and while the choice of word is not decisive, it is nevertheless noteworthy. His claim to familiarity, his 'stretta dimestichezza', with the subject of the book, strongly pressed in the dedication to the reader, is beyond doubt, as is the claim to have collected his material with great patience from the master himself, 'dal vivo oraculo suo'. Even in this dedication, the polemic with Vasari is implicit, as has been long recognised.[32]

Condivi declares his aim is twofold: to record the life and to record the work. He wishes to set the record straight; and here we at once enter into the world of ambiguity which surrounds Condivi's text, an ambiguity veiled by its seemingly simple language, plain narrative structure and the 'ostensible' author's own disclaimers. In a way entirely different from Vasari's partial survey, Condivi's account too is a very incomplete one despite its fascinating detail. In taking the opportunity to correct and make good Vasari's *Life* of 1550, the aim behind the book was biographical self-vindication, a literary act of *ex post facto* self-protection, one above all else (as long recognised) concerned to clear the artist's name over the protracted saga of his failure to complete the tomb of Pope Julius II who had died in 1513, exactly forty years before the appearance of Condivi's *apologia*.

That this was the overriding concern which lay behind the publication of the book is confirmed by the letter of 20 August 1553 written by Caro to a member of the court of Urbino, followed by a second one

---

[31] For Condivi's usage, see ibid., p. 30. For Caro's employment of 'corni' and 'corno' see *Lettere Familiari*, iii (1961), pp. 132, 136, 137, and 138. As pointed out to me by Giulio Lepschy, Caro and Condivi are uniquely credited with this usage in an architectural context in the Cinquecento; see S. Battaglia, *Grande Dizionario della Lingua Italiana*, iii (Turin, 1964), p. 790, no. 20.

[32] See Condivi, *Vita*, p. 4.

dated 17 November, after the book had been read in Della Rovere circles.[33] The earlier refers to the text's emphasis on the story of the tomb, and Michelangelo's explanations for its protracted history, his 'giustificazioni'. Caro concedes that much can be said against the artist, alludes to the role which successive popes had played in holding up progress with the project, and asks that Duke Guidobaldo della Rovere pardon him, 'e sarà cagione di prolungar la vita a quest'uomo singolare e anco di renderlo consolatissimo . . . .'.[34] The second letter again refers to the responsibility of others, the dead pope's executors, and two successive popes whom Michelangelo had served against his will, 'come esso dice, contra sua voglià'.[35] In both, Caro acts as mediator between the artist, close to his eightieth birthday, and the still unappeased Duke of Urbino. He implicitly confirms that the Condivi text is a *pièce justicative*.

We need not review here what the book refers to so unforgettably as 'la tragedia della sepultura', or the repeated charges of financial bad faith which had been levelled at the artist in both private and public. His unease over his vulnerability to such accusations is reflected in letters written decades before the appearance of the book. The issue continued to haunt him and his predicament became almost unbearably acute in the period immediately following the completion of the *Last Judgement* in the autumn of 1541. The long delay of Duke Guidobaldo della Rovere in ratifying what would prove to be the final contract between the family and the artist coincided with Pope Paul III's insistence that he proceed with painting in his recently completed chapel. In 1542, Michelangelo came close to breakdown and his desperation is manifest in the text of a letter of October, in which he declares, in a passionate *coda*, that all his troubles had been created by Bramante and Raphael, both dead for decades.[36] The crisis continued, as a notorious letter of Pietro Aretino to Michelangelo of 1545, later to be published, clearly shows. Duke Guidobaldo remained unreconciled.[37]

---

[33] For the earlier, *Lettere Familiari*, ii, pp. 153–4.

[34] Ibid., pp. 147–8.

[35] Ibid., p. 153.

[36] *Carteggio*, iv, pp. 150–5.

[37] Aretino's text is printed in *La Vita* 1962, iii, pp. 1260–2. Frustrated in his attempts to get a work out of the artist, Aretino writes: 'Ma se il tesoro, lasciatovi da Giulio acciò si collocassero le sue reliquie nel vaso dei vostri intagli, non è stato bastante a far che gli osserviate la promessa, che posso però sperare io?' Condivi's own repeated employment of the word 'infamia' when he turns to the tomb is very striking. We find it in the passage concerned with events following Julius's death (Condivi, *Vita*, p. 36), in the discussion of the situation after Clement VII's summons of the artist to Rome after 1530 (ibid., p. 44), and again when he describes the final stage of the 'tragedia' where he writes: 'E questo è quel di che Michelagnolo si duole, che in luogo di grazia se gli veniva, n'abbia riportato odio e acquistato infamia' (ibid., pp. 48–9).

Condivi's story is less the triumphalistic one of Vasari than that of an artist forever battling against adversity. There emerges from the later book the picture of a man consistently diverted from his true goal, less the protean creator than an agonised victim, surrounded by foes at the papal court when painting the Sistine ceiling, confronted by plaster that grows mould, wracked by physical discomfort, tormented by the incessant plotting of Raphael and the ceaseless importunities of Pope Julius. One or two passages in the book appear to reflect Michelangelo's letters written years earlier, and it seems possible that Condivi had access to copies.[38]

Vasari, writing his *Vita* in the later 1540s, had shown no understanding of the significance of the history of the tomb for the artist; indeed his account is extremely vague.[39] The story of the project runs so insistently through Condivi's book that, when he reaches the final phase, he actually apologises for dwelling on the subject at such length.[40]

But the issue of the tomb colours many other aspects of the *Vita*. On each occasion when Michelangelo takes on a new assignment, Condivi reports his deep unwillingness to proceed. One exceptionally striking example is the passage where he turns to the façade of San Lorenzo, assigned to Michelangelo by Pope Leo X and Cardinal Giulio de'Medici. The book dwells on his profound reluctance to accept the commission. We are told that the artist left Rome for Florence in 1516 grieving over being diverted from the tomb, 'piangendo'. We cannot reconcile the picture here presented with the artist's appropriation of the entire project for himself. His biographer goes so far as to stress that Michelangelo was compelled to shoulder the whole burden alone, '. . . sopra di se tutto quel peso . . .'. Yet there survives an angry letter of Jacopo Sansovino to the artist remonstrating with him over his

---

[38] For this portrayal as agonised hero, I am indebted to Paola Barocchi in *La Vita*, 1962, pp. XXV–VI.

[39] Wilde recognised that some of Vasari's remarks must have especially wounded the artist (*Six Lectures*, p. 12). Vasari even confuses Guidobaldo della Rovere with Francesco Maria.

[40] It has been suggested that Condivi introduced an erroneous statement that '*Prigioni*' were planned for the project of 1505, an error sanctioned by the artist himself (see J. Shearman in A. Esch and C.L. Frommel (eds.), *Arte, Committenza ed Economia a Roma e nelle Corti del Rinascimento* (Milan, 1995), pp. 224 and 240, n. 34). However, this ignores the fact that Vasari had referred to '*Prigioni*' for the first project in his own text of three years earlier, an account which cannot have been known to the artist himself before publication.

brutal exclusion of the younger sculptor from any share in the gigantic programme of statues.[41]

Again, episodes are mobilised to drive home the same message. Some of these are wonderfully vivid, such as that of the visit of Pope Paul III and a group of cardinals to the workshop at Macello de'Corvi just after the death of Clement VII in 1534. Paul is insistent that Michelangelo must continue with the project of painting of the *Last Judgement* on the altar wall of the Sistine Chapel. Cardinal Ercole Gongaza is reported to have remarked that the *Moses* alone was a sufficient honour for Julius II's tomb.[42] These details certainly came from the artist himself and do not strike one as invention. But the apologetic context is unmistakable. Michelangelo had been the prisoner of the popes, a thesis to which Caro returns in his letters of 1553. We are encountering the myth of the reluctant Michelangelo presented in his pupil's pages.

Despite the idiosyncrasies of the book, Condivi's narrative is dense with important information, much of it absent from any other early source and, of course, subsequently ruthlessly exploited by Vasari for his 1568 *Vita*. Particularly rich is his account of Michelangelo's youth, an emphasis certainly owing to Vasari's many *lacunae*. As already remarked, the book dwells at length on the young man's stay in Bologna. Whilst the dependability of Condivi's information is now frequently disparaged, much of it concerning Michelangelo's youth can be confirmed.[43] His remarks about the chronology of the Sistine ceiling, although persistently rejected by almost all modern art

---

[41] For Condivi's account, see ibid., pp. 36–7. For Sansovino's letter, see *Carteggio*, i, p. 291, where he bitterly remarks: 'E non mi ero avisto anchora che voi non faciesti mai bene a nessuno . . .'. Michelangelo's insistence here on presenting his own record of events must have been given greater urgency by Vasari's acute and antagonising comment, in his *Life* of 1550, that it was precisely his exclusion of collaborators which led to the consequent failure of the undertaking: 'Laonde Michele Agnolo si risolse di fare un modello e non volere altro che lui, in tal cosa, superiore o guida dell'architettura. Ma questo non volere aiuto fu cagione che né egli né altri operasse . . .'; Vasari, *Vite*, vi, p. 51.

[42] Condivi, *Vita*, pp. 46–7.

[43] It has recently been stated that, outside of Vasari's and Condivi's accounts, there exists no evidence of the direct youthful association of the artist with Lorenzo de' Medici; P. Barolsky and W. E. Wallace, 'The Myth of Michelangelo and il Magnifico' in *Source: Notes in the History of Art*, XII, 3 (1993), pp. 17–19; repeated in P. Barolsky, *The Faun in the Garden* (Philadelphia, 1994), p. 102. Yet for other evidence we need look no further than Sebastiano del Piombo's letter to Michelangelo of 27 October 1520, where he recounts how Pope Leo X (son of Lorenzo and exactly the same age as the artist) spoke of his being brought up with Michelangelo: '. . . et quando parla di vui par rasoni de un suo fratello, quassi con le lacrime algli ochii, perché m'a decto a me vui sette nutriti insiemi . . .': *Carteggio*, ii, p. 253.

historians, has, again, been confirmed by the recent restoration, even to the detail that Michelangelo began the histories with the scene of the *Flood*.[44] Nevertheless, we need to remain on guard. Domenico Ghirlandaio is dismissed as of no significance and Bertoldo's name in connection with the garden of San Marco is suppressed. Such silences owe to Michelangelo's wish to present himself as an autodidact—the pupil of nobody. Of necessity, given the circumstances, Condivi was dependant on one source alone. Again, the persistent concern with money must also come from the artist. We are told repeatedly how much the artist was paid for his works, a reflection of the old artist's anxiety about the fragility of his reputation.[45]

Another aspect of the book concerns the issue of the *non-finito*. We have only to open any illustrated account to be at once confronted by it. Michelangelo's chronic failure to finish his carvings had become, by the 1540s, a truth generally perceived, and preoccupation was not confined to the court of Urbino. Writing to Pierluigi Farnese at Piacenza in 1545, a member of the papal court close to Paul III unflatteringly describes both Michelangelo's obsessive concern to hold on to his income from the revenues derived from the River Po and to his failure to complete his projects: '. . . non vuol lavorare l'opere cominciate'.[46]

Most of Michelangelo's significant unfinished sculptures are omitted from Condivi's *Vita*. The only major exceptions are the *St Matthew* and the statues in the New Sacristy at San Lorenzo. We hear nothing about the two *tondi* begun for Bartolommeo Pitti and Taddeo Taddei, an omission all the stranger in that Vasari had referred to both of them in his *Life* of three years earlier. Vasari had, we may notice, specifically referred to their incomplete state: '. . . abbozzò e non finì due tondi di marmo . . .'.[47] Yet Condivi mentions, albeit with a confusion over the medium, the group of *Virgin and Child* of the same period as far away as Bruges. The group for the Mouschron, however, unlike the *tondi*, had been brought to the pitch of perfection at which Michelangelo aimed for his carvings. Many of the unfinished works were left out, it seems safe

---

[44] Condivi correctly states that half the vault had been painted when work broke off in 1510 and was revealed the following year. For his remark about the *Deluge*, see Condivi, *Vita*, p. 33, and for recent confirmation, F. Mancinelli in *La Cappella Sistina: la volta restaurata: il trionfo del colore* (Novara, 1992), p. 52.

[45] Condivi's remarks about what had been paid and spent in working on the pope's tomb are not persuasive. His statement that Michelangelo had spent all of the thousand ducats initially provided for materials at Carrara during Julius's lifetime is untrue.

[46] For the text of this extraordinary letter, see *La Vita* 1962, iii, p. 1463–4.

[47] Vasari, *Vite*, vi, pp. 21–2.

to conclude, because they were unfinished; whatever they may represent for modern admirers of the *non-finito*, for the artist they constituted failure. In other words, whereas Vasari's omissions in 1550 owe primarily to ignorance, Condivi's are deliberate and contrived.[48]

Perhaps Condivi's silence about the bust of Brutus can be explained in the same way; but in the case of this exceptionally strange omission, other considerations may have come into play. The bust was carried close to completion by Michelangelo, and was subsequently worked on by Tiberio Calcagni. We know that the work was undertaken for Cardinal Niccolò Ridolfi, the moral leader of the exiles implacably opposed to Duke Cosimo's regime and the man whom Condivi refers to as his own patron. Thus, the *Brutus* must have been known to the biographer.[49] The work is still most frequently dated in the late 1530s and related to the murder of Duke Alessandro de'Medici by his cousin Lorenzino, hailed as a new Brutus, in January 1537. The event was celebrated by the Florentine republicans whose hopes were subsequently to be cruelly dashed by the success of Cosimo. Nearly a hundred years ago, however, it was suggested that Michelangelo made the bust not to commemorate the assassination of the hated Alessandro, characterised in Condivi's text as 'feroce e vendicativo', but to honour the memory of the man who had done the deed, Lorenzino, himself cut down by Cosimo's agents outside San Polo in Venice in February 1548.[50]

This is an attractive idea, but another proposal is more plausible. Roberto Ridolfi suggested that this enigmatic sculpture could date from

---

[48] Condivi's most striking misstatement is over the identity of the true patron of the *Bacchus*, see, for this, M. Hirst in M. Hirst and J. Dunkerton, *Making and Meaning: The Young Michelangelo* (London, 1994), p. 29.

[49] That the *Brutus* was made for Ridolfi is stated by Vasari in the 1568 *Life* (*Vite*, vi, p. 104). This is confirmed by no less than the artist himself, in one of a series of comments he would later make on Condivi's text, discussed below, p. 80. Michelangelo is recorded as saying that 'per lui [i.e. Ridolfi] incominciai quella testa di quel Bruto che li donai'; see U. Procacci, 'Postille contemporanee in un esemplare della vita di Michelangiolo del Condivi,' in *Atti del Convegno di Studi Michelangioleschi* (Rome, 1966), pp. 279–94; the reference to *Brutus* on p. 292). Condivi's silence is even stranger when we recall that he himself was involved in making a bronze bust of Sulla for the cardinal's brother, Lorenzo. See the letters published by Milanesi cited above, n. 25.

[50] For this proposal, see F. Portheim, 'Beiträge zu den Werken Michelangelo's,' in *Repertorium für Kunstwissenschaft*, XII (1889), pp. 150–5. There are no strong grounds for dating Michelangelo's *Brutus* around 1539. Its block-like forms are, in fact, close to those of the 'Florentine Duomo' *Pietà* begun in the second half of the 1540s. The date of 1539 seems to have derived from the fact of Giannotti's arrival in Rome in that year.

the period when Giannotti composed his two dialogues to which I have already referred, in both of which Michelangelo makes an appearance. The second dialogue is substantially devoted to the topic of Dante's merciless treatment of Brutus in the *Inferno*, a long-standing problem for Florentine republicans since Landino's commentary on the poem. In the second edition of 1568, Vasari (who evidently knew nothing about the bust when preparing his 1550 text), even goes so far as to state that Michelangelo made the *Brutus* for Cardinal Ridolfi at Giannotti's instance.[51]

Roberto Ridolfi's suggested date of around 1546 for the dialogues and the bust could explain why the artist broke off work on it and why Condivi maintained his silence about it in the *Vita*. For a letter of Michelangelo's of October 1547, addressed to his nephew Leonardo in Florence, makes it very unlikely that the *Brutus* was begun after this date and at the same time accounts for its incomplete state. In this astonishing letter, Michelangelo disavows every connection with his closest Florentine friends in Rome, the *fuorusciti* who lived in constant danger from the agents of Duke Cosimo. It is a letter of amazing and even shocking disclaimers, one for the most part kept at arm's-length by the artist's biographers. Michelangelo has never had the hospitality of Filippo Strozzi's house when gravely ill; he has, indeed, only reluctantly (if at all) acknowledged the greetings of Florentines in the street. Yet this panic was not groundless; the letter is in reply to one of Leonardo's reporting imminent new moves on Duke Cosimo's part against the exiles.[52] In the light of this letter, I would suggest that the

---

[51] Ridolfi (*Opuscoli*, pp. 128 *et seq.*) proposed a connection between Giannotti's composition of his two dialogues and the making of the bust. He argued for a date of around March 1546 for the dialogues and suggested that they could have been planned for the artist's seventieth birthday and that the sculpture could have been the artist's reciprocal present to his friends. He did not, however, completely exclude that the bust might have commemorated Lorenzino (ibid., p. 130, n. 2). He persuasively reaffirmed the date for the dialogues in 'Antonio Petrei, letterato e bibliofilo del Cinquecento,' *La Bibliofilia*, XLIX (1943), p. 53. Unfortunately, D. J. Gordon, 'Giannotti, Michelangelo and the cult of Brutus,' in *Fritz Saxl (1890–1948) A Volume of Memorial Essays* . . . (London, 1957), pp. 281–96, did not know Ridolfi's arguments and his piece remains inconclusive. They have been given weight by T. Martin, 'Michelangelo's *Brutus* and the Classicizing Portrait Bust in Sixteenth-Century Italy', *Artibus et Historiae*, XXVII (1993), pp. 67–83.

[52] For the letter, *Carteggio*, iv, pp. 279–80. Dangerously ill in the summer of 1544, Michelangelo had been taken to Palazzo Strozzi to be nursed back to health in the rooms of Luigi del Riccio. The palace was in the Via de'Banchi and probably occupied part of the present-day Palazzo Niccolini. A notarial act involving the artist had been drawn up in Strozzi's courtyard as recently as March 1545; see E. Rufini, *Michelangelo e la Colonia*

artist abandoned work on the *Brutus*, so pregnant a political symbol, not for the bizarre reason offered by its later inscription, but because of fear. We may note that Lorenzino's murder followed Michelangelo's letter by no more than four months.

Condivi's suppression of the *Brutus* brings us back once more to the dependence of the biographer on the artist, and raises the last issue to which it is possible to allude here, the issue of how far the text accurately reflects Michelangelo's own words. For Karl Frey, Condivi's little book was literally an autobiography, 'seine Selbstbiographie'.[53] Despite the manifold reflections of Michelangelo's wishes and evasions I have tried to indicate today, I hesitate to endorse completely Frey's judgement. Frey had no chance, as we have, to take account of a remarkable fact, first revealed by Ugo Procacci in the 1960s, that Michelangelo, at a later date, made his own criticisms of and corrections to the *Vita* of his *discepolo*. Written into the pages of a copy of the *editio princeps* which Procacci owned, these marginal comments reflect how the old man regarded the text he had inspired. These *postille*, written in a cultivated hand which has still not yielded the secret of its identity, are quite varied in character. Some are relatively trivial corrections, some of great importance, some vividly indicative of the old artist's exasperation, some, like the correction to Condivi's hard words about Bramante, once more self-protective.[54] With the *postille*, therefore, we have one further twist in the story of the life that Michelangelo wished to present to the world, and, at the same time, a further problem in assessing the status of a biography which is so simple to read and so far from simple to penetrate.

---

Fiorentina a Roma (Naples, 1965), pp. 11–13. Duke Cosimo's new decrees against the *fuorusciti* were published in November, recapitulating previous measures (especially those of the Bando of 1539). For the text, see L. Cantini, *Legislazione Toscana raccolta e illustrata da Lorenzo Cantini*, I (Florence, 1800), pp. 363–5. Talking with declared rebels was proscribed, and the artist's extensive property holding in and around Florence could have been at risk. Even in Rome, the *fuorusciti* lived in real danger. See, for example, a letter of Cosimo's ambassador in Rome of 8 March 1542 where he reports that Piero and Roberto Strozzi could have been murdered four nights before: '. . . e posso dire di veduta che si poteva con una facilità e a man salva finire la guerra . . .'; quoted in *Legazioni di Averardo Serristori . . .* , ed. G. Canestrini (Florence, 1853), pp. 120–1.

[53] See *Le Vite di Michelangelo Buonarroto scritte da Giorgio Vasari e da Ascanio Condivi*, ed. K. Frey (Berlin, 1887), p. XXV.

[54] For these glosses and Elam's comments, see now Condivi, *Vita*, forthcoming.

## Appendix: Vasari and the Sistine Chapel

Some of the most problematic statements in Vasari's 1550 *Life* are those referring to Pope Julius II's wish to have not only the vault but also the walls of the chapel frescoed by the artist. Vasari in the first instance writes: 'Era già ritornato il Papa in Roma e, mosso dall'amore che portava alla memoria del zio, sendo la volta della cappella di Sisto non dipinta, ordinò che ella si dipignesse . . .'.[55] A little further on, he continues: '. . . Ma pure per commissione del Papa et ordine di Giulian da San Gallo fu mandato a Bologna per esso (Michelangelo); e venuto che e' fu, ordinò il Papa che tal cappella facesse, e tutte le facciate con la volta si refacessero; e per prezzo d'ogni cosa vi misero il numero di XV mila ducati.'[56]

While Wilde came to accept the accuracy of this information of Vasari and while, recently, its possible validity has been proposed with intricate arguments by Shearman, it seems to be true that Vasari's source for his statement (nowhere referred to in Condivi's *Life*) has remained completely undiscussed.[57] However, Vasari must have gained his information somewhere, and how he came to form his proposal is the more problematic in that no other source printed in the sixteenth century appears to refer to the much larger project to which he alludes. I should like to suggest here that he could have reached his conclusion from the evidence of a letter of Michelangelo's own.

The final text of this letter has not survived but two incomplete drafts do so, addressed by the artist in Florence to the man on whom he greatly depended at the papal court, Giovan Francesco Fattucci. The two drafts have been convincingly dated to December 1523 by the editors of the *Carteggio*; what is clearly Fattucci's reply survives and is dated 30 December.[58] These drafts have been repeatedly discussed in the literature, but the text of the lengthier one, published as the earlier in the *Carteggio*, must be reviewed once more. The artist's view of past events contained in it is, as we shall see, highly idiosyncratic. Turning to the chapel, Michelangelo first refers to a change in the programme of

---

[55] Vasari, *Vite*, vi, p. 33.
[56] Ibid., p. 34.
[57] Wilde expressed his acceptance in an unpublished lecture, 'Michelangelo and Raphael,' given at the Warburg Institute in March 1957. For the more recent arguments, see J. Shearman in K. Weil-Garris Brandt (ed.), *Michelangelo, La Cappella Sistina, Atti del Convegno Internazionale di Studi, Rome, March 1990* (Novara, 1994), pp. 29–36.
[58] For the drafts, *Carteggio*, iii, pp. 7–11 and for Fattucci's reply, pp. 12–13.

the project for the ceiling. He states that, after expressing his dissatisfaction with the earlier plan, Pope Julius allowed him a free hand to
paint what he wanted, down to the histories below: '. . . Allora mi decte
nuova chommessione che io facessi ciò che io volevo, e che mi
chontenterebe, e che io dipigniessi insino alle storie di socto. In questo
tempo, quasi finita la volta el Papa ritornò a Bolognia, ond'io v'andai
due volte per danari che io avevo avere, e non feci niente . . . Ritornato
a Roma mi missi a far chartoni per decta opera, cioè per le teste e per le
faccie actorno di decta cappella di Sisto, e sperando aver danari e finire
l'opera non potecti mai octenere niente . . .'.[59] The briefer draft alludes
to the change of programme, that is, its enlargement, and states that he
never received his proper payment for the larger programme; there is no
reference to cartoons for the 'facciate'.[60]

There exists a very real possibility that Vasari knew Michelangelo's
final and now lost letter sent to Fattucci and based his statement about
the frescoing of the chapel walls on it. That Vasari and Fattucci were on
friendly terms has never been recognised but is borne out by a neglected
and remarkable fact: that Michelangelo addressed his first surviving
letter to Vasari, to which I have referred above, not to the painter
himself but to Fattucci. Fattucci and Michelangelo had, so to speak,
exchanged places when this letter was written on 1 August 1550; the
artist was now in Rome, the cleric in Florence and a canon of the
cathedral. In writing to Vasari, Michelangelo adds a covering note to
Fattucci himself, interesting on several counts but of which the opening
words are our concern here: 'Messer Giovan Francesco, amico caro,
acadendomi iscrivere costà a Giorgio pittore, piglio sichurtà di darvi un
poco di noia, cioè che gli date la letera che sarà in questa, stimando che
sia amicho vostro . . .'.[61] It is important to note that this evidence of
friendship between Vasari and Fattucci dates from only a few months
after the appearance of the 1550 *Vite*.

A comparison of Vasari's remarks with the information in Michelangelo's longer draft goes a little way further in strengthening the
suggestion of dependence. In both texts, we find first a general reference
to the commissioning of the 'volta' and then, subsequently, the added

[59] *Carteggio*, iii, p. 9.
[60] Ibid., p. 11.
[61] *Carteggio*, iv, p. 344. The note to Fattucci was first published as long ago as 1923 in Frey
i, p. 290 n.

amplification that Pope Julius had also wanted the redecoration of the chapel walls.[62]

The hypothesis that Vasari could have based his remarks on the lost letter would explain why he persisted with the same statements in the second edition of 1568, despite Condivi's total silence about such a project; he could have presumed that he had the sanction of the artist's own words. To accept the hypothesis is, of course, to recognise that Vasari's dependability turns on that of Michelangelo's information.

A few further words about the contents of Michelangelo's longer draft seem, therefore, required. Michelangelo's whole preoccupation in writing to Fattucci was to attempt to justify his conduct over many years concerning the money he had received from Pope Julius II; the letter was prompted by a current crisis. However, his attempted self-exoneration extends further back, as far as 1503 when he had received the commission for twelve marble *Apostles* for Florence Cathedral and, in 1504, became engaged in the project to paint the *Battle of Cascina*. The draft which concerns us is replete with inaccuracies, all presented in self-defence; the artist's dependability or otherwise does not, in other words, rest only with what he writes about the Sistine Chapel. He states that he had transported to Florence most of the marble for the twelve *Apostles*, a remark with serious financial implications which the surviving documents do not confirm. He claims that he had undertaken to paint half of the Sala del Gran Consiglio in Palazzo della Signoria, a grossly misleading statement, made only worse by the added remark that he had made the cartoon for the work and had deserved appropriate remuneration.[63] As we have seen, he states in the passage quoted, that when Pope Julius II left for Bologna on 1 September 1510, almost the whole ceiling had been completed: '. . . quasi finita la volta.' His remarks about the issue of the tomb are also suspect. He writes that, following the pope's death early in 1513, Cardinal Leonardo della Rovere wished to increase the scale of the tomb.[64] This is contradicted in the account which would be published in Condivi's *Vita*, where we

---

[62] Vasari adds a postscript to his account, where he states that the artist continued to put his drawings for the walls in order after the completion of the vault and while working on the tomb of Julius II; *Vite*, vi, p. 50. Then malignant fortune intervened in the form of the pope's death. Different arguments notwithstanding, I find this passage (probably his own) irreconcilable with Michelangelo's flatly factual statement to his father of October 1512: 'Io ò finita la chapella che io dipignievo . . .'; *Carteggio*, i, p. 137. He does not use the word 'volta'.
[63] *Carteggio*, iii, p. 7. The *Bathers* cartoon was only for a part of his mural.
[64] Ibid., p. 9.

are told that in 1513 the executors considered the earlier scheme to be too big.[65]

Michelangelo's statements in this much cited text require, therefore, an approach of great caution. The remark in the longer of the drafts, that he had freedom to paint 'insino alle storie di socto' is difficult to reconcile with a project to redecorate the walls of the chapel without imposing a strained interpretation on the words he uses.[66] His remark about cartoons for the 'teste' and 'faccie' raises problems also. Its truth involves our believing that he proceeded to the last preparatory design stage for the walls when the second half of the vault still awaited its decoration, behaviour especially difficult to credit in the case of an artist who habitually left his design procedures to the latest possible moment.[67]

---

[65] Condivi, *Vita*, p. 36.

[66] Shearman (p. 31, n. 8) has suggested that this phrase, 'insino alle storie di socto' may be interpreted inclusively, and that the artist here refers to his assignment to paint wall narratives. But such an interpretation seems at odds with comparable examples of his own usage. Compare his request from Rome for the measurements of Florence Cathedral: '. . . da dove comincia la lanterna insino in terra . . .': *Carteggio*, iv, pp. 271–2. Or '. . . Le rivolte di decte alia dal mezzo in sù, insino al riposo di decta scala . . .': *Carteggio*, v, p. 43. Or again, in the same letter: '. . . dal mezzo in giù, insino in sul pavimento . . .' (ibid.). Or: 'Cioè decta volta, per osservare el nascimento suo insino di terra . . .': *Carteggio*, v, p. 117.

[67] For the fact that, when free to do so, Michelangelo never made designs until he had to, see M. Hirst, *Michelangelo and his Drawings* (New Haven and London, 1988), pp. 35–6. For the evidence suggesting that the artist only started to design parts of the second half of the ceiling as late as September 1511, see ibid.

*Proceedings of the British Academy*, **94**, 85–101

# Traps and Discoveries at the Globe

ANDREW GURR
*University of Reading*

NEAR THE CLOSE OF *As You Like It*, Rosalind tells Orlando how Celia and his brother fell in love: they 'no sooner met but they looked; no sooner looked but they loved; no sooner loved but they sighed; no sooner sighed but they asked one another the reason; no sooner knew the reason but they sought the remedy; and in these degrees have they made a pair of stairs to marriage which they will climb incontinent or else be incontinent before marriage'. *As You Like It* was the first play explicitly written for the new Globe, with its two stair turrets taking you up into the degrees on which the elevated audience in the galleries sat. The ascent into marriage by other degrees than those cited by Ulysses is one of many forms of climbing in that play. My subject is a few of the other manifestations of the different social altitudes in Tudor England, and their reflection in the vertical sociology of the Globe auditorium. In the process it is concerned, both metaphorically and literally, with the discoveries and the traps that come from studying the original venue for the plays.

To begin with metaphor, I am forced to stand somewhere between the discovery of the problematic and the trap of the speculative, gored by both horns of the theatre historian's current dilemma, where to the scholar 'speculative' is a severe pejorative, while to the critic 'problematic' is a term of praise. We recognise that for the historian there is no such thing as a fact that exists without a personal agenda and a subjective valuation attached to it, but that way life is too short. We all have to make some concessions to the illusion of factuality, refusing,

Read at the Academy 25 April 1996. © The British Academy 1997.

however transitorily, to admit that history is nothing more than Hayden White's fiction. To rejoice in the problematic means that negative capability rules, and speculation is everywhere, if not every thing. But the trap in Keats's concept of Shakespeareanism is that it inhibits any form of action, so no discoveries can be made. I used to enjoy speculating about the design of the original Globe, in the days when I was not being called on to advise the architects about actual details, or to assess the balance of probabilities in the exercise of best-guessing the evidence so as to reach some at least plausible conclusion that might help the architects to settle details such as where on the stage the two posts upholding the heavens were actually located.

For that reason if no other, so far as the current attempts to retrieve something of the original Shakespearean staging are concerned, I have had to abandon my own traditional preference for the problematic in favour of a distinctly irritable reaching after fact and reason. It is a positive capability that is forced on anyone who tries to tell architects and engineers what they ought to build. It concentrates the mind wonderfully into positive fact-finding, however fictional is the basis for so many of the facts, and however problematic the facts themselves may turn out to be.

The essence of the dilemma whose horns I have called the speculative and the problematic is partly a historical one. We have had nearly 400 years to develop our thinking about the verbal texts, even with the dubiously reliable forms in which they have survived. That has given us ample grounds for doing the kind of thing that Harry Berger celebrates so ardently, revelling in the self-evident riches which come from identifying the multitude of possible meanings that we can squeeze out of the basic words.[1] The 'pre-texts', the plays as originally staged, survive in no such detailed record, and they have until very recently been given far less attention. Above all they face the problem of being, in the current terminology, reductive. On stage, whether you are a bright young director inventing a new way of staging the old plays or are painstakingly trying to reconstruct Shakespeare's original concept, you have to make constant choices. Prince Hal's multivalent 'I do, I will' to pleading Falstaff had to be spoken originally in only one of its seven possible ways. Isabella, offered the Duke's hand twice without responding in the printed text, had to make her choice explicit in the pre-text staged at the Globe in 1604.

[1] In *Imaginary Audition: Shakespeare on Page and Stage* (Berkeley, 1989).

The pursuit of such questions is not a recanonising activity. Even if we could get enough confidence in the exercise to claim that we have identified the original staging of this or that scene or event in the plays, it can have only a limited value in today's theatres. The most we can do is to identify what collectively now seems to be something like the first ideas about the staging. In so doing we identify only the best shape, the best guesses, in the current calculations, marinaded in both the speculative and the problematic, part of a historical process of readings that will change and will and should go on changing. We can choose to ignore the authorial presence on stage and the author's authority behind the staging of *Measure for Measure* in 1604. We can choose to ignore the original staging of the end of *King Lear*, though I think that if we do we lose a lot of ripe speculation, a matter to which I will return at my own ending. If we ignore the intended staging, we forsake the pursuit of one distinctive reading of the plays, a reading which has its own value provided we do accept that there was a coherence and consistency in the mind that wrote all those plays, and that worked harmoniously in the original play-making team.

The metaphysical nature of the traps in this game, whatever discoveries it might be thought to offer, is fairly obvious, and I will not dwell on the pitfalls which lie in wait for us there. The practical discoveries are another matter. By using the new Globe stage on Bankside we are likely to learn a lot more about modern acting than we will about the original Shakespeare company's practices, but some of the questions are certainly getting sharpened, and framing a good question is an essential prerequisite to any sort of useful answer. But are they the right questions? We might illustrate a few of the more metaphysical discoveries by going through some of the practical traps and discoveries that lie in wait at the Globe.

In all this irritating reaching after fact and reason the essential problem with the texts themselves is that, given only the written record, we have to use at least some speculation to fix the uses that were originally made, or expected by the author to be made, on the stage—and that has its own problems. As Alan Dessen has frequently warned us, you might argue that when in *Richard II*, III. iii. 50, Bullingbrook says that his soldiers will 'march / Upon the grassy carpet of this plain' while he waits for Richard to respond from the castle, the stage floor must have been carpeted with green rushes, to signify grass. Or, equally speculatively, you could argue that it would not, because the words are there to signal what the audience's thoughts must piece out from the stage's imperfections. Still, we can assemble some pseudo-facts which might help us to determine which are the better and which the worse speculations.

To begin with, we know something about the sociology of the Globe auditorium, and its social orientation. We still tend, though, to underrate what one might call the vertical sociology, the physical affirmation of social differences which the design of these amphitheatres embodied. Those creatures for whom Hamlet invented the term 'groundlings'[2] walked into the playhouse at ground level, and stayed there, in the yard, for the play. Until 1600, a 'groundling' was a small ling or fish, a ground-feeding freshwater loach, with a huge mouth for sucking algae from stones. The small body behind the huge mouth made a wonder-fully patronising name for the gapers in the yard. Everyone else in the Globe's auditorium rose above them, literally, through Rosalind's 'pair of stairs' (the two stair turrets and their narrow doors through which everyone exited when the Globe caught fire), by and to the 'degrees', the benches in the galleries. From there they literally looked down on the understanders. Even the players had the groundlings at their feet, five feet below them. To the majority of playgoers paying to sit in the galleries, the yard was the place for porters and carters, servingmen and apprentices. You stood to watch the play only if you could not afford a seat and a roof over your head. The yard might even have a family of beggars in it, as John Taylor the water poet noted: 'Yet have I seene a beggar with his many / Come in at a Play-house, all in for one penny'.[3]

Opposite and high above that presence was the stage balcony, where, as Marston's cousin Everard Guilpin put it, you can 'See . . . him yonder, who sits o're the stage, / With the Tobacco-pipe now at his mouth', the gallant, the earl, the ambassador and his party. The best and most costly seats in the circuit of galleries, including what in the Fortune contract Henslowe called the 'gentlemen's rooms' to distin-guish them from the 'lords' rooms' on the stage balcony, were grouped close to and above the stage. With the citizenry and the middle level of affluence ranged round behind the yard in the 'twopenny galleries', the 'middle region', there was a clear hierarchy of affluence and social importance. Fletcher, writing *The Prophetess* in 1622 for the second

---

[2] *OED* cites Hamlet's as the first time the term was used to describe the audience standing in the yard. At about the same time, in a translation published in 1601, Holland's *Pliny* also identified the word as meaning a ground-feeding loach.

[3] John Taylor, *The praise, antiquity, and commodity of beggery, beggers and begging*, (London, 1628).

Globe, made Geta the clown talk of becoming the emperor or a senator in vertical terms:

> We Tilers may deserve to be Senators;
> And there we step before you thick-skin'd Tanners,
> For we are born three Stories high; no base ones,
> None of your groundlings, Master.[4]

His three storeys are the Globe's three levels of galleries, topped with the tiles which in 1614 had replaced the thatch of the first Globe. His joke echoes *Hamlet*'s gravedigger with his down-to-earth reference to the survival value of tanners' corpses. 'Groundlings', starting with Hamlet, became the standard term for Dekker and many others in subsequent years. Beaumont and Jonson, in calling the people in the yard 'understanding men', were more derisive but less actually dismissive. It is a nice question how far the lordly Hamlet, using the term in the midst of his sermon to the professionals on how they should act, was at the same time being quietly put in his own presumptuous place.

Socially, in the Globe auditorium the important customers were behind and above the stage, while the lowest level was around what we think of as the front. It was a steeply vertical sociology.[5] This raises such questions as whether the modern terminology, frontstage and backstage, is at all appropriate. Neither is a Shakespearean term. We know that 'upstage' and 'downstage' come from proscenium-arch days with their raked stages. But where is the 'front' of a circle, even one with such a vertical wall and a focal stage? The sociology of the Globe's auditorium suggests that we should question the cinematic terminology of 'front' and 'back', 'upstage' and 'downstage', and think rather of socially up and down, inside a cylinder.

The Inigo Jones drawings of about 1616 for an indoor playhouse, probably the Cockpit,[6] with its boxes flanking the stage and its degrees for equally privileged seating flanking the central music room on the balcony, reflect the Globe's auditorium apart from the yard rather more

---

[4] Fredson Bowers (ed.), *Beaumont and Fletcher, Dramatic Works*, 12 vols. (Cambridge, 1966–), ix, p. 238 (I. iii. 26–8).

[5] This question extends into the three gallery levels. The topmost level at the Globe needed a steeper rake and fewer benches than the lower levels, and was unlikely to have been as superior metaphorically as it was literally. But the middle gallery, which may or may not have been the 'middle region' where army captains might seat themselves (Henry Fitzgeoffery, *Satyres, and Satyricall Epigrams* (London, 1617), E8ᵛ) was where Henslowe located the 'gentlemen's rooms' at the Fortune, and they ranked next to the 'lords' rooms' on the stage balcony.

[6] See John Orrell, *The Theatres of Inigo Jones and John Webb* (Cambridge, 1985), ch. 3.

closely than we usually allow. They certainly affirm the grouping of the socially elevated around the sides and 'back' of the stage. So we should ask more carefully than we have up to now, which way or ways did the actors face? De Witt showed them in the Swan at what we call the 'front' of the stage, the lady and her waiting-woman sitting facing the crowd in the yard, and her steward making a leg to her from even closer to the understanders at the 'front' edge of the stage. De Witt's drawing is of a linear staging, and apart from the depth of its square stage on which the figures stand and its concern to feature the main architectural elements might have done for a proscenium stage. Paper is two-dimensional, whatever use we make of perspective. The *Roxana* and *Messallina* illustrations of the 1630s use the same disposition, influenced though they may have been by continental and 'proscenium' kinds of theatre. But was it normal at the Swan and the Globe for the players to place themselves with their backs to their best customers? Given the early auditorium's pricing and seating priorities, is our thinking not too linear, too shaped by the two dimensions of pictorial illustrations?

There is ample evidence that the early stages were thought of as having sides, but not much to say which was the back and which the front. The octavo of Jonson's *The New Inn*, written for the Blackfriars in 1629, and published in 1631 for the reader, has only one stage direction doing more than just tell us who Jonson wanted on stage for that scene. It launches the courtroom scene, III. ii., with this entry direction:

> *Prudence* usher'd by the Host, takes her seat of Judicature, *Nurse*, *Franke*, the two Lords *Beaufort*, and *Latimer*, assist of the Bench: The *Lady* and *Lovel* are brought in, and sit on the two sides of the stage, confronting each other.[7]

The judicature and its associated bench is central, and the two contestants are in flanking positions facing inwards. But was the central position meant to be facing what we would call the front, backed by the *frons scenae*, or backwards, towards it?[8] The ranks of seating alongside Juliet's balcony at the Globe, like the 'degrees' shown in

---

[7] *The New Inn*, III. ii. 1, in Jonson, *Works*, eds. C. H. Herford and P. & E. Simpson (Oxford, 1925–52), vi, p. 451.

[8] We might appeal to courtroom scenes shown on title-pages, like the woodcut on the title-page of *Swetnam the Woman Hater* (London, 1620), where the judge's chair is set with its back to a blank wall. We might adduce De Witt's view of the Swan's stage, with actors up 'front', forward of the stage posts, and nothing but a two-doored wall behind. However, the Globe and the Blackfriars stages had no blank wall, and a central opening in the *frons*.

Inigo Jones's plan, together with the flanking boxes at the Blackfriars, must have inhibited any sense that the standard viewing position had to be from the yard, or from the gallery places facing the tiring house where De Witt seems to have been positioned. The new Globe has already shown that De Witt's position was acoustically one of the worst in the whole house.

A vertical sociology and three-dimensional acting is nothing like so easy as pictorial staging and two-dimensional acting to camera, when the actors know where they have to face and direct their speech. At court, where Shakespeare's company performed at least twice every Christmas from 1594 up to the building of the Globe, with only one other company ever admitted to that lordly assembly, performing was easier than in the public playhouses. The royal target of the entertainment was always seated in 'front', facing the stage, marginalising the lords and ladies on the scaffolding at the sides. There was no such easy focus at the Globe. Since the top of the social hierarchy was grouped closest to the *frons scenae*, we ought to speculate whether at least some major set-piece scenes, and especially the plays-within-plays such as Hamlet's 'Mousetrap', might not have been staged facing away from the yard. Such a possibility has interesting implications for the mental alignment of the first audiences.

One of the largest questions about the symbolic or iconic functions of the original stage at the Globe is the use of the central opening in the *frons*. It is now normally called the 'discovery space' or 'alcove', but I prefer 'central opening', because it seems less value-loaded. Its apparent functions have changed since the Cranford Adams period of 'inner stage' theory, and thanks to the evident use for it in several plays it has survived all attempts to deny its existence on such grounds as that De Witt shows no such place at the Swan. There is good evidence from both the Globe and the Blackfriars that Shakespeare's company routinely used three openings in the *frons*.[9] It is logical to see it as the place normally fronted by the stage hangings, the arras through which spying Polonius is stabbed. Galatea in *Philaster*, another Globe play, uses it to peep through and to enter by, like Volpone at the Globe when he uses the hangings for his spying.

---

[9] *The Devil's Charter*, staged at the Globe in 1606, needs a 'study' and two flanking doors for its fourth scene. It makes more use of the central opening for shows and Alexander's 'study' than any other Globe play. See Bernard Beckermann, *Shakespeare at the Globe 1599–1609* (New York, 1963), p. 84.

The most obvious question about the central opening is its use for players to enter and exit by. Two references, one from 1592 and the other from 1638 or so, at opposite ends of the time-scale, suggest that clowns used to enter by first sticking their heads out through the hangings that fronted the central opening.[10] What that prompts me to ask is whether this tradition became a deliberate opposite, a carnival-esque parody, of the opening's normal use for ceremonial and porten-tous entrances and exits by authority figures. It is very tempting to see the many plays which used opposing sides, Yorkists and Lancastrians, Montagues and Capulets, Oberons and Titanias, as employing the two flanking doors for entries and exits by each side. That would have freed the central opening for the authority figures, the Duke of Verona, and Oberon with Titania once they had reunited, to signal the new unity by exiting at the close hand-in-hand through the central opening. The ending of *Two Gentlemen of Verona* makes the same signal: 'Our day of marriage shall be yours', says Valentine to Proteus, 'One feast, one house, one mutual happiness', and an arm-in-arm exit. By contrast, the departures in *Love's Labours Lost*, 'You that way, we this way', signal the absence of marital harmony by separate exits through the flanking doors in the closure of that disjunctive comedy.

Such possibly iconic uses of the central opening raise a question which can be tested by trying them out on a play which makes intri-guing use of oppositional parties, *Hamlet*. It includes the question where Claudius and Gertrude sit to view the 'Mousetrap', a question the answer to which has quite substantial repercussions through the rest of the text and its staging. Since nothing is said about it in the stage directions, the original positioning must have been routine, so we can look to other plays for a precedent. This is the unmarked country of practices that were too standard to be worth noting then, but which have been obscured by our own routine and unquestioning practices. Beau-mont and Fletcher's *The Maid's Tragedy*, also a Globe play, has a scene in Act I just like the staging of the 'Mousetrap' where a masque celebrates the marriage of the king's mistress, Evadne, to the young Amintor. Written in about 1611, probably for staging at both the Globe and the Blackfriars (its First Quarto in 1619 specified staging at the

---

[10] Thomas Nashe, *Pierce Penilesse*, 1592, 'A Tale of a wise Justice', in *Works*, ed. R. B. McKerrow, 5 vols. (London, 1904–10), i, p. 188; *Praeludium* to Thomas Goffe, *The Careless Shepherdess*, 1656, quoted in G. E. Bentley, *The Jacobean and Caroline Stage*, 7 vols. (Oxford, 1940–68), ii, p. 541, and iv, pp. 501–5. Goffe died before his play was restaged. The *Praeludium* was written for the revival at Salisbury Court playhouse in about 1638.

Blackfriars), its directions are distinctly more explicit than Shakespeare's for *Hamlet*. Knowing how intimately Beaumont and Fletcher played with their Shakespeares, their signifiers give us a fairly unambiguous measure for how the characters were disposed on the stage.

To start with, there are clear signs about where the ladies and the royal party were to be placed. The scene starts with old Calianax, performing the chamberlain's duties, making a fuss about keeping the crowd back behind the doors. A knock at one door heralds Melantius, calling for admission from '*within*'.[11] He enters with a lady, and is told 'The ladies are all plac'd above, save those that come in the Kinges troope'. Melantius then exits with her by the '*other dore*', and then returns into some by-play over keeping the crowd out, Calianax re-entering at the same time by the second of the two doors flanking the central opening. He quarrels with Melantius for placing his lady 'So neere the presence of the King'. Offstage hautboys then signal the arrival on stage of the king and his party, including Evadne and the forlorn maid Aspatia. Where the royal party position themselves on the stage to view the masque is the question which I believe the subsequent stage directions answer, and which should have copied the 'Mousetrap's' positioning.

The king on his chair of state orders 'Begin the maske', and after a few more lines of dialogue both of the substantive texts supply a heading 'The Maske', followed by the stage direction 'Night *rises in mists*'. Night, that is, enters via the stage trap. Cynthia enters subsequently, not by the trap, while later Neptune also '*rises*' like Night through the trap ('let me know / Why I ascend', he says to Cynthia). The next entrant, however, is Aeolus '*out of a Rock*'. This is evidently not the trap but a stage-level door or much more likely Polonius's arras. The central opening was the only space not used by the masque's spectators, and being curtained was the main resource for feature localities. Otherwise, one of the flanking doors would have had in some way to be signalled as a rock. Neptune orders Aeolus off to command the winds. He exits '*into the Rock*', and returns by the same opening with three of the winds. After the music and bridal songs to Hymen 'Neptune *descends, and the Sea Gods*' through the trap, and

[11] I use the text as given by Robert K. Turner Jr, in Fredson Bowers (ed.), *The Dramatic Works in the Beaumont and Fletcher Canon*, 8 vols. (Cambridge, 1970), ii, pp. 35–46. Most editors have adjusted the stage directions on the grounds that they are deficient, notably Theobald, in *Works*, eds. Theobald, Seward and Sympson (London, 1750).

Night and Cynthia then depart separately, Night saying, 'Ile vanish into mists', down the trap, and Cynthia, 'I into day', out of a stage-level door. To this the Second Quarto adds '*Finis Maske*'.

Night's and Neptune's use of the trapdoor at stage centre, while Cynthia entered and left by a stage door in the *frons scenae*, not to mention Aeolus using the curtained central opening, raises the question where Beaumont and Fletcher expected the royal throne to be placed for viewing this spectacle. It was not, evidently, in front of Aeolus's rock, facing out from the *frons* towards the trapdoor. So where was it?

Melantius took his lady offstage onto the balcony, where Calianax objects to her being 'so neere the presence'. That suggests the king's seat was close to the *frons* balcony. Calianax, however, is using status, vertical sociology. A soldier's common stale does not belong amongst the great in the royal 'presence', capable of looking on the king's face. I can only see the king's throne placed at what we with our two-dimensional thinking call the front of the stage, but facing 'back' towards the *frons*. The royal party is a substantial one, the entry direction specifying 'King, Evadne, Aspatia, *Lords and Ladies*', which must have meant at least three ladies and two lords standing or sitting alongside the king on his throne, plus Amintor and Melantius, who have entered already. That makes a stage audience of at least eight ready for the masque. They are evidently at a distance from the masquers, since Night when he arises in the mists (smoke?) from the trapdoor at centre stage says to Cynthia 'send a beame upon my swarthie face, / By which I may discover all the place / And persons and how many longing eies, / Are come to waite on our solemnities'. The stage audience is too many to be set inside the 'discovery space' or central opening, especially if that was required for Aeolus's entry from the rock. Even if not, the various entries of the masquers from the *frons* indicate that the royal party must have been positioned well clear of the *frons*, and so presumably not far from where King James customarily sat to view his masques, in the centre of the auditorium, facing the stage and its *frons*. That would place the royal party for *The Maid's Tragedy* in the nearest equivalent position on the stage, at the 'front' edge facing 'back', to the *frons*.[12] The position of the dais and throne there would entail a

---

[12] A similar disposition of stage audience for masques can be seen in other plays, such as *The Gentleman Usher*, II. i., where a carpet is laid down for the throne to stand on.

substantial loss of view for the groundlings, of course.[13] But that was another mark of the vertical nature of the society in the auditorium. It would give the nobles and gentry around the back of the stage a prime frontal view, not of the masque but of the king.

The texts of *Hamlet* give no help at all over its staging. In III. ii. 85–6, Hamlet tells Horatio to watch Claudius during the 'Mousetrap', and when he hears the trumpets and drums announcing the king's arrival says 'They are coming to the play. I must be idle. / Get you a place'. It is likely that the dais with its two chairs of state would be carried in as part of the royal procession, the guards carrying torches for the night scene, and attendants setting down the chairs for Claudius and Gertrude.[14] But where? Where does Horatio take his 'place' to watch Claudius, and where do Ophelia and Hamlet sit? With such numbers, it would work best in a setting like the *Maid's Tragedy* masque, with the royal party facing the *frons*, from which the players '*Enter*' for their dumbshow and play. Ophelia would be on the flank of the royal party, with Hamlet at a stage post by her and Horatio on the opposite side. Such a position would allow the elevated audience by the *frons* to see Claudius's face as Horatio does. More potently, it would reinforce the metatheatrical element that is so strong throughout the play, with the play-king now standing in the real king's place while the ostensibly real king joins the audience. The implications of such a positioning would be strengthened if for the first court scene, I. ii., Claudius's throne had been set in the stage centre or near the *frons* facing towards the yard, the position now taken by the players for the 'Mousetrap'. For a normative court scene, the elevated would have been behind the throne, seeing the king in his usual authority position, reflecting the view that any real courtier would have had at Elizabeth's real court. The second court scene, the 'Mousetrap', would displace him, putting actors in his place, so that the same courtiers in the audience can now study what they

---

[13] There is other evidence about the standard practice for such scenes. The opening of *Perkin Warbeck*, with its entry of the king in state, reports '*the King supported to his throne by Stanley and Durham*'. This was not a discovery, though it might have been a central entry from the hangings, since it requires some distance walking if the sickness of the king is to be made visible. Presumably it was an effortful struggle to reach a chair of state already positioned centrally or even 'forward', away from the *frons*. That says nothing about which way the throne would have faced, towards the yard or towards the lords' rooms.

[14] For an assessment of the chair of state, see A. Gurr, 'The "State" of Shakespeare's Audiences', in Marvin and Ruth Thompson (eds.), *Shakespeare and the Sense of Performance* (Newark, 1988), pp. 162–79.

know to be his false face. The elevated gentry would confront the king, not the 'Mousetrap'.

And what, then, about the third court scene, the finale with its other piece of play, Hamlet's duel? If for that Claudius was placed facing the *frons* as for the 'Mousetrap', with the duel conducted in the space between him and the *frons*, it would appear exactly like another mere piece of entertainment. If he returned to his official position facing the yard, as in the opening, with the duel staged between his throne and the edge of the stage fronting the yard, it would be the serious occasion that Claudius and Laertes know it to be. With less confidence than for the other two, I would guess it was the former.

Those three shifting positions are my reading of the staging intended for the main court scenes in *Hamlet*. They give priority to the great and their positioning. They admit the need for the groundlings to shift their positions in the yard if they wanted to view faces as Horatio is instructed to do. Most important, they make allowance for the lack of homogeneity in the different sections of audience at the Globe. The sociology of the Shakespearean audience was inevitably complex, as King James complained in *Basilikon Doron* when he spoke of the 'Hydra of diversely-enclined Spectatours',[15] the many-headed monster with one mind but unstoppably diverse in how, what, and where it saw everything. That diversity must have been reflected in the original staging. Or must it? Slippage from the literal to the metaphorical is all too evident in readings like these.

Now from discoveries to traps, and the diverse functions of the Globe's trapdoor in *Hamlet*. Few scholars doubt that it was used in both the first and the last acts of the play, as the entry-point for the ghost, and as Ophelia's grave. It was not directly employed at any other time in the play, but there is a case to be made that its symbolic presence was there throughout. It is, I would argue, significantly absent through the middle acts of the play. Stanley Wells[16] has sensibly questioned the common assumption that ghosts routinely came up through the trapdoor. He notes the procession of ghosts in *Richard III* which visit both of the sleeping commanders before Bosworth. Those eleven historic ghosts, including the innocent young princes, did not need the specific and traditional association of the trapdoor and its

---

[15] *The Political Works*, ed. C. H. McIlwain (Cambridge, Mass., 1916), p. 9.
[16] Stanley Wells, 'Staging Shakespeare's Ghost', in Murray Biggs (ed.), *The Arts of Performance in Elizabethan and Early Stuart Drama* (Edinburgh, 1991), pp. 58–65.

underworld with hell, and would more easily march on and offstage by the standard entry doors than come up out of the trap and back down once their speeches were delivered. He notes that these ghosts are unconventional, or at least not Senecan revenge figures, and suggests that their presentation may equally have been unconventional. On Caesar's ghost he agrees with Bernard Beckerman that an entrance through a door is more likely than through the trap, noting that it is premonitory rather than revengeful.

Over Hamlet's ghost he makes a strong case for a similar form of entry to those in *Richard III* and *Julius Caesar*. Even for the initial appearance, he argues that the soldiers and Horatio would sit at the front of the stage as far as possible from the tiring-house, so that the ghost can enter from there unobserved while Barnado is calling attention to 'yon same star that's westward from the pole'. Here I have to disagree. For the two soldiers and Horatio to sit and talk at the front of the stage with their backs to the ghost's entry would allow the ghost to emerge from the central trapdoor as readily as from the 'back' wall. If nothing else, his voice from under the stage ('old mole') in the final scene of the act while Hamlet is making the others swear to keep their knowledge secret, makes his exit downwards most likely, and therefore his entrance too. When first addressed, he stalks out of a door, and returns from it later, but his final exit when the morning light appears is down the trap. I would argue that the final act reaffirms that location for the ghost, when the trapdoor returns to play its part in the finale.

I think Wells's view that the ghost enters to Hamlet in Gertrude's closet through a normal stage door is correct, and that his exit from that scene 'out at the portal' marks a departure through the central opening where Polonius is still lying. The 'night-gown' that the ghost is wearing according to the First Quarto goes with a more normal, marital, patri-archal form of access than those of the first Act, although stepping past the corpse of Polonius would have been oddly resonant: murder has been domesticated. Portals in Tudor architectural language were impressive arched doorways, often not hung with doors, an image which best fits the central opening.[17] When Hamlet subsequently lugs Polonius's guts into the neighbour room he most likely follows the same route, closing the arras behind him. All three texts give Gertrude

---

[17] Shakespeare used the word twice before *Hamlet*, in *Richard II*'s reference to 'the fiery portal of the east' (III. iii. 64), and in Adonis's 'ruby-coloured portal . . . / Which to his speech did honey passage yield' (*Venus and Adonis*, 451–2).

no subsequent exit before Claudius enters to her, so she must remain behind for his hurried entry through a flanking door, which would keep the geography intact. The closet scene is an internal, domestic night scene, quite unlike the first appearance of the ghost in armour outdoors after midnight in the bitter cold. In her own chamber, Gertrude is the only person to whom he appears who cannot see or hear her husband. That obscuring is what serves to emphasise his supernatural character in this scene. Otherwise the domestic setting goes with his normal form of entry and exit. The domesticity is underlined by the undomestic corpse, and the night-capped husband who is a ghost.

A similar contrast of setting appears in the fifth Act's reuse of the trap for the gravediggers, who work in normal daylight. The scene works its way through different patterns of the ignorance which generated all the spying and lying of the first Acts. As usual, the audience is kept ahead of the actors. We can tell that the grave is Ophelia's, though Horatio, who has so oddly failed to tell Hamlet the news of her suicide, does not seem to realise it. The gravedigger comments on her right to Christian burial, anticipating the truncated ceremony of which Laertes later complains, and the similar interment of her father in hugger-mugger. Laertes invokes the stage's hierarchy of hell under the ground and the heavens over it when he tells the priest that 'A minist'ring angel shall my sister be / When thou liest howling'. She belongs above, not below. When he leaps into the grave-trap, all three of the Polonius family are joined as victims below ground.

There is a special feature of what follows on which I have commented before,[18] but it needs some reiteration here. Hamlet, witnessing Laertes plunging into hell, remembers where he first encountered the ghost. This prompts him to claim a new identity as his ghostly father by declaring 'This is I, / Hamlet the Dane!', the dead king of Denmark. So as a fell revenger he must take his father's place and join Laertes in hell.

It is easy to misread this claim and this encounter, and the role the trap plays in it. Osric for one misunderstands it, along with most editors, taking Hamlet's declaration that he was his father's ghost to be a claim that he should be the new King Hamlet, which is why he irritates Hamlet by keeping his hat respectfully in his hand when he comes to offer him the duel with Laertes. We cannot refuse to see these events in terms of Tudor iconography. Murder and revenge are hellish matters

---

[18] See A. Gurr, 'Shakespeare and the Visual Signifier', in A. J. Hoenselaars (ed.), *Reclamations of Shakespeare*, DQR Studies in Literature (Amsterdam, 1994), pp. 11–20

which belong below ground. News of murder first comes from below. Hamlet makes himself a murderer by killing Polonius, so in the final Act he belongs with revenging Laertes and self-murdering Ophelia, down the grave-trap. We might speculate what that does to the final scene, where the only failed revenger, Fortinbras, in his ignorance of the reality of events, orders Hamlet to be carried upwards, 'to the stage'. The Second Quarto makes him order all the bodies to be carried off thus, an obvious processional convenience given the quantity of corpses on stage by then. But we should wonder why the Folio and First Quarto both specify only Hamlet's body. Is he the only one not left to go down to hell? The stage, like the poetry of the sonnets, can claim to confer immortality, and 'the stage' is an apt term for his final resting-place. But, elevated above the ground where the trap and the graves were dug, it denies Hamlet's own expectation that as revenger he must lie in hell. Is this 'stage' ground-level, is it elevated above the groundlings, is it better than an underground grave? Verticality rules, even for corpses.

Let me conclude by offering a perspective in the form of a test case. Harry Berger claims that there are better riches to be found by reading the text than in the performance of Shakespeare. My claim is that the original performances contained more riches than Berger can be aware of. To illustrate that, I offer the use of coronets in the first stagings of *King Lear*, in 1605 and rather differently in 1611.

Crowns and coronets in *King Lear* provide a particularly challenging instance of the way the printed text inhibits the modern reader's access to the visual signals that do not appear in the original scripts. In the formal court scene that opens the play, Lear enters wearing the crown of his office, and sits on his throne as royal judge in his courtroom. The Quarto text supplies this stage direction: '*Sound a sennet, Enter one bearing a Coronet, then Lear, then the Dukes of Albany, and Cornwall, next Gonerill, Regan, Cordelia, with followers.*' The object carried before the king is a coronet, not a crown. Dukes wore coronets. The dukes of Cornwall and Albany would already have their own coronets on for this scene.[19] This extra coronet is Lear's game-play, a third piece of headgear for the surprise third ruler of the divided kingdom, whose arrival he announces at the outset: 'Know we have divided / In [not one, nor two, as Kent and Gloucester had been speculating, but] THREE our kingdome.' Dukedoms had died out under Elizabeth, so the existence of ducal coronets was new to England under James. By 1605 he had given one to his Scots cousin Lennox, and one each to his sons—the duchy of Cornwall to Henry, and of Albany, a Scottish title, to the infant Charles, giving them all precedence over Elizabeth's English earls. Shakespeare well knew the difference between a regal crown and a ducal coronet. In *The Tempest*, I. ii. 135, Prospero, when telling Miranda about what led to their being exiled on the bare island, notes the difference between his own ducal coronet as ruler of Milan and Alonzo's crown as king of Naples. The deal that Prospero's brother Antonio makes with Alonzo is to 'subject his [Antonio's] coronet to his [Alonzo's] crown.'

It is the lesser 'coronet', after Cordelia has annulled his plan to marry her to France or Burgundy and then split the realm between three coronet-wearing dukes, that Lear flings angrily down in front of the two remaining sons-in-law, Albany and Cornwall, as a visible icon for the impossibility of his plan. Splitting a golden circlet into two makes it unwearable. England is to be carved up impossibly between the Duke of Wales and the Duke of Scotland.

The insignia of this vertical sociology was something the Stuarts, and Shakespeare, knew better than we do. One of the marks of this play is the declension of authority from the crowned king in I. i. to his appearing in a hunting hat in I. iv. to being 'unbonnetted' in the storm in Act III, and then crowned with mad flowers. The crown disappears after I. i. as authority symbol, replaced by the two coronets of the dukes, before it descends at the close into the offer made by the sole remaining coroneted duke, Albany, to two coronetless earls, Kent and the new Gloucester. Albany's ducal offer to the earls at the end is a macabre renewal of Lear's opening division of the kingdom. It also marks a decline that is visible in the headgear, because while Albany's coronet was, in the original performances, visible on his head as a pale shadow of Lear's crown, the two earls have nothing golden on their heads. English earls did not wear quasi-regal headgear.

In the 1605 text it is coroneted Albany who makes the final speech, which implies that Edgar does not accept his offer after Kent has withdrawn. That would be sensible of Edgar, knowing what happened the last time such an offer was made, but it also leaves the remaining coronet firmly on the head of the Scottish duke, a fair reflection of the situation over the union of the two kingdoms in 1605. If it is Edgar who accepts the offer and makes the final speech, as in the 1611 or Folio version he does, the decline in authority from a single Scottish ruler to an English earl continues, and the local political application of the story to the question of union is lost. By 1611 that would have been tactful.

Even without getting entangled in the question of the two versions, we can see in this a visible on-stage record of the declension of status in rule through the play. Wherever we place the play in time, knowledge of the headgear used in the early performances can strengthen our sense of its local and specific application to its time. Harry Berger's point still has its application. By merging the discovery of early performance practices with knowledge of the text we augment the understanding that we can get from reading the text. Such insights would be lost on the modern stage. Modern audiences are trapped in ignorance of the Tudor and Stuart rules about royal and ducal headgear, and to restage the play using the original headgear would not tell audiences much that they might not already know from reading the text. But then, nobody has yet paid any attention to the declension from king to dukes to earls in the play, and that discovery, if discovery it is, I would claim has come from looking at the original staging. Every little helps.

There are traps and discoveries in any academic exercise. The circularity between the Globe's stage trap and the discovery-space, and the equivalent circuitousness both of access and of argument, make an exemplar for the games we use in which to exercise ourselves. Whether Hamlet's ghost leaves by the central 'portal' because he feels himself to be at home in Gertrude's chamber, and whether Hamlet is truly play-acting his father when by the trapdoor he calls himself Hamlet the Dane, are parts of the larger question of how symbolic we think the original staging of *Hamlet* was, and in consequence how we read so many of the indirections by which we have struggled for so many years to find directions out. I do think we learn more about the play, and about Shakespeare's mind, by studying such things than we do by rationalising the argument of the 'To be' speech, or even by identifying what is rotten in Denmark as a criticism of the royal chair. On such stage properties and their kin I rest my case.

*Proceedings of the British Academy*, **94**, 103–125

RALEIGH LECTURE ON HISTORY

# Politics and Manners from Sir Robert Walpole to Sir Robert Peel

PAUL LANGFORD

*Lincoln College, Oxford*

*Fellow of the Academy*

IN 1839 LORD MELBOURNE'S GOVERNMENT was re-established following the so-called 'Bedchamber Crisis'. His reconstructed Cabinet included several newcomers. One was the historian Thomas Babington Macaulay, who approached his duties with characteristic impetuosity. Indeed, as Lord Holland recorded in his Diary, he was presented to the Queen at Windsor and attended two Cabinet meetings before one of the other new members had even replied to Melbourne's invitation to join the administration.[1] This precipitate appearance at Windsor resulted in two unexpected embarrassments. The first concerned the Queen's daily cavalcade in Windsor Great Park, which ministers on duty at the Castle were expected to attend. Macaulay's horsemanship was not up to this test and he had to decline the honour, explaining that elephant-riding in India had left him unfitted for equestrian feats.[2] This was only a ripple of unease on the surface of court life but the second embarrassment is better known and was more awkward. While at Windsor, Macaulay wrote to his Edinburgh constituents, on notepaper headed Windsor Castle, a breach both of royal etiquette and good breeding. In this case the ripples spread beyond the Court and culminated in a Press campaign deploring the unsuitability of certain modern Cabinet

---

Read at the Academy 7 November 1996, at Edinburgh 26 November 1996. © The British Academy 1997.

[1] *The Holland House Diaries 1831–1840*, ed. Abraham D. Kriegel (London, 1977), p. 411.
[2] Ibid.

appointments. No lasting harm was done, but the episode retained a symbolic significance later recalled by Thackeray on Macaulay's death in 1859. Thackeray perhaps went too far in comparing Macaulay as champion of the middle class at Windsor to Napoleon dating his letters from the imperial palace of Schönbrunn after the Battle of Austerlitz, but he was in no doubt where the ultimate victory in the war of manners lay. 'That miserable "Windsor Castle" outcry', he wrote, 'is an echo out of fast-retreating old-world remembrances.'[3]

My concern this evening is to reconstruct a portion of that old world and to recapture something of the manners of politicians as they evolved between the two careers of two Sir Roberts, Walpole and Peel. During this period Britain invented a form of parliamentary government which was thought to have no parallel in contemporary experience and no precedent in recorded history. The constitutional implications were and are much debated. Less attention has been paid to the codes regulating the relationships of the men who lived through them. Yet what emerged between the Revolution of 1688 and the Great Reform Act of 1832 was a system of management, and management, as we are often reminded today, perhaps to the point of tedium, is a matter of style (or as the eighteenth century would have called it, manners) as well as technique. What was the distinctive style required of those who managed the modern British polity in its formative years? The question is an obvious one if only because the eighteenth century was itself so fascinated by manners and the structures that sustained them. Yet it is not often explicitly asked.

This may be because the evidence of public life is almost too voluminous to be comfortably managed. Moreover, some of the short cuts which suggest themselves turn out to be dead-ends. One such is the literature which consciously codified manners, a source which historians have used extensively for other purposes. Between the two Sir Roberts there was no shortage of such material, ranging from the courtesy books read by Walpole's contemporaries to the mass-market etiquette guides of Peel's day. Yet in this ocean of advice about how to behave, it is remarkable how little relates to politics. The most quoted of all such works, Chesterfield's *Letters to his Son*, though addressed by a statesman of the first rank to a young man intended for a public career, has little to say about political advancement and nothing about the conditions which prevailed at the time of writing, in the 1740s. The

---

[3]  G. O. Trevelyan, *The Life and Letters of Lord Macaulay* (2nd edn., London, 1886), p. 388.

occasional exception, such as Thomas Gisborne's *An Enquiry into the Duties of Men in the Higher and Middle Classes of Society in Great Britain* of 1795, offered only pious injunctions against 'unchristian behaviour' and in favour of the 'public welfare'.[4]

The deficiency is all the more remarkable when it is recalled that there existed an older tradition of public instruction on this subject. The so-called 'Book of Policy' was a distinct branch of courtesy literature, well known in England as elsewhere. Yet it disappeared at just that moment when a revolution in government might have made its revision and reissue pertinent. The eighteenth century possessed nothing similar. It had 'vade-mecums' for various officials, from magistrates to excise officers, but these were in the nature of professional manuals. They told the would-be administrator what to do, not how to conduct himself. Those publications which did offer instruction on this point were in the nature of moral tracts, often written by clergymen who had first aired them as sermons. Explicit guidance to young politicians on the make was rarely attempted. Politics was surely the only trade, craft or profession of which this was true. Historians of the early modern Book of Policy have noted that 'policy tends to drop out of the English courtesy tradition' and concluded that the eighteenth century had ceased to be interested in what they call the 'production of a social leader'.[5]

A pioneer in this field eventually appeared in 1836 with the publication of *The Statesman* by the poet and civil servant Henry Taylor. Taylor's advice described upbringing and schooling, making contacts and acquiring a leader or followers, cultivating an official language, conducting interviews, and so on. The author's intention is said to have been satirical, though he denied it in his *Autobiography*.[6] In any event, his advice was severely practical and plainly derived from his experience as a clerk in the Colonial Office. It ranged from avoiding the use of metaphor in official despatches to the placing of furniture in a Cabinet minister's room so as to minimise the discomfort to all parties when interviews did not go well. Taylor made no apology for the seeming triviality. 'These are not frivolous considerations where civility is the

---

[4] 2 vols. ( 2nd edn., London, 1795), i, chs 6, 7.

[5] J. E. Mason, *Gentlefolk in the Making: Studies in the History of English Courtesy Literature and Related Topics from 1531 to 1774* (Philadelphia, 1935), pp. 219–20, 252; see also, George C. Brauer, *The Education of a Gentleman: Theories of Gentlemanly Education In England, 1660–1775* (New York, 1959), pp. 61–2: 'For the eighteenth-century gentleman, the world seemed to imply mainly polite society, conversation, and social intercourse in general.'

[6] *Autobiography of Henry Taylor, 1800–1875*, 2 vols. (London, 1885), i, p. 202.

business to be transacted', he said.[7] The hostile reception accorded *The Statesman* helps to explain the previous neglect of the subject. To write on political advancement without appearing cynical on the one hand or satirical on the other was in truth difficult. William Maginn in *Fraser's Magazine* suggested that a better title for Taylor's book would have been 'The Art of Official Humbug systematically digested and familiarly explained'.[8]

Another stand-by of historians of manners, literary sources, are not more helpful. Clara Reeve's celebrated manifesto for the novel as a portrait of 'real life and manners' might lead one to expect that real politics would figure in such works.[9] It is true that novels of the period feature innumerable peers, MPs, and even ministers, but their political activities are rarely described. There was evidently a sensitive spot on the psyche of the eighteenth-century patriciate. It was quite feasible to denounce the horrors of political corruption in almost every form of polemic: parliamentary, journalistic, poetic. But to depict the effects on the lives of the gentlefolk who peopled the pages of fiction seems to have been thought too daring. When Maria Edgeworth attempted it in her book *Patronage* in 1814, she had an uncomfortable time. She seems to have repented of her temerity in this respect, observing in 1831 that to depict the 'ways of rising in the world . . . to say the best is very problematical in point of morality'.[10] By then, of course, political novels in the sense that we would recognise them had started appearing from the pens of Plumer Ward, Normanby, Lytton, and Disraeli, and thereafter there was no stopping them. 'No nation other than Victorian-Edwardian Britain has ever explored its elective institutions so extensively in fiction', it has been observed.[11] The contrast with Georgian Britain, which definitively empowered these elective institutions, is the more remarkable.

For a starting point then, I am driven to another source, the satire which was directed against the ruling manners, especially by the Augustans. It is of course little better than propaganda, but it does have the

[7] Ibid., pp. 58–9.
[8] 14 (1836), 393–8.
[9] J. Paul Hunter, *Before Novels: The Cultural Contrasts of Eighteenth-Century Fiction* (New York, 1990), p. 23.
[10] Maria Edgeworth, *Letters from England 1813–1844*, ed. Christina Colvin (Oxford, 1971), p. 508.
[11] George Watson, *The English Ideology: Studies in the Language of Victorian Politics* (London, 1973), p. 133.

advantage of highlighting some central issues. Let me select one example, that offered by Addison and Steele in their *Spectator*, of double interest because it was so influential in popularising fashionable ideas and because its authors were themselves active politicians. I have in mind *Spectator* 193, in which Steele pictures himself on a busy street, observing the variety of faces and persons, and speculating about one of the commoner classes to be encountered there, those 'whom we call good Courtiers, and such as are assiduous at the Levées of Great Men. These Worthies are got into an habit of being Servile with an Air, and enjoy a certain Vanity in being known for understanding how the World passes'. Steele traced their peculiar bearing to its ultimate source, 'that Market for Preferment, a great Man's Levée'. The levée (or 'levee' as I shall call it, in deference to the form of Franglais favoured at the time), had a long history and a close association with court life. Men of station not only attended the King's levees, but also held their own. Steele conducts us to one such to reveal a patron receiving his visitors. Colleagues and clients are fielded, flattered, and fussed over. The patron is not so much approachable as fawning in his anxiety to leave no supplicant unnoticed. For their part, his petitioners are equally hypocritical and even more offensively obsequious. Steele's concern in picturing what he called 'a direct Farce' is not only the obvious one, that free-born Englishmen were degrading themselves by such courtship, but also that it unmanned the patron himself. 'A Girl in new Ribbons is not more taken with her self, nor does she betray more apparent Coquetries, than even a Wise Man in such a Circumstance of Courtship.'[12]

In pursuing this theme, of men of power approaching each other and those they patronised, I am all too aware that I am scratching the surface of a rich subject. There are advantages, however. One is that it is specific to the political process. It would be easy to show that the manners of politicians changed with those of the Upper Ten Thousand as a whole; that, if you like, Peel's generation sported canes where Walpole's wore swords, shook hands where Walpole's showed a leg, danced waltzes where Walpole's performed minuets; but my question is about the manners required by participation in political life. Moreover, the effects are not limited to a handful of levee loungers. Steele estimated that one-third of the nation was locked into patron–client

---

[12] *The Spectator*, ed. Donald F. Bond, 5 vols. (Oxford, 1965), ii, pp. 256–60, 12 October 1711.

relationships. It was precisely the anxiety of the Augustans that parliamentary government had multiplied the opportunities for corruption and
therefore enslavement.[13] Steele's levee was emblematic of the nation's
plight, governed and governors. It was 'a Conspiracy of a Sett of Servile
Slaves, to give up their own Liberty to take away their Patron's Understanding'.[14]

The *Spectator* was not on its own. As the Hanoverian regime took
root, its opponents targeted style as much as substance. In prints and
journals the theme of Englishmen having to bow and scrape is common;
peers of the realm are humiliated, MPs appear as footmen. Walpole's
towering presence turned the political nation into a veritable Lilliput. Nor
was it necessary to be an enemy to see force in these charges. Walpole was
notoriously proud of his power. The magnificence of his Norfolk palace at
Houghton, the much-reported richness of its contents, from old masters to
mahogany privy seats, the pleasure that he took in his possessions, dress
and retinue, all suggested an uninhibited parade of status. The famous
congresses held at Houghton called to mind the provincial gatherings
mustered by great magnates of the past. Even in London, at Chelsea
and Downing Street, the appearance was of homage rather than companionship. Walpole's birthday was a ceremonial event second only to that
of royalty. When newspapers as far afield as Edinburgh, Amsterdam, and
Paris told of the nobility who attended his lodgings to congratulate him,
their readers can have been in no doubt that here was a minister who, for
all his dependence on a British Parliament, enjoyed the standing of a Sully
or a Richelieu, or to come closer to home, a Wolsey. Moreover the new
breed of Whigs who throve with Walpole—the Dodingtons, the Foxes,
the Winningtons—revelled in this atmosphere. The Walpole years were
years of unashamed triumphalism.

If this was a realisation of the fears of Addison and Steele's generation, it was, however, short-lived. During the decades which followed Walpole's fall, there was growing reluctance to show the full
extent of political power over others. This was displayed not least in the
language employed. When Walpole's son Horace published his
*Description* of Houghton's collections, he dedicated it to his father
with the words: 'Your power and your wealth speak themselves in the
grandeur of the whole building'.[15] Sentiments of this kind, even from a

[13] *The Spectator*, ii, p. 335, 5 November 1711.
[14] *The Spectator*, ii, p. 260, 12 October 1711.
[15] See Marcia Pointon, *Hanging the Head: Portraiture and Social Formation in Eighteenth-
Century England* (New Haven, 1993), p. 21.

son, would have seemed vulgar and offensive to subsequent generations. The Peels were proud of Sir Robert's country house at Drayton, and his art collection in Whitehall was scarcely inferior to Walpole's, but it is difficult to imagine his sons addressing him publicly in such terms. Wealth and power might be combined with a political career, might even result from it, but not as a matter of open avowal.

Earlier, there had seemed nothing tasteless about emblems of power. Walpole would have approved the modern maxim 'if you've got it, flaunt it'. Portraits show him in all his official glory, robed, ribboned, decorated. These appearances were not confined to the artist's studio. As the first commoner to be awarded the garter, Walpole took pride in wearing it in the Commons. His successors came to shun such displays. Lord North was, I think, the last premier regularly to wear his decorations in the House of Commons. For ministers who took pride in their representative credentials, such honours looked like a mixed blessing. The Younger Pitt was expected to nominate himself to the Garter but declined doing so when opportunity offered in 1788. Again, in 1790 when the King himself pressed him to do so, he preferred to honour his brother, the second Earl of Chatham.[16] Even in the Lords, Knights of the Garter abandoned their Blue Ribbons.[17] Such unobtrusiveness became a peculiarly English form of distinction, the most famous example perhaps being Castlereagh's sensational *un*adornment at the glittering Congress of Vienna in 1814.[18]

A simple indicator of change is the dignity of the Chancellor of the Exchequer, an office of state which was held either by the Prime Minister himself or by the leading minister in the Commons for much of the period between 1720 and 1850.[19] The gorgeous robes which went with the office gradually disappear in the portraiture of the period. Walpole delighted in appearing in them of course, in oils as in the flesh. So did his successors Henry Pelham, and Henry Bilson Legge, who not only posed in his robe but positioned the Chancellor's purse of office on an adjacent table. In the 1760s, George Grenville, Charles

---

[16] *Correspondence of Charles, First Marquis Cornwallis*, ed. Charles Ross, 3 vols. (London, 1859), i, pp. 361–2; John Ehrman, *The Younger Pitt*, 3 vols. (London, 1969, 1983, 1996), ii, p. 189.

[17] G. W. E. Russell, *Collections and Recollections of One Who Has Kept a Diary* (London, 1898), p. 91.

[18] *Roundabout Papers*, The Oxford Thackeray, ed. George Saintsbury, xvii, p. 377.

[19] Changing conventions can be traced most readily in the *Catalogue of Engraved British Portraits preserved in the Department of Prints and Drawings in the British Museum*, 6 vols. (London, 1908–25).

Townshend, and Lord North were all pictured in them: thereafter, there is a significant change. The numerous paintings and engravings of the Younger Pitt include only two of him wearing his Chancellor's robe. In others it is slung over a chair, or reduced to a flash of gold braiding in the chiaroscuro. Pitt's successors up to the 1850s were to dispense with it altogether. The sole exception seems to have been Vansittart, who had to fend off Canning's attempt to separate the possession of 10 Downing Street from the Exchequer, and took a proprietorial interest in the office.[20] Disraeli was also attached to his gilded robe of office, positively refusing to allow his successor Gladstone to have it, though convention required that it be passed from Chancellor to Chancellor.[21] The robe, believed to have been newly woven for the Younger Pitt, is still at his home of Hughendon today. Not even Disraeli, however, thought it appropriate to appear before his public in it.

Symbols of authority once considered unexceptionable, such as wands, sticks, maces, batons, bags, and purses of office, disappeared from view in political portraiture. Later, the despatch box provided the ideal means of suggesting the burdens of office rather than its perquisites or power. But that does not seem to have happened until the end of Peel's career and in the meantime even more discreet signals were employed. Politicians often appeared with pen and paper, but artists normally adept at using the written word as a visual device seem to have been wary of hinting at the contents of a paper borne by a politician. Close inspection does not reveal the commencement of a Treasury minute, or the sketch of a speech in Parliament, let alone something more interesting such as the words, 'Sir, I have the honour to inform you that His Majesty no longer requires your services'. There are a few exceptions but they are rare and the most striking, Pitt's portrayal as the 'Saviour of his Nation' with a copy of his Bill for the Redemption of the National Debt, which hung in Windsor Castle and was widely reproduced in engraved form, was in fact a posthumous work.[22] Few statesmen after 1750 had themselves depicted exercising their power. In the National Portrait Gallery one might take Georgian politicians for ordinary English gentlemen in their studies and libraries. There is not the same difficulty with judges, generals, and admirals.

[20] *The Diary of Henry Hobhouse (1820–1827)*, ed. Arthur Aspinall (London, 1947), p. 101.
[21] R. Blake, *Disraeli* (London, 1966), pp. 351–2.
[22] *The Holland House Diaries 1831–1840*, p. 16.

One innovation in self-portraiture there was. It became common to be shown addressing an audience, either the House of Commons or an extra-parliamentary body. Peel seems to have been the first so depicted during his lifetime in print form, and in his own Statesman's Gallery at Drayton, took pride in showing others in a parliamentary setting.[23] Of course, an orator is not as such exercising political power or disposing of patronage: he is merely a patriotic persuader.

The parliamentary context was crucial, for it was there that politicians rose and fell and there that the need to accommodate themselves to a wider body of opinion was felt. The House of Commons was no respecter of persons. When Charles Abbott entered the House he found MPs' inattention to the Younger Pitt, then a Premier of twelve years' standing, startling.[24] Those who knew Parliament were familiar with such irreverence, and prudent ministers did well not to let it irritate. Pitt's Secretary to the Treasury, George Rose, remarked that his complete want of any 'air of authority' was one of his greatest political assets.[25] Moreover, no attempt was made to adapt the rules of rank to the realities of power. Senior ministers in the modern departments of State featured low in lists of precedence, and junior ministers hardly at all, though royal household officers, many of them sinecurists, were guaranteed a good position on Coronation day. Foreigners were bemused by the mismatch between power and status. How, asked Léon Faucher, could Peel as Prime Minister rank below the most imbecile peer at a Court gala?[26] Those who did value status sometimes had difficult choices to make. It was said that the notoriously haughty Lord Durham, who boasted to Princess Lieven that he was descended from kings, chose the office of Lord Privy Seal because it allowed him to lord it over dukes and marquises.[27] The paradoxical understatement of power was often reflected in terminology. As Trollope's Madame Goesler remarked, a brilliant political career which commenced with a lordship, progressed to a presidency and finally attained the heights of a secretaryship sounded to the uninformed more like descent than ascent.[28]

[23] *The Private Letters of Sir Robert Peel*, ed. George Peel (London, 1920), pp. 6–7.

[24] *Diary and Correspondence of Charles (Abbot) Lord Colchester*, 3 vols. (London, 1861), i, 75–6.

[25] *The Diaries and Correspondence of the Right. Hon. George Rose*, ed. Leveson Vernon Harcourt, 2 vols. (London, 1860), ii, p. 293.

[26] Léon Faucher, *Études sur L'Angleterre*, 2 vols. (Brussels, 1845), i, p. 16.

[27] *Letters of Dorothea, Princess Lieven, during her Residence in London, 1812–1834*, ed. Lionel G. Robinson (London, 1902), p. 328.

[28] *Phineas Finn*, ed. Jacques Berthoud (Oxford, 1982), ii, p. 54.

Unpretentiousness in high office acquired an English connotation, enhanced by the manner in which Prime Ministers lived. Downing Street was symbolically unimposing. 'In a small German Principality such a house would be considered too mean for a porter's lodge', it was said, 'but in England we have not cared much to keep up appearances, wearing the star of our order within.'[29] It had the advantage of making criticism of Prime Ministerial grandeur difficult. Downing Street defied caricature, so humdrum and homely did it appear. Cartoonists showing ministers in their official setting before the heroic age of Whitehall office-building, were reduced to using unimpressive symbols of bureaucracy. Pitt on his way to open his Budget in 1796 was seen emerging from the Old Treasury arch, and when Fox was displayed knocking on the doors of power, the door was not that to 10 Downing Street, but the Treasury office.[30]

The Commons itself did not evolve a more pretentious code of manners for its members. In dress there was indeed a trend towards uniformity. Aside from the Speaker and his clerks, who wore what foreigners thought of as outmoded Spanish wigs, MPs were informally dressed. Back-bench and Opposition MPs gloried in the right to wear their most ordinary street clothes, to keep their hats on their heads, to wear outdoor boots. In this sartorial warfare they, not governments, were the winners. Ministers under George III grew self-conscious about appearing in formal attire. Canning, seconding the address in 1794, objected to wearing a dress coat for the occasion. 'But', he recorded in his diary, 'the Secretary of the Treasury averring that to come in a frock to second an Address would be such a departure from the established usage of Parlt as in these times to threaten the downfall of the constitution, I submitted'.[31] Ironically, Canning was remembered later by Disraeli as the last minister who 'always came down in silk stockings and pantaloons or knee-breeches'.[32] By the 1840s, differences in dress were matters of personal preference and not very marked then. Palmerston's famous sensitivity to his audience did not fail him in this

---

[29] *Autobiography of Henry Taylor, 1800–1875*, 2 vols. (London, 1885), ii, ch. 4.

[30] *Catalogue of Political and Personal Satires preserved in the Department of Prints and Drawings in the British Museum*, eds. F. G. Stephens and M. D. George, 11 vols. (London, 1870–1954), vii, pp. 8836, 8981.

[31] *The Letter-Journal of George Canning, 1793–1795*, ed. Peter Jupp, Camden Fourth Series, vol. 41 (London, 1991), p. 173.

[32] G. W. E. Russell, *Collections and Recollections of One Who Has Kept a Diary* (London, 1898), p. 158.

respect. As a young man he had been something of a dandy, but in his prime his dress verged on the casual.[33] By this time the absence of ministerial pomp presented a striking contrast with continental practice. Giovanni Beltrami was particularly impressed when he viewed Parliament in 1822. 'And the embroidered suits, the orders, the haughtiness, the stately repulsive air, of our ministers? No such thing! The ministers of England, often the arbiters of both hemispheres, are not distinguishable from the other members of parliament, either by their seats, their dress, or their manners.'[34]

There remained distinctions of dress, but none of them contradicted the underlying trend. County members uniquely enjoyed the right to wear their spurs, sustaining the pleasant conceit of the legislator who rode up to Westminster from the shires, and leapt from his horse to enter the chamber and speak for England; the officers of the House retained their lawyer-like robes and wigs; and military men were permitted to wear their uniform. Ministers, however, increasingly became indistinguishable from backbenchers, and politicians became indistinguishable from any ordinary gentlemen. As Constantine Phipps noted, there was logic in this. Once, politicians had represented the urbanity and sophistication of a metropolitan court, whereas ordinary MPs had represented the rusticity of the provinces. Silk and powder had confronted riding crops and round hats. Now all were united as members of a cohesive club, the gentlemen of England.[35] Certainly, views of Parliament in the 1830s displayed a body of men dressed in remarkably similar fashion. The same was true of the House of Lords, the dignity of the peerage notwithstanding. Legislators and governors were expected to look like other Englishmen of their class.

The resulting want of glamour could be disappointing. The most famous of all depictions of the eighteenth-century legislature, Copley's portrayal of the death of Chatham, lent colour and pomp to the scene by showing the peers debating in their robes. This was a gross solecism, also perpetrated by Bacon in his Westminster Abbey statue of Chatham.[36] Only on State occasions would the peers have been so dressed. Foreign visitors were dismayed by the unkempt appearance of Britain's

---

[33] William White, *The Inner Life of the House of Commons*, ed. Justin M'Carthy, 2 vols. (London, 1897), i, p. 2.
[34] *A Pilgrimage in Europe and America*, 2 vols. (London, 1828), i, p. 277.
[35] C. H. Phipps (later Marquis of Normanby), *The English in France*, 3 vols. (London, 1828), ii, pp. 289–90.
[36] John Taylor, *Records of my Life*, 2 vols. (London, 1832), i, p. 119.

legislators, and it was left to the French, when they invented their own brand of representative politics in the 1790s, to provide their lawmakers with robes and insignia. The very idea seemed un-English.

Demeanour for students of manners mattered as much as dress, and one of the common observations from the 1780s onwards was the growing coolness, reserve and circumspection which were thought to mark it. The alleged coldness and even repulsiveness of leading figures of the period are so often emphasised that it can hardly be merely a function of personality. Pitt the Younger, Lord Grenville, Lord Grey, and Sir James Graham were among the best-known examples of the tendency. Interestingly, in all these cases friends and biographers of these men found themselves having to emphasise that in their private capacity there was no sign of such coldness. Pitt, well-known for his off-putting manner, was apparently never happier than when he was romping with his nephews and nieces at home, or carousing with the friends of his youth. Grenville was described as 'in his outward manner offensive to the last degree'.[37] Yet his biographer Peter Jupp produces numerous instances of warmth and accessibility which impressed those contemporaries who dealt with him in a private or domestic setting.[38] According to Graham's biographer, at home he was the most congenial of men, but 'from the moment he crossed his own threshold appeared to assume a repellent air and mien, as though he were haunted by the fear of being intruded on'.[39] Of Grey it was remarked that 'he is reported to be as gentle and good-natured in private life, as in public he is stiff, arrogant, and supercilious'.[40] Here was evidently a need to provide the public with wholesome domestic images at a time when the moral imperatives of the home were hardening. But the tension between the constraints of a political existence and the release of private life may have been real enough. In Walpole's time, an open and engaging manner had been part of the conventional image of ministers of state; by Peel's, it was best kept for the fireside.

Confronting inferiors was different from associating with equals. But the trend was similar and towards a less assertive, more distant style of leadership. In fact the form of abasement which Steele had highlighted, the ministerial levee, was a victim of this change, though it still

---

[37] Philip Ziegler, *Addington* (London, 1965), p. 56.
[38] *Lord Grenville, 1759–1834* (Oxford, 1985), pp. 103–4, 295, 415–6.
[39] Edwin Hodder, *The Life and Work of the Seventh Earl of Shaftesbury*, 2 vols. (London, 1887), ii, p. 40.
[40] *Parliamentary Portraits* (London, 1815), p. 24.

flourished in the middle decades of the century, often irritating friends as well as foes. Walpole's supporter Hervey was embarrassed by the 'kissing, whispering, bowing, squeezing hands [which] were all acted' at his levee, and his enemy Argyle launched an astonishing public attack in the Lords on it in 1741, denouncing 'men whose birth and titles ought to exalt them above the meanness of cringing to a mere child of fortune'. 'This scene, my lords, is daily to be viewed, it is ostentatiously displayed to the sight of mankind; the minister amuses himself in public with the splendour, and number, and dignity, of his slaves; and his slaves with no more shame pay their prostrations to their master in the face of day, and boast of their resolutions to gratify and support him'.[41] After Walpole's fall, the followings of Walpole himself, Henry Pelham and Lord Carteret, could be reckoned by counting the carriages that waited outside their respective doors, conveniently, since all three lived in Arlington Street.[42] The Duke of Newcastle never stopped 'keeping levee' to use the proper phrase; in *Humphry Clinker* there is a memorable satire on it, as it still flourished in 1766, two years before Newcastle's death.[43] A little later it was still possible for Junius to deride levee-attending by an Opposition supporter as evidence of forthcoming defection;[44] but thereafter it fell into decay. Lord North was surely the last Prime Minister to be accused of bribing MPs at his levee, as Fox accused him in the Commons in 1781: 'Here Mr Fox personated the minister conversing with some dependent member of parliament, at his levee'.[45] Significantly, the levees which did flourish were given by those who were increasingly expected to be above party politics—the Crown itself and the Speaker of the Commons. In each case, attendance was transformed from an act of allegiance to a social privilege.

Patronage was ceasing to be an appropriate matter for public display. Ministers, far from advertising their services, retired or pretended to retire behind the protection of doorkeepers and secretaries. It suited politicians to portray themselves as victims of the patronage system

[41] Quoted Andrew Arthur Hanham, 'Whig Opposition to Sir Robert Walpole in the House of Commons, 1727–1734', Ph.D. thesis (Leicester, 1992), p. 92; *Parliamentary History*, xi, pp. 1185–6.

[42] *Letters of Horace Walpole*, ed. W. S. Lewis, xviii, p. 349.

[43] Ed. Angus Ross (London: Penguin, 1967), pp. 141–7.

[44] *Correspondence of Charles, First Marquis Cornwallis*, ed. Charles Ross, 3 vols. (London, 1859), i, p. 12.

[45] *The Speeches of the Right Honourable Charles James Fox*, 6 vols. (London, 1815), i, p. 364.

rather than its beneficiaries, disdaining personal approaches, deploring the necessity for petty calculation, and acting with extreme circumspection to all but close friends. Irish politicians seeking a career in London were warned that a less frosty Dublin manner was not helpful. Spring Rice was said to have made many enemies by his inability to fend off would-be clients, learning the hard way that cordiality was not a virtue in a Westminster politician.[46] Such claims had been made against not a few English ministers of the Pelhamite era, including the Duke of Newcastle. It was rarely made after 1800. Conversely, a minister such as Henry Pelham himself 'so honest and unreserved, that he has often been known to make a friend of the man, whose suit he has been obliged to reject' was held up for public admiration under George II, but under his successors the boast would hardly have been plausible.[47]

From the client's standpoint the art of pleasing in politics was reduced to knowing how to write a begging letter, not how to acquire the mien, carriage, and conversation of a client. In the diaries of impecunious young men it is possible to chart this shift. The naval officer Augustus Hervey in the 1740s regarded waiting on the great with cheerful cynicism as a necessary part of professional advancement.[48] Twenty years later Richard Cox, a clerk in the Navy Office, agonised about the propriety of courting his contacts among MPs, planning contrived visits with pretty address conned, as he put it, but eventually funking the whole thing.[49] Twenty years on again the young Bland Burges was embarrassed and angered by his father's insistence that he should pay court to a former Lord Chancellor, the Earl Camden.[50] These are, of course, merely individual instances and doubtless there were bumptious young men in the late eighteenth century as there had been earlier. None the less, the conventions of patronage were, I think, moving away from face-to-face contact between seller and buyer. The new, egalitarian sensibilities of the 1760s must have contributed to this withdrawal from public bonding.

Personal interviews with politicians were expected, at least in theory, to concern questions of policy, not patronage. Pitt was master

---

[46] *Autobiography of Henry Taylor, 1800–1875*, 2 vols. (London, 1885), i, p. 212.

[47] Alexander Jacob, *A Complete English Peerage*, 3 vols. (London, 1766–9), i, p. 352.

[48] *Augustine Hervey's Journal*, ed. David Erskine (London, 1953), p. 42.

[49] Charles Frederic Hardy (ed.), *Benenden Letters: London, Country, and Abroad, 1753–1821* (London, 1907), p. 70 *et seq.*

[50] *Selections from the Letters and Correspondence of Sir James Bland Burges, Bart*, ed. James Hutton (London, 1885), p. 51.

of the medium and acquired a reputation for knowledgeable handling of the diverse groups which lobbied Downing Street. This was the Great Man not as patron, but as legislator. Not everyone approved. In fact in 1800 there were complaints by MPs that the use of the Downing Street parlour as a kind of legislative ante-chamber was highly injurious to the dignity of Parliament.[51] Fifty years earlier the worry would have been about the jobbery that was going on within it.

There were alternative forms of gathering, of course. Some depended on the increasing influence of women in West End Society from the 1760s onwards. Routs, couchers, and evening parties of all kind fulfilled various functions, and by the heyday of the salons in the 1830s and 1840s it is conceivable that political hostesses were behaving more like Steele's Patron than their menfolk, though I wonder whether there were really many Phineas Finns who owed their rise to such patronage. In any event, such hospitality did not lessen the trend towards specialisation and segregation when men devoted themselves to politics, from Cabinet dinners all the way down to clubland politicking, culminating in the foundation of the Carlton and the Reform in the 1830s.[52] What these assemblies had in common was precisely what made them less objectionable in the *Spectator*'s terms. They were nominally gatherings of equals. They did not threaten the independence of the individual with courtly manners and hierarchies. This was a long way from the kind of patronising association envisaged in the early eighteenth century, when Henry St John's Brothers' Club had as its avowed object 'to reward deserving persons with our interest and recommendation'.[53] Creevey in old age recalled how as a new MP in 1802 he had declared allegiance not to a patron but to a party. In this way a young nobody 'became at once a publick man, and had a position in society which nothing else could give him. I advert particularly to such persons as myself, who came from the ranks, without either opulence or connections to procure for them admission into the company of their betters'.[54] A century before he would surely have had to brush up his skills as a levee-man.

[51] *Derby Mercury*, 24 April 1800.

[52] *Memoirs and Correspondence of Francis Horner, MP*, ed. Leonard Horner, 2 vols. (London, 1843), i, p. 253.

[53] Elizabeth Handasyde, *Granville the Polite: The Life of George Granville Lord Lansdowne, 1666–1735* (Oxford, 1933), pp. 114–5.

[54] *The Creevey Papers: a Selection from the Correspondence and Diaries of the late Thomas Creevey, MP*, ed. Sir Herbert Maxwell, 2 vols. (London, 1903), i, p. 224.

Men of power still needed followers, but the way they were described changed. The language of interest and connection gave way first to the language of friendship, implying reciprocity rather than dependence, and eventually to the language of party, implying common devotion to a principle or policy. Men of business had earlier been overtly the servants of a patron, even his secretary. They could be painted in Renaissance fashion as unequal but close companions, as Henry Legge was painted with Walpole, John Roberts with Henry Pelham, and Burke with Rockingham. A generation later such an avowal would have embarrassed both sides. I cannot find that the painfully loyal Rose was ever painted with Pitt. Early nineteenth-century politicians had their men of business of course, to draft their letters, research their interests, even write their speeches, but they were usually young, they were unequivocally employees and, in the case of the emerging parliamentary private secretaries, they were employees of the public.[55]

Summarising the changes I have sketched, we might think in terms of two models of statesmanship. One presents the statesman as courtier and courted, deriving respect from display, affable to equals and inferiors but not afraid to proclaim his superiority, uninhibited in his conduct, bold in his demeanour, and proud of his homage. The other reveals the statesman as orator and legislator, discreet in manner, unpretentious in appearance, reserved if not cold, keeping his warmth for his home and hearth, disdainful of men and their wants, devoted to public duties. Walpole and Newcastle could be portrayed as fulfilling the attributes of the first, Pitt and Peel those of the second. I do not pretend that individuals can be pigeonholed in this way, only that here were alternative sets of images and associations to fit changing requirements.

Foreigners were well placed to assess the resulting distinctiveness. Wendeborn was one of the first to affirm that British politics was breeding a kind of civility quite unlike that traditionally associated with the Court as a centre of power, one in which politeness and ease of conversation (in its widest sense) seemed less attainable. He also thought that official life was disabling in this respect. In his time, familiarity where inferiors were involved was more likely to be found among Opposition Whig aristocrats, whereas in Pitt's corridors of power condescension was not to be expected.[56] Whigs themselves

---

[55]  F. MacDonogh, *The Hermit in London: or, Sketches of English Manners*, 5 vols. (London, 1819–20), i, p. 28.
[56]  F. A. Wendeborn, *A View of England towards the Close of the Eighteenth Century*, 2 vols. (London, 1791), i, p. 17.

would have agreed. They often accused their opponents of being what Sheridan called 'stiffnecked and lofty'.[57]

There were more complimentary ways of putting it. Propriety, decency, modesty, were the approved terms for the coldness, correctness, and unpretentiousness which made modern statesmanship superior. At bottom this claim is to a higher virtue; it is about morals as much as manners. We think of the mounting certainty that public life had improved and was improving as Victorian, but its origins lie much earlier, with the generation which was born around 1760, entered public life around 1790, and summed up the lessons of a lifetime around 1820. One such was Robert Plumer Ward, who in his visionary political romance, *De Vere*, sought to distinguish, said, 'what men have been, not what they are. To look into the accounts formerly given by public men of themselves, as well as of each other, makes us tremble; and we are only consoled by the conviction that such accounts are deserved no longer. The whole Walpolian and Pelham school is at an end'.[58] This view commanded a consensus. Whigs and Tories disagreed about history as about everything else, but that the nineteenth century had achieved superior 'political honesty' came to be considered unchallengeable truth.[59] In the 1820s a spate of publications about eighteenth-century men and manners, Horace Walpole's *Letters* and *Memoirs*, Waldegrave's *Memoirs*, and Jesse's *Life of Selwyn*, reinforced the conviction.

That values changed in these years and that institutions were reshaped in consequence is indisputable, but the underlying realities of relationships are not so readily transformed. Reading Peel's correspondence with his Oxford friends in the 1820s, I cannot say that I find its substance unlike Newcastle's correspondence with his Cambridge friends in the 1750s, and Lady Salisbury's conversations with Peel and Wellington are not a world away from those of Hervey with Walpole or Queen Caroline. That nineteenth-century politicians were innately higher-minded than their predecessors would be difficult to prove, but what we can say is that regardless of vice or virtue, the fashion in which public figures met the requirements of their contemporaries was to a considerable extent a question of manners rather than morals. What was it about Georgian politics which made adjustments necessary?

---

[57] Henry Jephson, *The Platform*, 2 vols. (London, 1892), i, pp. 292–3.
[58] Robert Plumer Ward, *De Vere*, 3 vols. (3rd edn., London, 1827), i, pp. xii–xiii.
[59] Frances Anne Kemble, *Further Records, 1848–1883*, 2 vols. (London, 1890), i, pp. 153–4.

First, there is the sense of having to conform to a narrower definition of defensible behaviour. The results are best known in the realm of sexual morality, where conduct which would have been considered unremarkable in the mid-eighteenth century had either to be suppressed or kept secret by the mid-nineteenth. The same process of constriction also occurred in other matters. A favourite expression of the period, 'propriety', applied to all kinds of behaviour. One might suppose that the men I have been talking about, as members of a governing élite, would have been relatively free of constraints and not prone to feelings of social insecurity. Yet the truth was that not a few were either parvenus or regarded as parvenus. In any case there were so many gradations and nuances within a loosely defined genteel class that a sense of inferiority or superiority was easily engendered. Once gained, a reputation for unsociability could be ruinous. What wrecked the career of one of the eighteenth century's most promising statesmen, the Earl of Shelburne, was an unfortunate personal manner, attributed by some to a backwoods Irish upbringing which even two years at Christ Church could not correct. Moreover, those who did share the background and education of the *crème de la crème* were often younger sons, a class whose collective unhappiness and energy is one of the constants of British history. 'Dependence is the greatest curse in nature', complained William Grenville, younger brother of the Marquis of Buckingham and member of one of the wealthiest families in Europe.[60] Hardly a Robespierre, but as his biographer Peter Jupp argues, such feelings powerfully contributed to the alienation and distrust which marked his political relationships. There were many blue-blooded young men who believed themselves uniquely victimised by fate and a titled elder brother. And of course, when they gambled on a political career they were taking a risk, for the rewards were speculative. Other professions, the law for example, offered higher prizes and made less demands in point of personal behaviour. A succession of brutish Lord Chancellors—Northington, Thurlow, and Eldon—got away with manners which would not have been tolerated in ministers lacking the authority of the judicial bench.

I do not mean to imply that what was required was what was needed to impress the ladies of Almack's or cut a figure in Grosvenor Square. The plimsoll line of acceptable behaviour settled lower than that, around the level of the country gentlemen who stocked the backbenches

---

[60] Peter Jupp, *Lord Grenville, 1759–1834* (Oxford, 1985), p. 102.

in the Commons, or the metropolitan middle class whose opinions were so influential outside Parliament. That the ordinary backbencher could be representative of opinion at large is something which arouses the scepticism of historians, but it was an axiom of early nineteenth-century thought that at least when men and manners were being judged, that was the case. Edward Whitty, an experienced parliamentary reporter, unsmilingly advised aspiring statesmen to gauge their progress by selecting among the backbenchers one of the less distinguished intellects as what he called 'a foolometer'.[61] The chances were, he thought, that the reactions observed would be close indeed to that of the man in the street.

Not that the man in the street did not have his own input. It was the belief of many parliamentarians of Peel's era that they were subject to more intrusive scrutiny by the public at large than any preceding generation. Politicians often hold this view, of course, but in this case there may have been justice in it. Some dated the decisive change to the 1770s, when parliamentary debates became the staple fare of the newspapers, when the gossip columns swelled with the reported doings of West End society, when it became possible to identify the faces of prominent individuals in the cartoons of the day. Students of the so-called 'public sphere' assume a solemn interest in the public good on the part of the men and women who enjoyed the information revolution of the eighteenth century, but going by the newspapers, men and women were thought as fascinating as measures. The quantity of print devoted to the personal doings and characteristics of people in public life struck foreigners who encountered it as quite without parallel. When the King of Saxony visited England in 1844 he decided that this incessant 'prying and observation', as he called it, explained a style of statesmanship which contrasted with other modes he knew. 'The [British] statesman', he wrote, 'is not suffered to intrench himself behind . . . documents, but must come forth personally'.[62] English journalists themselves were aware that they were turning the private lives of statesmen into a form of public property. As the anonymous biographer of Lord Liverpool observed in 1827:

[61] *St Stephen's in the Fifties: The Session 1852–3: A Parliamentary Retrospect*, intro. Justin M'Carthy (London, 1906), pp. 301.
[62] C. G. Carus, *The King of Saxony's Journey through England and Scotland in the Year 1844*, trans. S. C. Davison (London, 1846), pp. 36, 157.

[I]n our own country, in particular, the value of this kind of property has
been duly estimated by the public. It is this which has thrown open the doors
of Parliament, and the deliberations of the Cabinet, sooner or later, to every
man in the empire, for the last fifty years. We have felt that our constitution
has a practical efficiency as yet unparalleled in any other country, for we
have watched its minutest operations: our most distinguished public men
have laboured throughout life, as it were, in a glass bee-hive.[63]

Politicians responded with a cult of personality which would have
puzzled their fathers and grandfathers. Walpole endured more abuse
from the Press than any of his successors, but only in stereotyped
images which made his personal behaviour almost irrelevant. It would
not have occurred to him that creating a set of publicly identifiable
characteristics was the means by which political success was to be
achieved. Yet this was the belief of the late eighteenth century. 'My
road must be through character to power', wrote Canning.[64] Recently,
John Ehrman has shown how the Younger Pitt became obsessed with
the public perception of his own character—with, in his own words
'character, not office'.[65] Perhaps he was an extreme case, but the sense
that politicians had become artists modelling their own reputation rather
than appealing to any particular patron, force or sectional interest, is
quite marked. It helps to explain many features of the post-1770s world.
The increased resort to political duels was surely a result of the priority
of preserving reputation at all costs. Perhaps, too, the incidence of
suicide among politicians, said to be higher in the early nineteenth
century than before or after, owed something to this dread of opinion;
and not least there was the horror of guilt by association, something
which had not troubled Walpole and his colleagues, but troubled many
who were touched by the scandals of the Napoleonic Wars. The period
had not invented the term 'deniability', but it certainly had the concept,
as Canning's secretary revealed in 1827 when he explained to a journalist that ministers must have it in their power to deny in Parliament
improper transactions.[66] Walpole and Newcastle had had a healthy
respect for the power of the Press, and did their best to manipulate it,
but never showed the genuine fear of it which afflicted later generations. No eighteenth-century owner of *The Times* would have been

---

[63] *Memoirs of the Public Life and Administration of the Right Honourable the Earl of
Liverpool* (London, 1827), pp. 1–2.
[64] Augustus Granville Stapleton, *George Canning and his Times* (London, 1859), pp. 66–7.
[65] John Ehrman, *The Younger Pitt*, 3 vols. (London, 1969–96), iii, p. 576.
[66] *Some Official Correspondence of George Canning*, ed. Edward J. Stapleton, 2 vols.
(London, 1887), ii, p. 370.

dined in 10 Downing Street as John Walter II was and, I suppose, most of his successors have been. To later generations it seemed that the social acceptance and political influence of newspaper editors went naturally together as achievements of the mid-nineteenth century.[67]

Politicians who did not work at their own character were punished by having it made for them, one reason why the art of modern political biography is effectively a creation of the Pitt era, and why the friends of retiring or deceased ministers attached importance to an early and authorised life. The long history of embarrassments caused by Cabinet ministers' memoirs begins, I think, with Stapleton's biography of Canning, suppressed at the insistence of his former colleagues in government, but eventually published in 1831.[68] It was not, however, necessary to be either a Cabinet minister or dead to find oneself described in print. From the 1780s there appeared compilations by parliamentary reporters, offering pen portraits of all the men whom they saw debating in Lords and Commons. Such material was overwhelmingly concerned with character, manners and oratory rather than what we would call principles or policy.

Two features of this flourishing branch of literature stand out. First, its authors were merciless in identifying idiosyncrasies. Accent, gesture, gait, dress, countenance, complexion, mannerism, were minutely delineated. Generally, the results match the impressions one might gain from unpublished sources, suggesting that publications of this kind did indeed provide a link between the member on the backbenches and the man in the street. Secondly, the manners approved by implication were those which I have tried to identify by other means this afternoon, gravity combined with modesty, unpretentiousness with dignity, manly reserve with gentlemanlike bearing. Rudeness, oafishness, clownishness, any form of what might be termed low manners, were devastatingly exposed, but equally, so was an excess of exhibition criticised. In these publications the reputation of being a fine gentlemen, or the most compleat gentlemen, or perfectly genteel, is implicitly condemned. It was not a disadvantage to appear as Peel was said to appear, 'conscious that the senate, not the ball-room, is his proper sphere'.[69]

[67] A Selection from the Diaries of Edward Henry Stanley, 15th Earl of Derby (1826–93) between September 1869 and March 1878, ed. John Vincent, Camden Fifth Series, vol. 4, (London, 1994), p. 200.
[68] Henry Reeve (ed.), The Greville Memoirs: A Journal of the Reigns of King George IV and King William IV By the late C. F. Greville, Esq., 3 vols. (3rd edn., London, 1875), i, p. 272.
[69] Sir Robert Peel, as Statesman and Orator (London, 1846), p. 16.

Was there an alternative to the trend which I have tried to sketch? Probably not, though the possibility of another cast of politician, demagogic on the American and French model, or (so to speak) camera-list on the German model, is worth considering. Demagogy never really threatened the gentlemanly ethic. Many Radicals prided themselves on their genteel manners. It was, after all, the populist Sir Francis Burdett whose idea of punishing the Irish nationalist O'Connell for his sub-versive activities was to move that he be expelled from Brook's.[70] In any case neither House of Parliament appreciated demagogic oratory, and the difference between the rhetorical styles which MPs adopted for Westminster and their electors was often noticed.[71] As for the evolution of an elite caste of governors, it showed no sign of happening. On the contrary, the amateurism of politicians grew stronger as the profession-alism of civil servants intensified. The result was famously described by Bagehot, when he observed that senior administrators 'regard the Parliamentary statesmen who are set to rule over them much as Benga-lees regard the English—as persons who are less intelligent and less instructed than themselves, but who nevertheless are to be obeyed. They never think of changing places any more than a Hindoo thinks of becoming an Englishman'.[72] We associate this mentality with Victorian Civil Service reform, but in fact the tendencies were there as early as the 1760s, when the separation of political from administrative func-tions was being increasingly urged. The tension between the two was less marked earlier, and there were administrators who proved adept as politicians. A good example would be the fourth Earl of Sandwich, a genuinely committed naval administrator and at the same time a poli-tician very much in the Walpolian mould, in fact almost an examplar of that type I tried to describe, flamboyant in public and private life, famously approachable by all classes, unconcerned by the criticism of others. His biographer Nicholas Rodger says he 'came as near to being a professional politician as a nobleman well could do'.[73] But as a profes-sional politician in the next generation, he would either have had to become a full-time administrator or change his tune, and, indeed, in his last years he looked outdated among a generation both less relaxed and

---

[70] *The Holland House Diaries 1831–1840*, pp. 330–1.
[71] Frederick von Raumer, *England in 1835*, 3 vols. (London, 1836), ii, p. 275.
[72] *Bagehot's Historical Essays*, ed. Norman St John Stevas (New York, 1966), pp. 175–6.
[73] N. A. M. Rodger, *The Insatiable Earl: A Life of John Montagu, 4th Earl of Sandwich* (London, 1993), p. 87.

less versatile. Politicians, in short, chose to remain gentlemen, exposed to a Parliament of gentlemen and a public of would-be gentlemen.

I suppose what I have been describing is in essence a shift from a court-based culture to a club-based culture, as the priorities of managing first Parliament and then public opinion exerted themselves. Foreigners had been struck by the resemblances between the Commons and a gentleman's club as early as the 1760s, and as William White, the doorkeeper who divulged the secrets of the life of the Commons in the 1850s, contended, it was precisely clubmanship which best described the individual manners and collective behaviour of politicians.[74] The understated style adopted in managing the club is a long way from the hype and hassle of management methods today. On the other hand, this particular club survived a turbulent time during which its counterparts in other countries were devastated by social revolution or demoralised by the rise of democracy. Perhaps Georgian politicians knew more about styles of management than their successors have sometimes supposed.

---

[74] *Lettere e Scritti inediti di Pietro e di Alessandro Verri*, ed. Carlo Casati, 3 vols. (Milan, 1879–80), ii, p. 92; William White, *The Inner Life of the House of Commons*.

*Proceedings of the British Academy*, **94**, 127–156

# Coleridge's New Poetry

## J. C. C. MAYS
### *University College Dublin*

THE LAST ATTEMPT TO COLLECT Coleridge's poetical writing, plays as well as poems, was in 1912. The 1912 edition, edited by Ernest Hartley Coleridge for the Clarendon Press,[1] proved remarkably durable but mistakes and omissions have become evident; also, expectations concerning the way poetry texts should be presented have altered in the intervening years. In EHC's edition, the poems were arranged in two categories: Volume I was made up of a main sequence of serious and achieved poems, and Volume II contained sequences of different sub-canonical forms and levels of achievement (epigrams, jeux d'esprit, metrical experiments, drafts and fragments).

The effect of the divided arrangement was to relegate Volume II material to a category where it appeared extra, optional, ignorable. The less literary and the less finished were bundled away and excluded, the implication being that there are higher and lower levels of poetic activity and those which fail to preserve decent poetic reputation are best ignored. The old edition was put together at a time when poetry aimed to be poetic in a late nineteenth-century, high serious or at least magical kind of way, and times have changed. The canonical/non-canonical separation is nowadays more contentious than helpful, and the poems in the forthcoming new edition are therefore arranged in a unified chronological sequence.

Read at the Academy 24 April 1996. © The British Academy 1997.

[1] *The Complete Poetical Works of Samuel Taylor Coleridge*, ed. Ernest Hartley Coleridge (Oxford: Clarendon Press, 2 vols. 1912; reprinted with corrections); hereafter 'EHC'. In the discussion which follows, to avoid confusion, I use EHC's titles even when I quote amended texts from the new *Collected Coleridge* edition.

Editors try to be accurate and informed and helpful. I think their role is subservient: simply to find appropriate ways to present textual evidence as it comes to light and surrounding information as it is relevant. Now my task is complete, however, it strikes me the *Collected Coleridge* edition involves more than repairs and improvements. I am persuaded that the poems which were previously unknown, or, if known, either have not been collected or were relegated to EHC's Volume II, will exert a powerful influence on the way the previously-known poems in Volume I are read. They are neither more nor less of the same; they constitute a different order of poetry whose encompassing requires considerable modification of some long-held views.

I stress there really is a lot of new material. Of the 706 poems in the *Collected Coleridge* edition, 257 are added to what is contained somewhere in the old one. The continuous sequence of 706 is surrounded by a penumbra of 133 poems and titles, some of which remove false attributions and others of which suggest attributions which none the less wait to be proved. If one supposes forty-three poems in the penumbral category could prove to be genuine, up to 300 new poems are added and about a third of them have never been published anywhere before. It is quite likely that many were known to EHC—he had access to notebooks, annotated volumes and other manuscript material[2]—but he was selective on principle. Not only did he assume the duty of presenting his grandfather in the form to which he believed his contemporaries would most positively respond, he thought it right to omit whatever might distract or not interest them.[3]

An example of this is provided by poems Coleridge wrote from late 1830 onwards. EHC positioned seven such poems in Volume I and three in different sections of Volume II ('Cholera Cured Before-hand' and 'To a Child' among *Jeux d'esprit*, and 'Epitaph of the Present Year on the Monument of Thomas Fuller' among *Epigrams*).[4] A number of

---

[2] The material available to EHC is described by George Whalley, 'Annex B: The Dispersal of Coleridge's Books' in George Whalley and H. J. Jackson (eds.), *Marginalia* (Princeton, NJ: Princeton University Press, 5 vols. 1980—; *Collected Coleridge* 12), I, pp. clvi–clxxiv.

[3] An interesting light on EHC's relation to surrounding literary standards is shed by his own *Poems* (London: John Lane, The Bodley Head, 1898). They can be compared with the more lively taste in poetry manifested by his fellow Coleridge editor, James Dykes Campbell.

[4] That is, compare EHC, I, pp. 487–92 and II, pp. 985–7, 975 respectively. A complete listing is supplied in Appendix A below.

misreadings and misunderstandings are easily corrected[5] and further improvements (e.g. more exact dating) can be made on the basis of further information.[6] EHC based 'Cholera Cured Before-hand' on two texts: I know of four. He based 'My Baptismal Birth-day' on two printed texts: five manuscripts must now be added. He reported one manuscript of 'Love's Apparition and Evanishment': six manuscripts have since come to light. So the story continues. The poems from the years 1830–4 in the old edition rested on a base of about twenty manuscript and printed versions. (It is impossible to be precise because EHC sometimes introduces readings from extraneous sources.) The same ten poems now rest on more than forty versions—that is, the textual base has doubled.

To the improved texts of these ten late poems, the new edition adds twenty-four more.[7] Eight of the twenty-four have been published (in *Collected Letters*, in academic journals, in early magazines) but the remaining sixteen have not previously been published in any form. Some exist in multiple versions (up to six, in one case), the majority in a single version. Only a couple are new in the sense they were previously unknown to anyone working on Coleridge: the larger number were known to the librarians in whose care they rested or to other Coleridge editors who drew them to my attention, they have exchanged owners in salesrooms, a good proportion must have been seen, as I said, by EHC; yet they are new in the sense that they are brought into relation

---

[5] In the three poems positioned in Volume II, for example, EHC (i) passes over a stanza-break between ll. 34–5 of 'Cholera Cured Before-hand'; (ii) derives the title 'To a Child' from James Dykes Campbell's 1893 edition, not from the *Athenaeum* text as the footnote suggests; and (iii) misreads several words in 'Epitaph on the Present Year' (the title properly continues 'or' [not <u>on</u>] 'a Monument'; 'though' in the last line should read 'then'; I think EHC also misread the tangled l. 7). Compare (i) *Collected Letters of Samuel Taylor Coleridge*, ed. Earl Leslie Griggs (Oxford: Clarendon Press, 6 vols. 1956–71), VI, pp. 917–18 and *Poetical Works* (London: William Pickering, 3 vols. 1834), II, pp. 142–4; (ii) *Athenaeum*, No. 3144 (28 January 1888), 116 with *Poetical Works*, ed. James Dykes Campbell (London: Macmillan, 1893), p. 467A; and (iii) British Library, C.44.g.1, rear flyleaves (also compare Campbell, 645B with EHC's version of this last: EHC had a touching respect for Campbell's editing and took over more than his titles).

[6] For instance, the group of poems written from towards the end of 1830 should include 'Inscription on a Time-piece'. EHC, II, p. 974 gives it as an 'Epigram', taking his text from *Literary Remains* (1844). It had in fact been included in the second edition of *Table Talk* (1835) as one of the poems 'accidentally omitted' from *Poetical Works* (1834); also, nine different manuscript versions are now known and affect the positioning as well as the make-up of the text; it dates from November 1830. 'Reason' and 'Forbearance', on the other hand, need to be removed from the 1830–4 group; that is, further evidence suggests earlier origins.

[7] Listed below in Appendix B.

with the other poems in a single undivided sequence for the first time. Whereas the old standard edition presents Coleridge's ten last poems (164 lines of verse) resting on twenty-three texts, the new edition replaces them with thirty-four poems (334 lines) resting on eighty-one texts—to which can be added six more poems with varying, lesser claims to authenticity.

As I will go on to describe, the picture changes because the additions are not simply more of the same: they supply what was suppressed or excluded. EHC's seven last poems—'Reason', 'Self-Knowledge', 'Forbearance', 'Love's Apparition and Evanishment', 'To the Young Artist Kayser of Kaserwerth', 'My Baptismal Birth-day' and 'Epitaph'—make up a rather solemn, one-directional sequence. When the poems which were relegated to Volume II or excluded altogether are reinstated, all is changed. It is at once apparent that EHC's divided presentation rests on a highly selective canon; the boundary-division between his first and second volumes collapses when the full amount of what Coleridge wrote is admitted. Newly-edited texts can be compared to refurbished pictures: to concentrate the same metaphor, when everything is allowed to enter the frame, the picture is transformed.

Coleridge was described as belonging to a 'new school' of poetry, along with Wordsworth and Southey, from the time of Jeffrey's review of *Thalaba* onwards.[8] The irony is, that in the process by which the 'new school' was incorporated into mainstream culture as the Romantic movement, Coleridge's contribution came to be seen, by himself as well as others, in a mainly Wordsworthian light. This nineteenth-century view of Coleridge is what the 1912 edition canonises and what the suppressed and excluded poems challenge. They upset the conventional story that he came into his own as a poet when he began to write in a more or less Wordsworthian way and later came to write a different kind of poem when he reflected on his inability to sustain such notes: they make the relation between the so-called 'canonical' and 'subcanonical' sorts of writing crucial instead. At the same time, Coleridge's poetry becomes of greater interest in its own right—that is, not simply to adorn a tale of a few miraculous successes followed by disappointment, 'Why is the harp of Quantock silent?'[9]—and on grounds other than those to which conventional appeal is made.

---

[8] *Edinburgh Review*, I: 1 (October 1802), 63–83.

[9] Wordsworth in a note to his 'Memorials of a Tour on the Continent, 1820', in *Poetical Works*, eds. E. De Selincourt and Helen Darbishire (Oxford: Clarendon Press, 5 vols. 1940–9; rev. 1952–9), III, p. 472.

The new Coleridge is different from the old in being more widely various, and, if he appears no less complicated, the complications are of a different sort. The relation to be understood is not between success and unsuccess but different levels of seriousness, varieties of address. Coleridge's whole poetry straddles a divide between exploration and meditation, on the one hand, and humour and satire on the other. The divide is not necessarily anguished, as some readers assume. He wrote poems of mystery in a literal sense, in that they utilise poetry to produce an order which at the beginning is unknown, and poems which are social and self-conscious and attempt different kinds of outcome. Such categories of poetry are not discontinuous, nor are the values they register. Understanding is not a matter of supplementing one category with the other but of perceiving how they thrive by virtue of their interconnectedness.

Walter Savage Landor was advised by his friend and future biographer, John Foster, to omit from a new edition of the *Imaginary Conversations* those which were on political and miscellaneous subjects, so as to heighten the specifically literary appeal of those which remained, but Landor resisted:

> There is a particle of salt in the very poorest of them which will preserve it from decomposition. Beside, this is to be considered, which nobody has considered sufficiently. If Shakespeare had written but *Othello*, the noblest of human works, he would scarcely have been half so great as the having written many dramas, even inferior ones, has made him. Genius shows its power by its multiformity.[10]

This is the burden of what I have to say, likewise, and the example of the poems Coleridge wrote from late 1830 onwards will supply the detail.

The twenty-four poems to be added at the end of Coleridge's poetic life are representative of the additions contained in the new *Collected* edition. They are made up of rewriting and altering, typically in marginalia. For instance, five lines pretending to be 'From a Manuscript Poem of Athanasius Sphinx' are written into Nehemiah Grew's *Cosmologia Sacra* (1701) and two lines *On an Ellipsis* are written into John

---

[10] John Forster, *Walter Savage Landor: A Biography* (London: Chapman and Hall, 2 vols. 1869), II, pp. 450–1.

Kenyon's *Rhymed Plea for Tolerance* (1833).[11] Lines are written in published letters and still-unpublished notebooks on subjects ranging from George Croly's *Apocalypse* and Reed's *Shakespeare* to a versified adaptation of Isaiah.[12] There are two sets of poems which were copied out against the demands of autograph-hunters; indeed the last in the new sequence is a sample of doggerel sent to a Mr Saunders a fortnight before Coleridge died.[13] There is a forgotten sonnet titled 'The Irish Orator's Booze' published in *Fraser's Magazine*.[14] There are poems over which Coleridge evidently took some care which exist in multiple versions, such as the 'Sonnet to my Tin Shaving-pot', and others such as a pair of commemorative word-cartoons of Lady Mary Shepherd at Cambridge which together extend to thirty-four lines but which were left in a notebook.[15]

The topics embraced by the additional poems are very much of their time. The adaptation of Isaiah departs from Coleridge's earlier interest, which was metrical—specifically hexametrical—and interprets the prophet in terms of contemporary imports from the East, the French as Philistines, Whig politicians, and so on.[16] The one poem with an explicit socio-political meaning which is included in EHC's edition—'Cholera Cured Before-hand'—is joined by several others on reform. Coleridge writes about the Irish in politics and literary politics, about doctors and their professional lives as well as doctors from the point of view of a long-suffering patient. He writes about neighbours and house-visitors, and his attitudes towards women and children are, for better or worse, those of his time; the poem EHC titled 'To a Young Child' is characteristic. He writes against bluestockings but finds the commingling of George Croly's intellectual and social pretensions no less ridiculous:

> The Keeper of the Seals inscribes my name—
> What? in the Book of Life? O better far—

---

[11] British Library, C.44.g.1, p. -5 and C.126.d.16, p. 3; compare *Marginalia*, II, p. 888 and III, p. 370.

[12] These are written in Notebook 54, fol. 22, Notebook 55, fol. 18ᵛ, and Notebook 52, fol. 23 (British Library, Add MSS 47549, 47550, 47547 respectively).

[13] See *Collected Letters*, VI, pp. 988–9. There is a facsimile in Sotheby Catalogue, 17 December 1981, p. 114 (lot 199); also a photocopy in British Library, RP 2277 (ii).

[14] V (July 1832), p. 721.

[15] The two sets of lines on Mary Shepherd are in Notebook Q, fol. 72–3, also 68ᵛ (New York Public Library, Berg Collection). The 'Tin Shaving-pot' poem is quoted in part below.

[16] Coleridge's literary interest in Isaiah was usually in the possibility of hexametrical translation. A new, thirty-seven line version dating from December 1799 (Victoria College Library, S MS F2.7) is included in the *Collected Coleridge*.

In the Book of LIVINGS! *This* now I call Fame
O Croley! born beneath auspicious Star![17]

Casual poems alternate with serious ones. Thus, 'Love's Apparition and Evanishment' appears between three savage lines on 'The Hunger of Liars' written in a notebook and thirty-six loosely-written lines beginning 'Oh! might I but my Patrick *love*' dictated to a medical assistant.[18] 'Epitaph' is sandwiched between 'Athanasius Sphinx' and a jokey apology for Abraham Wivell's half-length portrait:

'In truth he's no beauty!' cry'd Moll, Poll, and Tab,
But they all of them own'd He'd the Gift of the Gab.[19]

'Know Thyself' comes between the lines 'On an Ellipsis of John Kenyon's' and five lines in mixed Latin and English which Coleridge glossed as 'Hexamerised Gobbets, expectorated 3 Feby. 1833, at the 10th Hour A.M. by me, poor body-crazed Sinner'. In Lorna Arnold's translation, they go:

Rumbling in the bowels, laborious Breathing, Bile, troublesome
                                                              catarrh;
Hand on hand pressed hard across the Duodenum;
Gall, unhappy Cat whose name is purulent <u>Pus</u>,
Mucus, when we Sing—i.e. Miew! curse! with Wheezing;
And this common Cough = Hecking, Tuzzle and Tearing.[20]

One can easily appreciate what EHC achieved by passing over such lines and allowing only three carefully chosen examples into his Volume II.

The interpretation which EHC's choice imposes is that a serious poet at the end of his life writes about his coming end. The poet reflects on baptism, youth, lost love, truth, death, but seriousness is not compromised by levity. EHC's Coleridge does not indulge in outrageous rhymes and puns or write a poem such as the following, which acts out a drumming attempt to provide distraction from pain. It is headed,

[17] Notebook 54, fol. 22 (British Library, Add MS 47549). Here and elsewhere I have not recorded fresh starts and deleted words in quoting from manuscript. The editor of *The Literary Gazette*, William Jerdan, used his influence to obtain a suitable benefice for Croly, but in vain, and it was not until 1835 that Croly became rector of St Stephen's, Walbrook.
[18] 'The Hunger of Liars' appears in Notebook 51, fol. 5[v] (British Library, Add MS 47546); 'Oh! might I but my Patrick *love*' in a contemporary notebook-album in private hands.
[19] Versions of the lines are to be found in Arthur Coleridge, *Reminiscences*, ed. J. A. Fuller-Maitland (London: Constable, 1921), p. 43 and *Collected Letters*, VI, p. 969.
[20] The original lines were drafted in Notebook 54, fol. 19 (British Library, Add MS 47549).

'Substitute for swearing under the torture of Sciatic Rheumatism and
of equal virtue as a Charm':

> O Screams of Scotch Bagpipes! O Rub a Dub Dub!
> O Satan! O Moloch! O Bëelzebub!
> O Gripes Grapes and Barberries, acrid and crabby!
> Diabole diabolissime, abi! abi! abi![21]

No matter that the related 'Dialogue between a Nimble Doctor and a
Crippled Patient' is more representative of Coleridge's late verse than
the seven poems chosen by EHC which are recycled by the anthologists:

> D<sup>r</sup> Hop-o-my-thumb! my right Thigh's rheumatic.
> Yes, Sir, a plain case! tis a dolour Sciatic.
> D<sup>r</sup> Hop-o' my-thumb, that frisk on so skittish,
> *Sigh Attic* d' ye call it? No, by Jove! 'tis Great British.[22]

No matter that both sets of verses are indeed more representative of
Coleridge's verse overall: there are earlier 'Lines on the Cur, Arthritis'
and the second addition to the complete sequence is 'Fragments of an
Ode on Punning'.[23] Such poems are an embarrassment to the assumptions about poetry which the 1912 arrangement protects.

Coleridge did not go soft in the head in his later years; I mean,
additional poems of the sort I have been describing are distributed
through his career. 'Inscription on a Time-piece', drafted in November
1830, is anticipated by 'For a Clock in a Market-place' drafted in
1809.[24] The 'Tin Shaving-pot' repeats the celebration of a battered
tea-kettle at Christ's Hospital.[25] 'The Irish Orator's Booze' carries on
from poems published in the *Morning Post* in 1801.[26] The copying-out
of 'A Guilty Sceptic's Death Bed' for autographs in November 1832

---

[21] The first of six album epigrams copied in Coleridge's hand on 13 October 1832 (Victoria
College Library, S MS F2.15). The last line can be translated as 'Most devilish devil!
Avaunt! Avaunt! Avaunt!'

[22] The last of the six epigrams described in the previous note. The sciatic rheumatism for
which Coleridge was receiving treatment from J. H. B. Williams was the subject of two of
the other six epigrams.

[23] For the first, a letter to Thomas Poole dated 17 May 1801 (British Library, Add MS
35343, fol. 279), see *Collected Letters*, II, p. 732. The second appears in Notebook 42, fols.
71–2 and is as yet unpublished.

[24] Compare Notebook 48, fol. 6<sup>v</sup> (British Library, Add MS 47543) with Notebook L, fol.
22<sup>v</sup> (*The Notebooks of Samuel Taylor Coleridge*, ed. Kathleen Coburn *et al.* (Princeton, NJ:
Princeton University Press, 5 double vols. 1957— ), III, #3546).

[25] 'Monody on a Tea-kettle' is printed in EHC, I, pp. 18–19.

[26] 'Song to be sung by the Lovers of All the Noble Liquors Comprised under the Name of
Ale' and 'Drinking *versus* Thinking; or, A Song Against the New Philosophy' appeared in
the *Morning Post*, 18 and 25 September 1801, over a pseudonym.

was prompted by a recollection of 'Epitaph on a Bad Man' which had been published in September 1801.[27] So the dialogue continues across the years. The first version of 'Epitaph' was conceived in a form and spirit close to the epitaph Coleridge wrote for himself at Edinburgh in 1803.[28] 'Self-knowledge' can be read as a companion to or development from 'Human Life, on the Denial of Immortality'.[29] There is continuity between the new poems I have been discussing and the earlier writing.

The previous canon of Coleridge's published poetry had included one sort of 'bad' poem from the start and its early date was its excuse. The three-volume collections of 1828 and 1829 went back to the single-volume collections of 1796, 1797 and 1803, to which Henry Nelson Coleridge added poems from manuscript in 1834. The following lines from EHC's version of 'The Kiss' are representative:

> In tender accents, faint and low,
> Well-pleas'd I hear the whisper'd 'No!'
> The whispered 'No'—how little meant!
> Sweet Falsehood that endears Consent![30]

Judges are nowadays reprimanded for saying as much, and the different level of thinking in poems like *Christabel* is startling. But the point at issue here is that poems of a differently 'bad' sort, which family editors excluded for understandable reasons at earlier times, were written by Coleridge in abundance throughout his life. Their number and quality suggest the continuity of his career is not to be seen as sentimental prentice work, emerging into the Stowey *annus mirabilis*, before collapsing into drugs and metaphysics—as Wordsworth put it, ' "in blossom" only for four years—from 1796 to 1800'.[31] They require us to look again at the sort of poet Coleridge most prolifically and continuously was.

The 287 poems which make up the sequence of EHC's canonical Volume 1 form less than half of what he wrote and one must acknowledge that they were accompanied by a range of poetry different in quality and ambition from the beginning. It is not helpful to relegate

---

[27] 'The Guilty Sceptic's Death Bed' is one of five sets of verses now at Boston University (Special Collections). The earlier poem, drafted in Notebook 3½ (*Notebooks*, I, #625 fol. 120$^v$), was published over a pseudonym in the *Morning Post*, 22 September 1801.

[28] Located in EHC, I, pp. 491–2 and II, p. 970, no.61 respectively.

[29] EHC, I, p. 487 and I, pp. 425–6.

[30] 'The Kiss', ll. 21–4; EHC, I, p. 64.

[31] To Sir Henry Taylor; see his *Autobiography . . . 1800–1875* (London: Longman, 2 vols. 1885), I, p. 188.

the 'unserious' poems so as to contemplate the 'serious' poems without distraction. Poems like 'Epitaph' and 'The Pains of Sleep' and the 'Monody on the Death of Chatterton' make less sense when they are isolated in this way. The larger accompaniment comprises shards and fragments, and the additional completed poems are generally short, it is true, but they constitute a matrix, a substrate. It is not even accurate to describe the two modes as alternating. They are simultaneous; the additions supply the dominant continuum. It is difficult at first to understand how poems like 'Epitaph', 'The Pains of Sleep', and 'Monody on Chatterton' might arise from a background of continual poetic burbling but the effort is worthwhile. It enables one to appreciate qualities in the 'serious' poems which are otherwise obscured, and qualities in the merely rhyming, insistently punning poems which are equally worthy of attention.

I described the additional poems as 'merely' rhyming but the description requires qualification. We should note that, of the 334 lines of verse Coleridge wrote between the end of 1830 and his death, only five lines are unrhymed. His rhyming schemes usually follow a simple *aabb* or *abab* pattern; that is, his poems of all sorts characteristically rhyme merely. The most complicated instances among these late poems — 'My Baptismal Birth-day' and 'Love's Apparition and Evanishment' — only reshuffle regroupings of the same. Coleridge makes no attempt to use rhyme-patterns in counterpoint with complicated shifts of point of view, as Blake and Wordsworth do in their earlier quatrain poems. His rhymes do not provide a form to write into and against, like the more elaborate stanzas favoured by Keats and Shelley; they exist simply to carry meaning forward. Stress falls on the rhymes, and the effect is as often as not mildly surprising, but the effects are neither delayed nor complicated by other effects. The metrical pattern is typically some version of pentameter, with free substitutions. Rhyme enables the lines to move in a spontaneous, ad-libbed, associative way, constituting for the most part a kind of 'low boil' verse.

Such a use of rhyme constitutes an aural worry bead; or, better, an invitation to articulate: 'Rhymes seeks S. T. COLERIDGE,' he professed.[32] The insistent puns are part and parcel of the same manner:

[32] In William Upcott's collection of autographs gathered entitled *Reliques of my Contemporaries* (2 MS vols. 1830–3), II, p. 46 at New York Public Library, Berg Collection. Compare 'Written in an Album', l. 2; EHC, II, p. 972, no.70.

after all, puns are constructed of words whose sounds fuse in total rhyme as their meanings fly apart. The interrelated rhyming and punning of Coleridge's late poems is witness to continual resolution and dissolution of meaning. Sometimes the puns are technically complex. The conclusion of the Latin-English original of the lines quoted earlier in Lorna Arnold's translation runs:

> Mucus, cum Canimus—i.e. Miew! curse! with Wheezing;
> Ac hic et haec Tussis = Hecking, Tuzzle and Tearing.

A reader must translate 'Canimus' into 'we sing', and then 'Wheezing' back into 'we sing' to get the point. 'Mucus' is not simply 'Mucus', it is 'Miew! Curse!' This is perhaps what many of us expect from puns, and there are other unpublished poems in which Coleridge goes further, with triple puns in several languages in characters transliterated into other alphabets.

The interest is not simply bookish gamesmanship, however. In 'The Three Patriots: Cockney Snip, Irish Blarney, and Me', the rhyming-punning sets out a critical-political position in the month before the Reform Bill passed its third reading in the Commons:

> *Cockney Snip.*
>
> I'se a Rifforman!
>
> *Irish Blarney.*
>
> A Rafformer I!
>
> *Me.*
>
> And I write them both, a loud cry,
> And for this Riff-raff-form will live and die![33]

The mimicry sums up the coming together of divergent instinctive interests in a larger idea. It is satirical about the supporters and sympathetic to the general cause. Against such a background, the punning structure of the better-known 'My Baptismal Birth-day' is less likely to be overlooked:

> Is that a Death-bed, where the CHRISTIAN lies?
> Yes!—But not *his*: 'tis DEATH itself, *there* dies.

---

[33] In a letter to Charles Aders, 11 February 1832 (Cornell University, WORDSWORTH; *Collected Letters*, VI, p. 883).

'My Baptismal Birth-day' is based on the same punning coincidence of kinds of living and dying and the reversibility of categories as Donne's Holy Sonnet 6, 'Death be not proud . . .'. Even as Coleridge's pun heroically yokes together meanings in a final statement, the appositional grammar tempers its effect as a conclusion. A device which elsewhere blows up in a reader's face here lowers him more gently into the ground.

Puns are often effortful and pointless and they can also be sad, as in this last example. Perhaps late Victorians believed serious poets did not pun, but Coleridge was a contemporary of Charles Lamb and Thomas Hood and believed that, at the highest level, extremes meet. Like rhymes which draw attention to themselves, puns can be sombre as well as funny. They are 'strictly, in a philosophical sense, a natural expression of natural emotion'; 'Language itself is formed upon associations of this kind'.[34] Here is another previously unpublished poem from the years 1830–4 in which sounds clang shut like iron gates, and forms associated with light verse are freighted with anguish:

> Rack not my death-bed!—Silence! No replying!
> Ah stern Alternative—Nothing or Hell!
> Of this poor hope would'st rob me, that in dying
> I became nothing! Hark! that distant Yell!
> No! twas the Echo, that repeated—Hell.[35]

And here is a passage from another—'An Elegiac Plusquam-Sesqui-Sonnet to my Tin Shaving-pot'—in which the overlaying of sound becomes, diferently, a testament to tenderness:

> Thy Tears on the hot Hob
> Say, Iss! Iss! Iss! hard by the Top-bar reeks,
> And to each tear makes answer with a Sob!
> The Cambrian's Broth is none the worse for *Leeks*;
> *Rents* are the landed Noble's pride and glee;
> *Holes*, side or bottom, both to Man and Gun
> Are apt and seemly.—Would, twere so with *thee!*[36]

[34] *Lectures 1808–1819: On Literature*, ed. R. A. Foakes (Princeton, NJ: Princeton University Press, 2 vols. 1987; *Collected Coleridge* 5), I, p. 271; *Notebooks*, III, #3762 fol. 97. Compare Sylvan Barnet, 'Coleridge on Puns: A Note to his Shakespeare Criticism', *Journal of English and Germanic Philology*, LVI (1957), 602–9.

[35] 'A Guilty Sceptic's Death Bed' (Boston University, Special Collections).

[36] The version quoted here is from a fair copy in Coleridge's own hand, made in his 'Bed, book-room & sick-cage' at Highgate (on fol. 34 of Quarto Notebook at New York Public Library, Berg Collection).

This is all very well, I hear someone say. There are no doubt connections between these poems written at the same time. It is not altogether surprising that the collapsing rhymester of 'Lines on Lady Shepherd' ('With Sal Atticum corn'd, / With Paper-Spice pepper'd, / With Book-Garnish adorn'd— / Enter Lady Mary Shepheard—')[37] should employ simple couplets to turn the meaning of 'Know Thyself' inside out ('Ignore thyself, and strive to know thy God!'). After all, 'Epitaph' employs identical means to convert 'Death in Life' into 'Life in Death'. What, though, is the connection between this kind of writing and Coleridge's earlier poems? To stop beating about the bush, what about the 'Ancient Mariner' and 'Christabel'? What has 'Kubla Khan' to do with the kind of poetry represented by the categories excluded by EHC's old standard edition? The question is a fair one and I think it can be answered fairly. DEATH and LIFE-IN-DEATH entered Coleridge's poetry in the 'Ancient Mariner'. The continuity is real.

The connecting factor was long ago described by Kenneth Burke in an essay entitled 'Musicality in Verse'.[38] Burke writes about the marked consistency of texture of Coleridge's verse, and explains it with reference to habitual phonetic and grammatical patterns: alliteration concealed in cognate variation as in 'bathed by the mist', acrostic scrambling as in 'tyrannous and strong' and 'A damsel with a dulcimer', tonal chiasmus ('The ship drove fast'), patterns of augmentation and diminution. His detailed analysis makes evident that the kind of effects which give Coleridge's verse its characteristic sound are gained by versions of punning and rhyming such as I have been describing. Compare the changing of vowels within a constant consonantal frame in 'loud lewd Mirth'; or the repeating of one consonant while varying its partner with a non cognate variant ('glimmers with green light'; 'fluent phrasemen', 'in green and sunny glade'). The effects are subtle and, without going so far as to claim that the habitual patterns Burke describes were consciously striven for, Coleridge appears to have been aware of the reversals of direction they contained.

In the 'Ancient Mariner', the narrative establishes itself with preliminary interruptions and quickly settles into a mood of rising expectation

[37] ll. 1–4 in Notebook Q, fol. 72 (New York Public Library, Berg Collection).
[38] Appended to *The Philosophy of Literary Form* (Baton Rouge: Louisiana State University Press, 2nd edn. 1967), pp. 369–78.

which then peaks and goes into reverse. As the Mariner catches up with the implications of his crime, he begins again from an opposite attitude. 'The Sun came up upon the left' becomes 'The Sun now rose upon the right' and the reversal contains the argument of the poem: how to embrace this kind of oscillation, emotionally and metaphysically. The narrative as a whole attempts to bring into alignment the details of texture analysed by Burke to achieve some kind of rapprochement. Parts V and VI, in which Coleridge expanded on the first draft of his narrative,[39] contain writing whose rhyme and texture is as different as are the meanings the longer stanzas try to control. They appear to represent an attempt to trawl deeper in an attempt to achieve some resolution of the debate between the 'Two voices in the air', one stern and the other 'soft as honey-dew'.

'Christabel' takes on the argument broached in the expanded portion of the 'Ancient Mariner', through the metaphor of guardian spirits, at a self-consciously deeper level. Coleridge said his purpose was to 'have more nearly realized my ideal, than I had done in my first attempt'.[40] The lengthened ballad stanzas are expanded into rhymed paragraphs, and sound-effects are stretched across an even wider field of meaning. 'Christabel' engages the issues which emerged during the composition of the 'Ancient Mariner' and founders in the attempt. Part I sets out the problem of how innocence can be contaminated by an awareness of evil with such subtle force that there is no way to continue in the same terms. Coleridge attempted to continue the narrative, but the texture of the verse in Part II reveals the focus has been deflected to a more manageable level. The real issue is a situation; it can be wound into and better understood, but not sufficiently understood to unwind into a plot with a happy outcome. 'The reason of my not finishing Christabel', Coleridge is reported as saying, 'is not that I don't know how to do it; for I have, as I always had, the whole plan entire from beginning to end in my mind; but I fear I could not carry on with equal success the execution of the Idea—the most difficult, I think, that can be attempted to Romantic Poetry—I mean witchery by daylight.'[41]

---

[39] This claim rests on textual analysis in the new *Collected Coleridge* edition. See meanwhile Stephen Parrish, ' "Leaping and Lingering": Coleridge's lyrical ballads' in Richard Gravil, Lucy Newlyn and Nicholas Roe (eds.), *Coleridge's Imagination: Essays in Memory of Pete Laver* (Cambridge: Cambridge University Press, 1985), pp. 102–16 (109–12 esp.)

[40] *Biographia Literaria*, eds. James Engell and W. Jackson Bate (Princeton, NJ: Princeton University Press, 2 vols. 1983; *Collected Coleridge* 7), II, p. 7.

[41] *Table Talk*, ed. Carl Woodring (Princeton, NJ: Princeton University Press, 2 vols. 1990; *Collected Coleridge* 14), I, pp. 409–10 (1 July 1833). Earlier editions give a curtailed version under 6 July.

The relation between sound and meaning in the 'Ancient Mariner' and 'Christabel', and its radical originality, has been stated very clearly by the Irish poet, Brian Lynch.[42] He suggests that the quality which distinguishes such poems might have been dulled as much as nurtured by the drug dependency to which it is usually ascribed, and that their effects are related to what he calls 'a sort of prosodic automatism'.

> 'The Ancient Mariner', 'Christabel' and the other poems in the ballad form are visionary, but the sight is sound-dependent, driven by the senseless possibilities of English rhyme. (Have these poems ever been successfully translated?)

They make up a kind of poetry which is new in the English language, 'the first that ever burst / Into that silent sea'. Richard Holmes's new anthology makes evident the centrality of the ballad-mode and Holmes reminds us of its power to connect unexpected meanings in sometimes shocking ways:

> when Byron read 'Christabel' aloud at the Villa Diodati, one stormy night in June 1816, Shelley ran out in a fit and Mary Shelley began her novel *Frankenstein*.[43]

Coleridge's later poems are not, of course, engaged in the same issues in the same way. Verse is not being used to trawl for under-meaning; he is more accepting of mysteries which cannot be explained; he wrote allegories which map situations he had previously hoped to explore. The sound of chiasmus in later poems like 'Youth and Age' is balanced self-consciously in a way Kenneth Burke calls 'pointed'. Such a reversal as 'Flowers are lovely, love is flowerlike' contains the identical oppositions which sustain poems like the 'Ancient Mariner' and 'Christabel', but with an awareness that their mystery is not to be plumbed:

> FLOWERS are lovely; LOVE is flower-like;
> FRIENDSHIP is a sheltering tree;
> O the Joys, that came down shower-like,
> Of FRIENDSHIP, LOVE, and LIBERTY
>                         Ere I was old![44]

One has to reckon the same awareness contributed to the ironic reversal and deflation of the later punning, the later different uses of rhyme.

---

[42] 'Revelation of a Profound Metaphysician' (review of Richard Holmes; see below n. 43), the *Irish Times*, No. 44,494 (13 April 1996), Weekend: Books, 8.
[43] *Coleridge: Selected Poems* (London: HarperCollins, 1996), p. 68.
[44] 'Youth and Age', ll. 18–22. I quote from the version published in *Poetical Works* (London: William Pickering, 3 vols. 1828), II, pp. 82–3.

A corroborative example is provided by the following 'outgrowth' of 'Youth and Age' which Coleridge used for album verses:

> Dewdrops are the Gems of Morning,
> But the Tears of mournful Eve:
> Where no Hope is, Life's a Warning
> That only serves to make us grieve.[45]

The lines employ the same rhetorical formula which sustains the opening of 'The Irish Orator's Booze':

> Whisky is the drink of Erin,
> But of England foaming Ale:
> Where good drink is, Life is cheering
> That only serves to make us brave
>                               In our old age.[46]

The techniques which draw meanings together can put them asunder, whether tenderly or humorously. Chiasmus can divide as well as commingle. Echoes can be plaintive or hollow as well as resonant and magical.

As a last example of the continuity of Coleridge's poetic means, take 'Love's Apparition and Evanishment' (and I should warn that versions derived from EHC's edition and which include the 'Envoy' are misleading[47]). The poem returns to what many have identified as a theme connected with Coleridge's love for Sara Hutchinson but which, as a feeling, predates their first meeting. Though this poem invokes the 'sod-built Seat of Camomile' he built with the Wordsworths in October

---

[45] From a fair copy in Folio Notebook, fol. 2$^v$ (Huntington Library, HM 17299; *Notebooks*, IV, #5259).

[46] *Fraser's Magazine*, V (July 1832), 721.

[47] EHC, I, pp. 488–9 prints a mixed text, combining twenty-eight lines which were twice printed as a complete poem in Coleridge's lifetime with an 'Envoy' drawn from Derwent Coleridge's edition of *Poems* (1852) (in fact extempore lines written into Notebook 28, dating from April 1824: compare *Notebooks*, IV, #5146). The mixed version is reproduced by Stephen Potter (ed.), *Coleridge: Select Poetry and Prose* (London: The Nonesuch Press, 1933), pp. 127–8; Earl Leslie Griggs (ed.), *The Best of Coleridge* (New York: Thomas Nelson, 1934), pp. 131–2; Elisabeth Schneider (ed.), *Samuel Taylor Coleridge: Selected Poetry and Prose* (New York: Holt, Rinehart and Winston, 1951), pp. 161–2; John Beer (ed.), *Samuel Taylor Coleridge: Poems* (London: J. M. Dent, 3rd edn., 1993), pp. 487–8 (the incorrect pattern of indentation in Beer's ll. 1–4 incidentally derives from EHC, I, pp. 488–9, where ll. 2–3 straddle the page-break). The correct version is given by Morchard Bishop (= Oliver Stonor) (ed.), *The Complete Poems of Samuel Taylor Coleridge* (London: Macdonald, 1954), pp. 323–4; H. J. Jackson (ed.), *The Oxford Authors: Coleridge* (Oxford: OUP, 1985), p. 152; *The Oxford Poetry Library: Samuel Taylor Coleridge* (Oxford: OUP, 1994), pp. 152–3; Holmes (ed.), *Selected Poems*, p.221.

1801, the image of longing repeats the situation of 'Frost at Midnight' written at Stowey and set, earlier again, in childhood days at Christ's Hospital. It is written out of a deep sense of dissatisfaction and failure, yet in the late poem failure is accepted as a pre-condition of lasting satisfaction. The meeting of Love and Hope is situated at a distance from the observer, who reacts to it as if to a charade. The characters act out a trauma which is repetitive but in an unrealised way. The situation is nuanced by regret, but the will to intervene and change the situation is suspended.

One must recognise that 'Love's Apparition and Evanishment' reflects the grounds of Coleridge's Christian belief, his sense of the moral dimension of failure which distinguished him from Wordsworth and from most of his contemporaries. He was always a poet of weakness and fallibility in the Christian sense. In a note on Donne's Sermon VII he glossed Donne's observation—'as senslesse, and as absurd a thing to deny that the Son of God hath redeemed the world, as to deny that God hath created the world'—as follows: 'A bold but true Saying. The man who cannot see the redemptive agency in the Creation, has but dim apprehension of the creative power.'[48] Coleridge's sense of death in life and life in death is not simply a late orthodox obsession (he was never, in the obvious sense, even in later life, orthodox). The sense of personal inadequacy which extended to the necessity for redemption makes his art of failure different from modernists such as Beckett who have also explored the limits of unachievement.[49] I introduce this reminder because the moral dimension makes the style of these late poems different, too. Coleridge's puns are a kind of apology for failure: not a *tour de force* of self-advertisement, not even (as so often in Hood) painfully desperate. They are part of a style which has a more various human content than might appear and is not separate from the poems Coleridge has previously been known by. He was always a rhymester, sometimes a poet, and the qualities of one throw light on the other.

[48] *Marginalia*, II, p. 293. I am grateful to Miss Rachel Trickett for reminding me of this remark.

[49] My own essay, 'Coleridge's "Love": "All he can manage, more than he could"' in Tim Fulford and Morton D. Paley (eds.), *Coleridge's Visionary Languages: Essays in Honour of J. B. Beer* (Woodbridge: D. S. Brewer, 1993), pp. 49–66, is open to misinterpretation on this point.

The relation between poet and rhymester is the heart of the mystery. Only Keats among Romantic poets went in for the same sort of light verse, but poems like 'There was a naughty boy'[50] represent his Sidmouth mood (though this poem was written in Scotland). Helter-skelter anapaests were a holiday excursion for the poet who hoped to rival Milton and Shakespeare, whereas Coleridge the rhymester moved more variously (less hectically) and for a much longer period across a broader field. The diversity of Mangan's poetry is similar in kind but at the same time is less rich and has specifically Irish dimensions. I have argued it simply will not do to ignore Coleridge's rhyming, and there are more continuities than I have so far mentioned. I will add one other which has to do with textual matters. It was borne in on me while the evidence was accumulating and again only afterwards came to make sense. It connects with what I have been saying about reversals of meaning and the burden of self-consciousness.

When one attempts to confront the whole wide range of textual evidence, one is struck by the gratuitousness of Coleridge's three great poems. I mean, so much about them continues unknown, even while other evidence multiplies. Thus, Coleridge's movements can be plotted almost week by week, sometimes day by day, throughout 1797–8 but we do not know when he wrote 'Kubla Khan'. We have multiple draft versions of 'Religious Musings' and 'The Eolian Harp', but the first version we have of the 'Ancient Mariner' is the one printed in *Lyrical Ballads* 1798—that is, after it had expanded from a version of 340 lines to 658 lines—and the first versions we have of 'Christabel' and 'Kubla Khan' are presentation fair-copies. The three poems are gratuitous in that they appear without previous textual background.

One might overlook such a feature because there is a wealth of other material, but this is in fact a distraction because the material post-dates publication. In the case of the 'Ancient Mariner', it begins with annotated copies of *Lyrical Ballads* and proliferates with annotated copies of *Sibylline Leaves*; in the case of 'Christabel', there is a kind of pre-publication stage of fair-copies which circulated among enlarging circles of friends; and then, following book-publication in 1816 alongside 'Kubla Khan', copies were annotated in response to hostile reviews. The three poems share a distinctive textual history which is quite different from 'Lewti' or 'Alice du Clos' or 'The Destiny of Nations',

---

[50] *The Poems of John Keats*, ed. Jack Stillinger (Cambridge, Mass.: Harvard University Press, 1978), pp. 267–70.

the preliminary stages of which are separately represented by numerous tortuous drafts.[51]

The feature is not limited to the three great poems. No manuscript has been discovered for 'Frost at Midnight', whose complicated textual history is all post-publication. Nor is it limited to poems written during 1797–8, so many of which appear to have been composed out of doors, walking.[52] Two manuscripts of the verse 'Letter to Sara Hutchinson' exist but, typically, they both appear to be fair copies and their relation to one another is obscure. Negative evidence is inconclusive—materials may yet come to light—but the conclusion seems inescapable: Coleridge composed mainly in his head and wrote down what he composed at a subsequent stage. In a few instances, he retained poems in his head for more than twenty years. The so-far unpublished lines 'On Quitting Bristol for Nether Stowey: To Mr Maurice' were composed on New Year's Day 1797 and written down in 1828–9. 'The Ballad of the Dark Ladiè' was begun in 1798 but only written down in the years following 1827.[53]

The significance of the situation can be elucidated with reference to W. B. Yeats. Yeats seems to have been unable to think without a pen in his hand. His poems begin in a manuscript draft where handwriting is often nominal—that is, a squiggle serves to indicate what might later become 'this' or 'that'. Yeats seems on the one hand to have needed to write to bring to birth and at the same time to have been guided by the feeling that a legible hand is binding, that he was more free to make and remake himself while the components were not in fair-copy dress. The Cornell Yeats is a record of this primary phase which one could accurately describe as pre-textual. French editors classify such raw

---

[51] The tangle of rewriting in these later instances is recorded by James Dykes Campbell's type-facsimile, *Coleridge's Poems* (Westminster: Archibald Constable, 1899).

[52] The influence of Wordsworth can be added to the domestic reasons for Coleridge's composing out of doors *in ambulando* at this time. There are no working-manuscripts of such contemporaneous ballad poems written by Wordsworth as 'The Idiot Boy' and 'Peter Bell' either. Compare *'Lyrical Ballads', and Other Poems, 1797–1800*, eds. James Butler and Karen Green (Ithaca: Cornell University Press, 1992) and *Peter Bell*, ed. John E. Jordan (Ithaca: Cornell University Press, 1985). The new category of 'Hill Walking Poems' in Holmes (ed.), *Selected Poems*, pp. 133–56 should be read alongside the several recent studies of walking and Romantic poetry (e.g. by Jeffrey C. Robinson, Roger Gilbert, Anne D. Wallace). *Contra* Flaubert ('One cannot think and write, except sitting'), 'Only thoughts reached by walking have value' (Nietzsche).

[53] The manuscript of 'On Quitting Bristol' is at New York Public Library, Berg Collection; it is a fair-copy, not a draft. The 'Dark Ladiè' was first published in *Poetical Works* 1834; see below n. 55 on the fair-copy manuscripts.

material as *avant-texte*, German editors as *paralipomena*. The situation
with respect to Coleridge is different in late years as well as early. Brief
verses in notebooks and letters are often caught as they came but more
extended poems in multiple versions have characteristically been
evolved before the first writing-down. Coleridge's written revisions
operate in a post-textual situation.

There are eight manuscript versions of 'Inscription on a Time-piece'
(or nine, if one counts one which I have not been able to locate). There
are six manuscript versions of 'An Elegiac Plusquam-Sesqui-Sonnet to
my Tin Shaving-pot'. There are six manuscript versions of 'Love's
Apparition and Evanishment'. My point is the manuscripts of these
three late poems are not working-areas: they are re-runs, improved or
alternative versions produced for different occasions. They are witness
to someone who composed in his head and for the most part felt easy
writing out versions as a whole. Once Coleridge's poems entered print,
the story was different. Print freezes writing in an oppressive public
space in which an author possesses no special privilege, and the anxious
Coleridge was moved by antagonistic reviews to revise in a correspond-
ingly more constricted mental space. He added errata and footnotes,
marginal glosses and apologetic prefaces; he tinkered with alternatives
to passages which had caused displeasure or offence; but post-textual
intervention of this kind is a different order of adjustment from pre-
textual composition. It is reactive, indeed very often defensive, and the
revisions to 'Christabel', following the reviews,[54] provide the most
graphic example of how Coleridge wrote, at this stage of composition,
under a sense of threat.

Confirmation of the same feature is supplied by a habitual pattern
which at first appears odd. Coleridge kept his unfinished 'Ballad of the
Dark Ladiè' in his head for many years after composing it, as I have
said, but he first copied it down in albums of persons he did not know.
One album belonged to a friend of his daughter, the other to the wife of
a politician of whom he did not specially approve.[55] It is almost as if,
just because the unfinished poem was problematic, it was more

---

[54] Conveniently to hand in J. R. de J. Jackson (ed.), *Coleridge: The Critical Heritage*
(London: Routledge and Kegan Paul, 1970), pp. 199–247. Coleridge was most deeply
wounded by the reviews in the *Examiner* and the *Edinburgh Review*, which he assumed
were both by Hazlitt.
[55] That is, in the albums of Louisa Powles (Bodleian, MS Eng.Misc.e.181, fols. 9–12) and of
Lady Hannah Ellice (in private hands). He made another fair copy for an unknown person
(Yale University, MS Vault Shelves Coleridge).

available to be released when cast to the wind. Another intensely personal poem written in the 1820s which has to do with Coleridge's feelings for Sara Hutchinson, the previously-unpublished 'Thou and I', similarly appears to have been written down only once in the album of someone he did not personally know.[56] One recalls that the only manuscript of 'Kubla Khan', which he was again evidently anxious about, was copied for another autograph collector he did not know; and that the most elaborately annotated copy of 'Christabel' was abandoned in a lending-library.[57] Coleridge was inhibited by print, even by confronting himself in words, as he imagined himself being read with other eyes.

Another kind of confirmation is supplied by the different state of the manuscripts of Coleridge's writing in blank verse and rhyming forms. The working drafts of 'Religious Musings' and 'The Destiny of Nations' are complicated in a way matched only by the revisions of 'Love' and 'Alice du Clos' among poems in ballad-rhyming form, and they are special cases. Coleridge seems to have been specially inhibited as a writer of formal blank verse, which is why he persuaded himself it might be written in a more relaxed register as 'Poems which affect not to be Poetry', *Sermoni propriora*.[58] He was similarly uninhibited in the writing of dramatic blank verse, presumably because of practical exigency on the one hand and the demand to keep closer to spoken rhythms on the other. I think it can be argued from textual evidence that simple rhyme served as a mnemonic aid in the kind of composition Coleridge preferred. As the vehicle of hymns and popular ballads, it is not inhibiting in the way Miltonic blank verse can be. It supplies verse forms as unassuming as so many of Coleridge's subjects—kettles and shaving pots, arthritis and the naming of Bombay, bad German roads and a 'fill-a-sopha-col' game for Mary and Charlotte Brent—and it allows the juices to flow.

[56] Namely, James Keymer of Great Yarmouth. The mother of Coleridge's landlord, James Gillman, was a Keymer from Norwich. The manuscript is at the Pierpont Morgan Library (uncatalogued).

[57] The recipient of 'Kubla Khan' has been identified as Elizabeth Smith by Hilton Kelliher, 'The "Kubla Khan" Manuscript and Its First Collector', *The British Museum Journal*, XX: 2 (Autumn 1994), 184–98. The Ramsgate Library copy of 'Christabel' is described by Barbara E. Rooke, 'An Annotated Copy of Coleridge's *Christabel*', *Studia Germanica*, XV (1974), 179–92.

[58] Compare the subtitle and motto of 'Reflections on Having Left a Place of Retirement'. Also compare 'The Nightingale. A Conversation Poem'. The feature was long ago singled out for comment by George McLean Harper 'Coleridge's Conversation Poems' in his *Spirit of Delight* (New York: Henry Holt, 1928), pp. 3–27.

These several considerations return us to the point at issue. There is a connection between the spontaneous, ad-libbed, associative quality of what turns out to be the bulk of Coleridge's writing and his attitude towards writing down. Rhyme is already a form of 'outerance': a technical requirement which brings speech into neutral semi-public space. Rhyme has a senseless, self-sustaining life of its own which allows other things to happen. In *Biographia Literaria,* Coleridge quotes Petronius and Shakespeare on this point: 'Precipitandus est *liber* spiritus' ('The *free* spirit must be hurried onward') and ' "The man that hath not music in his soul" can indeed never be a genuine poet.'[59] Sense can be brought into alignment with rhyme in the most profound way—that is, sound can bring unconscious meaning to birth[60]—or rhyme can set itself against sense and laugh at it. The sound of light verse is neither less nor more complicated than the sound of serious verse: it is subtly complicated in the 'Tin Shaving-pot' poem in an evident way; 'Youth and Age' and 'The Irish Orator's Booze' march to the same tune. The difference between light and serious verse is produced by the mode of interchange between sound and meaning, even when the sounds are similar.

One might ask why Coleridge wrote down so much—lines, fragments, trial versions—when he found writing down could render the material less malleable, even inert. The answer is that though the stream of rhyming manifests the same inhibitions (puns, after all, are nothing if not self-conscious) it does so at lesser intensity. The situation of incessant versifying builds resistance to apology. He composed orally because '*writing a thing down rids* the mind of it,' even as it gives '*outness* to Thoughts',[61] but by writing so much, so variously, throughout his life Coleridge was not being wasteful. The writing which EHC either relegated to an appendix or omitted altogether kept open the possibility of movement. Such poems are enabling, they provide bridges, and they are of interest in themselves.

Coleridge is impossible to believe in simply as the author of 287

---

[59] *Biographia Literaria*, II, pp. 14 (quoting *Satyricon*, 118) and 20 (adapting *Merchant of Venice*, V. i. 83).

[60] As T. S. Eliot testified, writing about the 'auditory imagination' (*The Use of Poetry and the Use of Criticism* (London: Faber and Faber, 1933), pp. 118–19; and more recently Seamus Heaney writing about 'straining towards a strain, in the sense that the effort is to repose in the stability conferred by a musically satisfying order of sounds' (*Crediting Poetry* (Oldcastle: Gallery Books, 1995), p. 28).

[61] Detached thoughts recorded in Notebook 8; *Notebooks*, I ##1388, 1387.

canonical poems. The poems are separately authoritative but do not add up. One needs a sense of the matrix—their continuing, shifting, various background—to see where they come from and to understand them aright. Only the jostling variety of all 706 and more titles can communicate the creative evasiveness and inventiveness which is latent in the formally achieved poems. Just as Coleridge shifted from politics to theology to literary criticism to theory of science, and balked at domestic arrangements and romantic attachments and indeed any settled scheme, so his poetry is not contained in the high Romantic style. It moves from odes and elegies and blank verse to epigrams and satires and album verses without interruption. Chiasmus is continuous with punning and with rhyming. Streamy processes of association which conjoin complicated webs of reading also produce nonsense verses like the following sent to Wordsworth with the 'serious' *Nightingale*:

> And like an honest Bard, dear Wordsworth,
> You'll tell me what you think, my Bird's worth.
> My opinion's briefly this—
> His *bill* he opens not amiss;
> And when he has sung a stave or so,
> His breast, & some small space below,
> So throbs & swells, that you might swear
> No vulgar music's working there.[62]

If the new enlarged Coleridge at first appears incoherent because of these reversals of mood, I can only recommend standing further back to take in more meaning.

When I look at the new *Collected* edition of Coleridge's poetry, I imagine that its first readers will follow the course I followed myself. They are likely to be most interested in what I hope are more accurate versions of the poems they already know. Mistakes become evident in any edition after a length of time and fresh material comes to light. EHC's edition has been in print for more than eighty years and it is not surprising if readers interested in such things look forward to the rectification of errors which annoy them. I also anticipate that such readers will at first find the poems which have been added something of

---

[62] ll. 3–10. The lines are dated 10 May 1798 (Wordsworth Library, Grasmere, MS 14/1; *Collected Letters*, I, p. 406).

a distraction. Looking to read 'Mahomet' in its new, improved version, for example, they will find it embedded in a surround of forty epigrams translated from the German, at least a quarter of which will be totally unfamiliar. Looking to read the poem on Fulwood Smerdon, 'Written after a Walk before Supper', they will find it sandwiched between a new ninety-six-line poem in Greek and nineteen new lines in Latin.[63] To the extent that readers come to Coleridge's poems with established expectations, they will certainly be disconcerted.

My argument here has followed the stages of my own acquaintance. I think one begins as I described but later reaches a stage when Coleridge cannot be read in the old way any longer. One cannot simply relegate what turns out to be the larger part of his verse to a limbo-category, as previous editions have effectively done. All the verse he wrote has been brought into the new edition and it has, as I have tried to show, intimate connections with poems we thought we knew. Indeed, as I hope I have made clear, the connections oblige us to change our evaluation of both new and old. The change of perspective cannot be written off to literary history. It is true that the larger proportion of additional poems date from after Coleridge moved to Highgate, and the larger proportion of these are what might be called light verse, but they cannot be dismissed with mention of post-Napoleonic/pre-Victorian taste and a drum roll of the names of Reynolds, Hunt, Hood, Maginn. Coleridge's puns work differently from Hood's, his familiar manner is distinct from Hunt's, the different range of qualities represented by his sentimental verse was in place in the 1790s. Poems to the daughters of Highgate neighbours are continuous with the previously-unpublished 'To Miss Dashwood Bacon' written in Devonshire thirty years before.[64] Verses written during the album-craze of the 1820s cast a retrospective illumination on juvenilia like 'Kisses'.

The new material reveals Coleridge as someone who thought instinctively in verse, yet whose uncertain sense of worth allowed him a freedom and mobility in the medium denied to most contemporaries. Scott and Byron, for instance, were oppressed by obligations to the reading public; Wordsworth and Keats in their different ways were restricted by their ambition to succeed; Shelley's elevated sense of the

---

[63] That is, between the Greek-prize ode on the slave trade, 'Sors Misera Servorum . . . ', and 'Latin Lines on Ottery's Inhabitants' sent to George Coleridge in a letter.

[64] 'To Miss Dashwood Bacon' is to be found on fol. 7ᵛ of her Commonplace Book (Victoria College Library, uncatalogued). Examples of Highgate poems can be found in EHC, I, p. 482 ('To Miss A.T.') and II, p. 1009, no. 50 ('Elisa: Translated from Claudian').

poet's role was sometimes out of touch with the exigencies of domestic living. Coleridge wrote verse all the time, in the way Emily Dickinson did, but often socially as well as privately and therefore more variously. He used verse on occasions to draw out feelings he did not understand, at other times to sum up what he understood only too well. A range which extends from private meditation to hilarious sociability makes a ragged oeuvre. Some poems are polished like pebbles, others are scarred by anxiety and revision, the majority were cast upon the waters—sibylline leaves. Coleridge's rhymes make a stream which is always full and broad and which occasionally slows down over deeper currents. He emerges as the author not of three or thirty or even 300 poems, muddling in their difference, but of a body of 700 poems whose connected qualities derive from their variety.

What I mean is, as more evidence is brought to bear, the apparent raggedness of the whole body of Coleridge's writing becomes important in itself. I can think of no other writer whose collected poems contain such muddle, and yet it is not a muddle. Coleridge never struck any note simply. An early *jeu d'esprit* which EHC included in his main sequence of poems, 'A Mathematical Problem', and presumably reckoned could be excused as youthful high jinks, turns out not to be a simple literary exercise at all. The geometrical construction of an equilateral triangle simulates the democratic reasoning of those French calculators against whom Burke wrote: 'True; if the constitution of a kingdom be a problem of arithmetic.'[65] The most innocently literary-seeming poems turn out to be something else as well. We were long ago taught to see politics in the 'Ancient Mariner' and 'Kubla Khan'; they are also present in 'This Lime-tree Bower my Prison' and even in 'Love'. Few statements in Coleridge are entirely unqualified by other meanings, and, when he appears to be most in earnest, his reader should be most on guard.

In October 1832, after a sulphated hot-air bath treatment for sciatic rheumatism, after his skin then began to peel and he cut himself shaving, Coleridge wrote (or pretended to have written) the following 'Autograph on an Autopergamene' (autopergamene = self-parchment):

> Why, sure, such a wonder was never yet seen!
> An Autograph on an Autópergamene!

---

[65] *Reflections on the Revolution in France*, ed. Conor Cruise O'Brien (Harmondsworth: Penguin Books, 1968), p. 141. Compare EHC, I, pp. 21–4. Coleridge's poem participates in a minor genre of Cambridge undergraduate poems on the democratic triangle.

> A Poet's own Name, and own Hand-writing both,
> And the Ink and the Parchment all of his own growth—
> The Ink his own Blood and the Parchment his Skin—
> This from's Leg, and the other from's razor-snipt Chin—[66]

The poem was one of those taken up by journalists a while ago,[67] somewhat to my discomfort, but when I heard it read on the Irish radio and the newscaster finished off, with evident affection, 'There's old Coleridge for you!', I was made to think. Coleridge was never as respectable as his family wanted him to be: he has a maverick side which was cramped by conventional expectations. I believe he is the better poet because he was always more than a poet and because his serious side did not exist independently of his whole nature.

Perhaps so-called 'ordinary readers' always knew this: it is certainly contrary to much academic thinking, but I think the instincts of ordinary readers are right. When Coleridge's rhyming is accepted, he appears less solemn, more fun. He appears more sociable, as in Richard Holmes' biography,[68] but also more bookish at the same time; his arc is intellectually as well as emotionally wide. Coleridge does not sit as Shelley pictured him, 'obscure / In the exceeding lustre and the pure / Intense irradiation of a mind, . . . A hooded eagle among blinking owls'.[69] He gambols like the friend who made Dorothy Wordsworth and her brother laugh:

> Noisy he was, and gamesome as a boy;
> His limbs would toss about him with delight,
> Like branches when strong winds the trees annoy.
> Nor lacked his calmer hours device or toy
> To banish listlessness and irksome care;
> He would have taught you how you might employ
> Yourself; and many did to him repair,—
> And certes not in vain; he had inventions rare.

Not that he was devoid of a serious side:

[66] The version quoted here is from a letter to James Gillman dated 13 October 1832 at Princeton University Library (Robert H. Taylor Collection; *Collected Letters*, VI, p. 927 var). Coleridge copied out another version in a manuscript now at Victoria College Library (S MS F2.15).

[67] Nick Brooke and Tim Rayment, 'Don Finds 300 Coleridge poems', *Sunday Times*, No. 8894 (12 February 1995), 3; etc.

[68] *Coleridge: Early Visions* (London: Hodder and Stoughton, 1989).

[69] 'Letter to Maria Gisborne', ll. 202–4, 208; *The Complete Poetical Works of Percy Bysshe Shelley*, ed. Thomas Hutchinson (London: OUP, rev. 1945), p. 368.

He would entice that other Man to hear
His music, and to view his imagery.[70]

Wordsworth did not always picture Coleridge so. He came to judge him as a failed version of the kind of poet he was himself. 'Coleridge's twenty-sixth year was his "annus mirabilis", and . . . if he had not suffered himself to be drawn aside from poetry he must have proved the chief poet of modern times.'[71] I hope I have said enough to show the old myth will have to be replaced, I hope with something closer to William and Dorothy's earlier view. Coleridge colluded in the fiction of being a dead poet, as indeed he became in the Romantic sense. He meanwhile went on writing in ways not dissimilar from what he had written before and betimes. He was congenitally transgressive, he never succeeded in anything, according to one way success is measured, but he succeeded so much the better in others. The 'new poetry' in the *Collected Coleridge* edition will prove him to be a 'chief poet', in Wordsworth's words, in whom 'modern times' can delight.

# Appendix A

*The Complete Poetical Works of Samuel Taylor Coleridge*, ed. Ernest Hartley Coleridge (Oxford: Clarendon Press, 2 vols. 1912), I, pp. 487–92. Beginning with the last poem dated under 1830 and continuing to the end of the sequence.

*p. 487: 'Reason', 8 lines beginning 'Whene'er the mist, that stands 'twixt God and thee'; dated 1830; only text *On the Constitution of the Church and the State* (London: Hurst, Chance, 1830) [first coll *Poetical and Dramatic Works*, ed. Richard Herne Shepherd (London: Macmillan, 4 vols. 1877–80)].

p. 487: 'Self-Knowledge', 10 lines beginning 'Gnothi seauton!—and is this the prime'; dated 1832; only text *PW* (1834) [title from *PW* (1893)].

*p. 488: 'Forbearance', 16 lines beginning 'Gently I took that which ungently came'; dated ?1832; only text *PW* (1834) [title from *PW* (1893)].

---

[70] 'Stanzas Written in my Pocket-copy of Thomson's "Castle of Indolence"', ll. 47–54, 64–5 in *Poetical Works*, II, pp. 26–7.
[71] Aubrey de Vere, *Recollections* (London: Edward Arnold, 1897), p. 42.

pp. 488–9: 'Love's Apparition and Evanishment. An Allegoric Romance', 32 lines beginning 'Like a lone Arab, old and blind'; dated 1833; texts cited are *Friendship's Offering* for 1834, *PW* (1834), *Poems* (1852), *PW* (1893), *Letters* (1836), draft (in vol. 2 appendix) 'Now first published from an MS.'

p. 490: 'To the Young Artist Kayser of Kaserwerth', 15 lines beginning 'Kayser! to whom, as to a second self'; dated 1833; only text *PW* (1834).

pp. 490–1: 'My Baptismal Birth-Day', 14 lines beginning 'God's child in Christ adopted,—Christ my all,—'; dated 1833; texts cited are *Friendship's Offering* for 1834, *PW* (1834).

pp. 491–2: 'Epitaph', 8 lines beginning 'Stop, Christian passer-by!— Stop, child of God'; 9 November 1833; texts cited are *PW* (1834) and six mss—letter to Mrs Aders, 1833 (*Letters* 1895), letter to J. G. Lockhart, letter to J. H. Green of 29 October 1833, two versions in a copy of Grew's *Cosmologia Sacra,* in a copy of the *Todtentanz* which belonged to Thomas Poole (these last three in vol. 2 appendix, the *Todtentanz* from Mrs Sandford's *Poole* via *PW* (1893)).

Supplement this sequence with poems printed in vol. 2. Thus:

Insert before 'Love's Apparition and Evanishment' the lines EHC gives in II, pp. 985–6, no. 17 (under 'Jeux d'Esprit'): 'Cholera Cured Beforehand', 44 lines beginning 'Pains ventral, subventral'; dated 26 July 1832; texts cited are *PW* (1834) and letter to J. H. Green dated 26 July 1832.

Insert following 'My Baptismal Birth-day' the lines EHC gives in II, p. 975, no. 80 (under Epigrams): 'Epitaph of the Present Year on the Monument of Thomas Fuller', 10 lines beginning 'A Lutheran stout, I hold for Goose-and-Gaundry'; dated 28 November 1833; text 'Now first published from an MS.'

Insert following 'Epitaph' the lines EHC gives in II, p. 987 no. 19 (under Jeux d'Esprit): 'To a Child', 7 lines beginning 'Little Miss Fanny' dated 1834; text first published in *Athenaeum* 28 January 1888, first collected in *PW* (1893).

(The first and third poems listed, 'Reason' and 'Forbearance' in EHC, I, pp. 487, 488, are marked with an asterisk because they appear to date from earlier than the rest of these 1830–4 poems.)

## Appendix B

S. T. Coleridge, *Poetical Works*, ed. J. C. C. Mays (Princeton, NJ: Princeton University Press, 3 vols. forthcoming; *Collected Coleridge* 16). Beginning with the last poem dated under 1830 and continuing to the end of the sequence.

| | |
|---|---|
| 698 | 'On an Ellipsis of John Kenyon's' |
| *699 | 'E Coelo Descendit' |
| 700 | 'Splendida Bilis' |
| 701 | 'Latin Address to Christopher Morgan' |
| 701.X1 | 'Suggested Alterations in Thomas Pringle's "African Sketches" ' |
| 702 | 'Lines on George Croly's "Apocalypse" ' |
| 703 | 'A Motto for Reed's Shakespeare' |
| *704 | 'To Miss Fanny Boyce' |
| 705 | 'Doggerel Letter for an Autograph' |

(The first two of EHC's ten last poems are missing from this list and no. 672 has been added to it. The nine poems which appear somewhere in EHC are marked here with an asterisk. Note that a couple of poems have different titles.)

*Proceedings of the British Academy*, **94**, 157–172

# George Eliot: Immanent Victorian

## CATHERINE GALLAGHER
*University of California, Berkeley*

'YOUR SISTER'S A MASTER-MIND,' Joe Gargery tells Pip in an early chapter of Dickens's *Great Expectations*, 'a master-mind.' 'What's that?' Pip responds, almost sure that he is stumping his brother-in-law. But Joe is ready for that question, and answers 'with a fixed look, "Her." '[1] I won't make extended use of Dickens's novel in introducing the topic of George Eliot's art, although one is tempted to develop the analogy between George Eliot and Mrs Joe Gargery beyond their common nomination as masterminds, if only to note the masculine similarity of their first names: George, Joe. Mrs Joe's actual Christian name even turns out to be Georgiana. I, however, have opened with this conversation because it lightly raises a question that takes on considerable weight in George Eliot's fiction: how do we talk about the relationship between a general class of things and any particular instance of it? Dickens's joke turns on an ambiguity in the question, 'What is a mastermind?,' which can be interpreted to mean either 'What are the definitive features of any mastermind?' (the question Pip thinks will stump Joe) or 'What is an instance of a mastermind?' (the question Joe answers with the pronoun 'her'). Joe's is a valid (if ungrammatical) answer despite its comic circularity.

That very circularity, or tendency to point to instances when asked to discourse on the nature of a class of persons, I want to argue this afternoon, is coiled at the heart of the novel genre, whose earliest practitioners maintained that they were reforming the relation between

Read at the Academy 23 May 1996. © The British Academy 1997.
[1] *Great Expectations* (New York: OUP, 1989), p. 45.

general and particular. For example, when explaining the difference
between his satire (a satire employing truly *fictional* personae) and that
of the *romans scandaleuses* which were all the rage in the early eighteenth century, Henry Fielding declared, 'I describe . . . not an individual but a species.'[2] By a 'species', Fielding meant any category of
people. Like the other mid-eighteenth-century writers who invented the
novel properly speaking, he was trying to break the reader's habit of
interpreting characters as personal satires (or libels) on particular
individuals. The founding claim of the form, that which distinguished
novelists from libellers, was the insistence that the referent of the text
was a generalisation about and not an extra-textual, embodied instance
of, a species. Certainly, the novel provides instances, but it should not,
strictly speaking, refer directly to individual examples in the world. The
*fictionality* defining the novel inhered in the creation of instances, rather
than their mere selection, to illustrate a class of persons. A general
referent was thus indicated through a particular, but explicitly non-
referential, fictional individual.

The referential claim of the novel, its stake in the world outside the
text, therefore attaches to classes of persons, whereas the fictionality of
the novel, its disavowal of personal reference, defines the individual
characters. The novel is thus true in its generality even though all of its
particulars are merely imaginary. Indeed, practitioners asserted, the
novel's general applicability depended on the overt fictionality of its
particulars, since taking examples from among real people would only
confuse the issue of reference; *because* they had dispensed with the
individual referents, the novelists' characterisations could only have
referential value by pointing to what Fielding calls a 'species'.

This description of the novel—in which the type is the presumed
referent while individuals are presumed to be fictional—inverts normal
empirical ways of thinking about the relation between the real and the
imaginary, the sensual or experiential, on the one hand, and the ideational, on the other. Most novelists would have admitted freely that the
species is that which one never expects to encounter in actuality; it is to
be grasped only by an abstracting effort of the imagination. Individuals,
on the other hand, present themselves as the given data of the world.
The novel thus reverses the commonsensical empiricism that pervaded
the intellectual atmosphere of England at the time of its invention.

---

[2] *Joseph Andrews*, ed. Martin C. Battestin (Middletown, CT: Wesleyan University Press,
1967), p. 189.

Novelists took the abstract entity, the species or type, to be the given, the thing-in-the-world referent grounding the form, and conceded that their individuals are imaginary concoctions. We might say of the novel, then, that as a form it asserts not only the cognitive but also the ontological priority of the general over the particular.

Hence, the complexity of the general/particular relation in the novel goes beyond the usual epistemological puzzle of requiring categories to perceive facts but simultaneously requiring facts to create categories. The novel form for most of the eighteenth and nineteenth centuries gave an ontological priority to the type by promoting the fictionality of individual characters; but simultaneously it conjures as its own 'background' an empirical cultural understanding that the type is only a mental abstraction from more real concrete individuals in the world. Novel theorists since Ian Watt have been right to note the literary form's affinity with empiricism, but they have paid too little attention to the special turn it gives empiricist logic by invoking both an understanding that types are induced from persons in the world and a further awareness that its characters are deduced from types. It requires two sorts of individuals: those given in and those twice removed from an inferred world. If I might momentarily withdraw the circle analogy and substitute another, we could think of the form as claiming to be structured like a triptych, in which ontologically distinct categories of 'the particular' appear on either side of a category of 'the general', creating a centrality and solidity for the middle category not normally sustainable under the empirical assumptions that contrast the ideality of the type with the substantiality of the experientially available individual.

George Eliot, more than any other novelist, consciously exploited and explored these standard assumptions of her medium. Let me give you an example, from *Middlemarch*, of her construction of one of those triptychs. Characterising the heroine's uncle, Mr Brooke, the narrator comments,

> Mr. Brooke's conclusions were as difficult to predict as the weather: it was safe to say that he would act with benevolent intentions and that he would spend as little money as possible in carrying them out. For the most glutinously indefinite minds enclose some hard grains of habit; and a man has been seen lax about all his own interests except the retention of his snuffbox, concerning which he was watchful, suspicious, and greedy of clutch.[3]

---

[3] Ch. 1; passages from *Middlemarch* will be cited by chapter.

This initial description of the character proceeds from the particular individual, Mr Brooke, to the general category of persons by which we are to make sense of him: those glutinously indefinite minds enclosing hard grains of habit. The sentence making the transition from character to species begins with the word 'for', signalling that the sentence to follow will explain Mr Brooke by locating his type in an imputed world that precedes his invention. Then, as soon as the type, or referent, has been described, it seems to want experiential grounding, a want supplied by instancing someone belonging to the same species but sensually available: 'and *a man has been seen* lax about all his own interests except the retention of his snuffbox'. The 'and' beginning that clause tells us that we are continuing in the reference mode. Of course, it doesn't matter whether or not such a man has actually been seen, for we aren't exploring the truth of the narrator's claims here, only the structure of her rhetoric, which (to repeat by way of summary) assures us that Mr Brooke is not a copy of the man with the snuffbox but is rather a fictive instance of a class that has such real instances as the snuffbox clutcher.

Eliot here explicitly carries the reader through the arc of induction and deduction, deduction and induction that gives generalities weight and substance. The subtlety of such movements among referential levels, together with their frequency and seeming candour, the wave-like rise and fall from instances to generalities and back again, reassures the reader that *this* fiction is always proximate to the world, that we are never far from the referential bridge provided by the type. Eliot, though, is also the nineteenth-century novelist who is most sceptical about categorical thought, who turns her sharpest satire against those most apt to engage in it.

Indeed, the narrator of *Middlemarch* herself no sooner invokes a 'species' than she proceeds to dissolve it in qualifying subdivisions or expand it until its shape is no longer recognisable. In the passage about Mr Brooke, for example, we should notice that the general category to which the character supposedly refers begins as a mixed one: a man with benevolent intentions who is nevertheless stingy with his money. That is, he really belongs to two normally distinct categories which happen to overlap in his character. It is this perceived inconsistency that seems to require the narrator to make an explicitly referential gesture towards a more general category where the anomalous traits might be reconciled. That is, because Mr Brooke does not fit what we might call a 'stock type', the narrator needs to classify him under an unusual category. His full rubric might read: careless thinkers (that is, indefinite minds) who are, out of mere habit, very careful about certain items of their own property. But this category doesn't so much explain the coexistence of the traits as restate them, and the narrator finally justifies her character by pointing to someone in the world, the snuffbox clutcher, who is even less consistent than Mr Brooke.

Hence, on closer inspection, Mr Brooke's species—careless people who are habitually careful about some things—doesn't really seem to do much referential work. When sceptically attended to, it only asserts that there are eccentric careless people who have inexplicably rigid habits. The snuffbox clutcher, it will be noticed, has nothing else in common with Mr Brooke; nothing about him recalls the traits that at first seemed to conjure the species. He is neither benevolent nor stingy. Mr Brooke and the snuffbox clutcher are just two instances of generally careless people who aren't always careless. One might, therefore, say that they belong to a set of *category defiers* which the narrator, adhering to a formal demand of the novel, constructs as a class. A class constructed merely to accommodate random exceptions, however, might easily be read as a sceptical commentary on classification.

It would seem, then, that the passage under analysis assures us both that characters in the fictional world have the ontological ballast of general reference and that there will always be gaps between general types and individuals. That this should be so even when the individuals are characters made on purpose to illustrate types may at first seem puzzling, but we should bear in mind that it is only under these seemingly optimal conditions—the conditions of fictionality—that the problem of the general and particular can be fully discerned. For in the real world the problem will often be perceived as a gap between the nature of given things and the nature of concepts, or language, about them. But individuals in fiction are at least as conceptual and linguistic as types; they make no pretence to be the given data of the world. The inability of the class to account for the individual is thus more obviously a *logical* problem in fictional than in non-fictional discourse. As soon as the category of careless people who are both benevolent and stingy is figured in one Mr Brooke of Tipton Grange, who has a niece named Dorothea, many things about him are already irrelevant to the class of people he supposedly signifies. In novels it becomes possible to reflect on the fact that it is in the nature of examples generally to exceed that which they are supposed to exemplify.

Lest you suspect that the example I've chosen, that of an obvious

eccentric, too neatly fits my generalisation about the necessary superfluity in all instances, I'll supply one more descriptive triptych in which
the narrator asks the reader to find a living example of the type
represented by the character Mary Garth:

> [T]en to one you will see a face like hers in the crowded street tomorrow:
> . . .. [F]ix your eyes on some small plump brownish person of firm but quiet
> carriage, who looks about her, but does not suppose that anybody is looking
> at her. If she has a broad face and square brow, well-marked eyebrows and
> curly dark hair, a certain expression of amusement in her glance which her
> mouth keeps the secret of, and for the rest features entirely insignificant—
> take that ordinary but not disagreeable person for a portrait of Mary Garth. If
> you made her smile, she would show you perfect little teeth; if you made her
> angry, she would not raise her voice, but would probably say one of the
> bitterest things you have ever tasted the flavour of; if you did her a kindness,
> she would never forget it. Mary admired . . ..[4]

The description, like the person it describes, is self-consciously undistinguished; it illustrates well, however, the impossibility of remaining
for long on that threshold of typicality between fictional illustration and
persons in the world. Once the physical type is found, the passage
teeters for a moment between referencing through the imagined model
on the street, who is inside the novel but supposedly outside the fiction,
and realising the character of Mary Garth. In the movement between the
two sentences beginning with 'If', we can locate the segue: both are
written in the second person, direct address to the reader often signalling the onset of a triptych in *Middlemarch*, but the grammatical
resemblances between the two sentences only underline the automatic
way in which the passage slides, by the mere gravity of detail, into
fiction. Whereas the first sentence uses 'if' to name the conditions, the
physical characteristics, that would qualify a woman on the street to be
classed under the 'Mary' category, the 'if's in the second sentence
introduce increasingly narrative vignettes that, we soon realise, cannot
be predicated of the class. By the time we read, 'if you made her angry,
she would not raise her voice, but would probably say one of the
bitterest things you have ever tasted the flavour of', we know that
such an extraneous particular as a very sharp tongue has put us back
onto the side of the fictional, where characters are realised.

Individuated fictional characters, in other words, can never effi-
ciently refer to types which in turn organise individuals in the world.
To be sure, we might reduce their very excessiveness to a referential

[4] Ch. 40.

formula by noticing that it is typical of individuals to exceed types or depart from them; then the essentially referable thing about the specifics is just the very general fact that they are specific. Such a formulation verges on the absurd because it classifies individuals as things that depart from classifications. It nevertheless does yield some insight into the nature of novels by indicating why the extravagance of characters, their wastefulness as referential vehicles, is precisely what makes them seem real.

This point needs emphasis because a novel's realism is often assumed to be a matter of referential fidelity. When we analyse the nature of the gap between the general and the particular, however, reference and realisation appear to be quite distinct, whereas fictionality and realisation appear to be identical. Fictional characters may *refer* to people in the world by conforming to type, but they only *resemble* people in their *non*conformity. The impulse toward reference and the impulse toward realisation are thus not only separate but also deeply opposed, and their tension, rather than co-operation, might be said to define realism.

George Eliot masters this tension not by easing, concealing, or even self-consciously reflecting on it; she masters it, rather, by harnessing its energy and making it the dynamo of her narratives. She converts the strife between type and instance, between reference and realisation (a strife belonging primarily to characterisation), into a vigorous narrative friction between probability and surprise. Every novel may be bound to negotiate its plot between these rival narrative exigencies—between the all-too-likely and the unaccountable—but Eliot's give us the keenest awareness of what might be at stake in such negotiations. In *Middlemarch* especially, she conceives of the plot as driven by the competing needs to adhere to type and to deviate, to mean and to be, to have significance and to become real. There she takes the plight that belongs specifically to novel characters—that they are supposed to illustrate types from which they must depart—and makes it the central dilemma of a life story. She etches the heroine's plot quite precisely onto the outlines of the formal predicament we've been tracing, so that theme and genre, representation and its mode, coincide. When literary critics discover coincidences of this sort, we often conclude that the author is playfully exposing her artifice, giving away the representational game and admitting that her character is, after all, just a fiction. I would, however, like to pursue a different line of thought about this coincidence, for *Middlemarch*'s formal self-consciousness is not just a comment on some fundamental lack at the heart of fictions; it is, rather, a disclosure of their function. The remainder of this lecture will be devoted to convincing you that Eliot's fiction gives us something we might never otherwise experience: a *desire* to be real.

*Middlemarch* begins with the understanding that only the atypical can generate plot and only the exceptional can desire it. Witness this early description of Dorothea Brooke delivered by the astonished and uncomprehending chorus called 'rural opinion':

> A young lady of some birth and fortune who knelt suddenly down on a brick floor by the side of a sick labourer and prayed fervidly as if she thought herself living in the time of the Apostles—who had strange whims of fasting like a papist and of sitting up at night to read old theological books! Such a wife might awaken you some fine morning with a new scheme for the application of her income which would interfere with political economy and the keeping of saddle-horses: a man would naturally think twice before he risked himself in such fellowship. Women were supposed to have weak opinions, but the great safeguard of society and of domestic life was that opinions were not acted on. Sane people did what their neighbours did so that if any lunatics were at large, one might know and avoid them.[5]

This description not only implies normal behaviour for 'a young lady of some birth and fortune' by enumerating Dorothea's deviations, but also locates the place in which such norms are established: in the average, conventional, and conservative provincial mind as it calculates risk, specifically the risk of being impetuously awakened from rustic torpor. Initially, this voice has trouble even finishing statements about Dorothea because—well, who knows how her story might end? The first two phrases in the passage never complete themselves in a proper sentence but end abruptly in an exclamation point, as if 'sane people' were too startled to supply predication. Typifying is thus satirised here as an attempt at foreknowledge and at foreclosing the very possibility of unexpected events. Since novel readers are *ipso facto* in search of plot, the passage obviously implies our superiority in this counterposing of the conventionally typical and the narratable.

Eliot does not, however, engender a desire for realisation simply by threatening us with boredom and congratulating us on our desire to be surprised. After all, Mr Brooke, whose 'conclusions were as difficult to predict as the weather' is equally surprising, but we don't want to read a novel about him because his unexpectedness is merely random; it never holds out the promise of a new significance. A serious longing to be

[5] Ch. 1.

real, Dorothea's plot demonstrates, can only proceed from the exhaustion of the categorical mode; hence it must begin not in the semi-comical, dismissable classifications of rural opinion, but in types which command our respect: and so it does.

Before hearing the rural opinion about Dorothea, we have already encountered the category through which this fictional character is supposed to refer to the world. The novel's 'Prelude' has established St Theresa of Avila as the historical exemplar of a certain class of women who are not satisfied by the common occurrences of female destiny, women whose 'nature' demands an 'epic life'. Dorothea's characterisation begins with the induction of the type from that historical person: 'That Spanish woman who lived three hundred years ago was certainly not the last of her kind', we are told. '*Many Theresas* have been born . . ..'

But no sooner is the type—'Theresas'—named than it begins to dissolve, and its dissolution is linked not only to narrative but to fictional narrative. 'Many Theresas have been born', the sentence continues, 'who found for themselves no epic life wherein there was a constant unfolding of far-resonant action.' Between the subject of this sentence and its conclusion, we encounter a surprise: the many Theresas have not lived lives conforming to their species. For Saint Theresa, type and story coincided: after false starts and hindrances, we are told, 'She found her epos.' But the stories of all the other Theresas deviate from this norm; their lives do not result in any such coincidence of potential and actuality. Hence Theresa, oddly, becomes atypical of the category of Theresas; although they are conceived under her rubric, she is useless as a predictor of their destinies.

The passage does not, however, abandon its general pronouncements. Since the normal story prevents the realisation of the type, a new subtype takes shape, which the narrator calls 'latter-day Theresas'. All that can be said of the latter-day Theresa as a type, however, is that her story will deviate from a known heroic norm, and in her deviation she will become obscure. To speak of this type is therefore to resort to conjecture: the latter-Theresa has lived, we are told, '*perhaps* only a life of mistakes, the offspring of a certain spiritual grandeur ill-matched with the meanness of opportunity; *perhaps* a tragic failure which found no sacred poet and sank unwept into oblivion'. Since the failure to be a Theresa results in obscurity, the stories of how latter-day Theresas fail are unknown. As such they invite hypotheses, probable imaginings: 'perhaps . . . ; perhaps . . . .'.

Fictions, stories that begin with an implied 'perhaps', are certified
here as the only way to understand, not just a given 'species', as
Fielding would have had it, but the standard, socially and historically
determined, deviations from a species. These standard deviations,
moreover, lead us into the quotidian, and therefore the forgotten, and
therefore the conjectural, and therefore the *fictionally* specific. The links
established here between the mundane, the unknown, and the fictional
are crucial to the stimulation of narrative desire in Eliot's realism. We
should notice that they oppose the associations in the mind of rural
opinion between normalcy and complete foreknowledge: if the superficial provincial mind seeks ordinariness for its predictability, the serious realist seeks it for its uncertainty. It is, after all, no great
accomplishment to muster curiosity by promising tales of unusual
adventure. Eliot's task is more difficult: to convince us that what seems
familiar—the process by which people become ordinary—is in fact
radically unknown. She makes us curious about the quotidian because
of its very obscurity and defines the fictional by contrasting it with the
heroically *renowned*. Thus, even as she presents the departure of the
latter-day Theresas from their heroic type as a pity, and even as she
gathers up her instances of failure into new categories, Eliot uses the
gap between type and instance to create a momentum, an impulse
toward the prosaic that is indistinguishable from the desire to read a
fiction. To learn about the unknown through fictional particulars is to
resolve the mysteries of daily life: mysteries such as how could a
Theresa, in the very act of aspiring toward her type, become a drudging
wife-scribe to a provincial pedant?

In the 'Prelude' to *Middlemarch*, Eliot rouses our desire for fiction
by promising to show us just exactly how it is that one does not conform
to type. Classification, foreknowledge, and reference are the inevitable
framework of the novel, but the dynamic impulse established here is
towards fiction, unpredictability, and particular realisation. Curiosity
directed at a particular ordinary outcome, moreover, is stimulated
periodically by Dorothea's progress; she comes to occupy a series of
subcategories, each of which is in turn experienced as restrictive,
artificial, and potentially plot-obstructing. These stages of Dorothea's
plot can, indeed, be mapped onto the standard deviations mentioned in
the 'Prelude', as if to demonstrate that the subtypes, too, must be
instantiated, and, in that process, departed from. Dorothea must undergo
paradigm exhaustion; she must be, as we say in the vernacular, troped
out.

'Perhaps only a life of mistakes' is the hypothesis that looms over the novel's first Book, 'Miss Brooke,' which draws on one of the oldest novelistic types, the female Quixote, a visionary young lady who projects the ideal beings of her imagination onto very unlikely people. Miss Brooke even comes complete with a Sancho Panza—her sister Celia—and the structure of the plot is also true to form: it proceeds with ironic efficiency to demonstrate that the Quixote's failure is the result of her ambition. But every reader of *Middlemarch* will at once see the inadequacy of this model, and it takes no great critical acumen to begin to pile up the particulars that make Dorothea an exception to the quixotic norm. Not the least of these is the resolution of the first stage of her plot: instead of coming to her senses or proceeding to new adventures, Dorothea finds herself trapped inside the consequences of her first mistake, so that the novel segues from the proposition that she might lead 'perhaps only a life of mistakes' to the possibility that she could be 'perhaps a tragic failure'. Inside this hypothesis, too, however, the particulars of the tragedy eventually become anomalous. One potential agony, that she might knowingly waste her life completing her late husband's vain project, the worthless *Key to All Mythologies*, is supplanted by another when she seems condemned to live separately from the man she loves, and this apparently futile love—initially presented as a painful consequence of her quixotic mistake—transforms her into a different sort of heroine. In short, the details of her affliction force the plot to swerve from its trajectories repeatedly, to be retrieved by other general scenarios, or standard deviations, until the subcategories seem exhausted. Hence, when told in the novel's 'Finale' that 'our daily words and acts are preparing the lives of many Dorotheas', we would be perfectly justified to respond with a question like Pip's: 'But, George, what is a Dorothea?' By that point, the only truly satisfactory answer should be 'her'.

The effect of a curiosity impelled toward greater and greater narrative particularity should, in other words, finally yield a non-exemplary immanence, a minimally referential character, and yet it does not. Despite her compelling realisation and her overwhelming particularity, by the end of the novel, Dorothea's referential power has, if anything, increased, so that when the category of 'Dorotheas' replaces the former category of 'Theresas', we recognise it. For, as we noticed earlier, even the impulse towards the specific can be conceived in general terms, and in *Middlemarch* Eliot not only generalises the process of becoming particular but also assimilates it to both ethical and erotic drives.

Being-in-particular becomes not simply an end-point of narrative, but a value-laden desideratum, and it is Dorothea whose story gives the singular such gravity.

Because the *ethical* importance of particularising has long been noted by readers of Eliot, indeed, because Eliot's narrators themselves frequently underscore it, I'll only briefly sketch its well-known outlines for you. As Dorothea herself is realised by departures from type, so too does she learn to realise others by imagining their particularity instead of pressing them into categories. From a dark night of the soul which all readers of the novel will recall, the heroine awakens to a sympathetic understanding of errancy itself. She finds what heroism is left over for women in the modern world by an empathetic envisioning of the suffering of the very people who have just wounded her, Rosamond and Will Ladislaw. In short, realising in others what the narrator calls 'equivalent centres of self' is the supreme ethical act in Eliot's novels, and when the Dorotheas appear on the other side of the novel's final triptych, we understand that they might be women who spend their lives in feats of compassionate particularisation.

Eliot's *ethics* of realisation, however, have perhaps been over-emphasised; by stressing the ethical drive towards the particular, we have created an Eliot who seems moralistic to some modern readers; she appears all-too-Victorian, perhaps even sentimental in her earn-estness. Eliot can easily be caricatured as a lugubrious author who gives her novels gravity by weighing down the exuberance of narrative curiosity with moral strictures. To counter this caricature, which has, alas, survived a century of refutations, I will conclude this lecture by arguing that, especially in *Middlemarch*, Eliot's ethics are preceded and animated by an *erotics* of particularisation.

Long before Dorothea's dark night, a crucial moment of transforma-tion occurs. It is one of those nodes of transition between subtypes, but it represents more than the dawning of a further stage of mental awareness. It establishes a new vector of energy in the novel, one which pulsates through it to the end and enables whatever ethical resolution occurs. The moment I'm about to discuss, in which Dorothea becomes the last of the several subtypes of latter-day Theresas, marshals the powers of eroticism and produces a yearning towards embodiment.

The last thing to be said about the latter-day Theresas in the 'Prelude' is that 'their ardour alternated between a vague ideal and the common yearning of womanhood, so that the one was disapproved as extravagance and the other condemned as a lapse.' Dorothea's penultimate state is not that of the tragic but that of the *lapsed* Theresa, and it is in the transition between the two which Eliot stimulates a desire for realisation most intensely; it is also there that Dorothea's plot is retrieved for general reference by taking on almost the quality of a parable about becoming real. For although the lapsed Theresa at first seems just another standard deviation from the saint, she is in fact a dramatic enlargement of the referential category. Hence the narrator figures the transformation not as a gradual departure but as an abrupt metamorphosis, a sudden addition of species characteristics. The transmutation takes place when Dorothea is liberated from her oppressive sense of duty by learning that her husband had added a humiliating codicil to his will specifying that she would forfeit her inheritance if she married Will Ladislaw. The tumult of sensation that accompanies this revelation marks the 'alternation' (to use the language of the 'Prelude') from saintly ardour to 'the common yearning of womanhood'. The species change described in the passage I'm about to read, in other words, is not from one variety to another of blundering and suffering Saint Theresas:

> She might have compared her experience at that moment to the vague, alarmed consciousness that her life was taking on a new form, that she was undergoing a metamorphosis in which memory would not adjust itself to the stirring of new organs. Everything was changing its aspect . . .. Her world was in a state of violent convulsion . . .. One change terrified her as if it had been a sin; it was a violent shock of repulsion from her departed husband . . .. Then again she was conscious of another change which also made her tremulous: it was a sudden strange yearning of heart towards Will Ladislaw.[6]

The metamorphosis figure allows Eliot to imagine Dorothea as a passive plastic medium being reshaped from the outside. Even her own emotions seem temporarily external, as the syntax indicates. *She* does not yet exactly yearn toward Will Ladislaw, but instead is 'conscious of a change . . .: *it* was a sudden strange yearning of heart'. Yearning seems to be somewhere in the vicinity and will soon be lodged in Dorothea, but during her suspension between one species and another, while she is being remade as the 'type' who can own these feelings, all experience is momentarily alien. The species towards which she is metamorphosing, moreover, is unlike those she has previously instantiated; it is the 'common womanhood' of the lapsed

---

[6] Ch. 50.

Theresa. To metamorphose simply into 'woman', however, especially
in a text consistently contemptuous of generalisations about women, is
not so much to take on a specifiable new set of widespread mental
characteristics as it is to long for a particular man, to have a specific
desire. Eliot partly renovates Dorothea—in other words, makes her
'woman'—so that she can experience an utterly individual longing, a
yearning towards some one man. This, then, is the moment when the
very particularity of a desire simply refers to the particularity of
women's desires generally.

But this passage does even more than stretch the limits of referenti-
ality by temporarily decreasing the tension between class and instance.
With its language of being stirred by new organs, it indicates the sudden
eruption of erotic sensation in Dorothea; indeed, it implies the addition
of the very capacity for such sensation, the implanting of unaccustomed
vitals. The idea called 'Dorothea' is reshaped around a sexual and
reproductive core, so that the very notion of her 'species' takes on a
newly biological meaning. Hence, the striking widening of the 'species'
from tragically-failed Theresa to 'common womanhood' is simultaneously a shift away from 'character', in the usual sense of the word,
to physiological sensation. Dorothea, it seems, experiences not just a
reorganisation of her consciousness but its annexation of a desiring
body.

This crucial, metamorphic, realisation, therefore, strains towards an
incarnation, in which a specifically sexual human body is imposed upon
the character. Through it Dorothea obviously becomes the 'elevated'
type who descends onto the plain of everyday appetites, but she also
comes to signify just 'type'—ideality, fictional construct, the word itself
wanting to take on flesh. She stands, we might say, for all novel
characters in their demand for realisation, their demand that we think
of them as possessing the specificity of organic beings. Indeed, characters can only have the bodies we imagine for them, a fact the narrator
emphasises in telling us that Dorothea must be given her erotic womanhood by others: 'It had never before entered her mind that [Will Ladis-
law] could, under any circumstances, be her lover: conceive the effect
of the sudden revelation that another had thought of him in that light,
that perhaps he himself had been conscious of such a possibility'.
Dorothea's erotic body must be twice created: once by the other
fictional characters imagining it; and then again by readers conceiving
the effect of the characters' imagining. Dorothea does not take on flesh

and blood easily; and the harder it is to incarnate her, the more we want to do it.

This turn of desire in the novel certainly contains its own paradoxes and ironies, for the erotic pursuit of the particular is precisely what reproduces the biological species. The proximity between the urge of the species, in Darwin's rather than Fielding's sense of that word, and the specific longing of the character, moreover, might be said to squeeze out what had before seemed individual and unique about Dorothea. The passage and its aftermath in the novel, indeed, remind one of Feuerbach's contrast between 'species-being', which is always embodied particularity, and those modes of individualisation that create aloofness from one's kind. The turn towards the physiological, in other words, threatens to close the genre-defining gap between type and instance by redefining both. And yet such a narrowing also follows a generic imperative that the protagonist's being should come to resemble the uncharacterisable universal consciousness of the narrator and implied reader as the novel progresses. In the beginning, a novel heroine is an individual by virtue of her unusual characteristics, but by the end these should have been converted into the particularity of a unique plot, a story that can be told 'about' her, leaving the 'character' unencumbered by many of her earlier peculiarities. The extraordinary achievement of *Middlemarch* is to accomplish this turn towards generic consciousness through embodiment, a turn which produces, in its very erotic torque, an offshoot of regret: 'Her full nature, like that river of which Cyrus broke the strength, spent itself in channels which had no great name on the earth', the 'Finale' tells us. In short, this yearning for the real is not simple; it is philosophically and generically overdetermined, and it is mixed with melancholy; it is nevertheless desire.

The frequency with which one encounters figures like Dorothea in nineteenth-century literature—ideational, immortal, and spiritual beings impelled by amorous energy toward the state of mere humanity—indicates that Eliot was herself born along by a massive redirection of longing away from disembodied transcendence and toward embodied immanence. When we give ear to them, it seems as if the culture's imaginary creatures were sending up a lament for their missing bodies, demanding with Keats's Lamia, 'Give me my woman's form' or leaning out over the bars of heaven with Rossetti's Blessed Damozel and sighing for their earthly lovers. The animation for which all great art strives, I would argue, nineteenth-century writers want to accomplish by adding *flesh* to spirit. The end of art no longer seems to be transcendence, but immanence; matter is not in need of soul, but soul in need of matter. To enliven is not so much to inspirit as to embody, and it fell to the lot of George Eliot to instantiate this yearning most fully. As the English translator of Feuerbach, she was well-acquainted with the thesis that humans endow their gods, mere creatures of their imaginations, with their own most valued characteristics. Her own incarnation myth is a subtle revision of this idea: it gives us the disembodied spirit, the novel character, as a new sort of erotic, female Christ, who only craves to be us.

Because George Eliot makes us imagine not an independently living and breathing Dorothea, but instead an idea called Dorothea requiring that we conceive her bodily sensations to make her real, our very organic reality becomes newly desirable. Through Dorotheas, and perhaps in no other way, we can experience a longing for that which is already given as the basis of our being: our incarnate selves. George Eliot is the greatest English realist because she not only makes us curious about the quotidian, not only convinces us that knowing its particularity is our ultimate ethical duty, but also, and supremely, makes us want it.

*Proceedings of the British Academy,* **94**, 173–206

CHATTERTON LECTURE ON POETRY

# Yeats and Remorse

PETER McDONALD

*University of Bristol*

NEAR THE END OF JULY 1915, Henry James was busy soliciting on behalf of Edith Wharton, and addressed Thomas Hardy with a request for a poem to be written, sent, and received in just under a fortnight. Asking Hardy 'if you *can* manage between now and the 10th to distil the liquor of your poetic genius, in no matter how mild a form, into three or four blest versicles', James reassured the poet that 'It is just the stray sincerities and casual felicities of your muse that that intelligent lady [Edith Wharton] *is* all ready to cherish', and urged him finally to 'overflow, no matter into how tiny a cup'.[1] Responding (as requested) 'gently and helpfully', Hardy poured out a generous enough measure for *The Book of the Homeless*, Wharton's charity venture in aid of Belgian refugees: 'Cry of the Homeless', which was later to carry the subtitle 'After the Prussian Invasion of Belgium', filled up three eight-line 'versicles', two of them voicing the curses of the war's victims on the 'Instigator of the ruin— / Whichsoever thou mayest be / Of the mastering minds of Europe / That contrived our misery.'[2] In the final stanza, after the bitter wish from the 'victims', ' "May thy dearest ones be blighted / And forsaken . . . And thy children beg their bread" ', Hardy spoke in an authorial first-person voice, modulating the poem's curses into something more subtle:

Read at the Academy 31 October 1996. © The British Academy 1997.

[1] Henry James, *Letters: Vol. 4 1895–1916*, ed. Leon Edel (Cambridge, Mass.: Harvard University Press, 1984), p. 773.
[2] Thomas Hardy, 'Cry of the Homeless', in Edith Wharton (ed.), *The Book of the Homeless* (New York: Charles Scribner's, 1916), p. 16.

Nay: too much the malediction.—
  Rather let this thing befall
In the unfurling of the future,
    On the night when comes thy call:
That compassion dew thy pillow
  And absorb thy senses all
    For thy victims,
  Till death dark thee with his pall.

Whatever the extent of this poem's 'casual felicities', its concluding stanza appears to mark a moment when 'stray sincerities' enable the voice to return on the rhetoric it has entertained, and concede that it is in some ways 'too much'. In wishing 'compassion' on what this poem calls simply the 'Enemy', Hardy allows himself his own instant of corrective reflection. Writing to James on 8 August (two days ahead of his deadline), Hardy held on to his misgivings: 'I send the enclosed page, for what it may be worth, as not quite the right thing. . . . Anyhow I hope it may help, though infinitesimally, in the good cause.'[3]

By the time he published it in his volume *Moments of Vision* (1917), Hardy evidently felt that not every detail of his poem was 'quite the right thing', having refined the curses of its first two stanzas so that 'thy dearest ones' (now simply 'thy loved') are no longer just 'blighted / And forsaken', but 'slighted, blighted / And forsaken', thus giving a full measure of insult to the original injury.[4] Moreover, the final stanza is now voiced by the 'victims' rather than the poet, and instead of going back on a malediction that was 'too much', offers 'a richer malediction' in a future of 'compassion' that will no longer 'dew' but now 'bedrench thy pillow'. Although the poem's level of vitriol rises in revision, Hardy makes his own position more difficult to determine by assigning the last 'malediction' to voices not his own. Other contributors to *The Book of the Homeless* shared Hardy's revisionary impulse: W. D. Howells, for example, seems to have had early qualms about his 'The Little Children', where hapless infants are seized by 'The master-spirit of hell':[5]

---

[3] Thomas Hardy, letter of 8 August 1915, quoted in Thomas Hardy, *Complete Poetical Works*, Vol. 2, ed. Samuel Hynes (Oxford: Clarendon Press, 1984, repr. with corrections 1987), p. 505.

[4] Thomas Hardy, 'Cry of the Homeless: After the Prussian Invasion of Belgium', *Complete Poetical Works*, ed. Hynes, Vol. 2, pp. 296–7.

[5] William Dean Howells, 'The Little Children', in Edith Wharton (ed.), *The Book of the Homeless*, p. 17.

> through the shuddering air
> Of the hope-forsaken world
> The little ones he hurled,
> Mocking that Pity in his pitiless might—
> The Anti-Christ of Schrecklickeit.

Perhaps feeling that this too was 'too much', Howells attempted to withdraw the poem shortly after despatching it; yet the situation was too late to mend, as Edith Wharton was able to report:[6]

> He sent a ringing little poem to Mr. James, and when he wrote to recall it, Mr. James flatly refused, to my eternal gratitude. The poem is just what I wanted—and curiously enough, it is very much like the one which Mr. Hardy has written for me.

Whatever Howells's second thoughts about his shrill verses in the cause of 'Pity', the 'ringing little poem' fitted in well to the scheme of *The Book of the Homeless*, and was duly printed there, joining Hardy, James himself, and many others, among them W. B. Yeats.

Unlike Hardy (and Howells), Yeats provided a poem which, rather than just prompting later reconsideration, was *already* a kind of recantation of poetic 'meddling' with the times. The six lines, as they appeared in Wharton's book, carried the title 'A Reason for Keeping Silent':[7]

> I think it better that at times like these
> We poets keep our mouths shut, for in truth
> We have no gift to set a statesman right;
> He's had enough of meddling who can please
> A young girl in the indolence of her youth
> Or an old man upon a winter's night.

Sending the poem to the editor, Yeats regretted only that it was not longer;[8] in a letter copying the verses to James, he added some brief reflections:[9]

---

[6] Edith Wharton, letter to Sarah Norton, 10 September 1915, quoted in Alan Price, *The End of the Age of Innocence: Edith Wharton and the First World War* (London: Robert Hale, 1996), p. 66.

[7] W. B. Yeats, 'A Reason for Keeping Silent' in Edith Wharton (ed.), *The Book of the Homeless*, p. 45.

[8] See Alan Price, *The End of the Age of Innocence*, p. 63.

[9] W. B. Yeats, letter to Henry James, 20 August 1915, *The Letters of W. B. Yeats*, ed. Allan Wade (London: Rupert Hart-Davis, 1954), pp. 599–600. It is interesting to compare this with opinions expressed in a letter to the poet from his father J. B. Yeats, on 25 April 1915: 'On two subjects I want to share with you some of my wisdom, war versus art. The ego in man, the undying worm from whose [*word indecipherable*] he escapes in the mad and at heart utterly frivolous excitement of war or in the sane and beneficent and profoundly wise excitement of art and poetry.' See Richard J. Finneran, George Mills Harper, and William M. Murphy (eds.), *Letters to W. B. Yeats*, Vol. 2 (London: Macmillan, 1977), p. 313.

> It is the only thing I have written of the war or will write, so I hope it may not
> seem unfitting. I shall keep the neighbourhood of the seven sleepers of
> Ephesus, hoping to catch their comfortable snores till bloody frivolity is
> over.

Yeats's 'I hope it may not seem unfitting' is in a different key to
Hardy's more diffident 'not quite the right thing', for 'It is the only
thing I have written of the war or will write' gives the poet's 'hope' a
certain air of confidence. The appropriateness of 'A Reason for Keeping
Silent' to *The Book of the Homeless* is not, however, of the same kind as
that of Howells's poem, or of Hardy's; the silence it keeps about 'times
like these', and the distance it puts between itself and what the letter
calls 'bloody frivolity', might constitute not responsible detachment but
culpable uninterest.

   If Yeats was in some sense in error in the tone of his contribution to
Edith Wharton's book, his mistake was not one which acts of local
revision could make good. Nor is 'A Reason for Keeping Silent' an
isolated occurrence, a freakish mismatch between Yeats's particular
kind of imagination and the prevailing circumstances, for another short
poem, explicitly addressing the war, shares the same attitude towards
acts of 'bloody frivolity':[10]

   A Meditation in Time of War

   For one throb of the artery,
   While on that old grey stone I sat
   Under the old wind-broken tree,
   I knew that One is animate,
   Mankind inanimate phantasy.

The determined abstraction of this poem, which sends the reader
directly to Yeats's more esoteric concerns with its shorthand mixture
of Blake and neoplatonism, may sit uncomfortably with the facts from
which it seems to avert its gaze. All the more so, perhaps, when one
sees that the poem's first draft is in a notebook immediately beneath a
memorandum of a prophecy made by Olivia Shakespear:[11]

---

[10] W. B. Yeats, *The Variorum Edition of the Poems of W.B. Yeats*, eds. Peter Allt and
Russell K. Alspach (New York: Macmillan, 1957) (cited hereafter as *Variorum Poems*), p.
406.

[11] This note, with a draft of the poem lower on the same page, is in a notebook given to
Yeats by Maud Gonne in 1912, and now in the National Library of Ireland (NLI 30,358 fol.
58ʳ). A photographic reproduction of the page, with a transcription of the poem only, is given
in *Michael Robartes and the Dancer: Manuscript Materials*, ed. Thomas Parkinson with

A few days ago Mrs Shakespear said 'I was praying for the happiness of the souls of those that die in battle' (she had I know been moved by the preyeirs for this object ordered by the Grand Lama) & got the impression 'Peace on Feb 14' I want you to make a note of it

The prophecy was recorded on 9 November 1914; many more 'souls of those that die in battle' were to come to account before Yeats published 'A Meditation in Time of War' in *Michael Robartes and the Dancer* (1921). Whether Yeats took a just measure of such facts has seemed debatable, and it is still possible to find critics who take this poem, together with 'A Reason for Keeping Silent', as powerfully negative evidence against the Yeats 'who had denied a high degree of reality to the Great War, and who refused to write a poem about it on request'.[12]

In the weeks shortly before the Armistice, Yeats's American patron John Quinn wrote to the poet on the subject of the war, and on his part in its literature—too small a part, in Quinn's view:[13]

I never said to you before what I have said frequently to your father, and that was how much I regretted that you had not taken some part on the side of what I have always felt to be justice and right in this war, or at least have spoken some word for France or for the justice and right. . . . I do not mean

---

Anne Brennan (Ithaca and London: Cornell University Press, 1994), pp. 194–5. My transcription of Yeats's memorandum about Olivia Shakespear's prophecy differs slightly from that given by John Harwood in his *Olivia Shakespear and W. B. Yeats: After Long Silence* (London: Macmillan, 1989), p. 138. It is worth noting that the date 'Nov. 9, 1914' appears directly under the memorandum in Yeats's notebook (where the context seems to make a dating of the prophecy necessary); Harwood takes this to be the date for Yeats's note, and not for the poem which follows. Parkinson and Brennan, perhaps agreeing with this, do not include the date in their transcription of the poem. The other draft of a poem contained in the notebook (on fol. 68$^v$) is for 'The Rose Tree', and is dated 'April 7. 1917', and 'A Meditation in Time of War' might have been composed around this time. However, 'A Meditation in Time of War' has been dated as 9 November 1914 by some of Yeats's editors, following Richard Ellmann's 'Chronology of the Composition of the Poems' in *The Identity of Yeats* (London: Macmillan, 1954; 2nd edn. London: Faber and Faber, 1964), p. 290: see for example A. Norman Jeffares, *A New Commentary on the Poems of W. B. Yeats* (London: Macmillan, 1984), p. 207, and Daniel Albright (ed.), *W. B. Yeats: The Poems* (London: Dent, 1990), p. 238. If this short poem was composed *after* 1914, and perhaps a considerable time afterwards (Yeats did not include it in either the 1917 or the 1919 versions of *The Wild Swans at Coole*), then it may be in part a meditation also on the hopes for peace (however oddly received and expressed) of 1914, in the light of later events; its abstractions are therefore abstractions made *after* the facts, rather than in advance (and innocence) of such things.

[12] Declan Kiberd, *Inventing Ireland* (London: Jonathan Cape, 1995), p. 246.

[13] John Quinn, postscript of 22 October 1918 to letter dated 2 October 1918, *The Letters of John Quinn to William Butler Yeats*, ed. Alan Himber (Epping: Bowker, 1983), p. 192.

anything like making a propagandist of yourself or a journalist or anything of that sort, nor the reshaping of your mind and style. I merely mean some expression as an artist in the form either of prose or verse that your genius might take—some token that you felt that in this, perhaps the greatest struggle of all time, you had been on the side of justice and right.

Although Quinn did not demand any 'reshaping of your mind and style', he thought that change of some kind was in order for Yeats. Quoting the remark of Abbey Theatre actor J. M. Kerrigan that too many Irishmen are 'grave worshippers', Quinn urged Yeats to 'forget' those specifically Irish things which prevented a fuller act of contemporary remembrance:

> It is sometimes the highest wisdom to be able to forget. Of course some artists simply cannot make themselves over. For example Joseph Conrad, whose heart is, I know, all in the struggle on the side of right and justice. He has not given any artistic expression to it, except in the one contribution of 'Reminiscences in Poland in War Time' which was published in a book that Mrs. Wharton got up for France. I have not overlooked your little contribution to that book, but those five or six lines were quite unworthy of you and the occasion.

'A Reason for Keeping Silent' is much concerned with worthiness, both to itself and to its occasion; Quinn's criticisms here impugn that sense of what is appropriate in a fundamental way. The question of the war provokes for Quinn the imperative of artists having to 'make themselves over', a phrase which one would not address to W. B. Yeats without a degree of critical deliberation. As Quinn would have known well, Yeats's *Collected Works* of 1908 had included an epigraph in which the poet boasted of his powers of self-reinvention:[14]

> The friends that have it I do wrong
> When ever I remake a song
> Should know what issue is at stake:
> It is myself that I remake.

This friend, however, was quarrelling with Yeats's *failure* to make himself over in relation to the war, and thought he saw specifically Irish reasons for the poet's unwillingness to speak. Quinn's suspicion has been shared by Yeats's critics, and is voiced clearly in Denis Donoghue's declaration that 'The plain fact is that Yeats did not feel inclined to put his genius to work in England's cause.'[15]

[14] W. B. Yeats, *Variorum Poems*, p. 778.
[15] Denis Donoghue, *We Irish: Selected Essays*, Vol. 1 (Brighton: Harvester, 1986), p. 185.

Although it is perfectly possible to argue for the profound long-term effects of the First World War on Yeats's poetry, it would be hard to make a case for his having accepted Quinn's advice to provide some immediate 'token' of his support for 'justice and right' or to have 'spoken some word' that might not be construed as equivocal at the time. Yeats did, in fact, remake 'A Reason for Keeping Silent', but he altered the poem only in the direction of stiffer rhetorical grandeur, having the lines now announce themselves as 'On Being Asked for a War Poem', and disposing of 'We poets keep our mouths shut' in favour of 'I think it better that in times like these / A poet's mouth be silent'.[16] There is just one poet now, and the added sense of dignity, of the poem's worthiness of the poet, could have done little to increase Quinn's admiration of its appropriateness for the times. In fact, far from setting itself to be worthy of its occasion, the poem in question had always adapted occasions to suit itself: Yeats already had the lines when James wrote on behalf of Edith Wharton in July 1915, having written them early in February, with the title 'To a friend who has asked me to sign on his manifesto to the neutral nations'.[17] Some time after *The Book of the Homeless*, a holograph copy made its way into a college library in Massachusetts, as part of the response to an appeal on behalf of 'The Fatherless Children of France'.[18] In 1917 and 1919, the poem took its place in the two versions of Yeats's collection *The Wild Swans at Coole*. In all these (and, it could be said, in subsequent) appearances, the six lines spoke to different occasions; but the poetic stance, for all the poet's minor revisions, remained constant and unapologetic.

Ten years after the end of the war, Yeats embroiled himself in controversy when he rejected Sean O'Casey's play *The Silver Tassie* for the Abbey Theatre, and his reasons for dealing this blow to the playwright developed and consolidated those which had conditioned his writing a decade earlier. In what he described as 'a hateful letter to write', the poet did not flinch from spelling out the grounds of his condemnation:[19]

[16] W. B. Yeats, *Variorum Poems*, p. 359.
[17] See W. B. Yeats, *The Wild Swans at Coole: Manuscript Materials*, ed. Stephen Parrish (Ithaca and London: Cornell University Press, 1994), p. 219.
[18] See ibid., p. xiii for details of manuscript in the Dinand Library, College of the Holy Cross, Worcester, Massachusetts; another holograph fair copy was made by Yeats, and is now in the Burns Library of Rare Books and Special collections at Boston College (ibid., p. xii).
[19] W. B. Yeats, letter to Sean O'Casey, 20 April 1928, *Letters*, ed. Wade, p. 741.

> The mere greatness of the world war has thwarted you; it has refused to become mere background, and obtrudes itself upon the stage as so much dead wood that will not burn with the dramatic fire. Dramatic action is a fire that must burn up everything but itself. . . . Among the things that dramatic action must burn up are the author's opinions; while he is writing he has no business to know anything that is not a portion of that action.

O'Casey himself was unable to forget or forgive this: remembering Yeats's assertion in the letter that 'You are not interested in the Great War; you never stood on its battlefields', his indignation in the autobiography *Rose and Crown* (1952) was still fresh:[20]

> Oh, God, here was a man who had never spoken to a Tommy in his life — bar Major Gregory; and to him only because he was an artist as well as a soldier — chattering about soldiers to one who had talked to them all. . . . *Not interested* to one who had talked and walked and smoked and sung with the blue-suited, wounded men fresh from the front; to one who had been among the armless, the legless, the blind, the gassed, and the shell-shocked!

O'Casey's outrage, burnt in rather than burnt away with the passing of time, assumes that Yeats has wronged the plain facts of experience; Yeats on the contrary decided that the matter of fact had overcome the artist in O'Casey. Yeats's 'Pages from a Diary in 1930' returns to the controversy, now even more certain of its ground:[21]

> The war, as O'Casey has conceived it, is an equivalent for those primary qualities brought down by Berkeley's secret society, it stands outside the characters, it is not part of their expression, it is that very attempt denounced by Mallarmé to build as if with brick and mortar within the pages of a book. The English critics feel differently, to them a theme that 'bulks largely in the news' gives dignity to human nature, even raises it to international importance. We on the other hand are certain that nothing can give dignity to human nature but the character and energy of its expression. We do not even ask that it shall have dignity so long as it can burn away all that is not itself.

The implied violence of Yeats's recurring metaphor, 'burn away', replies to the rejected violence of the war as part of another tit-for-tat exchange in the poet's late manner between the English and 'We Irish'.

Yeats's later pronouncements regarding the war were not to change matters, and his most notorious remarks, in the Introduction to *The*

---

[20] Sean O'Casey, *Rose and Crown* (1952), in *Autobiographies*, Vol. 2 (London: Macmillan, 1981), p. 275.
[21] W. B. Yeats, *Explorations* (London: Macmillan, 1962), pp. 339–40.

*Oxford Book of Modern Verse* (1936) revealed an attitude hardened by the years, for which 'passive suffering is not a theme for poetry', and in which the situation of the war-poets excluded from his anthology was reshaped as 'some blunderer has driven his car on to the wrong side of the road—that is all'.[22] The poetry of war, it seemed, was anywhere but in the pity. Privately, Yeats was no more accommodating, and wrote of Wilfred Owen as 'all blood, dirt and sucked sugar-stick', conceding only that 'There is every excuse for him, but none for those who like him'.[23] Yet there were those who were unable to excuse Yeats for this, especially as another war cast its shadow over his words, and Stephen Spender's declaration that 'Yeats wrote by saving himself from the mud of Flanders'[24] was one sign of a reaction against his perceived irresponsibility. In 1915 and after, the poet had found his reasons for keeping silent; when the opportunity for redress offered itself, in the anthology twenty years later, Yeats only exacerbated the original affront.

On the face of things, Yeats emerges in this respect as a writer who is singularly lacking in the capacity for conceiving and articulating regret. However, the registers of regretful memory, or retrospective doubt and qualm, are central to a great deal of Yeats's best poetry, and find their focus in his poetic vocabulary with the word 'remorse', a term which denotes something *more* than regret, though also one which suggests significance other than the purely occasional or personal for that regret. For Yeats, remorse exists in the most intimate relation to the poetic impulse, and happens even in the textures of the poetry itself, in the soundings of words' returns on themselves and their sounds, through the structures of rhyme and of repetition; at the same time, remorse is a force against which the poetry exerts its own rhetorical counter-pressures. Sometimes, a victory of sorts is achieved, as in the concluding stanza of 'A Dialogue of Self and Soul':[25]

> I am content to follow to its source
> Every event in action or in thought;
> Measure the lot; forgive myself the lot!
> When such as I cast out remorse
> So great a sweetness flows into the breast

[22] W. B. Yeats (ed.), *The Oxford Book of Modern Verse 1892–1935* (Oxford: Clarendon Press, 1936), p. xxxiv.
[23] W. B. Yeats, letter to Dorothy Wellesley, 21 December 1936, *Letters*, ed. Wade, p. 874.
[24] Stephen Spender, 'Tragedy and some Modern Poetry', *Penguin New Writing*, 4 (March 1941), 147.
[25] W. B. Yeats, *Variorum Poems*, p. 479.

We must laugh and we must sing,
We are blest by everything,
Everything we look upon is blest.

'When such as I cast out remorse . . .': the reaction of an O'Casey to that 'such as I' may be readily imagined, and would not be disallowed completely by the knowledge that 'I' here does not represent (all of) the poet W. B. Yeats. 'Cast out' poses its own problems: one might cast out devils, but an emotion like remorse is not commonly understood as devilish, and Yeats's voice here seems all too ready to perform its own acts of self-forgiveness and exorcism in a manner quite incompatible with actual sorrow or regret. In his account of his own early writings in *The Trembling of the Veil* (1922), Yeats identified remorse as a problem:[26]

> For ten or twelve years more I suffered continual remorse, and only became content when my abstractions had composed themselves into picture and dramatization. My very remorse helped to spoil my early poetry, giving it an element of sentimentality through my refusal to permit it any share of an intellect which I considered impure.

When Yeats recalls his own younger sense of the inappropriateness of poetic abstraction to the matter of life and plain facts, he identifies a disabling remorse there; and this puts him in good poetic company, since he had claimed Edmund Spenser as 'the first poet struck with remorse' in his selection from that poet in 1906, where the demands of Elizabethan religion and policy were seen as responsible for the remorseful impulse to allegorise of 'the first poet who gave his heart to the State'.[27] The word 'remorse' sounds through much of the later Yeats, and in *The Winding Stair*, where the Self casts out remorse in its dialogue with the Soul, there is also 'The Choice', with its presentation of the alternatives of 'The day's vanity, the night's remorse',[28] and the poem 'Remorse for Intemperate Speech', with its final acknowledgement of the Irish 'Great hatred, little room' that 'Maimed us at the start'.[29] At the beginning of the sequence 'Vacillation', the destructive 'brand, or flaming breath' is given a double identification: 'The body calls it death, / The heart remorse.'[30] Announcing 'The first principle' in 'A General Introduction for My Work' (1937), Yeats declares that 'A

[26] W. B. Yeats, *Autobiographies* (London: Macmillan, 1955), p. 188.
[27] W.B. Yeats, 'Edmund Spenser', *Essays and Introductions* (London: Macmillan, 1961), p. 373.
[28] W. B. Yeats, *Variorum Poems*, p. 495.
[29] Ibid., p. 506.
[30] Ibid., p. 500.

poet writes always of his personal life, in his finest work out of its tragedy, whatever it be, remorse, lost love, or mere loneliness.'[31] The very late play *Purgatory* ends with the bleak prayer to God to 'appease / The misery of the living and the remorse of the dead'.[32] The meaning of Yeatsian remorse is clearly something other than simple regret, and its function is quite distinct from that of apology or reparation. The definition of remorse offered by the *OED* (*sb.*2a), 'A feeling of compunction, or of deep regret and repentance, for a sin or wrong committed', introduces elements that seem almost completely absent from Yeats's uses for the word. Most importantly, remorse for the later Yeats is something which has its dealings with the dead, and which can also describe the dead's business with the living.

To define Yeats's remorse in this way is to claim an intimacy between the word and those obsessions with spiritualism, magic, and esoteric and arcane traditions which run through almost the whole of the poet's writing life. However, such a definition also helps to locate this remorse historically, for it is during the First World War that Yeats, at the same time as he makes the breakthrough effected by and in the automatic script of his wife George, discovers remorse as a potent term in his imaginative vocabulary. If specific war casualties were bearing in on Yeats at this time—Sir Hugh Lane, perhaps, or later Major Robert Gregory—a much more numerous army of 'those that die in battle' could no more be ignored by the poet than they were by a public eager for the consolations of a belief in the afterlife, as exercised in the church or the seance-room. In the light of this, it is possible to see Yeats's writing about the war as including *A Vision* (1925) along with the many poems which, remorsefully and remorselessly, speak to, for, and sometimes against the dead.

By the time Lady Gregory's son Robert was killed in action on 23 January 1918, Yeats was already absorbed creatively in the dynamics of death and remorse. In his attempt at a pastoral elegy for Robert, 'Shepherd and Goatherd', Yeats had to hand a developed theory of the 'dreaming back' of the dead. In the poem, the process is misleadingly (though understandably in the circumstances) consolatory in its effect:[33]

---

[31] W. B. Yeats, *Essays and Introductions*, p. 509.
[32] W. B. Yeats, *Collected Plays* (London: Macmillan, 1952), p. 689.
[33] W. B. Yeats, *Variorum Poems*, p. 342.

Jaunting, journeying
To his own dayspring,
He unpacks the loaded pern
Of all 'twas pain or joy to learn,
Of all that he had made.
The outrageous war shall fade . . .

Behind this is a theme which, although it becomes elaborate in the automatic writings of 1917 and afterwards, had roots deep in Yeats's customary preoccupations. In *Per Amica Silentia Lunae*, finished just before George's communications began, Yeats gives the idea a high rhetorical polish, writing that 'The toil of the living is to free themselves from an endless sequence of objects, and that of the dead to free themselves from an endless sequence of thoughts'.[34] In 'Shepherd and Goatherd', Robert Gregory dreams back his life without pain or remorse, but Yeats knew that other thoughts beside these could be assigned to his ghost, and was to write a poem in 1920 in which these 'second thoughts' could be spelled out. By this time, Yeats is able to confront the dead with history, and demand remorse from both the dead and the living.

To measure the distance between Yeats's writings at the beginning of the war, and his attitudes by 1920 and the writing of 'Reprisals', is to encounter a number of plain facts lodged in history, which affected the poet in more and less profound ways. Of course, the significance of such historical matter is nothing like so plain: that the most catastrophic event in Irish history in the year 1916, for example, should have been ignored by Yeats seems unlikely. And yet the dead from the Irish and Ulster Divisions at the Somme are silent in Yeats's writing, and are silenced in much Irish history, while the dead of the Dublin insurrection of 1916 enjoyed, and continue to enjoy, a much more active afterlife. By the time of the poem 'Reprisals', the war had come to Ireland in the shape of the Black and Tans; Yeats voices anger and bitterness, forcing Gregory's ghost to face the brutal matter:[35]

---

[34] W. B. Yeats, *Mythologies* (London: Macmillan, 1959), pp. 353–4.

[35] The text of 'Reprisals' quoted here is that of the typescript which Yeats sent to Lady Gregory in a letter of 26 November 1920, as reproduced in *The Wild Swans at Coole: Manuscript Materials*, ed. Parrish, p. 423. The textual history of this poem is an involved one: its first publication was in *Rann: An Ulster Quarterly of Poetry* (Autumn 1948), in a text deriving from a MS fair copy in Yeats's hand (NLI 13,358), which went on to be the basis for the text of 'Reprisals' in *Variorum Poems* and some other editions. The typescript sent to Lady Gregory is regarded as more authoritative by Richard J. Finneran in *Editing Yeats's*

Yet rise from your Italian tomb,
Flit to Kiltartan Cross and stay
Till certain second thoughts have come
Upon the cause you served, that we
Imagined such a fine affair:
Half-drunk or whole-mad soldiery
Are murdering your tenants there . . .

A note in Yeats's hand on a draft of the poem records a remark made by
Gregory to the poet, that 'I see no reason why anyone should fight in
this war except friendship', and that 'The England I care for was dead
long ago'.[36] When he instructs Gregory's ghost to 'stay / Till certain
second thoughts have come', Yeats does so in the context of rethinkings
of his own, most clearly expressed in the opening of a manuscript
version of the poem:[37]

Some nineteen German planes, they say,
You had brought down before you died.
We called it a good death. To day,
Can ghost or man be satisfied?

To go back over things is not the same as being able to go back on them:
'We called it a good death'—and yet, as the poem ruthlessly records,
we were wrong. What is more (and what is worse), there is no going
back open to the voice in this poem, just as there is no possibility of
regret open to the ghost itself. A last couplet instructs Gregory to 'stop
your ears with dust and lie / Among the other cheated dead', advice
which echoes the bitter send-off given to Parnell in 'To a Shade'
(1913), 'Away, away! You are safer in the tomb'.[38]

In appearing to demand remorse from its subject and then, failing to
elicit this, giving him his marching-orders, Yeats's 'Reprisals' follows a
remorseless rhetorical course. In this sense, at least, it needs to be

---

*Poems: A Reconsideration* (London: Macmillan, 1990), pp. 147–51, where the matter of the
poem's early history is discussed in detail. It seems that a third version of the poem was
available to T. R. Henn, whose 1965 lecture 'Yeats and the Poetry of War' quotes in full a
text 'taken down from [Peter] Allt himself, in 1947, which seems to me far more Yeatsian'
(*Proceedings of the British Academy*, 51 (1965), p. 310, repr. in T. R. Henn, *Last Essays*
(Gerrards Cross: Colin Smythe, 1976), p. 89). However, Henn's lecture remains the only
source for this text of 'Reprisals'.
[36] This note is on the verso of a MS fair copy (NLI 13,583), and is quoted by Finneran in
*Editing Yeats's Poems: A Reconsideration*, p. 150.
[37] NLI 13,583, reproduced in *The Wild Swans at Coole: Manuscript Materials*, ed. Parrish,
p. 422.
[38] W. B. Yeats, *Variorum Poems*, p. 293.

distinguished from the poet's other Gregory poems, as Yeats himself knew: it was written to the moment, and for a purpose, 'because I thought it might touch some one individual mind of a man in power'.[39] The atrocities at which the poem bridles are those which it hopes it might help put an end to; bound originally for the *Nation*, and then for *The Times*, 'Reprisals' was written as a provocative poem, but the poet hoped that it would also provoke remorse among at least some of its English readership. Yeats was pleased with the poem, and had to have second thoughts forced upon him by Lady Gregory:[40]

> I cannot bear the dragging of R., from his grave to make what I think a not very sincere poem—for Yeats knows only by hearsay while our troubles go on—and he quoted words G.B.S., told him and did not mean him to repeat—and which will give pain—I hardly know why it gives me extra-ordinary pain and it seems too late to stop it . . .

It was not too late; the poem was stopped; and Yeats himself (whether remorsefully, regretfully, or forgetfully) did not include it in a future collection. Whatever the reasons for this occlusion, 'Reprisals' is a poem in which Yeats's imagination allows itself to become opportunistic, and in which the dead (whether Gregory in his 'Italian tomb' or the victims of the Black and Tans) are too simply pressed into service. There is a damaging sense in which 'Reprisals' cheats on the dead when it declares them to have been 'cheated', and the distortion which its (proper) outrage at the news from Ireland forces on the war is a part of that cheating which no amount of just intentions on the poet's part can make good. Lady Gregory thought it better that, in times like those, poets should keep their mouths shut—at least, if their words were to pay less than respect to either the truth or the dead—and Yeats may have come to agree with her. At any rate, the passive suffering which 'Reprisals' tries to force on Gregory's ghost was not a theme for Yeats's best poetry.

When Yeats wanted to engineer remorse in a public register, he insisted on 'second thoughts' as the trigger, and his own more private experiences lay behind this, suggesting as they did the possibilities (and the liabilities) of going back over the past. Again, the point at which the dynamics of personal regret and self-doubt begin to charge Yeats's

---

[39] W. B. Yeats, letter to Lady Gregory, 3 December 1920, quoted in Finneran, *Editing Yeats's Poems: A Reconsideration*, p. 151.
[40] *Lady Gregory's Journals*, Vol. 1, ed. Daniel J. Murphy (Gerrards Cross: Colin Smythe, 1978), p. 207.

work with energies of remorse comes during the war, in the flurry of ultimatums and decisions surrounding his marriage in 1917. Certainly, the Yeats who wrote to Lady Gregory on 19 September of that year was burdened by worries, about his love-life, the reasonableness of his own behaviour, and the intrusiveness upon all this of the war. With Maud Gonne and her daughter Iseult excluded from Ireland under the Defence of the Realm Act, the poet found himself in 'rather a whirlpool':[41]

> Poor Iseult was very depressed on the journey and at Havre went off by herself and cried. Because she was so ashamed 'at being so selfish' 'at not wanting me to marry and so break her friendship with me.' I need hardly say she had said nothing to me of 'not wanting.' Meanwhile she has not faltered in her refusal of me but as you can imagine life is a good deal at white heat. I think of going to Mrs Tucker's on Monday but may not as I am feeling rather remorseful especially now that this last business of the defence of the realm act has come.

The next day, Yeats reported that 'I am going to Mrs Tucker's in the country . . . and I will ask her daughter to marry me.'[42] Even this decisive (and successful) proposal did not put an immediate end to the poet's personal remorsefulness, and a honeymooning Yeats found himself 'in great gloom', and 'saying to myself "I have betrayed three people"'.[43] It is easy to say grandly of Yeats that 'The transformations of art . . . are closely bound up with betrayal',[44] but the enduring costs of such 'transformations' are more difficult to account for; and here, certainly, the meaning and role of remorse are at issue. With three people betrayed (Maud, Iseult, and his bride George), it is understandable that a pair of short poems from Yeats's period of 'gloom', subsequently titled 'Owen Aherne and his Dancers' (and thus put within the fictional orbit of *A Vision*), should figure remorse prominently:[45]

> A strange thing surely that my Heart, when love had come unsought
> Upon the Norman upland or in that poplar shade,
> Should find no burden but itself and yet should be worn out.
> It could not bear that burden and therefore it went mad.
>
> The south wind brought it longing, and the east wind despair,
> The west wind made it pitiful, and the north wind afraid.

---

[41] W. B. Yeats, letter to Lady Gregory, 18 September 1917, *Letters*, ed. Wade, p. 632.
[42] W. B. Yeats, letter to Lady Gregory, 19 September 1917, ibid., p. 633.
[43] W. B. Yeats, letter to Lady Gregory, 29 October 1917, ibid., p. 633.
[44] Stan Smith, *The Origins of Modernism: Eliot, Pound, Yeats and the Rhetorics of Renewal* (Hemel Hempstead: Harvester Wheatsheaf, 1994), p. 179.
[45] W. B. Yeats, *Variorum Poems*, pp. 449–50.

It feared to give its love a hurt with all the tempest there;
It feared the hurt that she could give and therefore it went mad.

In these lines, from the first of the poems, the Lover's dilemma is to be cornered by fear of emotional facts which are all too plain, and the Heart's apparent madness is presented as the result of being put in an impossible position. However, Yeats provides a companion poem, in which the Heart can have its say, this time in open opposition to the earlier verses assigned to the voice of the Lover. Now, the attitude is one that mocks the Lover's responsible worries: 'Let the cage bird and the cage bird mate and the wild bird mate in the wild.' Yeats begins and ends this second poem with the Heart's reckless dismissal of the Lover's misgivings, but he lodges a stanza of remorse, voiced for the lover, in the poem's midst:

'You but imagine lies all day, O murderer,' I replied.
'And all those lies have but one end, poor wretches to betray;
I did not find in any cage the woman at my side.
O but her heart would break to learn my thoughts are far away.'

'Owen Aherne and his Dancers' is not an overbalancing or a lopsided dialogue; although the Heart has the last word, it does not refute the Lover's accusation that 'You but imagine lies'. Instead, the Heart retorts by bringing to bear other home truths:

'Speak all your mind,' my Heart sang out, 'speak all your mind; who cares,
Now that your tongue cannot persuade the child till she mistake
Her childish gratitude for love and match your fifty years?
O let her choose a young man now and all for his wild sake.'

The air is thick with 'lies' in this debate, where each participant tries to force second thoughts upon the other. The poem's final exultation, in other words, resonates also with the echoes of self-doubt and remorse. The effect achieved by Yeats here has been described as 'disturbed and disturbing',[46] and this accounts accurately for the relative states of the two voices, one stricken with paralysis, the other goading and relentless in its mockery. Each side alleges facts against the other, and the facts lie plainly on both sides of the argument. However uncomfortable Yeats might have felt, his poetry was able to thrive in such an impossible position, and he sent the paired poems to Lady Gregory with the comment that 'they are among the best I have done'.[47]

[46] Elizabeth Butler Cullingford, *Gender and History in Yeats's Love Poetry* (Cambridge: CUP, 1993), p. 105.
[47] W. B. Yeats, letter to Lady Gregory, 29 October 1917, *Letters*, ed. Wade, p. 634.

In biographical terms, the breaking of this particular stalemate in Yeats's emotional life might seem miraculous; the poet himself would have applied that term, though in doing so he might have been rather more literal in intent, for George's automatic writing, which constituted the otherworldly intervention in 1917, did something decisive with some all too recalcitrant facts. Not least, the messages which George supplied spoke directly to Yeats's sense of remorse, and about it, in an idiom which enabled the poet to construct a system in which that remorse might find its place. On a personal level, George encouraged the poet to inspect his past—and especially the 'Crisis Moments' in his emotional past—in the light of ideas of character, fate, and passion which are developed from themes already present in his writing. One early communication enjoins both 'self knowledge' and 'anihilation [sic] of the concealed', and recommends 'confession':[48]

> [Question] What do you mean by confession.
> [Response] Confession is preceded by self knowledge—confession itself implies a need for human sympathy & expansion of the nature—the word is perhaps implying too much the idea of christian conf[ession] & repentance—I mean it as an acknowledgement of weakness or an acknowledgement of the need of all human beings for protection in one side of their nature . . .

The process of emotional defrosting which George's writing encouraged can be seen here, and its supernatural and symbolic accompaniments need to be understood partly as an idiom of reference which husband and wife shared. If 'repentance' was unhelpful at this stage (and also, in some ways, by this stage pointless), 'acknowledgement of weakness' was an area in which, increasingly, Yeats's creative strength lay. What was more, the crossing of 'self knowledge' with more esoteric concerns gave the poet's habitual preoccupations a new lease of life.

As usual, such vitality in Yeats exists in close proximity to, and attempts to draw its energy from the dead. In *Per Amica Silentia Lunae*, where 'The dead, living in their memories are . . . the source of all that we call instinct',[49] Yeats had already sketched out the lines connecting the dead, memory, judgement, and the self which George's automatic writing (and, in time, *A Vision*) would elaborate:[50]

---

[48] George Mills Harper (gen. ed.), *Yeats's Vision Papers: Vol. 1 The Automatic Script 5 November 1917–18 June 1918*, eds. Steve L. Adams, Barbara J. Frieling, and Sandra L. Sprayberry (London: Macmillan, 1992), p. 90. This message is dated 20 November 1917.
[49] W. B. Yeats, *Mythologies* (1962), p. 359.
[50] Ibid., p. 354.

> We carry to *Anima Mundi* our memory, and that memory is for a time our external world; and all passionate moments recur again and again, for passion desires its own recurrence more than any event, and whatever there is of corresponding complacency or remorse is our beginning of judgment; nor do we remember only the events of life, for thoughts bred of longing and of fear, all those parasitic vegetables that have slipped through our fingers, come again like a rope's end to smite us upon the face . . .

'Memory' is the medium in which 'passionate moments' come back on the self as they 'recur again and again'; the 'remorse' which figures here in Yeats's prose is the same remorse which becomes part of the process of 'dreaming back' explored in George's automatic script, where the whole idea of recurrence is elevated into a central principle of historical as well as personal fate. In the system which George and her husband developed, the destiny of the individual soul is to go back over its lives again and again, and the fate of civilisations is to re-enter cycle after cycle of growth and decay. Both processes are marked by moments of cataclysmic significance, which become the focal points for Yeats's poetic attention. While poems like 'The Second Coming' and 'Byzantium' emerge from Yeats's fascination with points of historical change, and attempt some measure of detachment from the scenes upon which they magnificently spectate, the poet's need to go back over the matter of memory, and the 'passionate moments' which found their place in the more personalised aspects of the symbolic system, make self-scrutiny and unsparing recollection necessary. Above all, in this supernaturally shadowed brooding on 'self knowledge', Yeats is able both to figure remorse in his writing, and to take his writing beyond remorse. Like his efforts to make good a creative detachment from the catastrophes of history, Yeats's inspections of and departures from remorse run the risk of seeming to outrun (culpably, for some of his readers) the plain facts, and to forget too readily or wilfully those loose ends of personal or public history which recur again and again, and come back, as it were, to smite him upon the face.

Yeats saw remorse as something distinct from action, and grew increasingly convinced of the need for art to include and forward action. Passivity, as Yeats understood it, could produce only an art of inertia, and this was a tendency he was able to detect retrospectively in some of his own early writing, and in that of his contemporaries. *The Trembling of the Veil* broods over the fate of a whole 'Tragic Generation' of artists whose defiance of things as they are carries with it a high cost in terms of inaction, self-delusion, and remorse. This is most subtly explored in

Yeats's depiction of Oscar Wilde, but is a theme which brings many of his contemporaries into the same fold. Accounting for William Sharp's belief in his own literary alter ego, for example, Yeats recalls how 'he had created an imaginary beloved, had attributed to her the authorship of all his books that had any talent, and though habitually a sober man, I have known him to get drunk, and at the height of his intoxication when most men speak the truth, to attribute his state to remorse for having been unfaithful to Fiona Macleod.'[51] Similar paralysis afflicts Lionel Johnson, 'who could not have written *The Dark Angel* if he did not suffer from remorse', and who, despite the fact of his alcoholism 'showed to friends an impenitent face'.[52] Going over the past in his autobiographical writings, Yeats sees remorse as a state producing paralysed repetition—or in the case of Ernest Dowson paralytic repetition: 'the last time I saw Dowson he was pouring out a glass of whiskey for himself in an empty corner of my room and murmuring over and over in what seemed automatic apology, "The first to-day."'[53] The cast of Yeats's 'Tragic Generation' go over and over the same things, as incapable of action in their lives as they are, being dead, for Yeats in 1922. Thus, when Yeats invokes Matthew Arnold against Owen and other war poets, it is the Arnold of the 1853 Preface, who stands in judgement on his own work, doing away with *Empedocles on Etna* on the grounds that 'the suffering finds no vent in action . . . there is everything to be endured, nothing to be done'.[54] By 1936, Yeats had found plenty for his own poetry to do; and one crucial thing done in the verse was the poet's listening to the sounds of his own endurance, and his ability to go back over those sounds.

It is no more than a truism to say that Yeats's poetry, from a very early stage, tends towards patterns of verbal and rhythmic repetition. However, there is a critical tendency to treat repetition in poetry as a device only, and an unremarkable one at that; whereas for Yeats (as for many other poets) such specifics of poetic texture are never simply formalities. In the matter of memory, with its possibilities of remorse, Yeats's poetry is especially prone and alert to recurring sounds. Even the contrived stasis of an early poem like 'He Wishes for the Cloths of Heaven' depends largely on the surprise effect of having what should be

---

[51] W. B. Yeats, *Autobiographies* (1955), p. 341.
[52] Ibid., p. 312.
[53] Ibid., p. 312.
[54] Matthew Arnold, Preface to *Poems* (1853), *The Poems of Matthew Arnold*, ed. Kenneth Allott, 2nd. edn., ed. Miriam Allott (London: Longman, 1979), p. 656.

the rhyme words repeat themselves exactly, so that 'Tread softly because you tread on my dreams'[55] comes to possess a certain intransigence of relentless (and perhaps remorse-provoking) suffering. In the later Yeats, such returns of sound carry strong and complex charges. In a draft of section V of the sequence 'Vacillation' (a section which initially bore the title 'Remorse'), the triggers for remorseful memory include 'a sound':[56]

> Blunders of thirty years ago
> Or said or done but yesterday
> Or what I did not say or do
> But that I thought to do or say
> A word or sound and I recall
> Things that my conscience and my vanity appall.

'A word or sound' can be caught up in the patterns of recurrence where remorse figures, and threatens the paralysis of memories stuck in the grooves of their own repetition. Again, the crises and resolutions in Yeats's personal life during the First World War produce poems in which repetition becomes a major force. In 'Broken Dreams', written for Maud Gonne in 1915, the element of repetition may be a force for a profound inertia, and the poem's coda-like conclusion seems to acknowledge as much:[57]

> The last stroke of midnight dies.
> All day in the one chair
> From dream to dream and rhyme to rhyme I have ranged
> In rambling talk with an image of air:
> Vague memories, nothing but memories.

This final line has become a kind of irregularly-returning refrain; finishing the poem with the line intensifies a sense that the voice has not gone beyond this point (nor wanted to get beyond it), and its recurrence becomes a kind of reassurance, with its internal repetition almost comforting. This measure of resignation (and, it may be, of passive suffering) has left behind the raw wounds present in early stages of the poem's composition, where Yeats remembered 'The lineaments that peirced [*sic*] my life with pain / Till it could have no life but memories'.[58] 'Broken Dreams', which ranges from repetition to

---

[55] W. B. Yeats, *Variorum Poems*, p. 176.
[56] Quoted in Richard Ellmann, *The Identity of Yeats* (1964), pp. 272–3.
[57] W. B. Yeats, *Variorum Poems*, p. 356.
[58] Holograph of 'Broken Dreams' (NLI 30,370 fol. 2ʳ), reproduced and transcribed in *The Wild Swans At Coole: Manuscript Materials*, ed. Parrish, pp. 186–7.

repetition, is a poem in which Yeats sounds out measures of resignation, but also one in which he takes the measure of such resignation, and balances against an imagined afterlife in which Gonne's beauty will be restored the small, actual imperfections ('Your small hands were not beautiful') which survive the vagueness of the 'memories'.

However problematic it may be in its context, the final line of 'Broken Dreams' echoes into other writings in which Yeats takes the measure of regret. On the back of one of the pages on which the elegy 'Shepherd and Goatherd' is composed, a fragment in four-stress couplets begins by hearing again the words and rhythm of 'Vague memories, nothing but memories', and paring them down:[59]

> Memories upon memories
> Have bowed my head upon my knees.
> A dying boy with handsome face
> Upturned upon a beaten place,
> A sacred yew tree on a strand
> A woman that holds in steady hand
> A burning wisp beside a door
> And many and many a woman more[.]
> And not another thought than these
> Have bowed my head upon my knees.

Yeats then alters his final couplet to produce 'Memories upon memories/ Have bowed my head upon my knees'. If the fragment has a connection with 'Shepherd and Goatherd' and Robert Gregory (as seems likely), it records a more personal corollary of the 'dreaming back' which the airman's ghost experiences in the poem proper, where 'He grows younger every second', so that 'The outrageous war shall fade';[60] here, powerful and inscrutable symbolic images are canvassed, but the paralysis of passive recollection takes over, leaving the voice to murmur over its 'Memories upon memories'.

There is another context for these lines, or at least a suggestive parallel for them, in Yeats's wartime writings. In the play *The Only Jealousy of Emer*, which was much on the poet's mind in the first year of George's automatic writing, and in fact featured on occasion as the subject-matter of the spirit communications, the character of Cuchulain

---

[59] Holograph, Berg Collection, New York Puiblic Library (Quinn (14)). The lines quoted here are on the verso of leaf 4 of the five leaves of draft for 'Shepherd and Goatherd': they are reproduced and transcribed in *The Wild Swans At Coole: Manuscript Materials*, ed. Parrish, pp. 418–9.

[60] W. B. Yeats, *Variorum Poems*, p. 342.

is depicted in relation to three female figures: his wife Emer, his mistress Eithne Inguba, and the supernatural Fand, a woman of the Sidhe. Given Yeats's anxieties over his having 'betrayed three women', the play's engagement with love, possessiveness, and renunciation is biographically loaded, as its author and his wife well knew. If the play's subject-matter is familiar, so is some of its language, as when Cuchulain's ghostly form converses with Fand:[61]

> *Woman of the Sidhe*   What pulled your hands about your feet,
> Pulled down your head upon your knees,
> And hid your face?
>
> *Ghost of Cuchulain*   Old memories:
> A woman in her happy youth
> Before her man had broken troth,
> Dead men and women. Memories
> Have pulled my head upon my knees.

As his body lies between life and death, Cuchulain's ghost is tempted away from the weight of recollection, the 'memories' which 'Weigh down my hands, abash my eyes'. While there is a recollection of 'Broken Dreams' here (and in the fragment relating to 'Shepherd and Goatherd' obviously relevant to the play), there is also the most glancing of allusions to another poem of 1915 in the word 'abash'. This poem, 'The People', remembers and restages an argument between Yeats and Maud Gonne, letting Maud's dignified reply face down and cast doubt upon the poet's pride and affected haughtiness; at the poem's conclusion, the voice of the poet is chastened again in its recollection of the original mistake:[62]

> And yet, because my heart leaped at her words,
> I was abashed, and now they come to mind
> After nine years, I sink my head abashed.

'Abashed . . . abashed' taps into the distinctive energies of poetic repetition: the poet is abashed twice—nine years ago and now—but he is also brought up against the word's sound again, and its reiteration makes audible a humiliation which has become a sticking-point. 'Abashed' comes back like a rope's end which smites the poet on the face. The Yeats who wrote these lines (unusually for one of his lyric poems, they are in blank verse) had learned much from listening to

[61] W. B. Yeats, *Collected Plays* (London: Macmillan, 1952), p. 291.
[62] W. B. Yeats, *Variorum Poems*, p. 353.

Wordsworth, the great English poet of repetition, in Ezra Pound's renditions during the wartime winters spent at Stone Cottage.[63] When 'abash' returns in *The Only Jealousy of Emer*, it comes in a different formal element, the ritualistic rhymed tetrameters in which one world converses with another; now, as Fand woos Cuchulain's ghost away from the vestiges of its humanity, memory must be erased altogether:[64]

> *Woman of the Sidhe*   Then kiss my mouth. Though memory
> Be beauty's bitterest enemy
> I have no dread, for at my kiss
> Memory on the moment vanishes:
> Nothing but beauty can remain.
>
> *Ghost of Cuchulain*   And shall I never know again
> Intricacies of blind remorse?

With 'Memory on the moment vanishes' the rhythm, for a moment, flutters out of its course, and the repetitive, four-beat measure in which memories recur seems, for a breath, to be loosening its grip. Cuchulain's question to Fand is sunk in the rhythm it hopes perhaps to leave behind when it forsakes remorse along with memory. Fand's last lines to Cuchulain promise a remorseless 'oblivion':[65]

> But what could make you fit to wive
> With flesh and blood, being born to live
> Where no one speaks of broken troth,
> For all have washed out of their eyes
> Wind-blown dirt of their memories
> To improve their sight?

Cuchulain, on the verge of vanishing forever with Fand, is reclaimed for humanity only by his wife Emer's last-minute decision to renounce his love. For Yeats, in the process of both inspecting and finding ways around his own 'Intricacies of blind remorse', the scene's incantatory rhyming towards and away from the hold of memory has a certain exploratory significance.

The rhythmic effects of repetition had always, in some obvious senses, been important to Yeats; his early poetry is often essentially incantatory, and years of effort, experiment, and thinking went into his practice, with associated excursions into the speaking of dramatic

---

[63] See James Longenbach, *Stone Cottage: Pound, Yeats, and Modernism* (New York: OUP, 1988), pp. 142–3.
[64] W. B. Yeats, *Collected Plays* (1952), p. 292.
[65] Ibid., p. 293.

poetry, and the virtues offered by Florence Farr's psaltery accompaniments. But the question of poetic rhythm's hold on reality changes and deepens as Yeats grows, and by the time of the First World War it has taken on new dimensions. Now the stakes are higher: memory, the dead, betrayal, action, and remorse are all implicit in poetry's rhythmic integrity, or its lack of integrity, but they are also concerns which might find blunter expression in the resistance put up to such poetry by an all too intrusive historical situation. When John Quinn chastised Yeats with 'It is sometimes the highest wisdom to be able to forget', he underestimated the complexity of the ways in which poetry remembers, and of Yeats's own knowledge (and experience) of this; whatever his *bona fides* on the subject of Ireland, England, and the war, Quinn's demand that Yeats do something 'on the side of right and justice' was too confident of what it took to be the facts of the matter. When Yeats writes 'Easter 1916', a poem in which the historical ironies of the insurrection's self-consciousness are given full rein, he does so with memory as his subject, and the poem concludes with the incantatory creation of memory, as the voice 'murmur[s] name upon name'.[66] 'Easter 1916' takes full measure of its dead and, in fundamental ways, questions them and subjects them to the forces of historical chance and irony; in creating their memory as a historical meaning, the poem shapes the dead into a deliberate, quasi-liturgical rhythm, sealed up behind the marble walls of the polished and emphatic refrain that structures and ends the poem. 'Changed, changed utterly' is built on a dead repetition, one which acknowledges grimly that, from now on, there will indeed be no change.

The dead of 'Easter 1916' are not the living men and women of Yeats's memory; like the dead in the poet's supernatural system, they have become a force to reckon with, 'living in their memories'. The poem's Irish context and meanings have this as their starting-point, but Yeats's procedure here derives also from his protracted encounter with the special demands of the dead as these presented themselves to him in wartime. Irish history makes the Dublin dead of 1916 an obvious source for much subsequent imagination and action; but Yeats's sense of the dead as a 'source', which conditions the poem, continues to develop in his writing, in ways which perhaps try to address Quinn's desire for something 'on the side of justice and right'. Yeats's equivalent to that phrase, when he describes the abstractions of *A Vision* as elements

---

[66] W. B. Yeats, *Variorum Poems*, p. 394.

which 'have helped me to hold in a single thought reality and justice',[67] has two sides to it, and summarises a process in which the dead are both accommodated and resisted. The place of remorse in this, and of the sounds and rhythms of remorse in Yeats's poetry, help to explain the poet's ambivalence about the dead as a 'source'.

Looking for the source of action was a habit well-known to Yeats, and one which he experienced in both personal and historical speculations. But when, in the Self's final stanza in 'A Dialogue of Self and Soul', 'source' is rhymed with 'remorse', the connection for Yeats is a matter of something more than either chance or convenience, and refigures earlier connections of the idea of 'source' and those of judgement and dreaming-back in *A Vision*. Of the personality at Phase 26, for example, Yeats says that 'His own past actions also he must judge as isolated and each in relation to its source; and this source, experienced not as love but as knowledge, will be present in his mind as a terrible unflinching judgment'.[68] Describing 'The Return', Yeats again fixes on 'the source':[69]

> During this state which is commonly called the *Teaching* he is brought into the presence, as far as possible, of all sources of the action he must presently, till he has explored every consequence, dream through. This passion for the source is brought to him from his own *Celestial Body* which perpetually, being of the nature of *Fate*, dreams the events of his life backward through him.

When the Self announces that 'I am content to follow to its source / Every event in action or in thought', it is preparing to quarrel in the most fundamental way with 'a terrible unflinching judgement'; defying the Soul in Yeats's 'Dialogue', the Self will also face down the dead by judging itself, forgiving itself, and casting out remorse. In the stanza's strong and supple construction, the rhyme for 'source' is deployed only to be rejected, and the connection of sounds is made only to be superseded by other, liberating forms of rhyming and rhythmic connection.[70]

The stanzaic nature of so much of Yeats's poetry from *The Wild Swans at Coole* onwards offers the poet opportunities of self-dramatisation, but

[67] W. B. Yeats, *A Vision* (London: Macmillan, 1937), p. 25.
[68] W. B. Yeats, *A Vision* (1925), quoted from *A Critical Edition of Yeats's* A Vision (*1925*), eds. George Mills Harper and Walter Kelly Hood (London: Macmillan, 1978), p. 112.
[69] Ibid., p. 225.
[70] See Peter McDonald, 'Yeats, Form and Northern Irish Poetry', in Warwick Gould and Edna Longley (eds.), *Yeats Annual* 12: *That Accusing Eye: Yeats and his Irish Readers* (London: Macmillan, 1996), pp. 216–17.

also presents him with a medium in which the rhetorical momentum can change in relation to the returns, postponements, confirmations, and surprises of rhyme. If the couplet, for Yeats, sounds out the dynamics of fate and inevitability, then stanzaic structures are those of freedom and action. In one sense, stanzaic forms give opportunities for Yeats to put remorse in its place, and it is this which the Self uses to its own advantage in the 'Dialogue'. In 'The Choice', a single stanza of *ottava rima*, the more expansive range of the 'Dialogue' has been compressed:[71]

> The intellect of man is forced to choose
> Perfection of the life, or of the work,
> And if it take the second must refuse
> A heavenly mansion, raging in the dark,
> And when the story's finished, what's the news?
> In luck or out the toil has left its mark:
> That old perplexity an empty purse,
> Or the day's vanity, the night's remorse.

Despite the appearance of insistently binary divisions, it is not clear that the poem acknowledges the reality of any choice at all: the intellect is not free to choose, but 'forced' to do so, and the terms of its choice are slewed towards 'the work'. However bitterly, the poem represents 'toil' and its consequences rather than any putative 'perfection of the life', and it follows the traces of this in its chain of rhymes, from 'work' to 'dark', to 'mark', preparing for a concluding couplet in which the plain fact of 'an empty purse' rhymes with 'remorse', and provides its own untranscendent gloss on that term. Furthermore, despite its internal division and balance, the last line presents 'the day's vanity, the night's remorse' not as alternatives, but as aspects of the same thing. 'The choice' is a poem about a choice long made, and not the presentation of a decision still open. Even so, the poem is alert to, and alive with second thoughts, not least in its freeing of the word 'remorse' from the associations with the dead that rhymes like 'source' might conjure. As Helen Vendler has noticed, Yeats opens up the last couplet by making 'perplexity' and 'purse' 'reinscribe the contest between the lofty and the vulgar dictions of the first six lines', whereas 'vanity' and 'remorse' 'belong to a single register of diction' and 'clash in content, but do not clash in plane'. The couplet does not rhyme like with like, and 'remorse' remains to that degree unstable, its work unfinished. On another level, 'The Choice' itself represents a second

---

[71] W. B. Yeats, *Variorum Poems*, p. 495.

thought, having been cut away from its original place as a stanza in 'Coole Park and Ballylee, 1931'. This adds its own weight to Vendler's summary of the last line, that 'the work one was so vain about in the daytime turns out to be, in the watches of the night, the cause of remorse'.[72]

The capacity of Yeats's poetry to return upon itself is the measure of its ability to speak to (and sometimes speak against) remorse. The process comes to its most extreme pitch in some of the late poetry, and in 'The Man and the Echo', where another dialogue takes place, the ambition to 'measure the lot' results in questions which articulate powerful self-doubt and regret:[73]

> All that I have said and done,
> Now that I am old and ill,
> Turns into a question till
> I lie awake night after night
> And never get the answers right.
> Did that play of mine send out
> Certain men the English shot?
> Did words of mine put too great strain
> On that woman's reeling brain?
> Could my spoken words have checked
> That whereby a house lay wrecked?

The full rhymes and the metronomic regularity of the verse here bring these lines very close to the measures of Yeatsian remorse, just as the poem itself is situated on the border between life and death. Like others of his dialogue poems, 'The Man and the Echo' makes itself listen to the voice of the dead, and here the voice of the Echo is dead indeed, repeating fragments of the living voice exactly. In so far as the poem attends to and joins in this repetition, it gravitates towards the state of remorse which is the domain of the dead; to the extent that it resists the recurrence and reiteration of painful memory, the poem finds an element of freedom and escape from what seem by now all but inescapable conditions. In a prose draft, Yeats pictured himself 'Worn down by my self torturing search', and wrote how 'Among this solitude I seek remorse', but struck out 'remorse' to replace it with 'escape'.[74] The

---

[72] Helen Vendler, 'Yeats and *Ottava Rima*', in Warwick Gould (ed.), *Yeats Annual* 11 (London: Macmillan, 1995), p. 32.
[73] W. B. Yeats, *Variorum Poems*, pp. 632–3.
[74] Transcription of holograph draft in Jon Stallworthy, *Vision and Revision in Yeats's Last Poems* (Oxford: Clarendon Press, 1969), p. 60.

words are true alternatives: one precludes the other, and Yeats's decision to choose 'escape' is what causes this poem's creative heart to beat. The particular freedom of 'The Man and the Echo' is its willingness to take stock of the worst possible things, the plainest and most humiliating facts, and still recognise that they are not the only facts, and that the living and individual will can yet, even here, pursue its thoughts towards active (and, finally, open) self-judgement. The remorselessness of the poem's self-interrogations is the guarantee of its escape from the deathwards pull of remorse. The extraordinary conclusion, in which 'I have lost the theme', takes the poem to places wholly unprepared for in its initial scenario of unsparingly ultimate questions:

> But hush, for I have lost the theme,
> Its joy or night seem but a dream;
> Up there some hawk or owl has struck
> Dropping out of sky or rock,
> A stricken rabbit is crying out
> And its cry distracts my thought.

'Seem but a dream' concentrates the grim closeness of the rhymes into a near-jingle, while 'struck' and 'rock', 'out' and 'thought' break free from close rhyme's air of inevitability. The repetition of 'cry' which happens internally in the last couplet is at the same time contrasted by the off-rhyming of 'out' with 'thought' (and also perhaps carries a faint recollection of the 'cry', 'cry' repetition in 'In Memory of Alfred Pollexfen', where the rhyme was—inescapably—with 'die').[75] 'A stricken rabbit is crying out' takes the poem's predominantly trochaic tetrameter (the metre of 'Under Ben Bulben') away from its rhythmic norm just as, at an earlier moment of assertion, the voice stretched the line's confines to accommodate:

> That were to shirk
> The spiritual intellect's great work
> And shirk it in vain. There is no release
> In a bodkin or disease . . .

Such moments effect releases of their own, and in order to hear them it is necessary also to hear the menacing enclosure and completeness from which they depart. Seamus Heaney has praised the poem's last rhyme, writing that 'The rhyme—and the poem in general—not only tell us of that which the spirit must endure; they also show *how* it must endure'.[76]

---

[75] W. B. Yeats, *Variorum Poems*, p. 360.

[76] Seamus Heaney, *The Redress of Poetry: Oxford Lectures* (London: Faber and Faber, 1995), p. 163.

The poem's final lines are lines enacting this exemplary escape, and not lines of remorse, where, as Jahan Ramazani has well characterised them, 'life disrupts the meditative progression toward death, calling the poet back with a cry of suffering'.[77]

There are, of course, many kinds of suffering, his own and others', to which Yeats might be called back; in his late work especially, he seems to have a high tolerance for the kinds of suffering that can be theorised as conflict and realised as war. The Self in 'A Dialogue of Self and Soul' speaks not just with a sword, but for the sword: ten years after that other dialogue in 'Owen Aherne and his Dancers', it echoes the Heart's 'who cares?' in its principled rejection of remorseful brooding, but adds to this a deliberate belligerence. A very early skeleton of the poem has the Soul as 'He' and the Self as 'Me', with the demand 'What use to you now / love and war[?]' being met with 'only the sword gives truth'.[78] Yeats's actual swashbuckling in 'A Dialogue of Self and Soul' is not, it hardly needs saying, quite so clearly defined as this, and it is an incautious reading of the poem which does not attend to the Soul's protracted silence at the same time as the Self's prolonged aria of victory which that deliberated silence permits. Nevertheless, the casting-out of remorse characterises a particularly heroic action for the later Yeats, one which he was not reluctant to apply to contemporary events. In 'The Municipal Gallery Revisited', the assassinated Kevin O'Higgins becomes one such heroic figure:[79]

> Kevin O'Higgins' countenance that wears
> A gentle questioning look that cannot hide
> A soul incapable of remorse or rest . . .

Whatever Yeats's attitudes towards the remorselessness of his friend's actions in the service of the Irish State, the poem takes O'Higgins as an example of the militant encounter of the living with the force of the dead. The otherworldly corollaries of remorse are still present in a draft of the stanza, in which Yeats begins by seeing 'Kevin O'Higgins eyes which on death and birth rest', then asks 'Kevin O'Higgins on what horizon stares?' The historical weight of O'Higgins's example is felt

---

[77] Jahan Ramazani, *Yeats and the Poetry of Death: Elegy, Self-Elegy, and the Sublime* (New Haven: Yale University Press, 1990), p. 199.

[78] Holograph fragment, National Library of Ireland (NLI 13,590 fol. 1$^r$), reproduced and transcribed in *The Winding Stair (1929): Manuscript Materials*, ed. David R. Clark (Ithaca: Cornell University Press, 1995), pp. 22–3.

[79] W. B. Yeats, *Variorum Poems*, p. 601.

fully when Yeats calls his friend 'That guilty and remorseless man' who
'that weary body bears'.[80] Yeats does not shirk the facts—but nor does
his finished version of the lines try to conceal them, insisting as it does
on what cannot be hidden. There is a certain remorselessness in the
poet's returning on the image of O'Higgins: 'guilty' is not summarily
erased from the lines, but is fully absorbed into 'incapable of remorse or
rest': the costs are real, and the poem knows that they have been borne
in full.

If Kevin O'Higgins's heroism consists for Yeats partly in his ability
to resist remorse, and so stare down the dead in his capacity for action,
'The Municipal Gallery Revisited' constitutes a more complex and
ambivalent 'action' in its own right. Here, after all, the figure of the
poet is brought almost literally to his knees by the power of memory:[81]

> Heart-smitten with emotion I sink down,
> My heart recovering with covered eyes;
> Wherever I had looked I had looked upon
> My permanent or impermanent images . . .

At first sight, this comes to within a hair's breadth of remorse, but the
voice keeps itself out of remorse's downward pull; in part, this is
something audible in the lines, which absorb repetition in order to
effect change: 'recovering' and 'covering', 'looked' and 'looked
upon', 'permanent' and 'impermanent' may sound like Yeatsian
close-textured incantation, but they are taking the measure of repetition
only to deny it its chance. In a poem concerned with understanding and
channelling the energies of the dead, the inertia of remorse is rejected in
both theory and action. What Yeats presents in the poem are not 'Vague
memories, nothing but memories', or those 'Memories upon memories'
that 'Have bowed my head upon my knees', but ordered, functioning
and available 'images' which, at the conclusion, he seems himself to
join, sure of the benevolence of his legacy. If there is a contrast to be
noticed between this and the more ambivalent legacy recorded in
'Easter 1916', where the verse concentrates into an almost threatening
sounding of the dead as a 'source', there is a difference too between
'The Municipal Gallery Revisited''s achieved and expansive poise and
the grim, marching rigour of other late poems, not least 'Under Ben

[80] Holograph draft in National Library of Ireland (NLI 13,593 (29)), as transcribed by
Wayne K. Chapman, ' "The Municipal Gallery Re-visited" and its Writing' in Warwick
Gould (ed.), *Yeats Annual* 10 (London: Macmillan, 1993), p. 166.
[81] W. B. Yeats, *Variorum Poems*, p. 602.

Bulben'. These things also are parts of the Yeatsian legacy, and in such contexts the overcoming of remorse (or the imperviousness to it) may seem too easily achieved.

To judge Yeats in such terms is to set his poetry in relation to a selection of plain facts, and to fix upon the poet 'that accusing eye' which, in certain moods, he was happy to invite. Irish criticism and Irish poetry have both registered profound difficulties with Yeats's work, and with the designs it seems to have upon a future which is, in part at any rate, our own time. There are readers of Yeats who regard his writings as a part of Ireland's cultural and political history for which, at this point in the century, critical remorse might be in order. In such arguments, there are always facts to be adduced, facts which Yeats may be said to have ignored, distorted, or wilfully denied. Such objections have ground in common with fundamental literary downgradings of Yeats's work as, in Yvor Winters's phrase 'a more or less fraudulent poetry'.[82] When Christopher Ricks, for example, notes Yeats's refusal to rethink a line from a poem of 1886, where 'peahens dance on a smooth lawn'[83] and then deplores his retort 'As to the poultry yards, with them I have no concern', he flings the plain facts about peahens in the poet's face: 'no amount of high and mighty scorn will undo the fact that a high price is paid by a poetry which invokes poultry and at the same time declares that it has no concern with the poultry yards'.[84] But the fact of peahens' behaviour and the fact of this 'high price' are not obviously facts of the same order, and Ricks's rhetorical sleight of hand itself misses (or bypasses) the facts both of what Yeats said and the context of his saying it. The quoted retort comes from Yeats at the age of twenty-three (itself a fact of some possible relevance, given the weight being attached to his remark), in a letter to John O'Leary written in the wake of a blood-thirsty review of *The Wanderings of Oisin and Other Poems* in the *Freeman's Journal*. As is fitting in a letter addressed to a much older man, and one whom the young poet regarded as a figure of authority,

[82] Yvor Winters, *The Poetry of W. B. Yeats* (1960), quoted in Elizabeth Butler Cullingford (ed.), *Yeats: Poems 1919–1935* (London: Macmillan, 1984), p. 124.

[83] W. B. Yeats, *Variorum Poems*, p. 77.

[84] Christopher Ricks, 'Literature and the Matter of Fact', in *Essays in Appreciation* (Oxford: Clarendon Press, 1996), p. 304. Ricks's source for his quotation from Yeats is A. Norman Jeffares's *Commentary on the Collected Poems of W. B. Yeats*, in its first edition (London: Macmillan, 1968): although this provides a reference to Yeats's *Letters* for the offending words, it does not supply direct information regarding the date of Yeats's remarks, or their context.

the tone is one of deference to authorities greater than that of the
periodical press:[85]

> The Freeman reviewer is wrong about peahens they dance throughout the
> whole of Indian poetry. If I had Kalidasa by me I could find many such
> dancings. As to the poultry yards, with them I have no concern—The wild
> peahen dances or all Indian poets lie. . . . That Freeman review will do no
> harm—It is the kind of criticism every new poetic style has received for the
> last hundred years. If my style is new it will get plenty more such for many a
> long day. Even Tennyson was charged with obscurity . . .

The facts of literature and the facts of a bad press are not to be
reconciled here: Yeats is defiant in settling for literature—for poetry
rather than poultry yards—and even dancing himself a little in his
rhetorical postures for O'Leary's benefit. Part of the letter's winning
quality resides in its boastfulness, and in the temerity of the young
Yeats mentioning himself and the (still living) Tennyson in the same
breath. It is less remarkable a century later for Ricks to align those two
poets, but when he goes on to register an instance of Tennyson's regard
for botanical accuracy as a fact which 'seems to me the more honourable position—and to have made for the greater poetry', the critical
consequences of this kind of respect for the facts begin to come into
view.[86] An older Yeats was even less ready to apologise for this order
of mistake, still less to attempt to go back on it, as when he noted that
'Henry More will have it that a hen scared by a hawk when the cock is
treading hatches out a hawk-headed chicken', and added the parenthe-
tical remark that 'I am no stickler for the fact'.[87] However, it would be a
poor reader who seized on this as evidence of the poet's culpable
disregard for the facts, since Yeats's irony (here, indeed, about the
poultry yard) is more subtle and more pervasive than a critical demand
for indiscriminate verisimilitude can comfortably acknowledge. In Ireland, the facts sometimes adduced against Yeats are different (and, it
may be, of a different order), while the canonical consequences are
altogether distinct, but the assumption that an 'honourable position'
(however that is to be ascertained or assessed) can 'make for the greater

[85] W. B. Yeats, letter to John O'Leary, 3 February 1889, *The Collected Letters of W. B.
Yeats: Vol. 1 1865–1895*, eds. John Kelly and Eric Domville (Oxford: Clarendon Press,
1986), p. 138. As the editors point out, Yeats was correct, in point of fact, on the subject of
peahens in Indian literature: 'There are . . . a number of descriptions of peahens dancing in
the poems of Kalidasa, the great Sanskrit poet of the fifth century.' If Indian poets do, indeed,
'lie' on this matter, Ricks's quarrel must be with them as well as with Yeats.
[86] Christopher Ricks, *Essays in Appreciation* (1996), p. 305.
[87] W. B. Yeats, *Mythologies* (1959), pp. 350–1.

poetry' is made in an unreflecting way by many who find Yeats less than satisfactory in relation to the truth as they see it. The kinds of remorse such readers demand are not forthcoming in Yeats's writings, and the remorse he does write of seems to them a hollow mockery of the real thing.

Demands like these tend to coarsen the reading of literature, and in particular of poetry. It needs to be observed also, in justice, that their insistence on the plain facts does not always coexist with a respect for facts that may be at variance with their arguments: one recent attack on T. S. Eliot, which concludes that 'like a true politician [he] never apologizes and he never explains' still prints a misattribution as a crucial part of its evidence, labelling this 'Wrong' in a footnote, without apologising, explaining, or taking stock of the damage done to the facts of the case.[88] In reading Yeats, the poetry's complex relations with facts, whether these are facts of the poet's private life or of the life of his times, are always critically relevant. Acknowledging this, and acknowledging the difficulty of understanding these relations with the necessary fullness, it is vital to add that the poetry itself is another fact in the matter, and that it too demands respect. To seek out and evaluate Yeats's uses for remorse is, in this sense, to take the measure of remorse *in* Yeats's poetry as well as *for* his poetry; this is to insist on form as something other than accidental or narrowly functional in literature and in literary meaning. In taking the measure of remorse, Yeats's poetry enacts what Geoffrey Hill calls 'that "return upon the self" which may be defined as the transformation of mere reflex into an "act of attention", a "disinterested concentration of purpose" upon one's own preconceived notions, prejudices, self-contradictions and errors.'[89] Such attention (an attention to form in its truest sense) is part of a fundamental respect for the facts, and finally it is bound up with that honesty about the facts of which Yeats was time and again capable. It was this capacity in Yeats to which T. S. Eliot responded when he wrote of the poet's 'exceptional

---

[88] Tom Paulin, 'T. S. Eliot and Anti-Semitism', in *Writing to the Moment: Selected Critical Essays 1980–1996* (London: Faber and Faber, 1996), p. 160. Paulin's laconic 'Wrong' (p. 151) refers to a misattribution of the authorship of an anonymous review in *The Criterion*; but cf. Paulin's 'Getting it Wrong', later in *Writing to the Moment*: 'The history of criticism is littered with tiny errors, huge *faux pas* and comic misquotations. What critic worth their salt has a clear conscience in this matter?' (p. 311). Paulin's conscience does not lead him to discuss the question of whether the Eliot misattribution is a tiny error or a huge *faux pas*: it may, perhaps, be more in the nature of a comic misquotation.

[89] Geoffrey Hill, *The Lords of Limit: Essays on Literature and Ideas* (London: André Deutsch, 1984), p. 155.

honesty and courage' and praised 'the honesty with oneself expressed in the poetry' in its 'revelation of what a man really is and remains'.[90]

Yeats's remorse should not be confused with his regret, or his sense of guilt with regard to things done or left undone in his private and public lives. Rather, Yeats's imagination settles on remorse, and is able to act upon it, as part of the attempt to 'hold in a single thought reality and justice'. The poet's returns upon himself, and the returns so insistently attempted by the dead upon the living, are themes which Yeats does not regard as separate, and together they constitute the underlying facts of, and conditions for his writing. The notion of 'the dead living in their memories' remains more than Yeats's eccentricity, however distinctively Yeatsian its expression; and in this sense, at least, the poet's Irish reception is especially alert to the specific dimensions of his continuing importance. Yeats's dealings with remorse are in tune with the kinds of honesty Eliot and others praised, for they do not allow emotion—whether it is regret, pain, humiliation, grief, or simple frustration—to overcome the proper freedom of poetic action. To take remorse as the measure of integrity is to understand the facts of art, and the facts of life, in altogether too plain a manner. For in serious terms, remorse is never enough: it has been said (against Eliot) that 'Remorse without atonement has its own equilibrium; introspection and the private acknowledgement of error do not always lead to amends being made'.[91] More simply, Geoffrey Hill has classed remorse among 'impure motives' for writing, when he postulates that 'a man may continue to write and to publish in a vain and self-defeating effort to appease his own sense of empirical guilt', and adds that 'It is ludicrous, of course'.[92] When such as Yeats casts out remorse, these facts continue to matter; and the poetry's reality goes on answering to, and answering for, its sense of justice.

[90] T. S. Eliot, 'Yeats' (1940), in *On Poetry and Poets* (London: Faber and Faber, 1957), p. 257.
[91] Anthony Julius, *T. S. Eliot, Anti-Semitism, and Literary Form* (Cambridge: CUP, 1995), p. 177.
[92] Geoffrey Hill, *The Lords of Limit* (1984), p. 7.

*Proceedings of the British Academy,* **94**, 207–228

ELIE KEDOURIE MEMORIAL LECTURE

# Harold Macmillan and the Middle East Crisis of 1958

WILLIAM ROGER LOUIS

*University of Texas*
*Fellow of the Academy*

ELIE KEDOURIE'S ANALYSIS of Britain and the Middle East was always based on meticulous and detailed research. But the distinction of his work lay in his critical and sustained examination of assumptions and calculations, and in his belief that British ministers and officials must be held accountable for their decisions. He was fully aware that the evidence could be read in different ways. Elie Kedourie's own assumption was that nothing was inevitable. My lecture this afternoon draws inspiration from his idea that the British in the aftermath of the Suez Crisis had choices, and that the consequences of initial decisions would be determined in part by further choices or decisions. In this process individuals and individual style played a major part. In the case of Harold Macmillan it is possible to view his ideas in 1956 as an alternative to those pursued by Anthony Eden, the Prime Minister, and to study the way in which Macmillan attempted in 1958 not to repeat Eden's mistakes. My comments are based in part on the Macmillan Diaries, which are not yet in the public domain though they along with Macmillan's other papers have been deposited in the Bodleian.[1] I should also at the outset mention that I had an ulterior motive

---

Read at the Academy 22 October 1996. © The British Academy 1997.

[1] I am indebted to Alistair Horne for allowing me to read the copies of the Macmillan Diaries in his possession. His biography, *Harold Macmillan, 1894–1956* (London, 1988) and *Harold Macmillan, 1957–1986* (London, 1989) remains the point of departure for a study of the Macmillan years. See also Richard Lamb, *The Macmillan Years 1957–1963: The*

for the choice of the topic which goes beyond Elie Kedourie and the Middle East. Along with other historians, I am engaged in the *Oxford History of the British Empire*. My own assignment is the dissolution of the Empire and I have been curious what I could learn about the larger subject by studying the crisis of 1958 in the Middle East. The crisis itself may be defined, from the British perspective, as Harold Macmillan's final confrontation with Nasser.

The current or prevailing historical judgement on Macmillan, especially among younger historians, is hostile. Sometimes this relates to his connections with the aristocracy and his Edwardian style, which gave the misleading impression of physical lassitude and intellectual laziness—misleading because Macmillan was exacting in all he did and demonstrated an intellectual mastery of the issues on which one would have perhaps to go back to A. J. Balfour to find the equivalent. Sometimes the hostility relates to his part in the Suez Crisis and the suspicion that Macmillan led a conspiracy to overthrow Eden. It is also connected with what is believed to be the lost opportunity to join the European Community in the late 1950s before de Gaulle had the chance to veto British entry. There is substance to the latter charge, though it could be levelled to a lesser extent as well against the leaders of the Labour Government at the end of the war: Attlee, Bevin, and Cripps. The sting in the indictment against Macmillan is not so much that he failed to guide Britain into Europe but that he turned to the United States in what is now thought to have been a rather hollow 'Special Relationship', and that he maintained Britain's pretence as a nuclear power, thus crippling the British economy. As to the charge that Macmillan was a conspirator, my judgement on the basis of reading various sets of private papers— those of Lord Salisbury and R. A. Butler as well as the Macmillan Diaries—is that this interpretation misses the essence of Macmillan as a political figure. Macmillan was a political adventurer who took extraordinary risks, but he also was usually politically adept. He has a lot to be held accountable for without the element of conspiracy, of which he was no more guilty than most of his colleagues.

---

Emerging Truth (London, 1995), which surveys archival sources not accessible to Horne at the time; and John Turner, *Macmillan* (London, 1994), which is especially useful on economic questions. Macmillan's own autobiographical account is *Riding the Storm, 1956–1959* (London, 1971). For recent assessments of Macmillan and issues of the Middle East, see Richard Aldous and Sabine Lee, *Harold Macmillan and Britain's World Role* (London, 1996); and Nigel John Ashton, *Eisenhower, Macmillan and the Problem of Nasser* (London, 1977).

The Middle East Crisis of 1958 was profoundly different from that of 1956. It had different origins and it was different in its nature, but it held the potential to become as severe. The Iraqi revolution of July 1958 was a watershed in the history of the Middle East and the region's relations with the West. It represented the overthrow of the old social and landed order and the virtual end of the British Empire in the Middle East, even though the British presence continued in Aden and the Gulf. In another sense the crisis marked the rise to the ascendancy of the United States as a Middle Eastern power in place of Britain. Two years earlier during the Suez Crisis, the British had attempted along with the French and with the help of the Israelis to restore European hegemony in the Middle East, only to be blocked by the United States. I shall briefly comment on the Suez Crisis in relation to the set of events in Lebanon, Jordan, and Iraq which triggered a similar confrontation with the leader of Egypt, Gamal Abdel Nasser, in 1958. The events of 1958 in a sense can be considered as a rerun of Suez, but with obvious and important differences.[2]

The two crises are intertwined and I would like to remind you of Macmillan's part in the Suez Crisis and how this is connected with the set of events in 1958. During the Suez Crisis Macmillan was Chancellor of the Exchequer. At the outset he took a more fire-eating stand than Eden himself. Macmillan took the lead in urging the overthrow of Nasser. He was the first to suggest to Eden that Israel should be brought into the alliance against Egypt. 'All history', Macmillan wrote, 'shows that Statesmen of any character will seize a chance like this and the Jews have character. They are bound to do something. Surely what matters is that what they should do is to help us and not hinder us.'[3] It is ironic that Eden's response to this suggestion was one of shock. Nor did it increase his confidence in Macmillan's judgement. Macmillan on his own initiative went ahead to discuss with Churchill, now in retirement, the possibility of an alliance with Israel. From Eden's point of view this was intolerable. He had his own plans to win Churchill's support during

---

[2] The best works generally on the 1958 crisis remain Malcolm Kerr, *The Arab Cold War 1958–1964* (London, 1965); and Patrick Seale, *The Struggle for Syria: A Study of Post-War Politics, 1945–1958* (London, 1965); see also especially Irene L. Gendzier, *Notes from the Minefield: United States Intervention in Lebanon and the Middle East, 1945–1958* (New York, 1997); Ritchie Ovendale, 'Great Britain and the Anglo-American Invasion of Jordan and Lebanon in 1958', *International History Review*, 16 (1994), 284–303; and Lawrence Tal, 'Britain and the Jordan Crisis of 1958', *Middle Eastern Studies*, 31 (January 1995), 39–57.
[3] Horne, *Macmillan, 1894–1956*, p. 401.

the Suez Crisis, and for Macmillan to meddle in the overall strategy by soliciting Churchill's views, which would have great symbolic significance, was a breach of confidence. Eden on one occasion wrote angrily that it was none of Macmillan's business. In any event it was an error of judgement on Macmillan's part. Macmillan now found the Prime Minister irascibly disposed towards him. '[T]his strangely sensitive man', Macmillan wrote, ' . . . thought that I was conspiring with C. against him.'[4] There was no love lost between Eden and Macmillan: each disliked and distrusted the other.

One wonders how Macmillan himself might have managed the Suez Crisis. He had bold ideas and was not inhibited by conventional concepts, as his Israeli plan indicates. He thought clearly and he delegated authority. He was daring to the point of recklessness, perhaps in retrospect a vital characteristic in such a venture as the Suez expedition. Macmillan's large ideas as well as his capacity to change direction are breath-taking. He was fascinated by the nature of the game down to the last throw of the dice.[5] He is the one person in 1956 whose boldness and flashes of insight might conceivably have enabled him to achieve a settlement satisfactory to Britain. Could Macmillan have co-ordinated the invasion with the Israelis as well as the French, moving quickly to achieve the objectives in Egypt before American and international pressures had time to build up? It is of course an unanswerable question, but it can be tested by his response to the crisis in 1958.

Macmillan was the single member of the Cabinet in 1956 who attempted to look beyond the crisis to see what might be the result of Nasser's fall. He preferred to regard it as a regional rather than as an Egyptian problem. Again there is significance for the crisis two years later. In a paper written for the Treasury in 1956, 'The Economic Consequences of Colonel Nasser', he concluded that without oil, Britain would be lost.[6] This was the short term problem. Over the long haul, he speculated in a letter written to the Prime Minister, a permanent arrangement would have to be made with the oil producing states of the Middle East. He proposed no less than a post-Nasser era in which a general conference, presumably with Egyptian participation, would agree to a broad plan for the economic development of the Middle East and would arrive at an equitable settlement of boundary disputes,

---

[4] Ibid., pp. 404–5.
[5] This is a prevailing theme in Keith Kyle, *Suez* (London, 1991).
[6] Horne, *Macmillan, 1894–1956*, p. 411.

including those of Israel. One way or another, the United States would be brought in to guarantee the arrangements and probably to pay for them. By contrast Eden seems to have devoted little if any thought at all to the prospect of a post-Nasser order.

Macmillan in 1956 believed emphatically that there was no alternative to defeating Nasser. 'If not, we would rot away.'[7] These were apocalyptic thoughts. From the beginning he had given the impression, far more than any other member of the Cabinet, of 'bellicosity . . . beyond all description' and of 'wanting to tear Nasser's scalp off with his own fingernails'.[8] Macmillan, however, misjudged the probable reaction of the American President, Dwight D. Eisenhower and the Secretary of State, John Foster Dulles. In a visit to Washington in September 1956 he had a long conversation with Eisenhower, during which the subject of Suez was not directly discussed. Macmillan, however, concluded that the Americans wished the British well, that the United States for a variety of reasons would not participate in an armed expedition against Egypt, and that secretly the Americans hoped that the British would succeed in their quest to topple Nasser. In the celebrated, indeed famous, reassurance that he gave to his colleagues in September, Macmillan proclaimed: 'I know Ike. He will lie doggo!'[9]

In the critical discussions leading up to the British and French invasion of Egypt in November 1956, members of the Cabinet discussed whether the invasion might 'do lasting damage' to Anglo-American relations. The minutes do not mention Macmillan's assessment that the Americans would acquiesce, but his earlier advice must have helped to reassure some ministers who believed that the Americans would tacitly support the strike against Egypt while for their own reasons they would refrain from being publicly associated with the move.

Macmillan now reversed himself. When Selwyn Lloyd, the Foreign Secretary, warned of an Arab oil embargo against Europe, Macmillan, as has been established from various accounts, threw his hands up in the air and said, 'Oil sanctions. That finishes it'. At the next stage, the day of the Anglo-French invasion, 6 November, Macmillan at this critical time reported that the reserves of sterling had been depleted by £100 million in the first week of November. This was a gross exaggeration

[7] Ibid., p. 410.
[8] Brendan Bracken to Lord Beaverbrook, 22 November 1956, Beaverbrook Papers (House of Lords Record Office).
[9] Kyle, *Suez*, p. 258.

(the real figure was £31.7 million), but in any event he conveyed his point that the run on the pound could spell disaster.[10] Macmillan now panicked. He believed that the time had come to quit. He had been influenced by the resignation of his Economic Secretary at the Treasury, Sir Edward Boyle, whose ethical as well as economic arguments had impressed him. Macmillan joined those who wished to halt the operation. 'First in, first out', was the phrase later used to describe his turnabout.

How can Macmillan's reversal be explained? First, it is clear that Macmillan was capable of colossal misjudgement based on perception rather than careful thought, as is evident from his mistaken impression of Eisenhower. Secondly, his ability to change his mind and reverse course reveals a highly strung and emotional temperament which swung from one extreme to the other, even as he managed to keep an unflappable exterior, to use the phrase which is historically associated with him. Macmillan was anything but unflappable. To keep his anxieties under control he would often collapse in bed and read novels and biography. During the Suez Crisis he read a novel by Jane Austin. During the crisis of 1958, for what it is worth, he read a biography of Palmerston.

Macmillan thus made two basic misjudgements during the Suez Crisis, one concerning Eisenhower, the other concerning sterling. As Chancellor of the Exchequer he certainly should have been prepared for the economic consequences of the invasion. He was not, and he greatly exaggerated the figures that he gave to his colleagues in the Cabinet. I do not, however, read this as sinister intent. I read it as a consequence of Macmillan's melodramatic temperament whereby he was apt to exaggerate his point and to choose inflated statistics or figures to prove his case. But there has been yet another charge beyond that of misjudgement and of failure as Chancellor of the Exchequer to prepare for the crisis. This is the accusation that together with R. A. Butler he conspired towards Eden's overthrow and managed to get himself ensconced as Prime Minister at Eden's and eventually at Butler's expense. This is a problem connected with the 1958 crisis because Eisenhower was centrally involved in it. In late 1956 after Eden's health had collapsed and he was recuperating in Jamaica, Eisenhower conducted discussions with certain people in the British Government and gave the impression that he would not favour the continuation of Eden as Prime Minister.

[10] Ibid., p. 464.

Eisenhower would now never again trust Eden. Macmillan took one of the initiatives in opening the talks. The others were Butler, who was the Lord Privy Seal (regarded by most as the apparent heir to Eden), and Lord Salisbury, the Lord President of the Council. They collectively carried on secret conversations with Eisenhower even before Eden departed for Jamaica.

There are all the elements of a conspiracy here, but as Elie Kedourie might have observed, the evidence is ambiguous and difficult, all the more because Macmillan destroyed his diary for the critical months of the Suez Crisis.[11] It is my sense that it was the sterling crisis, and not intrigue which motivated Macmillan in his effort to open discussions with the Americans, though the American Ambassador remarked that a move might be afoot within the Cabinet to remove Eden. Eisenhower made it clear that Winthrop Aldrich, the Ambassador, should never talk to Macmillan without Butler being present and vice versa. Eisenhower did not want the rumour to get about that he favoured one over the other. When Eden returned and decided to resign for reasons of continuing ill-health, the choice came down to Macmillan versus Butler. Macmillan emerged as the Prime Minister. Again, was there a conspiracy, with the American President at its centre? Did Eisenhower come dangerously close to intervening in British politics (one of his motives being that he did not want to deal any longer with Anthony Eden)? The evidence is more clear on the American than on the British side.[12] Eisenhower was careful to keep his distance but he needed to keep open channels of communication to resolve the Suez Crisis. Macmillan merely proved himself more politically agile in the struggle for succession, though he left the impression, which has tarnished his historical reputation, that he was devious as well as cunning, and not entirely to be trusted.

The circumstances of Macmillan's becoming Prime Minister had a direct bearing on the crisis of 1958 because Eisenhower, though he claimed impartiality, was clearly pleased. They had got on well during the war, when Macmillan had been Minister of State in the Mediterranean, and they would continue to get on well as they reshaped the special relationship between the United States and Britain. In 1957

[11] The case for the conspiracy is argued by W. Scott Lucas, *Divided We Stand: Britain, the US and the Suez Crisis* (London, 1991), ch. 27.
[12] See Cole C. Kingseed, *Eisenhower and the Suez Crisis of 1956* (Baton Rouge, Louisiana, 1995), pp. 140–1.

Macmillan made it clear that his priority was to restore good relations. In a series of meetings at Bermuda and elsewhere after he became Prime Minister, he was able to do this. Macmillan formed the judgement that Eisenhower prevailed in large decisions. He was a strong executive, in Macmillan's words, half king, half prime minister. He seemed to be a lonely figure without real confidants, though we know from American records that Eisenhower and Dulles shared common goals and discussed all matters easily and equally. It was true, as Macmillan surmised, that Eisenhower was a strong President who made his own decisions and that Dulles was always careful never to move beyond the bounds of Eisenhower's directives. Dulles was unpopular, legalistic, and argumentative, though he too had a side to him in private that was easy-going and congenial. If Eisenhower made the basic decisions, it was Dulles who implemented them and gave sustained attention to issues in a way that the President could not.

Dulles was both indefatigably persistent and determined not to let the situation in the Middle East deteriorate into what he called a power vacuum which might allow an expansion of Soviet influence. He was wary of American financial commitments but he believed that the United States now had to play a much larger part in the Middle East in the aftermath of Suez. For that reason Macmillan believed that the mantle of Anthony Eden had now fallen on Dulles. It was Dulles who had to take the initiative in trying to come to terms with Gamal Abdel Nasser and the forces of Arab nationalism. Dulles was not temperamentally equipped to find middle ground with nationalists such as Nasser who wished to remain neutral. 'Neutral' to Dulles conveyed a quality of *naïveté*, of ignorance of Communist methods, and of the danger of supping with the devil even with a long spoon. Nevertheless, from 1957 onwards one can detect in Dulles more flexibility and more patience with his allies, less rigidity and less doctrinaire views about Middle Eastern nationalists. In 1957–8 Dulles seems to have grown with the job. By the end of 1957 Macmillan recorded in his diary that Dulles now seemed to be aware that the 'Maginot Line' of NATO and other paper alliances would not in themselves provide a lasting answer to a changing and complicated world, not least in the Middle East. Eisenhower and Dulles, in Macmillan's view, by late 1957 'are now completely converted—too late—and wish devoutly that they had let us go on and finish off Nasser'.[13] We know from American documentary

---

[13] Macmillan Diary, 19 December 1957.

records that it is true that Eisenhower was perplexed at the way the British had abruptly ended the 1956 military operation, but we know too that he was obsessed with the idea that any future intervention in the Middle East in concert with the British would be regarded as the equivalent to the Anglo-French combination in 1956.

At the same time that Macmillan attempted to restore good relations with the United States, he also attempted to move closer to Germany and France. This was the period of the consolidation of the European Community of the Six, and the Free Trade Area of Britain and the Scandinavian and other countries known as 'the Seven'. Macmillan in 1957–8 was still committed to the Empire and Commonwealth though in these matters he proved to be capable of adjusting his views. He was a supreme pragmatist and especially in colonial affairs he was an agnostic. This is the key to his outlook as he presided over the dissolution of the British Empire. Ultimately he did not believe that the colonies were worth the cost or the trouble involved in retaining them in circumstances of colonial war—he was very conscious of the French problems in Algeria—and he hoped that the colonies could be converted into an informal relationship whereby Britain would continue both to benefit economically and to have defence links.

In 1958 he saw much more eye to eye on these matters with Adenauer than with de Gaulle. There are many entries in Macmillan's diaries about discussions with Adenauer on the problems of the Sixes and Sevens, on the problem of France and the United States, and on Adenauer as a man of stature who believed in a personal devil. No one could have lived under Hitler, Adenauer told him, without believing in the devil, especially since Adenauer's prison cell was immediately above a Nazi torture chamber. These sort of intimate conversations Macmillan did not have with de Gaulle. Nor did Macmillan have much hope that de Gaulle, when he returned to power in 1958, would be able to extricate France from Algeria. De Gaulle's success in Algeria and in the creation of an effective Franco-German axis in the European Community were the two major developments at this time which affected Britain adversely. It would be entirely unfair to blame Macmillan for things which others did not foresee. He was in fact representative of the view that Britain's future still lay with the Commonwealth and especially with the United States, but for his American proclivities he has in retrospect been severely criticised.

The year 1957 was the year that Britain exploded a hydrogen bomb at Christmas Island in the Pacific. The significance, Macmillan wrote in his diary, was that Britain was now truly a nuclear power along with the United States and the Soviet Union. De Gaulle of course drew the opposite conclusion: that Britain had only managed to become a nuclear power because of the Anglo-Saxon special relationship and therefore had cast her lot with the United States rather than with Europe, the same conclusion he had drawn from Suez. As a run-up to the crisis of 1958, it is important to bear in mind that nuclear testing and technology were at the forefront of everyone's mind. In October 1957 the Russians launched the space satellite Sputnik, which in Macmillan's mind caused the Americans to become unnerved and certainly less cocksure of themselves. It also meant that the Americans were now more disposed to co-operate with the British, even in the realm of nuclear weapons and of getting rid of the McMahon Act, which prohibited the sharing of nuclear information with other powers. 'It's a great comfort', Macmillan wrote in his diary in September 1957, 'to be working so closely and with such complete confidence with the Americans.'[14] On the British side, Macmillan detected a different reaction to the launch of Sputnik. The Queen made a speech saying that the Russians had launched a satellite 'with a little dawg in it'. The British public were far more exercised about the fate of the little dog than about the significance of the satellite and the Americans possibly losing their lead in technology, in space, and in the battle for the rest of the world.

In 1958 Macmillan continued to be concerned throughout the crisis in the Middle East with the question of the H-bomb, with a possible summit conference with the Russians, with the problems of the British economy, and above all with certain other regional problems which always appeared on what Macmillan called his 'worry list'. These included Cyprus, Malta, Yemen, and Syria in the Middle East itself, all of which were related to the general crisis, but beyond that Indonesia, where Sukarno was dealing with a Communist revolt in Sumatra, and Hong Kong where there was tension between the textile industries of the colony and Lancashire. These were all serious crises in themselves. Lord Salisbury, for example, resigned in early 1957 over the issue of Cyprus, and Alan Lennox Boyd, the Colonial Secretary, threatened to resign over the issue of Hong Kong. Yet the Middle East Crisis in 1958 did not become as all-consuming as the Suez Crisis had been two years earlier. Such was the magnitude of Suez that everything paled in comparison except in the last stage when the Hungarian revolution

---

[14] Macmillan Diary, 26 September, 1957.

began to seize headlines along with those of Suez. This then is a question: why did the crisis of 1958 not become a general crisis? The same elements of conflict were there and then some. Lebanon in the spring of 1958 at first appeared to be in danger of a Nasserite takeover; then in July came the Iraqi revolution, which proved to be not just another Middle Eastern coup but a major social and economic revolution. Was Nasser behind it? The decision had to be made whether or not to send in American and British troops to shore up Lebanon and Jordan lest they be swept up in the revolution and thus fall to Nasser. Yet there was no internal division in Britain as there had been in the case of Suez, nor was there a falling out of Britain and the United States. Above all the crisis in 1958 did not end in economic disaster. Macmillan of course played only a part in this but it is nevertheless remarkable that he, unlike Eden in similar circumstances, emerged unscathed. How did he manage to preside over what amounted to a series of crises without being consumed by confrontation with Nasser?

There were three chronological parts to the crisis of 1958 which I shall deal with in relation to the three geographical components: Lebanon in the spring of 1958 before the Iraqi revolution of July; Jordan in the aftermath of the Iraqi revolution; and the problem of Kuwait, which represents the dimension of oil.[15] I am not here dealing with the revolution itself, except to say that it was not anticipated by the British Government or by the British Ambassador in Iraq (though it was at lower levels in the Baghdad Embassy). Nor was there at any time any plan or any intention by the British to reoccupy Iraq. It was recognised at the time as a gigantic upheaval which had suddenly and permanently changed the landscape of the Middle East. What was not at all clear was whether Nasser in some way might have been responsible for the Iraqi revolution and intended to reshape Iraq as a sort of Egyptian satellite, and whether or not he was at the bottom of the trouble which had broken out in May in Lebanon.

What of Nasser? One might have thought that one of the lessons of Suez was that Nasser was neither a Hitler nor a Mussolini and that European analogies were misleading. But Macmillan continued to refer to Nasser as the Hitler of the Middle East and to Lebanon as Czechoslovakia. His political vocabulary was replete with phrases from the 1930s, not least 'appeasement' and 'dictators'. On that point he was

---

[15] On Kuwait and the crisis see Mustafa M. Alani, *Operation Vantage: British Military Intervention in Kuwait 1961* (Old Woking, 1990), ch. 2.

unrepentant. His underlying assumption was that Nasser, like Hitler, aimed at expansion and that he had to be confronted and made to desist, by force if necessary. Macmillan believed that Nasser was not merely a dictator of the 1930s vintage but that he was to some extent mentally unbalanced and thus, like Hitler, prone to unpredictable, irrational behaviour. Macmillan wrote in his diary before the Iraqi revolution in May 1958:

> A great crisis is blowing up in the Lebanon. Nasser is organising an internal campaign there against President Chamoun and his regime. This is partly Communist and partly Arab Nationalist.
>     Russian arms are being introduced from Syria and the object is to force Lebanon to join the Egyptian-Syrian combination. In other words, after Austria—the Sudeten Germans.[16]

Macmillan was writing before the Iraqi revolution. He concluded that 'Poland (in this case Iraq) will be the next to go'. He added that 'Fortunately the Americans have learned a lot since Suez'.

It is important to place Macmillan's ideas within the spectrum of British thought. One school held that Nasser did not fully control his own destiny because he had sold his political fortune if not his Arab soul to the Soviet Union. This was a view upheld by Sir William Hayter, who had recently been Ambassador in Moscow. In this estimate Nasser might be reckless, and perhaps even irrational, but any assessment of him had to take into account a certain amount of Russian control over his actions—even though he had suppressed Communism in Egypt and banned the Communist Party.

Another strain of British thought held that Nasser was not a Hitler or a stooge of the Russians but first and foremost an Arab nationalist who used the Soviet Union to achieve his own goals. This was a view upheld by Harold Beeley at the Foreign Office. He had long been a student of Egyptian nationalism and later became Ambassador in Cairo. In Beeley's view Nasser was essentially opportunistic and by no means in control of Arab nationalism, even though in the eyes of his followers he symbolised it. Beeley's Nasser was no demon but neither was he benevolently disposed towards Britain. He was hostile to British interests, especially those in oil. Nevertheless, it might be possible to avoid confrontation.

These interpretations were not necessarily contradictory, but it is useful to bear in mind that Beeley's, not Macmillan's, was closest to the

---

[16] Macmillan Diary, 13 May 1958.

historical reality. Nasser was essentially an Arab nationalist who used Russian and other external aid for what he believed to be Egypt's benefit. He was a charismatic orator whose rhetoric on Arab unity inspired his followers and caused Western observers to draw conclusions about his ambitions. His aims were not modest; but neither were they especially coherent. As later reports were to make clear, he was as baffled and frustrated by the course of events in 1958 as were the British and Americans.

The Lebanon Crisis took place against the background of the union between Egypt and Syria in January 1958. Though Iraq and Jordan had responded with a union establishing a federal link between their two states, it appeared as if Nasser or Nasserism, the ascendant Arab ideology, was on the march and that Lebanon would be the next victim. Arab nationalism sweeping the Middle East and aligned or backed by the Soviet Union was a real fear in Western circles in 1958. In early May there were strikes and violence in Beirut and other parts of Lebanon. The President of Lebanon, Camille Chamoun, was pro-Western, but the British and Americans did not believe that he was strong enough to hold his own against internal troubles and external aggression backed by Nasser.

In the wake of Suez the British could not take the initiative. It would now be up to the Americans, an ironic twist to the situation in 1956 when the Americans of course had protested against British and French intervention. The crisis, however, now differed in one very important respect. In 1956 the British and French had invaded Egypt in an act of war, if not in defiance of the UN Charter then at least setting it aside. This time the Americans, and the British, would be invited by the legally constituted Lebanese Government. Nevertheless the risks were substantial. Once in, how would the troops get out? The British Cabinet decided that unless troops went in the Lebanese Government would be overthrown and Lebanon would be taken over by Egypt. The British decided in favour of intervention, but only with a relatively small force in support of the Americans. Macmillan skilfully handled this stage of the crisis, conferring with John Foster Dulles every step of the way and keeping his colleagues fully informed. Lebanon was by no means his only preoccupation. In mid-May 1958 an impending railway strike engaged much of his attention and he also nervously watched the rise in the cost of potatoes and tomatoes as an index to politically unacceptable inflation. He observed mounting tension in France over the problem of Algeria. In colonial affairs both Cyprus and Malta needed careful supervision. Placing Lebanon in the context of his other over-seas preoccupations, he wrote in mid-May 1958:

> Lebanon still holds. Our forces are in readiness, in case the request for help comes. Malta is quieter—for the moment. Cyprus may boil over again at any moment . . .. France is in a turmoil—no one knows whether it will lead to the collapse or the revival of the 4th Republic. The only solid thing we have to rely on is the Anglo-American co-operation, which is closer and more complete than ever before.[17]

Troops were placed on alert. If the Lebanon crisis had come to a head, some 3,000 American and 2,000 British troops would have been deployed. British plans rested on the assumption that Nasser planned to annex Lebanon come what may, though he might play for time, letting the Lebanon crisis peter out and acting later when the Americans and British had lost interest or were preoccupied elsewhere. This was in fact what seemed to be happening, but then on 14 July 1958 news reached London and Washington that a revolution had broken out in Baghdad.

There is nothing like a revolution to concentrate the mind. After two months of deliberating about Lebanon, the British and American Governments now acted at once in response to the news that a group of young army officers in Baghdad led by Brigadier Abdul Karim Qasim had overthrown the monarchy and the Government of Nuri Pasha es Said. Though at first the situation was obscure, it soon became clear that members of the royal family had been executed and that Nuri had been killed while attempting to escape. President Chamoun in Lebanon immediately requested the landing of troops. The British, however, were now deflected to more urgent and more important matters: they needed to protect their clients' regimes in Jordan and Kuwait.

On the American side the ideas or apprehensions of Eisenhower and Dulles were apocalyptic. Dulles said that unless the United States supported Lebanon, 'we will suffer the decline and indeed the elimina-tion of our influence—from Indonesia to Morocco'. Eisenhower shared those thoughts: 'we must act, or get out of the Middle East entirely'. Macmillan believed that the final showdown with Nasser had now come. His response, however, was radically different from Eisen-hower's. Macmillan wanted to create an Anglo-American task force which would deal with the Middle East as a region. His initial ideas are remarkably similar to his response to the beginning of Suez—all or nothing. Only by a joint despatch of troops in Lebanon and Jordan could

---

[17] Macmillan Diary, 16 May 1958.

the Middle East be saved from revolution and resulting Communist takeovers. Eisenhower rejected Macmillan's grand scheme out of hand. It did not help matters when Eisenhower learned that Selwyn Lloyd, the Foreign Secretary, had allegedly remarked that the British wanted to involve the United States in a joint military operation to demonstrate that Britain 'had been right over Suez and America wrong'.[18] Macmillan said to Eisenhower over the telephone in characteristically emotional and tense language: 'I feel only this, my dear friend. . . . [I]t is likely that the trouble will destroy the oil fields and the pipelines and all the rest of it, and will blaze right through . . .. [W]e are in it together.'[19] He put forward the argument for dealing with the region as a whole in as sweeping and as encompassing a manner as possible. What he learned from Eisenhower, however, was that the United States would proceed step by step in consultation with Congress and as far as possible move forward in concert with the United Nations.

The Americans now moved into Lebanon; the British, into Jordan. There was a rationale to the separate moves. The US Government, in particular Dulles and Eisenhower, still did not want to be viewed publicly as acting with the British who had been aggressors at the time of Suez. The crisis created by the Iraqi revolution gave them the opportunity to intervene at the invitation at the Lebanese Government and without the British—or the French. Neither the Americans nor the British wanted to be associated with the French, above all because of the growing crisis in Algeria. Unilateral intervention by invitation from the two respective Governments of Lebanon and Jordan was a way of telling the French politely that they were not invited but that the British and Americans would keep them informed.

The British moved into Jordan initially with the strength of 2,000 men. A major problem arose immediately: no one had bothered to get Israeli permission for the overflight. The British and Israelis were not on the best of terms, and this was a major blunder. David Ben Gurion, who emerges from the crisis as one of the most consistent of the statesmen involved, had remarked earlier: 'The Lebanon was basically a democracy and would survive as such; Jordan was only the King and one bullet would finish him'—and the Jordan state.[20] Ben Gurion now

---

[18] Lamb, *The Macmillan Years*, p. 3. Lloyd denied that he had made the comment, though it would not have been out of character.

[19] Record of conversation, Top Secret, 14 July 1958, PREM 11/2387.

[20] As related in Sir Francis Rundall to Foreign Office, 19 July 1958, FO 371/134284. Reference to FO and PREM records refer to documents at the Public Record Office, London.

not unnaturally feared Russian intervention. Only after strenuous pressure from Washington did the Israelis grant permission for the British to overfly Israel on the mission to Jordan. For Macmillan it was an operation fraught with danger: 'no port, no heavy arms, and no real mobility'.[21] One of the greatest dangers was that the Soviet Union would regard Britain's reoccupation of Jordan as a step towards launching a counter-revolutionary attack against Iraq. It took great skill on the part of the American and British Governments to placate both the Israelis and the Russians, assuring them that the aim was not to reverse the revolution but to stabilise the regimes in Lebanon and Jordan.

Macmillan went through a stage of what can only be called extreme jitters. 'Sickening anxiety', he called it. 'God grant that we can avoid a disaster.'[22] It was at this time that he collapsed into bed and read the biography of Palmerston by Philip Guedalla. 'The style is irritating— almost unbearable', Macmillan wrote in his diary:

> But there are some good things in it. So much of the problems of 1850s resembled those of 1950s. The Russians, anyway, have not changed much— grasping, lying, taking everything they can, and only responding to physical pressure. Nor have the French changed much. De Gaulle is the Prince President. It is not so much the duplicity, as the vanity of the French which is so alarming.[23]

What worried Macmillan was the logistics of the British position in Jordan. 'Our force is too small for any real conflict—if, for instance, the Jordanian army deserts the King. Its only use is to strengthen the hand of the Government and provide an element of stability. The danger is that it might be overwhelmed.'[24] The British were entirely dependent on American transport planes for fuel and supplies. Macmillan was by no means the only one anxious about the outcome. John Foster Dulles had been sceptical from the outset about the British expedition in Jordan and feared that the United States would suffer the backlash of Arab sentiment. The Arabs would now view the Americans as well as the British of making another run on the Suez model and attempting to reassert Western hegemony.

Macmillan had to accept that the Americans would attempt to limit

---

[21] Macmillan to Eisenhower, 18 July 1958, *Foreign Relations of the United States, 1958– 1960: Lebanon and Jordan* (United States Government Printing Office, Washington, 1992), XI, p. 329.
[22] Macmillan Diary, 17 July and 1 August 1958.
[23] Macmillan Diary, 3 August 1958.
[24] Macmillan Diary, 1 August 1958.

the crisis to Lebanon, and, as far as possible, move forward in concert with the United Nations. He therefore tried to devise a course in harmony not merely with the United States but with the United Nations, where British motives were generally suspect. But this involved more than political manipulation in the General Assembly. Macmillan operated on different assumptions from Dag Hammarskjöld, the Secretary-General of the United Nations. What is surprising about Macmillan is perhaps not so much that he got it wrong about Nasser but that he got it disastrously wrong about Hammarskjöld. In 1958 the United Nations became a force in its own right in the Middle East and elsewhere, but Macmillan continued to regard UN politics as an extension of national politics and Hammarskjöld as an ineffectual yet irritating figure. Hammarskjöld emerges as a major participant in the 1958 crisis, much more prominently than most historians have previously allowed. Macmillan's response to him reveals much about Macmillan himself, and about the part that the United Nations would play not only in the Middle East but also eventually in Africa during the Congo Crisis in 1960 and subsequently.

The United Nations was little more than a decade old in 1958. It still commanded respect in a way that today is scarcely imaginable, in part because of the prestige of the Secretary-General, who in one sense took a minimalist attitude towards UN functions. If the United Nations were to survive, it had constantly to be on guard against taking on more than it could manage. Hammarskjöld strenuously resisted plans for converting the United Nations into a world police force or for taking on countries as permanent wards. In another sense Hammarskjöld saw the potential of the United Nations as an independent institution which might achieve peaceful solutions to international problems in a way that would complement or surpass the efforts of individual states, large or small, which were each locked in narrow visions of self-interest. Hammarskjöld worked relentlessly towards UN goals with creativity and resourcefulness. By careful calculation the United Nations might play a critical part in solving not merely the problem of Lebanon but even the more intractable problems of the Middle East. In Lebanon for example the United Nations might establish a permanent observation team. In Jordan it was a UN 'presence' which eventually facilitated the British withdrawal.

In all his affairs, Hammarskjöld held that absolute impartiality was essential. He embodied that attribute, although against the British his temper sometimes flared. Indeed, the British were perhaps the exception to his reputation for impartiality. He wrote to Selwyn Lloyd, the Foreign Secretary, about the Suez Crisis two years later but still in

incisive language which conveyed moral condemnation: 'The straight
line often looks crooked to those who have departed from it.'[25] He
could of course have been writing as well about Macmillan. Hammarskjöld had a suspicious frame of mind and a certain intellectual and
ethical condescension which won him enemies, especially among those
with equally strong personalities. An official on whom Macmillan
relied, Sir Pierson Dixon, the British Ambassador at the United Nations,
was only one of several to come into collision with Hammarskjöld. In
his attempt to remain unbiased towards all parties, Hammarskjöld
acquired among British officials a reputation, in Dixon's phrase, for
having a 'notorious penchant for the Egyptians'.[26] Regarding Hammarskjöld as hopelessly predisposed towards the Egyptians, Macmillan
did not until relatively late in the game recognise that the aims of the
United Nations and of Britain might be compatible, and that
Hammarskjöld had a creative part to play.

Contrary to the predominant view held in British and American
circles that Egypt or the United Arab Republic had inspired the insurrection in Lebanon, Hammarskjöld reckoned that Nasser had been wary of
Lebanese politicians using him to their own advantage. Hammarskjöld
held that Nasser had been drawn in reluctantly and feared great power
involvement. Contrary to Western assumptions, according to Hammarskjöld, Nasser suspected that the Syrians were using him to promote
their own aims. Hammarskjöld believed that the aims of the other
Western powers and those of Egypt were not as irreconcilable as the
British thought. If foreign influences were curtailed, and if the Lebanese
were left more or less alone in their own 'goldfish bowl', they would
devise their own solution.[27] On the exotic Lebanese goldfish bowl stirred
by foreign hands, Hammarskjöld and Macmillan could both agree.

Where they disagreed was the extent of possible Soviet influence
and intervention. Five days after the outbreak of the revolution in Iraq,
Nikita Khrushchev wrote to Eisenhower protesting against the 'armed
intervention' by the United States in Lebanon and by Britain in Jordan.
The Soviet records on Egypt in the 1950s are unfortunately still closed,
though scholars until recently have been able to get access to files on
many other subjects in Moscow. But we know from Egyptian records

---

[25] Hammarskjöld to Lloyd, Secret, 10 July 1958, PREM 11/2387.
[26] Dixon to Lloyd, Top Secret, 19 June 1958, PREM 11/2387.
[27] Many of these aspects of Hammarskjöld's thoughts are related in a conversation with
Cabot Lodge, 26 June 1958, *Foreign Relations, 1958–1960*, XI, pp. 175–80.

what Khrushchev said to Nasser: the Americans seemed to be acting irrationally and 'frankly, we are not ready for a confrontation. We are not ready for World War III'. Khrushchev said that if Egypt were attacked, Nasser would have to brave the storm. There was no other course because 'Dulles could blow the whole world to pieces'.[28] To prevent a conflagration in the Middle East, Khrushchev proposed a conference to be attended by the heads of government of the Soviet Union, the United States, Britain, France, and India. They would work out a solution to the Middle East Crisis. Khrushchev also suggested that Hammarskjöld participate. Khrushchev in many ways had more use for the Secretary-General than did Macmillan.

Macmillan devised a reasoned course of action in response to what he believed to be Khrushchev's purpose. Assuming that Khrushchev would act rationally—as always, as with Nasser, a large assumption in the British view—the British, correctly, did not think that the Soviet Union intended to go to war over Lebanon or Jordan, but that Khrushchev intended to make it clear that the Western powers must not embark on a counter-revolutionary invasion of Iraq. As the crisis approached its height in late July 1958, Macmillan gradually became convinced that there should be a United Nations solution.[29] This became his governing idea. He saw eye to eye with Hammarskjöld that Jordan, not Lebanon, was the heart of the problem. According to a record of a meeting with Dixon in New York, Hammarskjöld 'viewed our [British] presence in Jordan in a quite different light from the American presence in Lebanon'. The situation in Jordan was incomparably more serious. Dixon at the United Nations reported to Macmillan:

> [Hammarskjöld] . . . sees that a collapse in Jordan, bringing it within Nasser's sphere of influence would at once create an acute problem for the Israeli Government and would probably lead them to occupy the West Bank, with incalculable consequences for the peace of the area.[30]

[28] Brian Urquhart, *Hammarskjold* (New York, 1984 edn.), p. 278.

[29] See e.g. memorandum of conversation at British Embassy, 19 July 1958, *Foreign Relations, 1958–1960*, XI, pp. 340–3.

[30] Dixon to Foreign Office, Secret, 21 July 1958, PREM 11/2388. In a conversation between Macmillan, Dulles, and others, Dulles commented: 'The disintegration of Jordan would lead probably to the Israelis seizing the West Bank and this in turn would mean an Arab/Israel war with a very dangerous chain reaction in the international field. It was possible that Khrushchev could be made aware of the dangers of such an upheaval and might agree to co-operate to prevent it. This, of course, was presupposing that Khrushchev was motivated by reason. But there were grave dangers that both Khrushchev and Nasser were inclined to act spontaneously without any rational approach.' Record of meeting, 27 July 1958, PREM 11/2388.

Macmillan pondered various solutions. These were complicated, including Nasser's proposal for the division of Lebanon along the lines of Vietnam or Korea, though how Lebanon might in practice be divided seemed a rather scholastic point. Another proposal concerned the possible division of Jordan. Might the West Bank go to the United Arab Republic but with the pre-1948 state of Transjordan remaining independent? Would the Israelis allow the West Bank to taken over by Egypt? Would a truncated Jordan, in other words the Transjordan of the pre-1948 era before the incorporation of the West Bank, be economically viable? These were puzzling questions. According to the Levant Department of the Foreign Office:

> Transjordan would be politically more viable, and economically no more unviable, than the present Jordan—and cheaper to maintain. But what on earth would the West Bank do—except fall into Israeli hands?[31]

Other proposals included a neutralised Lebanon as a ward of the United Nations. Jordan might also be neutralised along the lines of Austria, and Kuwait might be guaranteed independence as a Switzerland of the Middle East.

The point of those frantic plans, some more realistic than others, was that the solutions would be found through the United Nations. Even so, Macmillan at first espoused only a half-hearted championing of the United Nations, with the transparent aim of acquiring support or at least the acquiescence of the international community that the British had so sorely lacked during the Suez Crisis. There was also the aim of using the United Nations as an instrument for protracting the negotiations, letting the participants blow off hot air and exhaust themselves. This was the tactic that John Foster Dulles had used in 1956 when he had attempted to let the crisis peter out through tedious negotiations. Macmillan wrote that it appeared unlikely that Nasser would take any 'desperate action' or that the new government in Iraq would precipitate a further crisis. The danger could be a coup in Jordan or a move against the Western interests in the Gulf.[32] Step by step Macmillan moved in the direction of fuller support of the United Nations to further British aims of stabilising Jordan and Lebanon and using the mechanism of the United Nations to allow British and American withdrawal. Macmillan had a lot to thank Hammarskjöld for in 1958.

The problem at the end of the crisis was to be sure that Khrushchev

---

[31] Minute by Robert Tesh (Levant Department), 7 August 1958, FO 371/133826.
[32] Macmillan to Dulles 27 July 1958, *Foreign Relations, 1958–1960*, XI, p. 405.

did not misunderstand the intent of Britain and the United States. They would not intervene in Iraq, but they would defend at virtually any cost their access to the oil in the Gulf. From beginning to end, the British aimed above all to preserve their position in the Gulf: they found to their great relief that the Americans agreed that this point had transcendent priority. After the outbreak of the revolution in Iraq, Selwyn Lloyd had flown to Washington. He reported jubilantly to Macmillan:

> One of the most reassuring features of my talks here has been the complete United States solidarity with us over the Gulf. They are assuming that we will take firm action to maintain our position in Kuwait. They themselves are disposed to act with similar resolution in relation to the Aramco oilfields in the area of Dhahran.They assume that we will also hold Bahrain and Qatar, come what may . . .. They agree that at all costs these oilfields must be kept in Western hands.[33]

Eisenhower himself wrote to Macmillan that, beyond Lebanon and Jordan, 'we must also, and this seems to me even more important, see that the Persian Gulf area stays within the Western orbit. The Kuwait-Dhahran-Abadan areas become extremely important . . .'.[34] Dulles entirely agreed: 'The thing we want to preserve is that Persian Gulf position . . .'.[35] With the oil of the Gulf remaining in Western hands, the loss of Iraq could be taken less tragically. Lloyd stated the problem at its most basic essential when he wrote of his agreement with Dulles: 'he was quite definite that the Gulf was the essential area, and that so long as we could hold it and its oil resources, the loss of Iraq was not intolerable.'[36] So it ended on a philosophical note. It could have been worse. British and American oil interests in the Gulf and Saudi Arabia were not challenged, Iraq continued for the time being to sell oil to the West, and the United Nations facilitated the departure of American and British troops from Lebanon and Jordan.

Apart from his case of the jitters, which was characteristic, Macmillan handled the Middle East Crisis of 1958 with panache and skill. He consciously avoided what he believed to be Eden's mistakes in 1956. He stayed in step with the Americans and he kept his officials as well as ministers informed at every stage. He weighed the evidence, he debated it, but he did not interfere in departmental affairs after

[33] Lloyd to Macmillan, Secret, 20 July 1958, FO 371/132776.
[34] Eisenhower to Macmillan, 18 July 1958, *Foreign Relations, 1958–1960*, XI, p. 330.
[35] Record of telephone conversation between Dulles and Eisenhower, 19 July 1958, ibid., p. 332.
[36] Lloyd to Foreign Office, Secret, 20 July 1958, PREM, 11/2388.

decisions had been taken. Again and again one is struck with the contrast with Eden. Yet one is struck also with the similarity. Both reasoned by analogy, both believed that Nasser represented the equivalent of a European dictator, that Iraq seemed to be a latter-day Czechoslovakia. Critics today have little sympathy with analogical reasoning and false comparisons, but it was entirely understandable that Eden and Macmillan would try to learn lessons from the great events of their age and would reason on the basis of their own experience. The difference between the two was that Macmillan had a much more agile and questioning mind. He questioned his own assumptions, he exaggerated his figures and facts, and he presented his case in public as often as not with Edwardian melodrama. In a sense the crisis of 1958 was a microcosm of the much larger and complex problem of the dissolution of the British Empire, in which Macmillan demonstrated the same characteristics.

*Proceedings of the British Academy*, **94**, 229–251

# Honour

### JULIAN PITT-RIVERS
*Directeur d'Etudes*
*Ecole Pratique des Hautes Etudes,*
*Vème Section Sciences Religieuses*

## Origins of Honour

THE WORD 'HONOUR' ORIGINATES from the Latin *honos*, the name of a god of war who endowed soldiers with the courage they needed in order to fight. Later, his name came to signify the gift of lands which had been earned by the victory or any other recompense given to those who had shown the quality of courage in battle which they owed to this bellicose divinity. From this basis the word extended the fan of its meanings in many directions: even as far as theology, or the 'honouring' of cheques or, in England, the Christian name for a girl.

The extension of its meanings has varied according to the uses made of the concept. It originated in a military society, but it found fresh applications as it elaborated its nature, soon becoming a mode of address and the title of a judge, for honour is a value which expresses a moral ideal, as well as a label for behaviour, and a social rank. As a moral value everyone would like to claim it and quite a lot of people are only too happy to criticise their neighbours for the lack of it. Hence it became grounds for discussion when individuals disputed the claims for its attribution or its loss. Thus a kind of social jursiprudence was developed around the subject, for example, in sixteenth-century Italy, where a notable work was published—*Il Libro del Cortegiano* (The

Read at the Academy 16 November 1995. © The British Academy 1997.

Book of the Courtier) by Baldassar Castiglione (Castiglione (1987) [1528]).

The criteria of honour vary not only according to the country and therefore the society and the culture, but according to the social status of the individuals concerned. To begin with, the honour of a man is not at all the same as that of a woman. It is true that there are certain fields of honour which apply equally to both sexes without any distinction: general moral obligations, financial or intellectual, honour in friendship, honour of one's word (*palabra de Inglés*, 'an Englishman's word', used to be said in Andalusia to mean 'word of honour'). A lie is a lie whether told by a man or by a woman, but the obligation to tell the truth is not the same under all the circumstances.

The 'honour of the family' is the same for both sexes, though the different sexes contribute to it in different ways. Honour depends also upon age. The honour of a young man is not the same as that of an old man, because the two are not expected to have the same physical force (honour, to be defended, requires, under certain circumstances, 'courage', which demands self-confidence in one's ability to fight, which can hardly be expected of the over-eighties.

## Collective Honour

Quite apart from these practical disabilities, however, there is a functional distinction according to sex. In Europe 'family honour' derives mainly from descent, that is to say from antecedents of both sexes, but in patrilineal societies, priority is given to the male line and descent from a female line is generallly invoked, rather as a supplement to descent through the father, than as having much value in itself, unless the descent through the mother happens to be considered socially superior (Pitt-Rivers 1954).[1]

Honour is, above all, a sentiment felt by the individual, it has been said, but it is often at the same time 'collective' in that it is shared by others, in the first instance by kinsmen as in family or lineage honour. In fact any social unit whose members recognise a common identity is likely to share a collective honour and a certain shared responsibility for it.

---

[1] These observations come from my own field notebook over the period of four years (1949–53) in Andalusia (with a concentration on the area of Ronda, especially Grazalema).

The honour of a family is one, but it is contributed to by members of both sexes whose individual honour is judged by criteria which are necessarily different—a conduct that is dishonourable for a woman is not so for a man, and vice versa. For a young man to show or imply that he is amenable to sexual relations with a specific girl does not dishonour him. For a girl the equivalent expression of such a desire does. For the same young man, to show that he is not prepared to fight to defend the girl from physical assault, dishonours him completely. To demonstrate the virtues proper to the other sex is not normally honourable. Hence the stigma attaching to homosexuality.

Courage is not expected, either from old men or from women. On the other hand, sexual purity is valued in women rather than in men and much more in the countries of the Mediterranean than in the north of Europe. This difference in the moral division of labour is clearly marked, and worthy of more attention than it has had.

To give an illustration, we may take Sicily as analysed by Maria Pia Di Bella (Di Bella 1992: 151–65; Pitt-Rivers 1992: 341 *et seq.*): masculine honour is referred to as the 'name' of the family: it is evaluated as the social status of the origins of the family, and to this is added the contemporary reputation of the menfolk. This is the masculine contribution to the family honour, while the feminine contribution (mainly more often negative than positive) is called the 'blood' and it depends upon the sexual purity of the women, such, at least, as it is known or imagined to be. Yet these same families, who have a different honour for each sex, have a common 'family honour', compounded of the two, for they all have the same 'name' and the same blood, and as Maria Pia Di Bella explains, it is the women of the family who exhort their men to fight to defend the family reputation, or to avenge it.

In Spain the identity of every person includes his place of birth, and this is entered in the municipal register. This is not just a bureaucratic means of identifying the population, but an internalised part of the personality of each member of the community, and, were he to move his place of residence, he would surely have, as his nickname, a reference to his place of birth. Thus, if he comes from another nearby *pueblo*, let us say, Ronda, he would be called *el Rondeño*—from further afield, by the name of his province, i.e. if he is from the province of Malaga *el Malagueño*, if from Cataluña, *el Catalán*. A man from Grazalema who goes elsewhere becomes *el de Grazalema* or *el Grazalemeño*, if he goes to another province *el Gaditano*, i.e. from the province of Cadiz. If he goes to the other end of Spain *el Andaluz* and this would be obvious to anyone by his andalusian accent. Of course, in Grazalema, I was *el Inglés*, though not to my face, since nicknames are never mentioned to their owners neither in their presence nor in that of a member of their family (which is just as well, since some are not very complimentary, and some frankly insulting). One dark night, on my way home to the farmhouse in la Ribera de Gaidovar where I lived, I was challenged to say who I was and I answered *el Inglés* whereupon I received a lecture to the effect that this was very incorrect of me because nicknames are not mentioned in the presence of their owners, and least of all by the person whose nickname it is.

Therefore, one shares a common identity with all those who are born in the same place, and it is inevitable that one should be conscious of sharing a collective honour. This common identity, however, is not all a joy, for the collective nicknames are also vehicles for injurious rhymes and sayings by those of the other *pueblos* of which I gave quite a few examples in my monograph on Grazalema (Pitt-Rivers 1954: 33). They are usually critical, if not insulting, and, if collective honour would lead only to listening to collective insults, it would risk causing a lot of trouble. But people are careful not to quote such a rhyme in the presence of one whom it might offend. A Spanish dictum defines the sources of honour: 'I owe my body to my king' (i.e. to fight for him), 'my soul to my God' (because He endowed me with it, and I hope it will return to Him), 'but my honour only to myself', a pretension which is firmly contradicted by the existence of a collective honour in which the rest of my family or whatever other collectivity such as my *pueblo* participates.

## Honour and Marriage

Moreover, while this dictum encouraged the theologians to claim that honour has its source in the religious conscience, it was a point of view which was popular with churchmen but not usually shared by the aristocracy. As we shall see, a more commonly expressed attitude among the nobility is found in the words of the hero of Tirso de Molina's play, *La Villana de Vallecas* (Tirso de Molina 1952: 792):

> My honour which I inherited from my father
> The best of patrimonies
> Which in Valencia was a mirror
> Of nobility and valour.

Yet neither in the dictum nor in the play is there any mention of the role
of his mother in the origins of his honour. If the transmission of
hereditary honour comes via the patriline, the legitimacy of identity
comes from the mother. Therefore the most dishonouring insult in
popular society is to question the morality of a person's mother.

Hence the ethical aspect of the family honour is, in popular cultures
in the Mediterranean and elsewhere, predominantly matrilineal and,
consequently, the worst insult that can be pronounced of anyone concerns not his own behaviour, but his mother's. To be *sin verguenza*
(shameless), i.e. without honour, is to have been born without it,
because one's mother had none. Honour in this sense has nothing to
do with patrilineal honour as social status, but as ethical honour it is
matrilineal. Honour in the sense of social status is patrilineal. Aristocratic titles are passed from father to eldest son, though in Spain, in
default of a son they pass through the daughter, and if she marries, her
husband assumes the title as well and thereafter it goes to the eldest
child. Consequently the noble Spanish families change their surname as
often as the title goes through a woman.[2] For this reason the honour of a
man in the Mediterranean area depends upon the virtue of his woman
and this means that, if you wish to bring total dishonour upon a man,
you attack not the mores of the man himself but his mother's, for the
lack of sexual purity casts doubt upon the value of his patrilinearity.
Since noble patrilineal birth, titled or not, is the seal of honour, then the
purity of one's mother is the guarantee of one's honour. Hence the
destruction of the honour of a man is centred upon the reputation of his
mother. If we examine the terminology of dishonour we find nothing
but the implication of illegitimacy, of the absence of an identity that can
give the person under examination the right to be somebody, regardless
of the lack of social distinction of his father. By a subtle but generous

[2] A law was passed by the Spanish Parliament at the beginning of the first Socialist
government in the early 1980s to the effect that since the equality of the sexes was
incorporated into the constitution, an elder child should inherit a title in preference to a
younger, regardless of their sex. A lot of noble sons with elder sisters saw their hopes of the
family title being dashed in favour of their elder sister (and, of course, her spouse or future
spouse), since when a daughter inherits a title in Spain her consort receives it also and in due
course their children, with the exception of *titulos de varonnie* which are limited to being
occupied uniquely by men. The king gave support to this law. This was understandable when
one considers that the majority of the nobility were *Tejeristas*, that is to say, sympathisers
with Lieutenant-Colonel Tejero of the *Guardia Civil* who, on 23 February 1981, occupied
the Parliament in an attempted *coup d'état* in order to reintroduce Fascism. The King, as
commander-in-chief of the Army, outwitted Tejero, by preventing the Army from supporting
him.

**Figure 1.** A modern illustration of Adam and Eve fabricated in Germany, purchased in Paris.

instinct the British monarchy lends its name to all those children who can lay no claim to any other but that of the family of the house of Windsor, the royal family.

Ethical standards expected of women are higher than those required of men, to whom much can be forgiven on account of their obligation to defend and to feed the family and their frailty in the face of feminine charm—after all, it was Eve who produced the apple or, if one prefers another interpretation, Adam, the cad, who had her pinch it, to give to him,[3] and has blamed her ever since—this at least is an attitude commonly encountered in the Christian Mediterranean. *Los hombres son todos sin verguenza* (all men are shameless) is sometimes heard from female lips in Andalusia.

This makes it possible to explain a variant of a Spanish insult utilised in Mexico which is not easily understood by Europeans, not even by Spaniards and it is as well that all should be warned: if, in a popular tavern, you hear an angry voice pronounce 'I am your father', do not wait to witness the family reunion, but get under the table quickly because the bullets are going to fly, for this is the crudest provocation that can be issued in Mexico. It is a variant of the Spanish 'son of a whore', but it is 'son of *la chingada*', that is to say 'son of the violated one'. Whereas the Spaniards attribute total dishonour to the lack of paternity through the scandalous conduct of the mother, the Mexican, sons of the Conquest, see it as the result of the violation of the mother by a descendant of a conqueror. The shameless one's mother has had no chance to prove her virtue: she was raped and to confirm this lack of a legitimate paternity, his aggressor is claiming to know, because he asserts 'it was I who raped your mother'. The only possible answer to such an insult is clearly patricide: hence my advice to the bystander to get under the table as briskly as possible.[4]

Honour everywhere in the world is not only a question of sentiments and reputations but of the structure of society. This is, thus, fundamental

---

[3] Quite a few pictures of the original couple show Adam with the apple in his hand which he has evidently received or which he is receiving from Eve. Cf. Rubens and Bruegel, *The Earthly Paradise*, Mauritshuis, The Hague; Lucas Cranach the Elder, *Adam and Eve*, and Albertinelli '*The Creation and Fall*', respectively of the Lee and Gambier-Parry collections, Courtauld Institute Galleries, London. Even modern naïve illustrations of this passage of the Book of Genesis stick to those of centuries ago.

[4] I have been asked, not without a hint of surprise, whether I have ever heard the challenge via the claim to paternity used, and I have to admit that I have heard it used but only in the absence of the would-be father on the part of the maligned one. It was a soliloquy to let off steam, so to speak. This made it unnecessary for us to get under the tables.

to the systems of marriage alliance as it is found among the peoples of the Mediterranean, and as indeed it must be, given the importance of the transmission of honour from the parents (Lévi-Strauss, *c.*1949: 52–65, 172–215; Peristiany 1976). Anthropologists seem to be agreed with Lévi-Strauss that endogamy reigns over this region, though it is not clear to me that they mean any more than that there are no *systèmes élémentaires* of kinship to be found there.

One must, however, distinguish at least between kinship endogamy and community endogamy, that is to say intermarriage between kin and intermarriage between neighbours (members of the same *pueblo*).

Kinship endogamy dominates the Islamic world and is very visible in the preference for marriages with the father's brother's daughter, the *bint el 'amm*. This preference is very evident in the high frequency of such appellations, as the late Emrys Peters, who studied no less than four different Islamic societies in the Mediterranean, pointed out. (Peters 1963: 1976). However, a careful calculation by John Peristiany, transmitted to me verbally at the time, showed that the number of possible father's brother's daughters available for demographic reasons, and neither too old nor too undesirable, was limited. So though this is a very prestigious marriage to make, nevertheless, it appears that it is understandably not a very popular one among the young today.

It is normal for the young bridegroom to address his father-in-law as *'amm* (father's brother), whether he is literally his father's brother or not. It is possible therefore that the statistics which failed to convince both Emrys Peters and John Peristiany were due to confusion caused by this usage of the courtesy title which was mistaken for a kin relationship. In fact throughout Islam the title of *'amm* is normally used by a younger man to address any older man to whom he wishes to show respect, and this is a common custom which has not diminished in modern times (Gélard, 1996).

None the less, it is to be noted that the preference for marriage within the patriline is a general tendency throughout Islamic society. There is also sometimes a certain Jewish preference for kinship endogamy. But such endogamy contrasts with Christians, who are forbidden to marry their close kin, making no distinction between patrilineal and matrilineal kin, but measuring kinship in degrees regardless of the lineage. The Greek Church requires the authorisation of the bishop in order to marry closer kin than of the seventh degree. Catholics require the bishop's authorisation for marriage with a first cousin and it can even on occasions be given to authorise marriage with a niece. The doctor of Grazalema while I lived there was married to his niece. The different churches of the Middle East all have slightly different rules, so one can only speak in general of tendencies to endogamy and prohibited degrees. The Maronites often choose to marry their father's brother's daughter and this they call 'an Islamic marriage'.

Community endogamy is inspired by rather different motivations. There is no preference in favour of marrying a cousin, quite the contrary. Consequently, it is precisely the marriage which is preferential in Islamic society that is potentially prohibited among Christians. As to the prohibition to marry outside the community, it was not stipulated by any rule other than the recommendation of popular wisdom which was traditionally expressed, for example, in Brittany and equally in the Basque country as *se marier dans la coiffe*, that is to say, to marry a girl who wore the same traditional head-dress of lace as one's mother. This was reinforced in Spain by the fact that sanctions were applied against boys who came from another *pueblo* to court a local girl. Moreover, a popular rhyme warned young men against seeking a bride in another *pueblo*: 'He who goes to seek a bride from outside is going to be deceived—or to deceive'.

In a *pueblo* in Andalusia or Castille such an outsider would be chased away with a shower of stones and, if the intruder persisted in his courting, in spite of this ill-treatment, he would be captured and ducked in the fountain of the *pueblo* until almost drowned. After that he was freed to continue his suit without hindrance, for having been baptised in the 'holy' water of the fountain of the *pueblo* he became an honorary member of the community (provided the girl's family made no objection). The ducking in the water of the *pueblo* was a ritual of some symbolic significance, for every *pueblo* believes that its own water is the purest in the world. I have never been in a *pueblo* where this was not the case and none was ever so brackish or salty that it was not asserted to be so by the locals. And the same is true in Castile, as Susan Tax Freeman's lengthy bibliography on Castile shows (Freeman 1970).

It is evident that the sentiment of the collective honour of the *pueblo* or the lineage is the basis of the traditional rules of endogamy in the Mediterranean, whether it is endogamy of kinship or of community. But it seems to have diminished in the last thirty years in Andalusia and perhaps further afield as well.

If the basis of the 'elementary systems of kinship' is the exchange of women, complex systems rest upon the refusal to exchange them. In order that a people should wish to exchange their womenfolk they must conceive of them all as humanly equal or at least equivalent. But when a society is hierarchised this ceases to be the case: one hopes to conserve the same breed and the conception of marriage changes; women become in the expression of Lévi-Strauss *les opérateurs du pouvoir* (persons through whom power is manipulated). Consequently, one no longer wants to give one's women away, save in order to establish a favourable alliance. To give one's daughters away badly puts the collective honour in jeopardy. The monarchs of Europe seldom gave away a daughter without a calculated political motive.

There are, then, two possible matrimonial strategies: the defensive and the aggressive. The 'defensive' consists of keeping one's daughters 'on the home-ground', as it were, marrying them to a cousin or to an ally or a subordinate of their father. The 'aggressive' consists of giving a daughter away to a powerful neighbour or of marrying a son to the daughter of such a person and establishing thus an alliance with a previously unallied family. King Solomon is the perfect illustration of both strategies: he married his daughters to his generals or to their cousins, but he himself married women who brought him an extension to his political power or wealth, of whom the most impressive were the daughter of the Pharaoh of Egypt and the Queen of Sheba herself, from both of whom he gained considerable material or strategic advantages.

## The Duel

It is often the case that one can best discover the essence of a concept by examining its negative form. Hence in order to understand the essence of honour one might do well to examine how dishonour is earned. There are obvious ways of incurring it: by demonstrating cowardice on the battle-field or by being accused of lying (for courage and truthfulness were the absolute requirements of nobility in the Middle Ages). Such dishonourable behaviour is likely to cause criticism and accusations to that effect. The man who wishes to defend his honour is likely to reply by denying them and to end up by issuing a challenge to a duel.

In medieval Europe the institution of the 'judicial combat' allowed members of the nobility to settle a difference with regard to a question of honour by fighting a duel which had to be authorised by the King. This ordeal was based on the supposition that God would judge and would ensure that victory should go to the righteous. The challenge to such a duel was called the *mentis* (i.e. the accusation of being a liar). Such a formula was conserved in the challenge to a duel long after the judicial combat had been abolished in French law by Louis IX ('Saint Louis'). Philippe Le Bel, grandson of Saint Louis, reinstated the judicial combat and, though it was subsequently abolished once more three centuries later when the Council of Trent (1545–63) forbade it, and though all forms of duelling were fobidden and punished savagely by Louis XIV (you could be condemned to the galleys even for being no more than a witness to a duel), the duel continued to be practised illegally (Thimm 1896; Billacois 1986).

Therefore it was in accordance with the rules conserved by custom for the simple reason only that gentlemen who considered that their honour had been blemished insisted on defending it at the risk of their life or of some most severe punishment. Indeed, it was not unknown for seconds also to be expected to fight, with the number of seconds limited to the same for each combatant, so that all participated, the duel ultimately resembling a battle between two armies.

The last judicial combat authorised by the King of France took place in 1547 and is commemorated by the name of the victor, Jarnac, who won against all the odds and a far superior opponent by a cunning, but perfectly legitimate, if unexpected ploy (Tricaud 1982). To win by a *coup de Jarnac* is today an expression still in common usage in France and it means to win by cunning rather than by superiority or strength.

Following the duel of Jarnac, King Henri II abolished the judicial combat as a legal measure requiring the royal assent and made the duel a crime. Far from putting an end to this custom it is precisely from this period, the mid-sixteenth century, that the number of duels increased in France, despite their illegality. During the seventeenth century which, it will be recalled, was a period of civil war between Protestants and Catholics in France, the number of duellists killed increased as did the treatises by lawyers and clerics condemning the practice.

Whether or not to allow duels to take place was discussed down the centuries and in general the state everywhere disliked to take the responsibility for allowing it, while at the same time showing itself unwilling to take action against those who violated the law by conforming to the custom whereby honour could be validated upon the field, that is to say, in a duel.

From then onward the duel flourished throughout Europe and, prior to the War of Secession, in the southern states of the United States where the aristocracy, the slave-owners, had a prickly sense of honour.

Unlike continental Europe, where feminine honour rarely extended to include such masculine practices, we have rich record of duels between women in Charleston (Thimm 1896).

In France, the duel continued to offer the solution to gentlemen whose honour had, they thought, been offended. Though not legal, it was not pursued by the law, on condition that nobody was killed, though even if somebody was killed it was sometimes recorded as 'killed by accident'. To fight a duel was accepted as a legitimate form of behaviour, particularly on the part of military men. In fact, in 1897 an officer of the French Army was revoked by the Minister of War for bringing a legal case against a man who had slandered him when, in the minister's opinion, he should have challenged his slanderer to a duel, i.e. he should have violated the law (Fabre-Luce 1974: 308). It was also during the last thirty years of the nineteenth century that Clemenceau fought a great number of duels, the first of which he won against a French officer who had, he thought, insulted him during a war trial following the Commune, but which caused him to be condemned to two weeks in prison. Others of his duels, all provoked by himself, included among his opponents the famous nationalist poet Paul Déroulède and the future president of the Republic, Paul Deschanel (Duroselle 1988: 423 *et seq.*).

In England the duel does not appear to have been pursued by the law very often. The system seems to have been somewhat similar in operation to that pursued in France. It was perhaps understandable that there should be no further action in the case of Lord Camelford, for he was notoriously quarrelsome; the *Dictionary of National Biography* records that he 'was killed in a duel wantonly provoked of one Mr Best, a noted pistol-shot' (Tolstoy 1978). The case fitted David Hume's complaint that one could risk in a duel one's life on account of some 'small indecency'. Perhaps Queen Victoria's disapproval of the duel, however, did more to make it unfashionable than either Hume's commentary or even Hogarth's *Marriage à la Mode*.[5] Loss of honour through cuckoldry had become less frequent than accusations of cheating at cards.

---

[5] London, National Gallery. A series of pictures representing the misfortunes of contemporary marriage in the mid-eighteenth century which shows the lover escaping out of the wife's window or killing the husband, or being killed by him.

## Honour in Literature

Honour has received ample attention in literature. In the seventeenth century, the Spanish 'theatre of honour' examined the problems presented by situations involving honour, such as: How to conceal your dishonour until you can avenge it? How to evade the situations when it is a royal prince who has seduced your wife (therefore you cannot do anything about it)? One of the plays of Lope de Vega,[6] *El mayor imposible*, suggests that it is a better solution to trust your wife's fidelity than to put her under lock and key with a broken leg—which is what a popular dictum recommended: *la mujer honrada con la pierna quebrada y la puerta cerrada* (the honourable wife with a broken leg and the door locked).

Shakespeare was not the only critic when Falstaff said that honour was nothing but wind, for already before him, the first picaresque novel in Spanish literature *La vida de Lazarillo de Tormés* (1554) explains that it is better to worry about getting enough to eat than about your honour. Lazarillo goes through a series of masters, starting with an indigent knight who sends him out to beg because he is penniless and then eats what Lazarillo has managed to collect for himself, and ending with a priest who sets him up in perfect felicity, married to the priest's mistress and eating to his full fill every day of the week.

From the end of the nineteenth century the theme of honour seems to be taken less and less seriously. Thus when in the 1930s the French playwright, Henri Bernstein[7] challenged the playwright and administrator of the *Comédie Française*, Edouard Bourdet, to a duel (because the latter had removed Bernstein's plays from the company's repertoire), quite apart from their *honneur blanchi*, both combatants were delighted with the publicity they were receiving from *Paris-Soir*. The first blood was drawn from the forearm of Bourdet by the author Bernstein, despite his seventy years of age and Bourdet's reputation as a duellist.

Another theatrical author to make fun of honour was Anouilh who, in *Ardèle ou la Marguerite*, presents a good bourgeois family gathered together for a reunion in their *château* where they are all lodged with

[6] Lope de Vega (1562–1635): Spanish poet and novelist; best-known playwright of the 'theatre of honour'; author of some 500 plays.
[7] Henri Bernstein (1876–1953): author of *Le Secret* (1913), a play which among others made him famous; known for his pride, he fought no less than twelve duels in his life.

the exception of the daughter's lover, who has to stay in the local hotel 'for the sake of appearances'. The jealous lover accuses her husband of seducing his own wife and ends by challenging the husband to a duel. The husband answers the challenge saying, 'If you really insist, we can find a quiet corner and try to puncture each other's forearms'.

In brief, honour as it was in former times, had become a subject of parody for the sophisticated, but that does not mean that it no longer existed at a more popular level. In 'street-corner society' its principles still function, as we can see in the following anecdote from London: a barrow-boy standing on the back of a bus gets his foot trampled on by a clumsy new passenger who has just got on. He says nothing, but as he gets off he catches the clumsy passenger a very sharp one on the shins. His honour is revealed to have been offended only by the gesture which avenges it. This is the conduct recommended by one of the plays of 'the theatre of honour' which shows how to conceal your dishonour until the moment when you can repair it. If the barrow-boy had had a coat of arms and a motto, this should surely have been '*Nemo me impune lacessit*'[8] which translated from Latin into modern very colloquial English might be given as 'Don't think you can pull a fast one on me and get away with it'.

The universality of honour is implied by this example, but others can equally be found and it is essential to recognise that the concept of honour can possess a multiplicity of meanings which can provide endless fuel for disputes and not only among anthropologists. Perhaps more interesting were those which separated the Church and the nobility of Spain in the seventeenth century.

Let us take, once more, as another illustration, a play of Tirso de Molina which was written in 1630, *Burlador de Sevilla y convidado de piedra* (The Mocker of Seville and His Stone Guest) on which more than a century later Mozart and Da Ponte composed the opera *Don Giovanni*. Unknown to the great majority of those who have seen either the play or the opera, it was in origin a major contribution to the polemic of the Church against the nobility—a fact which becomes more understandable when one considers that Tirso de Molina was, himself, a priest, like most of the other authors of the 'theatre of honour', and also that the phallocratic values of the nobility in those days tended to assume that their rank entitled them to the favours of any

---

[8] A popular motto of quite a few noble families of England and the device of the crown of Scotland.

pretty girl they fancied. Thus the deplorable verse of the Conde de
Villamediana, a Spanish poet of the seventeenth century (who this time
was not a priest):

> Tendran los que pobres son
> La ventura del cabrito
> O morir cuando chiquito
> O llegar a ser cabrón
>
> (Those who are poor
> Have the same fate as the kid
> Either to die young
> Or to grow up to be a cuckold)

## The Cuckoo and the Horns

If, as we saw, the sexual purity of women was so highly valued in the
Mediterranean countries, it was evidently in order to ensure the descent
of legitimately conceived children. This is amply illustrated by the
vocabulary of indecent insults: 'bastard' 'son of a whore', etc., and
all those that amount to the same. The deceived husband is the 'cuckold' in English, a word which derives from an ornithological image.
The 'cuckoo', the bird which lays its egg in another bird's nest, leaving
the other bird to raise the baby cuckoo. The image is most graphic. But
let's get at least our ornithology straight, if nothing else.

The cuckoo hen lays her egg somewhere else and plants it in the
mother thrush's nest when the right time comes (thrushes can't count up
to more than five) so the egg is slipped in later, and the mother thrush
does not recognise the fraud. The baby cuckoo grows faster than the
baby thrushes and as it grows, it pushes them all out of the nest and
remains the only heir to the thrush family: the most efficient confidence
trick in Nature. The analogy is obvious.

But where the anthropologists get interested, is that the cuckold is
not the cuckoo, but the unfortunate thrush who has been 'conned' into
raising a baby cuckoo, instead of a family of thrushes. It is not the
'guilty party' but his victim, who is the cuckold.

Now, the Mediterraneans do not use the ornithological image but
instead go on goats and their horns. To be a billy-goat is to be a
cuckold, and the horns are the symbol of dishonour. Hence the Spanish
term *cabrón* is a grave insult and this imagery is known in England or at
least was known in the seventeenth century. Shakespeare knew it and

probably quite a few modern British tourists do today too. But the horns are also the horns of the Devil, in the Christian interpretation, while in the pagan tradition they are the symbol of Pan, the deity of Nature. That the adulterer should be represented by the God of Nature is surely appropriate, but the same transfer is once more imposed. The horns are the symbol, not of the person whose taste for 'natural' activity has caused the marital infidelity, but of the lack of it, which appears to have been the cause of the wife's dissatisfaction with her husband. It is the *latter* who wears the horns, the symbol of the sexual enthusiasm which he lacks. This apparent contradiction can perhaps be given an explanation: one must not expect Culture to obey the rules of moral justice and the principles of Blackstone. It has other preoccupations concerned with the fate of the reproduction of society as a whole.

To find an appropriate analogy in anthropology we might refer to Evans-Pritchard's description of adultery among the Nuer of East Africa which creates a state of pollution, but 'it is not the adulterer but the injured husband who is likely to be sick'. A parallel also can be found in the first fruit ritual in South Africa: if the chief's right to the first fruit is violated, it is not the violator who is smitten by disease (Evans-Pritchard 1956: 189; Gluckman 1954: 12). In the same spirit the cuckold is responsible for satisfying his wife and if he has not done so, it is for Nature to set things right. She takes priority over Blackstone.

*Cabrón*, or billy-goat, is also used as a general invective for anybody of whom the speaker disapproves. Curiously enough, the only persons who do not use this word are the shepherds of their herd, they make the sign to repel the evil eye, the closed fist with index and little finger stretched out, like two horns. They themselves refer to the billy-goat of the herd as *el cabrito*, the 'kid', the diminutive form.

The word *cabrón* itself was not much used in the *vitos*,[9] the public mockings at night, when I witnessed them in Grazalema. In origin, in the nineteenth century, the *vito* was used to celebrate the remarriage of a widow. To remarry a widow is somehow to be not the first husband of the lady and therefore, as it were, a retrospective cuckold which perhaps explains the institution as well as its gentleness in that epoch. However, the ones which I witnessed were no longer provoked by the remarriage of a widow, for this practice had been dropped, but by an offence

---

[9] In English, the *vito* is the 'skimity ride' or 'riding', such as we can find in the novels of Thomas Hardy, *The Mayor of Casterbridge*, for example. For a comparative insight into the culture of cuckoldry in early modern France, see the classic study by Nathalie Zemon Davis.

against the mores of the *pueblo*; they were organised to mock, not a cuckold, but an unfaithful husband who had abandoned his wife and family to set up house with another woman. Yet all the symbols of cuckoldry were present; there we found the horns, the bells, the tins on a string, and above all, the rhymes composed in very local andalusian for the occasion of which I was able to record the texts from those who had written them. The victim besieged in his house had to listen, for his punishment, to these insulting rhymes, including injurious comments upon the woman with whom he was living.

In brief, the *vito* is a ritual impositon of dishonour which was even credited, on one occasion, with mortal results. Several years before I arrived in Grazalema, there was a famous *vito* whose victim showed unwillingness to defend his conduct or to excuse himself, but instead attacked his critics who decided in response to bring down the great 'bell of the snows', the bell used in the sierra by those who transported on muleback the ice-packs to Cadiz. The noise was so resounding that it could be heard as far away as Ronda and no one in the region could fail to ask in whose dishonour it was ringing. It rang for weeks and then something in the victim's heart burst and he died.

It is to be noted that *señoritos* did not attend the *vito* since they were not part of the plebeian community of the *pueblo*. Most of them in any case had sold out their lands and moved to live in Jerez or Seville. There remained only one landowner who lived permanently in the *pueblo* and he was called *el Señorito*, which was regarded as a nickname. Moreover he was the only *señorito* to have a nickname other than the function of a professional class such as 'the doctor' or 'the chemist', and he even had another one (not very often heard): *orejón* (fat ear).

## The Honour of the Honourables[10]

As I explained at the beginning of this essay, the notion of honour is associated with aristocracy, with 'noble birth', moral qualities

---

[10] The title 'Honourable' is a prefix to the name of a child of either sex of a baron (but not of a baronet), and this is normally appended in abbreviated form to the initials of any order the recipient may have received such as Knight of the Garter (KG), or Dame Grande Cross of the Order of the British Empire (GBE). It also features in a novel of the brilliant Nancy Mitford, who, in *The Pursuit of Love* (London 1945), gives a description of the children of a large and varied family of whom some were and some were not 'Honourables'. The 'Hons', aged betwen five and fifteen, decided to establish their rank and make it their privilege to hide in a certain cupboard (the 'Hons's cupboard), in which the 'non-Hons' were forbidden to hide when playing hide-and-seek.

supposedly being inherited together with the noble genes, special pre-
rogatives and social privileges being logically accorded to those thus
favoured, in the European countries.

Towards the end of my field-work in Spain I made the observation
that those whose claims to honour by their birth were the greatest,
appeared to have the least concern for their sexual honour and the
least apparent fear of dishonour which, as we have seen, is most
vulnerable through their women. Most aristocratic women were
allowed a far greater degree of freedom than the women of the
bourgeoisie. They could smoke, drink in public, drive a car, use
somewhat more liberal language, dress in a somewhat more international style, and they tended to know English—for the great 'sherry
families' of Jerez were largely interbred with Scottish or Irish
families and therefore Catholic in origin. It is understandable that
their sophistication should be greater, and with it the liberties they
should assume. In brief, they were more internationally-minded than
the middle classes, and this was not surprising, in view of the fact that
this was expected of them by their status, for which reason they had
been given in their youth British nannies and French governesses. But
the question was not to stop there, for thanks to the great anthropologist
and historian Julio Caro Baroja and the magnificent library founded by
his uncle, the eminent novelist Pio Baroja, I was able to have in my
hand a volume, published in 1729, which was of the greatest historical
value to me, entitled *El Chichisveo impugnado por* (impugned by) el
Rev. Padre Joseph Haro SJ. The *cicisbeo* was the institution of a friend
of the husband who, during his absences, keeps company with the wife
to ensure the protection of his honour.

The author, a Sevillian priest, was clearly against all forms of
modernity, especially the *cicisbeo* which included husbands allowing
their wives to receive homage, and even gifts expressing such homage,
from gentlemen other than themselves, and Father Haro feared the
worst: women would be climbing up on to chairs in no time, for in
this period in Spain, chairs were restricted to 'men only' and women sat
on cushions on the floor. Nor was he so wrong. As soon as his campaign
against the *cicisbeo* had made its mark, the women were up on to chairs
and his tirades appear to have served as predictions. Indeed, by the end
of the century the situation was the same in Palermo, where the morals
of the belles on account of the *cicisbeismo* were a scandal to the whole
continent and attracted the attention of German tourists, including
Goethe, and French *galants* (Pitrè [1904] 1977: 306–30). Later,

Stendhal, in his *Promenades dans Rome*, was able to observe that 'Love had not been slow to take advantage of the *cicisbeo*' (Stendhal 1955: 514), whether he was called the 'cavalier servant' or the *bracciere* (the man who gives his arm), or by any other name for the gentleman-in-waiting of a lady.

In 1829, when Stendhal was in Rome, the *cicisbeo* was still going strong, though he maintained that it had been eliminated from all except the backwoods after Italian mores had been enlightened by Napoléon. If, however, the regrettable adoption of this custom by Italian mores was to be attributed in origin to the Spaniards (who furiously denied this and maintained that it was introduced into Spain by the Italians, and like the pox, was bandied about between the nations of Europe), at least it could not end up, like the pox, by being blamed on the llamas of Peru. Stendhal dated its introduction into Italy as 1540, which might possibly suggest French or Spanish influence, but it seems most unlikely that it should have been Napoléon who had reformed the Italian mores of the upper class at that time. It could have been the Bourbon's influence, which had brought them the *cicisbeos*, if indeed the French mores had already adopted such a custom. We know at least that it was adopted in Seville by the date of Father Haro's publication, that is to say early eighteenth century.

In Italy, every well-off wife expected to be granted a *bracciere* to lend her a hand in public when her husband was otherwise engaged. He had to be of good family, to be a friend of the husband, and to have his approval, but his exact duties were not specified. What were they, these duties? It was not at all clear and I think it was not intended to be made so, if they had become what Stendhal thought. The official title of the *cicisbeo* was to defend the husband's honour while the latter was away, for whatever reason he thought he had a duty to be away. If Stendhal was right, it was obviously essential that the *cicisbeo* should be on good terms with the husband.

It is likely that he would be needed in a society where the motives for arranging marriages tend to be political or financial and where, as a result, the ages of the spouse tend to be somewhat unequal. When husbands marry at the age of fifty or more, they usually want to marry only a young woman and this young woman is likely to have interests which she does not always share with her husband, particularly if the marriage has been arranged for the financial interests of the family.

I cannot contain my curiosity to know whether the *cicisbeo* has ever been the fashion in England and if so, whether the institution was taken over by love, as Stendhal thought it had been in Italy.

It is possible that it could have been introduced under Charles I, but most unlikely. Certainly not under the Puritan reign of Cromwell, who distinguished between his own partisans (the 'Roundheads') as 'men of conscience', and the royalists (the 'Cavaliers') as 'men of honour', by which he meant 'honour as social status' (opposed to conscience). Thanks to Puritan mores, the theatres of London were closed for twenty years, but they were reopened as soon as the restoration brought back the King, and for ten years no jokes were made except about cuckolds—as the titles of the plays show: *The Golden Horn*, *A Horn for Cuckolds*, etc. and let us not forget *The Country Wife* by William Wycherley, whose hero had the bright idea of letting the rumour get around that he was impotent. He thus became extremely popular in the role of *cicisbeo* and, of course, it is only in the last act of the play that it is revealed that he was not at all what he was said to be. Yet we wonder where the author got his idea of the *cicisbeo* from, and if the *cicisbeo* was already introduced into England?

I don't think that such a well-organised arrangement to deal with the problems of married life, such as the *cicisbeo*, could ever have been generally adopted in England, but it was reported to me not so very long ago that a certain peer of the realm had reached a philosophical conclusion to the effect that, I quote, 'Best friend of husband is boyfriend'. I understood that to mean that he was well satisfied with the *cicisbeo* of this ménage.

A very remarkable novel, *Le Bal du Comte d'Orgel* (Radiguet 1924) was written by Raymond Radiguet and published after his premature death at the age of twenty in 1926. This was his second novel, confirming the success of the first one, *Le Diable au corps*. It was remarkable for many reasons, but most of all for the subtlety and sophistication of his perception of the aristocratic society of Paris in the 'roaring twenties'.

When the young and beautiful Countess d'Orgel reveals to her husband her love for their young friend who is their constant companion, one would expect, as the young man's rather less aristocratic mother suspected, that, in order to defend his honour, the count would try to put an end to their friendship with her son, but on the contrary, the latter is made to be the hero of the fancy-dress ball, planned by the count, and the countess must choose his costume.

Taken to this extreme, honour somehow becomes inverted. Sexual jealousy is an utterly unworthy reaction to be reserved for the middle classes. This seems to have been the count's attitude to the situation: [11] by showing jealousy he cannot but degrade himself. It is a point of view I have heard expressed occasionally in certain upper-class milieux, justified by the argument that one must defend the honour of one's wife, the mother of one's children. (In the case of Radiguet's novel this would not apply, since the countess does not have any children.)

## Honour, Power and *Mana*

Thomas Hobbes was certainly very much concerned with honour, yet, unlike many other philosophers and many theologians, he was not preoccupied with the fine sentiments which this word inspired nor the ideals which it represented, but with the mechanisms whereby it functions. Hobbes was concerned above all with power, and his interest in honour is inspired by his hope to explain that honour, quite apart from the self-satisfaction it may afford to one's ego, provides the road to power and how it can be used. He recognised that honour, rather like the *capital symbolique* of Pierre Bourdieu (Bourdieu 1979), represents a moral credit to be drawn upon by those who possess this kind of honour, whatever its source, which may be converted into power. As he put it, 'reputation of power is power' (Hobbes 1960: 56). Hobbes appears to have understood that it is culture which makes a society what it is, because it is the way in which people think that makes them behave as they do.

Therefore, in conclusion, we should reconsider the question which has rarely been asked, except perhaps by Marcel Mauss: can honour be brought into anthropology? Is 'honour' a cultural oddity of Western civilisation or is it a universal concept? Is it a concept necessary in order to discuss human society? Beyond the continuities of honour in the Mediterranean world as I have argued, we should recognise for example that Japanese culture must contain a sense of honour or it would not be possible to understand *hara-kiri* and the threat to commit it. *The Forty Samurais Without a Master*, so a Japanese friend told me, would be

---

[11] It has been suggested that the count was homosexual and, like his wife, was in love with the young man, although it is never made explicit in the text. Cf. Bernard Pingaud's preface in Radiguet (1983: 47–52). This interpretation is supported by the close relationship between Radiguet and Jean Cocteau, which could imply such a possibility, but does not necessarily indicate that this was the intention of the author.

incromprehensible without the Japanese sense of honour, this play being the equivalent in Japanese literature of *Hamlet* in English, though rather more costly in lives. Let us also recall that Marcel Mauss saw *mana*,[12] the magical power centred in the head of Polynesian chiefs and the source of their prestige and authority, as nothing other than the concept of honour in primitive society. Therefore my answer to Mauss's question whether honour can be brought into anthropology is yes, but on condition that it should be recognised as varying from one culture to another.

## References

Billacois, F. (1986), *Le Duel dans la société française des XVIe–XVIIe siècles: essai de psychosociologie historique* (Paris: Editions de l'Ecole des Hautes Etudes en Sciences Sociales).

Bonte, P. and Izard, M. (1992) (eds.), *Dictionnaire de l'ethnologie et de l'anthropologie* (2nd edn.) (Paris: Presses Universitaires de France).

Bourdieu, P. (1979), *La Distinction: critique sociale du jugement* (Le Sens commun; Paris: Edition de Minuit).

Castiglione, Conte B. (1987) [1528], *Le Livre du courtisan*, trans. with intro. by A. Pons (Paris: G Lebovici).

Davis, N. Z. (1965), *Society and Culture in Early Modern France* (Palo Alto: Stanford University Press; and (1987) Oxford: Polity Press).

Di Bella, M. P. (1992a), 'Name, Blood and Miracles: The Claims to Renown in Traditional Sicily' in Peristiany and Pitt-Rivers (1992), 151–65.

—— (1992b), 'Honneur' in Bonte and Izard (1992), 341–2.

Duroselle, J. B. (1988), *Clemenceau* (Paris: Fayard).

Evans-Pritchard, E. E. (1956), *Nuer Religion* (Oxford: Clarendon Press).

Fabre-Luce, A. (1974), *J'ai vécu plusieurs siècles* (Paris: Fayard).

Freeman, S. T. (1970), *Neighbors: The Social Contract in a Castilian Hamlet* (Chicago: University of Chicago Press).

—— (1979), *The Pasiegos Spaniards in No Man's Land* (Chicago: University of Chicago Press).

----

[12] In 1881, the missionary R. H. Codrington (who was also a linguist and an ethnologist) described the religious concept of *mana*, which he had identified as a form of spiritual power or symbolic efficacity suppposed to dwell in certain objects or persons in Polynesia and Melanesia. After ten years of correspondence with R. R. Marett, Professor of Anthropology at Oxford, and with Marcel Mauss, the leading anthropologist in Paris at that time, among others, it was accepted that *mana* was a powerful influence enjoyed by certain persons and things manipulated by spirits and ghosts. It was thought to be among other things the source of the power of chiefs located in their heads. Cf. Pitt-Rivers, *Mana: An Inaugural Lecture* (London School of Economics, 1974). See also Keesing (1992), an excellent entry on *mana* in Bonte and Izard.

Gélard, M. L. (1996), 'Honneur et Mariage en Kabylie et dans le Haut Atlas marocain', Diplome d'études avancées for the Ecole Pratique des Hautes Etudes en Sciences Sociales.

Gluckman, M. (1954), *Rituals of Rebellion in South-east Africa* (The Frazer Lecture 1952; Manchester: Manchester University Press).

Hardy, T. (1987), *The Mayor of Casterbridge*, intro. Dale Kramer (The World's Classics Oxford Paperbacks; Oxford and New York: OUP).

Haro, Padre Joseph, SJ (1729), *el Chichisveo impugnado*.

Hobbes, T. (1960) [1651], *Leviathan*, ed. Michael Oakeshott (Oxford: Basil Blackwell).

Keesing, R. (1992), 'Mana', in Bonte and Izard (1992), 440–3.

Lévi-Strauss, C. (1949), *Les structures élémentaires de la parenté* (Bibliothèque de philosophie contemporaine, Psychologie et sociologie; Paris: Presses Universitaires de France).

Mitford, N. (1945), *The Pursuit of Love* (London: Hamish Hamilton).

Peristiany, J. G. (1976) (ed.), *Mediterranean Family Structures* (Cambridge Studies in Social Anthropology; Cambridge and New York: CUP).

— and Pitt-Rivers, J. (1992) (eds.), *Honour and Grace in Anthropology* (Cambridge Studies in Social and Cultural Anthropology; Cambridge and New York: CUP).

Peters, E. (1963), 'Aspects of Rank and Status among Muslims in a Lebanese Village' in Pitt-Rivers (1963) (ed.), 159–202.

— (1976), 'Aspects of Affinity in a Lebanese Maronite Village' in Peristiany (1976) (ed.), 27–79.

Pitrè, G. (1977) [1904], *La Vita in Palermo cento e piu anni fa. Glorie e miserie della Palermo del'700*, Palermo, Il Vespro (ristampa anastatica), vol. I.

Pitt-Rivers, J. (1954), *The People of the Sierra* (London: Weidenfeld and Nicholson) and (1971) (2nd edn.) (Chicago: University of Chicago Press).

— (1963) (ed.), *Mediterranean Countrymen; Essays in the Social Anthropology of the Mediterranean* (Recherches méditerranéennes, Etudes, 1; Paris: Mouton).

Radiguet, R. (1983) [1924], *Le Bal du comte d'Orgel*, pref. Bernard Pingaud (Paris: Gallimard).

Stendhal (1955), *Promenades dans Rome* (Paris: Jean-Jacques Pauvert).

Thimm, C. A. (1896), *A complete bibliography of fencing and duelling, as practised by all European nations from the middle ages to the present day. With a classified index, in chronological order, according to languages (alphabetically arranged)* (New York: John Lane).

Tirso de Molina [pseud. Tellez, Fray Gabriel] (1952), *Obras dramaticas completas* (Madrid).

Tolstoy, N. (1978), *The Half-mad Lord: Thomas Pitt, 2nd Baron Camelford (1775–1804)* (London: Jonathan Cape).

Tricaud, F. (1982), 'Justice et Violence: analyse d'un combat judiciaire' in *La Violence: études thématiques* (Lyon: L'Hermès).

A. J. AYER

*The Sunday Times*

*Proceedings of the British Academy*, **94**, 255–282

# Alfred Jules Ayer
# 1910–1989

SIR ALFRED AYER, as A. J. or Freddie Ayer came to be known to some extent after 1970, was born on 29 October 1910. His father was Jules Ayer, a French-speaking Swiss from Neufchâtel, who had lived in England since coming here to join his mother at the age of seventeen. He worked for some years in Rothschild's Bank and as secretary to Alfred Rothschild, and died in 1928 at the time when A. J. Ayer was preparing to move from Eton to Oxford. He had married in 1909 Reine Citroën, who was of an Ashkenazi Jewish family from Holland. Her uncle André set up the car firm which bears the family name, and her father, David, was also in the car business and established the Minerva company. He rescued Jules from bankruptcy in 1912 and set him up in the timber business, where he seems to have prospered mildly. The grandfather appears to have been a larger presence in A. J. Ayer's early life than Jules.

Ayer was born in the family flat in St John's Wood and lived the solitary urban life of an only child of not very assimilated parents. In 1917 he was sent to a preparatory school at Eastbourne, which Ayer thought resembled the St Cyprians of George Orwell and Cyril Connolly, against which matches were played. He worked hard and was well taught, gaining the third classical scholarship to Eton in an examination he was sitting simply as a trial run for a later assault on Charterhouse. He recalls that he did not get on well with the other boys, attributing this in a clear-headed way to his 'unguarded tongue and propensity for showing off', characteristics which he continued to

© The British Academy 1997.

display, along with many more attractive ones, for the rest of his life. He also admits to boring his schoolfellows with his militant atheism, another lasting trait. All the same, he made some good friends and was well-regarded enough by his contemporaries to be elected to Pop, the Eton Society. He greatly disliked the Master in College, H. K. Marsden, but got on well with Dr Alington, the headmaster, Robert Birley and Richard Martineau. A very intense degree of specialisation in classics brought the reward of the top classical scholarship to Christ Church, Oxford, to which he went in 1929.

Despite the almost exclusively classical emphasis of his first twelve years of formal education, it left little direct imprint on him. At Oxford he did not take classical honour Mods. Instead of spending five terms on classics he took pass Mods. in one term, on a couple of books of Tacitus' *Annals* and Aristotle's *Nicomachean Ethics*. In the massive range of his publications between 1933 and his death in 1989 there is nothing whatever about ancient philosophy or an ancient philosopher, not even a book review. Plato and Aristotle do make a token appearance together in *Language, Truth and Logic* but then only in a parenthesis along with Kant, as part-time practitioners of 'philosophical analysis'. His mind seems to have been fully fixed and matured by his early twenties. His initial and, to a large extent, lasting preoccupation with the theory of knowledge never led him to reflect seriously on Plato's *Theaetetus* or *Protagoras*.

Ayer's involvement in philosophy seems to have come about suddenly and for no particular reason. It served no existing intellectual interest but appeared, rather, to fill a gap by providing some ideal material for his powerfully argumentative intelligence to work on. A master at Eton had run an informal class on the pre-Socratic philosophers. Before Ayer left school he had read Russell's *Sceptical Essays* (which contains very little philosophy proper) and had been led by a reverent mention of G. E. Moore in Clive Bell's *Art* to read *Principia Ethica*.

There was a certain narrowness to Ayer's mind which focused it sharply and contributed to its force. His lack of interest in ancient philosophy, which has just been mentioned, was part of a general indifference to the history of the subject. In practice he treated it as a contemporary phenomenon, or, at any rate, as a twentieth-century one. Hume and Mill he took seriously. The most ancient philosophers he wrote about at any length, C. S. Peirce and William James, died, respectively, in 1914 and 1910. There was no sense of temporal remoteness in his approach to any of them. For the most part the philosophers whose work commanded his attention were active when he was: Russell, Moore, Wittgenstein, Ramsey, Price, Carnap, C. I. Lewis, Quine, Goodman. Opponents, to the marginal extent in which he took explicit notice of them, were also contemporary: Broad, Ewing, Austin.

His interests were restricted in space as well as in time, being mainly confined to the English-speaking world and to the Vienna of the 1930s. His more or less perfect mastery of French did not induce him to study any French philosophers, apart from the special cases of Poincaré and Nicod, until an impulse of intellectual journalism prompted him at the end of the war to write articles on Sartre and Camus for Cyril Connolly's *Horizon*.

A further limitation, a little less conspicuous, was in the range of philosophical fields or topics on which he worked. Theory of knowledge was first and foremost, and, within it, the philosophy of perception in particular, but also our knowledge of the past and of other minds. Beside that he addressed himself at length to philosophical logic (the nature of necessity at first and later to reference, identity, truth, existence, negation, and the nature of individuals), the philosophy of mind (personal identity, the ownership of experiences), probability and induction, ethics (in a very generalised and schematic fashion), and the issue of the freedom of the will. He was not a practitioner of formal logic or, to any marked extent, of the philosophy of science, apart from essays on laws of nature and the direction of causation.

He had very little to say about the more concrete or human parts of philosophy: nothing on the philosophy of history, or of law, or of art, or of education. His only contribution to political philosophy until his very late book on Thomas Paine was a lecture on philosophy and politics which he delivered in 1965. Here he drew on memories of a course he had given in Oxford in the late 1930s, and set out a list of all the possible grounds of political obligation he could think of and found all but the utilitarian one wanting. He was a philosopher of religion only in the sense that a dynamiter is an architect.

These limitations are by no means peculiar to Ayer among philosophers of this century. There are, indeed, more extreme cases, although G. E. Moore is perhaps the only example of comparable eminence. Ayer is very different in this respect from his hero and model, the gloriously omnicompetent Bertrand Russell. Nevertheless, the fields he cultivated were the most philosophically fertile of his epoch, in part, no doubt, because of his work in them, and the philosophers to whom he gave his attention were those who pre-eminently deserved it.

The Oxford in which he began his study of philosophy at the start of 1930 was at a low ebb philosophically. Ryle wrote, 'During my time as an undergraduate and during my first few years as a teacher, the philosophical kettle in Oxford was barely lukewarm. I think it would have been stone cold but for Prichard'. The other two professors besides Prichard were idealists: H. H. Joachim, a gifted and stylish thinker who had given up direct contribution to the subject, and J. A. Smith, a capable Aristotelian scholar but only barely a philosopher. Prichard, together with the redoubtable H. W. B. Joseph, kept up the tradition of Cook Wilsonian realism, a form of intensely critical philosophising from which, for the most part, only negative conclusions emerged, such as that knowledge and moral obligation are both indefinable and irreducible to anything else. On the whole there was no constructive work going on in philosophy, only the carefully critical examination of philosophy which already existed.

Two philosophers of a much more animated kind were, however, present and beginning to make themselves felt: H. H. Price and Gilbert Ryle. Both of them had been enlivened by the influence of the altogether more vigorous philosophical world of Cambridge. Price, in bold defiance of Prichardian orthodoxy, spent a year there and returned a convert to the analytic pluralism of the early Russell and Moore and, in particular, to the theory that sense-data are the immediate objects of perception. Ryle acquired from close study of Russell and the *Tractatus* the conviction that the logic of our thoughts is obscured by the grammar of the language in which we express them. At the time he was teaching Ayer he published his celebrated account of philosophy as 'the detection of the sources in linguistic idioms of misconstructions and absurd theories.'

From his close and regular contacts with Ryle, Ayer acquired a great deal. In doctrinal terms he picked up a resolute commitment to the identification of the senseless, of unmeaning, idle talk. He was encouraged to indulge the bent he shared with Ryle for the bold and uncompromising dismissal of positions with which he disagreed. Even more important, perhaps, was Ryle's introduction to Wittgenstein's *Tractatus* and his suggestion that on finishing his degree, Ayer should go, not to Cambridge as he had planned, but to Vienna to study at first hand the activities of the Vienna Circle. From Price, more remotely and largely through the medium of the lectures which presented the contents of

Price's *Perception* (published in 1932), Ayer acquired his devout and persisting adherence to empiricism. Ayer's empiricism was a much more constricted one than Price's. Its emblem is the entry for 'experience' in *Language, Truth and Logic*, which reads 'see sense-experience'. The experience, which for Ayer is both the criterion of significance and the foundation of knowledge, does not extend to embrace moral or aesthetic, religious or mystical experience. Ayer would not have denied that there are states of mind which are properly so called; only that they have any cognitive import. He has so little to say about sensation's traditional partner—'reflection', introspection, self-consciousness—that a good case could be made for the view that he did not countenance it at all. In *Language, Truth and Logic* it is nowhere mentioned as such. Minds or selves are said to be 'reducible to sense-experiences' which hardly accommodates the thoughts, desires and emotions he casually attributes to them.

While still an undergraduate, Ayer read a paper to a society on the *Tractatus*, which he believed to have been the first public treatment of Wittgenstein in Oxford. This up-to-date enthusiasm nearly deprived him of his first in Lit.Hum. in 1932. The philosophy examiners marked him down with partisan disapproval. H. T. Wade-Gery, an ancient history examiner, seeing what was going on, marked him up. The narrow squeak did not worry his college, which had already appointed him to a special lectureship since they extended it for a third year and then, when that ended, to a research studentship on the strength of favourable opinions from Whitehead, Moore, and Price. Whitehead's was based on specimen chapters of *Language, Truth and Logic*, which was not yet published. Since he was not needed for teaching in 1932, he set off for Vienna with Renée Lees, whom he had just married.

He was generously welcomed by Schlick and the Vienna Circle, and sat in on their discussions. Back in Oxford in the summer of 1933 he gave a course of lectures on Wittgenstein and Carnap and settled down to the composition of *Language, Truth and Logic*, which was completed in 1935 and published by Gollancz in an attractive form the following year. In the years that remained before the war he did some teaching at Christ Church, regularly attended and contributed to the joint sessions of the Mind Association and Aristotelian Society each summer, took part in the foundation of *Analysis*, a platform for logical positivism in Britain, failed to secure permanent positions at his own college where he was edged out by Frank Pakenham (Lord Longford), and at Pembroke (where Collingwood's promotion to the chair of metaphysics had created a vacancy), met Carnap and Popper, and served as chairman of the microscopic Soho labour party. Early in 1940 he was called up in the Welsh Guards, so that *The Foundations of Empirical Knowledge*, on which he had been working since the completion of *Language, Truth and Logic*, could have its preface addressed from 'Brigade of Guards Depot, Caterham, Surrey' when it was published in April 1940.

The main contentions of *Language, Truth and Logic* are at once too well-known and too lucidly and forcefully set out in the book itself to need very elaborate exposition here. Metaphysics, conceived as a theory of a transcendental nature about what lies behind sense-experience is 'eliminated' by the application of the verification principle or, more precisely, by a very weak form of it which requires for the significance of a statement only that possible observations should be relevant to the determination of its truth or falsehood. Philosophy is an analytic undertaking, supplying definitions, not information about transcendent reality. Much of past philosophy is in fact analytic in character. The *a priori* propositions of logic and mathematics are necessarily true (or false) because of the linguistic conventions governing the terms which occur in them and are devoid of substantive content. Material objects are logical constructions out of sense-experience, as are selves or persons, but that does not imply that they are any less real than their elements. The elements themselves are neither mental nor physical. Propositions about the elements, that is to say reports of immediate experience, are not incorrigible since predication or classification of the given involves implicit comparison with what is not given. Probability is the degree of confidence it is rational to place in a belief, and rationality is defined in terms of procedures which have been found to be reliable. Truth, following Ramsey, is a logically superfluous signal of affirmation. Moral and religious utterances are both without literal significance, but for somewhat different reasons: religious ones because they are about the transcendent, moral ones because it is a fallacy to interpret them naturalistically and metaphysical to interpret them as referring to a transcendent realm of values. A brisk concluding chapter comes down on the side of empiricism against rationalism, of realism against idealism, and of pluralism against monism. In what is even by Ayer's standards an amazing feat of concision, the free will problem is solved in a few lines of a footnote.

The first thing to notice about the book is something that will ensure its place in the philosophical canon, at the expense of many more judicious and many more original books: its remarkable literary merit.

In its 60,000 words it covers a very broad range of philosophical problems, indeed pretty well the whole philosophical *table d'hôte* of its epoch, with considerable penetration, even if some carelessness, in superbly lucid prose, whose slightly glacial impersonality is mitigated by the book's bold and combative enthusiasm. In the sixty years since it was published, no philosophical book has combined its style, economy, and capacity to excite. It ranks for these qualities somewhere near Descartes' *Meditations* and Berkeley's *Principles*, and very close to Russell's *Problems of Philosophy*. What does differentiate these books from Ayer's is that they are original creations, where his is almost wholly derivative.

His 'elimination of metaphysics' is taken very largely from an essay by Carnap, with that phrase, in German, as its title. The identification of genuine philosophy with analysis was prefigured in the last chapter of Russell's *Our Knowledge of the External World* and was propounded in a strong, explicit form in various early writings of Carnap. The view that *a priori* propositions are analytic had, of course, been intimated by Hume and Leibniz, but had been unequivocally formulated in the *Tractatus* and, in a more straightforward fashion, by Schlick and Carnap in articles of 1930 and 1931. The idea that material things and persons are logical constructions out of elements which are neither material nor mental was adumbrated in Russell's *Our Knowledge of the External World* and *Analysis of Mind*, and elaborated in detail in Carnap's *Der Logische Aufbau der Welt*. Ayer's account of truth is a direct transcription from Ramsey. His provocative observation that since the statements that 'God exists' and 'God does not exist' are unverifiable both theism and atheism are meaningless is, a little surprisingly, credited to H. H. Price, who may well have thought it a *reductio ad absurdum* of Ayer's position. Ayer says of his emotive theory of ethics, 'I had in fact forgotten that a similar theory had been advanced as early as 1923 by C. K. Ogden and I. A. Richards'. That seems unlikely in view of the close verbal similarity between his 'we may define the meaning of the various ethical words in terms both of the different feelings they are ordinarily taken to express, and also the different responses they are calculated to provoke' and their '"(this) is good" serves only as an emotive sign expressing our attitude to *this* and perhaps evoking similar attitudes in other persons, or inciting them to action of one kind or another'. Of the book's main theses only its suggestive but sketchy remarks about probability, rationality and induction and the view that no empirical belief is incorrigibly certain are clearly his own inventions.

Neither of them survived intact for long. The incorrigibility of reports of immediate experience was admitted in *Foundations of Empirical Knowledge* in 1940, and reinforced in the preface to the second edition of *Language, Truth and Logic* in 1946, and in an essay of 1950: 'Basic Propositions' (in *Philosophical Essays*). When he came back to probability—in two short pieces of 1957 and 1961 and at greater length in *Probability and Evidence* in 1972—it was from a wholly new direction, starting from a critique of the logical relation and frequency theories neither of which was mentioned in the earlier treatment.

*Language, Truth and Logic* received a great deal of attention as soon as it was published, much of it fairly hostile. Intellectual, or strictly philosophical, criticism was most effectively brought to bear on Ayer's verificationism. His version of it, weakened, in the light of Viennese experience, to accommodate scientific laws, turned out to accommodate anything. Restated in a complicated, recursive form in the second edition, it was shown by Alonzo Church still to be deficient. A more general objection was that it seemed to condemn itself to insignificance, since it is neither empirically confirmable nor analytic. Ayer's reply that it is analytic, a conventional proposal to define 'meaning' in a particular way, allowed those hostile to its implications to propose another convention, compatible with their preferences, as he rather exhaustedly acknowledged. He did not come back to the subject until giving a brief and inconclusive survey of the controversy in 1973 in *Central Questions of Philosophy*. The theory that *a priori* and necessary truths are analytic was less damagingly criticised by defenders of synthetic necessary truth. In his second edition preface, Ayer effectively refuted the charge that his doctrine turned the necessary truths of logic and mathematics into empirical statements about the use of language. Before long, Quine's 'Two Dogmas of Empiricism' in 1951 argued powerfully and influentially that there was no clear distinction between analytic and synthetic truths. Ayer did not return to the topic, apart from a slightly dispirited section on it in *Central Questions of Philosophy*.

Other controversial positions taken up in *Language, Truth and Logic* were abandoned or qualified in the second edition of the book in 1946, in a substantial preface. His original view about our knowledge of ourselves and of the minds of others was asymmetrical, along the lines of Carnap's distinction between the 'autological' and the 'heterological' in his *Aufbau*. 'I am in pain' incorrigibly reports an introspection; 'you are in pain' is a more or less conjectural hypothesis about your actual and potential behaviour. It follows that 'I am in pain' said by me is compatible with 'you are not in pain' said by someone else at the same time about me, which is clearly absurd. The argument from analogy, which distinguishes an experience from the behaviour that manifests it, is tentatively reinstated. Drawing on Ryle's article 'Unverifiability-by-Me', Ayer argues that since it is only a contingent fact that an experience is part of the collection making up a particular person, it is not logically impossible that I should have had an experience which is in fact that of someone else. That was an idea he was to develop further.

His original conception of personal identity tied it conceptually to the identity of a person's body. A person is the totality of momentary complexes of experiences in each of which an organic sense-datum of a particular human body is an element. This seems gratuitous and implausible. Must I always have organic sensations when I am conscious, when, for example, I am preoccupied with a demanding intellectual problem? Although he continued to have a predilection for a bodily criterion of personal identity, he did not express it in its original form.

Another oddity that was bundled out of sight by the use of Ryle's suggestion was Ayer's initial adoption of C. I. Lewis's quaint theory concerning the meaning of statements about the past. The Lewis view, which Ayer took over, was that such statements are, despite appearances, really about the present and future experiences of our own which would, or could, empirically confirm them, such as future glimpses of documents. But, he came to think, it is only a contingent fact that I live when I do and not at some previous time. I could have witnessed the execution of Charles I and it is only a matter of fact that I did not.

Some of the shock effect of Ayer's version of the emotive theory of ethics was reduced by his amendment that moral judgements express attitudes, directed on to classes of actions, rather than immediate emotional reactions to individual actions. That made room for a measure of rational discussion in cases of conflicts of value. Is the approved or condemned action really of the favoured or unfavoured class? But, he held, disagreements about value, to the extent that they are rational, are always factual. Ultimate conflicts about values are not rationally resolvable.

A final watering down of the original audacity of *Language, Truth and Logic* concerned its reductivism, its conception of philosophical analysis as supplying logically equivalent translations of problematic statements into reports of immediate experience. He realised that this was a Utopian ideal. Material object statements are too 'vague' for the fit between them and any finite collection of sense-datum statements to be anything but loose. All the same, material objects statements have no content that cannot in principle be expressed in terms of sense-data.

Ayer's pre-war work in philosophy was completed in 1940 with *Foundations of Empirical Knowledge*, just as he was called up, and published six months later. It is mainly concerned with developing the fairly sketchy exposition of his phenomenalism in ten pages of *Language, Truth and Logic*. For the next five years he was to publish practically nothing, only an admirably lucid and unhackneyed essay on the concept of freedom in Cyril Connolly's *Horizon*. In the book's preface he very properly acknowledges his debt to H. H. Price's *Perception*. Rightly seeing that Price's book was the most judicious, thorough, and illuminating discussion of the problem of our knowledge of the external world then available, he dissented from it on an issue of method and one large point of substance. Ayer took philosophical propositions to be linguistic conventions or proposals, not statements of fact, and he rejected Price's idea that a material thing consists, over and above a 'family' of sense-data, actual and possible, of a 'physical occupant' as well, a ghostly residue of old-fashioned substratum, introduced to carry out the causal responsibilities of an unobserved material thing, all of whose component sense-data would be non-actual. Three of the book's five chapters are about the perception of material things, one concerns the 'egocentric predicament', and another is on the subject of a number of problems about causation, only loosely related to the book's main topic.

The first chapter meticulously sets out the case for thinking that all that we directly perceive is sense-data, based on the facts of illusion and hallucination. It ends with the startling conclusion that the sense-datum theory is simply an alternative language which it is helpful to employ for epistemological purposes. It is, no doubt, a conceivable alternative to the language of appearing. Macbeth could report his question-provoking situation in the words 'there appears to be a dagger in front of me', rather than the words 'I am experiencing a dagger-shaped sense-datum'. (He would be more likely to secure understanding if he did.) Ayer's view that we could call the objects of direct perception 'material things' if we made certain adjustments to our everyday assumptions would, if put into effect, have the ludicrous consequence that material things were private to particular observers, existed only momentarily (or, at most, discontinuously) and were of only one sensory kind (visual, tactual or whatever). Courteously criticised by Price (and, much later, less courteously by J. L. Austin), this idea soon vanished without trace.

This, however, was not essential to Ayer's main project, a phenomenalistic account of the 'construction' of material things out of sense-data, that is, of things that are public, continuous, and of several sensory dimensions out of things that are not.

The second chapter is devoted to giving a detailed account of the nature of sense-data. Since they are by definition that about which we are immediately certain in perception, they cannot appear to have characteristics which they do not have, or have characteristics which they do not appear to have. Their essential function is to be the infallibly known basis of all empirical knowledge. The assumption that empirical knowledge needs such a basis is never considered. In the final chapter on phenomenalism a loose, non-translational version of the theory is outlined. Material things are constructible out of collections of sense-data that resemble each other, occur in similar contexts, are systematically reproducible, and vary in accordance with the movements of the perceiver.

The discussion of the 'egocentric predicament' anticipates the treatment of propositions about other people's experience and of the past in the second edition of *Language, Truth and Logic*. The idea that the necessary privacy of experience is a matter of linguistic convention which has alternatives is set out more plausibly than the parallel contention about the publicity and continuity of material things. The somewhat miscellaneous chapter about causality effectively criticises G. F. Stout's 'animistic' and H. W. B. Joseph's 'rationalistic' accounts of causation. The law of universal causation is defended against arguments from miracles, free will, and quantum mechanics, rather by sleight of hand in the third case. But Ayer holds that the law is not necessarily true; it is, rather, a 'heuristic maxim'.

*The Foundations of Empirical Knowledge* has most of the merits of its predecessor. If it is, perhaps inevitably, less exciting, it is much less sweeping and much more argumentatively scrupulous. That is not to say it was not open to the serious criticism which it received in due course as the main target of Austin's *Sense and Sensibilia* (1962). Ayer's somewhat indignant reply—'Has Austin Refuted the Sense-Datum theory?' — is surprisingly effective in showing most of Austin's objections to be captious.

Ayer had a thoroughly enjoyable war, nearly all of it, not by his contrivance, well out of harm's way. He joined the Welsh Guards in March 1940 and was commissioned in September of that year. He was soon redeployed to intelligence work, which seems a sensible decision by the authorities, and found himself interrogating German prisoners in London, using the linguistic skill acquired for the purpose of learning from the Vienna Circle. He went to New York on behalf of SOE and made visits to Accra, Algiers, Italy, and the south of France. The chapter devoted to this part of his war service in *Part of My Life*, the first, and better, of his two autobiographical volumes, is aptly called 'More Cloak than Dagger'.

Early in the war, he and his first wife separated, although they remained quite close to one another. By then they had had two children. The separation enabled him to engage in what at one point he calls 'an active social life' and elsewhere, more bleakly, 'nineteen years of casual affairs'.

At the end of the war, after early demobilisation, he took up the fellowship to which he had been elected at Wadham. This was not to last for long. He was invited to apply for the Grote chair at University College London and did so, not because he was attracted to that college or its philosophy department, but because he liked the idea of living in London. London was not to disappoint him, which was just as well since his department was in a seriously debilitated state. It was accommodated in what he described in conversation as 'a couple of broom closets'. It had had no professor since 1944, when the eloquent John Macmurray had left, after sixteen years, to go to Edinburgh. There was a reader, a scholarly francophile, who used the return of peace as an opportunity for constant visits to the country he loved, and a Greek lady, with no discoverable academic qualifications, who had been Macmurray's secretary and had somehow mutated into an assistant lecturer. There were some half-dozen undergraduates and no graduate students.

Ayer responded energetically and successfully to the challenge. Within a few years his department had become one of the liveliest in the country. He brought Stuart Hampshire on to the staff and, later, Richard Wollheim. The department was soon strong enough to supply itself with excellently qualified lecturers of its own production: J. F. Thomson, John Watling, P. B. Downing, and the somewhat mysterious

A. H. Basson (later known, after a visit to the Sudan, as Anthony Pike Cavendish). The department developed an intense *esprit de corps* and this expressed itself at meetings addressed by visiting philosophers who were subjected, particularly if they came from Oxford, to fierce argumentative assault. His colleagues largely confined themselves to Ayer's topics, which, if not all that numerous, were central and important, and wrote in versions of his spare, expeditious, rather impersonal style. There was no servility about this however; he was exposed to his own sort of criticism. The atmosphere of the department in Ayer's thirteen years there is well caught in a novel by Veronica Hull (a pseudonym): *The Monkey Puzzle*. Ayer's fiddlings with his cigarettes and his watch-chain as he argued away on his feet are memorably recorded.

The social scene to which he had access in London was interesting and varied. The most eminent and admired constituent of it was Bertrand Russell, with whom Ayer began a long friendship at this time. That was counterbalanced by excommunication on the part of Wittgenstein, who had previously seemed quite favourably disposed. He was able to spend a good deal of time with scientists, which gratified him as a proclaimed defender of science. Ayer now began a protracted career of what may be called academic travel. He became an inveterate conference member and a frequent visiting professor in the United States, beginning with a stay at New York University in 1948. Always ready and vigorous in discussion, it is understandable that he should expend a good deal of time and energy doing something he did very well, however meagre its lasting value.

He began to make himself known to a wider public when his ideas, particularly on morality and religion, were attacked publicly. C. E. M. Joad in the *New Statesman* brought against him the traditional Socratic charge of corrupting the young, contending that the emotive theory of ethics led to Fascism. *Time* magazine joined in the hunt, interviewing him in a malevolent fashion when he was in New York. Narrowly considered, the charge is unwarranted. Philosophers have combined adherence to the emotive theory not only with Christian belief, but also with virtuous Christian practice, without evident inconsistency. Ayer himself had moral failings—most obviously vanity and sexual licence—but he was also generous, honest, and public-spirited, a practising utilitarian, as was only fitting in a professor at UCL. But emotivism, in his version, at any rate, rather than more decorous ones, does tend to suggest that morality is, in the end, a matter of arbitrary whim.

One public-spirited activity to which he gave a good deal of himself was the editing of two successful series of philosophical books. The more important of these was the Pelican series, mostly on individual philosophers, but some on general topics. Not all of them were good, but some were very good and very few were bad. The same judgement would be harder to support in the case of the International Library, published by Routledge, a resurrection of an earlier series, initiated by C. K. Ogden, under a similar title. From this time forward his enlarged reputation, with its marginally scandalous character, made him an effective public defender of various 'progressive' causes, notably that of removing the legal disabilities of homosexuals. His renown as a heterosexual amorist ruled out any suspicion of personal interest.

Ayer largely gave up philosophical activity—writing and publication, even reading and thought—during the war. He returned to the subject in 1945 most productively, perhaps invigorated by the pause. The first fruits of this were two substantial articles on the terminology of sense-data and on phenomenalism which sought to clear up some unfinished business left over from his earlier work on perception. Fresher and more interesting was his London inaugural lecture of 1947, 'Thinking and Meaning'. This is a bold piece of work and, for the most part, a new departure. It would seem that he had serious doubts about it afterwards, for he never arranged for, or perhaps even allowed, its republication. It does skate over some thin ice. It bears a very strong impress of the thinking at this time of his old tutor, Ryle; but that he was happy to admit, first of all by dedicating the lecture to him. It was to receive the privilege, unusual for an inaugural lecture, of article-length discussions soon after its publication by H. H. Price and J. D. Mabbott.

His procedure is to set up a theory of thinking with five constituents which are then subjected to a process of radical reduction or whittling down. There is, on this theory, the person who thinks; the instrument with which he thinks (his mind); the process of exercising this mind in thought, in various modes such as believing, wondering, doubting, and so on, this process being conceived as a series of mental acts; the medium in which the thought is carried on, that is to say words and images; and, finally, the object of thought, its meaning.

'In the first place', he writes, in a way which must have made his hearers sit up, 'I think that we can dispense with the mind'. What this comes down to is that the mind is no more than a class of mental events. His substantial point under this head is that thought needs no instrument, thinking is not done *with* anything, in the way that one sees with one's eyes. The fate that befalls the mind here could also have engulfed the person on Ayer's principles. It would decompose into the family of actual and possible sense-data making up a particular human body and the collection of mental events closely associated with that body.

After this throat-clearing the main event begins. Thinking in its various modes is not a process composed of introspectively identifiable mental acts. It is not an accompaniment of the use of symbols, but it is that use itself, in so far as it is intelligent or in so far as the symbols are used meaningfully. To do something intelligently, to think what one is doing, as we ordinarily put it, is not to do and to think as well, it is to do something with certain dispositions—for example, to correct, amend or adjust what one is doing, rather than plunging mechanically onwards. That was a position to be developed very fully in Ryle's *Concept of Mind*. That approach, as Ryle saw, works well with knowledge, belief, doubt, and their like, but, as he also saw, applies less adequately to what he called 'pondering', working things out in one's head. Since Ayer had no objection to privacy, that was not a problem for him.

What did concern him was to discern what the meaningfulness of our use of symbols amounts to. His main negative point here is that meaningfulness is not explained by the idea of abstract 'objects of thought': concepts or universals in the case of terms, propositions in the case of sentences. These expressions are dummies, unexplanatory synonyms for what they are alleged to explain. To say what a symbol means is 'to give it an interpretation in terms of other symbols', but that will not quite do. In the end the symbols, if descriptive, have to be related to 'actual situations'. Objects of thought, in the sense of a subsistent realm of Platonic meanings, have been avoided, but contact with the actual, non-symbolic world has been preserved.

Ayer was clearly not satisfied, for very long at least, by the doctrine of 'Thinking and Meaning'. He came back to the topic in 1958 in an essay on meaning and intentionality, which came to no very definite conclusion. The dissatisfaction may explain why the inaugural was never reprinted in any anthology or any of his essay collections.

The main fruit of Ayer's thirteen years at UCL were the essays in *Philosophical Essays* (1954), most of those in *The Concept of a Person* (1963), and *The Problem of Knowledge* (1956). Five of the twelve items in *Philosophical Essays* cover familiar epistemological ground in a familiar way, dotting *i*s and crossing *t*s. He defends his view that sense-data must appear what they are and be what they appear, and the connected theory that basic propositions, those which report sense-data, are incorrigible. Various difficulties in phenomenalism are confronted, far from successfully as regards the exclusion of reference to material things in the antecedents of the phenomenalist's hypotheticals ('if I were in the next room . . . '). The partial reinstatement of the argument from analogy as an account of our knowledge of other minds is worked out more fully. In another essay the same underlying idea— that past events and the experiences of others are not logically unobservable since it is only a contingent fact that they are past or somebody else's—is used to give a reasonable interpretation of statements about the past.

There is a conciliatory essay on the analysis of moral judgements, in which their ultimately non-cognitive nature is still firmly maintained and there is a characteristically lucid and clear-headed exposition of the principle of utility and its implications. It is not of merely expository interest. Ayer's own ultimate moral commitment was to the principle of greatest happiness and, to a rather admirable extent, his conduct conformed to it. He was largely devoid of those impulses of envy, spite, or malice which impel human beings to make others miserable. A final essay in this ethical group takes up the question of freedom of the will. In the spirit of Hume he says that an act is free not if it is uncaused, but if it has the wrong sort of cause. He then lists a few types of cause generally held to be exculpating and leaves it at that, without trying to find any common feature in these causes which might explain why they are taken to exculpate (such as that agents acting under their pressure would not alter their conduct if faced by the threat of blame or punishment).

The most original part of this early post-war work is Ayer's first incursion into philosophical logic, in essays on individuals, the identity of indiscernibles, negation, and Quine's ontology. A leading theme in most of these is that all the descriptive or semantic work of language is carried out by predicates. Following Quine's generalised version of Russell's theory of descriptions, Ayer holds that everything we want to say could be said in a purely predicative language, although it would be intolerably inconvenient. Lumping all predicates together it does not occur to him that spatio-temporal predicates, unlike others, make essential reference to individuals. The essay on negation is neat and original.

Why, apart from accidental linguistic form, is 'blue' positive and 'not-blue' negative? Could we not have called the latter 'eulb' and the former 'not-eulb'? Objections are briskly disposed of and a suggestion in terms of a formally defined characteristic called 'specificity' is proposed. 'Eulb' is not unlike Goodman's 'grue': invulnerable to formal attempts to prove its improper or secondary nature.

*The Concept of a Person and Other Essays* (1963) contains the best version of Ayer's doctrine about the sufficiency of predicates: an essay on names and descriptions. Another, on truth, defends the correspondence theory, shorn of the representational or pictorial embellishment with which Russell, partly, and Wittgenstein, wholly, adorned it, against coherence and pragmatist accounts, and against the accusation of triviality. The possibility of a private language is combatively defended against Wittgenstein's prohibition and, in his British Academy lecture of 1959, Ayer surveys the topic of privacy in general, usefully distinguishing four varieties. The long title essay criticises Sir Peter Strawson's view that the concept of a person is primitive and argues persuasively that an incoherence Strawson claims to detect in the theory that experiences are to be identified by the body to which they are causally related can be overcome. Two 'notes on probability' anticipate more far-reaching discussions in *Probability and Evidence* (1972). 'What is a law of nature' distinguishes law-like from merely accidental generalisations in terms of the different attitudes those affirming general statements have to them. Roughly, and as a first approximation, I treat 'all A are B' as a law if there is no property such that the knowledge that some A thing had it would weaken my belief that that thing was B. He does not ask the question as to when it is reasonable to treat general statements in this way. The book ends with a lively essay on fatalism, determinism, and the predictability of human action, and begins with a programmatic inaugural for the Wykeham chair at Oxford on philosophy and language. 'A study of language', he now maintains, 'is inseparable from a study of the facts which it is used to describe'. The sharp division between the conceptual and the empirical has become a bit blurred.

The most substantial product of Ayer's years in London was *The Problem of Knowledge* (1956). Brilliantly concise even by his standards—it is about 80,000 words long—it is a better account of Ayer's general position than the more comprehensive *Central Questions of Philosophy* (1973), since it confines itself to the epistemological issues in which he was most interested and in which he felt most comfortable.

An initial chapter sets out various more or less methodological preliminaries and concludes with a definition of knowledge: I know that *p*
if, and not unless, *p* is true, I am sure that *p* and I have a right to be sure
of it. This is more a schema than a definition. What confers the right to
which he alludes? It seems exposed to Gettier-style objections. And
what, one may unkindly ask, is the status of cognitive or epistemic
rights from the point of view of emotivism?

This is followed by a chapter discussing scepticism and certainty.
Philosophical scepticism is distinguished from the ordinary kind as
questioning not the evidence we actually have but the standards by
which evidence of that kind, however abundant, could support or
establish the conclusions drawn from it. He says that 'it is held' that
unless some things are certain, nothing can be even probable, and he
seems to hold that view himself since he assumes it, without examination, in what follows. He goes on to argue that *cogito* and *sum*, or,
rather, 'I think' and 'I exist,' are 'degenerate' propositions, in which the
verb is a sleeping partner; the conditions for the use of referring
expressions involved guarantee the truth of the statement containing
them. He considers the incorrigibility of reports of one's own current
experience. He now reverts to his original position 'that there is no class
of descriptive statements which are incorrigible' on the ground that one
can misdescribe one's experience and not all such misdescription is
merely verbal.

The most interesting part of the second chapter is Ayer's account of
what he calls the 'pattern of sceptical arguments'. All forms of philosophical scepticism point to a logical gap between the available evidence for a certain kind of belief and those beliefs themselves. No array
of singular statements entails a truly general statement; no collection of
experiences entails the existence of a physical object; from no con-
stellation of behaviour and utterance can it be validly inferred that
someone else is having an experience; from no assemblage of memories
and traces does the truth of any statement about the past follow. In each
of these cases (and others can be added) all the evidence for beliefs of
one kind is supplied by beliefs of another kind, but never conclusively,
there is always a logical gap. He distinguishes four ways of dealing with
problems of this kind. (There is, of course, a fifth possibility, that of
scepticism, but that is not exactly a way of dealing with the problem.)

The first way out is intuitionism, which denies that evidence of the
second sort is all we have to go on and claims that we have direct access
to the allegedly inaccessible items: direct realism about perception,

telepathic awareness of the contents of other minds, retrospective perception of past occurrences. Secondly, there is reductionism, which, denying the supposed gap, takes statements about the problematic entities to be translatable into statements about the uncontroversially accessible ones: the tactic of phenomenalism, 'logical' behaviourism, and the C. I. Lewis theory about knowledge of the past which Ayer had briefly espoused in his first book. Thirdly, there is the 'scientific approach', which attempts to bridge the gap by inductive reasoning, the point of view of causal and representative theories of perception, of those who take present memories and traces to make the existence of past events 'overwhelmingly probable' and those who take the argument by analogy to other minds to be acceptable. Finally, there is the 'method of descriptive analysis' which accepts the gap, neither tries to pull it shut from one end or the other, nor to bridge it, but, as he puts it, 'takes it in its stride'. This might seem irresponsibly blithe, a recognition of the correctness of scepticism together with a refusal to be affected by it. It might more charitably be viewed as an anticipation of the theory of 'criteria', that is to say, necessarily good evidence that falls short of entailment.

In the three remaining chapters, Ayer treats perception, memory, and 'myself and others'. In the first some familiar ground is elegantly covered, with the epistemic primacy of sense-data asserted as usual. But phenomenalism is now fully abandoned for the position that limiting cases of objects seeming to be perceived in all circumstances would entail the existence of the object in question. Such an ideal body of evidence is never in fact achieved, but the bodies of evidence approximating to it that we do have draw their evidential strength from it. He restates this conclusion in a form which was to satisfy him until the end of his career: 'in referring as we do to physical objects we are elaborating a theory with respect to the evidence of our senses'.

The excellent chapter on memory dispels a lot of Russellian confusion about images and feelings of familiarity and pastness. Memory-images occur, but they are dispensable. Habit-memory is simply having learnt something and not forgotten it. To remember that something was the case is to have a true (perhaps also justified) belief about the past. Event-memory is more of a problem. It is more than a true belief about one's own past but it is not quite clear what. Ayer does not consider the possibility of the extra factor being the causation of the belief by a past experience of one's own. The logical possibility of perceiving past events is handled as before. There is a good discussion of Dummett's question about whether effects might not precede their causes.

The final chapter on myself and others also covers some old ground in a familiar way (e.g. it is only a contingent fact that another's experience was his and not mine), but there is some interesting new material about personal identity.

In 1959, H. H. Price, Ayer's mentor and always courteous critic, retired from the Wykeham chair of logic in Oxford. His election led to something of an academic commotion. The three local senior philosophers on the electoral board voted against him. Ryle and J. D. Mabbott supported W. C. Kneale, the distinguished historian of logic, Ryle arguing, truly but perhaps not altogether relevantly, that 'Kneale had borne the heat and burden of the day'. Austin was for Sir Peter Strawson. Ayer was voted in by the vice-chancellor (Sir Maurice Bowra), Professor John Wisdom of Cambridge, and the two New College representatives. Ryle was very displeased and resigned from all the electoral boards on which he sat in protest. The fuss soon died down and his opponents did not seem to hold Ayer's victory against him. Price, when told the news, was delighted.

For the next nineteen years, until his retirement in 1979, Ayer occupied his chair and the fellowship at New College that went with it with considerable success. His lectures, delivered at high speed and argumentatively dense, were too demanding for the less committed of his undergraduate audiences, which tended to fall away sharply as the term went on. But he was of great value to Oxford's large population of graduate students in philosophy, most of them reading for the new, two-year degree of B.Phil. He energetically reanimated the professorial tradition in Oxford of the 'informal instruction', a weekly two-hour class, open to all graduates and to recommended undergraduates. He would select some recently published monograph or essay-collection, talk about it himself and then cajole members of the class to prepare papers on parts of the book for the remaining weeks. There were also his 'Tuesday evenings', when a group of younger philosophy tutors would meet in his rooms to hear and mangle a paper by one of them. At six o'clock strong drink would be served and under its enlivening influence the discussion would become at once more festive and more vehement. He was an admirable and very hard-working supervisor of graduate students, taking a great deal of trouble about their theses and their professional futures.

There was a non-metropolitan, donnishly respectable side to Ayer's character which flourished in New College. He had a fine set of rooms, looking over the college garden. He married Alberta Chapman (Dee Wells) in 1960 and lived with her in London, but he spent most week-days in term in Oxford and so was to all intents and purposes a resident. He dined regularly and brought in guests for common-room nights. For many years he turned out for the fellows' team in their annual cricket match with a team of the college choir school. On his first appearance he scored 74 not out, more than the rest of his team put together. His batting was very much in character: quick, bold, and militant.

In the two decades since *The Foundation of Empirical Knowledge* had seemed the last word in philosophy, the centre of the discipline had unquestionably moved back to Oxford, which, despite a philosophical population of unparalleled size, had been pretty much in eclipse since the early years of the century. Ryle and Austin had, in different but still cognate ways, developed a philosophical procedure remote from Ayer's deductive reasoning about propositions of high generality in which it was assumed that formal logic revealed the essential structure of thought and language, something inherited by Ayer from Russell. The linguistic philosophers of Oxford examined ordinary language and common (or common-sense) beliefs, rather than a logically regimented language and scientific knowledge. At the time of Ayer's arrival this was the consensus with which he was confronted, and it was expected that there would be an illuminating battle of Titans between him and Austin. Because of Austin's lamentably early death in 1960 this never happened. Other factors combined with Ayer's efforts to move the prevailing philosophical attitude into something more Russellian and formalistic: Quine's exhilarating year as Eastman professor in 1953–4, Strawson's move towards system in *Individuals* in 1959, perhaps some influence, to the advantage of scientism, from the 'Australian materialism' of Smart and Armstrong. In his years as professor in Oxford he could feel that the tide was turning his way and that he had helped to turn it.

He had little sympathy for the philosophy of the later Wittgenstein, although he never concealed his large debt to the *Tractatus*. Already in 1954, as has been mentioned, he had rejected the private language argument. Soon after coming back to Oxford he published a gleefully destructive attack on Malcolm's strange theory that dreams are not experiences but that to have dreamed is to be disposed to tell stories when one wakes up. Malcolm responded with some heat. Ayer's campaign culminated in his lively but slightly superficial book on Wittgenstein in 1985.

From the time of his return to Oxford, when he was nearing fifty, Ayer continued to be very productive, publishing thirteen books between *The Concept of a Person* in 1963 and *Thomas Paine* in 1988, the year before his death. There were three essay collections; two substantial surveys of important, more or less empiricist philosophers of the modern age (*The Origins of Pragmatism*, about Peirce and James, in 1968, and *Russell and Moore: The Analytical Heritage* in 1971); short books on Hume in 1980, Russell in 1972, and Wittgenstein in 1985; an idiosyncratic and rather disjointed history of *Philosophy in the Twentieth Century* in 1981, largely recycling material published earlier; slim volumes on Voltaire and Thomas Paine towards the end of his life; and two more ambitious works: *Probability and Evidence* in 1972 and *The Central Questions of Philosophy*, a statement of his ideas about practically everything, in 1973.

These books were, as always, very well written. No words were wasted; complex bodies of thought were lucidly expounded. But there were no major changes of view and no ventures into unfamiliar territory. The book on probability consists of John Dewey Lectures, delivered at Columbia University, supplemented 'in order to bring this book up to a respectable size', as he cheerfully admits, by a pretty lethal criticism of R. F. Harrod's attempt to solve the problem of induction and a concluding essay on conditionals. The Dewey Lectures start with a penetrating attempt to reinforce Hume's argument that no factual inference is demonstrative by way of the notion of an 'intrinsic description', under which every event is indeed logically distinct from every other event. Kneale's doctrine of natural necessity is dogmatically dismissed. Ayer distinguishes three kinds of probability (from Hume to Carnap, most philosophers get by with two): purely mathematical, as in the calculus of chances; statistical, based on frequencies; and epistemic, issuing in judgements about the credibility of particular beliefs. He repeats his earlier contentions that frequencies allow no judgements about particular events and that logical relation theories like Carnap's rely on an unclear and perhaps unclarifiable notion of 'total evidence'. Ayer's account of probability was convincingly criticised for its lack of familiarity with recent work in the field.

The two historical surveys are interestingly different. In the one on Peirce and James the two subjects are examined from a certain distance. Only a selection of their work is investigated, that part of it which mostly closely overlaps Ayer's own interests. In Peirce's case this means that rather a lot is left out. Fallibilism is mentioned, but only in passing; there is nothing at all about Peirce's critical common-sensism. Ayer considers Peirce's version of the pragmatic theory of meaning, his philosophy of science, where he rejects Peirce's vindication of induction, but expresses sympathy for his belief in objective chance, and his theory of signs, which receives the largest share of his attention. James's pragmatic theory of truth is objected to on fairly familiar lines. Ayer's main concern is with James's radical empiricism, which he sees as a rough, preliminary adumbration of his own account of empirical knowledge as composed of a primary system of sensible elements and a secondary system of theoretical constructions out of these elements (minds, common objects, the theoretical entities of physics). He seeks to replace James's large and sweeping constructional gestures with more detailed and explicit constructions of his own. He concludes by arguing that the constructedness of an entity does not, as James supposed (and in this Russell was to follow him), show that it is of an inferior ontological status to that of the elements from which it is constructed.

His treatment of Russell and Moore is much less distorted by his own preoccupations and supplies a much more comprehensive and balanced account of the subjects. That is obviously because he was much closer to them; their thought was part of the original constitution of his mind as a philosopher and most of his work took the form of developing or reacting against ideas he had found in them. The book is more clear-cut and decisive than that on the two American pragmatists. He begins with Russell's conception of philosophy as the analysis of most of what we think there is as logical constructions out of sensory data, a procedure authoritatively illustrated by Russell's theory of descriptions. The doctrines of logical atomism and neutral monism, in Russell's distinctive interpretation of them, are set out with the fluent concision that is derived from long familiarity. The view which Russell shared with James that logical constructions are not part of the ultimate furniture of the world is once again dismissed. In the case of Moore the early criticisms of the principle that *esse* is *percipi* and the doctrine of internal relations are largely endorsed; his defence of common sense is not. There is a very thorough examination of Moore's resolutely naïve but nevertheless scrupulously careful dealings with abstract entities such as concepts, universals, propositions, and facts, and of his ideas about the nature and seemingly paradoxical aspects of philosophical analysis.

Much of the material of these two books reappears in *The Central Questions of Philosophy* which was published not long after them. It is a little odd to find the militantly atheistic Ayer being invited to deliver lectures endowed for the purpose of defending natural religion which had, in practice, recently been the occasion, for the most part, for the presentation of large metaphysical systems such as Alexander's *Space, Time and Deity* and Whitehead's *Process and Reality*. Ayer complied in a negative way with both the principle and the practice of the series. His last chapter is devoted to undermining arguments for religious belief and his first to rejecting the claims of metaphysics, although more politely and less sweepingly than in his first youthful onslaught. On the whole, the book adds up to an admirable summary or textbook of Ayer's own mature philosophy, and, to some extent, of the kind of Russellian analytic philosophy of which he was such an able exponent. This modesty of aim and achievement may explain why it does not seem to have been reviewed in most of the main philosophical periodicals. A great deal of ground is covered in a very short space: most adroitly, perhaps, in the chapter on logic and existence, in which the main ingredients of logic, as well as set theory, are discussed, and also existence, identity, analyticity, and abstract entities. The once most ardent champion of the analytic-synthetic distinction puts up little resistance to Quine's dismissal of it. Having previously believed, no doubt under the influence of Russell, that common sense and physics give incompatible accounts of material things, he suggests here that a loose compromise is possible and that unobservable particles are literally parts of ordinary material objects. Although largely derivative from Ayer's other writings, there can be no book which covers so much of what really is, (or, at any rate, then was) central to philosophy than this. It is the most comprehensive, although not most exciting, introduction to Ayer's philosophy; it is a pretty good introduction to philosophy in general.

His *Philosophy in the Twentieth Century* was an attempt, he says, to provide a sequel to Russell's *History of Western Philosophy*, bringing the story up to date. It shares some of the qualities of its predecessor, being brisk and lucid as well as being selective—even more than Russell. Bergson, Alexander, and Whitehead, for example, are considered simply as they figure in Collingwood's *Idea of Nature*, an intriguing but unreliable peep-hole. Price appears only as sharing Broad's

interest in psychical research. The only non-analytic philosophers treated at length are James, a handful of phenomenologists and existenti-
alists, and Collingwood, who is considered at some length. Ayer
dutifully sets out some of Collingwood's extravagances, such as that
works of art are in the artists' minds, not on gallery walls, and that
history is the re-enactment of past thoughts, with an uncomprehending
bemusement worthy of Prichard or Moore. Added to brief versions of
Ayer's earlier treatment of Russell, James, and Moore is a substantial
account of C. I. Lewis, recalling discussions of him in the late 1930s
with Austin and others. A singular assemblage of philosophers of mind,
from Broad to Davidson, is handled in one chapter. A final one brings
the story pretty much up to date with Chomsky, Dummett, Kripke, and
Putnam. The book is not as amusing as Russell's and is not encumbered
with extraneous historical matter, indeed, it is minimally historical
about the people and ideas it does cover. Under a kind of Geneva
convention he discloses only the name, date, and professional positions
of his selected subjects.

Two of the best essays—on Austin's attack on sense-data and
Malcolm's theory of dreams—in the collection *Metaphysics and Common Sense* have already been mentioned, as has, by implication, a third
'On What There Must Be'. The best thing in *Freedom and Morality* is
an article 'Identity and Reference' in which Kripke's influential theory
of reference is taken to task. The only one of the three short books
which requires a mention is that on Wittgenstein. Apart from Ayer's
usual merits of clarity, concision, and what might be called transpar-
ency of argument—something particularly important in this case—it
has the virtue of being wholly unintimidated. Wittgenstein is treated
pretty much as if he were Bosanquet, the producer of strange utterances
in dire need of interpretation.

Activities outside Oxford were by no means suspended during
Ayer's years as Wykeham professor. He was a member of the Plowden
Committee on Primary Education and, for all his carefully nurtured
radicalism, dissented from its hostility to formal methods of instruction.
It was primarily for his services in this connection, and not for what he
had done for philosophy, that he was knighted in 1970. He was president of numerous progressive organisations, for the most part concerned with 'humanism' and homosexual law reform. For many years a
member of the Institut Internationale de Philosophie, he was its president from 1968 to 1971. This supplied lavish opportunities for attending conferences in more or less exotic places, a pursuit to which he was

strongly attached. At one of these, at Varna, a Black Sea resort in Bulgaria, in face of the total failure of repeated pressure on the button to obtain any room service, he voiced his dissatisfaction in a loud voice. The room's bugging system soon brought up an apologetic secret policeman in managerial guise.

In 1969 he was sounded by some fellows of Wadham about becoming warden and enjoyed thinking about the idea, both until he decided not to stand and, a little wistfully, afterwards. In 1977 he published *Part of My Life*, the first and better of two autobiographical volumes, taking the story up to his arrival at UCL. The second volume, *More of My Life*, which appeared in 1983, covered a shorter and less interesting period, finishing in 1963. He retired from his Oxford chair in 1978, on reaching the statutory age, but his election to a fellowship at Wolfson College gave him a toe-hold in the university for a number of years, which he made use of by regularly attending the Tuesday evening discussions. In 1979 he was elected to an honorary studentship at Christ Church, which was somewhat undermined by an unfortunate speech at some college occasion.

In 1981 Ayer and his second wife, Dee, were divorced and he married Vanessa Lawson. He and Dee had had one son, Nicholas, to whom he was devoted. He was extremely happy with Vanessa and she fell in splendidly with his characteristic style of London entertaining. He seems always to have lived in narrow houses where party guests flowed out of available rooms and on to the stairs. This time of very great domestic happiness did not last long since Vanessa died in 1985. With her he made an extended visit to Dartmouth College in New Hampshire in 1982. In 1987, without her, he made a similar visit to Bard College on the Hudson River.

Ayer was elected a Fellow of the British Academy in 1952 and was an active one. His 'Privacy' was the annual philosophical lecture for 1959 and 'Bertrand Russell as a Philosopher' the Master-Mind Lecture for 1972. He was awarded honorary degrees by Brussels (1962); East Anglia (1972); London (1978); Trent, Ontario (1980); Bard College (1985); and Durham (1988). There was a distinguished symposium on his work, *Perception and Identity*, edited by Graham Macdonald, to whose contents he replied with freshness and vigour in 1979. He also managed substantial replies to most of the contributions to the less distinguished volume dedicated to him in the Library of Living Philosophers, edited by Lewis E. Hahn, which was not published until 1992, three years after his death. The only serious monograph about his philosophy is that of John Foster, a most loyal, but penetratingly critical, admirer, which came out in 1985, in good time for him to enjoy it.

Ayer's health was generally good—perhaps surprisingly so for such a heavy smoker; steady, but not problematic, drinker; and, after his annual cricket matches in middle age, resolute avoider of exercise, apart from a little night-club-style dancing. But in the last few years of his life his health declined and he died on 27 June 1989. A curious medical incident occurred during his final illness. At one point he was thought to have died, but, to the surprise of those attending him, he then revived. His accounts of what went through his mind during the conscious part of this process left the question of the afterlife still very much open. He was looked after in his last days by his second wife, Dee, whom he had remarried shortly before his death.

Ayer's general intellectual enthusiasms were, like his philosophy, on the narrow side, but intense. He was extremely well read in the great male Victorian novelists: Dickens, Thackeray, Trollope, Wilkie Collins. He liked painting, but not very ardently. His comments on visits as a young man to the great collections of Europe are dutiful and rather banal, calling to mind A. C. Benson's remarks on Dickens in Max Beerbohm's *A Christian Garland*: 'He had for that writer a very sincere admiration, though he was inclined to think that his true excellence lay not so much in faithful portrayal of the life of his times, or in gift of sustained narration, or in those scenes of pathos which have moved so many hearts in so many quiet homes, as in the power of inventing highly fantastic figures, such as Mr Micawber or Mr Pickwick'. He loved the cinema and had at one time written film reviews. Music was for dancing to.

He was a faithful supporter of Tottenham Hotspur and, in something of the same spirit, of the Labour Party. He was the friend of many prominent Labour politicians and regularly spoke out in their and their party's interest. There was a kind of boyish mischievousness about his politics as about the vehemence of his attacks on religion which preserved them from any taint of rancour so that they were no obstacle to close and long-lasting friendships with Conservatives and Christians. Like Bloomsbury he thought personal relations much too important to be sacrificed to the abstractions of ideology.

He was undoubtedly one of the liveliest figures on the British philosophical scene in his time and, when he appeared on it, it was in need of enlivening. He was not a highly original thinker. His impact was due to the brilliance with which he arranged and expressed the ideas he had acquired from others. Perhaps his greatest intellectual virtue was his unremitting adherence to clarity and to rational argument. His work is without allusions, undeveloped suggestions, obscurity, and mannerism. Through his books and his teaching he set a fine example of intellectual discipline.

ANTHONY QUINTON
*Fellow of the Academy*

*Bibliographical note.* There are substantial bibliographies of Ayer's writings in two collections of essays devoted to his work. Much the better of the two is in *The Philosophy of A. J. Ayer*, ed. Lewis E. Hahn, (Illinois; Open Court, 1992). That in *Perception and Identity*, ed. Graham Macdonald, (Macmillan, 1979) (a better collection of essays) is very sketchy.

CAROLINE HAMMOND BAMMEL

*Proceedings of the British Academy*, **94**, 285–291

# Caroline Penrose Hammond Bammel
# 1940–1995

BY THE PREMATURE DEATH of Caroline Hammond Bammel, early Christian studies lost a major scholar, who had already achieved much and had many more things to tell us. She came of a family with a high academic background. She was born at Falmouth on 5 July 1940, at a time of dramatic peril for Britain in the world, and her eminent father had already gone from home to cope heroically with Hitler's war, soon to play a crucial role in Greece and the Balkans which he knew so well. So it came about that until she was five years old, his first-born had no opportunity to set eyes on him. When at the end of it all he came home, she had by then seen only a photograph of his head and shoulders, and it is on family record that her immediate reaction on her first sight of him was amazement that he was also endowed with legs. With the war ended and normal Cambridge university life gradually reviving, she was to find herself no longer an only child in what had hitherto seemed to be a one-parent family, but rather the eldest member of a lively quartet which in time would become a quintet.

No portrait of her could fail to say how important her family was to her. Beside her devotion to the acquisition of scholarly skills, there was a richly human side—delightful, indeed scintillating wit, sometimes gently teasing but never touched by malice—and the Hammond family share memories of peals of cheerful laughter together. Among her deepest pleasures was to be walking in the scenic splendours of the Elan valley in mid-Wales with its large reservoir, and this lovely valley was but one of many local areas and districts which she loved to

© The British Academy 1997.

explore. A favourite hobby was planning such walks. She also had high skill with drawings and ironic cartoons.

When in the coming of her fifties the grave medical verdict declared that a terminal cancer had begun its slow deadly work, a family assembly, after she had shared the serious and bitter news with each individually, was characteristically an occasion for indestructible courage and cheerfulness.

In October 1959 she arrived at Girton as an undergraduate to read for the classical tripos under Alison Duke. She was taught ancient history by a young Fellow of Trinity Hall, Robert Runcie. All her teachers found her to combine a self-effacing modesty with an acute intelligence of exceptional power. The mathematical system of old Cambridge in allocating marks in the Tripos according to the number of questions expected was not really clear to her, so that in her Tripos answers she succumbed to the temptation to write long and immensely learned answers and then ran short of time. In consequence she was not placed by the examiners in the first class—and was not the only brilliant scholar of her time (with a scintillating career ahead) who was to stumble at this fence. Nevertheless, she went on to undertake research, realising that to someone well equipped in Latin and Greek, in questions of text and palaeography, there was a wide field open before her in early Christian literature. So while she was trained to be qualified to teach Cicero and Vergil, her investigations took her beyond the canonical texts of the traditional classical syllabus.

A question that especially intrigued her was the continuity and discontinuity between the 'classical' Greek and Latin world and the new attitudes brought into being as people in the Roman Empire became Christian—which they did with a rapidity that astonished both sides of that debate. A year crucial for its consequences was spent in Munich as a Fellow under the Alexander von Humboldt Foundation. There she went to sit at the feet of Bernhard Bischoff, grand master of medieval manuscripts, Corresponding Fellow of the British Academy and of many other learned bodies. At first she found herself surprised and baffled by the fact that the main subject for his graduate seminar was the 'Lives of Saints'. Initially, she supposed that these often folklorish documents lay beyond her range or proper concern. She had not yet discovered the hard-headedness characteristic of Bollandist critical work on these voluminous documents. She was persuaded to attend, and immediately found herself riveted by Bischoff's methods and prodigious knowledge of his subject. From 1966 Girton College appointed her to a research fellowship. Two years later this was transformed into an official fellowship with a college lectureship, combining both classics and theology.

She had a well-filled timetable teaching undergraduates, especially in classics, but her research interests remained in the field of early Christian literature. As a thesis-subject for a doctorate she wanted to edit a text, and having already discovered Origen to be a figure of high interest, she embarked on a large project of soaring ambition which seemed only to become ever larger and more Everest-like over the many years that the work eventually demanded. The proposal was to plug a major gap in the critical editions of what remains of Origen's biblical commentaries, namely the abbreviating Latin paraphrase of his exposition of Romans produced by Rufinus of Aquileia in 406 in southern Italy, a work last seriously edited in 1759.

The search through the catalogues of manuscripts produced an alarming quantity of codices needing inspection and collation at least in part. Among them one was of particularly great importance, namely the fifth century Lyon 483 in half-uncial (Lowe, CLA VI 779), containing the first half, books 1–5, damaged at the beginning and end and with some other defects, but in date no great distance from Rufinus' autograph. It became possible to demonstrate that Rufinus' personal preferences, as mentioned in his writings, are reflected in the manner of punctuation and of citation, but especially in idiosyncratic *nomina sacra* with *dms* for *dominus, is* for *iesus* (never *dns* or *ihs*), the abbreviation *is* being extremely unusual but influenced by Greek usage attested from about 300 onwards. Rufinus had his circle of admirers and supporters, and not all the points in the contest went to Jerome in their vast quarrel which so distressed Augustine and others. Rufinus' works were lovingly copied in monastic houses which valued his achievements, and the scribes followed his precepts, set out in his preface to his translation of Origen, *De principiis*, and again in *Apologia contra Hieronymum*, i. 12. If his well-to-do friends Melania and Pinianus were helping to pay for the scribes making the copies, there would have been a certain expression of loyalty in the scribes' adherence to his principles.

A careful stemma was drawn up for the numerous other manuscripts. A codex from ninth-century St Amand, now at Copenhagen, includes a note on the first folio to the effect that the complete work of Rufinus was 'found in his library after his sudden death, unpublished and uncorrected'. This and several other ninth-century manuscripts illustrate the seriousness which the commentary on Romans commanded in the Carolingian age with its debates about predestination and grace.

Early Christian commentators followed normal ancient convention in citing a piece of the text being expounded before going on to offer interpretation, and the 'lemmata' of a Bible commentary provide crucial evidence for the type of text lying before the exegete. Rufinus seems to have had difficulty with Origen's lemmata, since he appears to have saved time by quoting only the first Greek words and then leaving it to the scribe to fill in the remainder.

Rufinus decided not to translate Origen's lemmata but provided his own Latin citations using his own manuscript of the Old Latin version. Thereby Rufinus' Latin paraphrase of Origen has preserved for us almost complete the copy of Romans in a manuscript of the *Vetus Latina* written towards the end of the fourth century or thereabouts. His codex need not represent the type of text current in the Aquileia of his youth, since he did not remain there but frequently travelled about. So his codex of the Pauline letters may have been picked up on his travels. In consequence of this procedure Rufinus preserves for us the text of an early manuscript of the pre-Vulgate Latin version of the epistle, which also turns out to be attested in the commentary of Ambrosiaster. From his reading of Origen Rufinus learnt the invaluable habit of recording variant readings between different manuscripts, and from time to time he takes occasion to compare the readings of his codex of Paul with other Latin manuscripts known to him.

The original Greek lemmata of Origen can in part be reconstructed from the content of the commentary.

The interest and importance of the research for the history of the Old Latin Bible gave the impetus to publish the fruits of her labours in the prestigious series of monographs, *Aus der Geschichte der lateinischen Bibel*, edited by Beuron Abbey under the aegis of the Heidelberg Academy. Her book of 551 pages mostly in small print appeared in 1985 with the great house of Herder in Freiburg im Breisgau. Five years later came the first volume of the critical edition of Rufinus, containing the first three books, with a promise of three further volumes to come.

Caroline Hammond had learnt fluent German from Mrs Stevenson, mother of her Tutor at Girton, Alison Duke, and was master of the language: 'That pupil of yours—she cannot make a mistake'. As a Humboldt Fellow in Munich she had been able to deploy her linguistic skill. In 1979 she married a Cambridge colleague in the Divinity

Faculty, Ernst Bammel, with a substantial house in Bonn and many German connections. German was the language they used together. So when the time came for her to publish the results of her researches, she decided to use German. Her husband used to say with pride that he never had to correct her. Several of her learned articles in journals also appeared in German.

In addition to the collation and assessment of the manuscript tradition, the commentary on Romans raised other questions. Rufinus expressly recorded that of the 15 *tomoi* of the original Greek of Origen, some had not been available to him, as he set about the task of reducing its length by about half as his friend Heraclius was asking him to do. At the end Rufinus appended a *peroratio* denying the right of malicious critics (Jerome is no doubt in mind here) saying that he ought to be giving his own name rather than that of Origen as the author of the commentary, so much of it is his own work. He goes on to admit that not all the books have been available to him. The booksellers' copies have been incomplete (*'interpolati'*, *not* meaning 'interpolated'). Some rolls were not to be had. It was always a factor militating against the complete transmission of Origen's biblical commentaries that they were relentlessly long; scribes became weary and felt sure that patrons would not wish to pay for so many *stichoi*, which in the case of the commentary on Romans would have run to 40,000. Rufinus filled the gaps with matter from Origen's other writings.

In 1899 E. von der Goltz published in the *Texte und Untersuchungen* NF II 4 a description of a tenth-century codex from the great Lavra on Mount Athos, where the scribe of the epistle to the Romans incorporated marginal notes recording the points at which Origen had begun the tomes of his commentary. A superior republication of this material came in 1932 in Harvard Theological Studies from Kirsopp Lake and Silva New. The marginal notes include the information that the eleventh and fourteenth *tomoi* were missing. Von der Goltz thought the marginalia of the same date as the Athos codex. The probability, however, is that they belong to early in the fourth century, first made by Pamphilus or Eusebius at the library of the Church in Palestinian Caesarea. Caroline Bammel spotted an unrecognised clue in Staab's *Pauluskatenen* (1926) and discovered a second witness to the marginal notes in a manuscript hiding in the Vatican library, Palatinus 204 s.xi, making possible a fuller publication of remarkable material.

Fragments of the original Greek of Origen also survive to be brought into the reckoning. Basil (*De Spiritu sancto* 29,73) has a piece on the divine being of the Holy Spirit. The historian Socrates (*HE* VII 32,17) recorded that 'in the first tome of his commentary on Romans Origen examined at length the use of the word theotokos'. Catena fragments from Vaticanus gr.762 s.x (a copy in Bodleianus Auct.E.ii.20), poorly edited by A. Ramsbotham in the *Journal of Theological Studies* 13 (1912), have been enlarged from Vindob.gr.166 s.xiv by Staab in *Biblische Zeitschrift* 18 (1928). The anthology of Origen on biblical interpretation made in fourth-century Cappadocia and called *Philokalia* has two excerpts. Above all there is the Tura papyrus, discovered in 1941 when the British Army had caves south of Cairo emptied of ancient rubbish to make a cache for ammunition. This gives excerpts of varying length from tomes 5–6, containing the commentary on Romans 3:50–5:10, and was written early in the seventh century or late in the sixth. The papyrus text received a masterly edition from the papyrologist Jean Scherer in 1957, who also provided the text with a partly contentious (and contested) commentary, sceptical of the integrity of Rufinus as a translator.

Caroline Bammel devoted a substantial section of her monograph of 1985 to an evaluation of the Greek papyrus, and some of its readings were incorporated into a verse-by-verse commentary on her monograph. But she did not need to be concerned with the problems inherent in the papyrus itself, where many excerpts cannot have been intelligible to the scribe himself a week later, so drastic is the degree of abbreviation and apocopation. A recent detailed study has appeared in the late Kurt Aland and H.-U. Rosenbaum's *Repertorium der griechischen christlichen Papyri* II (1995).

She decided not to include the Tura papyrus readings in her edition, where the Greek runs closely parallel to Rufinus. But she supplied a learned apparatus of parallels and possible sources in Origen or other writers.

It is a source of deep regret that the learned and tireless editor did not live to see her great edition completed. However, in 1996 the Vetus Latina Institut in Beuron and also the publishing house of Herder published a statement of firm intent to complete the printing. Books 4 and 5 are in proof; of book 6 the text and part of the apparatus are ready for the printer. The remaining four books of the whole can be edited from her *Nachlaß*, and the altruistic publishing house hopes to complete the work without undue delay.

Two volumes have been published gathering her papers and notes from learned journals, one from Variorum entitled *Tradition and*

*Exegesis in Early Christian Writers*, the second from Herder entitled *Origeniana et Rufiniana*. The latter volume includes a paper of central importance for the biography of Rufinus and the chronology of his career. The Variorum volume has its main weight either in papers on unity and diversity in the early Church or (a related theme) the varieties of biblical exposition found in these texts and their influence on the history of ideas.

Academic recognition came to her a little more slowly than one might have expected. She became a Reader at Cambridge, and was elected a Fellow of the Academy in 1994. In Germany more than one faculty of theology smiled upon the possibility of a call to occupy a chair, which would have been highly unusual for an English woman.

Initially she was a nervous lecturer, but she never delivered a lecture to undergraduates without being the soul of lucidity, fortified by handouts richly provided with the salient names and points. Youthful shyness yielded in time to the utmost firmness, and friends can recall quiet but formidable questions being addressed to paper-readers at learned seminars who seemed to her to be indifferent to some of the evidence.

Caroline Bammel's students were devoted to her, as she was to them. When first she became seriously ill with cancer, she asked herself what most mattered to her in life, and confessed that the answer was her friends and other people. The delayed sentence of death impelled her to throw herself ever more fully both into her teaching and research, and also into the life of her college and to seeing as much as possible of friends and family. When she realised that the end could not be far distant, a great burst of energy made her that year highly productive of papers in learned journals, including a meditation on death in the *Jahrbuch für Antike und Christentum* concerning this theme in ancient and Christian poetry.

Her husband, Ernst Bammel, well known especially for his learned articles about emergent Christianity, loyally supported her scholarship, and her marriage brought to her deep happiness, Bonn becoming her second home. Whatever of her was mortal now lies in the Bammel family grave at Kessenich by Bonn close to the Rhine. Ernst Bammel died on 5 December 1996 in Germany after a long illness.

She died, in strong faith, in Cambridge on 31 October 1995.

HENRY CHADWICK
*Fellow of the Academy*

A. F. L. BEESTON

Ramsey & Muspratt

*Proceedings of the British Academy,* **94**, 295–316

# Alfred Felix Landon Beeston
# 1911–1995

DURING THE LAST twenty-five years of Freddie Beeston's life he could, without hyperbole, be referred to as the most accomplished scholar of the Arabic language anywhere. He was also, by universal consent, the foremost student of South Arabian and the acknowledged Nestor of that discipline. Of general Semitics he was no mean practitioner, and his knowledge of Hebrew was good enough for him to quote (occasionally even to misquote) from memory passages of the Old Testament. When in charge of the Oriental Department of the Bodleian Library he felt obliged to familiarise himself with the rudiments of Chinese; and when asked, on departing for a conference in Hungary, in which language he would converse there, his reply was 'in Magyar, of course'. Yet he was the most modest, self-effacing, and unpompous of men; he preferred critical comment to encomia. While skilled in social intercourse as an inveterate college man, he liked above all else to talk shop on most aspects of language and linguistics.

Until his early fifties he wore his hair 'short back and sides'; thereafter he let it grow to shoulder-length, and his white straggly mane and partly unbuttoned shirts became a familiar sight all over Oxford. With his massive body and gargantuan appetite (he was both gourmet and gourmand—as he was a man of startling contrasts generally) he cut a Falstaffian figure. He had a penchant for formality and punctilious academic procedures which, at first sight, seemed to consort strangely with his fanfares of coughing and laughter (which would momentarily interrupt any academic discussion or conference) and with the chains of

© The British Academy 1997.

cigarettes constantly drooping from his mouth. By his students and colleagues and the large number of his friends he was much loved and indeed revered as a deeply learned man of singular genuineness, honesty and truth, without any airs, affectation, vanity, or arrogance. He was one of the last true Oxford characters with his entire career and virtually his whole life profoundly tied to, and associated with, this ancient seat of learning of which he became such a remarkable ornament.

Freddie (as he was almost universally known—at times even by those who would not address him in that manner) was born in London on 23 February 1911.[1] He was the only son (there was an elder sister who predeceased him) of Herbert Arthur Beeston (1872–1941) and of Edith Mary Landon (1873–1965). His father was apprenticed as an engineer (a term by which he described himself throughout), but he subsequently became a white-collar draughtsman in a firm of patent agents.[2] Freddie was greatly attached to his mother of whom he would speak occasionally with great affection. I remember vividly a meeting in 1965 of the Association of British Orientalists at the Queens' College, Cambridge, when we were having lunch together in hall. In the early stages of the meal a college servant approached high table and asked for Professor Beeston; he then handed him a telegram. As Freddie opened it, he changed colour and was absolutely stunned and shaking. When I asked him if there was anything I could do, he requested me to drive him to the railway station. *En route* he told me that his mother had

---

[1] Freddie Beeston left two short autobiographical fragments dealing with the early stages of his career and with the elements that caused him to become an orientalist. The first was published as the introduction to a Festschrift dedicated to him by the fraternity of continental *sud-arabisants* in *Ṣayhadica* 1987 (Paris, Geuthner). The second appeared in the *Oxford Magazine*, No. 122, Michaelmas Term 1995, and bears the following postscript by the editor: 'Happily, we had just accepted Freddie Beeston's account of his career shortly before he died'. Both versions reveal a considerable degree of overlap and are strictly confined to his scholarly life; they are characteristically reticent about all private and personal concerns. They will be referred to in the following pages together with some additions and minor corrections within the knowledge of the present writer.

[2] In the *Oxford Magazine* article (see above, n. 1) Freddie pays tribute to his father (and indeed both his parents) for being 'totally supportive and encouraging' once they had assured themselves that he was seriously set on his course of studying oriental languages. His father also gave him financial assistance when he had embarked on his D.Phil. research before his Christ Church and James Mew scholarships had been formally approved. Freddie's niece, Mrs S. Fuller, confirms Freddie's well-known reticence to discuss family or personal matters. I am greatly obliged to Mrs Fuller for her helpfulness in giving me access to many of Freddie's unpublished papers.

died; otherwise he was incapable of speech. In all the fifty-five years of our acquaintance I never saw him so moved and grieved.

Freddie received his secondary education at Westminster School, where he obtained 'a thorough training'[3] in Latin and Greek. The two classical languages remained throughout his life a primary aspect of his linguistic equipment; indeed he chose classics later on when he was obliged to 'approach oriental finals by way of Moderations in another Faculty'. 'From at least the age of ten' he displayed a 'passionate interest in foreign languages'. He had come across a 'school textbook of English grammar . . . which included an introduction with an account of the Indo-European languages' and their interrelationships. In his spare time he taught himself 'German in order to have access to scholarly work in that language'. The same applied to 'the rudiments of Arabic', for he had 'always had an inclination for specialising in something unusual and exotic'. 'I avidly scanned any language manuals that I could lay my hands on, from ancient Egyptian hieroglyphics to Spanish and Welsh, etc.—the more exotic the better . . . *My interest was in theoretical linguistics, in the structure of a language and its strategies for expressing ideas.* All this created in me a predisposition in favour of non-European languages'.

The penultimate sentence of the preceding paragraph (which I have italicised) seems to me the reflection of the mature scholar which, by an act of anachronistic inadvertence, he put into the mouth of the school-boy. But it is clear that from an early age Freddie displayed remarkably precocious talents in the study of languages and in philological (as it would have been called in the early to mid-1920s) analysis. Thus from the age of fourteen (when he gained his School Certificate[4]) he was not only a budding student of several Indo-European as well as of one or two oriental languages, but he also 'began to debate . . . the choice of a career'. He felt that a large number of occupations were closed to him from the outset: he had no manual skills and he considered himself deficient in numeracy which prevented him contemplating a career in

---

[3] Passages within quotation marks, cited without indication of source, are derived from the two autobiographical sketches referred to in n. 1.

[4] Freddie's attachment to Westminster School lasted throughout his life. He was there from 1923 until 1929 under the headmastership (1919–37) of Harold Costley-White, later Dean of Gloucester. Among Freddie's unpublished papers, now in Mrs Fuller's possession, is a piece of some eighteen closely typed pages entitled 'Westminster School sixty years ago' (written about 1983). He also attended the centenary dinner of Ashburnham House, Westminster School, in 1982 and made a speech on that occasion.

architecture to which he was otherwise drawn. He also had no confidence in his capacity (or indeed his desire) 'to influence or persuade
people' which ruled out the Bar. He thought he had 'a total aversion to
engaging in any sort of buying and selling whatsoever'. Then he read in
some magazine about careers in librarianship, an idea which appealed
to him.

The article in question dealt not only with municipal libraries but
included a full description of the various departments of the British
Museum Library as well as 'the qualifications required for each department'. He realised at once that any job in the Department of Oriental
Printed Books and Manuscripts (for which a degree in one or more
oriental languages was *de rigueur*) was precisely what he was seeking.
The only problem was that any such post was liable to occur only about
once in ten years. He now felt that he ought to set out on the choice of
language(s) in which to specialise. He determined that Sanskrit and
Persian, being Indo-European languages, were not sufficiently 'exotic'
to appeal to his taste. Ancient Egyptian, in his view, was too archaeologically orientated, although there are quite a number of Egyptolo-
gists, among them notably H. J. Polotsky, who had no interest in
digging. Freddie had already 'experimented' with Hebrew, but he found
that the only grammar (probably Davidson's) he could lay his hands on
was very old-fashioned and unsatisfactory.

He now hesitated between Arabic and Chinese. For the latter he
could only get hold of phrase-books which did not convey to him how
the language operated. For Arabic, on the other hand, he unearthed a
copy of 'Palmer's little Arabic grammar' in a second-hand bookshop.
So by sheer and somewhat fortuitous elimination it had to be Arabic. He
then set out to acquire as much Arabic as possible, although Palmer's
work was not exactly an ideal tool. But he also got hold of an Arabic
dictionary and a copy of the Qur'an which he 'demanded as prizes from
my school' (senior boys were allowed to make their own choice of
books as prizes).

He decided that he would go to Oxford; for reasons he was unable to
explain later in life 'Cambridge never entered into my calculations'. So
from an early stage during his school career at Westminster he expected
to obtain a degree in Arabic eventually and then 'sit down and wait
hopefully for a vacancy for an Arabist in the British Museum'. In due
course (1929) he entered the Honour School of Oriental Languages, on
a scholarship to Christ Church, to study Arabic as his major language
and Persian as a minor; the latter was one of the few languages that

could be combined with Arabic at that time. There was also an option to take an extra paper in one of a prescribed list of subjects, among which South Arabian epigraphy had been placed by D. S. Margoliouth, the Laudian Professor of Arabic. Freddie availed himself of this opportunity with great enthusiasm, for 'since the age of fourteen I had become fascinated with the South Arabian inscriptions in the British Museum'. This epigraphic material was in the past displayed in a room adjoining the Egyptian gallery; while the latter was always full of visitors, Freddie was usually alone in the South Arabian room.

He spent many hours copying South Arabian inscriptions whose lapidary style attracted him aesthetically (indeed it did so to his dying day) and whose mode of non-ligature writing offered no insuperable obstacles to decipherment. He subsequently came across J. Theodore Bent's *The Sacred City of the Ethiopians* (London, 1893), and from the appendix on the inscriptions of Yeha and Aksum by D. H. Müller he was able to make out the South Arabian alphabet and 'identify one or two words, but naturally the texts as a whole eluded me'. When he came to Oxford it was, therefore, a matter of great excitement to him that his principal teacher and master, Professor Margoliouth, had taken an interest in Sabaean epigraphy and had himself published several important texts. Freddie was the first to attempt (and indeed notably succeed in) the South Arabian option which made such an impact on his entire subsequent career. It will be realised that the South Arabian dialects are not part of the Arabic language but a separate branch of the Semitic phylum. After graduating he continued work on South Arabian and gained his D.Phil. with a dissertation on a selection of Sabaean inscriptions.

Freddie's attachment to, and admiration for, Margoliouth[5] was profound. The latter's impact on him was enduring. When on one occasion I was tempted, in a review article, to compare the former pupil's knowledge of the Arabic *language* with that of the erstwhile teacher, he was quite angry and urged me to omit that comparison. David Samuel Margoliouth (1858–1940) was a classical scholar and orientalist; the son of the convert missionary Ezekiel Margoliouth, he possessed (according to Gilbert Murray, his obituarist in the *DNB* and in the *Proceedings of the British Academy* 26 (1940) an 'exotic and vivid appearance'; and although the latter was 'not strikingly Jewish, he bore

---

[5] An exercise book of 1931 survives which shows Freddie's fine Arabic hand even at that early stage. There are several handwritten corrections and marks by Margoliouth in red ink.

about him some marks of Eastern origin'). He was a polymath and, again according to the great Gilbert Murray (ibid.), 'no scholar of his generation left so deep and permanent a mark on oriental studies'. I think this judgement ought to be understood and limited to 'within the British context'. It is interesting to visualise that from Margoliouth's appointment to the Laudian Chair of Arabic in 1889 until Freddie's retirement from the same Chair in 1978 only three incumbents (1889–1937; Gibb 1937–55; Beeston 1955–78) occupied this prestigious office over a period of 89 years, a succession of virtually unparalleled distinction.

When the young Beeston arrived at Oxford, he found that Margoliouth's 'teaching methods were considered slightly odd, but they suited me admirably', for he required no spoon-feeding, was already familiar with the rudiments of some Semitic languages, and expected independent work under some pressure and with stringent demands. He was less impressed with the teacher (an ex-Indian civil servant) and his offerings in Persian which Freddie managed to neglect (as far as that was practicable without damaging his degree prospects) in favour of Arabic and South Arabian. While still an undergraduate, in 1932, he had attended the International Congress of Orientalists meeting at Leiden, that famous centre of Arabic scholarship. There he met for the first time Mgr Gonzague Ryckmans, one of the most renowned of the then tiny fraternity of South Arabian experts. He and his nephew Jacques Ryckmans have made Louvain a focal point of these studies throughout the twentieth century. Freddie wrote of the 'immense debt' he owed to G. Ryckmans for the help and encouragement he gave him in pursuit of his Epigraphic South Arabian (ESA) researches, especially after the retirement and subsequent death of Margoliouth.

I find it strange, in view of the fact that Freddie's name and major scholarly endeavours are so intimately associated with ESA, that he should have thought, if only for a brief moment, of that immense work as a 'spare time' occupation and 'hardly otherwise than as a very arcane sort of hobby, just as someone might . . . become an expert in the works of a very minor mediaeval poet'. True, the Arabic language was his bread-and-butter subject, the nomenclature of his Chair, and the focus of some of his most cerebral disquisitions—and, of course, the point of contact with his students and his principal teaching. But his greatest international fame is almost certainly based on his very extensive South Arabian work over the past fifty years: texts, grammar, lexicography, etc. There is no question of 'hobby' or 'minor' here! The present writer's teacher, the late H. J. Polotsky, was uncharacteristically indignant when some reviewer referred to the neo-Semitic languages on which HJP had worked as 'peripheral'. In the same way Feddie could not possibly allude in similar terms to his own ESA research which had occupied more than half his lifetime. Indeed, in the very same column of the *Oxford Magazine*, where the above-quoted observations were published, we also find the following more balanced passage:

> These twin passions, for Arabic language and literature, and for the ancient Yemeni inscriptions, have dominated my life since the age of fifteen; and they have been aided to a remarkable extent by a series of lucky chances. To be paid for doing what one most enjoys doing is surely the most blissful state of life.

The study of South Arabian, in its manifold manifestations, has expanded enormously during the last two or three decades, in terms of substance as well as in the number of its practitioners. To this consummation the labours of Freddie Beeston, Walter Müller, and Jacques Ryckmans have made an immense contribution.

I must return to the earlier parts of Freddie's career. Still in the course of his undergraduate days he obtained an interview with the Keeper of the Oriental Department of the British Museum Library and set out to him his ambitions in oriental librarianship. The Keeper promised to get in touch with him when the prospect of a vacancy arose, but he made it clear that that might not happen for some time to come. So Freddie settled down 'cheerfully' to his D.Phil. research, supported by two scholarships and by his father, for the next two years (1933–5). And then the unexpected happened—as so often it does—when in the summer of 1935 two vacancies arose: the British Museum wrote to invite him to present himself to be interviewed for a post requiring an Arabist, while at the Bodleian Library the Keeper of Oriental Books had suddenly died. He was succeeded by the next most senior member of the department which left a vacancy at the more junior level. Bodley's Librarian informed Freddie that the Curators intended to ask him to occupy the junior position. Professor (Sir) Godfrey Driver did not yet hold the personal Chair of Comparative Semitic Philology (which Freddie somewhat prematurely assigns to him in 1935—*Oxford Magazine*, p. 5), but he was an influential personality within the Oxford establishment and a prominent Bodleian Curator. It was no doubt Driver (as Freddie rightly surmised) who intervened in favour of the young orientalist—as he was to do again, most effectively, exactly twenty years later. Driver had then, and retained ever after, a large measure of respect for 'young Beeston' (as he used to refer to him until Freddie was nearly sixty).

'Faced with the choice between the two jobs, there could hardly be any hesitation about opting for the Bodleian one'. First, it was certain and required no further interviews; secondly, it was much easier to complete his D.Phil. thesis at Oxford than elsewhere (which he did in 1937); and lastly, he had come to like Oxford during the past six years and considered it now his 'natural home'. Indeed it remained very much his home for sixty-six years, from 1929, when the young undergraduate arrived, until 1995, when the celebrated scholar died suddenly at the entrance gate to his college. Oxford could have had few alumni and senior fellows more single-mindedly dedicated to her intramural charms and traditions than this faithful son of hers.

Incidentally, he did attend ('just for the devil of it') the interview with the Civil Service Commissioners about the British Museum post. But when asked what he would do if he were not appointed to this job, he had to confess that he had a firm offer from the Bodleian Library. The chairman clearly felt that he was wasting their time.

Freddie remained at the Bodleian for precisely twenty years, but his work was interrupted by six years of war service when he joined the army in the Intelligence Corps, first as lieutenant, later as captain. In January 1941 he sailed from Liverpool, by way of the Cape, to Suez; and, after just a few days in Cairo, he went to Palestine where he was stationed for the duration of the war. Among the papers in Mrs Fuller's custody is an army diary penned by Freddie in 1941–2. This was the first time that he lived in an Arabic-speaking environment, though army life naturally prevented total exposure to that ambience. He learnt something of the Palestinian colloquial, but it was apparently not sufficient to quell a violent scene when the Palestinian cook ran amok in the mess kitchen.

In *Sayhadica* he reports two amusing experiences: in an Arab café at Haifa he got into a conversation with some young Arab students who 'shot' at him the question how he would construe the grammar of the quotation '*táaddadati l-asbābu wa l-mawtu wāḥidun*' ('numerous are the causes (of death), while death itself is unique'). Freddie was, of course, able to give a full syntactical explanation, in terms of *waw al-ḥāl* and *taqdir*, 'thus vindicating Oxford training'. On another occasion he was one of a boisterous group seeing off a friend at Lydda railway station, when one of a gang of schoolboys shouted at him in the local Arabic patois 'is it beer or whiskey that you have been drinking?' His immediate response was the literary Arabic *kilāhumā* 'both of them' which caused the boys a good deal of hilarity. While they knew the classical expression from school or from the Qur'an (Surah 17:24), they would never have used it themselves.

It was in Palestine during the war that I first met Freddie, at an intelligence briefing at Sarafand. We happened to be sitting next to each other, and I noticed at once his remarkable booming bass voice. He was nine years my senior and held an important orientalist appointment at the Bodleian, while I had just finished my studies in Semitic languages and was about to set out for service in Eritrea-Ethiopia. Whereas my name was *tabula rasa*, his seemed somehow known to me, though I could not immediately place it in any particular context. It was only a little while later that I realised that he was the author of an epigraphic appendix to H. St J. B. Philby's *Sheba's Daughters* which had been published two or three years earlier. I did not see Freddie again until I came to Oxford not long after the war to join (Dame) Margery Perham's Institute of Colonial Studies. He received me with his accustomed cordiality and soon after suggested that I might be interested in cataloguing the Bodleian's Ethiopic manuscripts that had been acquired since Dillmann's splendid catalogue of 1848, just about a hundred years before this proposal. I accepted with alacrity, both *per se* and for the financial help this work offered. Our collaboration then marked the beginning of a long friendship.

Freddie had returned to Oxford and to the Bodleian Library in 1946. Meanwhile the Keeper of the Oriental Department had retired[6] and Freddie had been promoted and appointed to the vacancy in his absence in Palestine. The keepership itself had been upgraded to the rank of sub-librarian. So by the age of thirty-five he had reached the apex of his career as an orientalist librarian. He was thoroughly satisfied with his job in the Bodleian and enjoyed it greatly. He 'threw himself' into a number of cataloguing enterprises (including the completion of the Ethiopic catalogue which was published in 1951). He considered that 'perhaps the most enduring service to the Library had been the acquisition of several particularly fine MSS at pretty reasonable prices'. In the early years (1946–8) after his return to Bodley's he kept a detailed diary of his private and official as well as scholarly concerns. His

---

[6] Thus correctly in the *Oxford Magazine*, tacitly amending the erroneous 'died' in *Ṣayhadica*.

service to the Library is commemorated in an obituary article published in the *Bodleian Library Record*, April 1996.

During his time at Bodley's he continued vigorously with his South Arabian researches, a steady stream of articles flowing from his pen. He also taught South Arabian texts occasionally and numbered among those attending his classes the present writer as well as A. J. Drewes (*Sayhadica*, p. XVIII). He forgot to mention that he also supervised the very successful D.Phil. thesis of Arthur Irvine (who later became Reader in Semitic Languages at SOAS) on South Arabian epigraphic material connected with irrigation techniques. To me it was a great pleasure when he was appointed (together with David Winton Thomas, Regius Professor of Hebrew in the University of Cambridge) examiner of my Oxford D.Phil. dissertation on the subject of the relationship of classical Ethiopic to the modern Ethiopian languages. Although neither of them was an expert in this particular subject, both had taken immense trouble and proved to be very knowledgeable and congenial examiners. I think he felt that the only drawback of his Bodleian appointment was the fact that in the library he could not indulge in his habit of chain-smoking cigarettes; I frequently observed, however, that on the short distance between the old and the new buildings of the Bodleian he would briefly light up and smoke part of a cigarette.

In 1953 the late Joseph Schacht, who had been Reader in Arabic at Oxford, left for the prestigious Chair of Arabic at Leiden (and subsequently moved to the United States).[7] H. A. R. (later Sir Hamilton) Gibb, the then incumbent of the Laudian Chair of Arabic, spoke to Freddie and others about the problem of finding a successor. He appears to have sounded him out, perhaps somewhat obliquely, whether he would be interested in this post. But to the Keeper of the Bodleian Oriental Department there were no obvious advantages, neither of promotion nor of finance, in such a move. The situation was quite different, however, when in 1955 Gibb departed for Harvard University and the Laudian Chair became vacant. Freddie entertained no thoughts of the succession, but Professor (Sir) Godfrey Driver, one of the principal electors, urged him in the strongest terms to apply—a request to which Freddie yielded with some reluctance and indeed trepidation.

After his application had eventually been submitted, 'in deference to Driver's bidding', I received a summons from the latter to come to

---

[7] Beeston's account of this matter contains a number of minor factual errors (*Sayhadica*, p. XVIII).

Oxford 'on an urgent and secret mission' (I was teaching at St Andrews University at that time) and was asked to let him have a short paper for the electors on Beeston's prowess as a teacher of South Arabian and as an examiner in Ethiopic. No easier or more congenial task had ever been entrusted to me. Some weeks later I got one of Driver's characteristic postcards which read:

> Dear U.,
> Isaiah 55: 11[8]
> Yours
> G.R.D.

I never doubted that Driver would succeed in the task he had set himself, and to the knowledgeable and the prescient it was the obvious and desirable denouement.

But the successful candidate himself, when told of the decision, had a feeling 'almost of alarm'; this appeared to be shared, Beeston continues, by a correspondent to *The Times* who criticised this appointment to the most prestigious Chair of Arabic in the world.[9] I penned a private note of protest to the writer of that letter and suggested that the time was bound to come when he would have to eat his words. I got no reply, but many years later that scholar invited me to lunch at his college; and before any greetings were uttered he said to me: '*touché*'. To my genuine sense of puzzlement he responded, 'You were right about Beeston! I wanted you to see me eat my words'. Nothing further was said on this subject.

Freddie's acceptance of the Chair of Arabic was not a decision taken lightly, but at forty-four he reckoned that this was his best chance, in mid-career, to take on a teaching and research appointment of a kind that was unlikely to recur. He later wrote (and at the time declared) that his 'equipment in Arabic was much less comprehensive than that of my illustrious predecessors in the Chair'. This *may* initially have been the case: Margoliouth was, of course, a polymath who had spread his wings over a vast area, while Gibb ('a daunting succession') had written a monograph on modern Arabic literature and was, above all, 'a very

---

[8] 'So shall my word be that issues from my mouth; it shall not return to me fruitless without accomplishing my purpose; it has succeeded in the task I set it'.

[9] Freddie's recollection of this letter to *The Times* is not quite accurate: 'G. Elwell-Sutton of Durham' (read in any event 'L. P. Elwell-Sutton of Edinburgh') was not the writer, but it was a much more distinguished scholar, in a different discipline, who neither referred to Beeston as a 'mere administrator' (*Ṣayhadica*) nor as a 'mere librarian' (*Oxford Magazine*) but as 'an antiquarian who does not speak colloquial Arabic'.

distinguished historian' as well as a man of affairs. In those fields
Freddie considered himself 'notably deficient'. Though Arabic language and literature cannot be studied without some basic knowledge
of Islam, the new Professor always refused to present himself 'as in any
way an authority on Islam as a religion or on Islamic history'. He
pursued this line unfailingly, and when some Arabist or Islamic scholar
was under consideration for election to the British Academy, Freddie
rigorously declined to offer an opinion on the Islamic aspect. Yet, Gibb
would have been the first to acknowledge that he was no grammarian or
linguist and that in that area of Arabic Freddie was his superior and
indeed became, with time, everybody else's as well.

Of great weight in his decision to allow his name to go forward for
the Chair was the prospect of a professorial fellowship at St John's
College (to which the Laudian Chair is affiliated), a privilege he valued
very highly: 'nothing in my career has given me more pleasure and
comfort than my membership of that friendly and generous society.'
Being unmarried he enjoyed that company of scholars and friends to the
full. Here he entertained his colleagues (and often their wives) in some
style and graciousness. He was knowledgeable on food and a dab hand
at cooking. As a guest he was always much appreciated, for he ate
unstintingly and with genuine discrimination. On occasion he would say
to me 'is it not time for me to have another taste of Dina's *zuppa di
pesce*?!'

While the Academy (to which he was elected in 1965, in the same
year as myself) was somehow slow to attach him to committees or to
admit him to its inner counsels and offices, his college made much use
of his manifold qualifications and allowed him to serve as Dean of
Degrees for twenty-six years. Few people can visualise the Sheldonian
Theatre without his gowned and ample figure with his long white hair.
At Oxford he was widely known and much in demand as a scholar as
well as socially. He also served with much aplomb on scholarly bodies
outside Oxford: he was elected to the Council of the Royal Asiatic
Society and was appointed to the Governing Body of the School of
Oriental and African Studies. He was assiduous in his attendance of
meetings, but his membership of the last-named body was not renewed,
no doubt because his scholarly conscience was unable to sanction one
or two aberrant decisions in areas where his particular expertise should
have carried crucial weight. He became the linchpin in the annual
Seminar for Arabian Studies whose foundation and prospering owed
much to his personality, drive, and devotion.

Freddie's teaching commitments in Arabic grew apace. In the pre-war and immediate post-war years the number of undergraduates reading Arabic had been very small. It was only in the fifties and early sixties that the large influx of candidates taking Arabic began. In Alan Jones and Donald Richards Freddie had two highly congenial colleagues of marked ability to whom he was devoted—and they no doubt to him. Later M. M. Badawi and F. Zimmermann, and subsequently Robin Ostle, lent further strength to this happy team. While the heavy teaching load 'put a severe strain on us all', Freddie was 'thankful to have had that experience . . . for I have found that teaching is an invaluable background to research; being obliged to present material in a way comprehensible to those who know nothing to start with clears one's own mind in a way that nothing else would do'. This recognition will be shared by all those of us who have been fortunate enough to have encountered undergraduates of a calibre to benefit from the type of instruction a scholar like Beeston was able to impart. Quite a few of us have met pupils or former pupils taught by Freddie and have been impressed not only with their standard in Arabic but especially with their esteem for their teacher's meticulous method of conveying knowledge—and indeed for his personality. Many of them have remained his friends.

In later years he was much in demand as an examiner of doctoral theses. If the subject and the candidate interested him, these examinations could be very prolonged. His attention to detail could on some occasions be such that it bordered on pedantry—if such a notion had not been quite alien to his character and general disposition. I remember at least one such doctoral inquisition which took place in my room at SOAS and stretched to close on six hours, only interrupted by lunch. It was not that he entertained doubts about the result but rather that his interest in the substance and the quality of the examinee's responses let him forget the effluxion of time—until in the end I had to explain that my room had to be vacated. Incidentally, the candidate concerned was (Professor) Simon Hopkins FBA.

As a reviewer Freddie was painstaking in the extreme. If the work under review was within the centre of his scholarly interests (and normally he only accepted commissions of that nature), he would scrutinise, analyse, and explore it to a remarkable extent. Such an examination could be severe, but it would always be just and directed *ad rem*, never *ad hominem*. He genuinely felt that his duty as a reviewer had not been properly discharged, unless he had explained to the reader and the author what the substance of his objections or assent was. Some potential reviewees were in fear of the impending avalanche, a few may have been aggrieved; but the proper reaction to so knowledgeable an assessment of one's work by so eminent an authority should have been gratification at such a fate. I remember well that I sent Freddie a passage of the typescript of one of my earliest books for comment. When I received his animadversions I included them as an extensive footnote *ad locum* (*The Semitic Languages of Ethiopia*, pp. 8 and 9). The reviews of the book which subsequently appeared almost invariably singled out Beeston's footnote for special praise and said fairly little about the rest of the book. His comments were an ornament to the book and enlightening to the reader and to myself.

My Beeston file containing correspondence from 1948 to 1995 forms a precious collection of Freddie's thoughts on many aspects of Semitic languages. Nearly all his letters deal with matters of scholarship and would make, if published, a valuable addition to his *oeuvre*. They are concerned with many disparate subjects over a wide range of Semitics, e.g. on Ge'ez (classical Ethiopic) orthography and in particular on variant spelling patterns of sibilants in epigraphic contexts as well as in MSS; and in the same letter questions on the advisability of acquiring certain MSS for the Bodleian (letter of 2 March 1951). Or: how to deal with a request by Sylvia Pankhurst for photographs of an Ethiopic MS which is inadequately identified (10 February 1954); some choice information about a collection (uncatalogued) of Ethiopic MSS in the possession of the London Library (9 June 1954). A long and very detailed letter on Ugaritic etymologies; on Sidney Smith's monograph on the history of the sixth century in Arabia; and on Caskel's Lihyan and Lihyanic (15 December 1954). On 13 April 1962 he writes about reviews of his *A Descriptive Grammar of Epigraphic South Arabian* (London, 1962, 1st ed.), of Littmann-Höfner's *Tigre Wörterbuch*, and about an Aden-based political officer who wishes to write on Mahri (modern South Arabian). All his letters are full of interesting ideas and ought to be more widely known; there are about a hundred of them and they decrease in frequency with my return to live at Oxford in 1970 when we could meet or speak on the telephone. Quite a few of his missives begin: 'Now that I've finished this (typescript enclosed), I feel thoroughly dissatisfied with it . . .' (21 March 1971). This is a typical example of Freddie's modesty and self-critical attitude to his own work. Over the next year or two I shall consider whether it might be possible to find a publisher for Freddie's correspondence on Semitic languages (cf. my edition of the late H. J. Polotsky's (Corresponding Fellow) Collected Letters, Stuttgart, 1992).

During his tenure of the Bodleian Keepership and, later, of the Chair of Arabic Freddie 'continued throughout it all to concern myself with research in South Arabian studies':

> I had only very limited time in which to do so. But my output in published articles is very large, and at the same time varied in quality. I have always held that a learned journal is the place not only for definitive results of research but also for a dialectical process in which hypotheses may be put forward for discussion, which may either validate or invalidate them. My total output in articles would hence need considerable sifting in order to extract what might possibly be regarded as an abiding contribution to the subject; the rest is better forgotten.
>
> In the earlier half of my time as professor, I produced little concerned with Arabic properly speaking, since I was preoccupied both with the day-to-day routine of teaching and with myself learning and gaining experience. It is only in the more recent years that I have published much in respect of Arabic.

I have quoted these passages from *Sayhadica* because they reflect accurately Freddie's self-effacing manner as well as his attitude towards the respective demands of teaching and publication. His (select) bibliography attached to *Sayhadica* covers the years 1937–86 but is very incomplete. His friend, Mr Michael Macdonald, is to publish a full bibliography in the *Proceedings of the Seminar for Arabian Studies*. My own library contains about a hundred items of Beestoniana, articles as well as books, but this, too, is very far from the complete tally. Most of his contributions have appeared in the form of articles, his preferred means of expressing his ideas (as he explains in the above-quoted extract). Even his books are not large tomes but relatively small volumes composed with considerable concision. Among the latter I would single out his *Baidāwī's Commentary on Surah 12, Written Arabic, The Arabic Language Today, Samples of Arabic Prose*, the important *Sabaic Grammar* (2nd ed.—which received a masterly review penned by no less a connoisseur than Walter Müller), and the *Sabaic Dictionary*, jointly composed with his colleagues Ghul, Müller, and Ryckmans. On the last-named work I have written a few pages of commentary in the Beeston Festschrift (*Arabicus Felix*—see below).

In terms of pure cerebral distinction his *The Arabic Language Today* (1970) stands out as a masterpiece which summarises in some 120 pages the salient elements of that highly complex and beautiful tongue. It is a slim and elegantly produced volume which represents something of a landmark in the study and description of a Semitic language. I do not know of any comparable work that manages, with such economy of language, to offer a reasonably full, succinct, and reliable introduction (couched in terms that are acceptable to the contemporary student of language) to any Semitic tongue. The editor of the series in which this work appears could not have made a better choice for the authorship of a modern book on the Arabic language. At a time when most Arabists have become *islamisants* and most Hebraists have turned into *Alttestamentler*, Freddie Beeston has adhered to the Arabist's first and principal concern, i.e. the study of the Arabic language.

It would undoubtedly have been easier to write a book twice the size of this volume, for the conciseness of formulation and economy of descriptive detail are apt to conceal the vast amount of thought and sheer intellectual effort that must have gone into the planning and execution of this work. The extreme succinctness makes it at times quite a difficult book to read, and I rather doubt whether it is appropriate diet for the novice. Essentially it tells us how the Arabic language works and how its operations relate to the underlying principles and theoretical bases. In the Arabic—as opposed to South Arabian—field, this is the present writer's favourite Beeston book.

In 1983 the Lidzbarski Committee (Spitaler, Rosenthal, Caquot, Ullendorff), on behalf of the Deutsche Morgenländische Gesellschaft, resolved to award the Lidzbarski Medal for Semitic epigraphy to Freddie Beeston. The decision was unanimous and was widely welcomed and approved. Beeston was, perhaps, the first scholar who received this medal in the most literal conformity with the testator's wishes, i.e. that it should be bestowed on someone whose principal work had been in epigraphy. The immediately preceding recipient had been H. J. Polotsky. The latter warmly concurred with the choice of the electors and expressed his pleasure that Beeston should be his successor. Such manifestations of approval were extremely rare and generally alien to the austere temperament of Polotsky who was always economical with praise. In a letter to the present writer (p. 110, top, of his Collected Letters, 1992) he said: 'I feel greatly honoured that Beeston should succeed me in the bestowal of the Lidzbarski Medal, although I must insist on my special position as the only Lidzbarski pupil in receipt of this honour'.

Polotsky's judgement, as the foremost Semitist of our generation, is particularly germane, for he expressed similarly complimentary feelings for Beeston's work also elsewhere: 'The feature (*naʻt sababiyy*) . . .

has been defined with greater precision by Professor A. F. L. Beeston;
. . . his description of this phenomenon in his *Arabic Language Today*,
94–5, and his comments therein contain practically all that needs to be
said on this topic . . . ; my present note is not to dilute . . . Beeston's
beautifully compact formulation . . .' (*Israel Oriental Studies*, 1978,
159). When I showed this passage to Freddie he was both pleased and
embarrassed, for he knew to value approval from that source. Unhap-
pily, circumstances conspired against my repeated attempts to bring
those two giants of Semitic scholarship together at the same place and
at the same time; both were, however, aware of each other's worth.

In n. 1 I have referred to the Festschrift in Freddie's honour published in *Sayhadica* 1987. In 1991, for his eightieth birthday, Alan
Jones, his close colleague, organised and edited another volume in
Freddie's honour, with contributions by his friends, colleagues, and
former pupils. It appeared under the brilliant and highly appropriate
title *Arabicus Felix* (punned on his second Christian name), *Luminosus
Britannicus*, and covered four areas of study in which Freddie had
shown a special interest: the Yemen, Arabic language and literature,
modern Arabic literature, and Semitica. There is also a lively introduction by Michael Gilsenan and an *envoi*, a *jeu d'esprit*, by Geoffrey
Lewis.

Gilsenan has splendidly caught the essentials of Freddie's remarkable personality in his fine essay:

> . . . He was a personage more exotic . . . than any of our Hadrami friends.
> He was clearly in his element too, this professor whose approachability also
> contained surely some quality of shyness and reserve. I mentioned to Freddie
> that I was due to go up to Pembroke College, Oxford, in October 1960 to
> read English, but I was thinking now of switching to Arabic . . . The
> invitation to come and see the Laudian Professor at St John's was warm
> and immediate. And so, with a chance and in this case unforgettable
> encounter, the course of one's life changed.
>
> Freddie sat down with the text of a pre-Islamic poem with all the relish of
> a wine connoisseur before a great claret. His eyes shone, notes and commen-
> taries were lovingly and meticulously scanned, metres established, subtleties
> of translation propounded, meanings elucidated. He was obviously . . . a
> lover of language, avid for learning, delighted by inquiry. Even a student like
> myself, temperamentally little inclined to the classical discipline, began to
> see that language need not be treated as 'dead' and that one could become
> enthused by these apparently arcane and abstruse topics of textual construc-
> tion.
>
> How many hours were spent in his room at St John's or in one of the large
> number of classes at the new Oriental Institute . . . with its wonderful

innovation of a shared coffee room? And did ever a professor spend so much time teaching undergraduates? . . . In my tutorials with him there were often agonising silences as he waited for me to translate. No spoon-feeding there, but a gentle insistence that one look at context and grammar and struggle for an answer. It was a very demanding form of teaching and often made a student sweat with embarrassed discomfort, or hope that a coughing fit would distract him, but it never did. . . .

. . . Gradually, the complete unpretentiousness, the manifest pleasure in and reverence for Arabic language and literature, and the terrifyingly lavish supplies of sherry or beer in a pub after a class gave us a greater awareness and appreciation of the person. That it was so was due mostly to the realisation that we mattered to him . . . and that he was not concerned only with high-flyers or the number of firsts and that students were central to his life, students and St John's College.

Freddie obviously took the rites and ceremonies of Oxford with the greatest seriousness. College, chapel, high table, these were central to his world, and he was courteous and generous in his invitations to students. That world in its higher reaches remained largely mysterious, but first nervous participations in high table as his guest were made easier by recognising the same delight as he took in travelling in South Arabia. . . . This was obviously not the stereotype of the bachelor don . . . devoted only to some obscure subject; Freddie was a mine of information and knowledge on any number of obscure subjects, but beyond that an immensely sociable man.

Gilsenan's portrait will be recognised as remarkably apposite and as offering a key to Freddie's personality, at once complex as well as revelatory. It would be hard to improve on this characterisation. All of us were also aware of his physical strength, of the exertions in travelling he undertook at the age of eighty-four, the number of publications— never decreasing in quantity or quality—the personal contacts, the academic and social engagements, the conferences and papers and reviews. We thought this amplitude of activities would go on for ever. Then, one day he telephoned me about a colleague's paper on Ethiopian names in Sabaic; would I let him have my candid opinion: 'but don't reply to my home address; don't write to Iffley but to St John's; I have returned to live in college, temporarily'. In reply to my question he said, in a matter-of-fact tone, 'I have contracted cancer of the colon, and it is easier to be in town for my visits to hospital'. This was a terrible blow, especially for a man who had never known any illness or weakness throughout his life. His friends rallied and visited him. He himself carried on fairly normally and certainly uncomplainingly. We spoke on the telephone frequently, mostly on matters of scholarship.

My wife and I were in Scotland during the first week of October 1995 when we saw the death announcement in the personal columns of *The Times* on 5 October. He had died on 29 September. Apparently, after a convivial evening, he went out briefly the following morning and on his return collapsed and died by the Porter's Lodge of St John's. For him it was a merciful death within the precincts of the college he loved; for his friends and colleagues it was a truly irreparable loss. *The Times* and the *Independent* had wonderful and very detailed obituaries on 6 and 7 October, respectively; the latter written by Donald Richards and the former (I would confidently surmise) by Alan Jones, both former pupils and devoted colleagues. The funeral service took place at St Mary Magdalen Church close by his college, a High Church service which Freddie, a devout Christian, favoured.[10] The congregation was very large, many standing in the aisles and overflowing outside the church. So many people wished to take their leave of this prominent Oxonian. There was genuine and widespread mourning. The memorial service took place in the same church some six weeks later; the address was delivered by Robin Ostle, Arabist and Fellow of St John's.

There were giants in the earth in those days (Genesis 6:4).

EDWARD ULLENDORFF
*Fellow of the Academy*

*Note.* The present writer is particularly obliged for information and documents kindly made available by Freddie Beeston's only surviving relative, his niece (daughter of his elder sister), Mrs S. Fuller of Witney, Oxfordshire. I also wish to acknowledge gratefully assistance given by the following: Sir Keith Thomas; Alan Jones; Donald Richards; Michael Macdonald; C. F. Beckingham; Miss Susan Churchill and Miss Rosemary Lambeth, both of the British Academy; M. M. Badawi; and Adrian Roberts of the Bodleian Library.

# Appendix

Nearly all of Freddie Beeston's correspondence was concerned with aspects of scholarship to the virtual exclusion of all private matters. I have referred to this in the main part of this memoir, but I thought it might be of interest to readers to have two specimens of his epistolary

---

[10] Very occasionally he would agree to deliver a sermon in St John's Chapel. One such address, dated 28 October 1973, survives in a typescript of five pages.

genre, one of his early period and one of a more recent vintage—
divided by some thirty years. I am appending these samples partly
because *le style c'est l'homme* and partly because the facts and opinions
described in them have not, as far as I know, been made generally
available.

65a St Giles
Oxford, 31.8.51

Dear Ullendorff,

Many thanks for your most valuable letter. I fear that there is no likelihood of
my paper being published in the near future, since it obviously needs a good
deal of recasting and polishing before it would be fit to print. If there is
anything in it useful for your work, you are welcome to use it; but if you
want actually to quote, I should prefer not to have this first preliminary draft
brought up against me, but will try and produce a second draft as soon as my
various commitments permit.

For the moment, I should merely like to discuss one or two of the points
raised in your letter.

(1) I would by no means oppose the statement that South Arabian colo-
nists brought the South Arabian alphabet into Africa (though I would be
reluctant to think that this could have been as early as 500 BC); nor would I
oppose the statement that South Semitic speech came into Africa from South
Arabia. What I do object to is the implication (which is certainly present in
Diringer's words, although he may not perhaps have intended it that way)
that it was the *same* wave of colonization which was responsible for both
developments. The two things seem to me to belong to quite different stages
historically.

(2) The mimation is irrelevant to our linguistic problem, because it is a
common Semitic feature, shared with other languages—Accadian, where it
is present in full force, and Hebrew where it has left some traces. The same is
true of the deictic *n* insofar as it is a component in various adverbial,
pronominal and conjunctional forms. These features are not specifically
characteristic of ESA. What *is* peculiarly characteristic of ESA is the regular
and extensive use of this deictic *n* as an affix to *nouns, in the function of a
definite article*. Since this usage has imposed itself on all the four ESA
dialects, which otherwise have indications of very diverse origins, and is
not found in other Semitic languages, it must be regarded as a linguistic
innovation in the ESA dialects. It therefore seems to me a wholly unsub-
stantiated hypothesis to conclude, on the basis of the presence of the deictic *n*
in Ge'ez adverbs, that Ge'ez has 'lost' a nominal termination which it once
possessed.

(3) I would agree that Ur-Ge'ez (if I may coin a term) must at some period
have been spoken in South Arabia; and also that the linguistic resemblances
between Ge'ez and ESA point to a period in which UG was in geographical

contiguity with the parents of the ESA dialects. It is doubtful, however, whether these periods coincided; and I find it difficult to believe that either of them can have coincided to any large extent with the period in which ESA is historically attested, otherwise, as I have said, the distinctive features of ESA which had the power to impose themselves on all the ESA dialects, would have spread to UG too.

(4) Your remarks on the influence of the Cushitic substratum are fully justified. At the same time, it is worth remembering that ESA itself was imposed on a non-Semitic substratum, which is ethnographically prevalent even today. Theoretically, one might perhaps envisage some of the differences between Ge'ez and ESA as arising on the Arabian side from the pre-Semitic Arabian peoples (this of course presupposes that the residence of the UG speakers in South Arabia was brief and transitional).

(5) As regards Ethiopic archaeology, you speak with authority. Nevertheless, the fact remains that in South Arabia, even without any systematic excavation, thousands of inscriptions of the seven centuries immediately B.C. have turned up; in Ethiopia they have not.

(6) In your final paragraph, on the motivation of the Ethiopic vowelled script, surely we are in complete agreement? You say that you cannot agree that the Ge'ez people should have behaved in very much the same way as the South Arabians, for the circumstances were completely different. This was precisely my argument, though put the other way round—that *because* the Ge'ez people did not behave like their South Arabian neighbours, *therefore* the circumstances must have been different.

I am off to Istanbul next week, but hope that we may continue this discussion, which to me at any rate is most profitable.

Yours sincerely,

A. F. L. Beeston

Dear Edward,                                                    15.9.81

As you know, in 1951 a campaign of excavation was undertaken at Timna' in the lower Wadi Bayhan (at that time in the Eastern Protectorate of Aden), the ancient metropolis of the kingdom of Qataban. This was done under the aegis of the 'American Foundation for the Study of Man', which in fact was created by and entirely financed by the subsequently deceased Wendell Phillips. Two epigraphists were invited to join the expedition, Professor Honeyman of St. Andrews and Professor A. Jamme (now of the Catholic University of America). These two did not, however, work in collaboration; they divided the area of the excavations between them and each assumed sole responsibility for the inscriptions discovered in his own sector. The inscriptions were recorded in the form of latex squeezes.

Jamme's portion of the finds has been published. Of Honeyman's share one single photograph, without any transcription or editorial work, was published in the Biblical Archaeologist for February 1952. The remainder has been ever since in Professor Honeyman's possession, without a particle of information of any kind about it being divulged to the learned world.

According to the very few people who have been permitted even a cursory glance at the collection of squeezes, it comprises several dozen substantial texts which must certainly be of the utmost importance for the study of the ancient history and language of Qataban. Experience at other sites makes it all too probable that, once unearthed, many of the original monuments will have been destroyed in subsequent years, or even if they survive may well have been dispersed and thus lost the indispensable link with their original archaeological setting.

On Professor Honeyman's removal from St. Andrews to the north of Scotland, this collection of squeezes was packed into a box (or boxes) and stored along with his library in a barn-like structure at his new residence. While one must deplore the fact that for thirty years the scholarly world has been denied access to these important materials, the situation now is even graver. He is said to be in hospital and apparently totally incapacitated physically; and there is an increasing danger that his library may be disposed of, and the collection of squeezes either destroyed by someone ignorant of their scientific value, or at least disposed of in some way which will make it difficult to trace their fate. Research on ancient South Arabia urgently needs these precious materials, and it is high time that some move should be made to safeguard them in some way which will ensure their presentation to the world. While it is true that latex itself is virtually indestructible, it is far from sure that squeezes will not progressively deteriorate the longer they are kept in boxes.

When next you go to Scotland, could you please discuss this with Honeyman?

Yours,
Freddie

CHARLES BRINK

*Proceedings of the British Academy*, **94**, 319–354

# Charles Oscar Brink
# 1907–1994

CHARLES OSCAR BRINK was born Karl Oskar Levy on 13 March 1907 in Charlottenburg, a town later to be incorporated within the city of Berlin. He changed his surname on 31 August 1931 and his first names in March 1948, having been known already for some time to English friends as 'Charles'. He died in Cambridge on 2 March 1994.

Between 1963 and 1982 Brink published three large volumes on those poems by Horace which concerned poetry itself. These gained for him an authority in every active centre of Latin studies. He was engaged on an edition of Tacitus' *Dialogus de oratoribus* and held the office of President of the International Commission in charge of the *Thesaurus Linguae Latinae* (*ThLL*) when he died. He wanted to be remembered above all as a Latin scholar. It should, however, also be recalled that by middle age he had won some eminence as a historian of post-Aristotelian Greek philosophy and that many credited him with having helped to move British study of ancient philosophy away from an exclusive concern with Plato and Aristotle.

Scholarship cannot claim Brink's whole person. He played a large role in the struggles which took place over the classical curriculum in English schools and universities during the 1960s and 1970s. He was for many years an influential member of the council of an ancient Cambridge college and could fairly be regarded as one of the founding fathers of a new one. When an account comes to be written of the contribution made from 1933 onwards to Anglo-Saxon science, scholarship and cultural life

© The British Academy 1997.

by men and women educated in Imperial or Weimar Germany, he will be seen as a figure of some significance.

Brink's courteous bearing struck everyone from those who taught him at school to those who only came across him for the first time when he was an old man. Beneath it lay not only a genuine respect for social convention but also a quite uncomplicated joy in the company of other human beings. In conversation he always steered the subject towards the interests of the other party. He did not like to talk about himself. A powerful ambition, directed at least as much by the causes he believed in and by the interests of friends he respected as by any kind of egotism, did not escape notice. In the political disputes of academe he never adverted noisily to his own aims but was wont to press hard particular points he thought might find favour with others. Strongly conservative though he was in personal behaviour, religious practice, and political opinion, he kept his eyes firmly on the present and his thoughts on the future. Straightforward intellectual disagreement drew him towards rather than away from the person of an opponent. His persistence knew no bounds. He had more close friends among his elders and juniors than among his contemporaries, but it cannot be denied he also had enemies. Not surprisingly, stories abound which are either unverifiable or demonstrably untrue. These tell more on the whole about their purveyors than about Brink himself, and they have been ignored in this memoir.

## Berlin

Brink's father, Arthur Levy II, and mother, Elise Misch, were the children of prosperous Jewish businessmen born in Berlin. Two years after Brink's birth, Arthur Levy moved from Charlottenburg to Berlin and registered as a lawyer (*Rechtsanwalt*) at the lower court (*Amtsgericht*) of the working-class district of Wedding. In November 1918 he was serving in the counter-intelligence section of the General Staff. At meetings in the barracks during the revolution he spoke strongly against the Spartacists. After he returned to civil life his career prospered. He was appointed a notary in September 1922. He enjoyed the respect of senior judges and regarded himself as a loyal citizen of Germany. He could never understand why in May 1933 he should have been stripped of his notaryship or in October 1938 forbidden all practice of law. Elise Misch is said to have been a woman of great intelligence, wide cultural interests, and open emotions. The two sons to the marriage were registered as being of the 'Mosaic' religion. The household maintained, however, few, if any, peculiarly Jewish customs. The musical, artistic, and literary culture of the Christian bourgeoisie enjoyed, on the other hand, more respect than it did in many an Evangelical or Catholic household. The young Brink (henceforth B.) played the piano from an early age.

The Lessing Gymnasium in Wedding, which B. entered in 1916, was a school of the type his father attended. It taught a large amount of Latin, Greek, and mathematics, far more indeed than it did German, history, geography, religion, French, and natural science put together. Parents who wanted for their children a career in the higher administration of the State, in the Church, in law, in medicine, or in the universities chose such a school rather than a *Realgymnasium* or an *Oberrealschule*.

B. did well in all his studies. A medical certificate had him excused from physical training. Those who taught him Latin and Greek were less enthusiastic in their praise than those who taught him German, history, and geography. He made a 'good' contribution to an *Arbeitsgemeinschaft* on German literature and a 'very good' one to another such group on philosophy. In what ways the approach to the German poets differed from that to the Greeks and the Romans it would be interesting to know. A Rabbi Dr Alexander rated B.'s knowledge of religion as 'good'. B. directed the school orchestra in a way which excited general admiration.

B.'s schooling ended in the summer of 1925. A coalition government under the chancellorship of Hans Luther, a man who had moved from administration into politics without joining a party, had been in office since 16 January. Paul von Hindenburg, a military man not identified with any party, had been elected President of the Republic on 26 April. The publication of the first volume of Adolf Hitler's *Mein Kampf* on 19 July had passed almost without notice. B. remained for a time undecided about a future career. He began to take instruction in musical composition, with thoughts of becoming an orchestral conductor—no totally fanciful ambition in the Berlin of the 1920s. In November he entered the Friedrich Wilhelm University with the intention of devoting himself in the main to philosophy. During the winter semester he attended the lectures of Werner Jaeger (1888–1961) 'on the foundations [*Grundlagen*] of humanism'. Jaeger's charismatic manner had a strong effect on him, as it had on other young men of an anxious and disturbed era. B. was to shake off much of Jaeger's influence, but he could still recall with admiration in 1961 'an ability to make an intellectual position a personal one between teacher and learner . . . to communicate himself, at a high intellectual level, when he taught'. He also went in that semester to lectures given by Paul Maas (1880–1964) on the metres of Greek poetry. In the summer semester of 1926 he listened to Ulrich von Wilamowitz-Moellendorff (1848–1931) on the history of the Greek language and to Eduard Norden (1868–1941) on the history of Latin literature. By the end of the academic year he was determined to become himself a professor of classical philology. He attached himself firmly to Jaeger, a scholar at the height of his powers and reputation in the late 1920s, and a personage of weight and resonance in high places.

A scholarship enabled B. to spend the summer semester of 1928 in Oxford. W. D. Ross (1877–1971), fellow of Oriel College and deputy White's professor of moral philosophy, who had been for some time on friendly terms with Jaeger, looked after the visit. B. found the atmosphere of the ancient English university more congenial than Berlin's and treasured the memory of the personal tutorials he received and the lectures he heard: on Kant from Ross, on Cicero from A. C. Clark (1859–1937), and on Roman history from H. M. Last (1894–1957). It was in Oxford that he came across for the first time both the poetry and the philological writing of A. E. Housman (1859–1936).

B. completed with the winter semester of 1928–9 the attendance at classes formally required of him by the Berlin philosophy faculty. In the Latin *vita* which accompanied the dissertation he submitted in September 1931 he listed as his teachers Jaeger, Maas, Ferdinand Noack (1868–1931), Norden, Wolfgang Schadewaldt (1900–74), Wilhelm Schulze (1863–1935), Eduard Spranger (1882–1969), Wilamowitz, and Ulrich Wilcken (1862–1944). The German *Lebenslauf* which he attached in May or June of 1933 to a number of copies of the printed version of the dissertation omits Maas from the list, and adds Franz Beckmann (1895–1966) and Richard Harder (1896–1957). One of the few things in his early life B. liked to talk about was his presence at the final meeting of Wilamowitz's seminar in the summer of 1929, but he hesitated to call himself one of the great man's pupils. He and Maas were to be fellow employees of the Clarendon Press between 1939 and 1941.

B.'s personal charm and social grace brought him many friends among the children of well-to-do Christian families studying at the

Friedrich Wilhelm University. He took a keen interest in political debate and often expressed himself critically about the economic policies of the coalitions which tried to govern Germany up to 30 May 1932. If he voted, it would, I think, have been for the Deutsche Nationale Volkspartei (DNVP) at federal and state elections, and for Hindenburg at the presidential elections of April 1932. The national question obsessed him. He came to think that a religion as well as a language, habits, and a culture defined an inhabitant of Germany as truly German, in other words as a member of the nation. Early in 1931 he joined the Evangelical Church of the Old-Prussian Union, an act which caused no breach with his family. On 31 August he gained permission to assume the surname 'Brink', an obsolete German name semantically associated with the land (*Brink*, a hilly piece of grassland), but phonetically similar to 'Ring', the original family name of both his grandmothers. Writing to a friend on 27 February 1933 Jaeger declared:

> Dr. Brink [Jaeger anticipated the formal conferment of the degree] . . . ist ein gebildeter, geistig feiner Mensch, nicht urkräftig, aber gewandt und elastisch, und intellektuell und künstlerisch hat er Niveau . . . Ich verschweige nicht, daß er Jude von Herkunft ist. Man merkt es ihm kaum an, wenn man es nicht weiß, zumal er bewußt sich davon loszulösen und in der deutschen Kultur und Nation aufzugehen strebt. Politisch denkt er ziemlich 'rechts'.

It would be easy to see worldly ambition as the motor of B.'s adhesion to Christianity. The teaching of Greek and Latin in Germany, as in other European lands, was part of a system of education which derived its authority from the churches which operated it. Secularisation did not destroy, indeed it helped to feed, the notion that a teacher of the German youth should be in some sense a Christian. Even in comparatively liberal Berlin the professoriate was reluctant to admit a Jew to its ranks unless he had been at least formally baptised. Nothing, however, in B. suggests the opportunist. He thought long and hard about the intellectual implications of his decision. He customarily emphasised that it was the Lutheran wing of the Prussian church—conservative in regard to theology, forms of cult, organisation, and relations with the state and the nation—to which he adhered. A suspicion of Calvinism and its spiritual descendants manifested itself in some 1932 remarks about the writings of Alfred de Quervains (1896–1968) on theology and politics (see bibliography, no. 2, *7) and remained with him all his life. Again, although he was to move ten years later from the Prussian to the Anglican church, the basic character of his churchmanship did not change, and no one who knew him in later life could doubt the depth of his religiousness. The character of his view of religion should not be overlooked in any consideration of his view of classics. He came to reject the romantic paganising of the subject's principal exponents and harked back to a time when Christianity and classical culture seemed to move in tandem.

In the summer of 1929, B. began to give Jaeger assistance with the editing of *Die Antike*, a journal which the latter had founded in 1925 for the purpose of providing men and women of the middle and upper classes with scientific knowledge of antiquity relevant to their intellectual lives, whether they had attended a humanistic gymnasium or had had some other kind of secondary schooling. Such was the confidence Jaeger came to repose in B. that he entrusted him with writing a bibliographical supplement (see bibliography, nos. 1 and 2). The second instalment appears to have been drafted, or at least to have received its finishing touches, after Franz von Papen (1879–1969) replaced Heinrich Brüning (1885–1970) as Federal Chancellor. At several points it went beyond the recording brief B. had been given. Scarcely concealed was a fear of the revolutionary movements on the extreme Right and the extreme Left, and a relief at the advent of a government which looked capable of containing them. B. declared that not just Germany but the whole of Europe faced a spiritual crisis fed by moral, intellectual, and artistic relativism, by tension between classes and groups unable to accept common norms, and by lack of respect for pastors, teachers and statesmen; that Germany's crisis was peculiar only because of the peculiarity of the relationship between German nation and state, in as much as the German working class had not effectively become part of the state until the revolution of 1918; and that the German nation lacked an intellectual and political stratum capable of giving general leadership and of steering the vigour of the masses onto sensible paths.

B.'s dissertation had started out as a paper delivered in Jaeger's seminar about the authorship of the *Magna Moralia*. It assumed that Jaeger and Richard Walzer (1900–75) had refuted the view of Hans von Arnim that what we have is an early work of Aristotle's heavily interpolated by an editor, and sought to show first how the verbal, phasal, and argumentative style of the treatise depended on and yet differed from that of Aristotle's genuine πραγματεῖαι, and second how its form related to that of the *Ethica Eudemia* and that of the *Ethica Nicomachea*. He hoped the results of his research might throw light on other works of the early Hellenistic period. Writing the dissertation took him about two years. Never one to shirk the tedium of prolonged labour if it seemed necessary, he supplemented the information provided by Hermann Bonitz's *Index Aristotelicus* with three perusals of his own of the entire corpus of Aristotle's alleged writings.

The examiners of the dissertation, Jaeger himself and Ludwig Deubner (1877–1946), graded it as an *opus valde laudabile*, i.e. below an *opus eximium* and above an *opus idoneum*. Deubner, in whose youth the schools still made their students write essays in Latin and the universities still required doctoral dissertations to be written entirely in that language, thought the quality of the obligatory Latin chapter quite mediocre considering the talent the author had displayed in the dissertation as a whole. On 21 April 1932 the philosophy faculty consented to the holding of an oral examination. For some reason the dissertation could not appear in *Neue Philologische Untersuchungen*, but a heavily abbreviated and economically printed form came in May 1933 from a small firm in Ohlau, Silesia (see bibliography, no. 3). By this time Arnim was dead. B.'s idea that the author of the *Magna Moralia* modelled its structure on that of the *Ethica Nicomachea*, inserting elements of the *Ethica Eudemia* in no very well thought-out way, has frequently been rejected. On the other hand his analyses of the style of Aristotle's πραγματεῖαι and that of the treatise in question remain definitive.

The result of his oral examination of 9 June 1932 must have disappointed B. Norden rated his performance in Latin as 'sehr gut' but Jaeger that in Greek as only 'recht gut'. With Spranger in philosophy and with Wilcken in ancient history the rating came down to 'befriedigend'. B. consequently graduated *cum laude*, i.e. better than *rite*, not as well as *summa cum laude* or *magna cum laude*. He did not abandon his ambition. The centre of his interests had never been in classical or archaic Greece; it had perhaps already moved from Greece itself to Rome, and from philosophy to literature. The *Deutsche Forschungsnotgemeinschaft* gave him a scholarship to pursue a general study of Tacitus' account of the Roman emperors in the *Annals* and the *Histories*, and in particular to compare this account with those extant in Greek and bring out its specifically Roman elements. Towards the end of the winter semester of 1932–3, B. decided to transfer his residence to Bavarian Munich. He was attracted by the fame of the *ThLL* and the presence in the Ludwig Maximilian University of Johannes Stroux (1886–1954), one of the few classical philologists of his generation with an orientation towards Latin and long a friend of Jaeger's. Norden was ageing and visibly tiring.

# Munich

The appointment of the leader of the revolutionary Nationalsozialistische Deutsche Arbeiter-Partei (NSDAP) Adolf Hitler as Federal Chancellor on 30 January 1933 did not alarm any of B.'s teachers. Some even welcomed it. They thought that the Army, the bureaucracy, and the men of the DNVP and the Deutsche Volkspartei (DVP) would tame the wild demagogue, and he in turn his followers. B. seems to have taken the same view. The implications of the 'Gesetz zur Wiederherstellung des Berufsbeamtentums' promulgated on 7 April were not as clear then as they are now. Nor were those of the threats uttered against Jews practising medicine and law privately. B. did not consider himself Jewish in any rational sense of the term and believed that men in government were rational beings amenable to rational suasion. He expected the anti-Semitic storm to pass.

Arthur Levy lost his notaryship at the end of May, despite vigorous support from Christian friends and colleagues, but was allowed to continue practising law. His other son remained a student of English philology at the Friedrich Wilhelm University. Jaeger and Norden had the previous month secured for B. a post as an assistant editor at the *ThLL*. This freed him from financial dependence on his father.

The period 1933–9 was an extremely productive one for the *ThLL*, twenty-four fascicles appearing as against the six of the previous seven years. A large grant made at the beginning of 1933 by the Rockefeller Foundation of New York and guaranteed for five years paid the salaries of seven extra assistant editors and enabled the executive committee to avoid questions about the racial origins of appointees. B. worked on articles in H under Georg Dittmann (1871–1956) and Heinz Haffter (b. 1905), in I under Johann Baptist Hofmann (1886–1954), in M under Hans Rubenbauer (1885–1963). He was put in charge of the institute's library on 1 June 1934, being already regarded as a lexicographer of unusual ability. At some point late in 1936 he was entrusted with the important group *homo*, *humanus*, *humanitas*. Clearly those in authority then thought his services could be retained indefinitely. As things turned out, Wilhelm Ehlers (1908–88) had to write up *humanus* and *humanitas*. Looking back on his life, B. frequently said he had learned more about philological research as an assistant editor at the *ThLL* than as a doctoral candidate in Berlin.

Those members of the NSDAP who moved in academic circles in Munich behaved affably towards Jewish colleagues. B. did not seek out their company, and he showed no curiosity about the regime's para-military parades. He talked freely to uncommitted colleagues, some of whom were surprised that a man of such elegant taste should seem to admire Hitler's ability to stir a crowd with his oratory. He kept a watchful eye on his family in Berlin and did what he could to aid his brother's plans to seek a career outside Germany after graduation. He was observed to be devoting an unusual amount of effort towards improving his English. He did not abandon the hope of eventually being able to take up a normal career in classical philology in Germany. Less ambitious fellow assistant editors smiled at his efforts to set up a group to read together Apollonius' Ἀργοναυτικά and his cultivation of professors at the university. In his free time in 1935 and 1936 he drafted for the *Real-Encyclopädie der Classischen Altertumswissenschaft* a number of articles including an account of the Athenian philosophical school founded by Aristotle (see bibliography, no. 5). This essay, still even today fundamental on the history of modern study of the school, was sent to the press, like others by 'non-Aryan' scholars, by the defiant Wilhelm Kroll (1869–1939). The editors of *Philologus* suppressed a contribution to the fourth series of the 'Beiträge aus der Thesaurusarbeit'.

At some point early in 1937 B. was informed that the *ThLL* could not continue his employment past the end of the year. Bernhard Rehm (1909–42), editor-in-chief since September of the previous year, nevertheless put on paper on 29 April, with the agreement of his predecessor Dittmann and all the senior editors, a statement about B.'s 'gründliche Kenntnis der Sprache, Fähigkeit zu einfühlender Interpretation, klare Erfassung der gegebenen Probleme, und größte Sorgfalt und Zuverlässigkeit'.

B. set about looking for posts in Switzerland, the USA, and Britain. Manu Leumann (1889–1977), once an assistant editor at the *ThLL* and since 1927 a *Fahnenleser*, could do nothing for him in Zürich, nor could Werner Jaeger, now a professor of classics in Chicago. W. D. Ross, now Provost of Oriel College, a Delegate of the Clarendon Press, and President of the British Academy, was aware of B.'s plight by 20 September. He told the Society for the Protection of Science and Learning (SPSL), from whom B. had also sought assistance, that he thought he could pay B. for contributions to the *Oxford Classical Dictionary* (*OCD*), which he was helping to edit on behalf of the Clarendon Press, but not enough to allow him to live in Britain. The SPSL, by now regarded with great suspicion by the German authorities, did what it could to help and put money at Ross's disposal on 18 January 1938. At this point it came to Ross's attention that Kenneth Sisam (1887–1971), Assistant Secretary to the Delegates of the Clarendon Press, wanted to make an additional appointment to the staff of the *Oxford Latin Dictionary* (*OLD*), then under the editorship of Alexander Souter (1873–1949) with J. M. Wyllie (1907–71) as his deputy.

Ross wrote to B. on 20 January 1938, inviting him to compose articles under his direction for the *OCD* and suggesting that a fulltime post with the *OLD* might soon become available. Sisam himself wrote on 28 February inviting B. to come to Oxford 'to join in consultation about the preparation of the *OLD*'. B. left Germany somewhat unsure of what awaited him in Britain. He arrived on 31 March.

## Oxford

Ross and others looked after B.'s material welfare, while Walter Adams (1906–75), the General Secretary of the SPSL, conducted negotiations with the Home Office and the Ministry of Labour about permission for him to stay in the country indefinitely. Sisam was finally able to write to B. on 25 May 1938 asking him to report forthwith for work under Wyllie's supervision. B. remained in the employ of the Clarendon Press until October 1941.

Souter and Wyllie did not long conceal their hostility to the newcomer. Nor did B. his shock at the simple-minded ideas about lexicography informing the enterprise. However, exile did not prove a total misery; the musical life of Oxford could not compare with that of Munich or Berlin but was not negligible, and B. was soon able to acquire for himself an upright piano. There existed too in the city a disinterested enthusiasm for philological enquiry shared by a number of those teaching classics in the university and some very distinguished refugees from Nazi Germany and Fascist Italy. As early as 3 June, B. was proposed for membership of the Oxford Philological Society.

The pogrom of the night of 9–10 November made it clear that all sections of German Jewry were now in the direst physical danger. B.'s parents lived in the *Rosenthalerstraße*, i.e. in the heart of Berlin's Jewish quarter. Already in the summer of the previous year B. had helped to get his brother out of Germany to complete his degree in Basle. The intention of the regime to bar Jewish lawyers from practice must have been known before the official announcement of 27 September. Switzerland had taken steps to block further Jewish immigration on 10 August, and temporary residents were left with no illusions about the possibility of being permitted to stay. Sometime between 3 June and 9 November, clearly with the idea of being able to accommodate his father, mother, and brother, B. moved to a larger residence in north Oxford, where he had first settled. After much effort he succeeded in getting his parents into Britain in April of 1939, his brother two months later. B. always liked to think that he himself came to Britain of his own volition. Ross and the SPSL concealed their charity. Until 1941 he seems to have expected his British sojourn to be a temporary one.

A rumour that B. had been invited to address the Philological Society on the subject of lexicography alarmed Souter and Wyllie. A formal letter came from Sisam on 10 November 1938 forbidding B. to discuss the *OLD* in public. When Souter retired under pressure from the editorship in June 1939, Cyril Bailey (1871–1957) was made senior co-editor with B. and E. A. Parker, a new appointee, directly under him, and Wyllie junior co-editor. Work on the dictionary officially stopped in October 1941. When Wyllie returned in 1945 as editor-in-charge he set the assistants he had been given to rewrite those articles which B. had drafted, eliminating everything *thesaurisch*. B. attended the party held to celebrate the issue of the final fascicle of the dictionary in 1982 and rarely betrayed his view of any aspect of the enterprise. What had upset him in 1938, apart from the arbitrariness of the chronological boundaries chosen and the failure to gather in an adequate amount of the relevant material, would have been the unwillingness of Souter and Wyllie to relate in any organic scheme the multifarious meanings they claimed to find in particular words.

B. already had a good command of English by 1938, but nevertheless continued an effort to perfect his pronunciation and to eliminate faults of grammar and idiom. He read with care English books and journals of every type, and studied closely the manners of the British people with whom he associated and made them his own. This did not always endear him to fellow immigrants highly critical of their new land or to Britons unsure of where they stood in a complex society.

In June 1940 the 26,000 enemy aliens 'about whom there might be some doubts' were rounded up. B. and his male relatives were held in the camp at Peel on the Isle of Man until 23 October. He gave lessons in Latin and Greek to fellow internees and assisted in the organisation of other activities. After his release he served as a part-time member of the Oxford Auxiliary Fire Service.

At the end of the Trinity term of 1941 C. G. Hardie (b. 1906), fellow and tutor of Magdalen College, a frequent attender of meetings of the Philological Society, ceased teaching in order to enter government service and arranged that B. should take over his college duties after the long vacation. By 1943 there were few undergraduates in residence, and B. also became senior classics master at Magdalen College School, where he remained until 1948. The position at Magdalen brought him membership of the university's faculty board of *literae humaniores*. In 1942–3 he took over from E. A. Barber (1888–1965), soon to become Rector of Exeter College, a course on Tacitus' *Histories*, one of the 'fully prepared books' of the Mods. syllabus, and repeated it every year until 1947–8.

Dons of the old Oxford type did not hesitate to farm out pupils to B., noting how resolutely he strove to overcome 'the handicaps of his German education' where both verse and prose composition were concerned. Auditors of his university lectures complained to each other about their 'dryness' but reported well to their tutors. He and R. S. Stanier (1907–80), the head of Magdalen College School, had a good opinion of each other. His relations with the younger boys were often turbulent, but those who passed through the upper forms remembered him with affection despite his proneness to talk over their heads on out-of-the-way subjects.

In April 1942, B. joined the Anglican church and married in Exeter College chapel Daphne Hope Harvey, whom he had first met in Oxford in the spring of 1940. Daphne was then a student of physiotherapy on leave from Guy's Hospital. Her father G. E. Harvey (1888–1962), who had been a member of the India Civil Service and was the author of a much-admired history of Burma, feared the possibility she might lose her British citizenship and for a time opposed the marriage. Daphne was as persistent as B. The marriage brought happiness to both, and they had three children: Adrian Charles (1944), Denis Hope (1946), and Stephen Arthur Godfrey (1950).

In 1941, while still at the *OLD*, B. began to review books for the *Classical Review*; in 1944 for the *Oxford Magazine*. Most were books on Greek philosophy. He handled quite coolly the second and third volumes of Jaeger's *Paideia: Die Formung des griechischen Menschen*, which appeared in English translation long before they did in the original German (see bibliography, nos. 10 and 12). The first volume had caused much private controversy when it appeared in 1934, and B. is said to have often defended its approach vigorously. He now declared the methods of *Geistesgeschichte* subjective and the results vague. None of Jaeger's broad historical concepts seemed quite to fit the actual historical figures to whom they were applied.

An article in the 1943 *Classical Review* touched on the interpretation of Tacitus, *Hist.* 1. 79. 3 (57, 67–9). This caused B. to offer the journal the next year a collection of examples of a variety of the figure of speech known as syllepsis which he had made while preparing his course of lectures on the *Histories* (see bibliography, no. 8). Two years later the *Classical Quarterly* published B.'s first substantial essay in English. In this essay he put together nine testimonia to and eleven fragments of the works of Praxiphanes 'Peripateticus' and demolished Rostagni's theory that Callimachus' views on epic poetry corresponded with Aristotle's (see bibliography, no. 11).

## St Andrews

In 1948, T. E. Wright (1902–85), senior tutor at the Queen's College, accepted the chair of humanity at the University of St Andrews in his native Scotland. A Mods. don of the old Oxford style, he had been disappointed in his ambition of becoming Provost of Queen's. B. accompanied him to St Andrews as a 'lecturer in humanity'.

St Andrews was in many ways the most English of the Scottish universities. A large proportion of the teachers of its faculty of arts came from outside Scotland, while those who were Scots tended to have done at least part of their studies in England. It recruited its students from a wide area, from England as well as from Scotland. In organisation, however, it had a character very different from Oxford's.

B. assisted in the teaching of the three Latin classes. One contained all the first-year students of the faculty of arts, a captive but far from docile audience who stamped their feet if they disapproved of any feature of a lecture. Tacitus' *Annals* and *Histories* and Cicero's correspondence were the texts B. had to expound to the Honours class. Pupils recall a slight diffidence of manner. Wright found him an effective teacher, a discriminating examiner, and a businesslike administrator, and spoke with some awe of his 'knowledge of books and bibliography'.

There was in St Andrews an intellectual life of some vigour.

B. established relations with a number of younger colleagues which lasted long after his departure, in particular with A. C. Lloyd (1916–94), who had been the lecturer in logic since 1946 and was to become professor of philosophy at Liverpool in 1957, with P. A. Brunt (b. 1917), who had been the lecturer in ancient history since 1947 and was to become the Camden professor of ancient history at Oxford in 1970, and with I. G. Kidd (b. 1922), who returned to St Andrews to become a lecturer in Greek in 1949 and was to be awarded a personal chair in 1987. From his time in St Andrews came three important contributions to the study of Tacitus: a detailed review of a book on the way Lipsius handled the text of the *Annals* (see bibliography, no. 17), a substantial article challenging the widely accepted notion that the text of *Annals* I–VI offered by cod. Florence, Bibl. Med. Laur. plut. 68. 1 required little correction from a modern editor (see bibliography, no. 20), and a shorter article affirming that *Visurgin* was a gloss at *Ann.* 1. 70. 5 and not the only one that had entered the text presented by the Medicean codex (see bibliography, no. 21). It was also in St Andrews that B. began to think of making an edition of Cicero's *De officiis*, *De amicitia*, *De senectute*, and fragmentary works like the *Hortensius*, and of writing a general book on the Roman statesman's philosophical output.

## Liverpool

In the course of the academic year 1950–1 the chair of Latin in the University of Liverpool became vacant. After Otto Skutsch (1906–90), a former colleague of B.'s at the *ThLL* who had left Germany in 1934, rejected the appointments committee's offer in favour of one from University College London, the committee turned to B.

Liverpool differed more from St Andrews than St Andrews had differed from Oxford. The faculty of arts had a very lowly standing in the university. Students came by and large from the local region, a region served by good grammar schools which sent their better products to Oxford or Cambridge. Many still took up Latin in the first year of an arts course, but for the most part only because of faculty or subject regulations and only so far as such regulations actually required. Few took up Greek. Rarely did anyone so distinguish himself as to be thought capable of continuing his studies elsewhere. The professoriate enjoyed an easy intercourse with the leaders of a still prosperous and self-confident commercial community.

Most of B.'s elder and contemporary colleagues had satisfied their academic ambitions or accepted their fate. The young were on the whole happy enough with what Liverpool had to offer. The choice of Cicero's *De officiis* as a text upon which to lecture to the senior Latin class was proof for at least one colleague that B. could not appreciate the nature of a Latin department of an English civic university. An observer from outside the classical area noted in him an energy for which Liverpool would never be able to provide a sufficient outlet.

Liverpool professors were expected to deliver an inaugural lecture to the university community soon after arrival. B. chose to treat not Tacitus or Cicero, Latin authors in regard to whom he could now claim a personal authority, but the classical poets, the centre in conventional thinking of Latin studies. In a lecture delivered on 11 February 1952 (see bibliography, no. 23), he affirmed the existence of an objective standard of excellence valid for all literatures and argued that a professor of Latin ought to concern himself not only with the Latin language and the culture from which Latin poetry sprang but also with the question of what made a particular 'great' Latin poem 'great'. Housman's notorious refusals of 1911 and 1933 to do in Cambridge what B. was now advocating in Liverpool he explained away as due to an unreconstructed romanticism arising from Housman's own practice of English verse and thus to a view of poetry which was too partial to apply to Manilius or Lucan or poets 'greater' than these. How he proposed to train students of Latin literature so that they might be able to judge what they read as literature he did not make clear. He touched gingerly on the composition of prose and verse, which in 1952 still dominated the British classical curriculum, suggesting that the practice did not suffice to prevent the student's judgement of any particular work from being dissociated from his sensibility.

The three years in Liverpool saw a winding down of B.'s concern with Tacitus. After penning a severe censure of an 849-page Italian volume on the historian (see bibliography, no. 24) he fell silent about him for more than thirty years. He continued on the other hand to occupy himself not only with the ethics of the Hellenistic philosophers, as his work on Cicero demanded, but also with other departments of their thinking. He and F. W. Walbank (b. 1909) found a common interest. In an article published in 1943 ('Polybius on the Roman Constitution', *Classical Quarterly*, 37, 79–113) the latter had divided the sixth book of Polybius' Ἱστορίαι into two layers, arguing that the bottom layer came from a first draft and the top one from a rethinking undertaken after the

sack of Corinth and the *coups d'état* attempted by the Gracchi. Around
that time he had begun work on the commentary on the substance of the
Ἱστορίαι which was to appear between 1957 and 1979. The analysis of
the Roman constitution which Polybius offered in the sixth book clearly
had a background in the theorising of the late third-century Greek
schools, and B. was able to persuade Walbank that what had come
down, while in certain respects incoherent, possessed a unity of plan,
and that the notion of two chronologically distinct layers was otiose. A
joint article by the two men appeared after B. had left Liverpool.

## Cambridge

In the course of B.'s second year in Liverpool it became clear that
Eduard Fraenkel would have to vacate Oxford's Corpus Christi chair
and that R. A. B. Mynors (1903–89), Cambridge's not very happy
Kennedy professor, would then be able to return to his maternal university. Classical teaching operated on a much larger scale in Cambridge than in Liverpool or St Andrews. The faculty rivalled Oxford's
in size. Students were numerous and serious. Many looked towards a
career of teaching classics in a school or a university. The subject
possessed a certain prestige despite the mathematical and scientific
bent of the university.

Applications for the vacant chair were called for 22 September
1953. B. was among the four applicants. Others did not conceal their
interest. The Board of Electors was divided between those advocating
'a real Latinist' and those looking for a man of 'variety and breadth of
experience and openness of thinking'. A national newspaper reported:
'there is no suitable candidate available'. Unanimity was eventually
reached on the election of B., who took up the post on 1 July 1954.

When chairs of Latin were established in England around the middle
of the nineteenth century, no agreement existed as to what a professor's
function ought to be. Housman told the University of Cambridge in
1911 very bluntly what he thought his duties were not. His two predecessors had said nothing of a general kind. Neither did his two
successors. B. had no doubt about where an area of academic study
definable as 'Latin' lay. In an inaugural lecture delivered on 1 February
1956 (see bibliography, no. 27) he marked out the area, surveyed what
had been done since Munro's time, and stated what he thought needed
to be done in the future. He called for more investigation of the

Renaissance codices of Cicero, Livy, Ovid, Juvenal, and others, for closer attendance to the lessons taught by Housman about textual criticism, for the making of large editions both textual and exegetical of both the major and the minor authors, for the collecting afresh of the fragments of authors admired in Antiquity but lost in the Dark Ages, for the cultivation of the history of Latin literature as a whole, with attention to Ovid, Cicero, Livy, and Seneca, as well as to Catullus, Virgil, Horace, Tacitus, and Juvenal, and for the granting of more respect to methodological developments in the other humane disciplines. None of this was controversial, however little had been achieved in the Cambridge of the previous two decades. Pregnant with future trouble on the other hand was a repetition of the demand he had made four years previously in Liverpool for the study of Latin poetry as 'poetry'. B.'s remark that 'Housman developed a kind of specialisation whose effect on Latin studies was not perhaps wholly beneficial' caused dismay among potential allies and brought joy to many who would prove in the long term to be enemies.

In his later years B. occasionally expressed a regret that Trinity, the college of his philological heroes Bentley, Porson, and Housman, had not elected him a professorial fellow. Gonville and Caius elected him on 18 February 1955 and gave him rooms. He brought in an already substantial personal library and spent his working day there. He threw himself into the life of the college in a manner unusual for a professorial fellow. The ancient rituals of the high table and the character of the company gave him genuine pleasure.

Caius was a rich college which had husbanded its riches well and maintained old ways more tenaciously than many Cambridge houses. Nevertheless some of the older fellows who had experienced the world outside Cambridge between 1939 and 1945 and most of those who joined the fellowship after 1945 thought a number of changes desirable. Not all wanted the same sort or the same degree of change. Discontent manifested itself first in 1950 in a move to reduce the status of the tutors and to enhance that of the research fellows. The demand for greater respect for, and greater expenditure on, research found an articulate supporter in B. More strongly than anyone else he took the view that the most important thing for an undergraduate was to be exposed to minds at work on the frontiers of knowledge. He did not know every detail of the recent history of Caius, but he had thought long and hard about what a college ought to be. He was elected to the Council of the college in October 1956 and remained there except for three brief intervals until

1977. He was a member of the Investments Committee from 23 November 1956 until the day of his death. When in 1958 the master, James Chadwick (1891–1974), appeared to be acting in a high-handed, if not totally unconstitutional, way, B. was vocal in his opposition. The mastership became vacant, and B. allowed his name to go forward. In one of the many ballots he missed election by four votes in an electorate of forty-nine. Some of the things said in the course of a bitter struggle surprised and hurt him. When the mastership became vacant again in 1965, B.'s name was much touted, but he perceived that he did not have sufficient support and backed the election of Joseph Needham (1900–95), a man with a very different outlook on the world from his own. He continued to be active in the internal politics of the college until the sudden death in 1975 of the economist M. J. Farrell (b. 1926), his constant friend and ally since 1958. The college made him a supernumerary fellow for life in 1974 and supported generously the publication in 1989 of a volume of essays written in his honour (J. Diggle *et al.* (eds), *Studies in Latin Literature and its Tradition*, Proceedings of the Cambridge Philological Society, supp. vol. XV).

B.'s refusal to slip into the background after the repulse of 1958 and his association with a group of members of council which planned its strategies and organised support throughout the college during the masterships of Nevill Mott (1906–96) and Joseph Needham gave a degree of offence which gossiping outsiders magnified. Reports that he had found himself at odds with the college's two senior classicists confirmed the hostility which many members of the faculty of classics early began to feel towards him.

When B. arrived in Cambridge, instruction in classics took place largely in the colleges. There were about sixty instructors forming a 'faculty'. Less than half of these held university appointments bestowed for scholarly distinction or promise. The overwhelming majority had come to Cambridge from a remarkably small number of English public schools and stayed there. The kind of instruction given had not varied significantly in over fifty years, and practical arrangements were made by mutual agreement among the instructors. The faculty possessed little geographical space of its own and had not developed anything of the corporate spirit to be found in the colleges or those faculties which operated from laboratories or taught large numbers in groups.

The university appointed professors in what were seen as the chief areas of advanced instruction and research and made lesser appointments in classics as a whole. It was usually through a professorship that an outsider entered the system. The readers and lecturers owed no allegiance to professors, as similarly titled instructors did in St Andrews and Liverpool. Only three of them could have been called professional Latinists, and they themselves would not have used such a term. Every member of the faculty, whether or not a university office-holder, felt a great confidence in his or her ability to write Latin prose and verse.

Between 1954 and 1974 much changed. More outsiders joined, and the faculty acquired a corporate spirit and even looked forward to having a building of its own. The spirit was a levelling one with which B. did not feel comfortable. He never gained the personal dominance that D. L. Page (1908–78) and M. I. Finley (1908–86) exercised in turn and perhaps never really wanted it. Two matters much debated by the faculty, the balance of university appointments in classics and the classical curriculum itself, aroused his special concern.

The body of university office-holders had not grown according to any conscious plan. B. made no secret of his feelings that the area of Latin as he defined it was under-represented, that the under-representation affected the health of the subject as a whole, both in the kind of original work coming out of Cambridge and in the kind of picture of the classical world students were being shown, and that in some other areas of central importance persons of insufficient scholarship and unsound educational aims were gaining preferment. When open hostilities began over particular cases many urged that for any vacancy the balance of specialisms should continue to be ignored and the best classical scholar available chosen. Some took the point about imbalance but demanded priority for the faculty's immediate teaching needs over the long-term interests of scholarship. B. and his colleagues rarely saw eye to eye over a particular case.

The curriculum was already at issue in 1954. Two newcomers from Oxford, D. L. Page and P. H. J. Lloyd-Jones (b. 1922) found fault with the pattern of teaching and examining which had formed their colleagues. Page got his way in 1956, when more general study of ancient literature, history, and philosophy was brought into the programme of the first part of the classical tripos and the specialist element of the second part was augmented. He resisted two further changes reducing the level of the knowledge of Greek required, but in vain. B.'s hostility to the traditional heavy emphasis on the practice of prose and verse composition and his advocacy of the 'critical appreciation of literature' helped to form the programmes in place by the time he retired. Many of the changes made he disapproved of, but he never broke rank publicly with his colleagues.

On one matter B. was able to persuade his colleagues with consequences universally recognised as fruitful. In 1963 at his instance the faculty board and the university press established a series of 'Classical Texts and Commentaries', each volume to contain 'an introduction, a text with apparatus, and a full commentary which discussed in detail textual and other problems'. B. remained the driving force among the editors until 1987. Over twenty-four years thirty volumes appeared, and a number which appeared after he left the editorial board owed much to his early guiding and goading.

It had grieved B.'s predecessor to find himself barred from the personal supervision of undergraduates. B. felt no such sense of deprivation. The kind of skill at which the best teachers of prose and verse composition aimed did not impress him as worth having. Neither of the lecturing tasks which had come to devolve on the Kennedy professor in connection with the second part of the tripos, the criticism of a Latin text—always since well before Housman's day one of a small number of poetic texts thought appropriate for students previously well drilled in verse composition and then being trained to read the scripts of the major witnesses of the text in question—and the general exposition of the work of the chief Roman representatives of one of the genres of classical poetry, enthused him. He never performed the latter task; the former he sometimes passed on to a junior colleague he knew to be working on a particular text. He believed firmly that what university students should be shown was wherever possible the thinking of a person actually concerned with a set of problems. His choice of a prose text for 1958–9 and 1959–60, Cicero's *De officiis*, a work which at that time he was still planning to edit himself, brought howls of protest from directors of studies. His initial scepticism about the value of palaeographical study at first degree level abated over the years.

B. rarely lectured on particular books to candidates for the first part of the tripos. He repeated a course on the philosophical content of Cicero's dialogues four times between 1956 and 1959. One on the metres of Latin poetry lasted in different shapes and sizes down to 1964. It owed much to the writings of Maas, Wilamowitz, and Hermann Fraenkel (1887–1977) on those of Greek poetry. Undergraduates schooled in verse composition found the approach more than a little off-putting. Between 1964 and 1973 B. took classes, sometimes alone, sometimes together with sympathetic colleagues, on both the theory and the practice of literary criticism. A class he ran in 1965–6 and 1966–7 in company with members of the faculty of medieval and modern languages as well as of that of classics on 'Senecan drama and its influence' reflected an increasing desire to free Latin studies from the stranglehold of classics. He had succeeded the previous year in persuading a number of Latinists to offer teaching orientated towards the late medieval, renaissance and early modern interests of students reading for other triposes.

Research students began to multiply in the late 1950s. B.'s undergraduate lectures attracted men and women of scholarly bent. He did not, however, go in for positive recruitment. Nor did he attempt to erect a seminar of either the German or the North American kind. His idea of what made a proper subject for initial research was an austere one: 'if critical scholarship aims at clearing up what is unclear there is only one kind of training which will serve that aim: that is concentration on a severely limited subject in a severely limited field' (see bibliography, no. 35, 776). He put up only with the kind of student who was capable of choosing such a field and doing the clearing up himself.

In 1954 both Britain's ancient universities demanded a knowledge of Latin from all matriculants. That demand helped to maintain a large role for the language in the curriculum of the better secondary schools and sheltered the study of Greek. By the end of 1958 plans were being made to create new universities and increase the size of all the old ones. No one seriously believed that the pool of outstandingly good students would increase, and there were fears among Oxford and Cambridge scientists that too many such students would be enticed to universities which did not require any previous study of Latin. Formal debate began in Cambridge with a discussion at a meeting of the senate on 24 February 1959 of 'the best method of retaining Latin and Greek among the subjects for university entrance, while at the same time terminating their compulsory character'.

Some members of the faculty of classics threw themselves into the debate from the beginning. B. inclined for a time to the view that what went on in the lower and middle school did not concern the university. Eventually he committed the prestige of his chair on the side of those who wanted Latin retained as a requirement for matriculation. On several occasions he argued that Latin was not yet in England a specialist preserve but, like mathematics, an important part of general education, having an educative power which other humane subjects lacked, and that it was in the interest of the whole university to keep an intellectually solid general form of education intact in the middle school. Some scientists were surprised at the way B. promoted Latin as an intellectual discipline rather than as a vehicle 'for studying the human condition'. A vote of the senate on 10 May 1960 left the abolitionists victorious.

The profile B. assumed in the struggle over Cambridge's matriculation requirements caused him to be invited to address the Association for the Reform of Latin Teaching in April 1960 about the debates in Cambridge (see bibliography, no. 31), and the Classical Association in the same month about those charges brought against the teaching of Latin in the schools which seemed to him to have some validity, namely an excessive concentration on the art of translating English into Latin and a neglect of the general educational interests of those who did not intend to carry their studies past the ordinary level examination.

B.'s enthusiasm for general education in the schools was genuine enough. It was, however, for the general education of those whose talent and rearing made them capable of pursuing intellectual activities at a higher than ordinary level. The needs of the humane disciplines, above all Latin, in the universities remained his chief concern. He took a deeply pessimistic view of the future of Greek and thought Latin itself could only survive if it lowered its formal standards and shifted its emphases. Advances in the humane disciplines could, in his view, be exploited by the schools to their advantage. On the other hand advances in pedagogical techniques, if there were any, or in those of communication did not seem to him likely to be of service in the universities.

B.'s chief ally in the Cambridge struggle, M. I. Finley, had a very different basic view of secondary and tertiary education. For him there were no deep trenches between the academic, the schoolmaster, and the publicist. He soon formulated a very different programme for the future. The *Sunday Times* published in March 1963 under the heading 'Crisis in the Classics' the substance of a lecture he gave several times in Cambridge and elsewhere in the course of 1962. Greek seemed to him to be finished in England's schools; Latin could be left, for those who wanted it, as a tool of instruction in the use of English, as a 'disciplinary grind'. In the universities on the other hand the traditional kind of course in classics with its heavy linguistic and literary base should, he recommended, be replaced by one which made use of English translations of the written record and historical interpretations of other kinds of record.

Already in 1961 B. had been enticed along with two academic Greekists, T. B. L. Webster (1905–74), and D. M. Balme (1912–85), by a number of practising teachers, administrators, and educational theorists, in particular C. W. Baty (1900–79, Her Majesty's Staff Inspector for Classics, then approaching retirement), and J. E. Sharwood Smith (b. 1921, since April 1959 lecturer in classics at the University of London's Institute of Education), to join with them in an effort to reform classical curricula. Webster, who had many contacts in the universities of the USA and the old Empire, and Balme, who had just returned to Britain after a spell as vice-chancellor of a West African university, shared B.'s alarm about the future, if not his kind of thinking about it. A new organisation, the Joint Association of Classical Teachers (JACT) and a theoretical journal, *Didaskalos*, emerged at the beginning of 1963. The place of ancient history in the school programme had been for some time a subject of debate, and B. drew the attention of his fellow reformers to the talent and zeal of Finley.

JACT occupied for some years a notable part of B.'s energies. He was president of the Association in 1969–71. By 1994 classics had become a very different sort of thing in the schools and universities of England from what it had been in 1963, and the Association had changed accordingly. B.'s first obituarists had to be reminded of the connection he had had with the Association.

As remarkable as the occupation with JACT was B.'s chairmanship of the Classics Committee of the Schools Council from when it was set up in October 1965 by the new Government of Harold Wilson until October 1969. B. had no sympathy with the general aims of this Government, least of all with those of its chief spokesmen on education, but he perceived the presence in it of dissension on fundamental issues and day-to-day priorities and believed, as he always had done, that the details of any policy whose implementation was actually attempted could be modified through patient argument.

B.'s association with the Cambridge Latin Course (CUP 1970–80), an elementary manual of instruction which received for a time a wide use in the nation's schools, was another example of his willingness to involve himself in any activity whose long-term contribution to the survival of the subject seemed likely to outweigh its immediately visible shortcomings. C. W. Baty, one of the architects of JACT, hankered after some new kind of course in classics which would receive general acceptance in the schools and the community at large, and the management of the Nuffield Foundation was willing to help finance the design of such a course. It was thought important that a university department of classics should foster the project. B. helped to design the proposal which the Cambridge faculty board eventually agreed to back, namely to 'investigate the problem of teaching Latin in the light of recent developments in linguistics and consider how a course on classical civilisation related to texts read in Latin might be constructed'.

In the years of his occupancy of the Kennedy chair, B. was not as much engrossed by the hurly-burly of administration and politics as many of his colleagues thought. He had the gift of being able, when he wanted, to abstract himself from secular concerns. There flowed from him a steady stream of scholarly publications, none of them ill-considered.

B. arrived in Cambridge still interested in the Hellenistic schools of philosophy but intent in the main on what the Roman statesman Cicero made of the teachings of these schools and on the textual problems of those of his dialogues which concerned ethics. A 1956 article (see bibliography, no. 26) argued that Zeno's ethical theory owed more to the Academic Polemon than to the Peripatetic Theophrastus. In a 1958 article on Plato (see bibliography, no. 28), however, B. called himself a 'student of Latin' and apologised for 'making bold to pronounce on Greek subjects'. When the *OCD* underwent revision between 1964 and 1966 he declined to amend the articles he wrote for Ross on Theophrastus and others (see bibliography, no. 16) or to permit them to be reprinted as they stood. On the other hand he continued to give encouragement and advice to the young men and women in Cambridge and elsewhere who started to interest themselves around this time in the philosophers between Aristotle and Plotinus, as he had done a decade earlier to I. G. Kidd in St Andrews.

The lectures which B. delivered for the benefit of candidates for the first and second parts of the tripos four times between 1956 and 1959 on Cicero's philosophical writing attracted only small audiences. The course he gave in 1958 and 1959 on the text of the *De officiis* for those taking the literature specialty of the second part involved him in unpleasantness with some of the college directors of studies. He abandoned the two projects he had begun in St Andrews. A review of a 1958 book (see bibliography, no. 32) shows how he would have himself gone about editing the remains of Cicero's *Hortensius*.

Other large projects came into mind and went. He found he shared some general ideas about the rhythms of the Latin language and its poetry with W. S. Allen (b. 1918) and proposed that they write a book together on the subject. He touched on these ideas often in the lectures he gave on metre between 1956 and 1964. Philological friends proved hard to convince, and he let Allen go his own way. An old plan to edit the first six books of Tacitus' *Annals* he was pleased to pass over to his talented pupil F. R. D. Goodyear (1936–87) in 1960. The defects he perceived in Mynors's 1958 edition of Catullus' poems tempted him from time to time to think of investigating the relations of the Renaissance manuscripts of these poems. D. S. McKie (b. 1952) was to take up the thought with B.'s encouragement in 1973.

In the course of 1959 B. decided to edit in the generous way advocated in his 1956 inaugural lecture those epistles in which Horace discussed literature. His study of the history of the Peripatos had familiarised him with the way the ancient schools of grammar and rhetoric as well as those of philosophy treated literature. Fraenkel's 1957 book on Horace said little about the epistles in question and yet suggested that there was much that could be said. A paper read to the Oxford Philological Society on 28 November 1958 on the old question of whether the *Epistle to the Pisos* possessed a coherent structure seemed to B. to have been received well.

B. consciously emulated a number of famous commentaries of the past: Bentley's on the whole of Horace (1706–11), Wilamowitz's on Euripides' *Herakles* (1889), Housman's on Manilius' *Astronomica* (1903–30), Norden's on the sixth book of Virgil's *Aeneid* (1903; a second edition of 1915 was much extended with material from the *ThLL*), and Fraenkel's on Aeschylus' *Agamemnon* (1950). The subject matter of the Horatian epistles had therefore to be explicated in every detail. Likewise the historical circumstances in which they were composed. The notion long fashionable among students of the modern literatures, that everything needed for the understanding and evaluation of a literary work is in the work itself, B. dismissed as obscurantist, although Fraenkel had occasionally paid it lip service. The text of the epistles had also to be established and its sense determined. Like Bentley and Housman, and unlike Wilamowitz, Norden, and Fraenkel, B. eschewed translation into a modern language. The progress of the *ThLL* made it possible, and indeed obligatory, in B.'s view, to give even more attention to the verbal style of the epistles than Norden had done to that of *Aeneid* VI. The epistles themselves had finally to be analysed and evaluated as whole poetic entities at least as far as the confines of the commentary form allowed. Here Bentley and Housman offered no guidance at all, Wilamowitz, Norden, and Fraenkel only a little. The doctrine of the 'new' critics, that the substance, organisation, and verbal style of a literary work could not be separated in the process of judgement received total adherence and contributed not a little to the frequent obscurity of B.'s exposition.

B. set himself to produce three volumes over fifteen years. Although he pursued the task with extraordinary single-mindedness it took him twenty-three. The structuralist theorising which began to sap the energies of the students of the modern literatures in the late 1960s and those of the classicists in the next decade did not bother him. The distractions of other areas of scholarship he resisted as far as friendship and courtesy allowed. Apart from two volumes of the planned trilogy, nothing appeared between 1963 and the day of his retirement which was unconnected with Horace or the genre to which the three epistles belonged. The essays on the theory that some of the argument of *Epist.* 2. 1 was with Varro (see bibliography, no. 36), on the literary quality of *Serm.* 2. 6 (see bibliography, no. 40), on the neglect of manuscript evidence in the discussion of various passages of the *Odes* (see bibliography, nos. 42, 44), and on the background to the comparison between Ennius and Homer alluded to in *Epist.* 2. 1. 51 (see bibliography, no. 49) made a strong impression.

The first volume of the trilogy appeared in 1963 (see bibliography, no. 37). It succeeded in illuminating the dark history of theoretical and practical literary criticism between the end of the fourth century BC and the last quarter of the first; likewise that of engagement with the *Epistle to the Pisos* from the late Middle Ages down to recent times. Not everyone, however, particularly in the Anglo-Saxon countries, was willing to find so much systematising in the *Epistle* as B. had found. G. W. Williams (b. 1926) affirmed a view of the poem's structure, or lack of structure, akin to the one urged by Antonio Riccoboni at the end of the sixteenth century. Others looked for sources either further away or nearer at hand than a treatise by Neoptolemus of Parium, the third-century BC poet and theorist referred to by Porphyrio and brought to life by B.

Twelve months after the volume was published, B. was elected to the Fellowship of the British Academy.

The second volume appeared in 1971 (see bibliography, no. 45). B.'s treatment of the relationship of the Horatian manuscripts and the history of the text in the introduction won general assent. The text he presented of the *Epistle to the Pisos* set the vulgate to one side and placed obeli against everything he felt he could not understand. It breathed much of the spirit of Bentley and little of that of Friedrich Klingner (1894–1968), the Teubner editor. Opinions were inevitably divided.

Two years after the volume was published, at the instigation of Carl Becker (1925–73), the Bavarian Academy of Sciences made B. a corresponding member.

## Retirement

Retirement from the Kennedy chair in June 1974 meant only that B. ceased giving lectures on behalf of the university and attending meetings of the faculty board. He continued to live in the centre of Cambridge, as he had done since 1958, and retained his rooms in Caius College. He listened to what still-active members of the faculty of classics had to tell him about current controversies and offered advice freely. He stayed in effective control of the Cambridge Classical Texts and Commentaries series until 1987.

The passion for music which preceded that for philology had never completely disappeared. Musical imagery appeared from time to time in B.'s scholarly writing. 'A poem', he declared in a lecture of 1965 (see bibliography, no. 40, p. 8), 'does not add up to anything that can be stated as a sum total in conceptual terms. In this regard a poem is like a piece of music—it evolves in time, as a time sequence'. Bach and Mozart were ever his favourites. He was nevertheless open to new experience: at a late age he took to Ravel and Shostakovitch. In 1975 he began to practice daily at the keyboard of a grand piano and to perform chamber pieces regularly with friends and acquaintances. The newly created office of chairman permitted him to impose some order on the Caius Music Society.

B. remained after retirement from his chair one of the trustees of the £10 million which David Robinson (1904–87), a successful Cambridge businessman, had offered the university for the foundation of a new college. Robinson had perceived in B. during an earlier but in the end unsuccessful negotiation with Caius a rare combination of realism and integrity. On the sudden death of J. W. Linnett (1913–75), the University's Vice-Chancellor, B. became Chairman of the Board of Trustees. He kept this office until Robinson College received a royal charter of incorporation in October 1985. He is credited with a large role in solving the main problems which beset the nascent college. When the

period of the trusteeship came to an end he was made an honorary
fellow. He remained an influential member of the Investment Committee, as in Caius, until his death.

1974 was B.'s seventh year as the British Academy's delegate on the
International Commission in charge of the *ThLL*. At every meeting he
had warned of the dangers which faced the enterprise, particularly those
which continuing slowness of production would bring. He advocated
improvement of the working conditions of the senior editors of the
dictionary, more contact with those studying Latin in the schools and
universities, and an increased recruitment of assistant editors from
outside Germany. A stream of helpful criticism of current methods
and procedures poured from him. He worked untiringly to persuade
the British Academy to support a British presence at the Munich
institute and sought out young scholars willing to spend some time
there. In 1978 he was elected a member of the Commission's Steering
Committee, in 1979 Vice-President of the Commission, in 1985 President. As President he proved to be much more than a figure-head. A
crisis in relations among those working in the institute in 1989 and 1990
was handled by him with firmness and a tact which calmed passions on
both sides of a bitter conflict. Just before he died he accepted a further
term of presidential office.

As B.'s visits to Munich grew more frequent they became as much a
pleasure as a duty. Longer than most of those who left Germany in the
1930s he had avoided going back. The first time he did so was in
December 1966 when he journeyed to Munich to consult the archive
of the *ThLL* in connection with his work on Horace. He renewed an old
friendship with Wilhelm Ehlers (1908–88), then editor-in-chief, and
made a new one with Peter Flury (b. 1938), later to be Ehlers's
successor. From 1978 many other old friendships were renewed and
many new ones made. Talking about and making music provided a
powerful social glue. B. came to use the German language again both
for private and for public purposes, although he insisted time and again
that he had come to think better in English.

The years of retirement brought to completion the scholarly enterprise of B.'s time as the Kennedy professor in a way that made clear the
virtues of every part of the whole. The third volume of the Horatian
trilogy appeared in 1982 (see bibliography, no. 57). Aspects of the
enterprise rekindled an old interest in the history of scholarship. A
much-discussed book and several articles resulted. Death caught him
in the middle of yet another enterprise large in its ambition.

Essays about the theory that Cicero's *De oratore* influenced the formulation of some of the arguments of the *Epistle to the Pisos* (see bibliography, no. 50), about the role given to reason and ethics in ancient theories of the nature of poetry (see bibliography, no. 54), and about the textual and literary criticism of Horace from the Renaissance to recent times (see bibliography, no. 56) preceded the appearance of the third volume of the trilogy. A further three, about the neglect of manuscript evidence in the discussion of various passages of the *Epodes* and *Satires I* (see bibliography, nos. 58, 63), and about an aspect of the reading of the *Epistle to the Pisos* in eighteenth-century England (see bibliography, no. 60) followed. The commentary on *Epist.* 2. 1 and 2 presented in the third volume showed no falling-off in quality from that on the *Epistle to the Pisos*. In an appendix entitled 'Horace's Literary Epistles and their Chronology; Augustanism in the Augustan Poets' B. grappled with the problem of how an artist could accommodate himself to the ideological pretentions of an authoritarian regime without sacrificing his inner independence. A draft version of the essay which B. kept seems to go back to 1975. At all events there remained with this draft a cutting of a newspaper obituary which described how the composer Shostakovitch had maintained a degree of intellectual liberty for himself under the Soviet regime. It is hard to read the published essay without sensing an unusually engaged mood. Rereading on the other hand will uncover an intense effort to avoid the influence of facile analogies from the world of recent experience.

Well before B. finished publishing all he had to say about Horace, signs of a reawakening interest in the history of scholarship began to appear. The grasp he showed in one of the chapters of the first volume of his trilogy of the five centuries of modern debate about the *Epistle to the Pisos* (see bibliography, no. 37, pp. 15–40) impressed even those who rejected the volume's principal theses. The surpassing quality of the critical work done on the text of Horace by Bentley and Housman — the latter's lecture notes were available in the Cambridge University Library to supplement the published essays — struck B. again and again as his own work proceeded, and he was ready to think more deeply about the historical circumstances in which the two great scholars went about their labours when an invitation came from the Scuola Normale Superiore di Pisa to deliver a series of lectures on the history of classical studies and textual criticism in England.

Three of the eight lectures delivered in Pisa in 1977 centred on Bentley and two on Housman. These sprang out of the reading and pondering of several years. The other three, on the scholars who preceded Bentley and those who came between the latter and Housman, B. devised for the occasion (see bibliography, no. 51). As soon as the Horatian trilogy was complete he set about revising the substance of the lectures for a book in English addressing both fellow practitioners of critical scholarship and educated laymen interested in general questions about the schools and the universities (see bibliography, no. 62). He replaced the account of Housman with one more suited to an Anglo-Saxon readership and, in order to clarify the context of the stance adopted by Housman towards the record of Antiquity, added one on how the educational use of the classics in the schools of the Victorian period influenced the character of classical studies in the universities. He broadened the base of his high estimate of Richard Porson and continued to treat W. M. Lindsay as unworthy of mention in the company of the likes of Housman. He maintained his refusal to discuss the English scholars of his own time or the current state of critical studies. An important change of view between 1977 and 1986 may be noted: he withdrew his earlier niggling at Housman's refusal to mix textual and literary criticism and even found in this refusal one of the springs of Housman's success in achieving what he set out to do (see bibliography: compare no. 51, 1222–8, and no. 62, pp. 160–7).

Unwillingness to speak about contemporaries eventually relaxed, at least where those who had predeceased B. were concerned. A lecture given in 1987 in Germany and in 1989 in the USA on the history of the relationship between classical scholarship and humanistic culture included in its purview the 'new humanist movement' led by Werner Jaeger in the 1920s. This he judged to have failed, as would, he predicted, any further effort in that direction. Humanistic culture could only thrive if there were in society and the body politic a similar potential to which it could appeal, and the industrial and technological society of Germany and the Anglo-Saxon countries showed little of that potential. Classics had, in his view, to restrict itself henceforth to what is scholarly, to seek to recognise what is the case, to attend to things as they are, and not mistake them for what they are not or for what we should like them to be.

An idea of making a modest edition of Tacitus' *Dialogus de oratoribus* for the use of undergraduates soon turned into something grander. Somewhere about 1982 B. decided he had enough life left in which to complete a general book on oratory at Rome in the first century AD and an edition of the *Dialogus* fit for his own Cambridge Classical Texts and Commentaries series. The lines along which he was thinking came out first in a review of a 1982 book on ancient theories about the rise and fall of oratorical skill (see bibliography, no. 61).

A paper completed towards the end of 1988 found in the *Dialogus*, with the help of Quintilian's *Institutiones oratoriae*, a number of exploitations of the substance of the Flavian rhetorician's *De causis corruptae eloquentiae* (see bibliography, no. 64). B.'s attempt to relate three works, one of which is lost and restorable only through consideration of the other two, and to base upon the hypothesised relationship a judgement about the third bears a certain similarity to his treatment of the *Magna Moralia* in relation to the *Eudemian* and the *Nicomachean Ethics* and to that of the *Epistle to the Pisos* in relation to Aristotle's *Poetics* and the treatise of Neoptolemus of Parium.

A lecture given several times between 1988 and 19 November 1991 argued that the *Dialogus* treated aspects of Vespasian's time necessarily ignored by the *Histories* and revealed on a proper reading much more of Tacitus' own attitude to the moral and political issues an individual of that time had to face than the *Histories* did. It neither proposed nor used any sophisticated model of the authoritarian regime as such and had to be published in a German periodical (see bibliography, no. 66). In the course of 1992 B. completed a collation of codices V, E, B, C, and Q of the *Dialogus*. This confirmed his view that the stemma divided two ways rather than three and that some of the variants could be regarded as transmitted rather than created through contamination. A paper on the issue was rejected by an American journal and ended up in the German *Zeitschrift für Papyrologie und Epigraphik* (see bibliography, no. 68). The final version of a paper dating the composition of the *Dialogus* to the reign of Trajan rather than to that of Nerva came from the typist on 24 January 1994. This one an American journal accepted (see bibliography, no. 72).

An element of great importance in B.'s scholarly life was the putting together of a philological library. He collected with great discrimination, and much could be inferred about the character of his scholarship from the items he had assembled by the time of his death. He wanted these to form the base of a distinct section of the library of Robinson College where they might aid the researches of serious scholars, but the college was prepared to take only such as might be of interest to undergraduates. The entire collection is now housed in the department of classics in the University of Tokyo.

H. D. JOCELYN
*Fellow of the Academy*

*Note.* For speaking or writing to me about Charles Brink I am grateful to: W. S. Allen; W. G. Arnott, Colin Austin; D. R. Shackleton Bailey; J. R. Bambrough; William Barr; Ralph Braunholtz; A. C. Brink; D. H. Brink; Christopher Brooke; P. A. Brunt; M. L. Burnyeat; Winfried Bühler; Francis Cairns; Sir Henry Chadwick; John Chadwick; R. G. G. Coleman; R. M. Cook; J. A. Crook; J. C. Dancy; R. D. Dawe; Josef Delz; James Diggle; Sir Kenneth Dover; Peter Dronke; Alison Duke; R. P. Duncan-Jones; Sir Sam Edwards; Mary Faris; Peter Flury; D. P. Fowler; W. H. C. Frend; W.-H. Friedrich; G. P. Goold; H. B. Gottschalk; A. S. Gratwick; Philip Grierson; J. B. Hall; E. W. Handley; Pauline Hire; Robin Holloway; P. M. Huby; A. G. Hunt; Rudolf Kassel; E. J. Kenney; I. G. Kidd; G. S. Kirk; Masaaki Kubo; A. G. Lee; Wolfgang von Leyden; A. C. Lloyd; Sir Geoffrey Lloyd; Sir Hugh Lloyd-Jones; A. A. Long; Ian McFarlane; D. S. McKie; J. S. Morrison; Kenneth Muir; R. G. M. Nisbet; Denis O'Brien; Sir Edward Parkes; John Pinsent; Jeremy Prynne; J. M. Reynolds; W. J. N. Rudd; D. A. Russell; J. E. Sharwood Smith; Wilfried Stroh; Gavin Townend; Ernst Vogt; F. W. Walbank; W. S. Watt; David West; M. M. Willcock; G. W. Williams; A. J. Woodman; J. R. G. Wright; and Sir Christopher Zeeman. Much help on general matters came from: Ernst Badian; M. St J. Forrest; Ian Kershaw; Dietfried Krömer; D. S. McKie; Eckart Mensching; and Arnold Paucker. Access to archival material was granted to me by: the Library of the University of Aberdeen; the Bodleian Library; Corpus Christi College, Oxford; Gonville and Caius College, Cambridge; the Humboldt University, Berlin; the Lessing Gymnasium, Berlin; the University of Liverpool; Magdalen College, Oxford; the Oxford Philological Society; the Society for the Protection of Science and Learning; the *Thesaurus Linguae Latinae*; the Warburg Institute; and the Widener Library.

# Bibliography

1 'Bibliographische Beilage I der Zeitschrift *Die Antike*' '1: Griechische und römische Autoren, Philosophie und Kulturgeschichte des Altertums'; '2: Archäologie', *Die Antike* 7 (1931), *1–*7, *7–*14.
2 'Bibliographische Beilage der Zeitschrift *Die Antike*' '3: Wirkungsgeschichte des Altertums, Humanismus', *Die Antike* 8 (1932), *1–*20.
3 *Stil und Form der pseudaristotelischen ' Magna Moralia'* (Ohlau, 1933).
4 'habrotonum', 'habus–haedus', 'hanappus–hardulatio', 'harenulces–harundulatio', 'hasena–hasse', 'haurio–haustus', 'homo', 'ignora–ignoratus', 'ileaticus–iliaria', 'ilicetum–ilicis', 'iligineus–ilisirica', 'illocabilis–illocalitas', 'immobilis–immorsus',

'maledulcis–malefio', 'malifatius', *ThLL* VI 3, fascc. 13, 14, 16; VII 1, fascc. 2, 3, 4; VIII, fasc. 2 (Leipzig, 1935–40).

5 'Peripatos', in W. Kroll and K. Mittelhaus (eds.), *Paulys Real-Encyclopädie der Classischen Altertumswissenschaft*, neue Bearbeitung begonnen von G. Wissowa, suppl. VII (Stuttgart, 1940), 899–949; articles on various members of the Peripatos in vols. XVIII 3–XXI 1 (1938–49).

6 Review of L. A. A. Jouai, *De magistraat Ausonius* (1938), *Classical Review*, 55 (1941), 103.

7 Review of F. J. C. J. Nuyens, *Ontwikkelingsmomenten in de Zielkunde van Aristoteles* (1939), *Classical Review*, 56 (1942), 31–2.

8 'A Forgotten Figure of Style in Tacitus', *Classical Review*, 58 (1944), 43–5.

9 Review of Aristotle, 'Generation of Animals', ed. A. L. Peck (1943), *Oxford Magazine*, 63 (9 November 1944), 51–2.

10 Review of W. Jaeger, *Paedeia: The Ideals of Greek Culture. Vol. 2. The Secrets of the Divine Centre* (1944), *Oxford Magazine*, 63 (8 March 1945), 195–6.

11 'Callimachus and Aristotle: An Inquiry into Callimachus' Πρὸς Πραξιφάνην *Classical Quarterly*, 40 (1946), 11–26.

12 Review of W. Jaeger, *Paideia: The Ideals of Greek Culture. Vol. 3. The Conflict of Cultural Ideas in the Age of Plato* (1945), *Oxford Magazine*, 64 (7 February 1946), 171.

13 Review of H. J. Drossaert Lulofs, *Aristotelis De Somno et Vigilia liber, adiectis ueteribus translationibus et Theodori Metochitae commentario* (1943), *Classical Review*, 61 (1947), 54–5.

14 Review of R. Hackforth, *Plato's Examination of Pleasure. A Translation of the Philebus with Introduction and Commentary* (1946), *Oxford Magazine*, 66 (29 January 1948), 246.

15 Review of V. Ehrenberg, *Aspects of the Ancient World* (1946), *Oxford Magazine*, 66 (20 May 1948), 466.

16 'Anacharsis', 'Arcesilaus', 'Bolus', 'Carneades', 'Clitomachus', 'Crateuas', 'Critolaus', 'Dio (1) Cocceianus', 'Diogenes (5)', 'Diogenes (6) Laertius', 'Eclecticism', 'Epicurus', 'Eudemus', 'Favorinus', 'Gromatici', 'Heraclides (1) Ponticus', 'Lycon', 'Menedemus (1)', 'Peripatetic School', 'Philon (3)', 'Philosophy, History of', 'Praxiphanes', 'Protrepticus', 'Pyrrhon', 'Sceptics', 'Sextus (2) Empiricus', 'Straton (1)', 'Theophrastus', 'Timon (2)', in M. Cary, J. D. Denniston, J. Wight Duff, A. D. Nock, W. D. Ross, and H. H. Scullard (eds), *Oxford Classical Dictionary* (Oxford, 1949).

17 Review of J. Ruysschaert, *Juste Lipse et les Annales de Tacite. Une méthode de critique textuelle en XVIᵉ siècle* (1949), *Classical Review*, 64 (1950), 120–2.

18 Review of César, *Guerre d'Afrique*. Texte établi et traduit par A. Bouvet (1949), *Classical Review*, NS 1 (1951), 183–5.

19 Review of Marcus Tullius Cicero, *Brutus. On the Nature of the Gods. On Divination. On Duties*, by H. M. Poteat, intro. by R. McKeon (1950), *Philosophical Quarterly*, 2 (1952), 269–70.

20 'Justus Lipsius and the Text of Tacitus', *Journal of Roman Studies*, 41 (1951), 32–51.

21 'Tacitus and the Visurgis: A Gloss in the First Book of the *Annals*', *Journal of Roman Studies*, 42 (1952), 39–42.

22 Review of D. de Montmollin, *La poétique d' Aristote. Texte primitif et additions ultérieures* (1951), *Gnomon*, 24 (1952), 379–81.

23 *Imagination and Imitation. An Inaugural Lecture* (Liverpool, 1953).

24 Review of E. Paratore, *Tacito* (n.d. [1951]), *Journal of Roman Studies*, 43 (1953), 145–8.

25 (With F. W. Walbank), 'The Construction of the Sixth Book of Polybius', *Classical Quarterly*, NS 4 (1954), 97–122.

26 'Οἰκείωσις and οἰκειότης. Theophrastus and Zeno on Nature in Moral Theory', *Phronesis*, 1. 2 (1956), 123–45.

27 *Latin Studies and the Humanities. An Inaugural Lecture* (Cambridge, 1957).

28 'Plato on the Natural Character of Goodness', *Harvard Studies in Classical Philology*, 63 (1958), 193–8.

29 Notice of Plotinus, *The Enneads*, trans. by Stephen MacKenna, rev. by B. S. Page, Pref. by E. R. Dodds, Intro. by Paul Henry (1956), *Journal of Theological Studies*, NS 9 (1958), 217.

30 'Tragic History and Aristotle's School', *Proceedings of the Cambridge Philological Society*, NS 6 (1960), 14–19.

31 'Small Latin and the University', *Latin Teaching*, 30. 7 (June 1960), 194–201.

32 Review of M. Ruch, *L'Hortensius de Cicéron: histoire et reconstruction* (1958), *Journal of Roman Studies*, 51 (1961), 215–22.

33 Review of M. Ruch, *Le préambule dans les oeuvres philosophiques de Cicéron. Essai sur la genèse et l'art du dialogue* (1958), *Gnomon*, 33 (1961), 159–62.

34 'Small Latin and the Classics', in *Re-appraisal: Some New Thoughts on the Teaching of the Classics*, suppl. *Greece and Rome*, II 9 (1962), 6–9.

35 Review of A. Michel, *Rhétorique et philosophie chez Cicéron. Essai sur les fondements de l'art de persuader* (1960), *Gnomon*, 35 (1963), 776–9.

36 'Horace and Varro', in *Varron*, Entretiens. Tome IX, Fond. Hardt, Vandoeuvres-Geneva 1963, 173–206.

37 *Horace on Poetry*: * *Prolegomena to the Literary Epistles* (Cambridge, 1963).

38 'Scansion: The Eye and the Ear. An Experiment', *Didaskalos*, 1. 1 (1963), 55–61.

39 Review of W. Wimmel, *Zur Form der horazischen Diatribensatire* (1962), *Classical Review*, NS 14 (1964), 161–3.

40 *On Reading a Horatian Satire. An Interpretation of ' Sermones' II 6* (Sydney, 1965).

41 'Horace and Empedocles' Temperature: A Rejected Fragment of Empedocles', *Phoenix*, 23 (1969), 138–42.

42 'Horatian Notes: Despised Readings in the Manuscripts of the *Odes*', *Proceedings of the Cambridge Philological Society*, NS 15 (1969), 1–6.

43 'Interpretation and the History of Ideas', in W. Schmid, *Die Interpretation in der Altertumswissenschaft. Ansprachen zur Eröffnung des 5. Kongresses der Fédération Internationale des Associations d'Études Classiques (FIEC) Bonn 1.–6. September 1969* (Bonn, 1971), 75–82.

44 'Horatian Notes II: Despised Readings in the Manuscripts of the *Odes* Book II', *Proceedings of the Cambridge Philological Society*, NS 17 (1971), 17–29.

45 *Horace on Poetry*: ** *The Ars Poetica* (Cambridge, 1971).

46 'A postscript to "Scansion: The Eye and the Ear"', *Didaskalos*, 3. 3 (1971), 485–91.

47 'Limaturae', *Rheinisches Museum*, nF 115 (1972), 28–42.

48 'Philodemus, Περὶ ποιημάτων, Book IV', *Maia*, NS 24 (1972), 342–4.

49 'Ennius and the Hellenistic Worship of Homer', *American Journal of Philology*, 93 (1972), 547–67.

50 'Cicero's *Orator* and Horace's *Ars Poetica*', *Atti del II Colloquium Tullianum, Roma 30 sett.–2 ott. 1974* (Rome, 1975), 1–12.

51 'Studi classici e critica testuale in Inghilterra', *Annali della Scuola Normale Superiore di Pisa*, III 8. 3 (1978), 1071–228.

52 Review of J. V. Cody, *Horace and Callimachean Aesthetics* (1976), *Gnomon*, 51 (1979), 60–2.

53 (With W. S. Allen), 'The Old Order and the New: A Case History', *Lingua*, 50 (1980), 61–100.

54 'The Impact of Rationality on Ancient Poetry', in *Proceedings of the fourth International Humanistic Symposium Athens 1978* (Athens, 1981), 105–16.

55 Review of W. Hering, *Die Dialektik von Inhalt und Form bei Horaz Gnomon*, 53 (1981), 231–5.

56 'Horatian Poetry. Thoughts on the Development of Textual Criticism and Interpretation', in W. Killy (ed.), *Geschichte des Textverständnisses am Beispiel von Pindar und Horaz* (Munich, 1981, Wolfenbütteler Forschungen 12), 7–17.

57 *Horace on Poetry:* ∗∗∗ *Epistles Book II: The Letters to Augustus and Florus* (Cambridge, 1982).

58 'Horatian Notes III: Despised Readings in the Manuscripts of the *Epodes* and a Passage of *Odes* Book 3', *Proceedings of the Cambridge Philological Society*, NS 28 (1982), 30–56.

59 (With F. W. Walbank [translation of no. 25]) 'Der Aufbau des sechsten Buches des Polybios', in K. Stiewe and N. Holzberg (eds.), *Polybios* (Darmstadt, 1982 [Wege der Forschung 347]), 211–58.

60 '"A great genius of our own" and Horace's *Ars Poetica* in the Eighteenth Century', *British Journal for Eighteenth-Century Studies*, 8 (1985), 67–78.

61 Review of K. Heldmann, *Antike Theorien über Entwicklung und Verfall der Redekunst* (1982), *Gnomon*, 57 (1985), 141–4.

62 *English Classical Scholarship: Historical Reflections on Bentley, Porson, and Housman* (Cambridge, 1986).

63 'Horatian Notes IV: Despised Readings in the Manuscripts of *Satires* Book I', *Proceedings of the Cambridge Philological Society*, NS 33 (1987), 16–37.

64 'Quintilian's *De causis corruptae eloquentiae* and Tacitus' *Dialogus de oratoribus*', *Classical Quarterly*, NS 39 (1989), 472–503.

65 Review of P. G. Naiditch, *A. E. Housman at University College, London: the Election of 1892* (1988), *Classical Review*, NS 41 (1991), 217–18.

66 'History in the *Dialogus de oratoribus* and Tacitus the Historian': A New Approach to an Old Source', *Hermes*, 121 (1993), 335–49.

67 'Paul Maas (1880–1964)', *Eikasmos* 4 (1993), 252.

68 'A Bipartite Stemma of Tacitus' *Dialogus de oratoribus* and some transmitted variants', *Zeitschrift für Papyrologie und Epigraphik*, 102 (1994), 131–52.

69 'Second Thoughts on Three Horatian Puzzles', in S. J. Harrison (ed.), *Homage to Horace: A Bimillenary Celebration* (Oxford, 1995), 267–78.

70 ' "Historical Reflections on Bentley, Porson, and Housman": Controversy and Reconsideration', in H. D. Jocelyn (ed.), *Aspects of Nineteenth-Century British Classical Scholarship* (Liverpool, 1996), 1–12.

71 'Rudolf Pfeiffer's History of Classical Scholarship', in M. Lausberg (ed.), *Philologia perennis: Colloquium zu Ehren von Rudolf Pfeiffer* (Augsburg, 1996), 46–56.

72 'Can Tacitus' *Dialogus* be dated? Evidence and Historical Conclusions', *Harvard Studies in Classical Philology*, 96 (1994 [issued 1997]), 251–80.

GRAHAME CLARK                    *Alexander Csáky*

*Proceedings of the British Academy*, **94**, 357–387

# John Grahame Douglas Clark
# 1907–1995

'IF ANYONE WERE TO ASK ME why I have spent my life studying Prehistory, I would only say that I have remained under the spell of a subject which seeks to discover how we became human beings endowed with minds and souls before we had learned to write'. So begins Grahame Clark's own account of his career.[1]

He was born on 28 July 1907, the elder son of Charles Douglas Clark and Maude Ethel Grahame Clark (née Shaw). The family was based at Shortlands near Bromley in Kent. Grahame Clark last saw his father in 1914 as Lt Colonel Clark left for France, the Near East and then India. His father died of influenza in 1919 as his ship entered Plymouth Sound. Clark was brought up by his mother and his guardian uncle, Hugh Shaw, for whom he had real affection. As a small child, he was introduced to archaeology by an elderly neighbour, a Mr Bird, who had a collection of flints from Yorkshire. Clark's own collection began soon afterwards, and his overwhelming interest was signalled to his mother when his pony arrived home riderless; he had spied some flints while out exercising the animal and had dismounted, gathered the artefacts, and forgotten about the beast.

Clark was sent to Marlborough, a school at the heart of prehistoric Wessex, with Avebury, Silbury Hill, and even Windmill Hill lying within the reach of an ambitious young boy. By this time, the family had moved to Seaford on the Sussex Downs where again there were great opportunities for observing ancient monuments and for collecting

© The British Academy 1997.
[1] 'A Path to Prehistory', unpublished manuscript, 1993.

stone tools. At school, Clark soon acquired the nickname of 'Stones and Bones', and he joined the Natural History Society. This brought him two advantages; he was excused games at least once a week in order to participate in Society activities, and he could engage in the pursuit of his two loves—the natural history of moths and butterflies, and flint collecting on the Downs. His first four publications, omitted from all the bibliographies usually consulted,[2] are reports on flint tools and weapons from the Marlborough and Seaford areas.[3] His first paper describes collections of flints with distribution maps, technological information and functional interpretations. As the 'weapons of war' (axes, arrowheads and spear points) only made up three per cent of the assemblages, and domestic tools (scrapers, borers, knives, etc.) made up ninety-seven per cent, 'the community must have been essentially a peaceful one'. From 1923 to 1926, Clark was one of the Society's leading scholars, collecting, guiding and lecturing on archaeology, and still engaged in study of the natural history of the area. It would seem, from this distance, that even at this early age he had begun to develop that intense curiosity about the ancient world that would drive him for the rest of his life.

Partly due to the academic stimulus offered by his school teachers, Clark resolved to study prehistory at university. Cambridge was the only English university to offer instruction in prehistory to undergraduates, so he sat for a scholarship at Peterhouse. Unsuccessful in the examination, he was none the less offered a place as pensioner of the college and arrived in 1926. He first took the History Tripos then moved across to the newly-created Faculty of Archaeology and Anthropology; meantime, his uncle Hugh Shaw came across to enquire of the Disney Professor, Ellis Minns, about the prospects of future employment for an archaeologist. Receiving the same reply that one would expect today, Shaw none the less agreed to the new venture when he saw Clark's fierce determination to study prehistory. Clark was thus exposed to the excitement of the 'Arch and Anth' Tripos, studying social and physical anthropology along with archaeology, for two years. Prehistory was taught by Miles Burkitt, but equally valuable was the instruction indirectly provided by Cyril Fox's *Archaeology of the Cambridge Region*,[4]

[2] G. Clark, *Economic Prehistory. Papers on Archaeology by Grahame Clark* (Cambridge, 1989); the bibliography in this book is incomplete in other respects although the omissions are minor. To the books can now be added *Space, Time and Man. A Prehistorian's view* (Cambridge, 1992).
[3] *Report of the Marlborough College Natural History Society* (1923), pp. 85–9; (1924), pp. 75–9; (1925), p. 114; (1926), pp. 73–5.
[4] C. Fox, *The Archaeology of the Cambridge Region* (Cambridge, 1923).

by J. Clapham's economic history and geographical research,[5] and by the Faculty's base in the University Museum of Archaeology and Ethnology. Clark was at once immersed in it all, walking daily by a huge totem pole from western Canada, past full-size casts of Mayan sculptures from central America, and proceeding underneath ethnographic hangings from the Torres Straits on his way to the lecture rooms. Across the court was the Botany School, and adjacent was the Sedgwick Museum of Geology. Among undergraduate books was Gordon Childe's *Dawn*,[6] and the new journal *Antiquity* was influential; visiting lecturers included Leonard Woolley, Grafton Elliot Smith, Gertrude Caton Thompson and Dorothy Garrod. Woolley was in the midst of his work at Ur (1922–34), Elliot Smith's *The Evolution of Man* was newly published (1924), Caton Thompson had just completed her survey of the North Fayum (1924–6) and was working on the sites as Field Director (1927–8), and Garrod had completed her excavations at the Devil's Tower, Gibraltar (1925–6), and was engaged in her survey of Southern Kurdistan (1928). Louis Leakey was also present, with news of his East African Archaeological Research Expeditions (1926–9). These scholars had an international awareness in contrast to the parochial west European view of Burkitt; here was the first inkling of a world prehistory.

Another omission from the standard teaching was any introduction to the ways by which prehistorians came into possession of the evidence. Burkitt was no excavator although he travelled widely to visit others' work. Clark was well aware of this gap and upon graduation he resolved to find instruction. An ideal teacher was soon to emerge, in Eliot Curwen who worked as an amateur archaeologist on the Sussex Downs.[7] In 1930 he and his son Cecil invited Clark to help in the excavation of a causewayed enclosure. This was good instruction in field techniques for Clark, although he had to learn to avoid certain subjects dear to his own interests; Curwen was a Creationist and would not tolerate hearing opinions that the world had a longer prehistory than 4004 BC. It was not the last time that Clark had to put up with people who had, to his mind, divergent and non-scientific views of the world.

Following success in the Archaeological and Anthropological Tripos (a First), Clark began research for a higher degree, and held a Hugo

---

[5] Clapham became Professor of Economic History at Cambridge in 1928 but had variously been a Fellow of King's College since 1898; his *Study of Economic History* appeared in 1929.

[6] V. G. Childe, *The Dawn of European Civilization* (London, 1925).

[7] E. C. Curwen, *The Archaeology of Sussex* (London, 1937).

de Balsham Studentship at Peterhouse (1930–2). He worked primarily on the Mesolithic industries of Britain, and when he published his first book, *The Mesolithic Age in Britain*, his supervisor M. C. Burkitt wrote the preface which included the phrases 'It is true that the cultures . . . were not so brilliant as those of Upper Palaeolithic date . . ... But at the same time though perhaps more miserable they are not at all despicable'.[8] Words such as these may or may not have encouraged Clark during his research.

At one of the Sussex enclosures, the Trundle, Clark met two people who were to become lifelong friends and advisers. Charles Phillips was teaching history at Cambridge, and Stuart Piggott was already engaged in his study of Neolithic pottery. Of the two, Phillips was the more influential; he had an uncanny eye for the landscape and soon involved Clark in a project to identify the traces of early communities in the hitherto unexplored rural landscape of Lincolnshire.[9] In Phillips's Austin car, the two men could drive into the prime areas, collect artefacts and map the sites, and return to Cambridge within the day. By evening, the finds were soaking in water, and Phillips's landlady was bringing macaroni cheese up the stairs to the team. Occasionally, Piggott would also be present, and Christopher Hawkes was there one day when extra supplies had to be summoned by a sharp tap on the floor. It was a good time for the men to debate how they hoped that British archaeology would develop. Clark was of the opinion that the archaeologists then controlling work were long on facts, miserably short on thought and narrow in perspective. No wonder Miles Burkitt put Clark up for election to the Society of Antiquaries of London in 1933, 'before too many enemies were made'.[10] Various Cambridge undergraduates were sometimes invited to sit in the back of Phillips's car on the Lincolnshire forays, T. G. E. Powell and C. T. Shaw among them, and doubtless they absorbed not only the experience of fieldwork but also the outspoken comments about their teachers.

Clark later joined Phillips in the excavation of a Lincolnshire long barrow, and one of the team was a young archaeologist Gwladys Maud (Mollie) White. Grahame Clark and Mollie White had already met, appropriately enough, in the University Museum of Archaeology and Ethnology. She came into the main gallery with a question for Miles

[8] J. G. D. Clark, *The Mesolithic Age in Britain* (Cambridge, 1932).
[9] C. W. Phillips, *My Life in Archaeology* (Gloucester, 1987).
[10] Clark served on Council in 1938 and again in 1946–7; he was Vice-President in 1959–62.

Burkitt about some Mesolithic object. Burkitt at once said 'you should ask Grahame Clark about that', and there he was, leaning over the balustrade of the upper gallery. Grahame Clark and Mollie White were married in 1936. Mollie gave up her job with the Welsh Commission and became an indispensable part of Clark's academic life as well as a source of immense happiness to him. Their honeymoon was spent in Norway and Sweden, visiting hunter-gatherer rock carvings recently studied by Gjessing;[11] they went on to Oslo to attend the Congress of Pre- and Protohistoric Sciences. Clark wrote an account of the carvings for *Antiquity* in 1937,[12] which helped him establish a long and good relationship with O. G. S. Crawford, founder and editor of the journal.

This period was crucial for Clark's future direction in prehistory. He was in regular contact with C. W. Phillips and the botanist Harry Godwin, both men later acknowledging Clark's influence on them as well, and Piggott was involved in even more serious discussions about the future of British prehistoric studies. It was agreed that Piggott would take on the Neolithic, Clark staying with the Mesolithic, and each had his own priorities for research, which were advanced through lectures and publications. Piggott modelled his later book on *The Neolithic Cultures of the British Isles* on Clark's concepts, especially in efforts to set the communities in an appropriate environmental frame. But Phillips was the prime source of inspiration for landscape archaeology, strengthened from a distance by Crawford. O. G. S. Crawford had already published his *Air Survey and Archaeology* (1924) and *Wessex from the Air* had appeared in 1928; these were influential books but Crawford's work as Archaeological Officer for the Ordnance Survey (1920–46) was more crucial for Clark's understanding of the potential of landscape archaeology. The writings of Cyril Fox were discussed as too theoretical and unyielding.

From this distance, it may be difficult to envisage the character of the archaeology of the period. Eager as Clark and Piggott were, to gain entry to the establishment they had to subscribe to the traditions of work and offer carefully-couched words of advice to their elders but not necessarily their betters. There were few significant excavations, and fewer still where methods were much beyond recovery of the most obvious structures and artefacts. At the stone circle of Avebury, all was well, as Piggott was employed as Assistant Director. The work was

---

[11] G. Gjessing, *Arktische Helleristninger: Nord-Norge* (Oslo, 1932).

[12] J. G. D. Clark, 'Scandinavian rock engravings', *Antiquity*, 11 (1937), 56–69.

directed and funded by Alexander Keiller,[13] and Grahame and Mollie Clark were invited for a visit. The site was viewed with mutual satisfaction, but dinner at Keiller's residence required full evening dress which neither possessed. Clark's somewhat worn trousers were of course collected by a servant at bedtime for cleaning and pressing, with the contents of its pockets laid carefully and symmetrically on the elaborate dressing table—a piece of string and a broken penknife.

As a junior research student, Clark found the time and the encouragement to publish his thoughts on a group of flint tools that he had long ago identified from the chalklands of southern England. His first professional paper, on discoidal flint knives, appeared in the *Proceedings of the Prehistoric Society of East Anglia* for 1928.[14] The Society was by then exactly twenty years old, and rather fewer of its members were resident in East Anglia than had been at the beginning; in addition, the mania for flint collecting was in decline. Clark was an active member of the old Society, as were Stuart Piggott, Christopher Hawkes and Charles Phillips. By 1933, their opinions had hardened and an effort was made to widen the scope of the Society's interests by dropping the East Anglian designation. It was not until the Annual General Meeting of 1935 that the crucial vote was taken; the principal supporter of the *status quo*, Reid Moir, had intimated that he would be absent and a small party, led by Piggott, made the journey from Avebury to Norwich in a borrowed car. The result was an overwhelming endorsement of the proposed change of title.[15] Clark was voted into the Editorship, Phillips became Secretary and the worn-out debates about the antiquity of man in East Anglia were at an end. It was ironic that Reid Moir gave a paper on 'worked flints' from beneath the Red Crag of Suffolk immediately after the Society had dropped its East Anglian title and just when the new generation were empowered to publicly dismiss the eoliths from further debate.[16]

---

[13] I. F. Smith, *Windmill Hill and Avebury. Excavations by Alexander Keiller 1925–39* (Oxford, 1965).

[14] J. G. D. Clark, 'Discoidal polished flint knives: their typology and distribution', *Proceedings of the Prehistoric Society of East Anglia*, 6 (1928), 40–54.

[15] G. Clark, 'The Prehistoric Society: from East Anglia to the world', *Proceedings of the Prehistoric Society*, 51 (1985), 1–13. The brief report of the AGM in *Proceedings*, 1 (1935), 162 can be amplified by the notice sent out to members beforehand, and a notice sent out after the event. These survive in the Society's archive.

[16] Burkitt was one of the few prehistorians who continued to give house room to eoliths, and in his *The Old Stone Age* (3rd edn., London, 1955) he was still arguing that 'the existence of Tertiary man seems incontestable'; in his University Museum collection he had labelled a flint flake from an impossibly ancient Crag 'this is a fine specimen', but of what we never were told.

The first meeting of the new Prehistoric Society was on 2 May 1935 at Burlington House, when nine members were present, and Clark was one of six speakers on recent archaeological research. In 1935, the Society had 353 members; by 1938, the total was already 668. The precarious nature of the finances, as evidenced in the accounts for the early years, never deterred the Council from its aim of publishing an annual *Proceedings*. In Clark's first year as editor of the new journal, 1,000 copies were printed even as the accounts showed an uneasy state, cash in hand £156. 4*s*. 7*d*., money owing £179. 2*s*. -. The confidence of Council in what it was doing must have been overwhelmingly strong.

Clark served as Editor of the *Proceedings* for thirty-five years, and worked to enhance its standing as a journal of international importance. Invited papers were secured from most of the rising stars of prehistoric studies (Piggott, W. F. Grimes, Glyn Daniel) as well as by the established leaders (Childe, Fox, Garrod, Curwen). Clark's aim was to promote prehistory as a subject and discipline in its own right, and to expose British readers to the European dimensions and, eventually, to the world. Although he had various Assistant Editors, among them Stuart Piggott and Kenneth Oakley, he never released his grip on the structure of the journal and rarely allowed a paper to pass to press without some alteration of style or content. Many papers went off barely legible, such was the rewriting between the typed lines.

In 1931, Clark was on the point of completing his book on the Mesolithic of Britain when he heard of a remarkable discovery made in the North Sea. From a depth of some twenty fathoms, a trawler had hauled up some moorlog containing a barbed antler point of Maglemosian type. This find, from the Leman and Ower bank, confirmed Clark's theory that the south-east of Britain had been colonised from lands across the present North Sea, at a time when there had existed a wide and welcoming plain between the higher lands of what were to become southern England and the north-west of continental Europe. Harry Godwin and his wife Margaret applied the new science of pollen analysis to the moorlog and dated it to the Boreal phase, just the period of the Maglemosian in Denmark.[17] Subsequent redating of the point to an earlier time is immaterial; the object stimulated great interest in and enthusiasm for Fenland research.

In the summer of 1932, Clark had seen enough Fenland landscapes,

---

[17] H. Godwin, *Fenland: Its Ancient Past and Uncertain Future* (Cambridge, 1978); original report, H. and M. E Godwin, 'British Maglemose harpoon sites', *Antiquity*, 7 (1933), 36–48.

and had sufficient knowledge of the limitations of the existing archaeological evidence, to take the lead in an act that has had a profound
influence on modern archaeology. He summoned a gathering of scientists, historians and archaeologists to a meeting in Peterhouse, and, with
Charles Phillips and Harry Godwin, the Fenland Research Committee
was formed.[18] The Committee brought the subjects of botany, geology,
geography, biology, history and prehistory together—almost certainly
for the first time—in a combined approach to a diminishing resource,
that of the Fenland of East Anglia. The Committee met three times a
year, at different Cambridge colleges, and under the influence of
competitive dinners the members could debate the programme of
work, and resolve to undertake the necessary tasks. One of the first
sites to be selected for work was Shippea Hill, a prehistoric site not far
east of Cambridge. Clark led the excavation, with Godwin in regular
attendance; the work was designed to explore the context of Mesolithic
and Bronze Age flints eroding out of a sand ridge mostly submerged by
peat. An enormously deep trench was excavated by labourers accustomed to working through damp peat, and the hole was stepped back;
even so, the photo of Clark at the bottom, with the peaty sides entirely
lacking shoring planks, is unnerving.[19] At a depth of 15 feet, Neolithic
material was found, and at 17 feet was the Mesolithic. The Bronze Age
occupation lay near the top of the sequence and Godwin was able to
examine both pollen and the sand-peat-clay sequences he had predicted.
From here, the Research Committee moved on to other sites, publishing
their results mostly in the *Antiquaries Journal*,[20] and in the short space
of a decade managed to imprint the idea that an ecological approach to
archaeological evidence was not only desirable at all times but essential
wherever and whenever conditions allowed the full panoply of disciplines to be applied. In terms of British archaeology, the Fenland work

[18] C. W. Phillips, 'The Fenland Research Committee, its past achievements and future
prospects', in W. F. Grimes (ed.), *Aspects of Archaeology in Britain and Beyond* (London,
1957), pp. 258–73.
[19] J. G. D. Clark, H. and M. E. Godwin, and M. H. Clifford, 'Report on recent excavations at
Peacock's Farm, Shippea Hill, Cambridgeshire', *Antiquaries Journal*, 15 (1935), 284–319.
[20] J. G. D. Clark, 'Report on an Early Bronze Age site in the south-eastern Fens', *Antiqua-
ries Journal*, 13 (1933), 266–96; H. and M. E. Godwin, J. G. D. Clark, and M. H. Clifford,
'A Bronze Age spearhead found in Methwold Fen, Norfolk', *Proceedings of the Prehistoric
Society of East Anglia*', 7 (1934), 395–8; J. G. D. Clark, H. and M. E. Godwin, and M. H.
Clifford, 'Peacock's Farm, (1935) see above, n.19; J. G. D. Clark, 'Report on a Late Bronze
Age site in Mildenhall Fen, West Suffolk', *Antiquaries Journal*, 16 (1936), 29–50; J. G. D.
Clark and H. Godwin, 'A Late Bronze Age find near Stuntney, Isle of Ely', *Antiquaries
Journal*, 20 (1940), 52–71.

did not make the permanent impression that Clark wanted; this was not due to an inadequacy of the approach, but was due in great measure to the general impression that the Fenland was a freak, unmatched elsewhere, both in its original and its current status, and thus ill-serving as a model. Time has shown how wrong that impression was, and how the opportunities were missed; Clark became well aware of this after the War.

*The Mesolithic Age in Britain* was published in 1932, and Clark obtained his Ph.D. the following year. His dissertation was not the same as his book, as in the former he covered the flint industries of the Mesolithic, Neolithic and early Metal Age. His collaboration with Piggott in publications began with a paper on the flint mines,[21] and continued soon after with a report on work on the Essex coastline.[22] Clark's interest in flint industries, so often ignored in considerations of his other, organic, archaeology, was always prominent in his many visits to museums and to sites throughout the world. His papers on microlithic industries in Britain and in western Europe served as landmarks for many years.[23]

By 1935 Clark had almost thirty papers in print. All were on British sites and subjects. He was elected to a Bye-Fellowship at Peterhouse in 1932 and one of his early tasks as a junior Fellow was to introduce the Abbé Breuil to High Table in College; this passed off well enough, perhaps in part because both Breuil, surprisingly enough, and Clark were of the same mind in asserting that in the Stone Age, Europe was no more than a small northern projection of the greater land masses of Africa and Asia. To this view not everyone agreed, especially most of the French prehistorians.

Clark set off in 1933, and again in 1934, on his first major study tours to northern Europe. His aim was to collect material relating to early human settlement and ecological change in the northern lands, and

[21] J. G. D. Clark and S. Piggott, 'The Age of the British flint mines', *Antiquity*, 7 (1933), 166–83.
[22] S. Hazzledine Warren, S. Piggott, J. G. D. Clark, M. C. Burkitt and H. and M. E. Godwin, 'Archaeology of the submerged land surface of the Essex coast', *Proceedings of the Prehistoric Society*, 2 (1936), 178–210.
[23] J. G. D. Clark, 'The classification of a microlithic culture: the Tardenoisian of Horsham', *Archaeological Journal*, 90 (1933), 52–77; 'Derivative forms of the *petit tranchet* in Britain', *Archaeological Journal*, 91 (1934), 32–58; 'A microlithic industry from the Cambridgeshire Fenland and other industries of Sauveterrian affinities from Britain', *Proceedings of the Prehistoric Society*, 21 (1955), 3–20; 'Blade and trapeze industries of the European Stone Age', *Proceedings of the Prehistoric Society*, 24 (1958), 24–42.

he visited Holland, Denmark and Germany, meeting three men in particular who influenced his work very significantly. Therkel Mathiassen was in mid-campaign on Mesolithic sites, J. Troels-Smith was engaged in refinements of pollen analysis, and Gudmun Hatt was studying primitive cultivation; most of their work was published three or four years later, but Clark was able to observe their individual environmental and ecological approaches in the field.[24]

But there were others at work too, and the sites visited included some from which inorganics were wholly absent. The fishing stations in particular, some in current use, and older examples then being investigated,[25] must have encouraged Clark in his quest to secure material for a major book. In 1936, *The Mesolithic Settlement of Northern Europe* appeared.[26] In this, he set out his aim—to put archaeology in the context of a totality of an ecosystem. He applied a battery of newly-developed and well-established techniques to the dating of the various industrial complexes so far identified over the vast territory of northern Europe, and he did not lose sight of the fact that environmental change in such a severe climate could have profound impacts on communities. Yet equally important to future work was his realisation that while he was dabbling with the lithic industries of the British Mesolithic, in Denmark his contemporaries were studying not only flints but also the wood, fibre, bone and antler artefacts surviving in the bogs. His chance to make the case for wetland sites to a wider public was made in his 1939 book *Archaeology and Society*, a wide-ranging essay on modern archaeology, its strengths and its weaknesses.[27] By this time, of course, the wave of nationalistic exaggeration was about to break upon Europe and the world. The book touched upon the threat, but concentrated on ancient economies, technology, housing, exchange of goods, and intellectual life.

[24] T. Mathiassen, 'Gudenaa-Kulturen. En Mesolitish Inlands bebyggelse i Jylland', *Aarbøger* (1937), 1–186; J. Troels-Smith, 'Stammebade fra Aamosen'. *Fra Nationalmuseets Arbejdsmark* (1946); G. Hatt 1937, *Landbrug i Danmarks Oldtid* (Copenhagen, 1937).
[25] e.g. I. Arwidsson, 'Några fasta fisken i Södra Bullaren från äldre tider', *Göteborgs och Bohusläns Fornminnesförenings Tidsskrift*, (1936), 92–122. Arwidsson's work here was only one of the family's contributions to Clark's development; Greta Arwidsson's later work at Valsgärde and Birka played a part in Clark's increasing interest in symbols of prestige - a far cry from the wooden stakes on the Bullaren Lake.
[26] J. G. D. Clark, *The Mesolithic Settlement of Northern Europe: A Study of the Food Gathering Peoples of Northern Europe During the Early Post-glacial Period* (Cambridge, 1936).
[27] Grahame Clark, *Archaeology and Society* (London, 1939).

Clark was appointed as University Assistant Lecturer in Archaeology at Cambridge in 1935, at an annual salary of £150. He worked under the Departmental Head, Ellis Minns, who had encouraged him throughout his undergraduate and graduate days. Minns gave Clark an offprint of his paper on 'The Art of the Northern Nomads' in 1942, inscribing it 'To Grahame Clark my most surpassing pupil'. In the Department, Clark could indulge himself by teaching the Mesolithic, by forays into the fields of Cambridgeshire and beyond, by serious involvement with the *Proceedings of the Prehistoric Society* and by a close acquaintance with the ethnographic collections of the University Museum. Here it was that he began to plan for major field projects, into the Fens with his Research Committee, and elsewhere for sites that would yield the sort of evidence he needed for his aim—societies in their true ecological setting. In 1937–8 he made a bad decision to excavate a Mesolithic site in Surrey, which yielded thousands of flints but little or nothing in the way of structures, and organic survival was poor.[28] He admitted later that he should have gone farther afield to the Somerset Levels where Godwin was already achieving much, and well-preserved sites were appearing.[29]

Several of the most successful of the students he taught soon ventured into archaeologically-uncharted lands. Thurstan Shaw, who graduated in 1936, became Curator of the Anthropological Museum of the Gold Coast (1937–45), and Desmond Clark became Director of the Rhodes-Livingstone Museum of Northern Rhodesia (1938–61). These men provided inspiration for Clark's eventual adoption of the world as his prehistoric theme. In 1939 he was able to anticipate the future with the unexpected (to readers) publication in the *Proceedings* of Donald Thompson's paper on the seasonal activities of the people of Cape York in Australia;[30] this paper had a profound effect on the editor and, had the war not intervened, he would have instigated a campaign in the Fens to try out his theory on the Mesolithic and Neolithic communities. By the time he could do this, the opportunity in the Fens had passed. He made a plea for the survival of the ancient heritage, in all its forms, in his 1939 book *Archaeology and Society*.

[28] J. G. D. Clark and W. F. Rankine, 'Excavations at Farnham, Surrey (1937–38): the Horsham culture and the question of Mesolithic dwellings', *Proceedings of the Prehistoric Society*, 5 (1939), 61–118.
[29] H. Godwin, *The Archives of the Peat Bogs* (Cambridge, 1981).
[30] D. Thompson, 'The seasonal factor in human culture', *Proceedings of the Prehistoric Society*, 5 (1939), 209–21.

While waiting to be called up for military service, he took lessons in Russian from Ellis Minns and apparently found this much less formidable than expected; deflation set in when presented with the poems of Pushkin, but his limited knowledge was put to good use later in life. In the RAF Volunteer Reserves he was first sent to Medmenham to the aerial photograph interpretation unit, and here he met again Stuart Piggott, Glyn Daniel, Charles McBurney and Dorothy Garrod (the new Disney Professor of Archaeology). Most of them were sent overseas, but Clark remained in Britain because of a health problem. In 1944 he transferred to the Air Historical branch in London; this allowed him to re-establish a home in Cambridge from where he commuted to work each day, writing on the train and editing papers for the *Proceedings*. He also found time for visits to art galleries in London, arousing an interest in modern art in which he could indulge later on. In great part stimulated by his pre-war travels, he also began to assemble material and thoughts on a new approach, that of an economic prehistory, one not based on typologies, and inorganics, but one more securely founded on seasonalities and organic survivals. Papers on bees, water, seals, whales, forests, sheep, fishing, and fowling flowed from his pen in the years 1942–8;[31] these short papers were revelatory to almost all archaeologists except those then working in the water-saturated sites of Denmark and north Germany. From here, the different work and emphases of Johannes Iversen and Albrecht Rust made Clark ever more determined in his ecological approach.[32] There had to be comparable opportunities in Britain, and all the necessary multi-disciplinary studies were ready to be mobilised.

At the war's end, Clark was made a full University Lecturer and helped Dorothy Garrod develop a new Part II in Archaeology for the

---

[31] 'Bees in antiquity', *Antiquity*, 16 (1942), 208–15; 'Water in antiquity', *Antiquity*, 18 (1944), 1–15; 'Seal-hunting in the Stone Age of north-western Europe: a study in economic prehistory', *Proceedings of the Prehistoric Society*, 12 (1946), 12–48; 'Forest clearance and prehistoric farming', *Economic History Review*, 17 (1947), 45–51; 'Sheep and swine in the husbandry of prehistoric Europe', *Antiquity*, 21 (1947), 122–36; 'Whales as an economic factor in prehistoric Europe', *Antiquity*, 21 (1947), 84–104; 'The development of fishing in prehistoric Europe', *Antiquaries Journal*, 28 (1948), 45–85; 'Fowling in prehistoric Europe', *Antiquity*, 22 (1948), 116–30.

These papers were reprinted in *Economic Prehistory* (1989).

[32] J. Iversen, 'Land occupation in Denmark's Stone Age. A pollen-analytical study of the influence of farming culture on the vegetational development' *Danmarks Geologiske Undersøgelse II R 66* (Copenhagen, 1941). A. Rust, *Die alt- und mittelsteinzeitlichen funde von Stellmoor* (Neumünster, 1943); *Das altsteinzeitliche rentierjägerlager Meiendorf* (Neumünster, 1937).

Tripos. Soon he was able to make another extended tour of northern Europe, this time to the far north with a Leverhulme Scholarship. He travelled up the west coast of Norway in a small boat which called at fishing villages in every fjord to deliver mail and stores. Clark could go ashore for daily supplies of milk and other food, and could observe how much the communities depended on the sea, their only means of travel, on fishing, and on preserving the catches for the long winters. From Norway and Sweden he travelled to Finland where his Helsinki hotel sheets were made of paper, and his coffee was brewed from parched grain, such were the reparation demands. This tour of 1947, and a later Australian visit in 1964, were probably the most influential on Clark's own evolution as a prehistorian. The Scandinavian visit allowed him to experience in part the wide landscapes, the environmental harshness yet also its richness, and to observe the seemingly primitive yet highly developed economic practices of the people both inland and coastal. He could hardly avoid noticing the wide use of organic substances for tools, nor the richness of folk culture; on a northern train he was rudely disturbed by a bunch of drunken travellers, which presumably added something to his appreciation of folk behaviour. He wrote a short account of the more archaeologically satisfying aspects of folk culture and prehistory in 1951.[33]

In 1950 Clark was offered a Fellowship at Peterhouse, which he held for forty-five years. Here in College he encountered a wide range of disciplines, among them the economic history of Michael Postan. Postan was Lecturer, then Professor, of Economic History at the University, and a Fellow of Peterhouse since 1935. His *Historical Methods in Social Sciences* had appeared in 1939, but it was his work towards *The Medieval Economy and Society* and *Essays on Medieval Agriculture and the Medieval Economy* (1973) that were the stimulus. Postan awakened Clark's interest in prehistoric agriculture that had remained dormant for some years, although Godwin had pursued the evidence from pollen analysis for some time for the Fenland Research Committee. The emerging Neolithic was important, but it did not alter Clark's own opinion of those who devoted themselves solely to the developed Neolithic, and especially those inclined to visit megaliths; these people were 'secondary archaeologists'. There may have been a deliberate attempt here to distance himself from certain of his colleagues, but

---

[33] J. G. D. Clark, 'Folk-culture and the study of European prehistory', in Grimes (ed.), *Aspects of Archaeology* (1951), pp. 49–65.

he said the same of the research students who went the way of the big stones.

As a University Lecturer, Clark was not always appreciated by his students. His lectures were generally considered to be rather poorly constructed, and he often wandered from the subject in hand. More than once he gave a detailed Part II lecture by mistake to a bunch of first-year students who may have felt happy to be considered able to take it, but who mostly could not understand what was going on. For those legitimately taking his courses on the Mesolithic or the beginnings of agriculture, the *post mortem* of the lectures would take place in a nearby coffee house, either 'The Bun Shop' or 'Hawkins' (both alas no more); here the delivery of the information was criticised, but no one would think of missing the lectures, and sometimes there was excitement when Clark would launch into an off-the-cuff description of a recent discovery that might even be relevant to the course of instruction. He never much ventured, throughout his many years as a prominent archaeologist, to get absorbed into popular archaeology. Glyn Daniel was very successful both in television and in writing for the public, and Clark must have felt unable to compete at this level. He mostly kept quiet about the public face of archaeology, with the occasional swipe at 'what might charitably be termed post-T.V. books'.[34]

In 1948, Clark was told about the discovery of some microliths at Seamer Carr in Yorkshire. He was already aware of a number of antler barbed points from Holderness, and hastened to the site. Here he found pieces of antler and bone sticking out from the side of a ditch. Godwin was appraised of the potential and he and Clark mounted an ambitious campaign in 1949–51.[35] The site, Star Carr, was explored with great care, and the organic material, for so long sought after by Clark, emerged in great quantities. The British Museum (Natural History) undertook the faunal analyses and introduced a vacuum chamber to ensure the continued preservation of the bone and antler. The story of Star Carr has been told so often, and the reinterpretations so frequent, that little needs to be said here. Inorganic flintwork could be seen in a proper subsidiary, yet still important, relationship to the bark, wood, bone and antler artefacts made and used by the occupants of a wooden

---

[34] J. G. D. Clark, 'Prehistory since Childe', *Bulletin of the Institute of Archaeology*, 13 (1976), 1–21.

[35] J. G. D. Clark, 'A preliminary report on excavations at Star Carr, Seamer, Scarborough, Yorkshire, 1949', *Proceedings of the Prehistoric Society*, 15 (1949), 52–65.

platform built out into the pool. Godwin's environmental analyses were crucial to the interpretation of the site, and Clark could assert with some justification that here was a British site to rival, indeed surpass, almost all of the Danish sites. The inventor of the radiocarbon dating method, Willard Libby, undertook to process a sample of the wooden platform and produced a date of 9488 ± 350 years before present; the site was on all counts the contemporary of Klosterlund in Denmark, where only flint and stone objects had survived. In the monograph of the site, published in 1954,[36] Clark produced a classic diagram showing how the Mesolithic group had exploited the animal, vegetable and mineral resources, for food, clothing, fire, tools and weapons, and adornment. He also made the point, again, that Quaternary Research was vital in any serious prehistoric research project, particularly those dealing with the Stone Age. Godwin had only recently assumed charge of the newly-formed Sub-Department of Quaternary Research in the Botany School and Star Carr was the best possible example of the great future that that institution was to have. For Clark, the successful use of the rich faunal remains in his interpretation, and the inspiring and entirely satisfactory radiocarbon date, were to remain with him as guides to future research projects.

Meanwhile, his more theoretical studies of subsistence practices and the exploitation of natural resources continued and an opportunity arose to bring his various papers together. Gordon Childe had retired as Abercromby Professor in Edinburgh and Clark was a candidate for the chair. Piggott was chosen and at once invited his friend and colleague to deliver the 1949 Munro Lectures in Scotland. Clark accepted, and the lectures appeared in printed form as *Prehistoric Europe: The Economic Basis*, in 1952.[37] To many, this is Clark's major triumph. The book went into various languages, including Russian; Minns would be pleased. In the same year, Dorothy Garrod made way and Clark was elected to the Disney Professorship in Cambridge. In the next year he took the Sc.D. degree at Cambridge on the basis of his published work. He was unsure about the degree, whether it should have been the Litt.D. or the Sc.D., but in part was persuaded towards science by the offer of a free scarlet gown of a deceased geologist; for a prehistorian, it was a fitting choice.

---

[36] J. G. D. Clark, *Excavations at Star Carr: An Early Mesolithic Site at Seamer, near Scarborough, Yorkshire* (Cambridge, 1954).
[37] J. G. D. Clark, *Prehistoric Europe: The Economic Basis* (London, 1952).

His 1953 Albert Reckitt Archaeological Lecture to the British Academy gave Clark an opportunity to express his economic prehistory in other ways, and foreshadowed the path he wanted to follow in his later writings. He used this lecture as one of the bases for his final manuscripts: '. . . economic progress, in the sense of a growing capacity to utilise natural resources such as we can trace in prehistory, marks stages in the liberation of the human spirit by making possible more varied responses and so accelerates the processes of change and diversification over the whole realm of culture'.[38]

In 1952 Clark broke out of Europe to attend the inaugural meeting of the Wenner-Gren Foundation for Prehistoric Research in New York. This brought opportunities for archaeological fieldwork in many areas of the world, and Clark was soon to benefit his students and others by Wenner-Gren activities. However, he set himself the task first of carrying out more local excavations, partly to test his observations on sites where skilful work had revealed surprisingly detailed information about settlements in particular. In Norfolk, first, he tested an Iron Age site but conditions were very poor.[39] Then in 1957–8 he undertook a major piece of excavation at Hurst Fen near Cambridge where, according to expectations, he might have found Neolithic house plans and settlement organisation along the lines of the sand-based Neolithic structures just across the North Sea. Although the site yielded vast amounts of flint implements and pottery, severe erosion of the Fen soils had removed all trace of structures. This was a great disappointment and the report on the site, as prompt as ever, was Clark's last excavation paper.[40]

Henceforth he was in analytical mode, and increasingly involved with committees both inside and outside the University. He served on the Ancient Monuments Board, on the Royal Commission on the Historical Monuments of England, on various management committees and councils, and continued to edit the *Proceedings*. He never took kindly to University politics or the machinations needed then, and now,

---

[38] J. G. D. Clark, 'The economic approach to prehistory: Albert Reckitt Archaeological Lecture, 1953', *Proceedings of the British Academy*, 39 (1953), 215–38. This quotation varies only in some slight degree from the published lecture, and is Clark's own annotated version which he aimed to present in his *A Path to Prehistory* (see above, n. 1), or in his *Man the Spiritual Primate* of which only one chapter, and various notes, exist in manuscript.

[39] J. G. D. Clark and C. I. Fell, 'The early Iron Age site at Micklemoor-Hill, West Harling, Norfolk, and its pottery', *Proceedings of the Prehistoric Society*, 19 (1953), 1–39.

[40] J. G. D. Clark, E. S. Higgs, and I. H. Longworth, 'Excavations at the Neolithic site Hurst Fen, Mildenhall, Suffolk (1954, 1957 and 1958)', *Proceedings of the Prehistoric Society*, 26 (1960), 202–45.

to ensure progress both structural (plant) and academic (staff); his time as Disney Professor and as occasional Chairman of the Faculty was propitious for augmenting his staff but he never bothered to work the system and press for new developments. Yet he was assiduous in encouraging every member of his existing staff to conduct research of almost whatever kind, and wherever in the world, and to help in its publication. One aspect of his Headship was widely appreciated; he never felt it necessary to have a formal Departmental meeting. Decisions for Faculty were made 'on the hoof' and communicated as and when necessary, or not at all. He was Chairman of the Faculty for three years and would race through the Agenda, overriding other Departmental Heads whenever discussion and decision seemed to be developing into debate. His aims for his Department were always clear—make time for study and research, and for graduate students, and for undergraduate teaching, in that descending order.

He had a succession of research students for whom he acted as supervisor or in other capacities, and he was immensely proud of their achievements. Some reflect wryly on the lack of real supervision of their subjects; Clark would often launch into a discourse on a totally unrelated topic, interesting perhaps but not much practical use for a student aiming to complete a dissertation on a specific subject, generally one suggested by Clark in the first place. His own graduate students went on to create new concepts in archaeological research or to direct major institutions in various parts of the world. More than one he sent off to new jobs in Africa or Australia, the recruit sometimes never having heard of the particular region or the precise subject which was to be the focus of research. Most survived the encounters, and were anxious to reciprocate when Clark, later on, began to travel the world[41] He suffered two terrible blows in his later years, with the deaths of David Clarke and Glyn Isaac, both Peterhouse men and world leaders in their fields. He took comfort in their accomplishments and those of the others, and while still Disney Professor he was assiduous in monitoring and encouraging the progress of all the graduates of his Department who participated in the expansion of world archaeology in the late 1960s and 1970s. Clark's famous map of the world, with its many coloured pins showing where the graduates had landed to establish outposts of the Cambridge school, was never prominently displayed,

---

[41] Clark wrote, often movingly, about his many students and their achievements in his book *Prehistory at Cambridge and Beyond* (Cambridge, 1989).

but he kept a mental image of the world with its Cambridge diaspora, and he could identify every region with its current 'holder', the work underway, and the latest publications emanating from the colonies. Of course he knew it was an exaggeration of the prominence of his school, but that was no hindrance to encouragement. Although his book *Prehistory at Cambridge and Beyond* appeared only in 1989, it reflected upon the flow of talent that had passed into and through Cambridge, with only a few remaining at home. Much autobiographical material appears in this book, and it shows Clark in a rightfully expansionist mode, and the pride which he had for the accomplishments of his students.

As Head of a prestigious Department and therefore on the receiving end of a succession of visitors to Cambridge, Clark used his College Fellowship to the full, and many a foreign archaeologist recalls dining at High Table where the talk could veer wildly from the quality of the food to University politics and inevitably to archaeology, without any noticeable break in the flow either of words or of food. Another divertissement for newcomers was a tour with Clark to visit local sites, or to travel together by car to meetings outside Cambridge. His abilities as the operator of a motor vehicle are legendary, and some of the stories told by former passengers are certainly true. Colleagues, visiting scholars and students all had variously unnerving experiences with Clark at the wheel of his Mercedes or other powerful car. Sudden braking, as a monument was sighted in the distance, created as much alarm to passengers as it did to the drivers of following vehicles; it was one way of picking up local terms of abuse. Clark's sense of direction was not often wrong but in any event there was little opportunity for anyone, especially a student, to suggest a change of course as the flow of words continued without respite. Many visitors recall with delight their times in the Fens with Clark; a few still shudder. Clark was wholly unconcerned with such matters, as one specific example may indicate. In the early 1960s, *en route* from Cambridge to Birmingham on the hitherto untried M1 motorway, and in driving rain, Clark placed his Mercedes firmly in the outside lane and rushed northwards at over 100 m.p.h, growling only as a very occasional Jaguar passed by on the inside lane. On approaching the Bull Ring, an innovative and terrifying ring road recently constructed, Clark handed over his only map to his newly-appointed Assistant Lecturer, suggesting that this would help us find our way into the city centre. The map was in an AA book of 1935 when, presumably, horse and cart were the order of the day. Cars, like bicycles and typewriters (but not his staff), were there to be used without respite until they were deemed unfit for the task; a new machine was then purchased.

Like most field archaeologists of the day, Clark was obliged to make most of his own maps, plans and drawings. He was surprisingly patient and talented at this, not so well able to create attractive artwork as Stuart Piggott could, but none the less entirely competent. His maps were invariably models of clarity. For the Star Carr report, he was able to take time to delineate over 100 barbed antler points and various pieces of bone and wood, in part because his literary activities were curtailed by a broken arm. The fact that Clark of all people was doing this kind of work amazed a small group of visiting Dutch archaeologists who were accustomed to assigning such tasks to draughtsmen; yet there was no better way to become acquainted with the artefacts. Photography was a craft never fully mastered and not often employed as a serious expression of the evidence. Site photography was a haphazard affair; at Hurst Fen he decided that a high elevation photograph was called for, but after trying to mount a contraption made of chairs and planks, he abandoned the attempt with the words, 'No, the loss to science would be too great'. Whether this referred to the potential damage to site or to archaeologist is unclear.

Clark was elected to the British Academy in 1951 and was Chairman of Section 10 (Archaeology) from 1974 to 1978. He was an active member of the Section but it was not until the late 1960s that he seized the opportunities to involve the Section and the Academy in major projects. Before that time, he embarked on a series of journeys to various parts of the world, rarely on holiday (apart from a Scandinavian visit in 1955) and often as a visiting lecturer or professor. He was the Grant MacCurdy Lecturer at Harvard in 1957, W. Evans Professor at Otago and Commonwealth Visiting Fellow in Australia in 1964, between which times he attended the Congress of Pre- and Protohistoric Sciences at Hamburg and Rome. A notable excursion to the Netherlands with the Prehistoric Society in 1960 allowed a group of recent graduates to observe the leading British prehistorians, Clark, Piggott *et al.*, in earnest and sometimes amicably heated discourse with W. van Giffen and his formidable graduates and associates P. Modderman, W. Glasbergen and H. Waterbolk. Clark was always held in very considerable respect by his contemporaries and it was not surprising to see even Piggott and his colleague R. J. C. Atkinson anxious to make a favourable impression on one of Clark's visits to their site at Wayland's

Smithy. Lounging in their directorial hut one day, drinking gin with a visitor, they were roused to frantic action when told that Professor Clark was walking up to the excavation. Clark did nothing to cultivate this superior position, but probably did little to undermine it. He was by far the most respected British prehistorian on the continent of Europe where his reputation was regularly enhanced by his visits and the encouragement given to young research workers in particular.

In 1961 Clark published the first edition of *World Prehistory: An Outline*, basing his syntheses in part on his own travels and visits, on the work of his own students, and to a considerable extent on his contacts in various parts of the world.[42] One of the basic elements of the book, and indeed essential for comparative studies, was the ever-wider presentation of absolute dates from all parts of the world. This was the master key that unlocked the doors of the world for Clark. It gave him the framework for the patterns of behaviour that he could deduce from the material culture observed, and it allowed him to speculate on contacts, influences and indigenous development. He pursued this in more detailed ways soon after his *World Prehistory* appeared. The first edition was flawed by omissions and some errors, as he well knew. But he also knew that some senior archaeologists could not find it in themselves to accept a theory of world prehistory, arguing that it was only possible to comprehend more specific, solid, site or landscape-based archaeology. Clark ignored such criticism because he knew the time had come to move outwards to the widest concepts of space and time. Almost at once, he began to reassemble the evidence and to augment it by his own research. A pleasant interruption to this was his installation as Commander, Order of the Danebrog, in 1961; as someone who had always looked to Denmark for both evidence and inspiration, this award was particularly gratifying.

In 1968 he was in Japan, Taiwan, the Philippines and New Zealand. In Taipei *en route* to some meeting or other, his host stepped into a bookshop and brought out a pirated copy of Clark's *Archaeology and Society*. This was not the only such unauthorised version of his books. But in this case, redress, if not financial then emotional, was secured in the Philippines. Clark was able to see the fabulous Locsin collection of

---

[42] G. Clark, *World Prehistory: An Outline* (Cambridge, 1961). It was about this time that he began to publish consistently under the name Grahame Clark rather than J. G. D. Clark. This was in part because J. D. Clark (Desmond Clark) was also actively publishing and some confusion could, and did, arise. In 1990 the laudation of the Erasmus Foundation cited the book *The Prehistory of Africa* as one of Grahame's major publications; it was Desmond's.

Chinese porcelain of the Sung, Yuan and early Ming periods, and was then invited to the Locsin estate where the excavation of a cemetery was in progress. The grave goods already found included Chinese porcelain of the Yuan dynasty (AD 1279–1368), and Clark was asked to continue the excavation of a grave where the labourers had dug down to the level of the burial. Lo and behold, he soon exposed some fine porcelain. Lunch was then taken under the palm trees, with white-coated waiters serving suckling pig on fine china. Upon departure, Clark was presented with a box containing 'his' excavated porcelain. A perfect day.

From 1964 to 1969 he travelled widely, not only to the east but also to Canada and America, and to parts of the Near East and central Europe. In Australia in 1964 on a Commonwealth Visiting Scholarship he had a particularly satisfying time, with a field trip into Central Australia with Norman Tindale. Here he could observe the aboriginal people's use of space in their hunting and gathering economies, and he could try to comprehend their complex cultural patterns; this visit was profoundly important for Clark's vision of prehistory. He generally made assiduous records of all his observations, but on this journey his notebook vanished into some crevice in the great outback; this loss may account for a slip of the pen in one of Clark's later publications where the Wombah midden appears as Wombat.[43] More importantly, Clark's observations of work at the stone quarries and long-distance distributions led him to an appraisal of traffic in stone axe and adze blades which appeared in 1965.[44] In New Zealand, as W. Evans Professor at Otago, Clark was intensely interested in the contrasting ways of life of the Maoris of the North Island and those of the South Island, due in good measure to the cultivation of introduced food plants in the North, and the implications therefrom for exchanges in materials and commodities. The impressions gained in Australia and New Zealand were to direct Clark in his future writings, not only in the *World Prehistory: A New Outline* of 1969,[45] but also in his later thoughts on symbols and interactions which appeared as lengthy essays in the 1980s.

---

[43] John Mulvaney has the last photograph of the book, and the reference is G. Clark, *World Prehistory: A New Outline* (Cambridge, 1969), p. 260.

[44] G. Clark, 'Traffic in stone axe and adze blades', *Economic History Review*, 2nd ser., 18 (1965), 1–28. He had already touched on this subject in his 1948 paper on South Scandinavian flint in the far north, *Proceedings of the Prehistoric Society*, 14 (1948), 221–32.

[45] G. Clark, *World Prehistory: A New Outline* (Cambridge, 1969).

In 1967 he received the Hodgkins Medal of the Smithsonian Institution, and in 1971 the Viking Fund Medal of the Wenner-Gren Foundation. These were followed by the Lucy Wharton Gold Medal from the University of Pennsylvania in 1974, the Gold Medal of the Society of Antiquaries of London in 1978 and the Chandra Medal of the Asiatic Society in 1979. He was a Corresponding or Foreign Member of a large number of European and American Academies.[46]

In 1969 he was Hitchcock Professor at Berkeley in California where his close friend J. Desmond Clark was based, and in his lectures he returned to the importance of basic archaeological evidence. Artefacts were the signposts of the course of prehistory, as everyone should know, but they were also the mechanism that distinguished humans from other animals. They signified the human capacity to identify and assign importance both to the everyday elements of prehistoric life and to the symbols of the thought processes that reflected forces beyond the grasp of humans. This statement served notice that Clark was not about to fall into the abyss of writing prehistory without evidence to back it up, but it was also a comment on those close at hand, both in America and in Europe, who were content to pick at the cherries and ignore the branches and trunk without which the fruit would not exist. The powerful theme pursued here, and in his Albert Reckitt Archaeological Lecture as long ago as 1953, was simple: economic progress empowered the human spirit. It was a theme that Clark continued to develop throughout his later years.

Clark did not devote as much research time to the Americas as he did to other parts of the world, but he made an impassioned plea to North American archaeologists when he made a tour across much of Canada in 1976. He commented upon the tendency of some current archaeologists to treat their subject as a science, and almost a pure science at that.[47] Clark stated that this view was misguided and 'it is also pathetic'. Natural science was a mere artefact of man, elaborate and expensive, and yet nothing more than a means by which man could comprehend and manipulate his environment; he might have included

[46] Royal Society of Northern Antiquaries (Copenhagen); Swiss Prehistoric Society; German Archaeological Institute; Archaeological Institute of America; Finnish Archaeological Society; American Academy of Arts and Sciences; Royal Danish Academy of Sciences and Letters; Royal Netherlands Academy of Sciences; Royal Society of Sciences, Uppsala; National Academy of Sciences, America; Royal Society of Humane Letters, Lund.

[47] G. Clark, 'New perspectives in Canadian archaeology: a summation', in A. G. McKay (ed.), *New Perspectives in Canadian Archaeology* (Ottawa, 1976), pp. 237–48.

culture in his argument. In this, he signalled his intention to devote time and writing to the development of his thoughts on the uniqueness of the human condition, and on the particular elements in the archaeological record that could most easily identify that state.

In the late 1960s, while writing two slighter books on *Prehistoric Societies* (with Stuart Piggott) and *The Stone Age Hunters*,[48] Clark took up a theme that was to develop into a major research project. By using the newly-available radiocarbon dates for the earliest agriculturally based communities throughout Europe and the Near East, he could produce a map that conclusively showed the spread of farming from the Near East into south-eastern Europe and across to the north and west.[49] This map, however refined and with a multiplicity of new spots, has never been seriously disputed although Clark was doubtless happy to accept minor adjustments and local innovations. But having secured the academic background and demonstrated the dynamics of economic change, he took steps to implement active research into the subject of early European agriculture. With the encouragement of the Sub-Department of Quaternary Research, Robert Rodden was despatched to Greece to begin a major excavation on the early Neolithic site of Nea Nikomedeia.[50] Eric Higgs, already attached to the Department of Archaeology and with practical experience of animal husbandry, went the same way and began investigations into earlier sites in the Aegean region.[51] Clark visited Greece and was inspired by what he saw. He worked with others in the British Academy to establish a Major Research Project on the Early History of Agriculture. A small committee was assembled in 1966, meeting in the same parlour in Peterhouse as had been used over thirty years before, when the Fenland Research Committee was established. Indeed, a majority of the new committee had been there at the earlier meeting. This initiated a major project that took much of Clark's time and energy, although Higgs was made director. The work

[48] G. Clark, *The Stone Age Hunters* (London, 1967).
[49] G. Clark, 'Radiocarbon dating and the expansion of farming culture from the Near East over Europe', *Proceedings of the Prehistoric Society*, 31 (1965), 58–73.
[50] R. J. Rodden, 'Excavations at the Early Neolithic site at Nea Nikomedeia, Greek Macedonia (1961 Season)', *Proceedings of the Prehistoric Society*, 28 (1962), 267–88.
[51] S. I. Dakaris, E. S. Higgs, and R. W. Hey, 'The climate, environment and industries of Stone Age Greece: Part 1', *Proceedings of the Prehistoric Society* 30 (1964), 194–214; E. S. Higgs and C. Vita-Finzi, 'The climate, environment and industries of Stone Age Greece: Part 2', *Proceedings of the Prehistoric Society*, 32 (1966), 1–29; E. S. Higgs, C. Vita-Finzi, D. R. Harris and A. E. Fagg, 'The climate, environment and industries of Stone Age Greece: Part 3', *Proceedings of the Prehistoric Society*, 33 (1967), 1–29.

done in Greece and elsewhere by the team was designed to explore the economic aspects of prehistory set within an ever-increasingly detailed palaeoenvironmental frame. Clark pressed for rapid publication of results, in a monograph series,[52] and provided much-needed encouragement and control at times of stress when the original aims of the project were threatened by the sheer speed of the work being done.

At the same time as he was demonstrating the spread of farming across Europe, and initiating the project, Clark took some of his British colleagues to task in a classic paper on the invasion hypothesis in British archaeology.[53] He could not accept that every innovation that appeared in the record had to be the result of new arrivals from the continent. That was too easy and, as he reiterated in the first Gordon Childe Memorial Lecture, 'it has tended in the past to inhibit research into alternative causes'.[54] His 1966 paper was not universally welcomed but it had the desired effect on the bulk of British prehistorians, who now looked more carefully before they leaped across the channel seeking originators for developments in these islands.

The Early History of Agriculture project absorbed much of Clark's emotions in the active years of its work. He was more content to see from a distance the work of his colleague Charles McBurney. McBurney's great excavations in North Africa and on Jersey absorbed much space and energy within the confines of the Department, and Clark had the greatest respect for the work of post-excavation analyses and the painstaking way by which McBurney put together the monograph of the Haua Fteah.[55] It was a happier relationship between the two than existed between Clark and the other senior figure, Glyn Daniel, but a working pattern was established with all and there can be little doubt that the Department offered an exciting spectrum of approaches to graduate students in particular. Undergraduates had their turn too, but only those who went the way of one camp or another had much hope of success in the Tripos; the rest left somewhat bemused by it all, with

---

[52] E. S. Higgs (ed.), *Papers in Economic Prehistory* (Cambridge, 1972); E. S. Higgs (ed.), *Palaeoeconomy* (Cambridge, 1975); E. S. Higgs, M. R. Jarman, G. N. Bailey, and H. N. Jarman, *Early European Agriculture* (Cambridge, 1982).

[53] J. G. D. Clark, 'The invasion hypothesis in British archaeology', *Antiquity*, 40 (1966), 172–89.

[54] J. G. D. Clark, 'Prehistory since Childe', see above, n. 34.

[55] C. B. M. McBurney, *The Haua Fteah (Cyrenaica)* (Cambridge, 1967). The Jersey excavations had to be published after McBurney's death: P. Callow and J. M. Cornford (eds.), *La Cotte de St Brelade 1961–1978* (Norwich, 1986).

Second Class degrees. Clark did better; he became Commander, Order of the British Empire, in 1971.

Although much absorbed with his travels and new experiences, and assembling vast quantities of new information in the late 1960s and early 1970s, Clark was always aware of his original base of research in Northern Europe, and of his environmental and economic approaches, and in his debt to the site of Star Carr. He was anxious that the evidence from Star Carr should be capable of reworking and although his excavation records were not stratigraphically detailed enough for intricate work patterns to be deduced, none the less the bulk of the material and its excellent condition permitted new appraisals over the years. Clark made an effort himself to expose new thoughts in a widely-quoted paper of 1972, subtitled *A Case Study in Bioarchaeology*.[56] This long paper, essentially a small book, was a very substantial reworking and rethinking of the data from Star Carr. The 1954 monograph had appeared soon after the field seasons ended, and Clark felt that he wanted to expose the evidence to new and more fully-considered thoughts. A major section of the paper, titled 'Bioarchaeological interpretation', allowed him to deal with environment, social context, seasonality, site territory and food supply. It remains a model of his own archaeological evolution up to the early 1970s.

In 1972, Clark was a Visiting Professor at the University of Uppsala, and he became once more absorbed into the study of the earliest traces of human occupation in northern Europe. He received a Filosofie Doktor (*honoris causa*) from Uppsala University in 1976, an award that gave him much pleasure in the recognition by a Scandinavian university of his contributions to prehistory. Equally satisfying was a Doctor of Letters awarded by the National University of Ireland in the same year.

In 1975, *The Earlier Stone Age Settlement of Scandinavia* appeared, in which Clark tried to bring together the evidence newly-acquired since his pioneering book of 1936.[57] Many new discoveries had been made, and new techniques applied to their elucidation, but the new book was not as warmly received as had been the first, and it was obvious to Clark that the task of identifying the significant developments in a land with which he was familiar, but in which he was not resident, was

---

[56] G. Clark, '*Star Carr: A Case Study in Bioarchaeology*' in *Addison-Wesley Modular Publication* (Reading, Mass., 1972).

[57] G. Clark, *The Earlier Stone Age Settlement of Scandinavia* (Cambridge, 1975).

beyond him; the pace of discovery was too great, and more importantly the new approaches made by a generation of Scandinavian scholars included concepts that Clark could not fully accept and therefore did not recognise in his book. He had planned a second book, *The Later Stone Age Settlement*, but did not pursue this as he would have been on less familiar chronological territory.

The multiplicity of scientific interests brought to bear on the Early History of Agriculture Project led easily enough to thoughts about the expansion of science-based archaeology, and Clark was instrumental in calling a meeting in 1972 between representatives of the British Academy, the Natural Environment Research Council, and the Royal Society. Archaeology and the natural sciences were debated in terms of equality of opportunity, but it was clear that the former would be the greater beneficiary of any union of resources. By 1974, Science-based Archaeology was on the agenda of the Science Research Council and in 1975 the Academy pressed for a solution to the problem of funding archaeological science from a wholly inadequate and inappropriate resource. In 1976, Clark assumed the Chair at the first Science-based Archaeology Committee, which consisted of a formidable array of scientists sympathetic to archaeology in one way or another. In 1980 he relinquished the Chair but by then major advances had been made, including the establishment of the Radiocarbon Accelerator Unit at Oxford. In that year, Clark gave the J. C. Jacobsen Memorial Lecture to the Danish Academy of Science, and he could point with some satisfaction to the results of the dating programme, on a world basis, and to the advances in an understanding of global environmental change.[58] These tools were essential in the efforts by archaeologists to comprehend the character and the pace of change within and between prehistoric communities.

Another abiding interest was in collecting porcelain. Clark had always been intrigued by Jomon pottery, not least by its early dating, and from 1968 when he had attended a Congress in Tokyo he became an avid collector of Far Eastern porcelain, some of it rare and extremely fragile. He probably took some amusement from the terrified looks on the faces of his students when they, invited to tea, were handed a piece, told its age (but not its price) and asked to admire it.

---

[58] In 1980, Clark was able to publish some of his thoughts about the relationships in 'World prehistory and natural science', the J. C. Jacobsen Memorial Lecture, *Historisk-filosofiske Meddelelser*, 50 (1980), 1–40.

At Peterhouse, where he was Master 1973–80, he and his wife entertained scholars from all parts of the world, and without exception the visitors speak of their joy at being received so warmly in such dignified surroundings. Clark felt passionate about the College, and firmly believed that anyone fortunate enough to become attached to a place of learning and Fellowship should accept an obligation to work towards the general good rather than holing up in a room for personal study alone. He has been described as 'an absolutely perfect Master of Peterhouse'. The College had such a hold on him that sometimes even prehistory had to wait; visitors who came during the Bumps were promptly bundled off with the Master to support Peterhouse. Clark would say: 'these things are important, we can't spend all of our time thinking about archaeology'. The College elected him to an Honorary Fellowship in 1980 and he continued to participate in College matters whenever possible. Welcome breaks from University and College politics were taken at Aldeburgh in Suffolk where he could sail his small boat in peace; rumour has it that he sailed as he drove. This time was a particularly happy one for him and Mollie. Gardening at his home in Cambridge was another interest and their Wilberforce Road garden had always been proudly displayed to a constant flow of visitors.

By the early 1970s, he was now wholly immersed in a world prehistory which he alone it seemed could grasp. His first two editions of the *World Prehistory* book had exposed the gaps in information, some real and some of his own, and he set to in 'the sanctuary of the Master's lodge at Peterhouse' to work up the material flowing into Cambridge through visiting scholars, and also the information he had accumulated on his world travels. He had a formidable card index system that allowed him to build up a body of evidence which he could search at will for the latest references, discoveries, personalities and above all concepts. Quotations were liberally sprinkled throughout the cards, and he was always generous in acknowledging help of any kind in the lengthy dedications and lists in his publications. Writing drafts of his papers and books was an ever-absorbing task and pleasure, and when one report went off to the press, another was promptly initiated at his desk in the Master's lodge or in the comfortable home he and Mollie acquired after 1980.

Clark was invited to India in 1978 by B. K. Thapar, Director-General of the Archaeological Survey. Thapar had spent some time in Cambridge and had provided Clark with material for his revision of *World Prehistory*. In India, Clark gave the first Wheeler Memorial

Lectures, on the contribution of Sir Mortimer to Indian archaeology. The two lectures, published soon after,[59] allowed Clark to expound on Wheeler's disciplined approach to field-work and to ponder on his legacy to Indian archaeology. Clark was generous in his praise of the first subject, but less so of the second; he felt that Indian archaeologists should now break out of the shackles that a too-rigid approach to fieldwork *à la* Wheeler might create. The chronologies had now been established, and it was time to ask more searching questions of the evidence. Of course, it was phrased well, as it had to be in the circumstances.

In 1977 Clark published the third and final edition of his book, *World Prehistory in New Perspective*.[60] This was a total rewrite of his previous efforts, was far longer and better constructed. It bore all the signs of a greater awareness of the prehistoric world in all its variety, and of the need to refine the information by more, and more-refined, research. Radiocarbon dating was extensively used to correlate events, if not on a world-wide basis, then at least on a continental frame. This book, like the other two editions, went into translations in various languages, but only the 1969 version appeared in Serbo-Croat. World prehistory is now beyond the capabilities of any one person, and although it may be said that any synthesis that tries to cover the world will, like a British Rail timetable, inevitably have gaps and missed connections, it is the chronology of Clark's work that is important. He it was who tried, and succeeded in part, to present the prehistoric world in such a way that the themes of humanity, of invention and innovation, of contact and stress, of a community of necessities, and of demonstrable variations in behaviour, were always before us. Understated in places, exaggerated in others, the humanity of the race was always implicit in his text. The place of the natural sciences, the cornerstone of much of Clark's own work, was there, of course, but it was the human condition that interested him.

There followed, in a way as anticlimax, other books, of essay proportions and thematic approaches. *Mesolithic Prelude* (1980), *The Identity of Man* (1983), *Symbols of Excellence* (1986) and *Space, Time and Man* (1992) were books designed for more general readership and helped to advance the archaeological and prehistoric causes that Clark

[59] G. Clark, *Sir Mortimer and Indian Archaeology* (New Delhi, 1979).
[60] G. Clark, *World Prehistory in New Perspective* (Cambridge, 1977). This book had 554 pages, in contrast to the earlier editions of about 300 pages.

still wanted to pursue.[61] *Space, Time and Man* drew heavily upon Clark's own *World Prehistory* but extended the enquiry into relatively modern societies. His premise was that once humans and other animals had exploited the spatial dimensions of their environments, and had successfully occupied their territories over time, a parting of the ways occurred. Only humans could perceive the dimensionality of space and time, by consciously and at times illogically expanding their spatial horizons, and by deliberately setting out to document the passage of time.

*The Identity of Man as Seen by an Archaeologist* was another essay directing attention to the features that distinguished humans from other primates, namely culture and cultural behaviour. The awareness of other times, of times long ago, of ancestors, and the quest for immortality, each necessitating attempts to try to grasp some conception of the cosmos, could be traced in prehistory, and delineated in ethno-historical societies. This book had a logical but less well-argued successor in *Symbols of Excellence*, subtitled *Precious Materials as Expressions of Status*, in which Clark's admiration for the artistic expressions of the Stone Age could be followed through time into the realms of modern societies in which extraordinary combinations of precious substances came to signify position and power. In the conclusion, he deemed it a privilege to be able to study objects that oozed status, and to thereby acknowledge the power that they conveyed to mere citizens of the state. Here, as much as anywhere else, Clark exhibited his own political proclivities, and why not? His great and good friend Gordon Childe had done the same from the opposite end and that had not disturbed their close relationship and mutual admiration. Both men subscribed to the view that it was essential for all people of whatever political hue to co-operate, or else to perish, and Clark's writings through the years carried that stark message—facing up to our predicament as self-conscious human beings was how he expressed it.[62] In 1976 Clark had been able to publish his view of Gordon Childe in a wide assessment of developments in prehistoric studies since Childe's death.[63]

---

[61] G. Clark, *Mesolithic Prelude: The Palaeolithic-Neolithic Transition in Old World Prehistory* (Edinburgh, 1980) should logically have been written decades before its appearance; *The Identity of Man as Seen by an Archaeologist* (London, 1983); *Symbols of Excellence: Precious Materials as Expressions of Status* (Cambridge, 1986); *Space, Time and Man: A Prehistorian's View* (Cambridge, 1992). Several of these appeared in translation and, in all, about a dozen of his books appeared in one or more of thirteen languages.

[62] e.g., in his Inaugural Lecture, *The Study of Prehistory* (Cambridge, 1954).

[63] J. G. D. Clark, 'Prehistory since Childe', see above, n. 34. In this essay, Clark gave no real indication of his friendship with Childe; their surviving correspondence speaks of a familiarity and warmth that does not come through in his publications.

In 1990, the Praemium Erasmianum Foundation of The Netherlands awarded its Erasmus Prize to Grahame Clark, and the citation referred to his interdisciplinary work, his interest in prehistoric economics, his definitions and descriptions of ancient societies, and his contribution to the Cambridge school of archaeology. In accepting the award, Clark at once identified the uses to which it would be put. The Prehistoric Society would administer a Europa Fund to provide an annual award to a Europa Lecturer who was judged to have made significant contributions to European prehistoric studies. And the British Academy would administer an endowment for a medal which would recognise achievements in prehistoric research. The first recipient of the medal was Clark's former colleague and collaborator Stuart Piggott, whose delight at the award was a reminder to those present of the long friendship of the two men. There followed, in 1992, a knighthood for Grahame Clark on the grounds of his lifetime of research and his leadership in the study of the prehistory of the world. In 1994, the emergence of the Macdonald Institute for Archaeological Research at Cambridge was witnessed by Sir Grahame and Lady Clark, and the Grahame Clark Laboratory for Archaeology was dedicated. At the time of his death on 12 September 1995 he was planning another book, to be called *Man the Spiritual Primate*, and sections exist for future research into arguably the greatest prehistorian of the twentieth century.

At the end of the day, how best to sum up the career and contributions of Grahame Clark? Much has been written, and more will appear, about his pioneering work in prehistoric economies, in the ecological approach, in the study of organic artefacts, in his initiation of science-based archaeology, in his Academy projects, and in his world view of prehistory. But perhaps above all else was the encouragement given to his own graduates and to all those he met in Cambridge or abroad, to pursue an archaeology that could bind the world together both in the prehistoric past and in the future, through the identification of a commonality of aspiration and endeavour.

On 10 July 1926, the young Grahame Clark delivered a paper to the Natural History Society of Marlborough College; the paper was called 'Progress in Prehistoric Times' and the Secretary of the Society reported: 'He knew his subject very well'.

JOHN COLES
*Fellow of the Academy*

*Note.* I am grateful to many people who have helped in the compilation of this Memoir. I am particularly grateful to Lady Clark who has provided many papers for me to read, and who has given me insights into Grahame Clark's life. Information and comments have been sent to me by many colleagues, and I am happy to acknowledge the assistance of the following: C. J. Becker FBA; J. D. Clark FBA; B. J. Coles; B. W. Cunliffe FBA; J. D. Evans FBA; P. Gathercole; B. Gräslund; N. D. C. Hammond; C. F. C. Higham; M. S. F. Hood FBA; R. R. Inskeep; I. H. Longworth; M. P. Malmer FBA; A. McBurney; C. McVean; P. A. Mellars FBA; P. J. R. Modderman; D. J. Mulvaney FBA; the late S. Piggott FBA; Lord Renfrew FBA; D. A. Roe; P. Rowley-Conwy; C. T. Shaw FBA; G. R Willey FBA; and Sir David Wilson FBA.

DONALD DAVIE

*Proceedings of the British Academy*, **94**, 391–412

# Donald Alfred Davie
# 1922–1995

DONALD DAVIE has an honourable place in the distinguished line of English poet-critics: Sidney, Dryden, Johnson, Arnold, and (by adoption) Eliot. The constructive interplay between the poetry he wrote and what he wrote about poetry is as substantial and impressive as that in any of his predecessors. In his critical views he was fiercely independent, always resisting fashionable opinion, championing unpopular or unread poets, opening up new avenues, making unexpected and forceful comparisons between writings from different countries and cultures. As a critic he lived dangerously, but he unfailingly opened up debate. In spite of some changes in direction, the threads of continuity in his work are strong and sustaining, and there is a real coherence in the large volume of critical writing he has left. His status as a poet has been steadily increasing; a number of his poems can stand by any written in his century for their strength and subtlety.

I

Academically, Davie was a wanderer between universities in England, Ireland, and the United States, spending indeed only ten years of his professional life as a university teacher in the United Kingdom. And yet, for this writer who constantly uprooted himself, the concept of roots was all-important; sacred, indeed. He very often returned in his writings to the humdrum life of Barnsley in Yorkshire, where he was

© The British Academy 1997.

born on 17 July 1922, and to his Baptist working-class inheritance. Both his grandmothers had been in service, and his grandfather had been a miner. But, as he described in his autobiography, *These the Companions* (1982), the family had 'bettered themselves' to the extent that he was frightened of 'rough boys' in jerseys and clogs. His father, a small shopkeeper, was a deacon of his Baptist chapel; his mother, self-taught, had become a certificated school-teacher, knowing by heart most of *The Golden Treasury*. The wide cultural gulf which nevertheless existed between the adult Davie and his parents never separated him from them. In his poem 'Obiter Dicta' he wrote of his father's love of sententious maxims—'the precepts that he acts upon, / Brown with tobacco from his rule of thumb'—and asked whether his own poems do more than 'snap the elastic band / Of rhyme about them.' Some of the ways in which his Baptist background was vital to him—though he was never a Baptist in practice—will be seen shortly.

Like so many of his contemporaries from similar backgrounds, Davie was well served by the pre-war grammar school system, and from Barnsley Holgate Grammar School a scholarship took him to St Catharine's College, Cambridge, in 1940, where he completed only his freshman year before volunteering for the Royal Navy. The best pages of his autobiography describe his time as a telegraphist in North Russia, ferreting a miscellany of books out of unlikely places—Maeterlinck, Borrow, Shaw, Sterne—and then at Archangel coming in closer contact with Russians, a girl-friend among them. This experience of Russia, constricted as it was, was vital to his intellectual career, and, writing nearly forty years later, he strongly conveyed the impact of foreignness on him at that time, 'the baby in a family of grown-up babies'. He later became a sub-lieutenant, but the autobiography passes over the later part of his more than five years' war-service, except for his marriage in 1945 to Doreen John, of Plymouth. That relationship was the mainstay of the rest of his life.

## II

Davie returned to Cambridge in January 1946 to complete his degree (1947) and to work towards his doctorate 'on an Anglo-Russian theme'. The greatest influence on him in those years was Leavis: '*Scrutiny* was my bible, and F. R. Leavis my prophet.'[1] In disowning Leavis in later

---

[1] *These the Companions*, p. 77.

years for ignoring non-English literature and for the unfairness of his judgements, Davie always praised Leavis for his insistence on literary criticism as fundamentally a moral activity. Nor could he bring himself to condemn the exclusiveness of Leavis's selection of acceptable authors. He joked about it. It saved so much time. There were 'whole periods and genres of literature which I not only *need* not read, but *should not.*'[2] But on a number of occasions he argued that even if Leavis had been wrong in his listings, it was no bad thing for a tiro to have a strong leader to guide him into literature at first, even if he has to be discarded later on.

There is no doubt that although he was very uneasy about it and constantly debated the matter with himself, Davie believed in the doctrine of literary election which inspired Leavis's criticism. That is to say, there are those writings, and therefore writers, who are moral and acceptable. All others are immoral and unacceptable. In an important interview in the Vanderbilt years (1987), Laurence Lerner pressed him on this point—that it is the duty of criticism 'to expose the false'. 'On this particular issue,' said Davie, 'I suppose I am impenitently Leavisite. I do believe that the good is the enemy of the best. The more expert, the more skillful the good, the mediocre, the more dangerous it is . . . . The second-rate is the enemy.'[3]

It is the business of criticism, then, not so much to provide a league-table of merit as to discern the impostors. 'All things foul would wear the brows of grace,' and it is necessary that they be exposed. In *These the Companions,* which is at times dominated by this debate, Davie defensively styles true critics 'prigs', and makes clear the link between true criticism and Calvinism.

> In the arts, as between the genuine and the fake, or between the achieved and the unachieved, there cannot be any halfway house. The Calvinist doctrines of election and reprobation may be false and brutal in every other realm of human endeavour; in the arts they rule.[4]

The necessary intolerance of those he calls 'puritan', such as Leavis and Yvor Winters, is contrasted with 'the serenely Catholic temper' of C. S. Lewis and Tolkien. In judging literature there is 'ultimately no room for compromise, . . . for "Live and let live".'

The debate arises early in the book in writing of the suspicions of his

---

[2] Ibid., p. 78.
[3] *Cumberland Poetry Review*, vol. 8, no. 1 (1988), 42–4.
[4] *These the Companions*, p. 170.

close friend Douglas Brown concerning those circles at Cambridge which (it later transpired) had provided recruits for the KGB. 'For Douglas spuriousness was seamless and indivisible.'[5] Falseness in literature may be not only the equivalent of political treason, it may be its signifier. If this overstates the argument against the mediocre in literature, it pointedly indicates that in his persistent advocacy of unfashionable writers Davie was being neither perverse nor led simply by taste. He was arguing against literary fashion which not so much represented as embodied false social, political, and religious attitudes and assumptions. The concept of 'the gathered church', which became so very important to him, was essentially the vision of a minority community living in permanent opposition to the values of the many. Within its confines as without, literature, conduct, and belief were indeed 'seamless and indivisible'.

## III

In 1950 Davie moved to Ireland to take up an appointment at Trinity College, Dublin. In spite of centuries of Anglicisation—in which TCD had been a leading agent—Ireland was in many ways a foreign country, and the discovery of its otherness, including poets like Austin Clarke almost unknown in England, was immensely stimulating. And the stimulus worked both ways. This is how Augustine Martin saw it:

> Dublin was a peaceful and relaxed city in the fifties and Davie loved it. The young poet was sufficiently exercised trying to introduce modern critical methods to his students and to the far less educable ranks of Dublin's critical literati. Indeed it could be said that Denis Donoghue at University College, Dublin, and Donald Davie at Trinity, in that decade dragged Irish literary study into the modern age. I recall the unexampled spectacle of undergraduates, myself among them, moving back and forth between the universities as one or other of these two happened to be lecturing.[6]

During the Ireland years, Davie published two very influential books of criticism and a volume of poetry. It is remarkable how *Purity of Diction in English Verse* (1952) established both the manner of his critical discourse and the substance of his critical preoccupations. A critical book by Davie was characteristically an argument developed in a series

---

[5] Ibid., p. 26.
[6] George Dekker (ed.), *Donald Davie and the Responsibilities of Literature* (1983), p. 55.

of brisk and succinct essays on discrete authors or writings. The reader is surprised to find each essay ending as its momentum increases, and is left at the end to consider how the wealth of interlinked suggestions, coming from so many different angles, creates the book's argument and confirms its conclusion.

The diction of verse is offered as something different from and inferior to the language of poetry, but this modest confession of a concern with something lesser turns out to be a rhetorical ploy. The diction Davie writes about is the language he wants. The operative words are restraint, sobriety, urbanity. The acme of this kind of poetry, written with a full sense of responsibility to tradition and to the known society which is its audience, is the eighteenth century, in Goldsmith, in Cowper, in Charles Wesley. The enemy of pure diction is metaphorical excess and the dislocated syntax of poets who live in a society which has itself become incoherent, and whose only utterance can be outbursts of personal emotion. Keats, Tennyson, and (particularly) Hopkins are attacked, as well as the symbolist tradition, for which 'dislocation of syntax is esential'. Milton is accused of 'egotism, individualism and arrogance', but Shakespeare remains outside the argument, except by inference. Two subjects which became of major importance for Davie make their appearance in this early book: the eighteenth-century hymn, and the poetry of Ezra Pound. In later life Davie said with characteristic self-deprecation that he began reading Pound on a tip from his head-master as he was preparing for Cambridge scholarship examinations: 'Not many of them [the other applicants] will be reading Ezra Pound.'[7] In 1952, though Pound's critical aphorisms are often quoted, the poetry remains beyond the pale. Davie has not at this time accepted Pound's distinction between symbolism and imagism. Pound's verse is 'speech atomized', and Davie says unhesitatingly what he was later to hesitate so much over: ' the development from imagism in poetry to fascism in politics is clear and unbroken.'[8]

'Restraint' in *Purity of Diction* means restraint. On the very first page of the book it is suggested that pure diction is achieved only by suppression. 'Words are thrusting at the poem and being fended off from it.' This idea of poetry as sacrifice rather than indulgence is central to Davie, and achieved fine expression in *A Gathered Church* (1978; the Clark Lectures for 1976): 'Art *is* measure, *is* exclusion; is therefore

[7] *PN Review 88,* vol. 19, no. 2, 4.
[8] *Purity of Diction in English Verse* (1952) (rev. ed. 1967), p. 99.

simplicity (hard-earned), is sobriety, tense with all the extravagances that it has been tempted by and has denied itself'.[9] This stands in direct and perhaps conscious opposition to Blake's Proverb of Hell: 'Damn braces: Bless relaxes', and his Voice of the Devil: 'Those who restrain desire, do so because theirs is weak enough to be restrained.' I introduce this central notion of poetry as self-denial as opposed to self-indulgence because of the postscript which Davie added to the 1967 reissue of *Purity of Diction.* There he said that the book was a manifesto for the poems which he had been writing at the time, and indeed for the poetry of all those like-minded writers who became known as the Movement. If the book overstated its case, it is because it was 'an angry reaction from the tawdry amoralism of a London Bohemia which had destroyed Dylan Thomas'. What he believed the poets of the Movement had in common was 'an originally passionate rejection . . . of all the values of Bohemia'. The identification of loose-living and poetic excess is striking and characteristic. Seamlessness once again.

Those of us who are old enough to remember the coming of the Movement will remember the relief with which we then applauded the cool, level-headed, intelligent, discursive poems to be found in Robert Conquest's anthology, *New Lines*, published in 1956, and including work by Davie, Amis, Jennings, Larkin, Enright, Holloway, Gunn, Wain, and Conquest himself—a very academic group. In 1959 Davie wrote a vitriolic attack on the Movement poets—himself included—for the 'craven defensiveness' with which they sold out to the demands of their educated audience. It seemed to him that they spent all their energy in achieving the right tone, instead of trying to know the world we live in.[10] It is difficult to accept this as a fair criticism of *Brides of Reason* (1955), unless it is a fault that these assured, clever, controlled poems continue to give their readers so much pleasure. It is true that too many of them are self-reflexive: are about writing poetry; but their world *is* the world we live in—as in 'Belfast on a Sunday Afternoon'. Their subtlety is often undervalued: the famous 'Remembering the 'Thirties' for example is trotted out as praising the 'neutral tone' of the Movement as against the disabling irony of the age of Auden. It does no such thing.

*Articulate Energy: An Enquiry into the Syntax of English Poetry* (1955) made Davie famous. It was a resounding success: its originality

---

[9] *A Gathered Church*, p. 26.
[10] Barry Alpert (ed.), *The Poet in the Imaginary Museum* (1977), p. 72.

and force were something quite new—'making syntax, of all things, a matter of living concern!' wrote Christopher Ricks, one of Davie's most consistent admirers.

> Most people [wrote Davie], if they think about the syntax of poetry at all, regard it as something neutral, in itself neither favourable nor unfavourable to poetry, a mere skeleton on which are hung the truly poetic elements, such as imagery or rhythm. . . . But a skeleton obviously has a great deal to do with the beauty or ugliness of the body it supports.[11]

Elsewhere, with change of metaphor, syntax is 'the very nerve of poetry'. It is hard to know whether to call the technique of his discourse poetic or forensic. He summons a host of witnesses, for or against syntax as it were: Fenollosa, Frye, T. E. Hulme, Nabokov, Yeats, Dylan Thomas, Yvor Winters, Edmund Wilson, Berkeley and Bergson, Pope and Pound. The power of the book is the resourceful fertility of producing these witnesses and throwing them into debate in a series of minimalist engagements.

'It will be apparent', the last chapter begins, 'that the impulse behind all this writing is conservative.' Those poets who know how to surrender to and to conquer words all at once, who submit in the syntax of their verse to what is considered normal in prose, are making 'a declaration of faith in the conscious mind, its intelligible structure and significant activity'.[12] The symbolist innovation, demanding the creation of meaning by the dislocation of syntax, brings us to the point where 'to write poetry or to read it, we have to behave like idiots'.[13]

For all its connections with Davie's later thinking, *Articulate Energy* was in many ways a conclusion. Davie spent the year 1957–8 at Santa Barbara in California. He met Yvor Winters, poet and critic, whose work he had admired for a number of years, and whose tight circle of admissible writers makes Leavis's exclusiveness look lax. Though the experience of California, like the experience of Russia and of Ireland, deeply affected Davie, it was not the cause of major shifts in his thinking which become apparent at the end of his Irish years. In July 1957 he gave two broadcast talks for the BBC, under the title of 'The Poet in the Imaginary Museum'. These talks take off from the contention of André Malraux that modernism is the result of the ready availability of the art of the past in all cultures through the new

---

[11] *Articulate Energy*, p. 67.
[12] Ibid., p. 141.
[13] Ibid., p. 146.

mechanical means of reproduction and preservation. Davie, although he argues that for literature print has served that purpose for centuries, asks what the poet of today is now to do when a single accepted tradition has been widened into 'the innumerable galleries' of the imaginary museum. He attacks the poets of the Movement for their parochialism, but he offers no programme in face of the 'unprecedented freedom' now granted to poets—except to praise Ezra Pound for his attempt to embrace international traditions ignored by contemporary English poets. In *Articulate Energy*, Pound was still on the wrong side of the fence.

## IV

In 1958 Davie and his family moved to Cambridge, where he stayed until 1964, becoming a Fellow of Gonville and Caius College. These were very productive years, concluding with his first book on Pound, *Ezra Pound: Poet as Sculptor* (1965). The title is explained by another broadcast talk which Davie gave in 1962, 'Two Analogies for Poetry'. The first analogy is poetry as music, an analogy developed by Pasternak; the second, preferred, analogy is poetry as sculpture. Davie derives from Adrian Stokes the argument that the two activities of sculpture— modelling and carving—are fundamentally different. To model out of clay is to produce something new. The one who carves stone is a humbler person, releasing what lies hidden in the stone. In poetry, the moulders are the symbolists, arrogant and presumptuous people inventing their own worlds. Now accepting Pound's distinction between imagists and symbolists, Davie enrols Pound among those who use language to reveal a reality which is not in the poet's head but is 'as fully and undeniably *out there*' as the block of marble in the quarry. It is impossible to maintain the analogy, because the block of marble for the poet is both language and nature, and some of Davie's most powerful and important poems derive from the tormenting uncertainty of the relationship between the two. But the point is made. There is the world of imagination and the world of reality: true poetry serves the latter. The polarities of poetry remain the same, although there are some changes in the poets.

There is nothing to my mind which so confirms Davie's lifelong commitment to the eighteenth century as his implicit acceptance of the Swiftian distrust of 'enthusiam' (as shown in *A Tale of a Tub* and *The*

*Mechanical Operation of the Spirit*). In both Swift and Davie there is nothing but contempt for the idea that inspiration could create the sublime. The source of inspiration is suspect, and what it produces is stylistically vicious. The whole tradition of the *furor poeticus*, in Plato (in the Ion), in Longinus, in Shelley, is repudiated. The imagination is anything but Adam's dream: it is individualist pretension. Truth has to be sought in tradition and the common forms.

An alliance bweteen stylistic opposites such as Swift and Pound looks unlikely, but in *Poet as Sculptor* Davie adduces G. S. Fraser and Yeats to establish Pound's allegiance to the values of the Enlightenment. In particular, 'Pound's whole philosophy of history is in the strictest sense "Augustan"'—like that of 'Pope and Swift'.[14] Above all the book lauds Pound for believing that reality is not something that we make, but is 'undeniably *out there*'.

> For Pound, color inheres in the colored object, it is of its nature; just as the carved or hewn shape inheres in the stone block before it has been touched; just as words inhere in the natures they name, not in the minds that do the naming. Not in painting any more than in poetry will Pound agree that 'it all depends how you look at it.' Nature exists as other, bodied against us, with real attributes and her own laws which it is our duty to observe.[15]

Davie's admiration for Pound was above all for his work as translator. Translation was a means of enlarging modes of feeling, countering narrowness and parochialism by making available the resources of other literatures. It was the primary bridge between cultures. To encourage translation as an academic discipline was one of the reasons Davie went to Essex. That Pound was a supreme translator, enhancing his own poetic being as he translated, was a primary reason for writing about him.

*The Forests of Lithuania,* the long poem based on the *Pan Tadeusz* of Adam Mickiewicz which Davie published in 1959, is not a translation but an adaptation. 'I have no Polish', said Davie, stating that he had founded his poem on the Everyman translation by G. R. Noyes.[16] But it served the same purpose as translation, bringing Mickiewicz into the consciousness of many English readers for the first time, and giving a quite new dimension to Davie's own verse. The poems of his second volume of verse, *A Winter Talent* (1957), had ranged from the domestic

[14] pp. 169–71.
[15] p. 158.
[16] *Collected Poems 1950–1970* (1972), *ad loc.*

and familiar to difficult and sometimes impenetrable meditations, of which the best are two water poems, 'The Fountain' (based on a passage in Berkeley) and 'The Waterfall at Powerscourt'. Here in *The Forests of Lithuania* is an ambitious long poem, admirably sustained. While the reader may wish that Davie had broken silence on the context of the several sections, what most impresses is the wonderful clarity and lucidity of the writing. There is a variety of metres in mostly short-line structures with intricate rhyming. If the poem fulfils Davie's ideas on diction, it is a fine tribute to them.

Davie's unpretentious critical work, *The Heyday of Sir Walter Scott* (1961), introduced as 'no more than a report on desultory reading over several years', was in fact an important venture in comparative criticism, establishing the international focus which was particularly his own. The authors he treats, sometimes in fairly rapid fashion, include Pushkin, Scott, Maria Edgeworth, and Fenimore Cooper—Russia, Scotland, Ireland, North America. The book seeks to examine 'what romanticism is . . . at least as it expresses itself in the novel'. It is particularly good on the collision of past and future in these novels and the Romantic concern about true community in contemporary society.

Finally from these Cambridge years, *A Sequence for Francis Parkman* (1961). These poems, further evidence of Davie's investment in North America and the eighteenth century, illustrate above all his talent for cultural geology; that is to say, his keen sense of the historical and geographical forces which shape cultures. Poems about Lasalle, Montcalm, Bougainville, Pontiac, show (wrote Howard Erskine-Hill) 'a preoccupation with exceptional enterprise and courage, but equally with betrayal, with the lost cause (French Canada), and disappointed ambition'.[17]

## V

In his autobiography, Davie passed in silence over his four years at the University of Essex, 1964–8, the 'four bad years',[18] except for one or two asides. But these were crucial years, creating a watershed in his life. His wife writes: 'His experience there changed his outlook on life forever.'[19] Because there has been much misunderstanding, the events of this period need to be looked at in some detail.

[17] *Donald Davie and the Responsibilities of Literature* (1983), p. 114.
[18] *Collected Poems* (1990), p. 164.
[19] Private communication.

Essex was one of the several new universities set up in the 1960s: York, Kent, East Anglia, Warwick, Lancaster being others. Albert Sloman, the Vice-Chancellor, caused controversy with the statement of his aims in the broadcast Reith Lectures, *A University in the Making* (1964). What he wanted to set up at Wivenhoe near Colchester was to be nothing like Oxford and Cambridge with their collegiate system but something resembling a North American university in size and a continental university in atmosphere. Academically he wanted interdisciplinary study, and, so far as literature was concerned, he wanted to break away from the dominance of English departments in the Arts Faculties of English universities and ensure that those who studied English literature were capable of reading other literatures. Sloman had been a colleague of Davie's at Trinity College, Dublin, before he moved to the Chair of Hispanic Studies at Liverpool. English literature at that time was not in itself a degree subject at TCD; it had to be studied in conjunction with another literature, ancient or modern. This 'comparative' background, taken with Davie's interests in Russian and North American literature, and his record and reputation, made him an ideal candidate for Sloman, and Davie became Essex's first Professor of Literature, to work with Jean Blondel, Professor of Government, in setting up a School of Comparative Studies.

Given Davie's literary interests, it is no surprise that he accepted the invitation. It is surprising, however, that one who found university and college administration irksome, and avoided it so far as possible, should launch himself into a situation where as head of department, dean of a school, and Pro-Vice-Chancellor of an entire infant university, he was bound to spend several years in planning, organising, and conferring. All the same, there is plenty of evidence that the early period of planning was exciting and pleasant.

The task of working out a curriculum involving collaboration between literatures and between literature and politics became extremely complicated because of university planning. On the one side there were restrictions, on the other expansion. The restrictions related to the 'areas' on which Essex decided to concentrate: Russia, North America, and Latin America. Each student was required to choose one of these areas to study in conjunction with Britain. Students without language qualifications who chose Russia or Latin America would be given a crash linguistic course in a preliminary year. No European country beside Russia was featured. When asked about the omission of France (for which he was not responsible) Davie would say optimistically that students knew French anyway.

Expansion very quickly brought sociology and art into the School of Comparative Studies. In spite of the difficulties, Davie and Blondel worked out a scheme by which all departments would collaborate in a common first year, centring on the Enlightenment and the twentieth century. Four subjects, four areas, and two major historical periods gave breadth rather than depth, and it is fair to say that the common first year might have been better at graduate level, or at least as a common *final* year at undergraduate level. As it was, the balance of the scheme was imperilled by the fact that most literature students did not have Spanish or Russian and, disinclined to accept the preliminary language year, flooded into the North American option. A more serious problem was that there was no opportunity for the study in depth of major areas of English literature, and those with particular interest in English literature might graduate in ignorance of large parts of it. The departments of government and sociology did not suffer in the same way. The common first year in the School of Comparative Studies was for them an attractive show-piece; and they were both able to extend and develop their own disciplines in a different school, the School of Social Studies. It would seem that Davie envisaged such an extension, for he invited a specialist in Shakespeare and drama to join him as a senior colleague, but in the event no provision was made in those areas.

The first students were admitted in 1965, and the programme began in full in 1966. The success of Davie's planning was in the graduate programme. He attracted a number of extremely able graduate students, many of them from Cambridge, among them John Barrell, Elaine Feinstein, Andrew Crozier, and George Hyde. He gave inspiration to the MA in Literary Translation by his own work with Angela Livingstone in translating Boris Pasternak, whose poetry had become the major influence in his own poetic career. Angela Livingstone has written an outstanding essay illuminating the Pasternak-Davie relationship,[20] and by using her work to identify poems influenced by Pasternak as well as learning about the proximity to the original of those which announce themselves as translations or adaptations, one can measure the extraordinary lift which the presence of Pasternak gave to Davie's imagination and the tread of his verse. Many of these poems are in the volume *Events and Wisdoms*, published as early as 1964. *The Poems of*

---

[20] *Donald Davie and the Responsibilities of Literature*, pp. 8–30.

*Doctor Zhivago,* translations with an introduction and commentary, appeared in 1965. The fruits of his Essex collaboration with Angela Livingstone are to be seen in an excellent selection of critical essays, *Pasternak: Modern Judgements* (1969), in which the prose is translated by Livingstone and the verse by himself.

Davie was also able (in those palmy days) to use university funding to help Essex become a centre where one could learn about new directions in the poetry of North America and Latin America. In particular, he brought attention to the work of the Black Mountain poets—Charles Olson, Ed Dorn, and Robert Creeley—by actually bringing Ed Dorn to Essex on a prolonged visit. He was patron to their English follower, Tom Raworth, and he promoted the work of poets such as J. H. Prynne and Roy Fisher who were sympathetic to the Black Mountain poets and to the Objectivist, Louis Zukovsky. With the presence of poets on the staff, among the students, as visitors for long stays or just to give readings, Essex must have been the liveliest place in England as a forum for the discussion of new lines in poetry.

However, in Stanford in California, they were discussing possible candidates to succeed Yvor Winters, the lonely poet and critic so much admired by Davie, who had set up a demanding and influential creative writing school. Davie's name was one—the only one—that could win the approval of both Winters and the faculty, and an approach was made.[21] In the early summer of 1967, Davie had told the Vice-Chancellor that he and Doreen were seriously thinking of emigrating, giving as his reason his disaffection with the intellectual climate of England. Some time later he told him of the Stanford approach and how much the invitation attracted him, at the same time expressing his disapproval of the amount of authority being given to students in English universities, including Essex. Just after the Christmas of 1967, he handed in his resignation, although this remained confidential.

The strain on Davie for having made his decision to leave Essex was evident in his reaction to proposals for change and development, which appeared to him as disloyalty towards the ideals underlying the curriculum. He expressed his fears for the future of the Essex system, though he knew that its maintenance depended to a large extent upon his continuing at Essex. In May 1968 the university erupted in violent student rebellion, which though it was perhaps not the worst in Britain was ideologically the fiercest and was certainly the most widely

---

[21] Interview with Davie, *PN Review 88,* 69.

publicised. To Davie the revolution was the manifestation of the social and political wrongheadedness he had spoken of to the Vice-Chancellor, and ever thereafter he gave the student disorders as his reason for abandoning Essex. The bitterness which he often expressed at his work being undone by the students was misplaced; it was not in any way the curricular structure at Essex which they were attacking; indeed most of the revolutionaries had been attracted to the university precisely by the blending of literature with politics and sociology which he had sponsored, and among those members of his department who supported the students were those who believed most deeply in the necessity for comparative literature.

The period of the revolution was wretched for Davie. As Pro-Vice-Chancellor he had to face at mass-meetings the jeers of students who minutes before had been cheering the fabricated news that Jean-Paul Sartre had sent a telegram applauding their insurrection. It is easy to understand the very bleak mood of many of the poems, and the jaundiced, sometimes splenetic mood in which he wrote about England, in the *Essex Poems* of 1969 and *More Essex Poems*. He concludes the depressed and defeated lines of 'Epistle. To Enrique Caracciolo Trejo' with the salute: 'I relish your condition, / Expatriate!'. When the news of his intending departure came out, many people expressed surprise that if student insurgence were his reason for leaving, California, in many ways the home of student unrest, should be his destination. To such people he frankly replied that he did indeed 'relish the condition' of being an expatriate: of not being responsible for what lies about you.


# VI


Doreen Davie writes of the ten years at Stanford as 'a happy interlude' although 'there was no thought of moving on'.

> We formed close and lasting friendships which still endure: Ian and Ruth Watt, Albert and Maclin Guerard, Janet Lewis (Yvor Winters' widow), George and Linda-Jo Dekker, friends from an earlier time; and twenty miles up the road in San Francisco, Thom Gunn.[22]

Davie was particularly happy with the creative writing course which he had inherited from Yvor Winters. It was a graduate course and the standard for admission was very strict. Demands were high, too; on

---

[22] Private communication.

teacher and pupil. And the bond created between teacher and pupil was strong. One of the essays in *Donald Davie and the Responsibilities of Literature*, by Harvey Oxenhorn, gives an account of Davie's methods and procedures, and is a warm tribute to the value of his teaching.

There are indeed many tributes on record to Davie's success as a teacher, from different periods of his career, at TCD and at Cambridge as well as in the USA: to his courtesy and patience, his learning, his generosity with his time, and to the unfailing stimulus he provided. It is certain that Davie's far-reaching influence on literary studies, particularly in the USA, is due not only to his writings but to his teaching at graduate level; to the dialogue of literary exploration which he opened up with each student he supervised.

Davie kept his relationship with England alive in many ways. By return visits lengthy enough for him to inscribe himself in every part of the country in his book of poems, *The Shires* (1974); by concentrating in a whole series of poems on the formative period of English imperial expansion in the eighteenth century; by committing his next major critical work almost exclusively to twentieth-century English poetry; and by being received in 1972 into the Episcopalian Church, which he had been attending since 1969.[23]

Davie had given a remarkable coda to *Essex Poems*. The title of the last poem, 'Or, Solitude' is the subtitle of Wordsworth's poem 'Lucy Gray' about the little girl who was lost on the fell and now is to be seen by travellers, a happy revenant who 'sings a solitary song'. Davie's poem is about an Iowan farm-boy who also was lost in the snow, and rides his horse alone 'for ever'. Davie can see the story as a metaphor of rural depopulation—but no more; and the short poem ends with a *cri de coeur*:

> The transcendental nature
> Of poetry, how I need it!
> And yet it was for years
> What I refused to credit.

The first line of this stanza was changed in later editions to read, much more cautiously and ambiguously, 'The metaphysicality / Of poetry, how I need it!' Whether it is named the transcendent or the metaphysical, the numinous does not in fact makes its entrance into Davie's verse until the brilliant, spare, mordant ironies of *To Scorch or Freeze*

---

[23] G. A. Schirmer, in *Donald Davie and the Responsibilities of Literature*, p. 130.

of 1988. His poetry remains for the time being directed, as he praises Hardy's poetry for being directed, 'into the world of historical contingency, a world of specific places at specific times'. The poems in *The Shires* are uneven in quality, but there are some remarkable evocations of places, of people, and of events. The poem on Sussex best illustrates his own position as returning exile. He and his family are now visitors, and he looks on all this Englishness with 'an alien poet's eye':

> 'Brain-drain' one hears no more of,
> And there's no loss. There is
> Another emigration:
> Draining away of love.

In a note to the poem 'Trevenen' in the *Collected Poems* of 1972, Davie said of the mass of information he had gathered about James Trevenen, the midshipman who sailed in the *Resolution* on Cook's last voyage, that he had thought of writing a closet-drama around him, but found he had no talent for the enterprise. As it is, this long, wide-ranging poem in octosyllabic couplets stands, with a poem on George Vancouver, in close relationship with *Six Epistles to Eva Hesse* (1970). This last is an ambitious venture about a collection of people from the seventeenth century to Victorian times, all associated with exploration and colonisation. It is cast as comedy, and the manner is light-hearted and bantering. The work as a whole refuses heroism, nobility, the teleologies of epic and romance, even the teleology of plot. Davie is dealing with those who, like Trevenen and Vancouver, worked in the shadow of greater men, or who were simply successors. There is Henri de Tonty, loyal lieutenant of La Salle, La Pérouse, following Cook and Bougainville in the Pacific, the obscure John Ledyard, also with Cook, and the obscurer Hargraves in Hudson Bay. What is celebrated is endurance, patience, above all loyalty. In spite of its Hudibrastic flippancy, the poem is working at the 'Abstracted potent lexicon / Of place, which helps us understand / Where, in some ultimate sense, we stand.' The indigenous peoples who were implicated in this 'where we stand' do not make their appearance, except for a brusque reference at the end of the fourth epistle to the myth of the noble savage.

The thesis of *Thomas Hardy and British Poetry (1973)*, is 'that in British poetry of the last fifty years (as not in America), the most far-reaching influence, for good or ill, has not been Yeats, still less Eliot or Pound, not Lawrence, but Hardy.' The book is perhaps the most trenchant and provocative of Davie's critical works, and perhaps the most severe and pugnacious. It is not always easy to follow the argument, as there seem to be a number of different battles going on at the same time, or, to put it another way, there are several maps in play, on each of which the relationships between poets are differently plotted, and the reader is not always sure which map is the right one to use at any given moment. It is impossible to summarise a book so complex in its discriminations. It is quite certainly about 'the responsibilities of literature', and poetry settling for less, and selling itself short. A basic theme is the now familiar one of observation of the real world against the creation of mental worlds. Hardy accepts life on the terms in which it offers itself and has to be coped with. But this lowering of the sights was a dangerous example to Larkin and others who followed, and turned Hardy's restraint into a surrender to meanness. The blame for this is in the moral cowardice and political irresponsibility of the English intelligentsia.

As in many of Davie's critical writings, one feels in the Thomas Hardy book a distinction between the fineness of close readings, moving through poems with an intelligence and sensitivity not to be matched in contemporary criticism, and the very different texture of the theoretical positions which are derived from these readings. And then again, the establishment of these critical positions is often in strong textural contrast with the political comminations linked with them. Again, if one senses as one must the close relationship between Davie's critical tenets and the poetry he was writing, one also feels so often that the poems he writes are of still finer grain than any level of his prose criticism. This seems to me particularly true on the matter so insisted on in the prose, fidelity to the world as it is, never put more bluntly than in *These the Companions*: 'the writer's sole duty is to report what was, *as it was*'.[24] There are three well-known poems of Davie's, one of them perhaps the best he ever wrote, which refuse the possibility of such confidence. 'The Hill Field', published in the 1964 collection, begins as an adaptation of Pasternak, but has entirely its own ending. A half-cut cornfield is described in a number of similes. Then the poet rounds on himself.

> It is Brueghel or Samuel Palmer,
> Some painter, coming between
> My eye and the truth of a farmer,
> So massively sculpts the scene.

[24] p. 80.

> The sickles of poets dazzle
> These eyes that were filmed from birth;
> And the miller comes with an easel
> To grind the fruits of earth.

Here it is the conventions of art, not true sight, which create art. In famous stanzas from 'In the Stopping Train' (the title poem of the 1977 volume of poems), it is words which film the eyes.

> Jonquil is a sweet word.
> Is it a flowering bush?
> Let him helplessly wonder
> for hours if perhaps he's seen it.
>
> Has it a white and yellow
> flower, the jonquil? Has it
> a perfume? Oh his art could
> always pretend it had.
>
> He never needed to see,
> not with his art to help him.
> He never needed to use his
> nose, except for language.

Finally, there is 'Having No Ear', from *The Battered Wife and Other Poems* (1982). This has to be given in full.

> Having no ear, I hear
> And do not hear the piano-tuner ping,
> Ping, ping one string beneath me here, where I
> Ping-ping one string of Caroline English to
> Tell if Edward Taylor tells
> The truth, or no.
>
> Dear God, such gratitude
> As I owe thee for giving, in default
> Of a true ear or of true holiness,
> This trained and special gift of knowing when
> Religious poets speak themselves to God,
> And when, to men.
>
> The preternatural! I know it when
> This perfect stranger—angel-artisan—
> Knows how to edge our English Upright through
> Approximations back to rectitude,
> Wooing it back through quarter-tone
> On quarter-tone, to true.
>
> Mystical? I abjure the word, for if
> Such faculty is known and recognized

As may tell sharp from flat, and both from true,
And I lack that capacity, why should I
Think Paradise by other light than day
Sparkled in Taylor's eye?

The doubts in this poem clearly have a much deeper concern than with the capacity of the true poet to tell the truth about the world. For one thing it is a transcendent world and not alone the human and visible world. But it is the inclusion of the truth of the critic with the truth of the poet that makes this such an important—and disturbing—poem. The faith which is shaken by the poem is in the proposition that the true poet speaks the truth, and that this truth is recognised and confirmed by the skill and understanding of the true critic. Recognising the preternatural skill of the piano-tuner, 'angel-artisan', and his own inability in *that* area, the poet-critic turns to question whether he indeed possesses that—must be *more* than preternatural—mystical skill for distinguishing the true from the false in religious poetry for which in the second stanza he thanked God, in a tone which surely derives from 'Holy Willie's Prayer'. Why should he have the presumption to think he is above other men blessed to determine and pronounce that what illuminates Taylor's writing is *lux aeterna* and not plain daylight? Obviously this self-accusation has no more logical justification than Hamlet's mortification at the Player's ability to weep for Hecuba. But this shaft of uncertainty and self-doubting might well be a gift from above.

## VII

In 1973 Davie was elected a Fellow of the American Academy of Arts and Sciences. In 1976 he delivered the Clark Lectures in Cambridge. These were published in 1978 as *A Gathered Church: The Literature of the English Dissenting Interest, 1700–1930.* There is here the accustomed energy in fighting an uphill battle against fashion and popularity as Davie meets prejudice against the dissenting tradition as implying philistinism, money-making and theological fierceness. Isaac Watts, the hero of the lectures, makes positive the negative virtues of restraint: simplicity, sobriety, and measure. His hymns are genuine tribal lays, belonging to the *hortus conclusus* of the dissenting communion (in which he insists the Unitarians have no right of entry). It is the decay of the best traditions of dissent in the early nineteenth century which has led to the association of dissent with fervour, iconoclasm, tastelessness, and the ignoring of the sacraments. George Whitefield is pitted against Mark Rutherford.

In 1978 Davie accepted an invitation to move to Vanderbilt University in Nashville, Tennessee. Doreen writes: 'As a poet, Donald was revered at Vanderbilt, as he was not elsewhere.' *Three for Water-Music* appeared in 1981, and *The Battered Wife and Other Poems* in 1982. This last is a collection richly varied in style, diction, subject and tone; poetry of great power and constant felicities. Of Howard Warshaw, for example:

> His work is what
> Stands, but as if on Easter Island, rude
> And enigmatic effigies, a lot
> Unsold at history's auction.

Davie was able to spend more time in England, in the house near Exeter which he and his wife had bought, and see more of their family. A return which gave him very great pleasure was to the annual Yeats Summer School at Sligo. He had been in at the beginning of that school, started in 1959 by his Cambridge tutor T. R. Henn, and he was a regular lecturer there in the 1960s. The school is affectionately described in several pages of *These the Companions*. Davie was invited back and served as Director of the school from 1982–4. In 1987 he was elected a Fellow of the British Academy; he took the keenest interest in its affairs and regularly attended all meetings until illness made travel from Devon too difficult for him. He was also made an Honorary Fellow both of Trinity College, Dublin, and St Catharine's College, Cambridge. In 1988, Davie finally retired from Vanderbilt and took up permanent residence in England.

Davie's extraordinary energy in his later years can be measured by the number of collections of essays, reviews, articles, and lectures which appeared. *Trying to Explain* (1979) combined English and American themes. *Dissentient Voice* (1982), centred on Browning, was based on the Ward-Phillips Lectures at Notre Dame in 1980. *Under Briggflatts* (1989) provided a wide survey of British poetry between 1960 and 1988. *Essays in Dissent* (1995) reprinted the Clark Lectures and the Ward-Phillips Lectures, adding a number of related writings, including the caustic 'A Day with the *DNB*'. Davie's anthologies are always ideological: to the early collection of longer eighteenth-century poems, *The Late Augustans* (1958), two important anthologies were added in his later years, *The New Oxford Book of Christian Verse* (1981), and the learned and attractive volume, *The Psalms in English*, published post-humously in Penguin Classics (1996).

Davie's last full-length critical book was *The Eighteenth-Century Hymn in English* (1993), which drew together many of the themes, and the poets, which had dominated his writing about the eighteenth century over the years. What he derives from the close-reading of well-known hymns by Watts is a matter for admiration in both the old and new senses of the word.

Davie's last volume of poems—the last, that is, published in his lifetime (there is already one posthumous volume and there may be more)—was *To Scorch or Freeze* (1988). They are largely religious poems, and in style and tone they represent a change of direction remarkable for a poet in his mid-sixties. The flexibility of the diction is very noticeable: it can be both dignified and undignified, formal and colloquial. His version of Psalm 45, 'Inditing a Good Matter', begins:

> I find nothing to say,
> I am as heavy as lead.
> I take small satisfaction
> In anything I have said.

Donald Davie died in Exeter on 18 September 1995. Few would dispute his position as the best critic of twentieth-century poetry. What is so remarkable about his output is its combination of breadth with depth. He insisted on denationalising the study of poetry in England by bringing in North America and Eastern Europe, and in America he made known the poetry of Britain. But it is not only correlation and internationalism for which he is important. If one reads through a collection of essays on British poets, such as *Under Briggflatts,* one is so impressed by Davie's attentiveness to the very wide range of writings with which he deals. Everything is so important to him! Everything is at stake in every line of every poem he writes about. Of course one cannot agree with him all the time. If his judgements appear too firm, or too severe, they all too often convict his dissenting reader of lazy reading.

A final note. Davie was a brilliant lecturer. He impelled attention, and his Yorkshire voice was clear in every corner. Even in important formal public lectures—as for example in Ann Arbor in 1965—he would carry with him a ruled hardback student's notebook in which he had written out his lecture in longhand. Often enough he would disconcert the audience by snapping the book shut before the expected time, leaving them, they might think in mid-air, to draw their own conclusions from what he had said.

PHILIP EDWARDS
*Fellow of the Academy*

*Note.* I am grateful to many people for the assistance they have given me. To Doreen Davie and George Dekker; to Sir Albert Sloman, Jean Blondel, Angela Livingstone, Richard Gray, Laurence Lerner, Henry Gifford, Gareth Reeves, Robert von Hallberg.

ESMOND DE BEER

*Proceedings of the British Academy,* **94**, 415–425

# Esmond Samuel de Beer
# 1895–1990

THE BRITISH ACADEMY possesses neither an achievement of arms nor a motto. Were it to make good what some might consider to be chinks in its armour it would be hard put to it to match the regal dignity of the coat of its sister Academy, the Royal Society, or the rigour of that Society's *Nullius in verba* motto. As regards the latter, the Academy's dedication to the advancement of humane letters ought certainly to set the tone; and of dedication to that noble aim there can have been no better exemplar than Esmond Samuel de Beer—not only by virtue of his monumental scholarly contribution (though few can match that) but also (and uniquely) on the grounds of his intelligent, munificent, and unostentatious patronage of arts and letters both in Britain and in his native and much-loved New Zealand.

At his death on 3 October 1990 in his ninety-sixth year (he was born on 15 August 1895 in Dunedin into 'the world's most southerly Jewish community') Esmond Samuel de Beer was one of the Academy's oldest Fellows, though, since his election dates from 1965 only, he was by no means its most senior member. Moreover, the modest temper and unremarkable figure of this arch-editor of two major sources for the social and intellectual history of seventeenth-century England—John Evelyn's diary and John Locke's correspondence—gave little clue to his exotic origins. Yet these were decisive: they provided the financial base for a life devoted to independent and unremunerated scholarship, and placed him in the same sadly minute (and probably now extinct) class as the wealthy Quaker banker, Thomas Hodgkin, who, like de

© The British Academy 1997.

Beer, never held an academic post but who left behind him a major work of scholarship—in Hodgkin's case the seven-volume *Italy and her Invaders* (1879–99).

In de Beer's case the financial base was an interest in a remarkably successful New Zealand enterprise established by his maternal grandfather, Bendix Hallenstein. Hallenstein was a German Jew from Brunswick who saw commercial possibilities in the South Australian gold-rush in the late 1850s, met in Melbourne an English girl, Mary Mountain, travelled to England, and married her at Alford in her native Lincolshire in February 1861. The couple returned to Australia and two years later sailed to New Zealand (and another gold-rush), settling at the southern extremity of the South Island. Bendix was clearly a very successful entrepreneur and became a leading figure in local commercial circles; he also served as Mayor of Queenstown and as a member of the Provincial Council. Mary remained an Anglican but the four daughters of the marriage were brought up in the Jewish faith. The second of these, Emily, married Isidore Samuel de Beer (a German Jew with no diamond connections) who became a director of 'Hallensteins', the family firm. Esmond Samuel de Beer was the second son of the marriage (his elder brother, Bendix, was killed in the First World War), and he and his two elder sisters, Mary and Dora, became beneficiaries of the large and growing family trust which was to underpin his life of scholarship.

Esmond de Beer always thought of Dunedin as 'home' and of London as his 'second home'. Dunedin was the place where he received his early education, but he ceased to live there in 1910 when his father's business interests brought him to London. The two boys were sent to Mill Hill School—an experience which he looked back on not without some regrets, though he admitted later that he owed a good deal of his education to his time there (Norman Brett James, the London historian, was an influential teacher).

In October 1914, when he entered New College as a commoner, de Beer became one of the first (apart from a dozen Rhodes Scholars) of the cohort of New Zealanders who were later to exert a powerful influence on the intellectual and administrative life of Oxford. Two years later he was a soldier and two years after that he was commissioned into the Indian Army. Active service ended for him at the end of 1919, and his Oxford undergraduate career terminated with an inevitable war degree in modern history in 1920.

On the face of it there was thus far nothing to suggest the life of scholarship which lay ahead: rather, a career in the family firm. But Ernest Barker, his tutor at New College, had marked him out, and already as an undergraduate he had been brought into touch with the man whom he always regarded as his mentor and exemplar, the Regius professor of history, C. H. Firth, and through him with the concept of research and with the study of the history of seventeenth-century England. Firth was the collaborator and continuator of his predecessor as Research Fellow at All Souls, S. R. Gardiner, whose massive history had ended with the Protectorate, and was an uncompromising (and tutorially unpopular) protagonist of the documentary and prosopographical approach to history. He also believed that historical studies should be illuminated by contemporary literary, artistic, and iconographic monuments—as was evident from his six-volume edition of Macaulay of 1913–15 with its thousand or so plates. Moreover, he was a wealthy man who commanded a fine personal library of seventeenth-century books, prints, and broadsheets. In all these aspects he prefigured de Beer, whom he doubtless came to see as his continuator (as he had been Gardiner's), and the eventual historian of Restoration England. In that he was destined to be disappointed: de Beer belonged temperamentally to the deductionist rather than to the inductionist school; he was more the investigator than the speculator, and it is not without significance that some years later he was to abandon a planned monograph on Charles II. Be that as it may, probably at Firth's suggestion (and certainly with his encouragement) de Beer proceeded to cover his academic nakedness by starting on an MA thesis (submitted in April 1923) at University College London, on the development of political parties under Danby, 1675–8. Much of the research was done at the Institute of Historical Research of London University, recently established by (and under the direction of) A. F. Pollard, Firth's successor in 1908 as Research Fellow at All Souls. Over a third of the text of this pioneer investigation is devoted to a list of original sources and to a biographical dictionary of Court Party members. Here his respect for the *Dictionary of National Biography* (to which Firth had contributed 200, and Pollard over twice as many biographies) is manifest—as is also the cool judgement of the twenty-eight-year-old scholar who wrote: 'The articles in the *Dictionary of National Biography* vary considerably in value; most of them could be supplemented; some of them ought to be re-written.' The critical de Beer, though by nature in the camp of those who regard accuracy as a duty and not a virtue, was as ever prepared to supplement criticism with co-operation: it is typical of him that among his earliest publications are contributions to the corpus of revised *Dictionary of National Biography* entries which Pollard regularly included in the *Bulletin* of the Institute from 1925 onwards. Between that year and 1943, de Beer published over ninety such contributions.

In the early 1920s de Beer was based in London and was able to accompany his parents and his sisters Mary and Dora on some of their travels in Europe, America, and Japan. It is at this period that his visits to art galleries and opera-houses refined his sensibilities and laid the foundations for the connoisseurship and intelligent collecting which developed on a large scale after the death of his mother (in 1930) and his father (in 1934). Their deaths meant that their incomes under the family trust devolved upon the next generation.

From 1926 de Beer had a base in Oxford where he continued his voluntary assistance to Sir Charles Firth and published occasional contributions on points of seventeenth-century British history. And it was there in 1929, when de Beer in his own words 'was hanging around Bodley at rather a loose end', that the New Zealand connection was to start the process of metamorphosing Sir Charles Firth's industrious and learned assistant into 'the prince of textual editors'.

Existing editions of the diary of John Evelyn—an essential source for the cultural, social, political, and religious life of seventeenth-century England—were known to be unsatisfactory since they all descended from an unscholarly printed text published in 1818 which was precariously based on inaccessible manuscript originals in the possession of the Evelyn family. By 1920 the combined efforts of A. T. Bartholomew, H. Maynard Smith, and Geoffrey Keynes had spurred the Clarendon Press into contemplating a more adequate edition and in 1921 the Evelyn family were persuaded to deposit the manuscripts in the Bodleian. By 1926 a transcript was available and Francis Meynell was showing an interest in producing a 'plain-text' Nonesuch Press edition to be printed at the Press using its Fell types. R. W. Chapman, the Secretary to the Delegates of the Press, himself a formidable textual critic, had suspicions about the accuracy of the transcript, and in February 1929 asked his Assistant Secretary, the philologist Kenneth Sisam (a sometime New Zealand Rhodes Scholar), whether he could suggest the name of someone who could cast an eye over it. Sisam thought that his fellow countryman, de Beer, was the obvious person for such a task and invited him to check the transcript. The document that he submitted left Sisam in no doubt about the competence of the reporter and the occasional unreliability of the transcriber (who read at one point 'vitals and sinewes' as 'rituals and sermons'). Chapman was evidently also impressed by de Beer's report (he described de Beer in a letter to Meynell of 19 March as 'a bigoted researcher' and 'a shy bird of independent means') and at the beginning of April Sisam opined in a note to Chapman that 'we should be well advised to commit our edition [i.e. the Clarendon Press edition] to de Beer with the help of Firth'. Meynell's Nonesuch Press project of a plain-text edition was not withdrawn until September 1931, by which time de Beer was being described as the 'heaven-born editor of the slap-up edition' (Chapman's words) of the diary which was to be his main (and unremunerated) occupation for the next quarter of a century.

Esmond de Beer came to his editorial task as a man of thirty-six with no academic affiliation and with not much more than a dozen sound and useful (if uninspiring) scholarly articles to his name. But he brought with him Sir Charles Firth's support and other advantages which it is safe to say no other scholar of his day could have matched. In the first place, financial independence and the *Sitzfleisch* necessary for an undertaking that would inevitably extend over many years. He had a passion for accuracy, and—most important of all—a realisation that the commentator on a seventeenth-century English diary must enter into the intellectual and cultural milieu of his diarist. The second-hand would not do: knowledge of contemporary culture, politics, literature, language, art, architecture, and travels as evidenced in particular in the publications of the diarist's day must be at the editor's fingertips. And with this in mind de Beer began to build up his 'Evelyn Collection', a background library of sources for seventeenth- and eighteenth-century studies most of which was eventually to enlighten readers in the Library of Otago University in Dunedin.

Enlightenment for the readers of the *Diary* was to come in the shape of some 12,000 footnotes which illuminated the first satisfactory text to appear since Bray's amateurish original edition of 1818. As a corollary of annotation on this Herculean scale de Beer also saw that the disparate information contained in both text and notes must be thoroughly indexed if it was to be fully exploited by the curious. In this he was ultimately following in the footsteps of another great editor, George Birkbeck Hill, who had pioneered indexing on the grand scale in his edition of Boswell (six volumes, Oxford, 1887), which was in the process of being re-edited in the 1920s and early 1930s at Oxford in the care of de Beer's great friend, L. F. Powell, by whom he was much influenced.

No less important in de Beer's eyes were his biographical account of Evelyn, the description of sources and editorial method, the bibliographical lists, genealogies, and other reference materials which occupy more than a half of the 300-page first volume. These, together with the index (but excluding the footnotes) account for nearly one-third of the pages of the edition's six volumes which were in the press from 1947 until their publication at the end of 1955 (at the then substantial price of fifteen guineas). With characteristic open-handedness de Beer arranged for forty copies to be presented to friends and others who had assisted him, including W. G. Hiscock, with whom he had been in disagreement and who had been unable to help him over access to important Evelyn correspondence at Christ Church.

The *Diary* was widely and favourably reviewed by seventeenth-century experts who could appreciate its value as a source and the industry and learning of its editor and annotator. A suggestion by the reviewer in the *English Historical Review* that there were cases of excessive annotation was neatly counterbalanced by the judgement of the *Times Literary Supplement* reviewer that 'the notes are never excessive'—and by the reflection that one reader's glimpse of the obvious is another one's useful addition to his (or her) stock of knowledge. An 'inexcusable' review in the *Spectator* (13 January 1956) suggesting that the *Diary* 'lacks human interest' and 'had been rendered almost unreadable by the Herculean scholarship of Mr de Beer' gave pain but could be dismissed on the grounds of illogicality—at least.

The 'heaven-born editor' was not allowed to rest on laurels which might have been regarded as crowning a life's work. A fellow New Zealander, Dan Davin, from 1946 to 1978 Deputy Secretary of the Clarendon Press, had him in his sights as a potential editor of John Locke's correspondence. The Clarendon edition of Locke's works (of which the correspondence would be the largest single component) had been the special concern of another of de Beer's New Zealand friends, Kenneth Sisam, who had been Secretary to the Delegates of the Clarendon Press from 1942 to 1948. Substantial materials for the edition had been acquired by the Bodleian since the 1940s (much with de Beer's financial support) but ten years later the correspondence lacked a competent and willing editor. Davin regarded de Beer, relieved of his Evelyn burden, as the ideal editor of the correspondence element of the edition. When approached, de Beer expressed a general willingness to take on what would certainly prove to be another unremunerated demi-life's work and typically, admitted to 'lack of qualifications in philosophy and Latinity'. The Delegates of the Press were unmoved by de Beer's modesty and he was appointed to edit the correspondence on 11 May 1956. The edition was to be his main preoccupation for the next thirty years.

Though de Beer was probably the only living scholar equipped and willing to undertake the task which now faced him, that did not mean that the task was an easy one—even for him. For one thing, he was dealing not with a small number of originals (as in the case of the Evelyn) but with several thousand individual documents, and since the edition was not merely of Locke's own letters, he was concerned with over 300 correspondents. Moreover, since Locke was a citizen of the seventeenth-century latinate commonwealth of learning and had spent time abroad, some of those correspondents were in France and the Netherlands. Locke's (and his correspondents') intellectual range could be described as universal—theology, medicine, geography, economics, law, politics, travel, and botany all came within their purview: their editor had to be prepared to assume pantomathy. Characteristically, de Beer built on his Evelyn experience, expanding his own personal library by acquiring original editions of the books and journals which would have been on the shelves of Locke's and his correspondents' libraries. As before, Otago was to benefit from the fruits of his collecting.

The editor was assiduous in collecting the texts. Originals were mainly in the Bodleian, the Public Record Office, and in the British Museum, but there were substantial groups of letters in Amsterdam, Copenhagen, New York, and Paris and de Beer's imagination and persistence even tracked down a letter in Moscow and a cache in the loft of a Belgian farmhouse. He was able to employ transcribers but all transcripts were checked by him against originals or photographs. Economical and informative headnotes and footnotes (often on obscure personalities and esoteric subjects) much concerned and tried him and, in 1962, six years into the project, he reported that according to his latest guess 'another 8,000 working hours' lay ahead of him. This chilling forecast proved to be an underestimate: the first of the eight volumes did not go to press until 1974, eighteen years since de Beer had taken on his task. The eighth and final volume of the letters was issued in 1989, leaving the vital index volume, on which de Beer had worked 'while there was light' (and generously subsidised), still unpublished.

After de Beer became engaged on the Locke edition in 1956 the flow of articles and reviews declined, but it did not cease. They were some-times stimulated by points of Locke annotation and concentrated on aspects of life in Restoration England. London topography remained an abiding interest and his only monographic publication (elegantly printed for him in 1936 by the Oxford University Press) was an edition of Evelyn's *Londinium redivivum*. He honoured his gremial links with the Institute of Historical Research and during the war years, when many of its staff were away, became its honorary librarian (and 'saviour', according to some). He published articles in the Institute's *Bulletin* and reviews in the Historical Association's journal, *History*, which were balanced and, if necessary, merciless. For example, in 1940, when reviewing four monographs on Cromwell's generals (de Beer was Vice-President of the Cromwell Association) three were dismissed as respectively 'leaving important questions unanswered', 'being an attractive substitute for historical novels', or eliciting the regret that 'so much work should be so unsatisfactory'; the fourth, on the other hand, was brusquely characterised as 'a masterly account'. The economy of phrase is typical of a man who regarded the presence of an exclamation mark at the end of a sentence as an admission of syntactical ineptitude.

In 1934, after the death of his father (his mother had died in New Zealand four years earlier), de Beer set up idyllic house in Sussex Place ('in the Regent's Park', in his phrase) with his sisters Mary and Dora. Here (and from 1964 in Brompton Square) he had a comfortable London base and was well placed to give his support to learned societies and institutions. He followed in Sir Charles Firth's footsteps in becoming a Trustee of the National Portrait Gallery and Vice-President of the Historical Association. He became President of the Hakluyt Society and of the London Topographical Society and served on the committees of the National Art-Collections Fund, the Friends of the National Libraries, the London Library, and (though by then a self-described 'atheist'), of the Friends of Lambeth Palace Library. All these organisations benefited not only from his counsel but also from his often grand-scale generosity—especially when subsidy was needed to support publication. His appointment (1965) as an independent member of the government Reviewing Committee on the Export of Works of Art, and the CBE which he received in 1969, were tributes to the respect in which the judgement of de Beer as a connoisseur was held. Other honours—honorary fellowships of New College, Oxford (1958) and of the Warburg Institute (1978), and the fellowship to which University College London, elected him in 1967, and honorary doctorates at percipient Durham (1956), Oxford (1957), and Otago (1963)—gave much quiet satisfaction.

Great scholarship and great financial resources are regrettably rare companions. In de Beer's case his means supported both a secure base and the possibility of devoting his life to the advancement of the cause of humane letters not only by his own researches but by strengthening institutions which provide the raw materials for the advancement of learning. Libraries, art galleries, and learned societies were the main beneficiaries of his carefully considered lifetime (and posthumous) support. In Britain the remarkable collection of New Zealand literature in the Library of the University of Essex is due to his subvention over many years. The placing of the collection in Colchester is explained by the presence there as librarian of Philip Long, once of the Bodleian, and the author of the catalogue of the Bodleian's Lovelace Collection of Locke materials whose purchase de Beer had supported. His sensitiveness to the desirability of a special collection of New Zealand literature being available in a British academic library certainly owed something to the fact that his cousin, Charles Brasch (whose Oxford career he had unofficially supervised in the 1920s), was the founder and editor of *Landfall*—the leading New Zealand literary journal which he supported financially. The Bodleian itself frequently benefited from his generosity on a scale that caused his name to be added to its lapidary Benefactors' Tablet (a rare exception to the principle of anonymity which he could not well oppose). Other British libraries, for example, the British Library, the London Library, the Library of the Courtauld Institute, and Lambeth Palace Library were also beneficiaries, but his chief concern was that the Library of the University of Otago in his 'home-town', Dunedin, should be well equipped for research.

The benefactor's sense of the practical is clearly evidenced by his subscription on Otago's behalf to the 263-volume catalogue of the printed books in the Library of the British Museum. His passion for contemporary sources is exemplified by his purchase in 1958 of Iolo Williams's library of some 2,000 volumes (mainly English eighteenth-century verse) which also went to Dunedin. He added to that in 1982 2,000 volumes from his own Evelyn working library including several hundred early guidebooks. His Locke collection of over 500 volumes followed in 1984 and monetary gifts amounting to over $NZ 170,000 followed in 1989. Such gifts, together with the anonymous establishment by himself, his sisters, and members of his extended family of three research fellowships (characteristically named not for the donors but for Burns, Mozart, and Hodgkins) placed the University of Otago in the first rank of New Zealand research centres in the humanities.

The field of benefaction which has caused de Beer, his two sisters (who died within a few weeks of each other at the end of 1981 and the beginning of 1982, leaving their interests to Esmond), and his wider Hallenstein family to be described as 'far away the greatest private patrons of the arts in New Zealand with gifts worth tens of millions of dollars', is in the area of painting and the graphic and applied arts. There was a family tradition of collecting: their father had built up a distinguished collection of Japanese prints, and de Beer and his sisters collected from the mid-1930s partly that they might be surrounded by beautiful objects in their London houses, but entirely with the aim of their eventually enriching and rounding-out the Public Art Gallery in Dunedin. As part of a carefully planned policy de Beer was systematically acquiring pictures and other art objects which, as the result of a survey which he had made of the Dunedin collections in 1963, he knew would fill specific gaps. Many of these works were purchased and sent immediately, others remained in the London home. When a 'gap-filler' came on the market, de Beer was prepared to pay as much as £20,000 for it, and as a result of this inspired generosity the Dunedin Public Art Gallery possesses works by, for example, Jacopo del Casentino (Landini), Zanobi Machiavelli, Marcus Gheerhaerdts the younger, Claude Lorrain, and Monet. Water-colours (including a Signac), old master and Japanese prints, and a few Russian icons made up the total of 172 works of art which reached the Gallery in 1982—the year of the break-up of the Brompton Square ménage. In that year de Beer, now eighty-seven and alone after his sisters' deaths, moved to a flat in north London, but he found the mechanics of living difficult. In March 1984 he entered a home for the elderly near Milton Keynes where, in spite of increasing deafness and before ultimate blindness precluded reading, he completed his work on the eighth volume of the Locke correspondence. His memory did not fail him: favourite pictures and operas stayed in his mind's eye and ear and he could find comfort in recounting to himself the texts of eighteenth- and nineteenth-century English novels. There he died on 3 October 1990.

During his lifetime de Beer had been unfailingly generous to members of his extended family and to needy scholars as well as to institutions. After his death his will showed his continuing and precise concern for the latter: thirty-six per cent of his estate (probated at over £1 million) went to the Library of the University of Otago; the

Dunedin Public Museum received six per cent, and the Art Gallery four per cent. Six British libraries and institutions received five per cent, and Mill Hill School, New College, University College London, the Institute of Historical Research, the Warburg Institute, and Durham University were other substantial beneficiaries of the posthumous generosity of a man who was not unmindful of the institutions which had formed or honoured him.

Of de Beer it can be said without qualification:

> He was reticent about himself and his own affairs and seldom expansive, but he had, and communicated, a sense of immovable confidence. He was completely loyal to his friends and to his side in any contention. He gave money generously to institutions and to people in need, often doing his alms in secret. In later life he had no religious beliefs. Having no liking for speculative thought, and considering how often minds are at the mercy of physiological processes or external accidents, he resigned himself to a kind of materialism; but lived up to an austere standard of duty.

The words are Sir George Clark's: they conclude his notice of Sir Charles Firth in the *Dictionary of National Biography*. The disciple did not shame his master.

JOHN SIMMONS
*All Souls College, Oxford*

*Note.* This obituary owes much to Michael Strachan's personal memoir: *Esmond de Beer (1895–1990): Scholar and Benefactor* (Wilby Hall, Norwich: Michael Russell, 1995), which includes my bibliography (now in need of revision). No. 156.1 in the bibliography (R. Notman's article in *Bulletin of New Zealand Art History*, xv (1994), 33–54) is an admirable survey of the de Beer patronage of the arts in Dunedin, and Keith Ovenden's recent *A Fighting Withdrawal: The Life of Dan Davin* (OUP, 1996) gives an insight into the 'New Zealand contribution' to the publication of the Locke *Correspondence* at pp. 290–2.

Relevant manuscript collections are in the Bodleian Library and in the Archives of the Delegates of the Clarendon Press at Oxford. I am grateful to their owners for access and for permission to quote—and to the Archivist of the Press, Peter Foden, and to its Librarian, Celia Clothier, for exemplary co-operation.

The photograph of de Beer, taken in the Brompton Square house in January 1976, is reproduced with the permission of Professor Walter Elkan, a great-grandson of Bendix Hallenstein.

GEOFFREY ELTON

*Stearn and Sons*

*Proceedings of the British Academy*, **94**, 429–455

# Geoffrey Rudolph Elton
# 1921–1994

## I

GEOFFREY ELTON BEGAN his inaugural lecture as Regius Professor of Modern History in the University of Cambridge with a genealogical *jeu d'esprit*. His chair had been founded in 1724 by an elector of Hanover who also happened to be king of England. In 1808 one Samuel Meyer Ehrenberg began to conduct a school at Wolfenbüttel, a few miles from Hanover but in the neighbouring duchy of Brunswick. Both George I and Samuel Ehrenberg were engaged in founding, in their different ways, dynasties: in Ehrenberg's case a scholarly Jewish dynasty which was to endure for five generations. In 1983, a descendant of the king-elector appointed to her ancestor's foundation the great great grandson of the original Ehrenberg. The elector of Hanover and the duke of Brunswick, both bearing the name of Guelph, had been, in a manner of speaking, cousins. And in 1983 it was found that the holders of the Regius chairs of history at Oxford and Cambridge were cousins too, for Geoffrey Elton's counterpart at Oxford, Professor Sir Michael Howard, is the son of a first cousin of Elton's mother.

Geoffrey Elton was born Gottfried Rudolph Otto Ehrenberg at Tübingen on 21 August 1921. His father, Victor Ehrenberg, was a classical scholar and ancient historian who withstood the damage of a sadly fragmented career to attain the great distinction acknowledged in his adopted England when, in 1966, he was awarded the Litt.D., *honoris causa*, of the University of Cambridge, the first refugee scholar to be so

© The British Academy 1997.

honoured. Victor was the son of a banker, Otto Ehrenberg, and the nephew of a professor of jurisprudence, Victor Ehrenberg, and of the economist Richard Ehrenberg, an authority on the Fuggers. He had studied architecture, in Stuttgart and London, before devoting himself to ancient history, working in Berlin under Eduard Meyer. In 1914, while serving on the Western Front, Ehrenberg began a notable correspondence with Meyer, whom he upbraided for his conservative, nationalist views.[1]

Geoffrey Elton's maternal grandfather, Siegfried Sommer, came from a more modest background, but married Helene Edinger, daughter of a wealthy merchant family of Worms. Helene was a talented artist, but her husband would not allow her to earn money through her painting. The portraits of her own family, for portraits were her forte, now adorn the Guildford home of Geoffrey's brother, Professor Lewis Elton (father of the writer and entertainer Ben Elton). The extent to which these cultured *haut bourgeois* families were assimilated into mainstream German society is indicated by the fact that the Sommers called their daughter, Geoffrey Elton's mother, Eva, after Eva in *Die Meistersinger*. If they knew about Wagner's anti-Semitism, it was not thought to apply to them. On the paternal side, Otto's son Hans, Geoffrey Elton's uncle, converted to Christianity and became a Lutheran pastor. But what happened on the maternal side of the family was the stuff of which history is made. Siegfried Sommer was sent as a child to school in Kassel, the only Jew in his class. Here his classmate and closest friend was the future Kaiser Wilhelm II. What he called the 'Experiment in Kassel' is described in detail by the historian of the youthful Wilhelm. Making extensive use of the Siegfried-Wilhelm correspondence preserved in the Ehrenberg family and now deposited in a Berlin archive, John Röhl writes: 'Der liebste Freund des künftigen deutschen Kaisers war Siegfried Sommer, der "junge Jude" aus seiner Klasse.'[2] No doubt the little Jewish boy was surprised to find that the boy he liked best, and who liked him, was the future Kaiser of all Germany; and we are surprised too, for the friendship suggests that Wilhelm was at this point in his life free from social and racial prejudice. After leaving school, Siegfried naturally addressed his future

---

[1] *Eduard Meyer-Victor Ehrenberg: Ein Briefwechsel 1914–1930*, ed. Gert Audring *et al.* (Berlin, Stuttgart, 1990).

[2] John C. G. Röhl, *Wilhelm II: Die Jugend des Kaisers 1859–1880* (Munich, 1993), pp. 233–9. See also Tyler Whittle, *The Last Kaiser* (London, 1977), pp. 45–6.

monarch as 'Eure Königliche Hoheit'. Siegfried Sommer was to become a judge of the Court of Appeal, but only after the Kaiser intervened to remove certain anti-Semitic obstacles to the advancement of his career. When Sommer died, in 1925, a wreath arrived from Doorn, the inscription simply 'from Wilhelm'. Geoffrey's mother grew up in the judge's house in Frankfurt, where she learned Italian through reading and translating Dante. In later life she was a published poet, writing in German and English.[3]

In 1929, Victor Ehrenberg was appointed to a chair of classics in the German University in Prague. A year or two later, an attempt to return to a chair at Tübingen was (fortunately) blocked by the anti-Semitic factor. Gottfried and his younger brother Ludwig were sent to the German Stephansgymnasium. Gottfried's education had started early. He was one week old when the 'Grundstuck seiner Bibliothek' was laid, a collection of *Deutsche Wiegenlieder* which still exists. At the age of seven, he wrote an account of a planet inhabited by teddy bears; and at twelve, having already written a play about the Spanish Armada, he wrote and acted in a drama called 'Das Attentat in Laufe der Zeiten', three tragic scenes devoted to Caesar, Gessler, and Wallenstein; and a comic final act about Dollfuss, played by the nine-year-old Ludwig sporting a large cardboard disc, the button which had deflected the assassin's bullet in the first attempt on the life of the Austrian chancellor. This was a proleptic play, since the second attempt, a year later, succeeded, with momentous consequences for Austria and, soon, for the Ehrenbergs. At about the same time, Gottfried wrote an heroical account of 'Die Erdumreisungs expedition' to Arctic Norway. He not only wrote it. He drew the illustrations and the maps, typed the text with perfectly justified margins, and bound it: a task resembling the youthful bookmaking exploits of the future Queen Elizabeth I of England. This book too survives.

In September 1938, the Munich Agreement was signed and Eva Ehrenberg, ever the practical brains of the family, persuaded her husband that the boys must begin to learn English rather than Greek, which was now an unaffordable luxury. The future Regius professor, whose inaugural lecture forty-six years later would be an apology for the study of English history, was now in his eighteenth year and preparing to sit his leaving examination, the Matura. Friends in Prague thought that to

---

[3] *Zweisprachig-Gedichte von Eva Ehrenberg* (Tübingen, 1971).

interrupt the boy's education at this critical juncture would be ruinous for his career. Eva Ehrenberg thought otherwise.

What happened next was improbable and, in Eva's account of it, miraculous.[4] In her childhood, Eva had shared with her friend Netty an English governess, Irene, who married a Mr Charnley, a Methodist minister. A lifetime later Netty and her Dutch husband were travelling on a train in Wales when they asked a fellow passenger, a clergyman, whether by any chance he knew Charnley. He knew Mrs Charnley and supplied an address. The couple travelled at once to Colwyn Bay in North Wales, where Mr Charnley was chaplain to Rydal School. This led to renewed contact with Eva in Prague, and, in the autumn of 1938, with the German schools and university undergoing Nazification, a letter from Eva to Irene Charnley, pleading for help.

Plans had already been made by the Society for the Protection of Science and Learning (SPSL) to bring Victor Ehrenberg to England, and to provide him with a grant of £250 for the first year. (This was the beginning of a long family association with the SPSL and with its secretary, the redoubtable Tess Simpson.[5]) But there was as yet no provision for Victor's family and the visa option would soon expire: hence Eva's *cri de coeur*, which was immediately answered. Mr Charnley spoke to the headmaster of Rydal School, J. A. Costain (the only academic to emerge from the well-known building firm), and a governors' scholarship was offered to Ludwig, it being assumed that Gottfried was too advanced in his schooling to be moved, or to derive any advantage from Rydal. But when the Ehrenbergs stoutly refused to leave Gottfried in Prague, the school agreed to accept both the brothers.

The family left Prague on 10 February 1939, travelling first to Frankfurt, where they tried unsuccessfully to persuade Eva's sister Elisabeth to join them. (Elisabeth would be shot by the Nazis in 1941; but Uncle Hans, the Lutheran pastor, was extricated from a concentration camp by the efforts of Bishop George Bell of Chichester and taken to England.) The family then made a short and unauthorised detour to Kassel to see Victor's mother for the last time. Himmler was in Kassel that night, and there were house-to-house searches. On 14 February the family arrived at Dover. When Elton came to publish his

---

[4] I am indebted to Professor Lewis Elton for sight of Eva Ehrenberg's account of 'The Emigration', which she sent to him on the twenty-fourth anniversary of the Ehrenbergs's arrival in England, 14 February 1963, translated from a published German text.
[5] *Refugee Scholars: Conversations with Tess Simpson*, ed. R. M. Cooper (Leeds, 1992).

last book, *The English* (1992), it was an expression of gratitude for that cloudless St Valentine's Day experience. In those later years, he would say that England was the country he should have been born into, an attitude reminiscent of the anglophilia in Max Weber, whom he despised and radically misrepresented. On St Valentine's Day 1939, so anxious was Eva that nothing should go wrong that she lied (the only lie she ever told?) about her sons' proficiency in English. It was also necessary to part with two of the twenty-eight pounds the family carried, as duty on the boys' bicycles, soon to be ridden up the steep mountain passes of North Wales.

At first the Ehrenbergs lived in a single room in Bloomsbury, with a gas ring in the corner, and later in a rented house in Woodlark Road, Cambridge. When the SPSL funding came to an end, Victor Ehrenberg secured a post as classics master at a school in Carlisle. From there he moved to King's College, Newcastle, where he replaced a lecturer called up for national service. In 1946, the lecturer returned, having written *The History of the ARP in the North East*, and Victor returned to school-mastering. But soon he succeeded Professor Max Carey at Bedford College in the University of London, where he would teach for the remainder of his career, for whatever reason denied the title and status of professor, which was surely his due.

It was on 20 February 1939 that Eva took Gottfried and Ludwig to Rydal School. The school housekeeper, still alive in the 1980s, remembered the arrival of 'the Ehrenberg boys'. 'They didn't have a word of English between them!' Within a matter of weeks, the boys were sitting mock School Certificate papers in English, with the help of a dictionary, and in June came the real thing, after coaching for Ludwig by Eva in *Paradise Lost* over the Easter holidays. (Eva continued to read and criticise everything that Geoffrey Elton wrote, up to two years before her death in 1973.) The boys not only pased their School Certificate in all subjects, but Gottfried won the school English essay prize, an achievement celebrated by Headmaster Costain in a *Manchester Guardian* article headed 'Triumph of a Refugee'. After four months of life in a country whose manners and customs Gottfried found 'absolutely strange', his English style left a little room for improvement: 'The course of events is not directable by our feeble hands, which arrangement is sometimes most fortunate, sometimes less.' Well, all this had been most fortunate.

In the first winter of the war, Gottfried was entered for a scholarship at Oxford and interviewed by H. A. L. Fisher. Elton later recalled that he had seen Fisher in New College a few days before his death, which occurred on 18 April 1940. But the interview must have happened in December 1939. There was to be no love affair with Oxford. Elton would later say: 'I've never been so pleased to have been *proxime accessit*.' He remained at Rydal, teaching German and studying for an external London degree. Now it was Victor who took on the role of coach, guiding Gottfried through his Special Subject in Roman history. Out of that experience came Geoffrey Elton's first publication, an article on 'The Terminal Date of Caesar's Gallic Proconsulate' (*Journal of Roman Studies* 36 (1946).) He took first class honours and won the coveted Derby scholarship, tenable at the University of London. He chose University College.

But first the war intervened, and some awkward choices. Should Gottfried join the Czech forces or the British Army? The Czech Government in exile wanted him, but there was marked anti-Semitism in that outfit. English naturalisation could not be taken for granted, while to choose the British Army could compromise any future the family might have back in Prague. The British option was to prove another of those most fortunate arrangements, for under a law of 1930 the Ehrenbergs were defined as Czech citizens of German nationality, and all German citizens were to be ethnically cleansed from Czecho-slovakia after the war, when the remainder of the family were natur-alised as British subjects. On joining the Army, Gottfried was given twenty-four hours to change his name, 'by Army Council Instruction'. He rejected Ellis as too Welsh (Elton was not over-fond of the Welsh), and Elliott as capable (like Ehrenberg) of being spelt in too many ways. So Elton it was. Geoffrey Elton saw action, briefly, at Anzio, and might have been sent to Burma but, instead, as a native German speaker, was transferred to Intelligence (Field Security), where his rank was sergeant, his posting Graz in Austria, and his function to debrief suspected Nazi prisoners-of-war. It was a position of unusual power for a young man, and it left him with a respect for law-enforcement which was intention-ally echoed in the title of one of his most notable books on Tudor history, *Policy and Police* (1972). According to Lewis Elton, it was the Army which turned his brother into an Englishman, even a 'super-Englishman', with a relative lack of interest in his former life and family history. With typical generosity, but also some indifference, he was content that all the family heirlooms which had come out of Prague with the Ehrenbergs, and they are considerable, should finish up with his brother Lewis and his family. The Army also taught Elton to drink and smoke.

## II

Geoffrey Elton had already met the Elizabethan historian J. E. Neale (later Sir John Neale) when a friend of his father at University College London pointed out that the UCL History Department had been evacuated ten miles along the coast from Colwyn Bay at Bangor. Professor Neale said that he would be glad to take Elton on as a research student when (or was it, Elton later wondered, 'if') he came back from the war. More most fortunate arrangements. When Elton reappeared in 1946, Neale's teacher and his predecessor in the Astor Chair of English History at University College, A. F. Pollard, was nearing the end of his active scholarly career. He died in August 1948. G. N. Clark remarked (in the *DNB*) that as a teacher Pollard 'relied rather on force than on sympathy', and for many years he had repelled all boarders who attempted to work in his own field, the reign of Henry VIII. Now, in the late 1940s, it was like Tibet reopening to foreign travellers after many years of exclusion. Warned by two of Neale's female students (who were only allowed to write MA theses) not to touch parliamentary history, or Queen Elizabeth, Elton told Neale that he would 'do Henry VIII, sir'. Neale said that in that case he had better get stuck into the *Letters and Papers of the Reign of Henry VIII*. Elton would allege that this was the only good advice he ever received from his supervisor.

Elton began his research in September 1946 and finished his thesis, 'Thomas Cromwell: Aspects of his Administrative Work', in record time, in September 1948, typing it himself on the same machine which had earlier been used to record that epic journey to the Arctic Circle. In *The Practice of History* (1967), Elton would later insist that the historian must master the relevant evidence in its totality and must devote himself to the task single-mindedly and to the total exclusion of all distractions. Elton seldom took a holiday in the ordinary sense of the word. But as a research student, he found that five hours in the Public Record Office was all he could take, so that in mid-afternoon he would go off to Lords to watch Denis Compton, an addiction to cricket having been acquired at Rydal. In later years, and well into his sixties, he was a very good squash player. 'Joinery' was listed as a recreation in *Who's Who*. Elton was a dedicated gardener, who nurtured a lawn with

an immaculate green nap to it which was one of the wonders of Cambridge. So it was not all work and no play. But beyond his garden, Elton
had no time for the open air and almost never went to the countryside.
Not for him R. H. Tawney's muddy boots. There is an almost total lack
in his work of that sense of place which is characteristic of so much of
the best (as well as some of the worst) of English historiography.
People, too, were often noticeable by their absence. *The English*
(1992) is not really a history of the English at all, but of their rulers
and of the state they were in.

It was Neale who told Elton that he could take Christmas Day
(1946) off—and Elton rested on Boxing Day too.[6] But Elton's stringent
disciplines were self-imposed and Neale need not have bothered. Elton
was to fall out with his supervisor, and even more with his shade, for his
attacks on Neale continued long after the older man's death and were a
necessary element of many of his public lectures, delivered in places
like New Zealand and Arizona to audiences of students who may
never have heard of Neale. (But Vivian Galbraith, Director of the
Institute of Historical Research in Elton's time, was a different matter,
and one of the few strong, personal, influences which Elton would
ever acknowledge.)

The feud with Neale was up and running as early as 1955, when I
was Neale's research assistant, while completing my own Ph.D. under
his supervision. And yet, as late as 1972, Elton could send Neale a copy
of his Ford Lectures book, *Policy and Police*, cordially inscribed with a
reference to the good old days, in Neale's seminar.[7] In the 1960s, when
Neale was known to be opposing his election to the British Academy
(Elton became an FBA in 1967), I even heard Elton described in public
as 'that young whipper-snapper'. He was in his mid-forties, and in mid-
career! The immediate circumstances were that Elton had alleged in
*The Practice of History* that Pollard had rarely darkened the doors of the
PRO. Later he would refer to Pollard's 'careful avoidance of
manuscript'.[8]

The quarrel, though notorious, remains mysterious. Was it based
entirely, so far as Elton was concerned, on a negative appraisal of Neale

---

[6]  G. R. Elton, *The Practice of History* (Sydney, 1967), p. 163, n. 1.

[7]  This copy of *Policy and Police* came on the market in 1996, part of the residue of Neale's
library. I am grateful to Raymond Kilgariff of Howes Bookshop Hastings for supplying me
with a photocopy of Elton's inscription, which reads: 'To Sir John Neale with best wishes
and in memory of happy seminar days. Geoffrey Elton'.

[8]  Elton, *The Practice of History*, p. 69; G. R. Elton, *F. W. Maitland* (London, 1985), p. 33.

as a scholar and academic power broker, or were there more personal reasons? Neale, like Pollard before him, was notorious for consigning to outer darkness those he thought not up to scratch. Whatever happened, in Pollard's time, to E. R. Adair, or, in the Neale years, to G. B. Harrison? But Neale knew that Elton was something else, and he backed him for his first job, at Glasgow, in 1948, and for his Cambridge assistant lectureship in 1949. This was effective patronage, for Elton was one of those rank outsiders who occasionally break into the introverted Cambridge History Faculty: by no means the first, since Walter Ullmann had arrived a few months earlier, and David Knowles had been made a university lecturer in 1946. In earlier years, Lord Acton, J. P. Bury, and M. M. Postan had all been, in their various ways, *arrivistes*.

In 1952, Geoffrey Elton was married to Sheila Lambert of Hartlepool, another product of the London History School. Sheila Lambert was and is a formidably learned historian in her own right, an authority on Parliament, the press, and press censorship. For a time she worked in close association with the legendary Lord Beaverbrook. Further legend has it that once at a conference in California, or some such place, an eighteenth-century legal historian, excited to find himself in conversation with Sheila Lambert, turned to Elton and said, 'Oh, is this your husband? What does he do?'

Cambridge was yet another most fortunate arrangement. Kenneth Pickthorn of Corpus Christi had taught the Tudors whilst doubling up as MP for Cambridge. Clement Attlee's abolition of the university seats took Pickthorn elsewhere and created the vacancy which Elton filled. So began forty-five years in a Cambridge which Elton was to bestride like a colossus. But at first he was insecure, without a college fellowship, and aggressive. Not everyone found him a breath of fresh air, although that is what he was. I arrived in the university to read history in the first term of Elton's appointment, but, knowing no better, never heard him lecture, learning my Tudors from Christopher Morris of King's. No one told me that I ought to go to Elton, but by the time the MP Tom Dalyell came up in 1952, Elton's fame, even notoriety, was established. Dalyell remembers that of the great names of those days (such as Knowles and Butterfield) 'none approached in certainty of historical opinion and pungency of historical prejudice Geoffrey Elton.' His lectures were unscripted and, in the 1950s and 1960s, crowded out; although in later years the off-the-cuff attacks on the many historians of whom Elton could not approve caused offence, and, ultimately, killed interest.

Elton had no postgraduate students until 1951 (Professor J. J. Scar-isbrick being the first), and as late as 1960 they could still be counted on the fingers of one hand. Soon after that there were enough swallows to make a summer, and the Cambridge Tudor seminar, meeting on a Tuesday morning, came into being, and still continues. In all, Elton supervised a total of more than seventy doctoral students, all but ten of whom completed their theses, and very many of whom still teach in the universities of three continents. It is a good question where the study of sixteenth-century England would now be without this massive input. The relationship between Elton and his doctoral students was exemplary. He never attempted to forge them into an Eltonian school, but offered not only rigorous supervision but the regular hospitality of 30, Millington Road, where Geoffrey and Sheila held open house every Sunday evening. (As the Artful Dodger sang it in 'Oliver': 'Consider yourself part of the family.') There was deep affection and much real grief when Elton died in 1994.

In 1954 Geoffrey Elton became a fellow of Clare, a college for which he had been teaching and directing studies. This was a much overdue election. Not long afterwards, Walter Ullmann was elected by Trinity, six years after his arrival in Cambridge. David Knowles, who campaigned for them both, suspected that colleges were afraid of being overwhelmed by two such dominant personalities. In an after-dinner speech, Ullmann would refer to Elton as his 'oldest and closest friend in the Faculty'. In spite of differences, 'nothing could and would shake our friendship'. Some colleagues were surprised when this warm tribute appeared in print in 1989.[9]

## III

It is high time to address Elton the historian. In 1953, his first book was published and had an immediate and huge impact: *The Tudor Revolution in Government*. The phrase of the title will not be found anywhere in the Ph.D. thesis on which the book was based. Legend has it that one of Elton's examiners, Professor C. H. Williams, filled with enthusiasm, had said at the viva: 'It seems to me, Mr Elton, that what you have stumbled across is—what shall I call it?—a kind of Tudor revolution in government!' Neale's advice to Elton to immerse himself in *Letters and*

---

[9] Elizabeth Ullmann, *Walter Ulmann: A Tale of Two Cultures* (Cambridge, 1990), p. 46.

*Papers* had not been wasted. But in those two years in the PRO, Elton had restored the documentary integrity of the original State Papers which the slavish deference to chronology of Victorian archivists and editors had disturbed, and from that rearrangement everything else followed. What Elton found these documents to contain was evidence that the 1530s constituted a great age of reform in the institutions and processes of English governance, a veritable revolution. In one decade, the English State took leave of the Middle Ages and entered a recognisably modern world. It attained full sovereignty, the sovereignty of the king in parliament, almost unchallenged authority within its own borders and marches, and a set of institutions which replaced the personal government and financial management of the king's household with a Westminster bureaucracy which had at its heart that progenitor of modern cabinet government, the Privy Council, and the king's principal secretary, no longer a clerkly body servant of the monarch but 'the chief national executive'. It was a grandly audacious thesis which was challenged at birth in the pages of the *English Historical Review* by Professor R. B. Wernham,[10] but which rapidly hardened into the new orthodoxy. It survived an onslaught in the pages of *Past & Present* in the early 1960s,[11] but not the heavy small-arms fire mounted in the 1980s by some of Elton's own pupils, a new race of 'revisionists'.[12]

Elton fought a series of rearguard actions and modified his views, while insisting to the end on their essential correctness. In a pamphlet on Henry VIII's minister of the 1530s, Thomas Cromwell, published as late as 1991, he conceded that he might have 'overstated [Cromwell's] systematic approach to the problems and represented him as newly creating a structure of government as though he possessed the powers of a god', while continuing to insist that Cromwell was 'a principled reformer of everything that came within his purview.'[13]

It was forty-five years since Elton had first discovered Thomas Cromwell in the archives and he was not done with him yet. It is odd that Cromwell's mental world and values were the subject of more than one article-length sketch, while a full-length biography was never

---

[10] *English Historical Review*, lxxi (1956), 92–5.

[11] G. L. Harriss and Penry Williams put the question 'A Revolution in Tudor History?' in *Past & Present*, no. 25 (1963). The resultant debate continued through nos. 26, 29, 31 and 32 of *Past & Present*, i.e. until 1965.

[12] Especially *Revolution Reassessed: Revisions in the History of Tudor Government and Administration*, eds. Christopher Coleman and David Starkey (Oxford, 1986).

[13] G. R. Elton, *Thomas Cromwell* (Bangor, 1991), pp. 31–2, 34.

attempted. But Elton did not believe in historical biography. Pollard had (almost) ignored Cromwell, the relevant entries in the index to his biography of Henry VIII reading 'anxious to make Henry despotic', 'anxious to make Henry rich', 'never in Wolsey's position': judgements, incidentally, which some revisionists now endorse. Cromwell had been portrayed unsympathetically in R. B. Merriman's two-volume *Life and Letters* (1902), still described in 1959 as 'the standard book on the subject', in Conyers Read's *Bibliography* for the Tudor period. Cromwell needed rescuing from his detractors, his true greatness recognised. Elton presented him as 'the most remarkable English statesman of the sixteenth century and one of the most remarkable in the country's history'.[14] As Cromwell was elevated, so his royal master was diminished, 'an unoriginal and unproductive mind'. Cromwell, not Henry VIII, was the author of the policy which broke with Rome, from which in a sense all else followed. In *The Tudor Revolution in Government*, Elton roundly declared: 'Cromwell, not Henry, was really the government'. The best evidence for this, which is open to challenge, is the constant presence of Cromwell's handwriting in the drafting and correction of parliamentary bills.

It became fashionable to say that Elton, the effective, tough but principled go-getter, formed Thomas Cromwell in his own image. Readers of Croce and Collingwood would almost assume that to have been the case. But, according to Elton, 'Croce and Collingwood were utterly wrong'. 'It is not true that every generation rewrites history in its own image.'[15] It could even be said (and was) that far from Elton planting his mirror-image Cromwell in the archives, Cromwell came looking for Elton. 'Elton did not go looking for Cromwell; Cromwell sought him out'.[16]

Cromwell was almost an incarnation of Elton's philosophy of history, which, however, was a term which he used pejoratively, as something 'which only hinders the practice of history'. In a late collection of lectures and papers called *Return to Essentials: Some Reflections on the Present State of Historical Study* (1991), we read of 'the burden of philosophy', which meant the theory which denies 'the very possibility

---

[14] G. R. Elton, 'Thomas Cromwell Redivivus', in his *Studies in Tudor and Stuart Politics and Government*, iii (Cambridge, 1983), 373.

[15] G. R. Elton, *Return to Essentials: Some Reflections on the Present State of Historical Study* (Cambridge, 1991), pp. 43, 67.

[16] Robert William Fogel and G. R. Elton, *Which Road to the Past? Two Views of History* (New Haven and London, 1983), p. 127.

of treating the past as having happened independently from the historian who supposedly is at work on it'. The past had really happened, the truth could be told about it (but only at the cost of Herculean intellectual effort), and its history must be studied and written on its own terms and even for its own sake, which meant 'giving the past the right to exist within the terms of its own experience'.

These views, no longer fashionable, were first elaborated on a general scale in *The Practice of History* (1967), usually read as a response to E. H. Carr's Trevelyan Lectures *What Is History?* (1964), but in fact frying several fish who were alive and well, swimming in the currents of Cambridge history and faculty politics at the time. It is a book full of good sense and advice for practitioners and consumers, teachers and students alike. If one were to point an enquirer in the direction of what historians do, and are best at, one would send them to this book, perhaps to be read in conjunction with Philip Sidney's *An Apology for Poetry*, where the historian is represented as bound to tell things 'as they were'. But Elton's brief for history was epistemologically shaky. The past may have had a real existence and it may be possible to establish the truth about that past. But to suggest that the historian does not in some sense invent his stories, if only by a selective process (and 'invention is a necessary part of rhetoric'), to propose that he can tell the whole truth about anything (although Cicero had so defined the historian's function), would not and does not wash. The past which brings itself to the historian's attention, Cromwell crying out from *Letters and Papers*, is also self-selecting. As Elton himself remarked, 'it may be that Cromwell appears to dominate his age so much because his papers have survived'[17] the accidental consequence of his attainder. Elton's parliamentary history canonised those parts of the archive which happened, fortuitously, to have survived.

Elton's uncompromising positivism and Germanic thoroughness invite comparison with Ranke. But he had little interest in or knowledge of a long-running debate in Germany about the meaning of Ranke's *wie es eigentlich gewesen ist*, and he had only contempt for grand theorists like Hans-Georg Gadamer, author of *Wahrheit und Methode* (1960). Ultimately, the sole purpose of studying history 'for its own sake' was (besides enjoyment) the intellectual training it provided, for sometimes

---

[17] G. R. Elton, *The Tudor Revolution in Government: Administrative Changes in the Reign of Henry VIII* (Cambridge, 1953), p. 5.

Elton was openly sceptical about any other social benefit it might confer.

But Elton's history cannot be defined, still less dismissed, as dubious epistemology. His austere insistence on the historian's 'that was' (Sidney), the ardour with which he attacked anyone with axes to grind, determinists, and teleologists, was at root a passion for liberty and order, rooted in his adolescent experience of ideological menace. Why else should he have hurled an apple across the Clare combination room in the early 1970s, after an awkward encounter with a group of trendy lefties? Hence the extremity of his reaction to the student insurgency of the late 1960s; and hence, too, the extraordinary attack on the meek and mild R. H. Tawney, which he made the centrepiece of his first inaugural, a very good man and a very bad historian. 'His history was not good, not sound, not right, not true.' Not since Peter Ramus in the sixteenth century declared that everything Aristotle had written was false had there been so comprehensive a denunciation of a revered guru.

Gadamer was German, but Elton's severest strictures were reserved for anything and everything French, and above all for French theory. Of Derrida, he wrote, memorably: 'the absurd always sounds better in French'. Of the battle of Pavia in 1525, he wrote: 'The better part of the French chivalry lay dead (a French habit this)'.[18] The language may have been a difficulty. Evidently Elton, for all his interest in legal history, was not at ease with the Law-French in which English legal business was conducted for many centuries, a fact not mentioned in *The English*; and he was evidently not a student of the plea rolls. It is on record that Elton conversed with the late Fernand Braudel in Latin.[19]

Elton's views were most applicable to the history of government and political institutions, least helpful to the study of ideas, or, as it might be, art, or religion. In *Political History, Principles and Practice* (1970) he came close to arguing that political history was the historian's true last, to which he ought to stick. The historian who was tired of politics was—like Dr Johnson's disillusioned Londoner—tired of life.

Yet no one was more adept than Elton at violating his own principles, and he had another side which, over and above the warmth of a

---

[18] Elton, *Return to Essentials*, p. 28; G. R. Elton, *Reformation Europe 1517–1559* (London, 1963), p. 81.
[19] J. H. Plumb, 'The Uses of History', in *The Making of an Historian: The Collected Essays of J. H. Plumb* (Hemel Hempstead, 1988), p. 289.

personality that was open to all comers, was ecumenically tolerant of many, to him, alien tendencies and interests. In a series of published conversations with a friend, a historian of a very different kind, the number-crunching R. W. Fogel, *Which Road to the Past?* (1983), Elton asserted: 'We are all historians, differing only in what questions interest us, and what methods we find useful in answering them'. Elton not infrequently denounced feminist history. Yet several practitioners of women's history, whose work he thought sound, enjoyed his strong support. Most of his colleagues in Cambridge (for example, Americanists and Africanists) attest that while publicly he obstructed the advance of their subjects in the tripos, they found him an encouraging colleague. He was also an outstandingly generous person, his generosity ranging from a return-of-post response to all correspondents, to finding good homes for the journals to which he subscribed but did not want to keep; and, above all, in the arrangements he made for his estate, under which all the royalties from his books were bequeathed to the Royal Historical Society.

Meanwhile, the serious work was advancing in the practical application of these methodological principles. A steady flow of articles on critically important details of Henrician legislation and similar topics appeared in learned journals and Festschriften and were reprinted in what became four volumes of *Studies in Tudor and Stuart Politics and Government*. At the other extreme of communication, Elton published in 1955 his first textbook, *England Under the Tudors*. The book was commissioned at the Anglo-American Conference of Historians of 1951, when the man from Methuen approached S. T. Bindoff, whose *Tudor England* in the Pelican History of England was then a runaway success. 'There's your man', said Bindoff, pointing to Elton. The book was written in eighteen months. It was not only the most widely-consumed and influential of all A level primers, on which most academic historians now working in a variety of fields cut their teeth. By obliging sixth-formers to work at something like university level it simultaneously set what were arguably inappropriately high standards in the schools and made it harder for these students to maintain their already well-informed interest in Tudor history when they were asked to repeat the experience of reading this book at university.[20] Much later,

---

[20] In the University Senate House, in 1966, Elton spoke of undergraduates who 'have done university work, as they think, at school therefore they come here to do school work at university' (*Cambridge University Reporter*, 96 (1965–6), p. 1018). Did Elton appreciate that these words were almost a piece of self-incrimination?

Elton would advise a younger colleague to write his textbook in his thirties: 'Firstly because you are young and zealous, and secondly because it gives you plenty of time to enjoy the royalties'.

*England Under the Tudors* was undergirded in 1960 by *The Tudor Constitution*, a collection of primary documents with critical commentary and apparatus, a demonstration in print and for student use of what history consisted of for Elton. Much later, in 1972, came the last fruits of those years shared between the PRO and Denis Compton's Lords: *Policy and Police: The Enforcement of the Reformation in the Age of Thomas Cromwell*. This, the most substantial of all Elton's books, grew from seeds planted in the 1940s, nurtured in a Cambridge Special Subject class in the 1960s, and harvested in the Ford Lectures of 1972. Through the pages of this book we look out upon the England of the Pilgrimage of Grace from behind Cromwell's desk. According to his critics, and especially to Sir John Neale's successor as Astor Professor, Joel Hurstfield, this was a book with too much of a taste for *realpolitik* for comfort. The London Carthusians were foolish enough to 'get themselves hanged'. Elton later complained: 'When I was younger I was often accused of judging the Tudor century by the standards and criteria which it itself employed, and I frankly cannot think of a more flattering comment'.[21] In 1973 Elton published his Wiles Lectures, *Reform and Renewal: Thomas Cromwell and the Common Weal*, which dealt with Cromwell's activities as a kind of social engineer. There was ambivalence here, too, for on almost the last page Elton admitted that some of the social aspirations of the 1530s remained pipe dreams which was 'just as well, for carried into effect they might easily have become nightmares. *Utopia* should stand as a warning of what life might become if earnest reformers ever really got hold of it'.

In 1977, Elton contributed a new Tudor textbook to the Edward Arnold series, 'The New History of England': *Reform and Reformation, England 1509–1558*. This was the high-water mark of his own revisionist phase, for it acknowledged many of the modifications made by his own pupils to his original vision of Tudor history. Dr David Starkey, for example, had drawn attention to the continuing importance of the inner sanctum of the royal court and of its highly personalised and factional politics, a perception damaging to the 'Tudor Revolution in Government' thesis. At about this time, Elton wrote an essay on the Pilgrimage

---

[21] Elton, *Return to Essentials*, p. 67.

of Grace (which still divides the experts on that event as to its merits) which interpreted this most threatening of Tudor rebellions as a displaced palace revolution. A revised edition of *The Tudor Constitution* in 1982 was no less reflective of a shifting agenda for Tudor historians.

Meanwhile, it should not be thought that Gottfried Ehrenberg turned his back on the history of his native Germany, or on the history of a Europe conventionally assumed to have excluded the history of England, or at least to constitute a distinct and different subject. G. N. Clark commissioned Elton to edit and contribute to the second, Reformation, volume of *The New Cambridge Modern History*, which appeared in 1958, with a new and substantially revised edition in 1975. Out of this involvement came a very successful European textbook in the Fontana History of Europe, *Reformation Europe 1517–1559* (1963), beautifully written and moving at a brisk and assured pace. This publication provides a suitable opportunity to discuss the thorny question of Elton and religion. David Knowles once said of a history of a particular monastery that it was 'without visible religion (like Geoffrey Elton's Reformation)'.[22] But this was very unfair. *Reformation Europe* was written within a very traditional mould. No one would now write a textbook on the sixteenth century which is so dominated by Reformation themes: Luther, Zwingli, the Anabaptists, Calvin, the Counter-Reformation, topics perceived as Ranke and the church historians understood them. Luther and Calvin were 'deeply religious men'. 'The Nation State' and 'Society' were mere appendices, Rosencrantz and Guildenstern to this religious Hamlet. There was no trace here of reductionist anti-religious prejudice. Elton was an active member of the *Verein für Reformationsgeschichte*, and retained a strong interest in Martin Luther, whom the genealogists will tell us was a kind of ancestor. In the quincentenary year of 1983 he lectured on the subject of Luther in several German universities. Yet distaste for religion as something which only contributed positively to civilisation in its most moderated and compromised forms was always present. Elton could hardly forgive Thomas Cromwell for having 'got religion', and would have preferred to have him as a secular proto-modernist. The appearance of the Yale edition of the *Works* of Thomas More encouraged Elton to

---

[22] Roger Lovatt, 'David Knowles and Peterhouse', in Christopher Brooke *et al.*, *David Knowles Remembered* (Cambridge, 1991), p. 118. Christopher Brooke would like me to say that Professor Knowles had a great deal of respect for Elton's learning and never supposed that his private correspondence would see the light of day.

run a Cambridge Special Subject based on these texts. Probably he was not best qualified to interpret More's religious ideals, austerities and intolerances. In fact, his was an effective piece of debunking, for which the saint of Chelsea was perhaps overdue. Yet Elton served his turn as President of the Ecclesiastical History Society (1983–4), to which he was always a good patron. Like his good friend Martin Luther, he might be called a *complexio oppositorum*.

So it was with those other large segments of social existence in past times, the law and finance. Elton addressed these matters, and to significant effect, but as it were from the outside. He did important work on Tudor financial administration, but wrote little on getting and spending, and was the first to admit that he did not really understand sixteenth-century accounting. His relation to legal history was more complex, and interesting. He was a very acceptable President of the Selden Society (1983–5), but his lecture to that Society in 1978 began: 'I am not a legal historian, I am not a lawyer.'[23] He and Professor John Baker had a fruitful and interactive professional relationship. Initially, Elton was reluctant to concern himself with the processes and traditions of non-legislative law formation, although Baker had some influence in this area. Elton remained convinced that the thought processes of lawyers and historians were poles apart. He found the characteristic teleology of lawyers 'intellectually impenetrable' and in 1989 told a gathering of American lawyers in Illinois that they did not think historically. Elton's most admired model and mentor was F. W. Maitland, for Maitland's legal history was real history, and vastly superior to the work of historians (like Pollard, in his estimation) who could not be bothered to grapple with the technicalities of legal documents: 'that understanding of the law which alone unlocks the records'. His book on Maitland, a portrait of a scholar whose work was done 'well, conscientiously, circumspectly, methodically', not what Elton wrote about Thomas Cromwell, was a kind of self-portrait.

It was Parliament with which Elton felt most at home, and for him Parliament was not a forum for politics but a machine for legislation, law-making for a law-abiding polity. Between 1974 and 1977 Elton was President of the Royal Historical Society and at the height of his powers. Three of his annual presidential addresses were devoted to what was called 'Tudor Government: The Points of Contact', and

---

[23] G. R. Elton, *English Law in the Sixteenth Century: Reform in an Age of Change* (Selden Society Lecture, 1978).

they were vintage material. The first 'point of contact' was Parliament, and it led to a dozen years of work and publication on the Tudor, and more especially the Elizabethan, parliaments, culminating in his last work of substantial and deeply-researched archival scholarship, *The Parliament of England 1559–1581* (1986).

Once again we detect ambivalence. In the preface to *The Parliament of England* Elton wrote: 'I am perhaps exceptionally relieved to be done with the Parliaments of Elizabeth' (but he was only half-way through!), adding that the customary concentration on what was, after all, only 'one of the Crown's instruments of government' was 'entirely misleading'. So what was the motive and purpose of this work? Partly to correct Sir John Neale's version of Elizabethan parliamentary history, although in the book and in his 1978 Neale Memorial Lecture 'Parliament in the Sixteenth Century: Functions and Fortunes', unlike those unscripted occasions, he was not lacking in courtesy towards Neale.

Of course the issue was not personal but concerned the true facts of the matter. Neale had worked from parliamentary diaries and speeches, many of which were his own original discoveries, to portray an over-politicised, over-confrontational House of Commons, which was engaged in a political and ideological contest with the queen that had distinctly teleological constitutional implications. Neale also took little account of the House of Lords. But bills and acts were what Parliament was about, not political issues, and bills and acts were what the historian of Parliament—with a Maitland-like serenity in the face of technical adversity—must concern himself with. Elton's position was extreme and untenable, for Elizabethan parliaments were also political occasions, and we are now in a tertiary phase of post-revisionism so far as this matter is concerned. Nevertheless, this was the most definitively scholarly account of the English Parliament to have been written for any period in its history.

## IV

The Cambridge to which Elton was initially marginal he came to dominate. In 1967 he was promoted to a personal chair and chose the unfashionable title of 'Professor of English Constitutional History'. It was thought by some that he would become master of his own or of another college, but those who knew him, and the collegiate scene, cannot think that there was much in this. He served his stints on the

General Board of the Faculties and the Council of the Senate, 'a body designed to teach men the mortification of the spirit'.[24] In the Faculty of History his dominance was not uncontested for 'there were giants in the land in those days' (Genesis 6:4). But those foolish enough to wager that Geoffrey Elton would not speak to every item on the agenda at a particular meeting of Faculty Board could expect to lose their stake. Usually he spoke first.

Much of Elton's span in Cambridge was enlivened by what Sir John Plumb has referred to as 'the never-ending progress of tripos reform',[25] a process (rather than progress?) from time to time central to the politics of the faculty. The pressures for change and diversification came from the expansion of historical horizons beyond as well as within Cambridge, very publicly, not to say stridently, celebrated in 1966 as 'New Ways in History', an escape from a cloud of alleged stultification which had settled over academic history in England for much of the twentieth century. We are talking about Elton's kind of history. Change was also promoted, naturally enough, by those with a vested interest in such relatively new subjects as American, Asian, and African history. Elton was in favour of a modest amount of American history, but not of 'Third World' studies. And there was also the steady advance of the 'new' social history. As Edward VII almost said, 'we are all social historians now'. Undergraduates, too, were all for change, and that, in 1970, somewhat surprisingly, tilted the balance for Geoffrey Elton.

Dr Kitson Clark of Trinity liked to call himself a 'midwife to radical reform', while changes were generally resisted by Sir Herbert Butterfield and, from the younger generation, were critically if less consistently scrutinised by both Plumb and Elton. Part of the question (which other universities found it easier to answer, or to circumvent) was whether English and European history should be taught in something like their entirety, or should give way to what we have learned to call a smorgasbord or 'pick-and-mix' syllabus. Elton would have said that more fundamentally it was a matter of how hard incoming undergraduates should be hit by 'real' history.

No other faculty in Cambridge chose to wash its slightly soiled linen as publicly. In 1965–6 and in 1970, there were Reports to the University from History, recommending substantial changes in the tripos, each of these reports reflecting years of discussion and committee work

---

[24] Elton, *Maitland*, p. 9.
[25] *Essays of J. H. Plumb*, p. 370.

within the faculty. Because the faculty was so evenly divided, or could be massaged into the appearance of a hung parliament, on both occasions the issue came to a Discussion in the Senate House and to a ballot, with the inevitable fly-sheets. Elton, unlike some other front-runners, felt the scandal of airing these matters in public and having to depend upon the arbitration of the university at large, which is to say, of the scientists. In June 1966, while insisting that he was not opposed to change as such, the tripos needed reforming, Elton spoke with passion against a new tripos 'directed against any proper standard of scholarship', 'which proposes to reduce the study of history in this University below the proper level of university attainment'. He spoke, as usual without script. 'I may have said things that I should have left unsaid': words quoted against him in 1970.[26]

In 1970, with Owen Chadwick the Regius professor but as Vice-Chancellor in the uncomfortable chair for the debate in the Senate House, the matter to be addressed, a critical refinement to the 1966 tripos, was whether the '1500 rule' should be rescinded, which would enable Cambridge undergraduates to avoid medieval history altogether, if they so chose. Elton had now changed sides, or so it seemed to the medievalists, headed by Walter Ullmann. Elton spoke as Chairman of the Faculty, and as the historian who had had most to do with student insurgency in the late 1960s. These were his declared motives for distancing himself from what he now called the 'apocalyptic' theory proposed by the opponents of change and defenders of the 1500 rule. 'I really think that the fears we have heard about the decay and the disappearance of medieval history are exaggerated, to put it mildly.' Elton claimed to have the best interests of medieval history at heart, and he was right to think that under the 1970 proposals those interests were not at risk, but it was widely suspected that he favoured the 1970 package (which also offered undergraduates an additional paper in English history) because it advantaged his own Tudor history. 'There has been some suggestion that this has been a product of a personal campaign or intrigue perhaps. I wish I thought I was as clever at intrigue as some people seem to have charged me with . . .'. Clever or not, the 1970 package was voted down by 203 votes to 93.[27]

By the time Elton reached his inaugural lecture as Regius in 1984

[26] *Cambridge University Reporter*, 96 (1965–66), pp. 627, 1013–28, 1292, 1591, 1605, 1830, 1852–3.

[27] *Cambridge University Reporter*, 100 (1969–70), pp. 1182–91, 1976, 2331–2.

('The History of England'), he made no bones about his disillusionment with what an age of supposed reform had done to Cambridge history. 'Our historical tripos now lacks all cohesion and with it any real understanding of what it is trying to do'. Options were said to have multiplied 'recklessly', 'bits of history', 'Mexico and Malawi'. 'We cannot be doing right when we send people into the world who have graduated in history and have never been made to feel the length of it'. Here he was right again, but the plea for 'a course built around a long stretch of English history' was not heeded. In 1996, those sitting a Part I paper on British history from 1450 to 1750 ignored the fifteenth and eighteenth centuries altogether. Out of more than eighty candidates, only one chose to answer questions on both the sixteenth and seventeenth centuries. Elton must have turned in his grave.

There was also the politics of professorial elections and Crown appointments, which aroused more public excitement than we have witnessed in more recent years. If there were giants in those days, there were also some giant egos. In 1963, Elton and Plumb were favoured as leading candidates for the Chair of Modern History, which Butterfield had vacated on his promotion to the Regius Chair. However, the prize went to Charles Wilson, who had been thought of as the most suitable occupant of the Economic History Chair. Again in 1968 Elton and Plumb were passed over, when the Crown appointed Owen Chadwick to succeed Butterfield as Regius. It was widely assumed that Elton's hour would come in the due course of time, which it did in 1983, rather late in the day, since he was by then only five years away from retirement.

Even in 1983 there were fears that the right decision would not be made, for with (the then) Mrs Thatcher in Downing Street, a nakedly political appointment seemed possible. Few doubted that for the Crown to appoint anyone but Elton would be a kind of affront to the historical profession as a whole. Three professors of history in a university in the north-west of England even took the unusual step of writing to Number Ten to say so. They need not have worried. The Prime Minister was well advised, and always seems to have played with a very straight bat when it came to academic appointments. There was almost universal relief and pleasure in Cambridge, while from Oxford A. J. P. Taylor wrote to say that Elton was the only Regius in his lifetime who commanded his wholehearted approval. Elton came from a hospital bed and an operation for detached retina to deliver his inaugural. For once, he had a written text, and now he could not read it. But soon he got into his stride and within fifty minutes had managed to offend almost everybody in the hall. A colleague remembers: 'God was in his heaven, Geoffrey was still himself, and all was right with the world.'

Further stories could be told about the History Faculty building and about Clare College. The proposal to spend a great deal of money on a purpose-built home for the Faculty of History on the Sidgwick Avenue site was a late item on the agenda of a board meeting presided over by Butterfield in 1961; almost 'any other business'. But as early as 1949 the question had been put, from the central administration of the university, whether the Faculty of History 'could conveniently be accommodated on the Sidgwick Avenue site'. To take study leave is always risky. When, early in 1965, Elton returned from leave to find that he was no longer a member of the relevant committees, he wrote with some bitterness of having worked 'for some eight years on the whole question of a building for the faculty'. But he was soon back in the saddle. In 1962, Elton had appeared before the Sidgwick Avenue Commiteee as a representative of the Faculty of History. By April 1963, he was a full member of the Committee and appears to have played, with Professor Moses Finley, the critical role in the selection of James Stirling of Messrs Stirling and Gowan from the three rival bids for the architectural contract. Stirling's was the only bid within the target sum of £238,000, and the Committee wondered, as well it might, whether, 'having regard to the character of their building', not to speak of questions of maintenance, the Stirling and Gowan estimate was realistic. It looks as if Elton was the key player on 23 April 1963, when it was decided to recommend the award of the contract to Stirling, and when the Committee heard an explanation of how Stirling proposed to turn the building through an angle of 90 degrees in order to bring it wholly on to land not owned by Mrs Eaden Lilley of 11, West Road: a fateful decision for those destined to spend their entire working lives within the building, exposed to the merciless summer sun beating on the glass of what was now to be the west side of the triangular building.

By the summer of 1968, the building was complete, inviting comparison with glass houses designed for giraffes at the zoo or palm trees at Kew, not to forget an ingenious architectural contrivance of Jeremy Bentham. It is admired by students of architecture from all over the known world, but for those who have to work in it, in all weathers, it is not a friendly place. Writing to his Chairman, Otto Smail, about the proof for an invitation card to a grand opening which never happened, Elton wrote: 'At least the card—like the building itself—looks *different*! . . .

I expect you've heard of the latest troubles—water everywhere.' Unfortunately, this was not the last of these aqueous troubles.

Oddly enough, the many small seminar rooms which are a feature of the Stirling Building, without a single lecture room as such, were designed to accommodate those many little 'bits of history' of which Elton was to complain in 1984. In 1961–2, the faculty had specified that it would need two lecture rooms to hold 250, three to hold 150, and so on. The Stirling Building was supposed to be complemented by a purpose-built block of lecture-rooms on the same site. But in 1966 it became horribly clear that this was not going to happen, and the then secretary of the Faculty Board, the future Professor Sir John Elliott, wrote a letter of protest to the Old Schools: which was answered, negatively, seven months later: 'very little prospect of a second block of lecture-rooms'. Never mind. Soon students ceased to form lecture audiences of 150, let alone 250. However, all's well that ends well. In September 1968, the Seeley Library, the largest single-subject history library in the world, was moved into the new building, Geoffrey Elton and a small army of volunteers doing the physical work of putting the books on the shelves, while the Chairman, Otto Smail, drove the books across Cambridge in a van.[28] Elton (whose father, we must not forget, was trained in architecture) would never hear anything said against Sir James Stirling's striking if dreadful building. The first meeting of the Faculty Board to be held in the new boardroom was dramatically interrupted by the entrance of a posse of firemen with helmets on their heads and axes in their hands, the smoke detectors having been activated when Elton and Professor Sir Harry Hinsley lit up their pipes. Hinsley did not best please Elton with his remark that the smoke detectors at least had worked.

Clare College takes us into more architectual politics. Elton was the principal proponent of the Forbes Mellon Library which now fills up Clare's Memorial Court, obstructing the vista to the University Library. There was stiff opposition to the scheme on aesthetic grounds, and, as the man who had engaged Stirling (Arup was to be the architect on this occasion) Elton was not altogether comfortable. The Governing Body decided to go ahead by a single vote. As a sweetener, Elton disclosed his intention to bequeath his own library to the college, which in due course he did. Clare, however, was unable to accept the gift, and the books, under the terms of a further clause in Elton's will, and through

[28] Archives of the Faculty of History, Bay 3, Boxes 1, 2.

the good offices of the Royal Historical Society, are now to be found in the Borthwick Institute of Historical Research of the University of York. Elton would have been upset by these posthumous manoeuvres, for he was a very staunch college man, entertaining his guests in the college, usually to lunch, almost daily. Some of those younger historians whose careers he advanced, even while he had little or no interest in their work, he helped for no other reason than the Clare connection. An example is Peter Lake, now the holder of a distinguished chair at Princeton University. Making the after-lunch speech on the day Cambridge conferred on him the honorary degree of LLD, Elton boasted about his college as one of the first to admit women, and then, characteristically and off-the-cuff, caused offence by wondering whether that had been a good idea after all.

In the republic of letters beyond Cambridge, Elton was a more active and creative citizen than any other historian of our age. As President of the Royal Historical Society, his creativity was outstanding, bringing the RHS into a new age of usefulness to all members of the profession, and not least its younger members. The monograph series 'Studies in History' was his brain-child, created to enable suitably talented Ph.D.s to publish their theses. He was the editor of the series to the very end. The RHS *Annual Bibliography of British and Irish History* which was launched in 1976 ('Publications of 1975') was not merely invented by Elton; for many years he edited it, on his own typewriter. Thinking of the books which even Elton did not write, there are those who regret the many hundreds of hours spent on that useful enterprise. These bibliographies had grown out of a bibliography of British history, composed in German, which Elton had contributed to *Historische Zeitschrift* as a *Beiheft* to that journal, which was later rendered into English as *Modern Historians on British History 1485–1945: A Critical Bibliography 1945–1969* (1970). Elton was taken aback by the *naïveté* of someone who supposed that he had actually read all the 1,351 items which this bibliography contained.

The list of public services Elton performed is very long. He founded and presided over the List and Index Society which from 1965 made widely available a long series of essential guides to the public records, not only in the PRO, but, in the case of one of these volumes, the Channel Islands. At one time he was simultaneously editing major series for five leading publishers. For twenty years he presided over the annual gatherings of 'Senior Historians' at Cumberland Lodge. From 1981 to 1990, he served as Publications Secretary of the British

Academy. He had a close connection with the Wiles Lectures in Belfast, which he himself gave in 1972. He was a frequent visitor to the United States, and held visiting professorships at Pittsburgh in 1963 and Minnesota in 1976. There were also visits to Australia where, taken out of Sydney in a car to see the Blue Mountains, he saw them and asked to be taken home. All these occasions were well but sensibly lubricated with Glenfiddich or (a later, American discovery) Jack Daniels. College history societies who competed to lionise the great man knew that not the least of the arrangements which had to be made when they entertained him was a liberal supply of these substances. It was on these occasions that he was at his most informal, and robust.

Many honours came Elton's way. He was the recipient of no less than five Festschriften, including one from his American friends, another from Australia and New Zealand, and others reflecting his interests in parliamentary and European history respectively. Honorary degrees were conferred on him by the universities of Glasgow, Newcastle, Bristol, London, Göttingen, and Cambridge. The last was a particular cause of pleasure, for since Elton was already a Litt.D. of the Univesity the degree awarded *honoris causa* was the LLD, Maitland's degree. In 1986 came his knighthood.

The files of letters received on such occasions are very indicative of the man he was. Professor A. G. Dickens wrote: 'You have worked harder than any other British historian for the young and even not-very-brilliant'. He was echoed by Sir Richard Southern: 'You have done more for English history than anyone living—more to help the young in their early struggles, and more for the health of our subject—words would fail me to express it all'. C. S. L. Davies thought that the knighthood ought to have been 'the Earldom of Essex' (Cromwell's ultimate honour, ultimate, we recall, in that it prepared the way for his execution!—which was probably not the point that Davies wished to make!). With very few exceptions (such as Tam Dalyell MP), those who wrote were fellow-historians. It does not appear that he mixed very much outside his own university and his own profession. He was indeed the historian's historian, for all his impact on generations, tens of thousands of school as well as university students of the subject, men and women now in Parliament, or running the Gas Board, or the National Lottery. At conferences devoted to his memory and intellectual legacy, held in Washington DC in October 1995, and in London, at the Institute of Historical Research, in March 1996, it was remarkable to observe how almost every facet of Elton's work was subjected to radical and sometimes devastating criticism, while no one doubted for a moment that this had been a great man, and a great historian. As Dr John Morrill has written: 'For at least thirty years everyone else defined their own position in relation to his.'

PATRICK COLLINSON
*Fellow of the Academy*

*Note.* I must above all thank Lady Elton and Professor Lewis Elton for their indispensable assistance; and acknowledge the anecdotal contributions, help, and corrective advice of many colleagues, including especially: Professor John Baker; Dr George Bernard; Dr Margaret Bowker, Professor Christopher Brooke; Dr Christine Carpenter; Professor Peter Clark; Dr Christopher Haigh; Dr Patrick Higgins; Professor Sir Harry Hinsley; Dr Clive Holmes; Dr Richard Hoyle; Arnold Hunt; Dr Ronald Hyam; Dr Peter Linehan; Professor David Loades; Dr Rosamond McKitterick; Dr David Morgan; Dr John Morrill; Dr John Reeve; Professor Jonathan Riley-Smith; Dr Roger Schofield; Professor R. W. Scribner; Dr Jonathan Shepard; Professor Quentin Skinner; Dr David Smith; Professor Frank Walbank; and Dr Keith Wrightson. None of these correspondents can be held responsible for the somewhat sideways appraisal which this memoir makes of Sir Geoffrey, a historian 'whose shoe-latchet I am not worthy to unloose' (Luke 3:16, Tyndale version).

# Bibliography

A full bibliography of the writings of G. R. Elton, excluding reviews, a total of 158 items, will be found in *Law and Government Under the Tudors: Essays Presented to Sir Geoffrey on his Retirement*, eds. Claire Cross, David Loades, and J. J. Scarisbrick (Cambridge, 1988), pp. 257–64. To this should be added, for the period 1987–1992:

'A New Age of Reform?', *Historical Journal*, 30 (1987), 709–16.

'Tudor Government', *Historical Journal*, 31 (1988), 425–34.

'The History of Parliament: Myth and Reality', *Platt's Chronicle*, 1988.

*Thomas Cromwell* (Bangor, 1991).

*Return to Essentials: Some Reflections on the Present State of Historical Study* (Cambridge, 1991).

*The English*, 'The Peoples of Europe' (Oxford, 1992).

MOSES FINLEY                    *Edward Leigh*

*Proceedings of the British Academy*, **94**, 459–472

# Moses Finley
# 1912–1986

THE DEATH OF MOSES FINLEY on 23 June 1986 was as unusual as the life that preceded it. In effect he died on the same day as his much-loved wife, Mary, who had been the close companion of his entire academic career, from the days when both were graduate students studying ancient history at Columbia University. There was something moving and symbolic about the fact that a few hours after the ambulance had taken Mary from the house, he himself suffered a massive heart attack and, although pronounced dead only the following day, never regained consciousness. News of his death was followed by a flood of telephone calls and letters from eminent scholars around the world, each of whom registered a sense of deep, personal loss. Although he could be fierce with his enemies, friendship and loyalty to his students and colleagues were two of his most attractive attributes.

It is the richness of Moses Finley's personal experiences and what Arnaldo Momigliano termed his 'formidable intellectual heritage' which in retrospect continue to astonish. The Finklesteins had origins deeply rooted in Jewish history, including ancestors (on his mother's side) among the Katzenellenbogens, one of the grand central European and Italian rabbinic families since the sixteenth century, which produced the great Maharal of Prague, creator of a *golem*. His early education at Central High School, Syracuse NY, was intended as a preparation for training as a rabbi at the Jewish Theological Seminary. His younger brother tells how at his bar mitzvah, instead of the conventional platitudes of thanks to his family, he delivered a learned

© The British Academy 1997.

historical study of the ceremony. Quite when or why Moses changed course is unclear, and it was no doubt a slow process, but it culminated in the alteration of the family name to Finley some time after he had reached the age of 29.

Momigliano, a fellow Jew and the oldest of his European friends, who had known him since 1934, said that he had rarely heard Finley talk of his Jewish background. The violence of the renunciation, he believed, explains his blind spot in ignoring the importance of Jewish attitudes to slavery. My own experience, although later and briefer, is that, despite personal encounters with anti-Semitism when he first arrived in Cambridge, Moses spoke and wrote freely of Judaism—but more as a humanist with ironic detachment. Surveying Christian historiography in the *New York Review of Books*, for instance, he ridiculed pious attempts to eliminate collective Jewish wickedness from Western culture: 'Are we to undertake a great campaign . . . ,' he asks, 'beginning with Bach's *Passion According to St John*, the words and music together? The dead past never buries its dead. The world will have to be changed, not the past.' Discussions of the history of Jewish resistance did not bring out any passion for Jewish nationalism; rather his dislike of 'religious exclusiveness and alienness, in a world which otherwise found room for all varieties of cult and belief.'

The French word 'formation' is a better description of the extraordinarily varied influences at work on the young Finley in the next decade, since much of it came from beyond formal education. Instead of the Jewish Seminary, he went to Syracuse University, where at the precocious age of fifteen, he graduated *magna cum laude* (Phi Beta Kappa) in psychology (major), French and English (minors). From there he went to Columbia to take an MA two years later in public law, which included a dissertation entitled, 'Justice Harlan on personal Rights with special reference to due Process of Law'. During this period he met Mary Moscowitz, his future wife, who was awarded her MA in the same year, having qualified in both Latin and Greek, after which she continued as a fellow at Columbia and abroad until 1932. Moses meanwhile left Columbia to work as a clerk in a legal department of a large corporation, but after six months he declared, 'I had had enough', and he found a post for the next three years as a 'fact-checker' on the editorial staff of the *Encyclopedia for Social Sciences*. The experience this gave him in a wide range of current thinking in social sciences was to serve him well, although he claimed its main benefit was insight into the fallibility of the good and the great.

While checking facts for the Encyclopedia, he returned to Columbia to work for A. A. Schiller as research assistant, mainly, as he said, 'on history and theory of public opinion', while concurrently enrolling for a doctorate in ancient history under W. L. Westermann, who was then writing his great study of ancient slave systems for Pauly-Wissowa. In 1934–5 he became a research fellow, which he combined with part-time teaching duties at the City College of New York, a post he held until 1942. In 1937 he joined the Institute for Social Research, formerly the Institüt für Sozialforschung of Frankfurt, which, under threat from the rising tide of Nazism in the Weimar Republic, had removed itself with its director, Max Horkheimer, to quarters generously provided by Columbia. For two years Finley worked as an editor, translator and reviewer of books on philosophy, criminology, sociology, law, and ancient history, acquiring an awesome range of professional skills as well as a close working acquaintance with many of the Jewish radicals who were to influence the next generation of Americans—what has been described as 'the only interdisciplinary aggregation of scholars, working on different problems from a common theoretical base, to coalesce in modern times'.

One can only guess at how precisely each of these experiences affected Finley. He himself claimed that two major influences of his academic formation in this period came from fellow students—Wesley Mitchell, who opened his eyes to economic politics, and Ben Nelson, a sociologist who also worked with him in the Institute and introduced him to the works of Weber. This is not to diminish, however, the value of Schiller's knowledge of ancient law and Egypt or Westermann's interest in slavery, both of which exhibited themselves in the later Finley repertoire. From the galaxy of stars in the Institute he clearly acquired his Marxism (or 'Critical Theory', as it was termed for sensitive American ears). But theirs was the liberal Marxist dialogue of the *Gründrisse* against the deadening effect of Stalinist orthodoxy, the history of consciousness above historical materialism, which were the themes embraced by the Frankfurt group and which Finley found in later years earned him as much abuse from traditional Marxists as from the conservative Right.

Perhaps the most important lessons he absorbed from the Institute were a preference for brief critiques over large, definitive books, the importance of debate through dialogue and provocative argument, and above all the importance of studying ancient history not as a series of isolated, specialist monographs but as subjects related to an overarching political economy. Although in these pre-war years he was beginning slowly to make his mark as an ancient historian under Westermann's influence through a few cautious articles, the bent of his mind is more evident in the reviews he produced for the house journal of the Institute. 'The study of ancient history', he said in a review of Victor Ehrenberg's *Ost und West*, 'has reached an impasse. Unless the basic postulates are shifted, no real advance is possible. Most historians, seeming unaware of this dilemma, continue to flounder in positivistic analysis and the eternal reiteration of the glory that was Greece and the grandeur that was Rome.' He quoted with approval Farrington's words (later repeated in *Greek Science*), 'The struggle between science and obscurantism is a political one', and insisted that ancient science could only be discussed by reference to the slave economy.

The war years are something of a blank in Finley's career. Although he apparently continued to retain the fellowship in history at Columbia, his attention was diverted to what he called 'war relief agencies'. But in 1948 he was appointed to his first university teaching post at Newark College, Rutgers University. In retrospect it seems that this year was a turning point in his academic career. His decision to return to his Ph.D. studies resulted in the book *Land and Credit in Ancient Athens*, completed in 1951 (published 1952), a study of Athenian boundary stones (*horoi*) on hypothecated land and in many ways the kind of specialist monograph which Finley had criticised, although some scholars still think it to be his finest work. In it he challenged the prevailing notion of a large underclass of indebted Athenian poor in the fourth century and he was able to cast important light on the functioning of the law and credit institutions.

At the same time he found his teaching at Rutgers hampered by his intense dislike of the ancient history textbooks available for the large, non-specialist classes he was required to educate. It was this that led him to contact Pat Covici at the Viking Press, a man on intimate terms with many of the great American literati of the day, such as John Steinbeck, Saul Bellow, and Arthur Miller, who was to be a major influence in his life. In 1950, with Covici's encouragement he hatched an ambitious proposal to produce a 'Portable on Greek Civilization', containing selected texts that would reflect 'the gamut of thinking *and acting* [MIF's italics] on the broadest range of materials'. The portable was intended as the material for a history of Greek civilisation that would carry on 'to the end of the Roman Empire and include, among other things, the Greek impact on Judaism and Christianity'. Above all, he underlined, this would not be just a textbook but a book 'written to be read'.

The final outcome was totally unexpected. It says much for the tolerance of Covici that after three years of correspondence and declarations of good intentions, Finley finally admitted that he had been unable to make progress beyond the first chapter on archaic Greece. Despite a mass of scholarly articles and books on Homer, he said, he could not find a single short work which gave 'a thorough, systematic and consistent picture of Homeric society'. Here for the first time was a need where he could provide in practice what he had complained of as lacking in ancient historical writing, a readable, brief account of an ancient society which entered into dialogue with modern scholarship beyond the confines of ancient history. His enthusiasm was fired and *The World of Odysseus* was born. 'The damned thing is in my blood,' he wrote to Covici. 'I even dream of paperbacks.' By 1954 the book was ready for publication.

Meanwhile, Finley was engaged in another interdisciplinary project at Columbia, where Karl Polanyi had taken up a visiting professorship from 1947 to 1953, inspiring a group of scholars to study the economic aspects of historical growth. The result was a collection of seminar papers edited by Polanyi and C. M. Arensberg, *Trade and Market in Early Empires* (1957). No one doubts the enormous admiration that Finley felt for Polanyi nor the profound influence of Polanyi's theory concerning the relationship between the economy and society, and his desire to liberate historians of early societies from ideas of production and exchange implanted by the industrial revolution. But the course of the relationship between the venerable Hungarian exile and the young American blood did not run entirely smoothly. Although Polanyi read *The World of Odysseus* in manuscript and Finley in turn read what was probably Polanyi's first draft of *The Livelihood of Man*, their correspondence betrays a tension and unwillingness on both sides to accept criticism. Finley, for instance, expressed himself 'flabbergasted' at Polanyi's dislike of the 'Greenwich village immaturity of tone' in *The World of Odysseus*, particularly in some of the passages on 'high-school sexuality'. Polanyi found some of the frank and trenchant remarks about his interpretation of Aristotle and the economy hard to take. Finley eventually refused to publish the text of his seminar contribution, 'Aristotle on exchange' in the proceedings and he later made public in a paper, 'Aristotle and economic analysis' published in *Past and Present* (1970), his dislike of Polanyi's non-market view of classical Greek society. Twenty years later he wrote, 'I discovered that these studies [of Polanyi's seminar] . . . were more misleading than illuminating for my purposes. . . . The intrusion of genuine market (commercial) trade . . . into the Greek world . . . render(s) the primitive models all but useless' (Anthropology and the Classics', in *The Use and Abuse of History*, ch. 6).

The astonishing thing is that in the years 1951–4, during which Finley was conducting large and immensely popular lecture courses at Rutgers, he not only finished and published *Land and Credit*, delivered from scratch *The World of Odysseus*, wrote papers and numerous long letters connected with Polanyi's seminar, and was giving serious thought to a major study of Greek property institutions (for which he left two outlines, although it was never written), but he was at the same time under emotional pressure from the Senate Committee on Internal Security led by Senator McCarran (better known for its association with the name of Senator McCarthy). The committee was investigating the activities of the Institute for Pacific Relations (IPR), in the process of which Karl Wittfogel alleged that Finley had been running a Communist study group in his house in 1938–9, the period when he had been most closely associated with the Marxist-orientated Frankfurt Institute. No doubt he was also regarded with suspicion for his activities at Columbia when he had helped organise the Committee for the Defence of International Freedom, encouraged by senior academics such as Franz Boas.

The climax came with a summons in late 1952 to appear before a subcommittee, where, although denying activities with the IPR or running a Communist cell, he declined under privilege of the Fifth Amendment to answer allegations about his past membership of the Communist Party. His refusal was backed by a university review committee but rejected by the University Board of Trustees, who ruled that unwillingness to testify before a Senate committee was grounds for automatic dismissal. The ruling was voted upon and carried by a full assembly of the university. From 1953, therefore, Finley was unemployed.

Fortunately for him, his academic reputation was by now established. Momigliano in 1954 recognised him as 'the best living social historian of Greece' and offers of visiting lectureships in Britain resulted, partly through his friendship with Professor Tony Andrewes at Oxford. That in turn led to invitations to apply for posts at both Oxford and Cambridge, election to a lectureship at Cambridge in 1955 and a fellowship at Jesus College two years later. In 1962 he took British citizenship; in 1964 he was appointed Reader; and in 1970 he succeeded A. H. M. Jones to the sole Chair of Ancient History in the university. In 1971 he was elected a Fellow of the British Academy, followed in 1976 by his appointment as Master of Darwin College and a knighthood in 1979. Although he retired in that year from his chair, he continued as Master of Darwin until 1982, being responsible in his time for establishing the annual Darwin Lecture Series in 1977 and inspiring the important Darwin Centenary Conference on Evolution, whose proceedings were published in 1983. Both attracted wide audiences and eminent speakers from a variety of disciplines, thereby contributing to the growing reputation of the college as a centre for postgraduates.

Although Finley was writing extensively on a wide variety of subjects in the first decade of his period in Britain, it is fair to say that most communications were in the form of quite short articles and edited papers, many of them deriving from conferences and popular broadcasts which made his name widely known beyond the university classics faculty—*The Greek Historians* (1958), *Slavery in Classical Antiquity* (1960), *The Ancient Greeks* (1963), *Aspects of Antiquity* (1963). This is not to ignore the book on *The History of Sicily*, produced in 1968 in tandem with Denis Mack Smith, and *Early Greece. The Bronze and Archaic Age* (1970), which became another popular paperback. But his most influential works were yet to come and it is, perhaps, significant that it was the renewal of his American connections which stimulated the first of them. Nominated as Sather Professor of Classical Literature at the University of California, he also accepted an invitation to return to Rutgers University to deliver the Mason Gross Welch Lectures in what was officially described as a righting of a past wrong. This was his first, triumphant return to American soil after nearly twenty years. Both were duly published in 1973, the first as *The Ancient Economy* and the second as *Democracy Ancient and Modern*.

True to the precept he had learned in his early years, Finley presented these books as 'dialectical discourses'—that is to say, provocative and radical challenges to received wisdom about the nature of the ancient market and the function of political élites. They were explicitly intended as dialogues between the ancient and modern world, a task for which he was by his training supremely well equipped and for which the lecture form provided an ideal vehicle. Three other books followed the same pattern in rapid succession. In 1978 an invitation by J.-P. Vernant to the Collège de France allowed him to return to the subject of slavery in four lectures published under the title of *Ancient Slavery and Modern Ideology* (1980). In 1980 he delivered the Wiles Lectures in Belfast before a mixed audience of ancient and modern historians and political scientists, subsequently published as *Politics in the Ancient World* (1983). And in 1983 his retirement from full-time lecturing was honoured by an invitation to deliver the annual J. H. Gray Lectures in Cambridge, later published as *Ancient History. Evidence and Models* (1985), which summed up his historiographic creed.

*Evidence and Models* brought his published books (apart from collections of articles) to a round dozen and his works were translated into at least ten languages (including Catalan). Abroad he was fêted like a popstar in the popular media and in the quality Press like a visiting politician with full page interviews in *La Repubblica* and *Le Monde*. In Britain, although his reception was more restrained, the entry in *Who's Who* of the academic honours and positions showered upon him makes impressive reading. Outside the circle of classical faculties he had become probably the best-known living ancient historian either in Britain or abroad. It was he who insisted on and became convener of the ancient historical section in the International Economic History Conferences. In Cambridge University he played a dominant role in the History Faculty and became Chairman of the Social and Political Sciences Committee, giving to ancient history a respect it had lacked.

As with any complex personality, it is impossible to sum up the academic contribution of Finley in a few words. But it helps us to understand his achievement if we recall the state of ancient history in Britain in the 1950s and early 1960s. In an article, 'Unfreezing the Classics' in a *Times Literary Supplement* of 1966, he complained bitterly about the isolation of ancient history outside Britain, fixed as it was in the tradition of classical philology. Ancient historians never published in the *English Historical Review*. Weber's studies of Roman agriculture were practically unknown and no English translation existed. It was difficult, he said, to find what were the debates which excited ancient historians, who, instead of discussing the nature of the Athenian Empire, were writing 'sentimental piffle' which often revolved around the dates of stonecutters.

Momigliano, who had taken up the chair of Ancient History at University College London, chose the 'crisis' in Greek History as the subject of his inaugural lecture in 1952 to voice the same disquiet. While public interest was turning more and more to social and economic history, ancient history was in intellectual bondage to German abstractions—causing 'the divorce of the study of Greek political ideas from the study of politics' (Finley's words, reviewing Momigliano). No history existed of the Athenian empire, no history of Greek agriculture, only out-of-date studies of Greek trade, no history of Greek political theory after Aristotle nor of historiography after Thucydides. The wrong kind of history was occupying the energies of ancient historians. 'Too much historical research', said Momigliano, 'was being done by people who do not know why they are doing it.' Writing for the American Social Science Research Council in 1960, Finley summed up: 'Ancient history is unique in western history in that its professional practitioners are by long tradition often men who are not in the first instance historians but . . . who call themselves classicists.' The historian's task was not merely to recover lost data but to understand—which was to generalise.

It is not hard, therefore, to see why Finley's intellectual formation rebelled against this suffocating climate and turned much of his writing into a crusade. Nor is it difficult for even a first-year undergraduate to recognise how much had changed by the time he died. Here I pick out only three areas where his contribution to historiography seems clearest. They are all of a parcel and themes which he repeated throughout his life. First, his attitude to 'facts' and sources; secondly, his use of models; and thirdly, his devotion to total history.

One of the deadening effects of the philological background, he believed, had been that classicists rarely reflected upon historical problems outside those posed in the ancient texts, from which they had formed their basic assumptions in their school-days. Ever greater refinement of the Greek and Latin sources might improve the 'superstructure' of understanding but rarely led to re-examination of the 'substructure', which had to be stimulated from outside. Inevitably, therefore, he had a strong antipathy for Rankean scientific historicism and the notion that value-free facts and truth could be distilled from the sources. He was relentless against history that was mere 'fact grubbing' or 'butterfly collections', reserving a chapter of his final book for a savage denunciation of the whole concept of 'How it really was', which could never be more than illusory. 'Accuracy and truth', he declared, 'are not synonymous.' In this campaign against what he called 'latter-day antiquarianism' he reserved his special ire for learned monographs of city-histories, not because the aim was intrinsically wrong but because it was impossible to achieve with data that was not susceptible to analysis.

Finley's attitude closely mirrored the prevailing view of what came to be called the French *Annales* school. H.-I. Marrou, for instance, in 1954 was stressing that the initiative in historical research did not belong to the document but to the historian and that ever closer study of documents did not bring answers, since history was not a police enquiry. Yet it is probably a fair guess that when Finley came to Britain few modern and almost no ancient historians had even heard of the *Annales* school, despite some notable exceptions. Finley, by contrast, had already learnt one of the central tenets of the school, when he wrote *The World of Odysseus*, that a historian must generate his own data. The text of Homer did not yield up its secrets simply by closer study of the text nor by applying recent research in archaeology but by using the conclusions of modern anthropology and in particular those of Marcel Mauss. His book immediately attracted the attention in Paris of the rising scholar, Pierre Vidal-Naquet, and a lifelong friendship was forged which did much to bring Finley's work into the mainstream of scholarship in France far sooner than in Britain.

The same solutions were not, however, available for archaic Greek history, where he produced a much less satisfactory book than *The World of Odysseus*. Anthropology, he argued in this case, could not open doors to every society. But he also had an instinctive suspicion of oral tradition and the kind of Lévi-Straussian religious 'bricolage' or arguments from 'mentalité', techniques in ancient history most closely associated with the works of Vernant and Dumezil, which were (and still are) used to reconstruct an age where the written sources are so fragmentary. The reluctance may have derived from his close association, dating from his Institute days, with Herbert Marcuse and Walter Benjamin, who were then writing about political manipulation of ideology and creation of political myth. This, in Finley's opinion, was the central obstacle to writing a history of the archaic period in either Greek or Roman history—'the irrecoverable losses of data, or conflation of data, manipulation and invention'. His inaugural lecture in 1971, after election to the chair in Cambridge, was devoted to the same theme, a demonstration of how a political myth was created in Athens in the fifth century, analogous to what had happened in the America of Jefferson.

Ultimately, of course, this was a counsel of despair for many periods of antiquity where no contemporary sources existed, which Finley made no attempt to hide. It was not that he rejected the importance of ancient sources; on the contrary, he asserted, they were the only means of selecting a valid historical problem. But all depended on the nature of the sources. The sources must contain what he described in an important programmatic essay, 'Myth, Memory and History' (1965), as an historical or historiographic 'interest' or process. You cannot write a social or economic history of Greece *from* Thucydides, he argued, but you cannot write a social or economic history of Greece *without* Thucydides. Inscriptions and archaeology, however abundant, were not enough.

The emphasis was on 'history' and 'politics'. One could discuss 'problems' using the resources of archaeology, myth, and poetry, just as Finley himself was perfectly prepared to use the text of Homer and colonial myths to study alienability of land in ancient Greece. But it was not possible to write a history of those societies, only to discuss their structures. To write history it was necessary to have sources which found their explanations in an historical narrative which was 'human and secular and, in particular, political'. If there is some justice in the criticism that he undervalued the force of religion in the ancient city, we must never lose sight of the fact that Finley, the historian of society and economies, saw them essentially in the context of politics.

The second major contribution by Finley was in his use of models, which was an obvious corollary to his attack on the use of sources. Writing in 1977 on 'Progress in historiography', he was blunt. 'The evidence propounds no questions. The historian himself does that . . . (by) the construction of hypotheses and explanatory models.' His objection to Ranke's theory of value-free history was that all history was a form of ideology, since no historian was capable of detaching himself from the thought-set of his environment, and it was more honest to be explicit about one's preconceptions. The model, or Weber's 'ideal type', was just such a means of explicit declaration. It was a simplified means of structuring reality which mediated between particular phenomena a coherence which was sometimes lacking. Because, however, it was simplified and never found empirically, the construct was bound to be Utopian.

The failure of his critics to appreciate the function of a model led to frequent attacks and misunderstandings, nowhere more so than in his model of the ancient economy. But, said Finley in the second edition of *The Ancient Economy*, 'it is not a serious objection . . . to evoke a particular passage of an ancient author or a specific case of economic behaviour, unless it can be reasonably argued that the passage or the case represents more than a passing exception.' Even though much had been written about Weber by the time Finley wrote his last book in 1985, and although many pupils and colleagues by then freely admitted the success of his method, he returned to the theme, since he believed that the model was persistently misunderstood or ignored by ancient historians, most especially in recent books on urban history.

It comes as a surprise to us, therefore, (and to Finley himself, he claimed) that in the final chapter of his last work his dislike of Weber's schematic model of legitimate domination, when applied to the *polis*, and Weber's élitist views of Athenian democracy led him to believe that 'the deployment of models can become too abstract, too schematic.' Just as in his earlier change of approach from the study of *The World of Odysseus* to the study of archaic Greece, he now called for 'different strategies according to the nature of the evidence.' 'Not even my stress on non-mathematical models', he added, 'is meant to imply an exclusive approach or procedure.' Exactly what these different procedures might be, he did not make clear, and certainly all that he said about historiography throughout his career gave the impression that the model was everything. The attack on Weber was not, in any case, despite his claim, on Weber's methodology but on Weber's classification. In reality, I suspect, Finley, the natural rebel, was renouncing his own position as an infallible *papato laico*, since the devil was already on the run.

Perhaps the most important historiographic contribution Finley made was his insistence that history could not be studied by compartmentalising it into politics or economics or social studies, but only by acknowledging what Marc Bloch called 'the total historical fact' and what he himself called 'all-pervading factors'. The texts of history were not restricted to the ancient historical authors but included drama, epic, law, and philosophy, as well as art and archaeology, on all of which Finley wrote with authority. For this his early multi-disciplined training had equipped him superbly well, apart from his personal passion for the theatre, which he attended regularly, and music, of which he possessed a massive collection of records. But most particularly he was served by his association with the extraordinary array of talents gathered in the Mandarin society (as Martin Jay calls it) of the Frankfurt School, from where during its brief sojourn at Columbia, fifty young scholars in different faculties became professors in American universities, inspired by the holistic vision of society they had learned from their mutual association.

Apart from a rejection of vulgar Marxism and the rigidities of the class society, which Finley learnt from this group, there is little doubt that he also inherited their obsession with the problem of why the poor and deprived did not behave in a revolutionary manner—why, for instance, the German proletariat accepted Nazism but not Communism—and the problem of authority and control of society. It was this which stimulated Finley's interest throughout his life in revolution, demagogues and democracy. Momigliano rightly observed that Athens was the ideal context in which to work out the problem through the unification of social, economic, and political history. Here it was possible to explain freedom by slavery; to reject the élitist views, propounded by Mosca and Pareto, that democracy only worked through mass apathy and non-participation, or that it was dominated by emotional demagogy, or that there was some innate good sense in the Athenian people, if one followed Hannah Arendt, which persuaded them to hand over power to experts. Finley's unromantic response to such theories was that the system worked through rationality, based upon promises and programmes, not charisma. His aim broadened in *Politics in the Ancient World* to demonstrate how popular politics worked—or were 'invented', as the French title was translated. But his intention was misunderstood by some critics who believed, with some justice, that he had reduced all ancient politics, particularly those of Rome, to the operation of Athenian institutions.

One final effect of *histoire totale* was the stress placed upon the 'embeddedness' of economies in social structures. Although the term was never used, as far as I know, by Finley, there is no doubt that Polanyi's influence led him to perceive that markets were not invariably a form of economic organisation and that economics did not invariably determine society and culture. But he met stiff opposition from both orthodox Marxists and classical economists, who dismissed him as a Primitivist. The absurdity of the label can be seen in the Jane Harrison Lecture of 1972, when Finley distanced himself from the societies studied by most anthropologists. But his vision of Athens was paradoxical. On the one hand, it was the measure of democracy in the twentieth century, yet on the other, so specific in its alterity that modern comparisons simply distorted the truth. The modernity of the message lay in the organising principles and the nature of the problems—the principle of embedded economies and of political rationality or the problem of the relations between rich and poor.

But the very success of Finley has obscured the magnitude of his achievement. Many of the historiographic citadels he was storming have fallen and the debates have moved on. The status of the text is no longer disputed between Rankeans and structuralists but elevated to the level of a discourse between author and reader. Models are taken for granted and have given way to semiotics. Social and economic histories have given way to religious, cultural, or gender studies. I do not know whether Finley would have approved or not, although he was by nature sympathetic to innovation. But he scented danger in privileging any one form of history: 'Human behaviour cannot be reduced *only* to structures and symbols. . . . Overt behaviour is as legitimate a subject of systematic enquiry as the unconscious structures beneath.' Above all he insisted on the political dimension of every enquiry, without which any historical research was in danger of being reduced to mere antiquarianism.

C. R. WHITTAKER
*Churchill College, Cambridge*

*Bibliographical note.*   Apart from the papers of MIF which are held in the Faculty of Classics, Cambridge and in Darwin College, Cambridge, surveys of his work or the period in which he worked appear in the following books and articles:

M. Jay, *The Dialectical Imagination. A History of the Frankfurt School and the Institute of Historical Research* (London, Boston, 1973).

Introduction by B. D. Shaw and R. P. Saller to M. I. Finley, *Economy and Society in Ancient Greece* (London, 1981).

C. R. Whittaker, 'Qui êtes-vous, Sir Moses?', *London Review of Books*, 8.4 (1986), 10–11.

A. Momigliano, 'Moses Finley and Slavery: a Personal Note', in M. I. Finley, *Classical Slavery* (London, 1987).

R. Di Donato, 'Appendici dalle carte di M. I. Finley', in *La Città Antica/La Cité Antique* (*Opus* VI/VIII, 1987–9), 261–323.

ARTHUR GOODHART                    *Ramsay & Muspratt*

*Proceedings of the British Academy*, **94**, 475–487

# Arthur Lehman Goodhart
# 1891–1978

ARTHUR LEHMAN GOODHART, one of the outstanding common lawyers of the century, was born in New York on 1 March 1891, and died in London on 10 November 1978, aged eighty-seven. For nearly sixty years he lived and worked in England, but despite his Anglophilia and his thorough acclimatisation here, he remained throughout a citizen of the USA, and unmistakably American. For over fifty years, nobody had a greater influence on the development of the common law. This resulted mainly from the steady flow of his writings, but also from his teaching, his committee work, and his easy relationship with many leading figures in the law. Though England was the main beneficiary, the whole common law world profited.

His inheritance was rich. He was endowed with ability, public spirit, modesty, and generosity, as well as material wealth. His grandparents were all born in Europe and emigrated to the USA in the 1830s and 1840s. His father, Philip, was born in Cincinnati, but as a young man he went to New York, where in due time he became a prominent member of the New York Stock Exchange, in partnership with his brother. He was a kind and gentle man who died in 1944 at the age of eighty-eight. Arthur's mother, Harriet, was a sister of Irving Lehman, who became Chief Judge of the New York Court of Appeals, and of Herbert Lehman, who, after being Governor of the State of New York from 1932–42, became Director-General of the United Nations Relief and Rehabilitation Administration (UNRRA), and then from 1948–56 a US Senator who was one of Senator Joe McCarthy's most resolute adversaries. Harriet

© The British Academy 1997.

was small, serious, dominant, and rather fierce; and she too lived to be eighty-eight, dying in 1949. Her father and one of his brothers had been shopkeepers in Alabama, and through accepting payment in cotton instead of cash they had become cotton brokers. After the end of the Civil War, the brothers became established in New York as general commodity dealers, and from that they progressed into merchant banking. By the end of the century Lehman Brothers had become one of the leading merchant banks in New York.

Arthur was the third and youngest child of Philip and Harriet. They were devout Jews, but members of the Reform wing, which had discarded the dietary laws and other minutiae of the Talmud. At an early age Arthur abandoned any religious belief or observance; but throughout his life he remained very much concerned with Jews and Jewish causes, and in his latter years his support for the State of Israel tended to the fanatical. His upbringing was in a brownstone house on 88th Street, just west of Central Park, and next door to the house of Harriet's sister and her family. He went to day-school in New York, and then to Hotchkiss School, a well-known preparatory school in northern Connecticut. From there he entered Yale, graduating in 1912 with high honours. At Yale he was popular with his fellows, and was the first Jew to be elected a member of Alpha Delta Phi. For this, the Yale Chapter was suspended by the national organisation. He became an editor of the *Yale Literary Magazine* and other Yale periodicals, and graduated with high academic honours, a Phi Beta Kappa. His athletic activities were limited by poor eyesight, but he was a good cross-country runner. He enjoyed lawn tennis and, after he had come to England, real tennis.

Arthur had been intended to join Lehman Brothers. Fortunately, his father had come to admire British bankers, and so in 1912 Arthur was sent to Trinity College, Cambridge, to read economics. When he arrived, his tutor, Morley Fletcher, told him that the Trinity economics fellow was away for the year. 'If you really want to read economics, we will have to send you to a young don at King's called Keynes. But nobody thinks him very sound; why don't you read law instead?' This advice fell on receptive ears, for although Arthur had not read law at Yale, he had gone to Professor Arthur Corbin's classes on the law of contract, and this had convinced him that law was a subject of 'the most profound interest'. So at Cambridge he began to read law, with H. A. Hollond as his director of studies. Hollond had been a fellow of Trinity for only three years, and was still in his twenties; but he was to play a significant part in Arthur's life. A close friendship which was to last sixty years soon sprang up between them.

Goodhart greatly enjoyed his two years at Cambridge; and this did not prevent him from getting a First in Part II of the law tripos. Among his contemporaries at Trinity, Lawrence Bragg and George Thomson, both to be Nobel prize-winners in physics, became his lifelong friends. Some time later, when they were young bachelor dons, they hired a sailing boat in the Solent for a cruise along the south coast, and there was a series of disasters which, in retrospect, Goodhart enjoyed recounting.

With the outbreak of war in 1914, Goodhart joined the Officers' Training Corps, and later volunteered for the Army; but he was refused a commission on account of his nationality. He then returned to the USA, and after passing the New York State Bar examinations, he became an assistant corporation counsel for New York City in 1915. When his country entered the war in 1917 he joined the US Army, and became a captain. At the end of the war he went to Poland as counsel to the US Military Mission. Out of this visit came his first book, *Poland and the Minority Races* (1920), which was particularly concerned with the position of Polish Jews. By this time Hollond had suggested that Goodhart should teach law at Cambridge, and the percipient eye of Will Spens of Corpus Christi had recognised his ability. The result was a law fellowship at Corpus and a university lectureship in law in 1919. He was also called to the Bar by the Inner Temple, which he had joined in 1912. He never practised in England, but settled down to teaching.

In 1921 Goodhart became secretary to the Vice-Chancellor of the university, a post which he held until 1923. But another event in 1921 was to have greater significance in his life. This was the foundation of the *Cambridge Law Journal*, with Goodhart as its editor for the initial four years. This venture was largely due to his initiative as well as his substantial financial support. In the USA it had long been common for law schools to publish learned periodicals. An outstanding feature of these publications was that although the articles and book reviews were written by established lawyers on the academic staff and elsewhere, the notes on recent cases were written by students in the law school. Selection as one of the student editors of the law review, and so as one of its contributors, was a hallmark of distinction, both in the law school and beyond. The *Cambridge Law Journal* was established on this model. But somehow this system of student case-notes never really flourished in England. Despite notable exceptions, and the presence of names later to become highly distinguished in the law, by 1954 the system had come to be replaced by one of case-notes written by senior members of the faculty and others. Nevertheless, the *Journal* achieved an immediate and sustained success, due in no small part to Goodhart's flair for obtaining articles of a high standard.

Another significant feature of those early years in the law was Goodhart's choice of subject. By inclination and nature he was a common lawyer. His heart was in tort and contract, with some crime and constitutional law; yet he made jurisprudence his subject. A university lecturer in jurisprudence had been killed in the war, and so had left a vacancy in that subject. As a subject, jurisprudence can be almost all things to all men. It may be analytical, anthropological, comparative, ethical, general, historical, normative, particular, post-modernist, sociological, and realist, and, more recently, feminist. None of these labels really fitted Goodhart, though 'analytical' was *proxime accessit*. He seldom soared to the rarefied heights of jurisprudential abstraction, and remained firmly in the world of living law. He became not so much a professor of jurisprudence as a jurisprudential professor of the common law. There is no difficulty in making law seem complex and obscure, and many succeed. Without being simplistic, Goodhart's simplicity of utterance matched his clarity of thought, and brought him nearer to judges and practitioners than any academic lawyer before him. His approach was to subject the common law to his formidable powers of jurisprudential analysis and then to apply his sturdy common sense and reason to it. For him, principle never lost sight of the practical.

In 1924 Goodhart married Cecily Carter, of Beaulieu, Hampshire. A notable beauty, she had gone up to read history at Newnham in 1919, a little belatedly on account of her having volunteered for factory work during the war. Goodhart's family accepted his marriage to a gentile without dissension, and the American husband and English wife with their three sons (1925, 1933 and 1936) became a truly Anglo-American family. Goodhart's frequent (and often extended) visits to America left untouched his affection for England.

A major step in Goodhart's life was his appointment as editor of the *Law Quarterly Review*, in 1926, when he was thirty-four. The *Review* had been founded in 1885, mainly by Sir Frederick Pollock. From 1885 to 1919 he was the editor of the first learned legal periodical in the common-law world. It was followed in 1887 by the *Harvard Law Review*, and then by many other American journals; but in England it remained unique until the *Cambridge Law Journal* appeared in 1921. Pollock's successor, A. E. Randall, died suddenly in 1925, and Goodhart was his obvious successor. He remained editor for fifty years, the last five as editor-in-chief, with P. V. Baker as editor. His run was unbroken except for 1929 while he was a visiting professor in the Yale Law School and P. H. Winfield deputised for him. His editorship of the *LQR* and the body of his contributions to it were the outstanding achievements of his life in the law.

He was a discerning and open-minded editor, accepting contributions over the whole range of law even when he disagreed with them or lacked interest in them. But he was insistent on maintaining a high standard, and looked for tenable originality and lucid presentation. Nothing was rejected out of hand. The good, the bad, and the indifferent were all considered, at a cost of time and patience which was sometimes increased by giving advice and encouragement to the inexperienced. With himself, he could be downright. A hint of fallibility would sometimes be met with a pause, and then a flat 'No—it's wrong'. In discussion, he would put his point directly and reasonably, often ending with a characteristic sound, 'D'there'. This was as eloquent as Puff made Lord Burleigh's shake of the head in *The Critic*, and meant: 'I think this deals with it, but let me reflect for a moment, and meanwhile tell me what you think about it'. His editorship was very personal, with no supporting staff except a combined assistant editor and book review editor; and his correspondence and his contributions alike were all in a handwriting which remained bold and clear throughout. After the war, visiting American lawyers, with the establishments of law reviews in the USA in mind, would sometimes ask to see the *LQR* offices; and it pleased him to say that the nearest thing to an editorial office was an armchair in the assistant editor's chambers[1] where each quarterly issue was put together.

In 1931, an unexpected vacancy occurred in the chair of jurisprudence at Oxford which had once been Pollock's. Goodhart had published no book on law which could support an application. He speedily assembled thirteen articles of his, ranging far and wide in their sources and their substance. Four had appeared in the *Yale Law Journal*, three in the *Cambridge Law Journal*, and singletons in the *LQR*, the *Cornell Law Quarterly*, the *Canadian Bar Review*, the *New Zealand Law Journal*, the *Buffalo Law Journal* and *Cambridge Legal Essays*. These formed his *Essays in Jurisprudence and the Common Law*, the book by which he was best known. The title of the book matched the chair by putting jurisprudence first, but in its substance the common law

---

[1] Mine for nearly twenty-five years, and then Paul Baker's.

predominated. His *Three Cases on Possession* from the *Cambridge Law Journal* analysed cases on the possession of objects found in or on land in a way that still exerts influence sixty years later; but it was one of the Yale contributions, *Determining the Ratio Decidendi of a Case*, that was a jurisprudential classic from the start. The question was how to distinguish the *ratio decidendi* of a case that would bind all courts of an equal or lower status from mere dicta which would not. At the core of the article was the proposition that the principle of a case was to be found not in the reasons or rule of law set out in the judgment, but by determining the facts treated by the judge as being material, and his decision as based on those facts. In doing this, the reasons given by the judge was a guide to which of the facts he considered to be material. Over the years this contention attracted much critical appraisal and reappraisal.[2]

With the publication of this book and other support, Goodhart was elected to the chair and also to a fellowship at University College that went with it. At thirty-nine, the main course of his life was settled. As a lecturer, he was deservedly popular. He was direct, clear and audible, with touches of his own style of humour (sometimes mordant) and a measured pace that carried both the quick and the slow in thought. There was no lack of critical evaluation and lines for further thought, but unlike some lecturers he never sought to pass off the law that should be as being the law that was. He held the attention of his audience throughout.

In 1935, after he had become established in Oxford, Goodhart joined Lincoln's Inn *ad eundem*. He had taken over Pollock's chambers in the Inn, and Hollond had recently been elected an honorary bencher there. Less than three years laters, quite exceptionally, Goodhart too was elected an honorary bencher. This was to prove significant to the law.

When war came in 1939, Goodhart remained in Oxford and continued with such teaching as there was. He joined the Home Guard, and as Chairman of the Southern Region Price Regulation Committee he played his part in enforcing price controls. When the USA joined the war he did much for the short courses in law that were provided for American and English officers awaiting the invasion of France, and he also was vigorous in promoting Anglo-American relations among the many other Americans in the country. Both during the war and after, he

---

[2] See e.g. Goodhart (1959) 22 *Modern Law Review* 117; Cross and Harris, *Precedent in English Law* (4th edn., 1991), ch. 2.

was sent on lecture tours and missions to America in aid of Britain; and he tirelessly wrote, spoke and broadcast in furthering understanding on both sides. To his delight he was made a KC in 1943. No appointments had been made since 1939, and in the list of twenty-four he was one of four non-practising barristers, known at the Bar as 'artificial silks'. Goodhart's appointment was very properly acclaimed; indeed, it was probably unique. Under the Act of Settlement 1700, s. 3, no person 'born out of the kingdoms of England Scotland or Ireland or the dominions thereunto belonging' was to be capable of being a Privy Counsellor or MP or of enjoying 'any office or place of trust either civill or military'; and clearly New York in 1891 was not 'thereunto belonging'. If the point had emerged, Goodhart would have relished silk that was illegal as well as artificial. To his great pleasure further recognition came in 1948 when he was aptly made an honorary KBE; but neither at home or abroad did he seek to use the 'Sir'.

In 1951 a new phase of Goodhart's life began. He was elected Master of his college, the first American to head a college at Oxford or Cambridge. Under the Oxford system he was obliged to relinquish the chair of jurisprudence that he had held for twenty years. Despite earlier portents, he had expected this step less than nearly everyone else. He proved to be an outstanding Master. He combined respect for tradition and a reforming zeal with an amiable but firm leadership that avoided differences on policy degenerating into lasting animosity; and with his genius for personal relations he earned the affection of all. The Master's Lodgings became a centre of wide and generous hospitality for all members of the college, from freshmen to honorary fellows, and for many others as well; and the college servants became devoted to him. In all this Cecily played a large part. Each of them engaged fully in all forms of college life, and they were zealous in their pastoral care. When the time came, the college extended Goodhart's tenure to 1963, the maximum possible extent. His portrait by A. R. Middleton Todd RA which hangs in the hall shows him as he appeared for decades, save that it sadly lacks the twinkle in his eye.[3]

While he was Master, his work on the *LQR*, both as editor and as contributor, had gone on unabated. He had also continued to make visits abroad to give lectures or attend conferences, and in 1959 he went on a noteworthy lecture tour of Australia and New Zealand in company with Lord Justice Pearce and Justice Harlan of the US Supreme Court. After

---

[3] So also the photograph reproduced above.

he retired he made many more visits abroad, and the improvement in air travel encouraged short visits as well as long. These visits included being a visiting professor at the law schools of Harvard, the University of Virginia, and McGill, and being a scholar in residence at the New York City Bar Association.

Goodhart never wrote or edited a legal textbook. His work as a legal author is to be found almost entirely in his articles and notes in learned legal periodicals, particularly the *LQR*. His 'notes' were miniature articles, ranging from half a page or less to five pages or more; and some notes grew into articles in the writing. Most of the notes and articles were based on recent decisions of the courts; for him, these were the life of the law.

The contrast with writing or editing legal textbooks is sharp. So much law is static, both settled and well settled; and a major part of the work of writing or editing textbooks, though worthy, tends to be time-consuming and tedious. There are also the inelastic bonds of the space available, as contrasted with the flexbility of notes and articles. Above all, notes and articles confer liberty to concentrate on the law as it lives and develops and sometimes retrogresses: and this became the centre of Goodhart's life in the law. He was a tireless and economical worker who enjoyed working, and wasted no time on trivialities. When he could, he put up his feet for half an hour after lunch in order to extend his working day by two hours or more in the evening.

Goodhart's notes were models of concise relevance. Though they ranged far and wide in their subjects, style and approach, most of them fell within a pattern. Usually they began with a sentence that set the scene and caught the interest. Then the facts of the case and the decision were set out economically before turning to a critical appraisal of the decision and its consequences. Criticism was constructive, and laudation not uncommon. The note took the reader to the heart of the case in a tithe of the time needed for reading and digesting the judgment. Some of the notes were bread-and-butter notes, doing little more than welcoming a significant decision and putting it in context; but the great majority provoked thought. Those attending his postgraduate classes on recent cases at Oxford were often given a preview of impending notes. Discussion was encouraged, and sometimes it led to useful revisions. The notes were written in English English, with only an occasional transatlantic reverter, such as 'in back of' for 'behind'. The style was simple and direct, with no attempt at fine writing, but sometimes a

Puckish quirk or a sardonic flick. Some of his articles ranged over a wider field, but the general style was the same.

Goodhart's notes and articles embraced the whole of the common law. Tort, contract, and crime predominated, but constitutional and administrative law, international law, company law, divorce, and much else besides were also represented, with equity and land law the more notable absentees. The concentration was on English law, but many other jurisdictions made their contributions, not least the USA. Apart from 1929, while Goodhart was a visiting professor at Yale, the flow was unbroken. At varying intervals over fifty years well over sixty articles were published. The index to the *LQR* lists thirty-six (though a few were less than articles) and there were many others, including twelve in the *Cambridge Law Journal*, five in the *Yale Law Journal*, and four in the *Modern Law Review*. On the other hand, the notes in the *LQR* appeared in every issue with unfailing regularity. Usually there were between fifteen and twenty pages of them, though rather less in the latter five years when Goodhart was editor-in-chief instead of editor. In mere volume, Goodhart's notes and articles equalled several textbooks; but in concentrated and relevant penetration they amounted to much more. Although he was a judicious book reviewer, he contributed relatively little, usually on books concerned with America.

Over the years a number of books or booklets by Goodhart were published: usually they were prints of lectures. His 1947 Lucien Wolf Memorial Lecture was published in 1949 in an extended form (74 pp.) as *Five Jewish Lawyers of the Common Law*. This consists of deft sketches of Judah Philip Benjamin Q.C., Sir George Jessel M.R., Louis D. Brandeis J., Rufus Isaacs (L.C.J. and ultimately the first Marquess of Reading), and Benjamin Nathan Cardozo J. In the same year the Benjamin N. Cardozo lecture that he gave in 1948 appeared as *English Contributions to the Philosophy of Law* (34 pp.). His Hamlyn Lectures for 1952 were more substantial. They were published in 1953 as *English Law and the Moral Law* (151 pp.). In this, he examined and sustained the general thesis that the public recognition of a duty to obey the law was based less on force or a fear of punishment than on reason, morality, religion and inherited tradition; that was over forty years ago.

As an editor of books, Goodhart produced Pollock's *Jurisprudence and Legal Essays* in 1961. He selected, edited and introduced, in some 230 pages, substantial parts of Pollock's *First Book of Jurisprudence*

(1896), *Essays in Jurisprudence* (1882), and *Essays in the Law* (1922), seeking in piety to revive writings that were out of print. He also, jointly with Professor H. G. Hanbury, undertook the massive burden of editing and completing volumes 13–16 of Holdsworth's *History of English Law* (1,725 pages in all). Most of the material was in typescript or barely decipherable manuscript; but much had to be added to finish it. The publication of the four volumes between 1952 and 1966 completed a work of which the first volume had originally appeared in 1903.

For long, Goodhart was the most influential academic lawyer in England. Today, it is easy to forget how small and remote the world of English academic law was when Goodhart first came to it. Oxford and Cambridge had indeed been joined by four other universities during the nineteenth century, with five more by 1920, but the total number of those teaching or reading law was, by today's standards, tiny. Intending lawyers often accepted advice to broaden their minds at university by reading any subject other than law. In contrast with today, few solicitors were graduates, and many preferred (some vehemently) to have as articled clerks those who were straight from school, untainted by academe; the *tabula* must be *rasa*. Legal periodicals were severely practical, addressed to the needs of practitioners, and legal textbooks were in like case until Pollock and others began to write law books of academic stature towards the end of the nineteenth century. Practitioners held academic lawyers in low esteem. 'A jurist', said Lord Bowen, 'is a person who knows a little about the law of every country except his own'. And, added A. V. Dicey, 'jurisprudence is a word which stinks in the nostrils of a practising barrister'. In England (but not the USA) there was a rule that the work of a living author could not be cited in the courts as an authority, though this could be evaded in some degree by counsel 'adopting' the work 'as part of his argument'. This nineteenth-century attitude was still alive in the 1920s, despite all that Pollock had done; but thirty years later it was dying, and Goodhart had played a large part in the change. Academic lawyers rarely mingled with judges in easy informality, and most honorary benchers rarely attended their Inns; but despite the claims of Oxford, Goodhart was often in Lincoln's Inn, especially at lunch, and this opened new doors. Knowing the author sometimes changes the impact of the printed page. Lord Evershed and Lord Pearce (as they became) were soon warm friends, and Lord Denning and Lord Simonds were also benchers, with many other judges and judges-to-be. Other friends were Lord Greene, Lord Wright, and Lord Diplock, all great names in the law.

More than any other academic lawyer, Goodhart was equally at home with judges and practitioners, bridging the previous gulf between the two worlds both at home and abroad.

Through his writings and his membership of committees, Goodhart was in large part responsible for many important changes made by the courts, the legislature or administrative action. Eight examples may be given, four of them in tort. Hospitals were made liable for the negligence of their doctors and nurses while exercising their professional functions even though the hospital managers had no control over them. A person's liability for a negligent act no longer applied to all the consequences, but only to those that were reasonably foreseeable. A person who is injured while attempting to rescue a third party from a peril negligently created by another, such as a runaway horse, is now not prevented from recovering damages on the ground that he had been under no duty to act but had voluntarily undertaken the risk. The liability of an occupier of land to those who are injured while lawfully on it now depends on a common duty of care instead of fine distinctions between invitees and licencees.

Other changes are that a company can no longer escape liability for acts done by its servants on the ground that the acts were *ultra vires* its objects. The rule that appellate courts must be slow to disturb findings of fact made by a judge who has seen and heard the witnesses now applies with less force to findings of fact if they are really mere inferences. When quashing a conviction (e.g. on technical grounds) the Court of Appeal is no longer unable to order a new trial where the interests of justice require it (Goodhart's partial success in his lifetime became complete after his death). Lastly, for over forty years all decisions of the Court of Appeal (and not only those that appear in law reports) have become available for all by transcripts being made and filed.

Goodhart gave much time to a wide range of committees and other bodies. At various times he was President of the American Outpost; the International Association of University Professors; the Society of Public Teachers of Law; the American Society; the Pedestrians Association for Road Safety (with the pleasure of being addressed by a Japanese correspondent as 'The Honourable President of the Streetwalkers Association'); and the Selden Society. He was a Vice-President of the British Academy, and of the Pilgrims; Chairman of the International Law Association; and a governor of the Atlantic College at St Donat's Castle. As a member of the Royal Commission on the Police, he made a dissent which sought the establishment of a national police force. He was also a member of many important committees, including the Committee on Law Reporting (with a dissent which advocated more comprehensive law reporting and better indexes), and committees on monopolies and restrictive practices, Supreme Court procedure (with its series of reports), company law revision, and alternative remedies. He was also a zealous foundation member of two of the Lord Chancellor's major standing committees, the pre-war Law Revision Committee and the post-war Law Reform Committee (whose first report, in 1953, surprisingly cost a mere £10. 7s. 6d. to print and publish). To his various committees he brought innate good timing, and contributions made with a force of reasoning that was enhanced by their moderation in presentation.

His honorary degrees were numerous and far-flung. The USA led the field, with a dozen honorary LLDs from California, Cincinnati, Columbia, Dartmouth College, Harvard, New York, Pennsylvania, Princeton, Tulane, Wesleyan University, Williams College, and Yale. There was one in each jurisdiction in the United Kingdom (Edinburgh, London, and Queen's University, Belfast), and also one each from Australia (Melbourne) and Canada (Dalhousie); and he had an honorary D. Litt. from Cambridge. He was also an Honorary Fellow of Trinity, Trinity Hall and Corpus at Cambridge, and Nuffield at Oxford; and on retiring as Master of his college he became an Honorary Fellow Extraordinary. In 1952 he was elected FBA, and ten years later he was a Vice-President of the Academy.

He was a man of an exceptional generosity that was both discerning and imaginative. He was always concerned to see that the need was real and the provision wise and effective. He became the greatest benefactor that his college had had in its life of over seven centuries, and he was also the cause of munificence by members of his family and others. Amongst other additions, the college is grateful for the Alington Room, the Goodhart Building and Quadrangle, the Magpie Building and the Parson's Almshouse; and Helen's Court and Cecily Court preserve the names of the sister and wife of a Master who is held in great affection by the college. In honour of his eightieth birthday the Arthur Goodhart Visiting Professorship of Legal Science at Cambridge was established in 1971. This percipient foundation enables foreign lawyers of great distinction to be in residence at the university for a term or more, with ample provision of a house, a secretary and travelling expenses for them and their families. Goodhart's unostentatious generosity could be found in many other fields, some of them small and private; and he was also generous with his time and advice, as many of the young remembered as their careers advanced.

Goodhart had little interest in the arts, and none in music. His interest in literature soon narrowed down until he read little except on law, politics (in the wider sense), and current affairs. One of the last of his articles in the *LQR* was a long and convincing assault on the English Press for its attack on the findings of the Warren Commission on the assassination of President Kennedy. In his latter years he became engrossed in two diverse attempts at the virtually impossible: a defence of President Nixon over Watergate, and a justification of Israel's annexation of the West Bank. Hospitality apart, he was simple in his tastes and style of life. There was moderation in everything except his driving urge to work and carry out his duties in abundance, and his gift for friendship. In all that he did, he lived his life to the full, and without stint.

Goodhart died after suffering a severe stroke. He was survived by Cecily, for over six years, and by his three sons. They became Sir Philip, an MP for thirty-five years; Sir William, the Chancery silk; and Professor Charles, FBA, the economist. He also, to his and their delight, had fourteen grandchildren.

R. E. MEGARRY
*Fellow of the Academy*

*Note.* For assistance in person or in print, or both, I am greatly indebted to: His Honour Paul Baker QC; Mr George Cawkwell; Lord Diplock; Sir William Goodhart QC; Professor F. H. Lawson FBA; Lord Redcliffe-Maud; and *The Times.*

ROBERT HAMILTON

*Proceedings of the British Academy*, **94**, 491–509

# Robert William Hamilton
# 1905–1995

It is the persons of an ancient society even more than its works and art that can enlighten and reward the curiosity of an archaeologist.[1]

ROBERT HAMILTON was the least well known of a remarkable trio of Oxford contemporaries who, in the 1920s, more by accident than by contrivance, entered upon careers in Near Eastern archaeology through which they were to define the British contribution to it for a generation. In background, character and achievement they were very different, though they were to be lifelong friends. Sir Max Mallowan (1904–76)[2] and Dame Kathleen Kenyon (1906–76)[3] became public figures, whilst Robert Hamilton, by preference, remained a private man, though his contributions to the subject were no less fundamental for being less spectacular. They were field archaeologists in the grand manner, he was an imperial civil servant and museum administrator by profession, a scholar and an architect *manqué* by inclination. 'I find architects are nearly always interesting and there is always something to say to them'.[4]

---

© The British Academy 1997.
[1] Robert Hamilton, *Walid and his Friends: An Umayyad Tragedy* (Oxford Studies in Islamic Art VI, Oxford, 1988; hereafter *Walid*), p. 9.
[2] David Oates, 'Max Edgar Lucien Mallowan, 1904–1978', *Proceedings of the British Academy*, 80 (1991), 499–511.
[3] A. D. Tushingham, 'Kathleen Mary Kenyon, 1906–1978', *Proceedings of the British Academy*, 71 (1985), pp. 555–82.
[4] R. W. Hamilton, *Letters from the Middle East by an Occasional Archaeologist* (The Pentland Press Limited; Edinburgh, Cambridge and Durham, 1992; hereafter *Letters*), p. 77.

## Ancestry, Education, and Archaeological Apprenticeship, 1905–31

He was born on 26 November 1905 and died on 25 September 1995 within sight of his ninetieth birthday, alert in mind and active in body until almost the end, true to the Scottish ancestry in which he took such quiet pride, not least his paternal great grandfather. Sir William (Stirling) Hamilton (1788–1856) was Professor of Logic and Metaphysics in Edinburgh University from 1836 until his death, a man memorably recalled in Carlyle's briefest *Reminiscence*.[5] To anyone who knew Robert Hamilton, phrase after phrase in this masterly sketch bridges the generations:

> . . . his ancestor, Hamilton of Preston, was leader of the Cameronians at Bothwell Brig, and had stood by the Covenant and Cause of Scotland in that old time and form . . . . A fine firm figure of middle height; one of the finest cheerfully-serious human faces, of square, solid, and yet rather *aquiline* type . . . .He was finely social and human . . . . Honesty, frankness and friendly veracity . . . a strong, carelessly-melodious, tenor voice, the sound of it betokening seriousness and cheerfulness; occasionally something of slightly remonstrative was in the undertones, indicating, well in the background, possibilities of virtuous wrath and fire.

In a chance encounter in Teheran in 1961 with an Iranian studying in Edinburgh he assured him that the city was 'indeed the Athens of the North, partly made so by the erudition of my own great-grandfather'.[6]

His father, William Stirling Hamilton, had been born in Edinburgh. Like his son, he was a scholar of Winchester and a demy of Magdalen College, Oxford, where he took a first in Greats in 1892, passing second in the Indian Civil Service list in the same year. He served his time in the Punjab. His mother was born in Aberdeen, daughter of G. R. Elsmie, who had a distinguished career in the judiciary of the Indian Civil Service. 'She was a good artist in water colour and other media and also a good player of the violin and piano.'[7] It was to her that Robert Hamilton owed his talent as a draughtsman and his lifelong love of music, both as listener and as performer.

He began his education at the tender age of four at Girton Hall

---

[5] Thomas Carlyle, *Reminiscences*, ed. Charles Eliot Norton (Everyman University Library, 1972), pp. 381–6.
[6] *Letters*, p. 205.
[7] All quotations without attribution are taken from brief handwritten notes about his life deposited by R. W. Hamilton with the British Academy in November 1990.

School, Torquay, 'accompanied by a nurse, my parents being then in India'. From 1911–12 he himself spent a year in India, where his father was then Director of Agriculture, briefly experiencing as a young child the life of the Raj both on duty in the plains at Lahore and relaxing in the highlands at Simla. Throughout the First World War he was a boarder in Copthorne School at Crawley in Sussex, 'of which the founder and headmaster was Bernard Rendall, a classicist of Cambridge, brother of Montague Rendall, of Winchester; former Corinthian footballer and formidable martinet. Conditions at Copthorne during the First World War were austere in the extreme, discipline severe, but the teaching of football, Latin and Greek both intensive and successful.' His love and mastery of the classics were lifelong and his rigorous training in them was for ever reflected in the clarity and concision of his English prose style. To his early drilling on the football field he owed his physical resilience and his enduringly trim physique.

In 1919 he went on to Winchester, 'where life and company in the semi-monastic chambers and hall of College appeared luxurious and delightful after the deprivation of all comforts and agreeable diet at Copthorne'. When he returned to Oxford a generation later a number of his contemporaries at Winchester, such as C. F. C. Hawkes, William Hayter, J. N. L. Myres, John Sparrow, and C. E. ('Tom Brown') Stevens, were once again to be of the company, from time to time engaging in verbal sparring that had the edge of old fires rekindled. In 1924 he went up to Magdalen College, Oxford, where he was to be elected a fellow in 1959, as a demy. He was an outstanding classical scholar, gaining Firsts in Mods. and Greats. When the time came to go down in 1928 he had no clear idea of a future career. His father, who believed that the end of British rule in India was in sight, advised him not to follow in his footsteps. As fate would have it he was to choose another branch of the Imperial Civil Service that was to survive barely a year longer.

'Influenced by Leonard Woolley's entertaining accounts of archaeological work in the Middle East I joined the British School of Archaeology in Jerusalem, with a Senior Demyship from Magdalen.' It was his father who had called his attention to Woolley's *Dead Towns and Living Men: Being Pages from an Antiquary's Notebook* (1920) at an opportune moment. Within a very short period of time he was now to be brought into contact with the small group of people who were to forward his career, to serve with and under him, and to stimulate his research interests over the next twenty years in Palestine. His association with the British School was to be lifelong as a trustee, council member, and editorial adviser.

In 1929 and again in 1930 he joined the joint Yale University and British School of Archaeology in Jerusalem excavations at Jerash in Jordan, organised by J. W. Crowfoot, Director of the School. This dig resulted in Hamilton's first published report, in collaboration with Crowfoot, in the *Palestine Exploration Fund Quarterly Statement* (1929), recounting the discovery of the remains of synagogue, with interesting mosaic pavements, beneath the remains of a church built in AD 530–1. It briefly anticipated the best of his later work. His archaeological apprenticeship was then varied by serving as a 'volunteer', from 24 June to 10 July 1929, at Megiddo, where P. L. O. Guy was directing the Chicago University excavations on some of the now renowned Iron Age buildings. From November 1929 until April 1930 he excavated for the first and only time in his career in Egypt, at Meydum, where the Eckley B. Coxe Expedition from the University Museum, Philadelphia, directed by Alan Rowe, was working in the area of the famous IVth Dynasty pyramid, first seriously studied by Petrie in 1891. His colleague as 'archaeological assistant' was C. N. Johns, soon to become a very close friend, sharing his interests in the history of architecture, particularly of the Crusader period.

Hamilton's archaeological career began in earnest in 1930–1, when for six months he 'accompanied R. Campbell Thomson as sole assistant for excavations at Nineveh, travelling to Iraq by the Oriental Express, six days in the train from Calais to Nisibin (terminus at that time)'. At Nineveh he was in charge of processing the pottery and whatever classical inscriptions might be found. He was also closely involved with the supervision of numerous untrained Arabic-speaking workmen with whom, according to Mallowan's later report, he was a 'regular little spitfire.' In such a forcing house his command of colloquial Arabic rapidly improved. It was to become remarkable, though little used after 1948, except at Nimrud, but he was an amateur student of classical Arabic until the end of his life, with a deep love of the language and its early literature. Although wholly out of sympathy in later years with what he regarded as an excessive attention to pottery in conventional archaeological practice and publication, he still spoke with pleasure over thirty years later of drawing the painted and incised late prehistoric pottery found at Nineveh. These drawings, published in the *Liverpool Annals of Archaeology and Anthropology* (1932), are among the earliest and best published examples of his skills with pen and pencil.

## The Years in Palestine, 1931–48

Hamilton greatly impressed Campbell Thompson, whose warm recommendation carried great weight in 1931 when he applied for a post in Palestine under the British Mandatory administration. Although still well under thirty years of age, he was duly appointed Chief Inspector of Antiquities. As G. R. Driver, who had been his Lit.Hum. tutor at Magdalen a few years earlier, recorded in his reference for Hamilton's application for the Keepership of Antiquities in the Ashmolean Museum in 1956, 'he made his mark by his wide knowledge, keenness and efficiency . . . . His career was meteoric . . . in 1938 (he was made) Director of Antiquities at the age of 32 or 33 years. The fact is that he was in a different class to any other available candidate—and there were several.'[8] This period of his life allowed him to exercise his special talents in an environment which he found wholly congenial and which gave him the responsibility and scope to develop simultaneously as an administrator, as a field archaeologist and as a scholar.

Professionally this was for him his golden age, always recalled with affection and not a little regret that he had been forced at the end to abandon it. It was also memorable for his marriage in 1935 to Eileen Hetty Lowick, by whom he had a daughter and two sons before the Second World War, and a son and a daughter after it. In 1992 he dedicated his *Letters from the Middle East* thus: 'These old letters are rededicated now, with all the love left unexpressed in this revival, to her who received most of them originally.' As Oleg Grabar[9] has remarked, 'He was too, a family man who could hardly be dissociated from his wife Hetty and his children.'

Much of his life in the Mandate Department of Antiquities was a round of routine administrative duties, but it was at this time that he first established his credentials as a potential museum curator and undertook the excavations and building surveys upon which his academic legacy was based. When he was appointed to the Ashmolean Museum's staff in 1956, his immediate grasp of its needs, architectural and curatorial, was such as to lead many to assume that in Palestine he had been a professional museum curator. It was an excusable misapprehension since the Palestine Archaeological Museum, later to be known as the Rockefeller Museum, after the donor of the funds to create it in 1927, was the modern building to which he was most attached. He always

[8] Archives of the Ashmolean Museum, Oxford: R. W. Hamilton: Personal File.
[9] Obituary in the *Independent*, 6 October 1995, 22.

referred to it with great respect as his ideal design for a museum. The offices of the Department of Antiquities were an integral part of the museum. It had been inaugurated by Ernest T. Richmond, his predecessor as Director of Antiquities and designed by Austin S. B. Harrison, with monumental lettering in the galleries by Eric Gill. The curator was J. H. Iliffe.

In G. R. Driver's words,[10] 'it was Mr Hamilton who built it up into its position as a Museum known all over the world. He made the bulk of the collections, organised their arrangement, got together and trained a staff, partly English, and partly Palestinian. I know the Museum well and can say that, although its collections are as yet small as compared with those in European Museums, it is (or was) one of the best kept and best arranged of all museums known to me, thanks almost entirely to Mr Hamilton, who is a master of the technique.' It was opened to the public in 1938. Hamilton's concern extended to its garden, often mentioned in his letters home as the Mandate came to an end, with an appreciation that reveals his enduring love of gardening. In recalling Jerash as late as 1993, what he remembered was that 'in the springtime it was covered with cyclamen, asphodels, lovely wild flowers'.[11]

The future of the museum particularly concerned him by the close of 1947, as his term as Director of Antiquities came to an end with the Mandate. He was always fiercely critical of British policy at this time; but he managed to steer the museum tenaciously and successfully into the hands of an international board of trustees endorsed by the United Nations Commission. 'You know, making the plans for establishing the Museum independently is subtly undermining my resolution to leave it . . . '.[12] Ironically his last visit to Jerusalem, in November 1966, coincided by chance with the nationalisation of the museum by the Jordanian authorities. 'There is a sort of feeling that my apparition and lecture and so forth might be a factor somehow lubricating and tidying over the transition of the Museum—however I think that it is confined to the minds of the British. The Arabs have no misgivings, except only Aref (the Director elect), who knows himself to know nothing of museums of antiquities, and wants technical advice'.[13] Within a year the museum had passed, with East Jerusalem, under Israel's control.

---

[10] See above, n. 8 for source.
[11] Interview in the *East Anglian Daily Times*, 20 February 1993, 30.
[12] *Letters*, p. 53.
[13] *Letters*, p. 211.

Hamilton was that relative rarity in the archaeological world, not only a rapid publisher of exemplary concise reports on his excavations, but also a perceptive and persistent interrogator of his evidence and its significance in human terms. His publications are distinguished by acute observation and careful study combined with continual comparison and deduction. He never shirked debate, indeed he encouraged it to the point where one sometimes wondered in his later works how far his tongue was into his cheek. Oleg Grabar, who as a young man collaborated on the study of Khirbat al Mafjar, notably of its paintings, remembered 'the quality of the notes he (and others) had left in the archives of the Palestine Archaeological Museum, in Jerusalem . . . . In albums and boxes there were . . . stored drawings, photographs, observations of all sorts on Mafjar and on many other Palestinian remains by a man of intelligent devotion to his task.'[14]

One of his first tasks in Palestine was a rescue excavation at Tell Abu Hawam in 1932–3, the last in a series initiated by the Department of Antiquities a decade earlier. His report on rather less than six months' work is a forgotten landmark in archaeological reporting in the Near East. It set standards new to the region for work on a complex, if small, tell, that even now are not as commonly observed as they should be. His basic stratigraphic divisions were tested decades later by fresh work and found in the main to be sound, whilst his concise study of the pottery and small finds were models for the time.

His report contains a memorable statement of a fundamental principal of excavation:

> The conventional use of 'strata' in the analysis of the formation of a mound suggests a history divisible into static phases in each of which the life and culture of the last are definitely superseded. The history of fact is not so divided. In Jerusalem today a twelfth-century building stands in good condition and in active use while its twentieth-century neighbour, already a rubbish heap, will soon be a ruin. Similar conditions doubtless marked the evolution of an ancient site, and a certain complexity in the structural remains, is the result. Stratigraphy is the attempt to simplify or schematize that complexity so that it may be used to co-ordinate intelligibly the associated material. Where the architecture has little intrinsic merit the plans are still necessary as the framework within which the essential historical relations of one object to another are preserved. The main purpose of what immediately follows is to define, with greater precision than plans and levels alone can convey, the degree to which the stratification may be trusted as a true index of chronological relations amongst the excavated material.[15]

[14] Obituary in the *Independent*, 6 October 1995, 22.
[15] R. W. Hamilton, 'Excavations at Tell Abu Hawam', *Quarterly of the Department of Antiquities of Palestine*, 4 (1935), 1.

Although retrospectively criticised as a 'strange definition of stratigraphy',[16] it is in fact a classic statement, unmatched elsewhere even by Reisner for its brevity and clarity, of how the so-called 'architect-archaeologists' in Palestine conceived their purpose. It was a method to be superseded twenty years later, when Kathleen Kenyon demonstrated at Jericho the rather different and more effective methods of stratigraphic excavation pioneered by Mortimer Wheeler. But Hamilton from the outset in Palestine had mastered the best procedures of his day, technically far better than anything done at Nineveh.

Throughout his Directorship he undertook rescue excavations from time to time, usually reporting them briefly in the *Quarterly* of the Department, to the same consistently professional standard. None compares in significance to the work at Tell Abu Hawam, but his excavations against the north wall of Jerusalem in 1937–8 (reported in 1944) are enduringly relevant to the contentious question of the line of the northern wall of the City in the first century AD. They were reported with his customary precision, greatly easing the task of Hennessy in 1964–6, when he undertook a follow-up rescue excavation in the same area.[17]

Restoration and preservation work usually involving some minor excavation, reported in the *Quarterly*, was to lead to the two most notable of his publications apart from *Khirbat al Mafjar*. Both exemplify his primary scholarly achievement, the description and analysis of individual major buildings. *The Church of the Nativity at Bethlehem* (1947) might well have been no more memorable than his *Guide to Samaria-Sabaste* (1944), workman-like but routine, were it not for an outstanding discussion of the mosaics, printed in a smaller script so as not to distract the tourist into what he regarded as essential, if technical, controversies. Accepting that his views were new and thus at times debatable, he presented the case on the basis of the evidence as he knew it first hand so others might judge for themselves as they stood with the book in hand in the Church itself.

*Structural History of the Aqsa Mosque* (1949) is, by contrast, an enduring major monograph stimulated by the demolition and reconstruction of the middle and eastern aisles of the Aqsa, and related work

---

[16] H. J. Franken and C. A. Franken-Battershill, *A Primer of Old Testament Archaeology* (Leiden, 1963), p. 26.

[17] J. B. Hennessy, 'Preliminary Report on Excavations at the Damascus Gate, 1964–6', *Levant*, 2 (1970), 22–27.

by the Department, in 1938–42. This is a building no less remarkable than the Church of the Nativity, but of renowned architectural complexity as the result of frequent rebuilding over the centuries. Once more the strength of the book is in the detail, in the description and analysis, which endures, allowing readers in subsequent generations to use his meticulous, step by step dissection of the structure, for different reconstructions of the sequence of work and new chronological phasing. It has been overshadowed by the more monumental *Khirbat al Mafjar* and the associated publications, but in many ways it is a better basis for assessment of his special contribution to the archaeological and historical study of architecture. The Aqsa, however intricate its history, is a standing monument; Khirbat al Mafjar is the dismembered skeleton of one, where the quest for the creator almost came to eclipse the reconstruction of his creation in Hamilton's study of it. But that belonged to the next phase of his career.

## Nimrud and Oxford, 1948–56

The end of the British Mandate was a watershed in Hamilton's career, abruptly separating him from a world he loved and way of life in which his special talents had been exercised to the full. He was rescued through the good offices of Mallowan from 'minding geese and hens and a garden'[18] in Suffolk by the offer of a fellowship of the British School of Archaeology in Iraq combined with the post of Secretary Librarian of the School, founded in 1932 as a memorial to Gertrude Bell. His first duty was to provide the School with the physical base in Baghdad that it had so far been without. He left England for Iraq late in October 1948, just over six months after his enforced departure from Jerusalem. He had a number of friends and acquaintances in Baghdad, not least Seton Lloyd, then Technical Adviser to the Inspectorate General of Antiquities and his wife Hydie, who helped him to establish the school in a fine old Turkish house in the centre of the city. All was ready in time to receive Max Mallowan, with his wife Agatha, for the first season of his renowned excavations at Nimrud in 1949, where Hamilton joined them.

G. R. Driver, now as Chairman of the Oriental Faculty Board at Oxford, had already inaugurated procedures for appointing Hamilton to

---

[18] *Letters*, p. 64.

a personal lectureship in Near Eastern archaeology. This was not the first such possibility to be mooted, as Mallowan had earlier suggested to him a comparable appointment in the Institute of Archaeology in London University. He was then, and remained, surprisingly diffident about his competence to offer formal lecturing and teaching. 'I am *amateur* in archaeology; if I take the job (in London) I should have to masquerade as a *professional*. As Director here (in Palestine), it is quite all right to be an amateur—that is all Richmond was; but a lecturer must really know the stuff.'[19] The London job went to Kathleen Kenyon. Driver, who knew his man better than he appeared to know himself, was not to be gainsaid. After the first season's excavation at Nimrud was over, Hamilton accepted the lectureship in Oxford offered a month earlier. 'My engagement with the Oriental Faculty required a certain amount of lecturing each year; but was so agreeably relaxed that I was able to accept a standing invitation from Max Mallowan to join his continuing excavations which took place year by year at Nimrud in the Spring'.[20]

Hamilton's contribution to these excavations, about which he never wrote anything himself, was in every sense complementary to Mallowan's. 'I do some surveying and drawing as well as sharing with Max in the general supervision of the work'[21] where his colloquial Arabic was an additional asset. In his *Memoirs*, some twenty years later, Mallowan recalled his old friend and colleague thus: 'I have rarely met a more modest, talented and self-effacing man. He was gifted for drawing, a surveyor, and kept the architectural record . . . . A natural recluse, he was by nature a philosopher and I think would have been equally happy as a metaphysician and gardener. Although ready to be sociable his friendship had to be excavated and he was possessed as it seemed of a deep inner melancholy'.[22]

This perhaps too closely reflects the circumstances at Nimrud in which the two men were most often together for extended periods. In the community and *en famille* a warmer and more open personality was evident. However, he rarely wasted words, on paper or in speech, and this could be misleading as those of his letters written in a relaxed mood, published and unpublished, make clear. 'Digging (at Nimrud) is

[19]  *Letters*, p. 54.
[20]  *Letters*, p. 105.
[21]  *Letters*, p. 95.
[22]  M. E. L. Mallowan, *Mallowan's Memoirs: the Autobiography of Max Mallowan* (London, 1977), p. 246.

the one thing that can transport me back to my youth, and I almost (not quite) recover the feeling of sunshine, and freedom, and absence of worry, and interest, which I had at Jerash and those places in 1929.'[23]

Despite the fact that he was 'filled with dismay at the prospect of having to lecture in learned circles about archaeology'[24] he gave his first two courses at Oxford in 1950. In the seven years during which he was a University Lecturer he gave twelve courses in all, usually two a year, save for one a year in 1952–3 and three in 1951. Three themes recur: the material evidence for the religion of Canaan and Israel, the Phoenicians, and early Muslim architecture. He also gave single courses on Early Christian archaeology in Palestine (1956) and on the art of the Caravan Cities (1952). The lectures on aspects of Old Testament archaeology provided for undergraduates reading Hebrew or theology; but the attention he gave to the Near Eastern architecture in the first millennium AD were not directed to any syllabus requirement, but opened up new areas of archaeology in Oxford, closely related to his own research in these years as he prepared his major work on Khirbat al Mafjar. His lectures, combining sober thought with sound scholarship, were always delivered with clarity and fluency, spiced with irony and wit. Anyone who heard him in a lecture hall must regret that he never got round in these years to writing the general books on the Umayyads and on Jerusalem, which he lightly referred to in later years as passing fancies.

Formal university teaching, particularly at a time when there was little demand for what he had to offer, never really suited him. It was not then surprising when, early in September 1956, he applied for the Keepership of the Department of Antiquities in the Ashmolean Museum, about to fall vacant when Donald Harden moved to the London Museum. He was supported by strong testimonials from G. R. Driver;[25] from C. J. Gadd, a former colleague at Nimrud, then Professor of Assyriology in London University, who noted that 'his ability as an organiser and as a director of workmen was very evident'; and from Mallowan, who pointed out that 'here we have a man of rare and exceptional talents of which the University is at present making insufficient use.'[26]

---

[23] *Letters*, p. 95.
[24] *Letters*, p. 99.
[25] See above, p. 495.
[26] See above, n. 8.

He took up the Keepership in the Michaelmas Term 1956. He was to remain at the Ashmolean until his retirement in 1972. In October 1962, on the retirement of Sir Karl Parker, he succeeded as the senior departmental keeper to the Keepership of the whole museum. He was the last holder of this post, created in 1683. On his retirement Sir David Piper was appointed to the newly created office of Director. In 1960 he became a Fellow of the British Academy.

Although his major work *Khirbat al Mafjar: an Arabian Mansion in the Jordan Valley* was not published until 1959, when he was well established in the Ashmolean, its production really belongs to the years of his lectureship, when he returned three times briefly to Jerusalem, in 1949, 1952 and 1953, to work on the finds from the site. By 1949 Gerald Harding, as Director of Antiquities in the Hashemite Kingdom of Jordan, 'had already, before the time of my visit, secured from America a promise of finance and had invited me to work on publication of the site and its remains. The money was to serve not only for the costs of printing and publication but also for restoration and photography and for draughtsmanship'; he was to secure more funding from Rockefeller later.[27]

Recurrent plundering of the site for stones attractive to builders had originally called attention to the group of ruins in the Jordan Valley near Jericho known as Khirbat al Mafjar. The ornamentation of some of the stonework, particularly, had caught the eye of archaeologists. The Department of Antiquities initiated excavations in 1934, directed in the field by Dimitri Baramki, one of the four Palestinian Inspectors of Antiquities in the Department, who also published the preliminary reports. He was later to take a doctorate at London University and to be Professor of Archaeology in the American University in Beirut. Hamilton's priority in 1948 before he had to leave Palestine, apart from the Museum, was 'to finish the dig at Mafjar and get as much of the record completed as possible.'[28] By the end there was friction between him and Baramki, which he much regretted. It was almost inevitable. The differences in ability, education and status were far too great to be the basis for a continuing partnership in research; the more so when their lives developed so differently after 1948 and their temperaments were so different. 'What is important is that Khirbat al Mafjar is the only true early Islamic palace to be published, but that

---

[27] *Letters*, p. 103
[28] *Letters*, p. 33.

Hamilton never ended his affair with it.'[29] For over half a century it was a recurrent preoccupation.

Four major articles complement the final volume as they deal with various parts of this remarkable building—the baths, the sculpture, the mosaics, and the carved plaster—in ways not wholly superseded by the final volume. They sum up the work he undertook during his rapid trips to Jerusalem and Jericho from 1949–53 whilst firsthand study was still possible for him. The monograph *Khirbat al Mafjar* (1959), in his own words, 'became an indispensable source for the study of the earliest Islamic art and architecture'. The judgement stands, not least since description and reconstruction may easily be separated from interpretation as in all his major works.

This study is a masterpiece of reconstruction in three dimensions of earthquake debris in four media—stone, plaster, mosaic, and paint—which had provided the original structure and extremely elaborate decoration of the building. As he acknowledged, many others had contributed over the years, not least G. U. S. Corbett, architect to the Department of Antiquities, who had taken part in the final stages of the excavation. He had provided not only most of the often remarkable drawings for the volume, but also 'the help which it has been to ponder and argue with him many elusive but, as they have often proved, not insoluble problems.'[30] Oleg Grabar contributed the chapter on the paintings. Hamilton drew it all together with clarity and style.

It remains true that:

> The variety of materials represented, and the wealth of detail in construction and ornament which time and chance have preserved, place the ruins of Khirbat al Mafjar amongst the richest of available sources for the secular architecture of Palestine at a critical and fleeting moment: a moment when the reviving stimulus of religion and empire, of wealth and passionate will, under the Umayyad Caliphs seemed about to transform, by a new synthesis of Greek and Asiatic genius, the millennial art of Hellenistic Syria.[31]

Debate and controversy enters in with Hamilton's enduring conviction that, although an inscription fixed construction in Hisham's caliphate, the whole nature of the building was entirely out of keeping with what is historically known of his character. 'It is the character and career of al Walid, the poet, the hunter, and the drinker, much more than Hisham,

---

[29] See above, n. 9.
[30] R. W. Hamilton, *Khirbat al Mafjar* (Oxford, 1959), preface.
[31] Ibid., p. ix.

the censorious, the smasher of lutes, which can suggest and illuminate the origins of al Mafjar'.[32] He argued the case with increasing conviction and ingenuity over the next thirty years, ever seeking new clues to resolve the question. For many the case remains open; but, whatever the final answer may be, it may not be doubted that affirmation or contradiction will depend largely upon data provided by Hamilton in his occasional papers and in this monograph.

## The Ashmolean Years, 1956–72

The most revealing episode in the last decade or so of his working life was a visit to Iran in January 1961, after just over three years in the Ashmolean, with the prospect of securing appointment as Director of the Antiquities Service there. Until then this post had been held by French citizens. Now the Iranians sought a British candidate for an appointment which had to be endorsed by the Iranian Parliament. They hoped to secure financial sponsorship from the United Nations for the post. 'I have had three very hectic days and am pretty well exhausted with talking to innumerable elegant and civilized gentlemen, and hearing how many **un**civilized and **un**gentlemanly gentlemen have a hand in my affairs . . . this is a task which will try me out in my own estimation in a degree which neither Palestine nor the Ashmolean could.'[33] In the event negotiations collapsed when he refused to accept a clause in his contract, inserted by the UN bureaucracy, which 'subjected the person appointed to the superior authority of Persian officialdom'.[34]

He was to return briefly to Iran in 1970–1 on the eve of his retirement, when Mallowan persuaded him to join the British excavations at Siraf directed by David Whitehouse. There he combined surveying ruins in the vicinity of the excavated areas with overseeing 'excavation of a large destroyed building which looks like a custom's shed, or wharf or warehouse . . . this is a very large empty building, full of chunks of its own structure thrown about by an earthquake'.[35] Fortunately, a few of his workmen spoke Arabic; but on the whole it was not a rewarding experience. Neither his expertise nor his interests

[32] Ibid., p. 105.
[33] *Letters*, p. 204.
[34] *Letters*, p. 207.
[35] *Letters*, p. 230.

were fully engaged by the work on this his last field trip, indeed his last visit to the Near East.

He wrote relatively little in these years and then normally only essays for volumes in honour of old friends. Publication of his season excavating in the Great Mosque at Harran in 1959 with David Storm Rice, establishing its plan and largely Ayyubid date of construction, was aborted by the director's premature death. His specially commissioned report in English and French on the state of the Islamic monuments in Algeria, undertaken in 1968, remains an unpublished government document, presented to the Minister on his final day in the country. '(He) was introduced to me as (*mirabile dictu*) unable (presumably in fact unwilling) to speak any language but Arabic. Confronted with this emergency, my mind made the desperate switch from French to very rusty Arabic, in which my scrambled compliments were rewarded by my overhearing (as I truly believed) one of my audience expressing a preference for my manner of speech—I supposed he meant a Palestinian accent—over that of "the Egyptians"!'[36]

In the Ashmolean he always took a controlling interest in the acquisition of objects for the Department of Antiquities, enjoying visits to the major London showrooms, where he executed wonderfully rapid sketches of desirable objects in a notebook, and relaxed conversations over lunch with his colleagues about what was or was not to be pursued in the forthcoming auction, followed by library research. These were the days when such an acquisitions policy was not frowned upon and keepers still had a free hand. The publication of objects, however, rarely appealed to him and an editorial request from a friend was usually needed to secure one. It is not surprising then that the most characteristic and important paper of these years was *Jerusalem: Patterns of Holiness* written in honour of Kathleen Kenyon,[37] in which he explored the motives which impelled first a Jew (Solomon), then a Christian (Constantine) and then a Muslim ('Abdul Malik) to establish shrines in Jerusalem. In many ways it is to be regretted that in retirement he did not pursue the lines of thought he opened up here into the major study of Jerusalem he was so well equipped to write, for his heart remained there and his firsthand knowledge of its monuments and the literature about it was almost unrivalled at the time.

[36] *Letters*, p. 218.
[37] P. R. S. Moorey and P. J. Parr (eds.), *Archaeology in the Levant: Essays for Kathleen Kenyon* (London, 1978), pp. 194–201.

Constitutionally his Keepership of the Ashmolean Museum was in many ways the most eventful decade in its history since Arthur Evans had virtually refounded it on the Beaumont Street site some sixty years earlier. It began with the implementation of a newly revised statute governing the museum, which formally created two new departments, of Coins and of Eastern Art, to add to the existing Antiquities (and Cast Gallery) and Western Art departments and concluded with university legislation enshrining the recommendations of the *Brunt Report* (1967). That had been significantly modified in some respects by his vigorous and forcefully argued opposition to the proposed new policy of internal centralisation and unification at the expense of traditional departmental autonomy.

> The new plan rests on the theory that the Ashmolean is one, and should be administered as a unity. The old principle was that archaeology and the study of fine arts are distinct disciplines, applying different methods and aims to their subjects and calling for specialized direction . . . . The University should not be hypnotized by cant of 'Unity'; nor by stale analogies from municipal and government museum bureaucracies. The working ties between each Ashmolean department and the Ashmolean library are far closer than any that link the departments themselves. Yet no-one has preached 'unity' at the library or opposed its separation from the museum. The unity of the Ashmolean is true of its building; it is true of the library and its collections; but when cited of the collections themselves it is an academic catchword and no more.'[38]

His firm conviction, clearly based on his personal experience, that the roles of a museum curator and a university lecturer were distinct, requiring different aptitudes, experience and training engaged him in a long-standing debate in Oxford which continues. Pragmatic as ever, he argued in respect of proposals in the *Brunt Report* that: 'If curators were to undertake regular teaching then **either** the Museum must appoint more staff **or** the reorganization and cataloguing of the collections (which enable scholars to use them) and their eventual publication, together with any revival of fieldwork (entailing more publication), would be indefinitely delayed.'[39] To choose this second alternative, in his view, would be a deplorable reversal of policy in the museum.

In the event, the museum's purpose was formally redefined from 'to facilitate and assist study' of its collections to 'to assist in relevant teaching and research within the University'. At this stage archaeology

[38] Archives of the Ashmolean Museum, Oxford: The Brunt Report: Keeper's File 1966–8.
[39] Ibid.

and art-history were still struggling for recognition within the university's curricula, at most taught at diploma level, despite powerful advocacy by the holders of newly founded professorships. The subsequent emergence of fully-fledged degree courses, at a time of severe economies in staffing, has accentuated the dilemma which Hamilton had so acutely appreciated.

He also had to cope with the first real signs of the gradual emergence of the Ashmolean from the closed world of the university into the public arena. In the museum's relations with the city and the county, Hamilton, drawing on his long experience as a government official, was both constructive and dutiful. He appreciated and forwarded attempts to create new institutions, the Oxford City Museum and the County Museum at Woodstock (originally joint) and the local Oxford Archaeological Unit (originally the Oxford Excavation Committee), a pioneering enterprise. These were to satisfy fresh and growing demands for the independent promotion and proper development of local archaeology and history which had long been under the museum's wing. 'My recollection of him is of a member who made valuable contributions to the various matters to be expected on the creation of a new Museum Service from scratch and was well liked, which is confirmed by the warmth of the Committee's minute on receiving his resignation on 11.10.1972 . . . unlike the usual terse note.'[40]

Hamilton always seemed to know instinctively when it was best to stand back and when best to fight for what he saw as the museum's best interests. In a crisis, internal or external, he was a tower of strength, pragmatic and direct. If he offered support, he could be relied upon to carry it through; if he could not, he told you so. Once his mind was made up on the merits of a case, he was a staunch advocate or a redoubtable opponent, as the case might be. On committee he said little, but rarely without noticeable effect. Many were surprised, in view of his quiet manner in public and his economy with words at meetings, to discover how well-informed he usually was as much about the official as about the unofficial activities of his staff of whatever rank.

## The Suffolk Years, 1972–95

Retirement to Suffolk, where his family had spent the Second World War and where he joined them briefly in 1948, came easily to him. He

---

[40] Ashmolean Museum Archives: R. W. Hamilton: Personal File: Letter from John Edwards, former Deputy Town Clerk of Oxford, dated 17 December 1995.

was by then out of tune with the museum policies he was obliged to pursue, disenchanted by current trends in archaeology and saddened by the continuing strife in the Near East. He turned to music and gardening, reading and writing for recreation. Whether it be playing the piano, wielding a garden instrument, pen, or pencil, he always enjoyed doing things with his hands. Although it had been his greatest academic achievement to make Khirbat al Mafjar the best known of all Umayyad buildings through his meticulous record and analysis and reconstruction of the material remains of its structure and remarkable decoration, he still sought to convince his learned colleagues that its creator was not the Caliph Hisham, but rather Walid ibn Yazid, whose libertine lifestyle in his view better explained the idiosyncrasies of the building as he had reconstructed it. In a final monograph, *Walid and his Friends: An Umayyad Tragedy* (1988) he combined early Arabic literary and poetical accounts including Walid's own, which he read and translated with occasional help from A. F. L. Beeston, to recreate the daily life of Khirbat al Mafjar as he imagined it. As his editor Julian Raby noted, in apologising for 'Walid's fleshy appetites' as revealed by Hamilton, 'This is a tale not only of physical and emotional excess, but of gross religious irreverence. Let those who are offended read this as a moral tale. It begins with a tragedy—an earthquake which ruins Walid's palace—and ends with a tragedy—Walid's own assassination. Let these tragedies be viewed as the twin vengeance of God and man.'[41] 'To which I might add', Hamilton remarked in a letter accompanying a presentation copy, 'my own for one or two slightly vulgar bits in the text, which you might think could well have been omitted—however, the Arabs in those days were not so sensitive.'[42] The debate about Khirbat al Mafjar will continue with the implicit tribute that without Hamilton's fine published documentation in the first place, as in other cases, it could never be sustained.

Hamilton's career was of its time. It is inconceivable sixty years later. It is now fashionable to denigrate imperial archaeology which at its best, as exemplified in Hamilton's work in Palestine, was based on a common purpose shared between the expatriate administrators and their

---

[41] *Walid*, p. 8.
[42] Personal letter, 7 December 1988.

local assistants, who so often went on to be their successors. By great good fortune he found from the outset a career equal to his talents and demanding of them in a region famously rich in the monuments of antiquity and early modern times. He took them, the people, their language and heritage, to heart. He did as much as anyone in his time and place to see that the legacy with which he had been briefly entrusted was passed on not only in better repair, but also better known. In the Department of Antiquities of Palestine and later in the Ashmolean Museum, Oxford, he was a remarkable steward, decisive, dedicated and direct.

P. R. S. MOOREY
*Fellow of the Academy*

*Note.* In this memoir I have drawn heavily on close personal acquaintance with Robert Hamilton, as a junior member of his department in the Ashmolean Museum from 1961–72 and on occasional conversations and letters in his years of retirement. All other debts are acknowledged in the footnotes.

DONALD HARDEN

*Proceedings of the British Academy*, **94**, 513–539

# Donald Benjamin Harden
# 1901–1994

DONALD HARDEN, the world-wide authority on ancient glass, master exponent of Phoenician history and culture, Keeper of Antiquities in the Ashmolean Museum and Director of the London Museum, died on 13 April 1994. His life was devoted in equal measure to archaeology and museums; artefacts—rather than excavations—were the focus of his scholarship.

## Family and Early Life

Donald Benjamin Harden was born in Dublin on 8 July 1901, the elder son of the Revd John Mason Harden and Constance Caroline Sparrow. The first Irish Harden, Major John Harden, came from Essex, where he was recruited into the Parliamentary Army, went to Ireland in 1649 and was amongst those paid off in land as part of the Cromwellian settlement. The Hardens were traditionally Church of Ireland clergymen, and schoolmasters. John, Donald's father, was born in Dublin 3 July 1871. He attended the Rathmines School and was a Scholar of Trinity College Dublin from 1890, graduating in 1892. He won prizes in Greek, Syriac, Chaldean and Hebrew. John Harden was ordained in 1895; he was chaplain to the Female Orphan House in Dublin 1899–1901. John had married, in 1896, Constance Sparrow of Clonmel, and Donald was born at the Parsonage of the Orphan House.

In 1903 John took up the post of Principal of the Training College

© The British Academy 1997.

for the Ministry of the Lusitanian Church, in Oporto, Portugal. John's second child, Joan, was born in Oporto in 1905. In 1907 John was appointed Headmaster of the College of St John at Kilkenny; their third child, Alan, was born there in 1909. Donald attended the college from 1909 to 1914. After seven years at Kilkenny, John became Vice-Principal of the London College of Divinity, Highbury; Donald was sent to Westminster School as a day-boy: he was an Exhibitioner 1914–16 and a King's Scholar 1916–20, taking his School Certificate in 1917 with six credits. Donald was a member of the Debating Society, and of the Officer Training Corps; he rowed, and was a keen stamp-collector: an early sign of his classificatory instincts. Donald was awarded an Exhibition to Trinity College, Cambridge, and went up in 1920.

Donald's brother and sister were graduates of Trinity College Dublin: both predeceased Donald by some years; Alan left a son, Brian, who has worked on the family history. Their father returned to Ireland in 1922 as Chaplain and Headmaster of the King's Hospital, Dublin, and was Bishop of Tuam, Killala and Achonry from 1927 until his death on 2 October 1931. He was awarded the degrees of LLD and DD. His obituaries describe him as a brilliant scholar and easy to approach. Many of his father's traits—his scholarship, devotion to duty, approachability, aptitude for languages—can be seen in Donald's career.

At Trinity, Donald read for the classical tripos. He was a Bell Scholar in 1921 and a Senior Scholar in 1922. His mentors were Ernest Harrison and Donald Robertson, FBA 1940, Lecturers in Classics; Arthur Cook, FBA 1914, Reader in Classical Archaeology, and Sir William Ridgeway, FBA 1904, Disney Professor of Archaeology. Harden was misadvised to take Part I in one year, achieving only a second class in 1921. Robertson and Harrison apologised, saying that he was near to the line of division, but he obtained a first class in Part II in 1923, including papers in Special Group D (Archaeology). He was top of the archaeologists, just missing a distinction. He was awarded the Walker Prize for a 'diligent and hardworking scholar'.

## Rome, Carthage and the Phoenicians, and Aberdeen

### Tarantine terracottas

Harden was relieved to hear about his First, and hoped to stay in Cambridge for post-graduate studies, but on 20 June he was awarded a travel grant from the Craven Fund to study terracotta figurines from Taranto. Ridgeway wrote to Harden on 23 June, 'You seem to me to have the right turn for archaeology.' The subject was clearly suggested by Cook, who was interested in the religious aspects of terracotta figurines.

Harden spent a month studying terracottas in the Department of Greek and Roman Antiquities in the British Museum and left London in October 1923 for Rome, where he would be based at the British School at Rome, whose Director was Thomas Ashby, FBA 1927. Harden found accommodation at the Pensione Rubens, where Arnold Mackay Duff was also lodging; Duff, of Oriel College, Oxford, was researching for his B.Litt. thesis. Harden worked on terracottas in Naples Museum and then Taranto. In early February Harden visited Sicily, for the terracottas in Syracuse and Palermo. Duff joined him there, and they toured classical sites before sailing for Tunis. Harden spent the summer of 1924 writing up his findings, giving special attention to the cults revealed by the figurines, but he published only a short article, in 1927, on the Artemis Figurines.

## Carthage

An increasing amount of excavation took place in Carthage during the last quarter of the nineteenth century, with Cardinal Lavigerie's appointment of Father Alfred-Louis Delattre, of the Order of the Pères Blancs, as Curator of the new museum in 1878—'the Ancient God of the place', as Belloc described him in 1925. Most of the excavations were on Roman sites, since Punic finds proved elusive.

The scientist Jules Renault carried out excavations on Juno Hill in 1920 and 1921, until his death in May of the latter year. During 1920 he was assisted by the energetic and imaginative American explorer, writer, and archaeologist Count Byron Khun de Prorok, who was of Central European origins; born in Mexico in 1896, he had a colourful career on expeditions to northern Africa, central America, and Arabia. Before his death, Renault had asked de Prorok to continue his excavations: these were carried out in 1922 and 1923, accompanied by the first use of cine-films in archaeology.

De Prorok asked Ashby for recruits for his 1924 Carthage season; Duff expressed interest, and Harden sought advice from Ridgeway, as it would affect his Craven grant. Ridgeway replied, 'Go over to Carthage and excavate . . . sure Craven not object . . .'. So Harden and Duff arrived in Tunis on 27 February 1924, and helped to prepare the excavation headquarters at the Villa Amilcar in Sidi Bou Said. De Prorok arranged a memorable trip through Tunisia by car in April.

## Precinct of Tanit

It was lucky that Harden was recruited for the 1924 excavations since it was then possible to investigate the Punic levels. Limestone stelae, bearing symbols associated with the cult of Tanit, began to appear on the market in 1921; clandestine digging was discovered in the Salammbô district, close to the western shore of the rectangular port. Intermittent excavations were carried out during 1922 with help from the Service des Antiquités, its Director, Louis Poinssot, and his assistant, Raymond Lantier. Many stelae were found, with Punic urns containing the remains of child sacrifices. Four stratigraphical levels, from the eighth century BC to the fall of Carthage in 146 BC, were elaborated by Poinssot and Lantier, who took over the site in 1923. De Prorok assisted in these 1923 excavations. For 1924 he purchased the land and brought in the Abbé Jean-Baptiste Chabot, an expert on inscriptions, as his French co-director. Work lasted from 30 April until 24 May; 468 urns were found. Harden recorded nine main urn types: already pottery seems to have been his main interest. But relations with Chabot were strained: the Abbé would not sanction the removal of dumps which prevented the digging of new ground, so de Prorok took advantage of Chabot's absence one day to have these removed and dumped in the sea.[1] The excavation was stopped after further dissension. Harden records Chabot as being intractable, but the Count 'is awfully decent and obliging'; Poinssot had denigrated de Prorok the day Harden arrived. De Prorok published only an interim report.[2]

## Aberdeen 1924–6

Harden returned to Cambridge in June 1924 to discuss his future. The general advice was that he should not spend another year at Cambridge; Harden agreed: after seven months abroad, he had little interest in

[1] Review by John L. Myres of Byron Khun de Prorok, *Digging for Lost African Gods* (1926), *Geographical Journal*, 68 (October 1926), 353.

[2] Byron Khun de Prorok, 'The excavations of the sanctuary of Tanit at Carthage', *Art and Archaeology*, 19.1 (January 1925), reprinted in *Annual Report of the Board of Regents of the Smithsonian Institution* (1925), pp. 569–74.

Cambridge life. He applied for lectureships in classics at Durham, Reading, and Manchester. Manchester was looking promising when on 4 September Harden was advised that there was a post at Aberdeen, giving lectures on Classical authors: 'they are prepared to nominate you'. Harden accepted, and was appointed Assistant in Latin in the Department of Humanity from October 1924, a post he was to hold for two years, advancing to the grade of Senior Assistant. Harden was happy here, giving his first lectures on Seneca and Horace's satires. Alexander Souter, FBA 1926, was Regius Professor of Humanity; he gave Harden considerable encouragement in pursuing his Punic studies. As Robert Getty said in his 1952 British Academy obituary, 'young scholars could wish for no better start in their careers than Souter's Humanity Department'. In his later years, Harden retained his love for the classics, continuing to read them in the original tongues.

## Carthage 1925

Souter released Harden for three weeks at Easter 1925, to attend his second season at Carthage. The University of Michigan at Ann Arbor had started a programme of Near East Research under its Professor of Latin Language and Literature, Francis William Kelsey. De Prorok had met Kelsey to interest him in the Precinct of Tanit project; Kelsey wanted to take part, but requested that de Prorok first carry out a trial season in 1924. The spectacular results of 1924 showed the importance of the site, so a joint Franco-American staff was assembled, including Delattre, the Abbé Chabot, and American supervisory staff.

In March 1925 Harden travelled out to Carthage, visiting Sicily to study the Punic urns from Motya. He reached Tunis on 8 April, to work in the Bardo Museum on Punic urns. On 20 April Harden happened to be visiting the site, the day before he planned to leave, when Kelsey told him to go down into the trench at once to have the urns photographed *in situ* and to supervise their removal. Harden wrote 'as I was the only man at his disposal who even professed to know anything about pot, Kelsey finally made me the astounding offer of entrusting me with the report on all the pottery from the site and have it published with the rest of the Michigan report, too good a chance to be missed'. But relations with the French were difficult, and Poinssot, who could be very plain-spoken, now sent Kelsey 'two insulting letters full of unfounded accusations'. The French stopped the excavations on 6 May. There was a great rush for Harden to record the 1,100 urns found that season and store them before leaving on 14 May. Kelsey published a preliminary report in 1926;[3] unfortunately, with his death in 1927, no final report was published; Harden wrote a twenty-four-page study of the lowest stratigraphy, with a plan; this and other records are preserved in the University of Michigan archive.

Harden spent the 1925 summer studying Punic urns in earnest. Thomas Ashby had given Harden steady support following his change from terracottas to Punic urns, and wrote to him on 22 May: 'do you want to read a paper on the subject of Punic urns to the British Association at Southampton in August'. Parts of Harden's lecture, on 'Recent excavations in a Punic precinct at Carthage', were incorporated in Kelsey's 1926 report.

By December 1925 it was clear that there would be no 1926 excavation, so Harden decided to visit the Mediterranean in the spring, looking for parallels to the Punic urns found at Carthage. He studied collections in Malta, Sicily, Sardinia, and Italy.

## Commonwealth Fund Fellowship 1926–8

It was still thought that the French authorities would release to Ann Arbor 500 of the Punic urns found in 1925, and Kelsey invited Harden to go over for two years to study them. Harden considered possible sources for a grant: Kelsey's colleague, Professor Robert Mark Wenley, then Director of the British Division of the American University Union in London, recommended the Commonwealth Fund. Harden was awarded a fellowship on 9 June, to spend two academic years at Ann Arbor writing up the Punic urns from the Precinct of Tanit as his special study and to 'obtain through travel some knowledge of the United States.' The Fund, based in New York, had been founded in 1918 by Mrs Harkness, widow of Stephen Vanderburg Harkness of Standard Oil. In 1924 their son, Edward S. Harkness, suggested that the Fund should establish a fellowship programme for 'British students of unusual promise and ability to study in America'. Harden was the only Commonwealth Fund Fellow, until the 1960s, whose subject was archaeology. Harden left Southampton on 11 September 1926 for New York.

The urns from Carthage had never arrived, and Harden had diverted

---

[3] Francis W. Kelsey, *Excavations at Carthage 1925: A Preliminary Report* (New York, 1926), pp. x, 51; VI plates. Also published as a Supplement to *American Journal of Archaeology* (1926).

to the study of glass, but he was asked to give a lecture (published 1927) in December to the Twenty-Eighth General Meeting of the Archaeological Institute of America at Harvard, on Punic urns. Harden also lectured at Ann Arbor to the University Classical Journal Club on his April 1924 Tunisia trip, and to the Annual Meeting of the American Oriental Society, Middle West Branch, in March 1928, at Urbana, Illinois, on Punic urns from Malta, Sicily and Sardinia.

Harden made good use of his vacations. At Easter 1927 he attended a conference in Chicago and toured Michigan. In the summer he spent three months travelling west to see the national parks (with Leiv Amundsen, who remained a lifelong friend) and explore the southwest Pueblo; in December he visited New Orleans. Harden's diary gives insights into his social life: he attended the Episcopalian Church and took part in their evening discussions; his main evening activity was bridge, varied by attending musicals, plays, and concerts. He played pool, handball, squash and tennis and was a keen observer of the American scene.

## Carthage 1933 and later

Harden was well aware that his 1927 publication 'did not do justice to the well stratified 2,000 plus urns found in the four seasons.' In November 1933, therefore, he revisited Carthage and completed his study and classification of the urns, the results being published in 1937.

Soon after Harden's 1933 visit the French resumed excavations in the Precinct; the Americans returned in 1975–9 with an expedition directed by Lawrence Stager. These excavations have not been adequately published, though there has been a recent summary:[4] Harden's two articles remain the only full account of Punic urns from Carthage; subsequent work has confirmed his chronology. Serge Lancel, the head of the French 1970s project at Carthage, said in 1992[5] that 'it is to Harden that we owe a decisive improvement in the stratigraphic perception of the tophet'.

In the 1970s Harden was a member of the committee supervising the British participation in the UNESCO excavations at Carthage. His valedictory visits came in 1976 and 1978 at the invitation of Lawrence Stager, who also called to see him in London: Harden was much touched by this gesture.

[4] Hélène Bénichou-Safar, 'Les fouilles du Tophet de Salammbô à Carthage: Première partie', *Antiquités Africaines*, 31 (1995), 81–199.
[5] Serge Lancel, *Carthage* (Paris, 1992), trans. as *Carthage: A History* (Oxford, 1995).

## The Phoenicians

'Carthage and the Phoenicians have never been far away from my thoughts, though often for long years the research has had to be laid aside', wrote Harden in 1962. For nearly forty years he returned intermittently to Punic matters, reading extensively and reviewing publications on the Phoenicians. In 1948 he published his 'Phoenicians on the West Coast of Africa' and in 1950 visited Malta to report on what could be done to advance Phoenician research there.

The culmination came when Glyn Daniel commissioned Harden to contribute a volume to his 'Ancient Peoples and Places' series. Harden took advantage of his 1955 Leverhulme Research Fellowship tour to visit Beirut, Byblos, Tyre, Sidon, and other Phoenician sites and museum collections. The book was published in 1962, and rapidly established itself as one of the best general studies of the Phoenicians. *The Phoenicians* epitomises Harden's clear, well-informed style of writing, his classical scholarship everywhere apparent.

There were so many printing errors that a revised edition had to be issued in 1963. The 1971 Pelican edition embodied substantial revisions; Harden had many problems with getting his corrections carried out. The final edition in 1980 contained further revisions. *The Phoenicians* was translated into Italian, Spanish, and Portuguese; it has been widely used as a source-book by scientists working on a remarkably diverse range of topics.

## Mediterranean imports

Another Mediterranean interest was ancient imports into Britain. Harden published papers in 1950 and 1951; the text of his 1960 update is in the Society of Antiquaries Library: his main concern was Italic and Etruscan finds of the first millennium BC.

# Glass Researches

## Ann Arbor

The possibility that Harden might change from the study of Punic urns to glass during his Commonwealth Fund Fellowship at Ann Arbor was first broached by Kelsey in a letter of 9 July 1926: 'in case the urns do not come promptly would you not like to work over our Egyptian glass?'. When Kelsey met Harden and Whittemore Littell, of the Fund's Education Division, in New York on 27 September it was agreed that Harden should work on the Romano-Egyptian glass from Karanis in the Askren Collection, and then on that from the 1924–5 Karanis excavations by the University of Michigan. He 'avidly accepted the unexpected challenge after falling into the assignment quite by accident' and was set on his major life's work: the study of glass.

Harden's diary and letters record how he started his research on glass. He arrived at Ann Arbor on Friday, 1 October 1926 and already, on the Monday, was making 'a half-hearted attempt to start on my own subject by reading the article on glass in the *Encyclopaedia Britannica*'. This would have been the 11th edition of 1910, which included an eight-page section on the history of glass, written for the 9th edition (1879) by Alexander Nesbitt; it was revised for the 11th edition by Henry James Powell. Harden was told to read two works in German on the history of glassworking: a chapter by Blümner[6] and the three volume work by Kisa.[7] Although Harden could read German, these were heavy going; Kisa was about the only general book on glass then available. Harden also found a sixteen-page article by Morin-Jean.[8]

## Karanis glass

Harden then started sorting the Askren Collection of 333 vessels into groups, with drawings of the 'variants of type', and tried to work out the relative dating of the various types. By the end of term he was enquiring about taking a Ph.D., and the Commonwealth Fund agreed. He had to prepare for examinations in French and German, and on Latin and Greek authors, as well as an oral examination covering classical archaeology. Over the years, Harden learnt at least half a dozen languages, a talent perhaps inherited from his father. In the December vacation he visited glass collections in Toronto, Boston, New York, and Philadelphia. Kelsey returned early from Karanis; he had a long talk with Harden but died suddenly on 14 May 1927, so Harden was left very much on his own during his second year working on the glass. He

---

[6] 'Die Fabrikation des Glases', in Hugo Blümner, *Technologie und terminologie der Gewerbe und Künste bei Griechen und Römern*, IV (Leipzig, 1887), pp. 379–413.
[7] Anton Kisa, *Das Glas im Altertume*, 3 vols., Hiersemanns Handbücher, (Leipzig, 1908).
[8] Morin-Jean, 'Vitrum', in Charles Daremberg, Edmond Saglio, and Edmond Pottier (eds.), *Dictionnaire des antiquités grecques et romaines*, V (Paris, 1905), pp. 934–49.

completed his catalogue of the Askren Collection in late June. He had hoped to go to Egypt for the 1927–8 season at Karanis, to study the glass as it was excavated, but the Commonwealth Fund refused to sanction this as 'too divergent from the whole scheme of the Fellowship and would interfere with the fundamental purposes.'

Karanis (Kôm Aushîm) was one of the larger Graeco-Roman settlements in the north-east corner of the Fayûm, south-west of Cairo. In the 1920s a local doctor, D. L. Askren, collected large quantities of glass which formed the basis of Harden's first year of research. The University of Michigan excavations led by Kelsey, with Professor Enoch E. Peterson as Field Director, started in 1924–5 and continued until 1935. For his thesis, however, Harden was able to study little but the glass from the first season. Karanis had a population of about 4,000 at its peak between the second and fourth centuries AD. Mud-brick houses were well preserved, with many artefacts left behind as the buildings were abandoned and rebuilding took place at a higher level. There was therefore good stratification, and it was also possible to separate the finds from the various properties.

Harden set about studying the glass methodically, sorting that from each room into types and fabrics, and entering the information on to cards. He relied on his own classification instincts: only limited reading was possible as so little had been published. The classification, which was purely morphological, was based on minor differences in shape, technique, decoration, and colour. By the end of March 1928 Harden had picked out fifteen houses for detailed study. In mid-April he was much heartened to receive a seventy-page account from Amundsen in Karanis, describing the latest finds of glass, which confirmed many of his conclusions. Harden's work on the Karanis glass owed much, as he later acknowledged, to the advice of Amundsen. Harden's copy of his thesis is now in the British Museum Department of Greek and Roman Antiquities. He passed his oral examination on 28 May and sailed home from Montreal on 22 June.

Harden's thesis 'Roman glass from Kôm Aushîm in the Fayûm' was just a synopsis of his earliest thoughts on the Karanis glass and its significance. His visit to the excavations was arranged for October 1928–February 1929; he made only this one visit (not two as reported elsewhere). Having returned from America in July, he worked on glass in the British Museum, then left for the Fayûm. Harden was disappointed in his time at Karanis, as the main impetus of the excavations seems to have been lost following the death of Kelsey. More seriously, most of the work was on disturbed levels so he never saw much stratified glass actually being excavated. The dig finished mid-February 1929 and Harden visited Luxor and Aswan, before returning to take up his post as Assistant Keeper at the Ashmolean.

Between 1929 and 1935 Harden enlarged and revised his thesis, taking into account glass from excavations at Karanis up to 1929; the result, *Roman Glass from Karanis* (1936) was a startlingly original work, the first full-scale publication to treat systematically, and on a basis of all types of evidence, the glass from a single important site. Modestly described in the preface as a 'catalogue', it is rather a treatise on Roman glass from Egypt and, more importantly, a description and definition of the subject's fundamental methodology. It was a milestone and became a model for volumes such as Gladys Davidson's report on the Corinth glass[9] and Christoph Clairmont's volume on the glass vessels from Dura-Europos, on the Euphrates.[10] Clairmont acknowledged Harden's volume as a 'source of deep and profound inspiration'. The basic dating still stands but, as was pointed out by (Sir) Laurence Kirwan,[11] the end date of *c*.AD 460 is rather early. The text has stood the test of time and remains a standard work of reference.

## 1930s glass research

The Karanis glass had given Harden a felicitous start and, settled in Oxford from 1929, he soon became known as an authority on glass of Roman age in the West. Glass from excavations all over Britain was sent to Harden in confident expectation of meaningful reporting, resulting in a stream of contributions to excavation reports over the next fifty years.

Harden's first publications on glass, however, were reviews in 1930 of M. L. Trowbridge's *Philological Studies in Ancient Glass* (Urbana, 1930) in which he criticised her archaeological blunders, at the same time recommending the book as an indispensable compendium of literary and linguistic evidence. During the 1930s Harden combed the literature for references to Roman glass and was an avid explorer of existing collections in museums at home and abroad. Between August

---

[9] Gladys Davidson, *Corinth XII: The Minor Objects* (Princeton, 1952), pp. 76–122.

[10] Christoph W. Clairmont, *The Excavations at Dura-Europos: Final Report IV, Part 5: The Glass Vessels* (New Haven, 1963).

[11] Laurence P. Kirwan, review of D. B. Harden, *Roman Glass from Karanis* (1936), *Antiquaries Journal*, 17 (1937), 90–2.

1939, when the Ashmolean Museum objects were packed, and his departure to join the Ministry of Supply in September 1940, Harden spent much time in the Bodleian Library searching for glass references of all periods, thus consolidating his remarkable encyclopaedic knowledge.

## Major excavation reports

In 1947 he published a study of the glass from the 1930–9 excavations at Camulodunum: this essay, with its dual approach of studying glass from excavations in conjunction with material in museums, is the foundation of the study of first-century AD glass in the West. As Jenny Price comments[12] it 'was the first rigorous study of a large assemblage of glass from a Romano-British archaeological site to be published. . . . This report has remained an essential reference tool for all glass historians working on early-to-mid-first-century material and has been very influential for generations of students of Roman glass.' Another seminal publication of excavated material was Harden's 1971 report, with Jenny Price, on the glass from Fishbourne, which showed that the first colourless glass table wares in the Roman Empire started to appear between AD 65 and 70. This was absolutely new, and is still widely quoted.

## British Museum catalogue

In June 1946 Bernard Ashmole, FBA 1938, Keeper of the Department of Greek and Roman Antiquities at the British Museum, invited Harden to prepare a descriptive catalogue of its Greek and Roman glass. The Ashmolean released Harden for several periods to work in the BM. In 1953 he was awarded a Leverhulme Research Fellowship to study the BM glass in more depth: between January and May 1955 he travelled widely to obtain broader knowledge of the ancient glass in the eastern Mediterranean and North Africa. But, with his appointment to the London Museum in 1956, he had to postpone further work until after his retirement. From July 1971 until 1988 Harden spent two-thirds of his time in the BM producing a catalogue *raisonné*, with full discussions

---

[12] Hilary E. M. Cool and Jenny Price, *Roman Vessel Glass from Excavations in Colchester, 1971–85*, Colchester Archaeological Reports, 8 (1994), 1. This monograph is dedicated to the memory of Donald Harden in recognition of our debt to his scholarship.

of the historical and archaeological background. In 1974 Veronica Tatton-Brown was appointed as his Research Assistant, and the *Catalogue of Greek and Roman Glass in the British Museum: Volume I* was published in 1981. Between 1983 and 1987 Harden drafted the text for volume II, while Mrs Tatton-Brown wrote the catalogue entries. But already in 1979 she was being diverted to other tasks; Harden himself was busy keeping up his wide contacts, replying to letters, examining glass sent to him, and seeing visiting scholars. After the considerable work involved in 1986–7 in preparing his essays for the 'Glass of the Caesars' exhibition catalogue, he no longer went into the BM, so volumes II and III of the BM catalogue, although still in progress, have not yet appeared. When Harden left the BM, Martine Newby catalogued his glass papers, now in the BM archive.

## 1950s and 1960s research

Harden's reports (1959 and 1963, with Jocelyn Toynbee) on the Rothschild Lycurgus Cup were the basis for more recent assessments of cage cups. His researches culminated in three presidential addresses to the Royal Archaeological Institute, in 1967–9, on Pre-Roman, Roman, and Post-Roman glass. Harden was always willing to take new finds and other people's research into account and change his opinions when necessary. It is one of the hallmarks of his remarkable, broadly based scholarship that he was in touch with the leading practitioners of the subject throughout the world, both personally and in their publications. Zahn, Fremersdorf, Lamm, Fossing, Eisen, Morey, Trowbridge, Thorpe, Rademacher, Haberey, and Simonett are names which recur constantly throughout his correspondence and the bibliographies of his own work (as well as those of subsequent generations), and their research enhanced his own, while his insights often surpassed those of his sources.

During the late 1940s and early 1950s Harden began to think about glass from post-Roman contexts in Britain in relation to continental material, publishing a seminal article in 1950. In 1956 he expanded this in *Dark-Age Britain*, the Festschrift that he edited for Leeds, his former head at the Ashmolean. In the same year he took part in Ralegh Radford's excavation of a Saxon glasshouse at Glastonbury. In 1968 he was the leading member of a team who prepared the BM exhibition, 'Masterpieces of Glass'; Harden contributed notably to the catalogue and gave a magisterial survey of medieval glass in the West.

## Glass organisations

After the war Harden rapidly became recognised internationally. In 1950 he attended in London a meeting of international scholars working on glass, initiated by Ray Winfield Smith, the American collector whom Harden had known since 1935. In June the International Committee for Ancient Glass (ICAG) was formed, with national committees to provide support. Harden attended annual meetings in Belgium, Germany, and France, lectured at two of them and chaired meetings of the British Committee. As there was no central finance, the ICAG never made real progress, but it did allow scholars to meet.

In 1958 the Journées Internationales du Verre was founded by Joseph Philippe at Liège with the support of the local authority: this effectively replaced the now moribund ICAG; Harden was elected Vice-President, and, as the natural representative to speak on behalf of members, was President from 1968 until 1974.

Meanwhile, in the USA, the Corning Museum of Glass was opened in 1951. In 1957 Ray Smith published his catalogue of its exhibition 'Glass from the Ancient World', formed from his own collections. His short general history of ancient glass was largely based on discussions he had had with Harden over some twenty years. In 1959 the Museum started the *Journal of Glass Studies*; the 1975 volume was published in Harden's honour, with a short bibliography by Dorothy Charlesworth[13] and an appreciation by Robert Charleston.[14] In 1983 Harden became an Honorary Fellow of the Museum and was the first recipient of the Rakow Award. The paper he read is a masterly survey of the development of glass studies, providing the framework for many of the events recorded in this memoir.

In 1987, at the age of 86, Harden played a major role in mounting his crowning achievement, the ambitious international exhibition 'Glass of the Caesars' held in Cologne, Corning, London, and Rome, 1987–8, which combined unique objects from the Corning Museum, the British

[13] Dorothy Charlesworth, 'Bibliography of the works of Donald B. Harden', *Journal of Glass Studies*, 17 (1975), 14–22.
[14] Robert J. Charleston, 'In Honor of Donald B. Harden', *Journal of Glass Studies*, 17 (1975), 11–13.

Museum, the Römisch-Germanisches Museum in Cologne, and Italian museums. Harden contributed much of the introductory material for the catalogue, a model of its kind; as he said in the introduction, 'no item is, surely, worth including in an exhibition if it is downgraded by not being illustrated in the relevant catalogue.' During the exhibition the Society of Antiquaries of London held a seminar on Roman glass,[15] at which he made an endearing farewell speech, including the notable phrase 'as I said in 1933, and see no reason to change my mind'.

Harden was an inspiring presence behind the formation of the Bead Study Trust in 1980, and gave Peggy Guido a lot of support when she was setting it up. In the early years he was particularly helpful when the publication of regional catalogues of the Beck Collection was mooted.

## Ashmolean Museum: Assistant Keeper 1929–40

### Appointment

David Hogarth, Keeper of the Ashmolean since 1909, died on 6 November 1927. E. Thurlow Leeds, Assistant Keeper since 1908, was appointed Keeper and began to seek an assistant. Two letters from Stephen Glanville to Leeds suggest Harden for the post; Harden did not get wind of the possibility until July, writing to Leeds on 1 August 1928 'a post in the Ashmolean Museum certainly does appeal to me very much'. Glanville had suggested that Harden might work for a trial month at the Ashmolean before going to Egypt; Leeds agreed and Harden went to Oxford in August to organise their 400 Roman bronze pins and brooches, as well as Roman terracotta lamps. His work must have been satisfactory, as Leeds was prepared to wait for him to take up the post on his return from Egypt in April 1929. Harden was appointed as Assistant Keeper in the Department of Antiquities, for five years from 1 April. So started Harden's long professional museum career, which was to last over thirty-six years.

### Achievements at Oxford

Harden was well suited to the demands of a department which covered so wide a range of periods and civilisations. He wrote a short note on

---

[15] Martine Newby and Kenneth Painter (eds.), *Roman Glass: Two Centuries of Art and Invention*, Society of Antiquaries Occasional Paper, 13 (1991).

the glass from the Ashmolean/Field Museum excavations at Kish, in Iraq, in 1934, but it was clearly part of his duties to report also on the Sumerian and Sassanian pottery; his publication of the Sumerian pottery was a landmark for Middle Eastern pottery studies, considering the social aspects many years before these were generally recognised.

Harden never allowed the prehistory and history of Oxfordshire to be neglected. He regarded it as vitally important that the Ashmolean should be responsible for the investigation and excavation of local sites. He took part in several excavations including the Abingdon Anglo-Saxon cemetery in 1934, and the Ditchley Roman villa in 1935. Harden became Secretary of the Oxford Architectural and Historical Society in 1931, and, in 1936, was instrumental in launching its new periodical, *Oxoniensia*. Although his name does not appear, Harden was mainly responsible for the editing; he wrote the preface in volume I and the notes for the first four volumes. It was here that he developed the meticulous editorial skills for which he became highly respected, not least twenty years later when *Medieval Archaeology* was launched.

In 1939 Harden rearranged the Ashmolean's Near Eastern collection, but war clouds were looming: in March 1938 Leeds had arranged for selected antiquities to be stored at Chastleton House; on 25 August the Museum closed, and a band of staff and volunteers began packing under the direction of Harden. During the phoney war, Harden helped Grimes excavate a barrow on a new airfield at Stanton Harcourt, editing the report for publication in 1945.

## Marriage

Harden's first wife was Cecil Ursula Harriss, the eldest of three daughters of James Adolphus Harriss (1861–1919) and Caroline Prynne (1863–1942), both of Cornish origin. James Harriss had been a missionary in India before becoming Curate of Swansea, where Cecil was born on 18 July 1895; from 1906 until his death he was Perpetual Curate of St Andrew's, Oxford.

It was pure coincidence that both Donald's and Cecil's fathers were clergymen, as by this time neither went to church regularly. They were introduced by a friend in common, St John Gamlen, a solicitor at Lincoln's Inn, who had a lifelong interest in medieval antiquities. They were married on 6 July 1934. Their daughter, Georgina, was born 3 January 1936; she has inherited her father's editing instincts, albeit with different interests. A magazine editor and journalist, she has held a succession of editorial posts with *Vogue*. She married Anthony Boosey, of Boosey and Hawkes, in 1960.

Cecil was admired for her style, her perspicacity, and humour. Few realised that she often suffered physical pain as the result of a childhood accident. She took great pride in Donald's work, her devoted support giving him a confidence he had earlier lacked. She helped Donald with his publications, proof-reading and advising on style, which he greatly valued. Cecil enjoyed entertaining, and she and Donald were always respected for their generous hospitality (a rare talent in Oxford!).

## War Service 1940–5

### Warwick and London

Harden was released for government service on 31 August 1940, and joined the Ministry of Supply in Warwick Castle as a Temporary Principal in the Raw Materials Division, with responsibility for paper supplies: his great joke was that he kept the war effort going by supplying lavatory paper. The family moved to a flat in Warwick: one of their main memories soon after arriving was of enemy bombers flying over, and then seeing the sky red from fires burning in the Coventry raid. In 1941, his peacetime interests far from forgotten, Harden arranged archaeological lectures for his colleagues.

In June 1942, with the setting up of the Ministry of Production, Harden was transferred to London. From June 1943 for five months he had responsibility for leather during the visit of the United States Leather Mission; he was Secretary for all their joint meetings. He was promoted to Assistant Secretary in December.

With the start of the liberation of Europe, the Supplies to Liberated Areas Secretariat (SLAS) was set up in the Ministry of Production, with Harden as one of three Assistant Secretaries. He had responsibility for Italy and the Balkans.

### 1944 mission to Italy

Now came the most notable passage in Harden's Civil Service career: a secret mission to Italy in October 1944. The Hyde Park Declaration had been issued on 26 September, following a meeting between Churchill and Roosevelt at the President's home, stating that efforts were to be made to rebuild the Italian economy. A mission, comprising two Americans and two Britons, was sent to Italy to work out details with Allied Headquarters, in the Palace of Caserta near Naples, and the Allied Control Commission in Rome; this was to be done in consultation with Harold Macmillan, the British Resident Minister. The two Americans were from the Combined Civil Affairs Committee (CCAC) of the Combined Chiefs of Staff. The British Ambassador in Washington nominated Adam Denzil Marris, also on the CCAC, and described by Macmillan as 'a very clever man'. London designated Harden to represent the civilian departments.

Harden spent three weeks in Italy, from 8 October. He familiarised himself with the local position, prepared a path for the mission discussions, and had meetings with Macmillan. Macmillan's *War Diaries* record Harden's description of a 'terrific dispute going on in London about Italian civil affairs and a raging interdepartmental war—chiefly between the War Office and the F.O.' On 15 October the mission drove to Rome with Sir Anthony Rumbold, Macmillan's Second Secretary; details of the rehabilitation programme were worked out, and the mission returned to Naples on 22 October. The next day it drafted the proposals for supplies to Italy: Harden did this, with Rumbold's help.

Macmillan was very selective in his diaries and seems to have regarded Harden as a background civil servant figure. But Harden's diary demonstrates that he played an important part in the mission. He records that Macmillan agreed the drafts; Macmillan, however, commented in his diary that they seemed rather complicated and he would try to redraft them. The rest of the story comes from Macmillan, who writes on 25 October, 'I redrafted the Italian supply stuff for tomorrow's meeting in Rome', and then, in Rome, 'After a very good and sensible discussion, *all* my plans and drafts were approved. Now for action in London and Washington!' In adopting the mission's results as his own, Macmillan pays a perhaps unintended compliment to Harden's efforts. Harden stayed on at Caserta for another week, to assess local conditions. He kept to his job very resolutely, rarely diverting to archaeology.

Following his return to London, Harden continued for nearly another year with the SLAS, his responsibilities extending to Romania and Bulgaria and later to Scandinavia, the Netherlands, Germany and Austria. He was released on 1 October to take up his new post at the Ashmolean. Harold Macmillan's official biographer, Alistair Horne, has described how Macmillan was made by the Second World War: sent by

Churchill to North Africa, he never looked back; so, too, did Harden's career prosper, the administrative expertise then developed bearing fruit in many of his future endeavours.

## Ashmolean Museum: Keeper of Antiquities 1945–56

Leeds should have retired as Keeper of the Museum in 1942, but he kept the Museum going through the war, despite ill health. He wrote on 21 December 1943, on the occasion of Harden's promotion to Assistant Secretary, 'your promotion from what may be termed civilian inefficiency to such heights of competence will unquestionably stand you in very good stead, for this trade of ours does need plenty of calm business-like capacity which I have never possessed'. Leeds clearly hoped that Harden would succeed him as Keeper of the Department of Antiquities, which he held jointly with the Keepership of the whole museum. Harden applied for the post of Keeper of Antiquities in March 1945 and was duly appointed.

Harden had to face the major task of reorganisation; he undertook this with energy and commitment. Harden did most of his research at home, as he did not have time while he was in the museum: he often stayed after hours chatting with the staff, catching up with administration and walking round to discuss improvements. He had many contacts with foreign scholars, but Oxford dons were relatively rare visitors to the museum. Harden helped young people in the museum; visits to schools for lectures, and from schools to the museum, were encouraged. He was President of the Oxford Architectural and Historical Society 1952–5 and a Vice-President until 1990.

## London Museum: Director 1956–70

### Appointment

The question of a successor to Gordon Childe as Director of the University of London Institute of Archaeology in 1955 was a contentious one. The Chairman of the Directorship Committee, Sidney Wooldridge, wrote to Harden, asking, 'would you be willing to consider putting forward your name, probably we will agree to recommend you'. However, he had to report on 6 October that Peter Grimes,

Director of the London Museum, had been appointed, after a long and troublesome debate, by a majority vote.

Ironically, six months later Grimes wrote to Harden that he was 'inviting a small number of individuals to submit themselves for interview' for the post of Director of the London Museum, then in Kensington Palace. Harden was appointed and took up the Directorship on 1 December 1956, on the understanding that the Trustees would support his aim to amalgamate the London and Guildhall museums.

## The Museum of London

Harden proved to be the right man for the job: very receptive to new ideas; a great committee-man, most important at this juncture of the museum's history; and never discouraged by the numerous setbacks on the long road towards amalgamation. His friendship with Norman Cook, Keeper 1950 and, from 1966, Director of the Guildhall Museum, led them to collaborate in establishing the new Museum of London. Harden's skills in administration and committee work suited him to take part in the complicated negotiations.

The first plans were made in February 1959, and a draft constitution was approved in 1961. In 1964 the architects, Philip Powell and John Moya, were chosen, and a Museum of London Bill prepared. The Act was passed in June 1965, and Harden was appointed Acting Director of the new Museum of London, working from Kensington Palace. Lord Harcourt was appointed Chairman of the Board of Governors. Harden worked closely with his Chairman, whom he had known since he came to London. Unfortunately, frustrating bureaucratic delays held up the project. In Harden's words, it suddenly entered into 'a state of suspended animation'. In December 1968 new sketch plans were ready, but construction could not start until April 1971, after Harden had retired in June 1970. The Guildhall and London museums were finally amalgamated on 1 June 1975.

Harden raised the London Museum's attendances from 158,000 in 1959 to 290,000 in 1970, an increase of over eighty per cent. This was helped by several important exhibitions and temporary displays. He managed to persuade the Treasury to raise the grant for purchases from £3,000 to £8,000 in 1970, and extracted from that body an increase in staff of one-third; this made it possible to set up a Schools Service and appoint a Field Officer.

## Second marriage

Harden's first wife, Cecil, died in December 1963. In May 1963 Donald and Cecil had been on a Swan Hellenic cruise, with Donald as one of the lecturers, and they had been booked to go on another in May 1964; Donald was understandably loath to go alone but was persuaded to, especially by his daughter Georgina. On this cruise he met the McDonald family: Dorothy May, her sister, brother-in-law, and niece. Dorothy was born in 1911, the elder daughter of Daniel Herbert McDonald, a chartered accountant in Melbourne; she was the co-owner of the Ormiston School for Girls in Melbourne. Dorothy and Donald immediately formed a rapport; the McDonalds came on to London after the cruise and Dorothy became engaged to Donald.

They were married on 1 April 1965. For nearly thirty years Dorothy looked after Donald, and was very supportive of him; she discouraged his traditional pattern of retiring to his study after dinner. She persuaded Donald to take up church-going again, worshipping at St Mary's, Bryanston Square, where he became a churchwarden. Dorothy died eight months after Donald, in December 1994.

## Honours and Appointments

Harden was appointed OBE in the 1956 New Year Honours, while still at the Ashmolean, and was advanced to CBE in the Queen's Birthday List of 1969. He was elected an Honorary Fellow of the British Academy in July 1987. He was a member of the Ancient Monuments Board for England 1959–74 and of the Royal Commission on Historical Monuments for England 1963–71. He was a member of the German Archaeological Institute from 1960 and was appointed to the Executive Committee of the British School of Archaeology in Iraq, representing the Society of Antiquaries of London, 1948–84; he was also a member of the Council of Management of the British Institute of Archaeology at Ankara, representing the Society for the Promotion of Roman Studies, from the foundation of the Institute in 1948 until 1964. He was on the Council of the British School in Jerusalem from 1955 and a member of the Faculty of the British School at Rome 1957–61. Harden was external examiner for several University Archaeological Departments and external assessor of Civil Service Appointments Boards for posts in the Ancient Monuments Inspectorate and in the Royal Commission on

Historical Monuments for England: all reflect his wide interests and influence in the 1950s and 1960s.

## Archaeological Organisations

Harden joined the *Museums Association* in 1933 and, throughout his career, was a dedicated supporter. He was particularly concerned with the training of museum staff: in 1947 he set out the need for a proper scheme of professional education and training, which has still not totally come to pass. He was Secretary of the Association 1949–54 and Chairman of the Educational Committee 1954–9; he edited the Association's *Handbook for Museum Curators*. He was President 1960–4 and Chairman 1968–70 of the Directors' Conference of National Museums.

The *Carnegie UK Trust* (CUKT) began to make improvement grants to museums in 1925. Harden was appointed a committee member in 1950, and was Chairman 1961–9, of the joint Museums Association/ CUKT Committee that helped the CUKT to administer these grants; he carried out many museum inspections.

Harden attended meetings of the *British Association for the Advancement of Science* (BAAS), Section H Anthropology, for forty years. After the war, Section H was, for a dozen years or so, renamed Anthropology and Archaeology at Harden's instigation; at the first post-war meeting in 1947 he delivered a paper on Romano-Egyptian lamps, and for the next five meetings he was Recorder of Section H. In 1950 he returned to his Punic interest, lecturing on Maltese archaeology. He was Section H representative on the Council of the BAAS, 1950–6. For the Oxford meeting in 1954, Harden was Chairman of the Publication Sub-Committee which arranged publication of *The Oxford Region: A Scientific and Historical Survey*. Harden's time at the BAAS culminated in 1955 when he was President of Section H. In his presidential address on 'Anthropology: a scientific unity' he argued, diplomatically using the phrase 'we anthropologists', for archaeology and anthropology to come together at a time when they were drifting apart. Harden did another stint on Council 1962–5. His main achievement at the BAAS was in bringing younger people on to the Section H Committee.

Harden was elected a Fellow of the *Society of Antiquaries of London* in March 1944, having been proposed by Leeds. For forty years there was hardly a volume of the *Antiquaries Journal* which did not contain some reference to his giving lectures, exhibiting at ballots, and publishing papers and reviews. Sir James Mann appointed him as his first choice for Vice-President in 1949; he served on the Council and as Vice-President until 1953. He had the rare honour of being appointed a Vice-President for a second term, 1964–7. Harden was the longest serving member of the Publications Committee. His contributions to committees were distinguished by a shrewd and well-balanced approach, sometimes trenchantly expressed. Harden was presented with the Society's Gold Medal in 1977, followed by a dinner in his honour. His last major appearance at the Antiquaries was at the 1987 seminar on Roman glass, which was marked by a party at Burlington House, at which, dapper and bow-tied, he spoke with undimmed sprightliness. His final visit to the Antiquaries was for a tea-party on his ninetieth birthday in 1991.

Following his long editorship of *Oxoniensia*, his editing of *Dark-Age Britain* confirmed his editorial expertise. So when (Sir) David Wilson and I were discussing the formation of a medieval society, it seemed natural to turn to Harden. He was immediately enthusiastic and wrote on 11 November 1956, 'I have long had it in mind that a new periodical covering the later British fields of archaeology is necessary'. Harden obtained the support of the establishment, including the Society of Antiquaries. He persuaded its President, Sir Mortimer Wheeler, to chair the initial meetings, enabling the *Society for Medieval Archaeology* (SMA) to be formed in a period of less than six months. The first paper in the first volume of the new journal was an article by Thurlow Leeds.[16] His editorship of *Medieval Archaeology* created a journal of international stature; he could take justifiable pride in its being adopted by Professor Michel de Bouard, in 1971, as the model for its French counterpart *Archéologie Médiévale*. Harden had a real love of the editorial role, and would talk freely of the pleasures and problems involved in the task. He was President of the SMA 1975–7.

Harden was elected as second President, 1950–4, of the *Council for British Archaeology*. He was an efficient President, who put the interests of the Council before his own; with the administrative experience of his wartime days, he did a great deal to get things done. His 1952 presidential address stressed the importance of the co-ordination and co-operation of local archaeological societies, following the Council's

---

[16] The late E. Thurlow Leeds, ed. Sonia Chadwick, 'Notes on Jutish art in Kent between 450 and 575', *Medieval Archaeology*, 1 (1957), 5–26.

*Survey and Policy of Field Research.*[17] He pointed out that it was easy to plan, but hard to implement, research without the necessary drive. This led to the formation of six Research Committees in 1953, setting the tone of the CBA for forty years.

Harden became a member of the *London and Middlesex Archaeological Society* in 1957. He was elected to the Council the same year and was President 1959–65. His five presidential addresses covered the wide range of his interests: the London Museum; prehistoric trade between Britain and the Mediterranean; ancient glass-makers; the Phoenicians; and the modern museum.

He also joined the *Royal Archaeological Institute* in 1956. He was a member of the Executive Committee 1960–3, a Vice-President 1963–6, and President 1966–9.

## An Appreciation

All through his life Harden's encouragement of young people was particularly marked. Arnold Taylor, who went up to St John's College in 1930, recalls that to 'a young committee member of the Oxford University Archaeological Society, Harden, together with his ever-revered master at the Ashmolean, Thurlow Leeds, and Nowell Myres, Student of Christ Church, were the three senior members of the university who, by their experience and contacts, linked the generality of the Society's undergraduate membership to the active outside world of archaeology and antiquities. My abiding memory of Dr Harden, as I would then have spoken of him, is of his friendliness and approachability.' Martyn Jope recalls that 'From 1936 the Ashmolean with Harden seemed to provide a second home in Oxford where I was made welcome at any time.'

The number of similar cases must be almost endless. It must suffice to record my own experience. I first met Harden at the British Association meeting in 1948, when I was about to go up to Cambridge to read archaeology. From this point Harden was the main mentor in my career. He encouraged me to take up medieval research, and later recommended that I apply for a job in the then Ministry of Works. At my interview he was the external assessor: by drawing me out on my

---

[17] Council for British Archaeology, *Survey and Policy of Field Research in the Archaeology of Great Britain* (London, 1948).

interest in deserted medieval villages, and later asking me to lecture at the BAAS meeting in 1952, he concentrated my thoughts and persuaded me to take up this subject as a major research topic. This led to the formation of the Deserted Medieval Village Research Group and forty years of excavation at Wharram Percy.

Although Harden encouraged students in many subjects, it was those interested in glass who benefited most. Robert Charleston, when he went up to New College in 1935, had a consuming interest in glass, which was actively encouraged by Harden. After the war, Dorothy Charlesworth came up to Somerville; at Harden's suggestion, she took up the study of ancient glass, and worked for him at Oxford and London. She went on to publish many reports on excavated Roman glass. Jenny Price had always been interested in glass as her family were glass-workers in Stourbridge; Harden heard about her 1966 work on the glass from Masada and invited her to help him with the Fishbourne report; 'Harden was very welcoming to me, and spent a lot of time discussing my material. More than anyone else, Harden was my patron and supporter during my postgraduate years and my early career in archaeology.'

When Harden started reporting on glass in the 1930s he was the only English-speaking expert. The fact that there are now so many practitioners is due entirely to his prompting of others to take up the study of glass, and his success in establishing the principles of classification, description and dating. There can be no more fitting tribute than the following appreciation by Martyn Jope, who knew Harden for nearly sixty years:

Harden served archaeology very well in many ways. His major contribution to archaeological scholarship must be seen in his lifelong topic of research, ancient glass; in this he was an acknowledged authority world-wide, and one whose *oeuvres* still command full respect. From his first introduction to ancient glass as a worthwhile research topic at Ann Arbor, Harden proved to have an innate feel for this elusive and fascinating material. His first major work, the account of the glass found during the first five seasons' work at Karanis, is a consummate and gracious volume, set forth with great clarity. Harden seemed from the start to have an instinctive faith in ancient glass as a meaningful cultural and dating index, and he set out on a long journey to use it as such in the service of pre- and proto-history. He soon realised that knowledge of changes in composition and manufacturing processes was much to be desired, but after a few years he began to see that a very large data-bank of element analysis would be needed. He must have foreseen that this could hardly come in his time (long though it turned out to be), and that he had therefore to formulate and apply his own judgement criteria. By great good fortune his mind proved exactly suited to the task.

What were the special attributes which gave Harden his never-failing masterly feeling for glass? He had an empathy with this infinitely malleable material, its texture, its reflections and its evanescent colours. He was fortunate in serving his apprenticeship with a self-contained body of material from a unitary source like Karanis; his years of study of this gave him the necessary discipline. He had a quiet mind, calm and unrufflable, such as is perhaps responsible for the cream among all scholarship. Harden easily made human contacts and soon became internationally known, so that he acquired a very wide experience of glass and glass study in many countries. His work on glass has firmly held its authority; if we wish occasionally to modify a conclusion, it is but to take account of new evidence. Harden was responsible for showing that glass can be used as a highly meaningful tool for the study and dating of human civilisations, a view being now very much enforced by the conclusions from current refined technology of element analysis.

Robert Charleston, in his 1975 appreciation[18] described a wise and generous counsellor of outstanding candour and common sense, practical and energetic; a generous host; a loyal and warm-hearted friend. 'The unaffected laughter without malice, the white hair, the pipe, the bow tie, are all treasures in affectionate recollection by his many friends.'

Harden died on 13 April 1994, aged 92. The funeral service was held at St Mary's, Bryanston Square, on 20 April. A memorial service was held in St James's, Piccadilly, on 11 October 1994. The address was given by Michael Robbins, whose own distinguished career in transport had been combined with archaeological society and museum positions; he joined the Board of Governors of the Museum of London in 1968, just before Harden retired. He was also an Old Westminster, which gave him a pleasing bond with Harden. Robbins summed up Donald Harden's long and fulfilled career when he concluded 'we saw the man's extraordinary industry, his decent humility in the face of

---

[18] See above, n. 14.

evidence, his helpfulness and courtesy to colleagues and students, his cheerfulness in private life. For those qualities we all respected him; as for those of us who had the good fortune to know him at all well, we indeed loved him'.

JOHN G. HURST
*Fellow of the Academy*

*Note.* I am greatly indebted to Harden's daughter, Georgina Boosey, for her help and for making available the family history and her father's papers; also to the Society of Antiquaries for allowing access to Harden's diaries, notebooks and correspondence (MS 967). I am grateful for the contributions and other help from his colleagues, particularly Kenneth Painter, Jenny Price and Veronica Tatton-Brown on glass, and generally Donald Bailey, Beatrice de Cardi, Joan Clarke, Max Hebditch, Marjorie Hutchinson, Jocelyn Morris, Michael Robbins, Roger Moorey, and Arnold Taylor. I am also indebted to Martyn Jope for his tribute to Harden's leading role in glass studies, and for other material.

The completion of this memoir would not have been possible without the continued help of my colleague from the Wharram Percy Research Project, Richard T. Porter, who not only researched several topics (especially the background to Harden's 1944 mission to Italy) but also took pains to correct my drafts and edit down the large amount of information collected. I am grateful to my typist, Wendy Gilding. A more detailed text, of some 21,000 words, together with background material, is in the possession of Mrs Boosey; there are also copies of the detailed text in the libraries of the British Academy and the Society of Antiquaries of London.

Obituaries appeared in the *Daily Telegraph*, 21 April 1994; the *Guardian*, 3 June 1994, by Jenny Price; the *Independent*, 29 April 1994, by Kenneth Painter and Hugh Thompson; *The Times*, 3 May 1994, by Robert Charleston; other obituaries include: *Oxoniensia*, 59 (1994), iii–iv, by Joan Clarke, stressing Harden's time in Oxford; *Journal of Glass Studies*, 36 (1994), 143, by David Whitehouse; *Medieval Archaeology*, 38 (1994), 182–3 and *Medieval Settlement Research Group Annual Report*, 9 (1994), 52, by John Hurst; *British Archaeological News*, NS, 14 (June 1994) 11, by Jenny Price.

In 1975 Dorothy Charlesworth published a basic bibliography of Harden's publications in the *Journal of Glass Studies*, 17 (1975), 14–22. This was followed in 1991 by a full bibliography of his research papers, compiled by Martine Newby, in M. Newby and K. Painter (eds.), *Roman Glass: Two Centuries of Art and Invention*, Society of Antiquaries Occasional Paper, 13 (1991), xi–xxix. Full details of the dated references given in this memoir to Harden's publications will be found in this 1991 bibliography.

RAGNHILD HATTON

*Proceedings of the British Academy*, **94**, 543–553

# Ragnhild Marie Hatton
# 1913–1995

THE DEATH ON 16 May 1995 of Professor Ragnhild Hatton has deprived us of one of the foremost historians of early modern Europe. Ragnhild Marie Hanssen was born on 10 February 1913 in the Norwegian port of Bergen, a centre of trade and shipping which had always had far-flung international contacts and been exposed to a wide range of foreign influences. This relatively cosmopolitan background was to influence permanently the tone and direction of her life, making her always markedly international in her interests. Yet though she spent the whole of her working life in Great Britain (apart from numerous though usually relatively short visits to the United States in her later years) she retained always many of the characteristics—forthrightness, good humour, and generosity—of her Norwegian ancestry. She came from a well-to-do family with shipping interests. After ten years at a Norwegian private school for girls and three at the Bergen Katedralskole, where she was a gold medallist, she entered the University of Oslo in 1932 and graduated from it with a master's degree in 1936. By then, although she had at first contemplated a career in medicine, it was clear that history was to be her dominant intellectual interest. In the same year she married Harry Hatton. This not merely made her a British subject by marriage but was the beginning of a partnership whose obvious happiness impressed all who knew her and which was broken, after more than half a century, only by the death of her husband in 1989. The marriage was soon followed by the birth of two sons.

The demands of motherhood and the disruption of the war years

© The British Academy 1997.

meant that an academic career had to be postponed for a considerable time; but her deep interest in her subject and the energy and drive which she possessed in such full measure (and which sometimes threatened to intimidate those whose acquaintance with her was relatively superficial) ensured that her gifts then found full if slightly belated expression. In 1949 she was awarded a Ph.D. by the University of London; and throughout her life she was to feel and express gratitude to two of her teachers at University College: Professor G. J. Renier who supervised her graduate work, and Professor Mark Thomson. Both of these were strong (in the case of Renier it might perhaps be said eccentric) personalities; and both had considerable and enduring influence on her. In the same year she was appointed to an assistant lectureship in the London School of Economics, the institution to which she was to contribute so much and to which she remained faithful for three decades until her retirement in 1980.

LSE was then entering a period of vigorous expansion; but like British academic life in general it had still not recovered completely from the effects of the war. Moreover, neither the field in which the young assistant lecturer was beginning to be a specialist, the history of early modern Europe, nor the general approach to history which she was beginning to develop, wide-ranging and with strong cultural and biographical interests, had as yet put down roots in the school, in spite of all its intellectual energy and open-mindedness. In economic and social history there was already a distinguished record of achievement founded on the work of outstanding scholars—R. H. Tawney, Eileen Power, T. S. Ashton, and the younger F. J. Fisher. The international relations of the nineteenth and early twentieth centuries were in the capable hands of Sir Charles Webster; but though a commanding figure he was a somewhat remote one, often taken away from the school by government business. (However Professor Hatton found him noticeably, even surprisingly, understanding of the problems facing a woman teacher who was also bringing up a young family: she always remembered him with affection.) There was much first-class teaching at LSE; but a rounded and balanced history degree of the kind available in British universities in general and in other colleges of the University of London was still only a small element in the work of the school. It was an important aspect of Ragnhild Hatton's achievement to play a leading part in developing the role of political, diplomatic and intellectual history at LSE and to make it one of the leading centres in Britain for the study of the history of international relations. Her progress up the academic ladder was steady—Lecturer in 1950, Reader in 1958, and finally Professor of International History in 1968.

She contributed to LSE and to the world of historical studies both through teaching and through research, writing, and publication. In the essential and often time-consuming tasks of administration also she took her full share. She was a conscientious member of LSE committees and of the university Board of Studies in History. In 1968, when student unrest seemed for a moment to pose a significant threat to the functioning of the college as a teaching organism, she was one of a small group to whom the then director, Sir Walter Adams, delegated considerable powers to act, if necessary, on his behalf—a convincing tribute to the reputation for balance and common sense which she had by then earned. In 1974–8 she acted as Dean of the Faculty of Arts, an essentially honorary post in whose ceremonial aspects she none the less took much pleasure. Yet to her, all this was always secondary. She was a remarkable teacher and an outstanding scholar and writer. It was in these fields that she made and deserved her reputation.

As a teacher she conveyed above all an impression of energy, an energy which at times could appear almost overwhelming. A striking appearance, a loud voice, a ready smile and great personal charm, a considerable physical presence, and an obvious desire to communicate the information and ideas which so fascinated her, all combined to give her some of the aura of a Valkyrie, though always a benevolent one. More than any other university teacher I have known, in an experience extending over four decades, she obviously and strenuously wanted her students to learn. She even resorted occasionally to the dangerous expedient of lending them books of her own (which were almost always, though I think not quite invariably, returned). With her graduate students in particular she took immense trouble. Draft chapters were read and corrected with great care and returned, with a speed few supervisors then or now could match, accompanied by copious comments and suggestions for improvements, usually typed in her own distinctive and somewhat erratic style. She had also an ability to treat every aspiring young doctoral candidate as an individual, with needs and problems of his or her own which called for individual treatment. Over the years, as they became established in the academic world and built up significant bodies of published work of their own, her better graduate students came to form what can, without excessive stretching of the term, be called a definable school of writers on the history of early modern Europe. They included H. M. Scott, Derek McKay,

H. L. A. Dunthorne, and Peter Barber. Her interest in and kindness to students in a non-academic context also impressed all who knew her. For many years she and her husband did much to encourage the LSE sailing club; and her hospitality was remarkable and widely renowned. The charming though rather inconvenient house in Campden Street which she and Harry occupied for most of their married life saw much generous entertaining, in which her very considerable talents as a cook played an important role, and from which her colleagues bene-fited at least as much as her students.

Yet it is, inevitably, as a researcher and writer that she will be remembered by those who did not know her personally. In some ways she was a thorough subscriber to the now dominant drive towards specialisation in historical research. She had an active interest in the history of the Baltic in the nineteenth century, supervised a number of graduate students working in the area and probably contemplated a book on the movement for Scandinavian union which was strong in the middle decades of the century. But it is by her writing on the half-century from 1680 to 1730, the period which she made her own and on which she became an acknowledged expert, that she will be remembered. Within that period she ranged remarkably widely. At different times she threw light on the history of many different parts of Europe and several very different leading individuals. Her interests embraced the whole continent: she never confined herself to a single country or even any single region of Europe. Her Norwegian background gave her, as the native of a small and traditionally neutral country, a freedom from national prejudices and the ability to take a cosmopolitan and supra-national view of the great-power struggles which bulked large in much of her writing. Her command of languages, to which her Nordic origins again undoubtedly contributed, was wide, impressively so to colleagues too often confined to French and a little barely-adequate German. Her range of personal contacts with European and American scholars was remarkable and hardly to be equalled by any other of her British academic contemporaries: the seminar in the international his-tory of the seventeenth and eighteenth centuries which for many years she conducted at the Institute of Historical Research allowed her to bring to London many foreign scholars who would otherwise have remained mere names to her graduate students and even her academic colleagues, an interchange which had stimulating effects on both sides. Her generous and outgoing personality made her a significant link between a British historical world still often somewhat insular and a wider one; and many of the scholars she invited to London were or soon became her personal friends. Moreover, though her teaching at LSE was concerned with international relations and her own interests drew her in that direction, the seminar interpreted that term in a very liberal sense, so that a remarkable range of topics in government, political ideas and even the history of religion figured in the papers it heard and the discussions which followed.

Her first published book, *Diplomatic Relations between Great Britain and the Dutch Republic, 1714–21* (London, 1950), a printed version of her Ph.D. thesis, was merely a foretaste of what was to come. A relatively narrow subject treated in great and meticulous detail, a text dense with information and lavishly equipped with footnotes, published in a small edition for the Anglo-Netherlands Society, the book is a good example of the printed thesis, a genre more common in the 1950s than the harsh realities of publishing make it today. Yet even here there were indications of the width of view which was to mark all her work. As well as diplomatic relations in a limited and conventional sense, the study of negotiations, treaties and alliances, the thesis gave considerable attention to the way in which the relations of states were influenced by the physical difficulties of communication between them in that age, and by their efforts to gather intelligence on each other's policies and dominant personalities. Information-gathering of this kind was a subject which never ceased to interest her. Four years later there appeared in Stockholm a small documentary publication, *Captain James Jeffereyes' Letters from the Swedish Army, 1707–09*, which again was of specialised and rather limited interest, though presented with the thoroughness and scholarship which was to mark all her writing.

Already, however, she was hard at work on the book which was to make her name, the magisterial biography *Charles XII of Sweden* (London, 1968; New York, 1969). Charles, the warrior-king of Sweden and perhaps the most spectacular and dramatic ruler of his age, has also been the most sharply criticised. For generations he had inspired a very extensive and often highly polemical literature in Swedish; but no large-scale and up-to-date treatment of his life existed in English and even Swedish historians had tended to shy away from the perils and temptations of a full-scale biography. The book therefore filled an important gap in the historiography of the early eighteenth century, and its appearance was an event of importance. Professor Hatton made no secret of her admiration for the king, and may now and then have been somewhat too willing to give him the benefit of any doubt as to the wisdom of his actions—for example, in her discussion of the peace proposals made to him in 1707 by his great adversary, Peter the Great of Russia, and his rejection of them. Nevertheless, she was always fair in her judgements, neither ignoring the arguments of Charles's critics nor glossing over his failings and weaknesses. In particular she showed that he was a good deal more than the unreflecting and narrow-minded militarist of most conventional accounts and that he had a real interest in improving the Swedish administrative system which, in more favourable circumstances, might have allowed him to rank as an early 'enlightened despot'. Large in scale, balanced in its conclusions and based on extremely wide knowledge of the huge Swedish historical literature, this book broke new ground in the English-speaking world and established Professor Hatton's reputation as one of the leading historians of early modern Europe. Its appearance in a Swedish translation (not, a little surprisingly, until 1985) was an inevitable recognition of its importance.

Almost simultaneously she showed the range of her interests and knowledge by publishing another book, very different in scale and subject-matter, her *Europe in the Age of Louis XIV* (London, 1969; French trans., Paris, 1970). Some good judges consider this her best book, or at least her most characteristic one. A brief treatment of a very large subject, it shows more than anything else she wrote the breadth of her interests. Its discussion of the cultural life of the age, stimulating and penetrating given its small compass and one of the best sections of the book, is supplemented by a wide and varied selection of illustrations, most of them chosen by herself. The depth of reading in a wide range of languages on which the book is based is again unmistakable and very impressive. As one reviewer pointed out, it is 'that rare thing, a truly European history of Europe'. In its structure and emphases it also reveals her personal interests and even idiosyncracies. Throughout it shows her concentration on the individual, whether monarch or peasant, on his beliefs, assumptions and reactions to the demands of his age, rather than on the over-arching impersonal forces which to so many scholars now seem the essential motor driving history. A view of history which was impersonal and purely analytical, and therefore almost inevitably to some extent quantitative, never held any attractions for her: it is noticeable that the book, though it shows her interest in social history and the day to day life of individuals, pays little attention to economic history. It can be argued that in this respect her view of her subject was traditional, even old-fashioned. She realised that the

*Annales* school in France and its admirers had made important contributions to the way in which history was studied and written, for though she wrote little on historiography she thought deeply about it; but for her the detective work which is an essential part of the historian's craft was at its most absorbing when it was applied to the life of a specific individual.

The same strengths and limitations can be seen in her next book, *Louis XIV and his World* (London, 1972). Here again personalities, sketched vividly but with balance, are central, while the more impersonal forces which made up the environment in which they had to act receive much less attention. The book, understandably in view of its title, is focused very much on Louis himself, and his personal and family life; and once more, as in the case of Charles XII, Professor Hatton's sympathy with the central character in her story is apparent. This sympathy never becomes partisanship; but it may be argued that in her discussion of the revocation of the Edict of Nantes in 1685 she is again inclined to give Louis the benefit of any possible doubts, and that she perhaps overstates his moderation in the complex negotiations of 1698–1700 over the Spanish Succession. Nevertheless, wide-ranging knowledge, a continual search for fairness and balance, and warm human sympathies are evident throughout. In one important respect, moreover, she helped to spread a more realistic view of the Sun King. She was one of the first historians in the English-speaking world to throw doubt on the traditional view of the French monarchy in the seventeenth century as increasingly absolutist, and to stress the gulf which usually existed between the claims of royal propagandists and the limits which local, corporate and traditional rights set to the effective exercise of royal power. The book also showed that her interests were now broadening to include a notable one in the courts of rulers and their political and social significence. It was only fitting that she was asked, a few years later, to write the chapter on Louis in the composite volume edited by Professor A. G. Dickens, *The Courts of Europe: Politics, Patronage and Royalty, 1400–1800* (London, 1977).

Her work on Louis XIV, to her considerable pleasure, allowed her to indulge an interest which meant much to her—that in the use of illustrations, very often chosen by herself, as a means of making a period or a personality come alive for the general reader and even for the relatively expert one. She always believed, as she said in a published lecture, that 'much can be forgiven for good illustrations' and spent much time and effort in seeing that, when publishers permitted, her own were as good as possible. To her, one of the joys of the biographical approach to history, as she openly admitted, was that it gave her an excuse for visiting many possible sources of illustrations—galleries, palaces and collections of all kinds. Artefacts (a term she disliked) such as pictures, ceramics, tapestries, and jewellery, were to her important guides to the assumptions and outlooks of the groups which ruled early modern Europe. The economic pressures which, as time went on, forced even those publishers willing to contemplate the inclusion of illustrations in their books to reduce their number and increasingly to shy away from the use of colour were a source of real regret to her.

Professor Hatton's last large-scale work, her *George I: Elector and King* (London and Cambridge, Mass., 1978; German trans. Frankfurt, 1982) has many of the characteristics of her earlier publications. Like her *Charles XII*, it is a biography, but a biography of a ruler whose historical importance had not hitherto been reflected in the treatment of him by English-speaking historians (or indeed in the case of George I by historians writing in any language). Her desire to present a full and balanced picture of a distinct personality can be seen in the fact that a large part of the book, well over one-third, deals with George as elector of Hanover, before he rose to a new level of importance by becoming king of England in 1714. Again, the width of view and depth of research are unmistakable; and in this case the use of a wide range of archives, in different countries and languages, is particularly important. George I was never popular with his English and still less with his Scottish subjects; and until the appearance of Professor Hatton's book this meant that his reputation had been influenced excessively by the comments, usually unfavourable and sometimes downright spiteful, of contemporary writers of memoirs and diaries. From this her work rescued him once and for all. As with Charles XII and Louis XIV, her sympathy with her subject, that continual and often fruitful temptation of the biographer, is apparent; but as always it is kept within bounds and tempered by an essential objectivity and sense of balance. In one important respect in particular this sympathy had a constructive result. Professor Hatton showed convincingly that in Britain George ruled as well as reigned and was far from being as ineffective, as much of a nonentity, as traditional accounts had tended to make him.

Her books, therefore, make up an impressive body of work, the product of sustained effort and meticulous research extending over four decades. But she was also an energetic and painstaking editor of the work of others: none of her contemporaries in the historical world did more to inspire and see into published form collections of essays by different authors, always of high quality and usually focused on a relatively well-defined theme or issue. The first of these, *William III and Louis XIV: Essays 1680–1720 by and for Mark A. Thomson* (Liverpool and Toronto, 1968), which she edited together with her friend Professor John Bromley, was a generous albeit posthumous payment of the debt which she always felt she owed Professor Thomson. This collection also included one of the most important of her own essays, 'Gratifications and foreign policy: Anglo-French rivalry in Sweden during the Nine Years War'. In this she showed that the presents and payments to ministers and favourites given by foreign governments, so widespread a feature of international relations in early modern Europe, which had usually been written off by historians as mere crude bribery, were in fact something considerably more subtle and nuanced and a more or less recognised part of the diplomacy of that age. Two years later there appeared the more wide-ranging and less clearly focused *Studies in Diplomatic History: Essays in Memory of David Bayne Horn*, co-edited with Professor M. S. Anderson (London, 1970), and this in turn by two further collections; *Louis XIV and Europe* (London, 1976) and *Louis XIV and Absolutism* (London, 1976). Both of these were important, most of all in making accessible to the English-speaking world work by French scholars which might not otherwise have been given the attention it deserved. The second in particular brought together essays, some of them commissioned for the volume, by an impressive range of experts. These threw light not merely on such general questions as the definition of absolutism and its development in seventeenth-century France but also on the court and intellectual development of Louis, the administrative mechanisms through which he ruled and different aspects of the economic history of his reign. Such a collection illustrated once more Professor Hatton's width of interest within her chosen period, her truly European outlook on her subject, and her remarkably wide range of European academic contacts. Her most ambitious undertaking as an editor, however, was to inspire and supervise from 1975 onwards the series 'Men in Office', published by Thames and Hudson, in which eight volumes appeared over the next five years and a ninth in 1983. Here again her personal approach was clearly visible. Each volume was biographical and made extensive use of illustrations. Each dealt, at moderate length but with wide perspectives and using materials in a variety of languages, with an important figure in the history of early modern Europe: the Emperor Charles V;

Philip II of Spain; Frederick the Great; Peter the Great. (*George I* was originally meant to form part of this series but became too long and detailed to fit easily into it.) The authors she coaxed into writing for this series, French, German, Spanish and American as well as British, showed once more how international her range of scholarly contacts now was. Her achievement as an author was very substantial; but she might well have produced more, and at least equally important published work of her own if she had been less active as an editor. Her long-standing interest in Louis XIV might have been the foundation of a biography to compare with her *Charles XII*, while she hoped for many years to produce a large-scale study of the 'northern crowns' which would place the Scandinavian states and indeed the entire Baltic area in their European context, and show their importance in the whole European picture during the period which she had made her own. She left at her death a considerable body of unpublished writing in various states of completeness; and it is gratifying to think that some of this at least may eventually appear in published form.

Her middle and later years saw her importance as a scholar become increasingly widely recognised and the range of her circle of international academic contacts widen. From 1964 onwards she visited the United States frequently and with great enjoyment, combining the holding of a series of visiting professorships (notably at Ohio State University and the University of Kansas) with travel in which she was accompanied by her husband. This introduction to American academic life owed a good deal to her oldest friend, Professor Andrew Lossky, whom she had first known as a fellow graduate student in London in the later 1930s. She became a foreign fellow of the American Historical Association in 1979 and received an honourary degree from Ohio State University in 1985. The Scandinavian directness, even bluntness, and the outgoing and good-humoured approach to life which so marked her, made it easy for her to fit into a North American environment and she looked forward very much to her visits and the new friendships to which they led: as they became more frequent in the 1970s and early 1980s they were to her a source of real and lasting pleasure. Four years after her retirement, in 1984, LSE, to which she had contributed so much over so many years, made her an Honorary Fellow. The cosmopolitanism and international outlook which marked all her work meant that formal recognition in several European states also came in growing measure, notably and understandably from Scandinavia. She had become a Corresponding Member of the Swedish Vutterhetsakademi as early as

1954, while in 1983 she was made a knight, first class, of the Royal Norwegian Order of St Olav. To be honoured in this way by her native country gave her particular pleasure, which was shared by her Norwegian relations. In 1986 she became a commander of the Swedish Royal Order of the Northern Star: two years earlier she had also received the French Palmes Académiques. The last of this catalogue of formal recognitions of her work was her election as a Senior Fellow of the British Academy in 1993.

The years which followed her retirement were clouded by the long illness of her husband, who died in 1989. This ended an exceptionally close and happy companionship of more than half a century. Throughout the whole of their life together Harry shared to the full his wife's efforts, hopes, and successes, and gave her never-failing support and encouragement. They were well matched in their determination to enjoy life and their liking for travel and good food; while the fact that she never learned to drive meant that he became a valued source of practical help by acting on numerous occasions as her chauffeur. Harry, who had been intended for the Navy and was a keen and adventurous sailor, inspired his wife with some of his own enthusiasm for the sport, though she never pretended to his expertise in it. To the students and colleagues, so many of whom enjoyed their hospitality, either in London or at the cottage they acquired at Paglesham, near Burnham-on-Crouch, the strength of their marriage and their devotion to one another was unmistakable.

Ragnhild Hatton's life, therefore, was rich and productive both personally and intellectually. With her death we have lost an outstanding historian. We have also lost a teacher who inspired her students through the help and encouragement she gave them in lavish measure and the high standards she set them. Most important of all, we have lost someone whose generosity, good humour and even occasional quirks and idiosyncrasies earned her the warm affection of a host of friends.

MATTHEW ANDERSON
*University of London*

*Note.* I am most grateful for the help given by Dr Hamish Scott and Dr Robert Oresko in the writing of this memoir.

There is a very complete bibliography of her work in Robert Oresko, G. C. Gibbs, and H. M. Scott (eds.), *Royal and Republican Sovereignty in Early Modern Europe: Essays in Memory of Ragnhild Hatton* (Cambridge, 1997).

**DAVID LEWIS**

*Jane Bown*

*Proceedings of the British Academy*, **94**, 557–596

# David Malcolm Lewis
# 1928–1994

DAVID LEWIS, the outstanding ancient Greek historian and epigraphist of his time, died of myeloma at his home in Oxford on 12 July 1994, aged 66.

Lewis was born on 7 June 1928 in Willesden, Middlesex (Outer London). His grandparents were all part of the Jewish immigration from the Russian Empire in 1883–1900, one from Warsaw, the rest from Lithuania. Little is known about the families, except for a probable connection with Aron Alexandrovitch Solts (1872–1945), member of the Soviet Communist Party's Central Control Commission, and friend and eventual victim of Stalin.

Lewis's parents were born in the United Kingdom and were educated in good East London schools. His mother, the daughter of a furniture manufacturer with a small workshop, stopped her education on the verge of a degree course on deciding that she would not enjoy teaching. His father, the son of a general dealer, left school in his matriculation year in a fit of wartime restlessness, and after a brief spell in accountancy, spent the rest of his career with an auctioneering firm which he did much to expand, and which eventually took over the West End firm of Phillips. His memory for detail was encyclopaedic and legendary. In early married life he supplemented his income with book-dealing; the house was always full of books.

Lewis himself started school in a local elementary school with classes of fifty, but transferred at eight to a small but efficient private school. The attraction of this for his mother was that it offered more

© The British Academy 1997.

possibilities for physical exercise to a badly co-ordinated child; that it also started French and Latin immediately was a later discovery. From here he moved on to City of London School (CLS) with a scholarship. This was in September 1939, and the greater part of his school career was spent billeted round the town in Marlborough, Wiltshire, site of a famous boarding-school; here the two schools had an uneasy symbiosis. Intellectual life was lively and a compensation for absence from home. The ethos of CLS and some of its contrasting classical masters, such as the enlightened C. J. Ellingham, have been described in various writings of Lewis's senior Kingsley Amis, who remarks in this connexion that the CLS teachers were 'imitable eccentrics almost to a man'[1] and puts this down not just to the stylising effects teaching has on behaviour but to the nature of the adolescent observer 'for whom all grown-up behaviour is so fantastic as to defeat discrimination'. An acute, but amused and tolerant, facial expression was characteristic of Lewis in middle age, and one can imagine that, for a teacher, a veneer of blustering eccentricity might be a useful mechanism of defence against such very observant observers as the youthful David Lewis. But CLS did not merely provide an entertaining spectacle of spectacle-chewing pedagogues, it imparted civilised values. Amis's *Memoirs* praise the school for freedom from every sort of prejudice and factionalism. There was just one public attempt in Amis's time at anti-Semitism and it was a frostily received failure. 'Differences of class, upbringing, income group and religion', wrote Amis, 'counted for little. In particular, although perhaps fifteen percent of the boys were Jewish, not a single instance of anti-semitism [with the exception noted earlier] came to my attention in the seven years I was a pupil there. The academic teaching was of a standard not easily to be surpassed, but more important still was that lesson about how to regard one's fellows'. There was an assumption that the classical side was the only side for a bright boy; Lewis started Greek at eleven. Mathematics was not neglected, though science was. By present-day standards, much was expected linguistically, and the Classical Sixth's standard diet of unseen translations came from old papers set for the 'Ireland' at Oxford. In later life Lewis recalled that 'ability to construe through a brick wall was the ideal, but a wide range of reading was also encouraged'. The regime, which had once turned out Prime Minister H. H. Asquith, produced in Lewis's day not only a series of top civil servants, but three Oxford teachers of

[1] K. Amis, *Memoirs* (London, 1991), pp. 26, 34.

ancient history, Peter Fraser, James Holladay, and David Lewis. In addition, Michael Jameson, later of Philadelphia and Stanford, was four years ahead of Lewis at CLS, and just remembers him from 1939 or 1940, when Lewis 'must have been eleven or twelve and made an impression even then', but apparently only as being one of two 'tiresome young squirts in a break between classes'. More than fifty years later, at the beginning of his contribution to Lewis's Festschrift, Jameson was to acknowledge how much he had learnt from the honorand,[2] the tiresome young squirt of 1939.

Lewis went up to Corpus Christi College, Oxford, in 1945, again with a scholarship. He was aged only seventeen, and there was no certainty that he would be allowed to remain for more than a year, but in the event he took Mods. and Greats in the usual way (1947 and 1949) and got Firsts in both; one of his examiners in 1949 was his future collaborator Russell Meiggs. Corpus, then as now, was a tiny college, particularly strong in classics. In 1994, Lewis contributed a chapter to *Corpuscles* (a collection of Corpus undergraduate reminiscences edited by Brian Harrison), and a new copy of the book was lying around in the family home at Ferry Pool Road a few days before he died. His Mods. tutor was Frank Geary, whom he found old-fashioned and uninspiring; most of what he learnt during Mods. came from E. R. Dodds and Eduard Fraenkel, then professors of Greek and Latin respectively. It was Fraenkel, for whom Lewis had a very warm personal regard and who was *ex officio* a fellow of Corpus and a friendly and encouraging influence to the undergraduate classicists, who by example convinced Lewis that he had an academic future. If Mods. was a disappointment, Greats was another matter. In those days, and indeed until 1972, the syllabus consisted of philosophy and ancient history, with no option of offering literature instead of one of the other two subjects. To a young man with Lewis's extraordinary brain, philosophy was not a problem; he was taught by Frank Hardie and (out of college) Paul Grice. But his true intellectual milieu was on the other side of the school, in ancient history. Here his tutor Frank Lepper provided, as Lewis later recalled, a rigorous training in how to deal with facts, and he 'caught the bug of the most exciting developments of the days in the relationship of Attic epigraphy to the Athenian Empire'. There is a revealing sentence in

[2] M. H. Jameson, 'The Ritual of the Nike Parapet', in R. Osborne and S. Hornblower (eds.), *Ritual, Finance, Politics: Athenian Democratic Accounts Presented to David Lewis* (Oxford, 1994), pp. 307–24, at p. 307n.

*Corpuscles* to the effect that Lepper 'found me messes to clear up and I enjoyed clarifying them'. There is a sense, as we shall see, in which this description sums up Lewis's entire academic career—clearing up messes dumped on his desk by other people. A puzzled undergraduate letter to Marcus Niebuhr Tod of Oriel was the origin of a long association with Benjamin Meritt: in 1974, at the beginning of his contribution to the Meritt Fetschrift, Lewis wrote that it was 'just twenty-five years since Meritt answered a piece of undergraduate scepticism of mine, sent on to him by Tod, with infinite thoroughness and courtesy'.[3] For the rest of his life Lewis was warmly attached to Corpus, to which as we shall see he returned as a Junior Research Fellow: even when at Christ Church he regularly took in Corpus undergraduate pupils for the minority fourth-century BC option in Greek history.

Academic work was important to him at this stage but it was not everything, any more than it was in later life. He had interests ('intellectual rather than ambitious' as he admitted in *Corpuscles*) in the Liberal Club and was back-handedly grateful in retrospect to the Army for saving him from standing for Parliament in the Liberal debacle of 1950. His other main extra-curricular interest was in the Jewish Society. This was at the time of the end of the Palestine Mandate and the creation of Israel: he chaired a meeting at which he 'narrowly averted the lynching of Max Beloff, who had been suggesting that there was something to be said for British government policy'.

There followed two years of national service. Rather unwillingly, he found himself with the Royal Army Education Corps (RAEC), but always acknowledged later the value of a compulsory spell of administration as an Assistant Brigade Education Officer in Germany, organising the distribution of newspapers and examining the 'licensed illiteracy' of the Army Certificate of Education, Third Class. A long campaign with superiors about what the RAEC really ought to be doing eventually landed him in a more Oxford situation, sitting in Rhine Army HQ as the only second lieutenant on the establishment, with his general reading and attempts to learn Russian interrupted once a week by frantic preparation to produce current affairs hand-outs. These were and are impressive not just for their range, shrewdness, and prescience (two foolscap pages on Indo-China, dated April 1951, are a particularly good read, as is a kind of Platonic dialogue on the US

---

[3] D. M. Lewis, 'Entrenchment-clauses in Attic Decrees', ΦΟΡΟΣ *Meritt* (1974), pp. 81–9, at p. 81. From this point on, all references are to work by Lewis unless stated.

Constitution), but for their accessible English prose style. Accessibility was not to be a feature of Lewis's more specialist writing, but in the last years of his life, when writing for the *Cambridge Ancient History*, he showed that he had not forgotten the RAEC apprenticeship in the production of crisp, clear and interesting English. It was during this period that he made his one attempt to get off the academic path by enquiring what the BBC might offer along these lines.

In 1949 the University of Oxford had awarded Lewis a Craven Fellowship, which carried an obligation to spend part of the year abroad. But it was not until 1951 that this possibility of overseas study became a reality, when he applied for and got a Jane Eliza Procter Fellowship which enabled him to go to Princeton University for the year 1951–2; at the same time he was, unusually, awarded membership of the Institute for Advanced Study nearby—the 'Mecca of Greek epigraphy' as he put it later—where he was allocated an office. He certainly did plenty of epigraphy. His Princeton supervisor A. E. ('Toni') Raubitschek recalls that Lewis tried to spend most of his time with Benjamin Meritt at the Institute: 'I had to call his attention to the terms' [of the fellowship]. His letters home to his parents reveal that he also had epigraphic discussions with the doyenne of archaic Greek inscriptions, L. H. ('Anne') Jeffery, who happened to be at the Institute that year and had a study close by; but Lewis seems to have been slightly in awe of her at this stage and he paints a strange picture of her in his letters home, as of a formidable recluse. During the Christmas vacation, supervisor Raubitschek and his precocious British pupil took a walk on the Graduate College grounds. Lewis said, 'How about getting a Ph.D. with you?', and Raubitschek told him he was sure he could get him a (Princeton) fellowship for the following year. Lewis said, 'No, this year', and refused to be deterred when Raubitschek pointed out the hurdles ('preliminaries', exams, a dissertation). As for a dissertation, Lewis suggested 'The Peace of Nikias' or 'The Indirect Tradition of Thucydides'. Raubitschek said, 'Nikias is easy'. Lewis: 'Then I do the other!' And he did. Almost every week Raubitschek got a chapter on an author: 'Thucydides in Isokrates', 'Thucydides in Plato', 'Thucydides in Aristotle', and so on. He got his degree on time, and went on to be an usher ('Honorary Assistant Sergeant-at Arms to the West Virginia Delegation') at the 1952 Eisenhower-Taft Republican Convention in Chicago. Though the Peace of Nikias was spurned at this stage, it is worth noting that in 1957 Andrewes and Lewis published their 'Note on the Peace of Nikias'.[4] This short and elegant study, the conclusions of which still stand, took its origin from a typically brilliant observation of Lewis that ten of the seventeen names of Athenians, listed by Thucydides at v. 19 as having sworn to the Peace, are in the official tribal order. The immediate occasion for the publication of this piece was surely the publication in 1956 of the relevant volume of Gomme's *Historical Commentary on Thucydides*, which missed the particular point and generally showed little interest in personal names; but one wonders how much earlier (?1951) Lewis had thought of the basic idea for the article.

But the option chosen in Princeton was 'The Indirect Tradition of Thucydides' and the eventual thesis, called *Towards a Historian's Text of Thucydides*, was recommended for acceptance by the Department of Classics in May 1952: not many theses of this quality can have been written in less than five months. Little of it got into print directly, apart from 'Ithome Again',[5] an attempt to solve the worst problem of Thucydidean chronology, that of the mid fifth-century helot revolt, by an ingenious supposition: that a Hellenistic scholar, who got his history from Ephorus, used that history to 'correct' the text of Thucydides. In 1977 Lewis virtually retracted this article, saying he had 'long since ceased to believe much' of what he said in it.[6] But note 'much': the retraction surely applied only to the particular argument about the numeral at Thucydides i. 103. 1. We have no right to think that he repudiated the dissertation as a whole (a view I have sometimes heard expressed). The contrary can be proved: in *Gnomon* 1966, when reviewing Kleinlogel's *Geschichte des Thukydidestextes im Mittelalter*, he explicitly directed the reader to 'see in general my Princeton dissertation, *Towards a Historian's Text . . .*', and recapitulated one of his particular 1952 suggestions.[7]

The main argument of the dissertation was that the text of Thucydides as it has come down to us suffers from officious 'emendations' by

---

[4] *Journal of Hellenic Studies*, lxxvii (1957), 177–80, esp. n. 7.

[5] *Historia*, ii (1953/4), 412–18. Some of Lewis's 1953 work has since got into print indirectly, either via his own reviews or in other ways: see below, n. 7.

[6] *Sparta and Persia* (Leiden, 1977), p. 46, n. 135.

[7] *Gnomon*, xxxviii (1966), 136, discussing Thuc. ii. 25. 1, cp. pp. 44–6 of the dissertation; see also *Journal of Hellenic Studies*, lxxvii (1957), 329 for another authoritative and highly technical review of a book on the text of Thucydides (Hemmerdinger). It is relevant to the question what value did Lewis attach to his dissertation, that he was prepared in after years to make it available to commentators on Thucydides; see e.g. K. J. Dover, *Historical Commentary on Thucydides*, vol. iv (Oxford, 1970), p. 237.

Hellenistic scholars who were familiar with, for example, the poems of Homer and the history of Ephorus, and who misapplied this familiarity. The approach is perhaps best explained by an example which draws on more than one kind of tradition: Lewis's ingenious handling of Thucydides iv. 107. 3. Thucydides here mentions Oisyme in north Greece; the equivalent passage of Diodorus (xii. 68. 4) has Syme, which has usually been emended to Oisyme, partly because Stephanus of Byzantium quoted Oisyme from Thucydides and this seemed to guarantee the longer form of the name. Now, tribute quota-list no. 21 contains a place called Syme in what, from the historical or geographical point of view, was 'extremely strange company' (in fact, in a northern context, whereas the well-known Syme was an island off Caria). Lewis suggested that the Carian Syme and the Syme of list 21 were distinct places, and that the latter was Thracian. 'I am not trying to create two towns where one had stood before. I suggest that the same town had, side by side, two names. Οἰσύμη has fifth-century warrant from Antiphon, Σύμη I suggest from the quota lists . . .'. There were, Lewis suggested, two alternatives:

> a) It is possible that Thucydides wrote Οἰσύμη, that Ephorus thought he knew better and wrote Σύμη. To confute this we do not need the negative criterion of the absence of ὀνομαζομένη or καλουμένη. Ephorus is quoted by Harpocration as having used Οἰσύμη in the fourth book. He is hardly likely to have changed his opinion later. b) It is however quite likely that he transcribed a name from Thucydides without thinking about it too clearly. On this hypothesis Thucydides, who knew this area as well as any Greek of the fifth century, wrote Σύμη. This will have been an idiosyncrasy not found elsewhere in literature and possibly the Alexandrians may have considered it a mistake. This will have been made easier by the fact that Οἰσύμη is no ordinary name. It was identified with the Αἰσύμη of Iliad VIII 304. This implies that the vast body of theorising on the Homeric corpus touched the name. I suggest that at some time this theorising affected an ancient editor's views on the text of Thucydides.

That Lewis did not publish his dissertation in full should not be taken as evidence that he had a low view of it (though he made dismissive remarks at the time and later): publication frenzy is recent, and has been partly caused by pressures on individuals and institutions which hardly existed at the beginning of the 1950s. In any case, Lewis's main preoccupations soon moved towards the more purely epigraphical— though the example above shows him interweaving epigraphic, historical, and literary arguments in a way which already puts us on notice that this was a scholar who refused to separate the epigraphist's

job from that of the historian, a cardinal Lewis belief, to which I shall
return. To conclude on Lewis's textual work: as recently as 1995, a
scrupulous and excellent monograph by Karl Maurer on interpolation in
Thucydides[8] cited Lewis's thesis and referred to 'uncertain, but still
very interesting possibilities' raised by it, specifically the idea discussed
above, that the indirect tradition preserves some good Thucydidean
material lost from the direct tradition; a few pages later Maurer says
that 'the best review of Kleinlogel's book is that by D. M. Lewis'. It
should not be doubted that Lewis's contribution to the study of the text
of Thucydides was not merely ingenious but important.

Lewis divided the next two years (1952–4) between Oxford and
Athens. He was a Senior Scholar at New College, which provided a
small stipend, supplemented by his Craven Award. The choice of
college was enhanced for Lewis by the presence in it of H. T. (Theodore) Wade-Gery and and of Antony Andrewes, who was to succeed
Wade-Gery as Wykeham Professor of Ancient Greek History in 1953;[9]
Lewis had from Princeton been in negotiation with both men, and also
with H. M. Last, the former Camden Professor of Ancient Roman
History. The connection with Tony Andrewes was the beginning of
an exceptionally close and warm working friendship which ended only
when Lewis wrote Andrewes's obituary for the *Independent* and for
these *Proceedings*[10] (by then he had already, in 1987, written the
Academy obituary of Anne Jeffery,[11] and had long discovered her great
personal charm, so rectifying the callow and utterly wrong impression
of her which he had acquired in 1951–2. His only other obituary of any
sort[12] was of Benjamin Meritt and was published in the *Independent*, 14
July 1989; all these were written within a very few years of each other
and though the undergraduate Lewis had attended lectures by Andrewes

---

[8] K. Maurer, *Interpolation in Thucydides. Mnemosyne*, supp. cl (Leiden, 1995), pp. 204, 220,
n. 7. This book contains other favourable references to Lewis's dissertation. At p. 75, n. 30,
however, Maurer declined to follow Lewis all the way in his positing of systematic
interference, by Hellenistic editors, with the text of Thucydides.
  For Lewis's effortless command of Thucydidean textual issues see also *Sparta and Persia*,
p. 101, n. 74.

[9] In fact, Wade-Gery was to be elected to a Senior Research Fellowship at Merton College
on his retirement in 1953, but was surely part of the New College furniture in Lewis's time.

[10] *Independent*, 15 June 1990; *Proceedings of the British Academy*, 80 (1993), pp. 221–31.

[11] *Proceedings of the British Academy*, 82 (1987), pp. 505–16.

[12] There is a mystery about an obituary of Eduard Fraenkel, not listed in the list of his own
publications which Lewis prepared towards the end of his life, and not found among his
papers by Peter Rhodes, but mentioned by Lewis when considering candidates for inclusion
in his volume of *Selected Papers*. It is published in no obvious or even not so obvious place.

and no doubt also by Jeffery, all three relationships seem to have originated at the personal level in what for Lewis was the academically crucial year 1951–2.[13])

From New College, Lewis made long visits to the British School at Athens (BSA) where he worked in the city's Epigraphic Museum and in the Agora Museum. (This took him to the other side of the world from Princeton physically, but was not really an academic depature because of the magnificent collection of paper squeeze-impressions of Attic inscriptions in the Institute for Advanced Study. It was on these that he had worked with Meritt in what is now called the Meritt Library, though the fifth-century squeezes themselves were taken by Meritt to Austin, Texas, on his retirement in the 1970s.) Lewis later recalled that he was able to acquire a firsthand knowledge of the resources of these two Athens museums 'in a more casual and easier atmosphere than greater governmental restrictions have since made possible'.

The work he did at the BSA appeared in the School's *Annual* for 1954 and 1955 in two articles unassumingly called 'Notes on Attic Inscriptions' and 'Notes on Attic Inscriptions II'.[14] No address is given; the reader is intended to assume that work published under the auspices of the School was done from that address. The two epigraphic articles are a miscellany: some of the twenty-nine studies are very short, and some are very much *pour les spécialistes*. Nevertheless, they announced to the scholarly world, instantly and convincingly, an addition to the topmost flight of Greek epigraphists. They are also and primarily the work of a *historian* applying epigraphic method. To reread them is to be impressed above all by their range. The first of the two collections opens with a re-edition of the so-called Praxiergidai inscription (now *IG* $1^3$ 7), a mid-fifth-century BC text which guaranteed the religious privileges of an old and proud Athenian *genos* or family. Lewis's suggested restoration of a word meaning 'things decreed' in the third and fourth lines did indeed fit the line well, as Lewis modestly claimed. That, however, was not all. He continued, 'I suggest an implied assertion by the *demos* [people] that even the oldest privileges depend on the will of the people'. The historian speaks. Lewis's succinct observation has since been developed elsewhere and by others, above all by his

---

[13] One other important influence should be mentioned, that of A. M. Woodward, whose work Lewis admired greatly; see Lewis and Woodward, 'A Transfer from Eleusis', *BSA*, lxx (1975), 183–8.

[14] *BSA*, xlix (1954), 17–50; and l (1955), 1–36.

subsequent graduate pupil, J. K. Davies, who in more than one place compares the democracy's treatment of the Praxiergidai with the reforms associated with the name of Ephialtes, who in the late 460s stripped venerable institutions of their political and judicial privileges and insisted that what they retained, they retained by the permission of the sovereign people.[15]

The opening study in the second Attic collection, that of 1955, deals with Aristophanes: it contains Lewis's famous suggestion that Lysistrata was 'deliberately modelled' on the real-life priestess of Athena Polias, Lysimache. Forty years later, this idea has held up well, though recent commentators are shy of the strict implications of 'modelled', and tend to insist that we are not dealing with an identification like that between Kleon and Paphlagon in the *Knights*.[16] The piece is interesting for Lewis's intellectual biography, not just because it illustrates his precocious range ('Who was Lysistrata?' has only religion, in the broadest sense, in common with 'The Praxiergidai'), but because it illustrates its author's lifelong facility for seeing in a flash how new evidence could help solve old problems. In this instance, the new evidence was the grave epigram for the priestess of Athena Nike, Myrrhine, now *IG* 1[3] 1330. J. Papademetriou had suggested a link between this Myrrhine and the character of that name in the *Lysistrata*. Lewis's 'Lysistrata' also illustrated his co-operative tendencies; he was always ready to work with others and—as with Papademetriou—to show them courteously how their ideas could be taken much further. This was to make him in the course of time the ideal collaborator, the ideal scrutineer-in-advance of books and articles, and the ideal graduate supervisor. In a selfish world, however, it was a cast of mind which was to slow down his advancement.

An authoritative and virtuoso appendix to this section (which started

---

[15] J. K. Davies, *Democracy and Classical Greece*[2] (1978, 2nd edn., 1993), pp. 57–8; *Cambridge Ancient History* v[2] (1992) 300, cp. P. J. Rhodes (another Lewis pupil) at p. 70, n. 27, of the same volume, in the chapter on, precisely, Ephialtes. It is a pity that Louis Robert in the *Bullétin Épigraphique* 1955 (no. 84) chose to report 'The Praxiergidai' as merely a contribution to the study of the topography of the Acropolis. For reservations about the Praxiergidai point see R. Parker, *Athenian Religion: A History* (Oxford, 1996), pp. 124 *et seq.*

[16] See the editions of the play by J. Henderson (ed.), *Aristophanes' Lysistrata* (Oxford, 1987), pp. xxxix–xl; A. Sommerstein, *Aristophanes: Lysistrata* (Warminster, 1990), p. 5; note also D. M. MacDowell, *Aristophanes and Athens* (Oxford, 1995), pp. 240–2. Richard Rutherford reminds me that Lewis's concern for the literary aspect of the identification should be stressed: 'he is concerned to ask also what this [the identification] does for our appreciation of the *play*, and makes points which matter for any interpreter (p. 3)'.

with Aristophanes) gives and discusses the evidence for priestesses of Athena Polias through the fourth century and the Hellenistic and Roman periods; included here are some serious contributions to the prosopo-graphy of Roman Athens. Exchanges with R. Syme, evidently as with an equal, are duly acknowledged, on such points as the identity of Roman individuals from the second century AD.[17]

The twenty-seven other pieces include an epigraphically-based essay on the career of the atthidographer Androtion,[18] and an examination of the fourth-century problem of the epistates of the proedroi (when did the proedroi replace the prytaneis as presidents of the Council and Assembly?)

1954 brought the need for Lewis, now twenty-six, to decide between the succession to Geoffrey de Ste Croix in his Ancient Economic History post at the London School of Economics, and the gamble on an Oxford career represented by a P. S. Allen Junior Research Fellow-ship at Corpus. He chose the latter, and was the first holder of the title. During his one year there he did some teaching, and his pupils included his brother Philip, then in his fourth year. In *Corpuscles*, David was to record that Philip 'stayed behind after their first Greats revision class to tell me with some emphasis that for the first half hour I had not earned my keep'. David also noted that this Corpus teaching gave him a 'pretty false idea' of what undergraduate teaching was like, a typically round-about way of saying that his pupils were exceptionally good.

In 1955 he moved to the Greek History tutorship at Christ Church, which had been turned down by the first choice, M. I. Finley, who took a Cambridge lectureship in preference. The outgoing tutor was R. H. Dundas, a historian of a different generation and a very different attitude to publication; in a piece for the Christ Church Annual Report for 1955, Dundas wrote of Lewis's learning as 'positively unseemly. He has published articles; and will publish many more.' In fact, and despite this patronising tone, Dundas was very kind and helpful to Lewis on the

---

[17] It may be observed at this point that when Elizabeth Rawson wrote in 1985 that 'Roman historians and Greek epigraphists do not always talk to each other as much as they should' (E. Rawson, 'Cicero and the Areopagus', *Athenaeum*, lxiii (1985), 44–66 at 44 = *Roman Culture and Society* (Oxford, 1991), p. 444) the grateful accompanying footnote makes it clear that David Lewis is emphatically not included in the implied indictment.

[18] See, however, G. L. Cawkwell, 'Notes on the Social War', *Classica et Medievalia*, xxiii (1962), 34–49. It was characteristic of Lewis's generosity and intellectual scrupulousness that he later spoke of this correction of one detail as having exposed a 'major howler' in his own study.

latter's arrival; Lewis had expected hostility from that quarter because of his religion.

For the next thirty years, until he was appointed to a personal professorship (1985), Lewis taught Greek history, from the archaic period to Alexander, to Christ Church undergraduates; he remained a Student (i.e. Fellow) of Christ Church until his death. Most Oxford tutors in this field were and are expected to teach both Greek and Roman history, but until Lewis's change of status, Christ Church was fortunate and rich enough to have two tutors in ancient history; the other was for Lewis's first twenty years Eric Gray, an expert in Asia Minor and its epigraphy, who was replaced in 1977 by Alan Bowman, a historical papyrologist. Christ Church in Lewis's time was a great centre for the documentary study of the ancient world: from 1965 the literary papyrologist Peter Parsons was also Student of Christ Church (and Regius Professor of Greek from 1989 in succession to Hugh Lloyd-Jones). The remarkable result was that in the decade-and-a-half from 1980 the following books were published by Christ Church scholars: Lewis's *Inscriptiones Graecae* (3rd edn.); Parsons and Lloyd-Jones, *Supplementum Hellenisticum*; and Bowman's *Vindolanda Tablets* (with J. D. Thomas: 1983).

But though Lewis was by nature a collaborator, his only Christ Church collaboration was with his colleague as literary tutor, John Gould (Student of Christ Church from 1954–68). In 1968, the year of Gould's departure to the Chair of Classics at Swansea, they produced a revision of Pickard-Cambridge, *Dramatic Festivals of Athens*. This, and the collection of Greek historical inscriptions which Lewis published with Russell Meiggs (also 1968), were, at least until his involvement in the *Cambridge Ancient History* in the last phase of his life (from 1979), the part of Lewis's scholarly output most obviously geared to the needs of undergraduates and their teachers. Both works surely grew from Lewis's own teaching activities as a college teacher and university lecturer. This is therefore a good point at which to consider Lewis as an undergraduate teacher and lecturer.

As we saw, the Corpus pupils whom Lewis taught (and continued to teach for fourth-century history) were exceptionally bright. Christ Church was and is a different sort of place—not just rich, but large, and at that time more aristocratic in tone and intake than any other Oxford college. Such a social milieu was bound to produce a wide mix of ability, and it was just as well that Lewis was not only clever but by nature tolerant and kind. Even so, there were undergraduates who found him hard to keep up with: his manner of self-expression was always economical or even elliptical. For his part Lewis confessed (in a letter of reply to an older friend who wrote in 1985 to congratulate him on his promotion to the personal Chair) that although he had mixed feelings about the change of status, he was on the whole glad that he would never again have to 'listen to another ß+ essay on the hoplite theory of tyranny'.

At Christ Church, Lewis was secretary to the governing body for many years and is remembered for his instant and accurate recall of detail, particularly on matters of finance (he was for many years a valued member of the Committee on Investments). John Sparrow, the Warden of All Souls, used to divide university academics into those who could have been something other than dons, and those who could not. There is no doubt that David Lewis could have had a successful career as a civil servant in some exacting department like the Treasury, or as a merchant banker or barrister (like his brother). And yet, as we have seen, his only attempt to explore a non-academic career was his 1951 approach to the BBC. As far as I know he made only one broadcast, to be considered below. Though he took that opportunity to state, early in his career and emphatically, his position on important matters of epigraphic principle, it is hard to think of him as a broadcaster *manqué*. It would not be absurd to regard him as an administrator or professional financier *manqué*, but that is not the right expression because his college and above all the Jewish community in Oxford (see below) received some of the benefit of that special mix of acumen and organisational talent; his skills as an organiser were not fully seen in a purely academic context until his work as editor and eventually senior editor of the classical Greek volumes of the *Cambridge Ancient History*.

College teaching was only one part of his teaching duties: from 1956 he was also university lecturer in Greek epigraphy. He gave practical classes on epigraphy from time to time both in this capacity and later as professor; but he did not develop, or seek to develop, a school of Greek epigraphy in Oxford. The way he passed on his epigraphic knowledge at the local and didactic level (as opposed to publication) was different, namely by supervising historical dissertations which had an epigraphic component. This was surely by preference, and reflects his conviction that history and epigraphy are inseparable. I shall reserve an attempt to assess Lewis's supervision of graduates, the area of instruction in which above all he excelled, until I reach the 1970s and his professorial period

(1985–94); although that is an artificial postponement because Christopher Ehrhardt,[19] Albert Schachter,[20] John Davies, and Peter Rhodes had all passed through his hands by the beginning of the 1970s.

In addition to his obligation to lecture on epigraphy, he had to lecture on Greek history generally and regularly gave courses on Demosthenes (separate courses on the public or political speeches and—under the title 'Some Athenian Attitudes'—on themes illustrated by some of the private speeches[21]) and on classical Athens. He was never a communicator of the frothy or theatrical type, so that some undergraduates found his lectures too concise and demanding to be, in the Thucydidean phrase, immediately pleasurable, while conceding that if you took good notes and worked through them later, the profit was permanent and immense. The lectures were like concentrated orange juice: you had to add water. But some of my Balliol contemporaries found 'Athenian Attitudes' refreshing and frank in their treatment of aspects of sexual and social life not normally covered in the Oxford lecture-list at that time.[22] In any case, he seems over the years to have made more concessions to his audience, and half-way through his final lecture series, which was on a selection of texts from 'Meiggs and Lewis' and which he courageously insisted on giving although he had known for several months that he was dying, one of my undergraduate pupils told me they were the best lectures he had ever attended. (He went on to ask me whether the lecturer was anything to do with the Lewis of 'Meiggs and Lewis', a point David had modestly not made clear.)

Dundas's announcement of Lewis's appointment described him as unmarried, but this was not to be true for much longer. As early as his Princeton year he was finding it necessary, in letters home, to deny rumours, put about by well-meaning but inquisitive New York City relations, that he was engaged. In 1958 he married Barbara Wright, daughter of the eminent physiologist Professor Samson Wright. In 1981 he was to describe Barbara, in the preface to the second fascicle of

---

[19] Ehrhardt wrote a B.Litt. thesis (a shorter dissertation than that required for a doctorate) on 'The Third Sacred War' (1961).

[20] Schachter's *Cults of Boiotia*, still not quite complete, began life as an Oxford doctoral dissertation supervised by Lewis.

[21] These lectures were centred round the person of Apollodorus, the son of Pasion (on whom Lewis's graduate student, J. C. Trevett, was to write his dissertation in the 1980s). They are included in a collection of unpublished papers which has been deposited in libraries in Oxford and elsewhere.

[22] I am here indebted to a letter from Richard Jenkyns, dated 14 March 1996.

*Inscriptiones Graecae*, as the 'mainstay of my life', *columen vitae meae*, and *The Jews of Oxford* (1992) is dedicated to 'Barbara, who always asks the right questions'. It was a happy marriage to a generous, impulsive and talkative partner (Miriam Kochan's address at the memorial service rightly spoke of Barbara's 'intelligence and dynamism'), and a happy family life: Joanna was born in 1959, followed by Isabel (1961), Helen (1963), and Eve (1968). Up to this point, David had been an intense worker at all hours: his Princeton letters record long sessions of bridge with fellow-addicts, followed by expiatory bouts of academic work into the small hours. Life in Corpus and Christ Church, as a living-in bachelor, cannot have been very different. From 1958 on, that all changed. The work and the productivity never flagged, but an absolute divide was placed between the working day and the time set apart for family and normal life. When he brought work home, he never shut himself away but could read and write against household noise and activity; he worked five days a week; and was essentially a nine-to-seven man. There was a rich domestic life to entice him home punctually ('home' was first Old Road, Headington, then Charlbury Road, and finally 1, Ferry Pool Road): helping with the children's homework (he learned New Maths for this purpose); gardening; games of scrabble. Music, especially opera, was an interest which, unlike bridge, he never abandoned, except that in adult life it was as a listener not a player (he had played the piano competently in youth but let it lapse). In other ways, too, the Lewis household was not a silent one; it was a friendly, hospitable (the Lewises regularly held Sunday lunch-parties for Christ Church pupils, and there were many academic and other visitors from outside Oxford), interested in other people's doings, and noisy with laughter and simultaneously conducted conversations. He lived long enough to be a grandfather twice over, with the arrival of Isabel's two children (1992 and 1993), and this was an enormous source of pleasure and quiet pride. By the time the grandchildren arrived, Isabel was in Israel, and this gave further reason and opportunity for visits to a country where the Lewises had many friends. David enjoyed travelling, and adventurous holidays were an important part of family life. He took to camping in his forties. He was not really happy travelling alone, and had a less than idyllic time on a visit to Sicily without Barbara in the late 1980s as odd man out in a commercially organised archaeological tour group, conscientiously looking at sites and terrain in connection with his chapter on Dionysius I for the *Cambridge Ancient History* vi. Surprisingly, it was not till the summer of his sixtieth birthday that Barbara and David visited Turkey and David set himself with characteristic thoroughness to read up modern Turkish history in preparation, though the Turkish language defeated him.

Distractions and non-academic activity on this scale (and I have not yet said anything about his work for the Oxford Jewish community) might have slowed down the output of a less disciplined worker, and a less quick mind. Not David Lewis. But hard work and acumen alone will not make an epigraphist in the full sense, that is, an editor of *new* inscriptions. For that, a connection with an excavation is necessary. Lewis's opportunities came to him from the American excavations in the Athenian city centre or *agora*, not from the British school, whose excavations have always tended to be on prehistoric sites. Of the sites excavated by the British in the post-war period, only Chios was likely to turn up classical Greek inscriptions, and George Forrest had already been booked as the dig epigraphist there. In any case, Lewis's interests were at this stage essentially Athenian. The connection with Benjamin Meritt was therefore crucial, because Meritt was responsible for the publication of the epigraphic material from the *agora* and passed important texts to Lewis. The relationship with the American School's excavations went well beyond this; it is clear from extensive correspondence over many years between Lewis and Homer Thompson, the field director of the *agora* excavation, that the Americans consulted the Lewis oracle across a range of issues going well beyond the purely epigraphic, taking in, for example, architectural history and the likely siting of individual monuments.

Lewis's first big publication of American material was in *Hesperia* (the journal of the American School of Classical Studies at Athens) 1959. Three separate articles appeared under his name; the most substantial in terms of bulk was 'Attic Manumissions', but a second and shorter piece, a publication of a new fragment relating to the Lesser Panathenaia, was wider-ranging and more controversial; here Lewis displayed his outstanding ability to derive far-reaching historical conclusions from small epigraphic indicators.[23] Other *Hesperia* articles followed: one of them, in 1979, was written in collaboration with R. S. Stroud. It was the publication of a new fragment of an Athenian decree honouring Evagoras of Cyprus and enabled Lewis to combine

---

[23] The text mentioned a five percent tax on the 'Nea', 'a specific and well-known area of state land'; for the subsequent controversy over the identification of this see L. Robert, *Hellenica*, XI–XII (1960), 294 and Lewis's brief rejection of Robert, *Hesperia*, xxxvii (1968) 374, n. 18. On Lewis's view the tax was on produce, and constituted evidence that such a tax did not disappear with the Peisistratids (*Hesperia*, xxviii (1959), 244).

his epigraphic skills with that interest in Persia which found most obvious expression in *Sparta and Persia*, 1977.

The indivisibility of history and epigraphy was implicit in all these periodical publications, some of them at first sight highly technical. In 1959, the year of the first *Hesperia* articles, Lewis expounded his beliefs to a wider audience, in a Third Programme radio broadcast called 'Testimony of Stones' and subsequently published in the now-defunct *Listener* magazine.[24] The talk was in fact a review of A. G. Woodhead's *Study of Greek Inscriptions*;[25] though acknowledging the usefulness of the book, Lewis objected to the author's tendency to speak as if an epigraphist were a distinct class of person. 'We must, however, ask whether the epigraphist is a distinct specialist. As soon as the scholar starts thinking about the content of his inscription, he is outside the area of pure epigraphy. He will stop thinking as an epigraphist and start thinking as a historian of politics, economics, religion or whatever . . .. Why after all should we stress the medium through which facts and texts are transmitted?' Lewis added to this an autobiographical remark, very relevant to his lectures, noted above, on Demosthenes and to his collaborative revision of Pickard-Cambridge's *Dramatic Festivals*: 'I myself do a good deal of work on Athenian inscriptions of the fourth century BC, but what goes most naturally with these is not late epitaphs from Anatolia, or Hellenistic dedications from northern Greece, but the speeches of the Athenian orators of the period'. The talk concludes with a plea that scholars should cease to talk of the field of epigraphy and should realise instead that every branch of classical scholarship involves inscriptions and they may have to know how to use them. This is far and away the clearest statement known to me of David Lewis's view of his own life's work. There is a similar, but less transparent and forthright, statement in the short paper on August Boeckh which he delivered in 1967 to the Fifth International Congress of Greek and Latin epigraphy, and published in the conference *Acta* in 1971. He quoted with approval Boeckh's view that epigraphy is not an art or a discipline at all, because its subject-matter is not uniform; and he commented, 'I am sure that it is good for us to be made to wonder from time whether epigraphy exists'.[26] He ended that paper by saying

---

[24] *Listener*, 20 August 1959, 281 and 284.

[25] Cambridge, 1959; rev. ed. 1981.

[26] 'Boeckh, Staatshaushaltung der Athener, 1817–1967', in *Acta of the Fifth International Congress of Greek and Latin Epigraphy, Cambridge, 1967* (Cambridge, 1971), pp. 35–9, esp. p. 39. For a rather similar point see Jowett's *Thucydides*, rev. W. H. Forbes and E. Abbott (1899), p. x (from the introductory section 'On Inscriptions of the Age of Thucydides').

'we should all have our *Hellen*, individual or communal' — a reference to the synthetic book which Boeckh planned as the crown of his studies.

Boeckh never wrote his *Hellen*, but he did launch the project which he saw as a preparation for *Hellen*, a mere means to an end. The 'means' was the great corpus of the Greek inscriptions (*Corpus Inscriptionum Graecarum*). Lewis's 1967 decision to hang his reflections on Boeckh was not fortuitous: since 1962 he had himself been part of the *Inscriptiones Graecae* project, the successor of *CIG*. In that year, as Lewis was to put it in his own 1987 memoir of Anne Jeffery,[27] 'a small cabal persuaded Professor Klaffenbach of the Berlin Academy that I was the person to organize a new edition of *Inscriptiones Graecae*, I, the volume containing Attic inscriptions to 403 BC'.

There is no one or obvious point at which an obituarist should deal with a project which was to last from 1962 to 1994. When Lewis accepted the job he was either thirty-three or thirty-four, young for such an honour and responsibility. When copies of the second fascicle reached the libraries he was approaching sixty-six and dying. Half a life for *IG* 1³.

The new edition was in fact the third; Hiller von Gaertringen's so-called *editio minor*, really a second edition, had been published in 1924. Much had happened since then, most obviously the finds from the American *agora* excavations, but also (as he explained in the preface to the first fascicle) the development of 'architectural epigraphy' by scholars like W. B. Dinsmoor. 'Architectural' here means that you pay attention to the monument as a physical structure, as opposed to merely concentrating on decipherment of the letters. In the 1990s this tendency has been taken further still, as scholars insist on the monumental character of much ancient public epigraphy and even ask how much of it was meant to be read at all. In the 1993 conference honouring David Lewis, his one-time pupil John Davies asked 'how many people before the 20th century AD do we suppose ever brought a step-ladder in order to consult the top lines of the First Stele of the Tribute Lists?' Davies cited Rosalind Thomas, who in turn has remarked of Athens' fifth-century Coinage Decree that it was intended 'to intimidate as well as communicate, to impress as well as to record on stone'.[28] We never

---

[27] See above, n. 11; see pp. 513–4.

[28] J. K. Davies in *Ritual, Finance, Politics* (see above, n. 2), p. 212; R. Thomas, 'Literacy in Archaic and Classical Greece', in A. K. Bowman and G. D. Woolf (eds.), *Literacy and Power in the Ancient World* (Cambridge, 1994), p. 44. For a more extreme position see C. Hedrick in *Ritual, Finance, Politics*.

discovered in detail what Lewis thought of this scholarly shift (the editors of his Festschrift hoped to extract from him a reply to the papers, but he fell ill almost immediately). What the 1981 preface makes clear is that Lewis was alert to the big shifts of direction and found them exhilarating. (In the same way his reaction in 1990 to the new technique of laser enhancement—see below—might have surprised those who expected outright hostility merely because the technique threatened to dislodge traditional datings.) Nevertheless, the 1981 preface also makes clear that he did not accept (*'etiamnunc firme repellimus'*) the whole-sale down-datings of Harold Mattingly. (It should be remarked here that this controversy, unlike that between Lewis's teacher Meritt and W. K. Pritchett, was always conducted on both sides with respect and absence of personal rancour, and this characterised other arguments Lewis conducted, for example that with Margaret Thompson on Athenian New Style Coinage[29]).

The preface to the first fascicle of *IG* 1 was dated 1976, five years before eventual publication. The material had been basically completed and passed to Berlin by as early as the summer of 1972, but Klaffen-bach's successor, E. Erxleben, wanted and extracted full rather than minimal exposition of the texts. The book was a work of collaboration—in particular the tribute lists (nos. 259–90) were the work of Meritt and M. F. McGregor, and other old friends like Jameson and Raubitschek contributed—but Lewis's part was easily the largest: as with the *Cambridge Ancient History* many years later he was both a hands-on editor and a large-scale contributor. At the end of four pages of critical discussion in the *Classical Review*, Michael Osborne con-fessed 'the foregoing are essentially matters of detail, and they repre-sent utter minutiae in so massive an enterprise'. He was right to predict that *IG* 1[3] would be 'not so much popular as indispensable to studies of fifth-century Athens'.[30]

In the Jeffery memoir Lewis remarked 'fighting the public inscrip-tions through to publication as a first fascicle in 1981 had not been

---

[29] *Numismatic Chronicle* ii, 7th series (1962), 275–300 and 290–2.

[30] *CR*, xxxii (1982), 255–8 at 258. It can be added that the third edition of *IG* I represents a massive contribution to the history of scholarship; see for instance no. 1453 (from the second fascicle) for Lewis's mastery of the history of the texts and of their interpretation. The age of Boeckh (i.e. *CIG*) and of the first and even second editions of *IG*, were pioneering days; but by the late twentieth century an epigraphist who handles central texts like the Coinage Decree needs to be not just a historian in the sense insisted on throughout the present memoir but a historian of his or her subject—that is, a modern as well as an ancient historian.

easy'. The second fascicle, partly for reasons to do with Anne Jeffery's own state of health, was harder still. It carries the publication year 1994 and its preface is dated February 1993. Lewis's sentence quoted above, about the cabal who sold his name to Klaffenbach, continues: 'I needed collaborators and was in particular certain that I could not move a step without Anne'. He goes on to explain why it was that, although she had readily agreed to handle the bulk of the private texts, they were still unpublished in 1987: the trouble was, the material needed rethinking and reworking, partly in order to meet the standards of Erxleben who, as we have seen, wanted fuller presentation; and towards the end Anne Jeffery herself no longer had the health or the heart for this job. What emerges only slowly from Lewis's account is that he himself was left 'tidying for publication'. (This is a typical Lewis story: to my knowledge, more than one of the chapters in the *Cambridge Ancient History* volumes for which he was responsible as senior editor were pretty extensively rewritten by Lewis himself, but there is no hint of this in the relevant volume.) As the preface and (at greater length) the 1987 memoir makes clear, the difficulties were not merely practical: there was a serious and fundamental problem about the dating of inscriptions before and after 480, the year of the Persian sack of the Acropolis: this is the problem of the so-called 'Perserschutt'. The 1993 preface records a curious kind of death-bed confession by Anne Jeffery that her criteria for distributing material before and after 480 had been unsatisfactory; evidently, the resulting need to allocate the material more reliably was met by Lewis himself, a task calling for finesse in the highest degree. But her contribution had been large and the second fascicle appears under the joint editorship of Lewis and Jeffery, with the help of E. Erxleben, 'adiuvante Eberhard Erxleben'. The achievement represented by the first great fascicle of *IG* 1$^3$ was surely the main reason why Lewis was honoured with corresponding membership of the German Archaeological Institute (1985).

Big team projects such as that described above are commonplace in the academic life of the 1990s, but they were less usual in 1962. (An obvious example from Lewis's own field was the collaborative four-volume *Athenian Tribute Lists* which appeared between 1939 and 1953, and in which even so individual a scholar as H. T. Wade-Gery submerged himself.) It was typically far-sighted, and typically modest, of Lewis to grasp at so young an age the important truth that there are severe limits to what even the sharpest and most industrious scholar can achieve in one lifetime. F. Jacoby had produced fifteen fat volumes of the fragments of the Greek historians by the time he died in the late 1950s, but that was barely three-fifths of the whole task he had set himself back in 1909; an international team has only recently (1994) set to work on the remaining portions. As a Jewish refugee, Jacoby had at one time been kept going by the hospitality of Oxford and Christ Church; did Lewis have in mind this local lesson in what a single dedicated genius can and cannot do?

There is further and more significant evidence that from an astonishingly early point, Lewis saw his life's work as a collective enterprise, in fact as the direction of a kind of one-man research programme. I say 'more significant' because *IG* was after all an idea put to him by others, it was not an initiative of his own. It can be shown, I think, that from very early in his career, perhaps already in 1959, he had in his head an interlocking set of thesis topics for future graduate students, amounting to no less than a programme of research into the history of classical Athens. This is extraordinary enough (not many supervisors outside the sciences start off with a defined and related set of thesis topics to be parcelled out for years to come); it was and is even more extraordinary that he succeeded so brilliantly. There was an element of luck: how could anyone have foreseen that in his first few years at Christ Church he would be presented with two graduate students of the calibre of J. K. Davies and P. J. Rhodes? 1959 was the year in which he suggested the Athenian liturgical (i.e. propertied) class to John Davies as a 'focus for attention'[31]; and in 1963 he suggested to Peter Rhodes the subject of *his* dissertation: the Athenian *boule* or Council of Five Hundred.[32] The 'master-plan' is not just my own fanciful retrospective imposition of order on random events. Looking back in 1984, in an unpublished paper delivered at Birmingham called 'M. H. Hansen on the Athenian Ecclesia', he said, with a characteristic mix of tentativeness and firmness (and perhaps irony?):

> it is not totally clear whether my activity has any overall plan to it, but if it ever has had, it was certainly at least once along the lines that John's original thesis, now happily all in the public domain,[33] on the propertied families and Peter's work on the *boule* needed completing first by one more book on the non-assembly features of the Athenian constitution, i.e. on the strategoi and other elected officials, and finally another on the workings of the assembly

[31] See J. K. Davies, *Athenian Propertied Families 600–300 BC* (Oxford, 1971), preface.
[32] See P. J. Rhodes, *The Athenian Boule* (Oxford, 1972), preface.
[33] A reference to J. K. Davies, *Wealth and the Power of Wealth in Classical Athens* (New York, 1981), which supplemented the gazetteer cited above, at n. 31.

itself. It was here that a yawning gap in Athenian studies, mostly filled with platitudes, existed when Mogens [Hansen] began his work.

In other words, Hansen had pre-empted a topic earmarked for some future Lewis pupil, but that was one potential Oxford thesis which could be struck off the list: Lewis could only offer (with applause) some comments on detail, and that he went on in Birmingham to do. As for the other project (the *strategoi* (generals) etc.), that too was done outside Oxford, by R. Develin in his *Athenian Officials 684–322 BC* (Cambridge, 1987); but there is certainly Lewis input throughout, as the preface acknowledges, and as I remember from a visit to Lewis's rooms in Christ Church at the time he was working through the draft typescript.

As we have seen, Lewis's main work on the first fascicle of *IG* 1³ was done in the decade 1962–72; but this was not the only book he was working on during these years. In 1968 and 1969 he published two books, both of them collaborative. The first to appear was 'Gould and Lewis', the revision of *Dramatic Festivals of Athens*, Pickard-Cambridge's last and posthumously published book (1953). The work of revising *DFA* was 'essentially completed in the late summer of 1964'. Lewis greatly expanded and improved the epigraphic material, particularly the appendices to chapters 1 and 2 (on the festivals) and 7 (on the Artists of Dionysus). Chapter 7 itself was pretty thoroughly overhauled and now represents an important contribution to Hellenistic and even Roman cultural history. It was above all the deficiencies of this section of the 1953 book which made a new edition desirable from the epigraphic point of view. Jeanne and Louis Robert, in the *Bulletin Épigraphique* 1954[34] were harsh about the non-Attic material. They commented that Pickard-Cambridge used inscriptions extensively, and that they were conveniently reproduced—as far as Attica went. 'Mais toutes les fois qu'on sort d'Athènes, la documentation est vieillie soit *passim* soit spécialement dans le chapitre final', which, as they said, reproduced some texts from Teos with grave errors and 'phrases inextricables'. Lewis not only put all that right, but widened the geographical sweep of the relevant epigraphic appendix considerably. (It was thus a little ungenerous of the *Bulletin* not to notice the 1968 revision at all.)

This was not the whole story, however, nor (for students of Athens and Attic drama) the most important one: the second edition improved and rearranged the first throughout, in ways which the 1968 preface

---

[34] *Revue des études grecques*, lxvii (1954), *Bull. Épig.*, no. 54.

handily summarises. What the mere list of changes in that preface imperfectly brings out is the tactfully-executed but crucial shift of direction in the direction of the political. Not only was the paragraph on the politics of *choregoi* (p. 90) new; so too was the change in what the preface—too blandly and modestly—calls the 'account of theatrical taste' at pp. 274 *et seq*. It would be better to say that the problem of political comedy was now confronted directly, in some paragraphs which read far more incisively than their 1953 predecessors. 'To put the question in a concrete form', the revisers asked, 'how could *Knights* win first prize without, apparently, Kleon's position being affected in the least?' It was to this precise question that Christopher Carey attempted an answer in his 1993 contribution to the Lewis conference.[35]

Simon Goldhill, in his contribution to the conference in honour of David Lewis, put $DFA^2$ alongside Fraenkel's *Agamemnon* as one of the books which changed his academic life;[36] he added, almost incidentally, that he made much use of it as a work of reference. Its value as a reference-work is clear from the need for a second revision in 1988 (this not only provided, for example, new epigraphic material on the festivals and some exciting new evidence for Aristophanic costume, but also, at p. 364, a valuable new section on political censorship, a topic oddly omitted in the two previous editions; this carries still further the extension of the book in a political direction). Goldhill was, however, right to speak of the book as much more than a dry compilation of the evidence. His own paper addressed one of the most controversial questions addressed by the book in both 1953 and 1968: did Athenian women attend performances at the theatre? (In 1968, however, the question was no longer confusingly put, because it was now prised apart from the separate question of attendance by boys.) The urgency and topicality of the question has been underlined by the poet and playwright Tony Harrison in an interview:

> Were women present at theatrical performances? Now why is that not one of the main questions being asked about Greek drama, considering the context? It would make all the difference between a stag party and a mixed party; it would make the sexual hostility of the plays understandable . . . I found a reference pointing to the fact that, if women were admitted, they sat separately from the men, which again creates a different kind of expectation. One

[35] See *Ritual, Finance, Politics* (see above, n. 2), pp. 69–83.
[36] S. Goldhill, 'Representing Democracy: Women at the Great Dionysia', in *Ritual, Finance, Politics* (see above, n. 2), pp. 346–69 at p. 346.

of the techniques of the stand-up comedian, who knows how to relate to his audience, is the way he polarises the audience sexually.[37]

For anyone interested in such questions, $DFA^2$ is the first recourse. For Lewis's biographer, $DFA^2$ is important as showing that his insistence that history and epigraphy are inseparable could equally well be expressed as a proposition about epigraphy and literature; or rather, we could say that Lewis's conception of history took in literature—and religion: the Dionysiac content of the book makes it an essential handbook for students of some of the main Athenian festivals. The only feature of the book which we might regret in 1997 is its relative inaccessibility to the Greekless reader. In their 1968 preface, Gould and Lewis wrote 'we offer no apology for the continued prominence of Greek text'. Fortunately, this problem has now been solved by Csapo and Slater, who have provided translations of the primary material.[38]

Though Goldhill, on the page I have already quoted, generously called $DFA^2$ 'really a new book', the revisers would have deprecated that description: however much they had improved on Pickard-Cambridge, his name alone appears on the spine. By contrast, Russell Meiggs and David Lewis, *A Selection of Greek Historical Inscriptions to the End of the Fifth Century BC* (1969) definitely superseded M. N. Tod's volume i, and was 'in no sense a new edition of Tod's work', though the authors deliberately preserved his title for the new book. The preface, from which I have just drawn, ends with the following charming sentence, after a string of acknowledgments: 'we should also compliment one another, for we have found a surprising measure of agreement and our few differences of opinion have never escalated'. The most obvious and explicit of these differences is on p. 184, concerning the dating of no. 67, the contributions to the Spartan warfund: *c*.427 (Meiggs) or much later, perhaps even 396–5 (Lewis)? The two datings are juxtaposed, but Lewis evidently bowed to his collaborator's view; his own would have excluded the text from the volume altogether. It would on Lewis's 1968 dating have had to wait for the replacement of Tod's fourth-century volume (once planned by Lewis himself for his retirement and now to be carried through on rather different lines by Robin Osborne and Peter Rhodes). In any case, this

---

[37] See Neil Astley (ed.), *Tony Harrison: A Critical Anthology* (Newcastle, 1991), p. 243, part of a 1983 interview with John Haffenden and reprinted from *Poetry Review*, 73 (1984). The 'reference' here is presumably Ar. *Pax* 962 *et seq.*, discussed at $DFA^2$, p. 264.

[38] E. Csapo and W. J. Slater, *The Context of Ancient Drama* (Ann Arbor, 1995).

is one text where Lewis was able, in the revision which (like that of $DFA^2$) appeared in 1988, to point to new fragments of the stone which made Meiggs' date preferable.[39]

There was hard work to be done for ML, as the book has come to be called, and Lewis did some of the necessary work on squeezes during another visit to the Institute for Advanced Study at Princeton in 1964–5. But it must also have been fun choosing the sixteen new texts: their discovery was after all (p. vi) the main avowed reason for producing a new book rather than a new edition. The first six inscriptions were all new since Tod's book of 1933, although (for instance) the oath of the settlers at Cyrene (no. 5) had been known since the 1920s, so that Tod could have used it if he had wished. One of the newly included texts, the 'Themistocles Decree' (no. 23), nowadays attracts scholarly interest for reasons other than those which seem primarily to have led Meiggs and Lewis to print it: not so much as a factual corrective to Herodotus on the events of 480 as because it is a palmary example of invented tradition about the Persian Wars. Other exciting new texts threw light on Athenian relations with Carthage (no. 92) and life in Attica away from the city of Athens itself (no. 53: from the deme of Rhamnous). There were losses too, such as the two inscriptions which dealt with the amphictyonies of Delphi and Delos: Tod nos. 39 (*IG* $1^3$ 9) and 85 respectively. Thucydides' neglect of this important aspect of fifth-century life is bad enough without compounding it.[40] But the date and interpretation of the very fragmentary *IG* $1^3$ 9 are controversial, and the commentary on ML 62 contains valuable compensating material on Delos and its amphictyons, although that text does not actually use the word. Other excisions must have been painful: a Thucydidean such as Lewis must have felt a pang at the jettisoning of Tod no. 72 (*IG* $1^3$ 83), the Quadruple alliance between Athens, Argos, Mantinea, and Elis, cp. Thuc. 5.47. But no one can fail to be grateful for the exemplary discusson of such complex topics as the use of the tribute lists (nos. 39; 50; 75).

[39] See p. 312 of the 1988 revision (slightly different on this point in the paperback reissue of 1989) and the *Cambridge Ancient History*, vi$^2$ 28, n. 17. Still more recently, Ionian War dates for this inscription have been argued for, above all by M. Piérart, *Bulletin de Correspondance hellénique*, cxix (1995), 235–82 (an article which is dedicated to the memory of David Lewis, and whose first footnote reports Lewis's unpublished flexibility on the dating of the inscription; it may be that Lewis would have accepted Piérart's dating).

By 1988 Russell Meiggs of Balliol had only a short time to live and left the work to Lewis; see the latter's reference to 'my ever generous and trusting colleague' in the preface to the revision.

[40] See *HSCP*, xciv (1992), 169–97.

Like *IG* 1$^3$, and like Meiggs' 1972 book *The Athenian Empire*, ML rejects the wholesale downdatings of H. Mattingly and is to that extent conservative on Attic letter-forms at least; but Meiggs may have felt more strongly on this point than did Lewis (note in any case such discussions as p. 121 on ML 47, where the rejection of Mattingly is by no means confident or doctrinaire). The book was fully collaborative and it is hard to guess who wrote what; but work on such a book has to start somewhere and the two scholars divided the inscriptions among themselves. Thus I remember asking Lewis in about 1990 why the ML date for no. 74, the Delphic thank-offering of the Messenians at Naupactus, is given without explanation as '*c.*421 BC' whereas Tod had put it '425 BC' (i.e. Tod thought such a dedication at Delphi could have been made during rather than after the Archidamian War); the answer, roughly, was that Meiggs had been responsible for that one. This being so, it seems reasonable to suppose that Meiggs had first go at the imperial inscriptions.[41]

I hope it is abundantly obvious, from what I have said already, that Lewis had a collaborative gift amounting to genius. This was perhaps most successfully displayed in his supervision of graduate students—the area of teaching in which above all he excelled: he was, in a word, professional about it. 'Collaboration' is perhaps not quite the word for even the closest graduate supervision in historical studies, but Lewis supplied his ideas and material to his students with the same automatic open-handedness that a scholar might show to a co-author or a co-editor with whom he was to share equal credit. No doubt there have been other supervisors of whom similar things could be said; what made Lewis so remarkable was the quantity and quality of the ideas and material so supplied. When I began research myself in 1974, Keith Thomas asked me, at dinner in my then college, who was my supervisor. When I told him, he commented, 'Ah yes, Lewis, the man who writes other people's books for them'. We have seen that there is a literal sense in which this was true, because Lewis (with others) *re*wrote books by Tod and Pickard-Cambridge, and some of the skills of revision are transferable to supervision: in both operations, one of the things most needed is a good nose for what is worth keeping and what should be discarded. But

---

[41] See e.g. p. 226 on no. 75, 'serious objections' against West's dating, cp. *Athenian Empire*, p. 340. But 'imperial inscriptions' is a broad concept and presumably ML 63, which discusses Lewis's own published views and has a paragraph of argument against Mattingly, is the work of Lewis.

Lewis was an adder and a multiplier, not just a subtracter. Above all—
and here for the first time in this memoir I speak with firsthand
experience, having on good advice asked for Lewis as a supervisor in
early 1974—he *raised your game*, simply by making you aware that his
standards were so high. Although as we have seen he was remarkable
for having a clear general idea in advance of the graduate topics which
needed to be done, nevertheless he did not give any help along the way
about what particular aspect of the topic might be tackled next or at all;
to that extent he was the least *dirigiste* of supervisors. Peter Rhodes,
although his thesis topic was suggested by Lewis himself, received
equally little direction beyond an initial set of suggestions for reading.
Nor, although I lived only a couple of hundred yards away, did I find his
conversation (which was alarmingly omniscient for a postgraduate rusty
on Greek history after more than two years qualifying for the Bar, and
which left too many gaps in thought to be supplied) as profitable as his
written comments on a draft. These, as anyone who ever showed work
to Lewis will confirm,[42] were pure gold. They could themselves be
highly elliptical and concentrated, but at least you had them there as a
possession, and could spend the next day or two slowly working
through them, to your immense profit. This should not be taken to
mean that he was impersonal or unsupportive; the opposite was true.
He could be calming and witty at the same time. I once sent him an
over-excited and anxious letter after what I was afraid must have
seemed a non-productive period, concluding with a promise that a draft
of a new chapter of my thesis would be on its way to Christ Church in a
week or so. I got a postcard back which read, 'I await your chapter 4
without impatience'. Even at the time I could appreciate the marvel-
lously ambiguous phrasing of this piece of reassurance.

It may be thought that the above account errs by treating him as too
little of an independent scholar. Was all his work, it may be objected,
team work? What—to be specific—about his one sole-authored academic book on a classical topic, *Sparta and Persia* (1977)? I do not
think the general objection a damaging one even if it were true, but in
any case it misses what I think is an essential point: Lewis was, I
suggest, keen on delegation, co-operation and sharing not because of
some inbuilt academic gregariousness (his widow testifies to his groans
over many years about the demands of *IG* in particular) but precisely

---

[42] Not just historians either. For the debt owed by a close literary colleague note C. Macleod,
*Collected Essays* (Oxford, 1983), p. 20, n. 1; p. 52, n. 1; p. 139, n. 56.

because he knew how little one scholar can do in one working lifetime. His own premature death shows how right he was—in a way; and yet, in another way, how much he *did* do! As for the specific objection, *Sparta and Persia* demonstrates that in the rare case where a topic could not be farmed out to a pupil he would do it himself.

Let me explain this. Here, at the risk of being autobiographical rather than biographical, I think I can throw light on the immediate genesis of *Sparta and Persia*. Part of the book's origin[43] undoubtedly lay in the help Lewis was giving to Tony Andrewes in the 1960s and 1970s, when Andrewes was working on the difficult book 8 of Thucydides, with its satrapal Persian material. (We recall the Corpus undergraduate of many years earlier, for whom Frank Lepper found 'messes to clear up'.) Andrewes' letters to Lewis from this period survive, and it is clear that very complex and detailed matters were being intensely discussed between these two heavyweights. So much indeed is clear enough from the published final volume of the *Historical Commentary* (1981); but the correspondence shows that Lewis himself was deeply engaged with the doings of Tissaphernes, Pharnabazus and the Greeks who had to deal with them. So when a graduate student (myself) appeared at the end of 1973 with an expressed wish to do something on Persia and the Greeks, Lewis put him to work on the subject-matter of what was eventually to become *Sparta and Persia*, that is, on a study of the complex diplomatic history of the late fifth-century Greek and especially Spartan involvement with the satraps of western Asia Minor. This, however, lasted only about six months, because in summer 1974 I was diverted into studying Mausolus and his dynasty by becoming aware, thanks to Peter Fraser, of the then recent (1972) epigraphic material from Labraunda published by Jonas Crampa; this was shortly to be followed in autumn 1974, after my switch of subject, by the discovery of the trilingual inscription from Lycian Xanthus ('if you haven't read the new *CRAI*' ran a postcard from David Lewis, 'drop everything and do so'). The excuse for introducing Mausolus and

---

[43] But only part. In an unpublished lecture delivered at Chicago in 1993, he recalled that 'it was Aramaic evidence from Egypt, Driver's Arsam archive [i.e. G. R. Driver, *Aramaic Documents of the Fifth Century BC* (Oxford, 1957)] which, in 1957, prompted my first publication related to Persia [i.e. 'The Phoenician Fleet in 411', *Historia*, vii (1958), 393–7]. It needed the quantity of new material provided by Hallock's Fortification Tablets [R. Hallock, *Persepolis Fortification Tablets* (Chicago, 1969)] to get me going at all seriously'. The chatty and smooth-paced Chicago lecture is of interest as disclosing Lewis's own linguistic qualifications in the relevant languages: 'patchy Hebrew' (this was certainly much too modest) and some Elamite, in addition to Aramaic.

myself into this memoir is that I believe that David Lewis decided to write *Sparta and Persia* only after the point in summer 1974 when it was clear I was going to stray away from the topic which he had decided needed investigating. As a result he realised he would have to do it himself, so he did, and much better than I could or would have done.

*Sparta and Persia* was given as the Donald Bradeen Memorial Lectures in autumn 1976 at Cincinnati, Ohio; before that he tried parts of it out on a small lecture audience in Oxford (summer 1975). I remember the Oxford audience as being very small, and as including Robin Lane Fox and myself; apart from that I have only my notes on the lectures themselves—useless for academic purposes, because so soon superseded by the book. The lectures were not easy listening but I do not remember learning so much so quickly from any other lecture course in my life. The Cincinnati invitation was given and accepted when Bradeen, with whom Lewis had worked on the funerary inscriptions from the *agora*,[44] was still alive; but by the time Lewis arrived Bradeen was dead.

The book has established itself as a classic. It was slow to do so, partly (one suspects) because of its absolutely uncompromising presentation: a slim, dark red volume, not issued by a promotionally minded university press[45] but by Brill of Leiden; no dust-jacket; no subtitle; no chapter titles (though the running heads were informative); long footnotes containing untranslated Greek; few reviews.[46] Nevertheless it was and is an exciting and original book. The first two chapters introduced Persia and Sparta: the Sparta chapter took for its subject-matter some more or less traditional themes to do with the structure of Spartan society and the nature of Spartan decision-making and transformed them. The opening and matching Persia chapter was revolutionary in more obvious ways, exploiting as it did, and for the first time in an account aimed at Greek historians, the evidence of the Persepolis Fortification Tablets, which were to occupy Lewis on and off in the remaining twenty years of his life. One of his last published essays, called 'The Persepolis Tablets: Speech, Seal, and Script',[47]

[44] See *Classical Quarterly*, xxix (1979), 240–6.
[45] The book was offered to neither Oxford nor Cambridge, as Hilary O'Shea and Pauline Hire confirm. (Publication was evidently by special arrangement. The book does after all describe itself as *Cincinnati Classical Studies*, vol. i, and was published with the financial support of the Classics (Sample Fund) of the University of Cincinnati.)
[46] Nothing, for instance, in *Classical Review*.
[47] In Bowman and Woolf (see above, n. 28), pp. 1–15.

exploited the tablets from the point of view of literacy, and some material, still unpublished at the time of his death, has been absorbed into a study by Christopher Tuplin.[48] *Sparta and Persia* uses the tablets for the understanding of the Persian economy and political system, and in order to trace the movements of high-ranking personnel: these movements are traceable via their allocations of rations. The results are usually unspectacular in detail (although Lewis was able to illuminate the career of a figure known as 'Datis the Mede', well-known from Herodotus and the Lindian Chronicle, in a short follow-up article in 1980[49]). But the whole discussion is a superb demonstration of what a 'gift-giving' society (in the sense in which twentieth-century anthropology has taught us to understand that notion) was really like at the level of detail—though the book contains no references to such theoretical discussions.[50] Equally, the book does not explicitly acknowledge, what was surely true, that some of Lewis's fascination with the Persepolis material flowed from the same sources as had his youthful fascination with the Athenian tribute lists: this was concrete, nuts and bolts, epigraphic evidence for imperialism otherwise known only from generalised data in literary sources: Thucydides in 1952; Herodotus in 1977.[51]

The structure of the rest of the book is essentially narrative, covering the second half of the fifth and the early part of the fourth centuries BC. It would be too much to say that it solves a problem per page, but twenty years on, it is possible to gauge the book's importance by the way whole learned articles and even books[52] have been generated and stimulated by suggestions advanced in it. Thus a single page in *Sparta and Persia* called into existence a 'Treaty of Boiotios' of 407 BC, to solve certain diplomatic puzzles of that period and of the 390s; this has been much discussed since 1977.[53] A single footnote in the book offered a solution, in terms of Thucydides' narrative technique, to the

---

[48] Forthcoming.

[49] *JHS*, c (1980), 1941 *et seq.*

[50] Note, however, 'Persian Gold in International Relations', *Revue des études anciennes*, xci (1989), 227–34 at 227: 'although it did not attract the attention of Marcel Mauss, the master of the subject, the Achaemenid Empire in fact constitutes a textbook case of a gift-centred economy'.

[51] See 'Persians in Herodotus' in *The Greek Historians, Literature and History: Papers Presented to A. E. Raubitschek* (1985), pp. 101–17, and his postscript to the 1984 reissue of A. R. Burn, *Persia and the Greeks*.

[52] Note the tribute in the preface to E. Badian's *From Plataea to Potidaea: Studies in the History and Historiography of the Pentecontaetia* (1993), p. ix.

[53] See the *Cambridge Ancient History*, vi[2] 65, n. 89, for references.

problem of Artaxerxes I's death-date: Matthew Stolper then took this up in 1983 in a full-length article.[54] The essential point was that Thucydides (iv. 50) could anticipate his own narrative—a technique which narratologists call 'prolepsis'—by some considerable margin, and finish off an incidental episode before reverting to the main story-line. If *Sparta and Persia* was illuminating about Thucydides, it was no less so about Herodotus: witness for instance the observation (p. 148) that one of the themes of Herodotus' *History* is that the Persians gradually discover what the Spartans are like. More than any other of Lewis's works, *Sparta and Persia* manages to combine its author's normally separate spheres of expertise: Greek history and historiography; Greek epigraphy (see, for example, p. 129, n. 132: Evagoras); and the study of the newest evidence from and about Achaemenid Persia. Even the Jews are there—surprisingly perhaps, given the book's title (see pp. 20 and 51, n. 5, Nehemiah; cf. p. 153, n. 118).

Despite the actual publication date of 1977, 1976 was really the year of *Sparta and Persia* (the preface to the book is dated November 1976, and the lectures were given that autumn), and was thus a year of international professional success for its author; but it was also a year of local professional disappointment. At the beginning of 1976 it became clear that the Wykeham Professorship of Ancient (Greek) History at Oxford, due to fall vacant after a long tenure by Tony Andrewes at the end of September 1977, would be filled without a gap of the kind now familiar. Only two candidates were considered by the electors: David Lewis, and George Forrest, who was elected in May 1976, after a very short meeting indeed, and without the holding of interviews. The preference of M. I. Finley, the Cambridge elector, then at the height of his influence, seems to have been a, or even the, decisive factor; he apparently[55] considered Lewis to be ruled out as a mere epigraphist. If this memoir has not been completely useless, it should have prepared the reader to reject that assessment. On the other hand, George Forrest was certainly the more successful and charismatic

---

[54] M. Stolper, *Arch. Mitt aus Iran*, xvi (1983), 23–36, developing *Sparta and Persia*, p. 71, n. 140 (a suggestion offered by Lewis as an *alternative* to that in his text). The implications for Thucydides' narrative technique were noted by Andrewes, *Historical Commentary on Thucidides*, v. 366.

[55] I am indebted to the reminiscences of Peter Brunt, himself an elector (he was Camden Professor of Roman History at the time, but a notable Greek historian as well). The other electors (apart from the Vice-Chancellor and the Warden of New College, to which the professorship is attached by university statute) were G. E. M. de Ste Croix, H. R. Trevor-Roper, and C. M. Robertson.

communicator of the two (his undergraduate lectures were famously well attended in the 1950s and 1960s, and he had published two sparkling books in recent years, one called *The Emergence of Greek Democracy* (1966) and one *A History of Sparta* (1968). Both were lightly documented but crammed full of ideas, and both were politically *engaged*, as books about ancinet history rarely are. But Lewis had been an FBA since 1974 and was already a figure of international and magisterial distinction, to whom one automatically looked for a lead in seminars and conferences. If the electors were unaware that *Sparta and Persia* was on the way (and astonishingly, it does seem that they *were* unaware), the fault was partly Lewis's own. In a letter to a senior friend in America dated 9 January 1976, he asked in the briefest possible way for a reference for the Wykeham job, and made no mention of projects in hand, although the book as we have seen had been tried out on an Oxford audience as early as summer 1975. The referee in question therefore wrote to the electors in admiring but rather apologetic vein about Lewis's failure to produce a book of his own, and about how he preferred to revise other people's work.

Lewis took the rejection calmly, as far as the outside world could see; to his referee in the US he wrote a laconic note of the result, added thanks for support, and ended, 'I do not find myself greatly disturbed or distressed'. But he was privately shaken, and did seriously contemplate moving to the US at this time. The possibility had arisen a few years earlier, with the retirement of Ben Meritt from his professorship at the Institute for Advanced Study; at that time Lewis had declined to be considered for the succession to Meritt. His wife says one of his reasons for staying put at that earlier time was that he 'did not want his children to grow up in Nixon's America'. It is good to be able to record that in 1985 Oxford University offered Lewis a personal professorship, and that he greatly enjoyed the professorial role. From that point on he lectured more, as his duties required; he took on more graduate students and over a wider range of topics. It would be parochial to say more on this topic, but his chairmanship of the reformed 'Oxford Classical Monographs' series helped to bring many Oxford classical and historical theses to publication.

His professorial duties enabled him to shine as an extremely effective 'committee man', for instance in 1991–2 as Chairman of the Literae Humaniores Faculty Board (a notoriously fractious and unwieldy body which includes philosophers and literary specialists, as well as ancient historians). His gifts for administration, however, were not confined to the Oxford academic scene. We shall see what he did for the Oxford Jewish community; and in London he was highly valued for his work for the British Academy. The Secretary, Peter Brown, recalls that he 'took the Academy *seriously* and was loyal to it and personally forthcoming to us here. He chaired its Ancient History section, he served on Council, and he was one of the three "wise men" who reviewed the Academy's Research Projects.'

Not long after the professional reverse of 1976–7, Lewis became involved in the large-scale historical project which was to last the rest of his life, and through which he was to reach out to a wider audience than ever before: the *Cambridge Ancient History*. He became an editor of and contributor to volume iv, which covered the later sixth and early fifth centuries BC; Lewis's own contribution was on the later Pisistratids (Pisistratus himself had been covered by Tony Andrewes in volume iii, part 3 (1982)). John Boardman writes that Nicholas Hammond 'got David in on *CAH* iv mainly with an eye to the future, wanting someone on the spot to cope with the core history and not wanting to go on himself'. So much for the motives of his editorial colleagues; what of Lewis's own? One wonders if he agreed (albeit reluctantly; see below) because something inside him compelled him, at just that time of his life, to assert as unequivocally and publicly as possible his credentials as a mainline historian rather than 'merely' an epigraphist. But the letter from Lewis to Jeremy Mynott of Cambridge University Press dated 18 July 1979 merely says 'my conversion stems from the beneficial effect on my pupils' Solon essays caused by reading the Solon chapter' [i.e. Tony Andrewes' material, in draft].

Lewis's own chapter in volume iv is tightly argued and fairly short (16 pp.; contrast the following chapter by Martin Ostwald: 44 pp.); but it packs a lot in and is notable for its attention to religious aspects.[56] However his contribution did not stop there because his editorial input was considerable: thus he made large-scale but self-effacing improvements in the long opening chapters on the Persian Empire and its neighbours. This was, as I have already noted earlier, even more true of the volumes of which he was senior editor, namely volumes v and vi, covering the post-Persian-Wars fifth century, and the fourth century, respectively. The title 'senior editor' is not one which appears on the title pages of the *Cambridge Ancient History* volumes; but for each

---

[56] And is duly cited in the notes to the appropriate pages (pp. 86 *et seq.*) of R. Parker, *Athenian Religion: A History* (see above, n. 15); see also the preface to that important book.

volume there is a primary organising individual and taker of initiatives, on to whom much of the donkey work falls. Pauline Hire of Cambridge University Press recalls Lewis's initial reluctance to get mixed up with the *Cambridge Ancient History* at the editorial level at all: it was clear to her that his chief reason was that he knew how much work would be involved if he did it properly (and being Lewis, he was not capable of doing anything in any other way). He did the job, he did it properly, and he did it so as to win from the experienced Pauline Hire the description 'my perfect editor'.

Volumes v and vi are, together with *IG* $1^3$, Lewis's historical memorial. The two volumes were designed as a pair (a conception symbolised by John Boardman's accompanying plates volume, which covers volumes v and vi together). Thus the regional studies in volume vi are intended to cover the fifth century as well as the fourth, and the religious material in volume v draws (as the preface to volume vi points out) on 'later sources'. Lewis himself wrote no fewer than four chapters for volume v, all of them on absolutely central topics in this most central of all the Greek volumes of the *Cambridge Ancient History*. A lifelong interest in historiography generally, and in Thucydides in particular, gives special authority to his elegantly written opening chapter on the written sources (note the suggestive remarks on Thucydidean selectivity at p. 5). As in volume iv, his gift for compression was at a premium (see especially the treatment at pp. 111 *et seq.* of the so-called First Peloponnesian War, a topic which Lewis had handled elsewhere[57]) but the writing is trenchant and authoritative, and there is no crabbedness or obscurity about his meaning. And some of the material, like the account of the run-up to the main Peloponnesian War, is ample and almost leisurely. Some initial reactions to this magnificent volume were oddly negative (I think of Peter Green in the *Times Literary Supplement*), but M. H. Jameson, reviewing the book more judiciously and at the perspective of four years after its appearance,[58] wrote more cordially and correctly that Lewis's 'sure, subtle and restrained inter-weaving of the evidence of inscriptions into the narrative of political and military events is one of the major achievements of this book, an achievement in which Peter Rhodes and Davies, scholars who have worked closely with Lewis, also share'. Note the careful and correctly

---

[57] In the Festschrift for M. F. McGregor, *Classical Contributions*, ed. G. S. Shrimpton and D. J. McCargar (Locust Valley, NY, 1981), pp. 71–8.
[58] *Class. Journ.*, xci (1996), 193–6.

balanced emphasis here, on both the individual achievement of Lewis the scholar and on the vicarious achievement of Lewis the teacher and collaborator.

The final, fourth-century, volume vi was published after Lewis's death, but he had by early 1994 corrected proofs of his own chapters and missed seeing a bound copy by only a matter of weeks. Again, the overarching conception was to a great extent Lewis's, and I know of two chapters, ostensibly written entirely by other contributors, which looked very different before Lewis put his editorial hand to them—one indeed he virtually rewrote, the other he annotated creatively. Of his own two chapters, chapter 2 on 'Sparta as Victor' (i.e. on the aftermath of the Peloponnesian War) took him back to 'Sparta and Persia' country, with a bonus in the form of an elegant treatment of the Thirty Tyrants. The other (chapter 5) is on 'Sicily 413–368' and could hardly be more different. It includes the tyranny of Dionysius I and includes sections (see especially pp. 153–6 on the character of the tyranny) written in a racy style next to which, for instance, his own handling of the death of Theramenes in chapter 2, looks abrupt and dead pan. This chapter is, with the possible exception of his *Encyclopaedia Britannica* article on Pericles,[59] the closest he got to writing in a popular manner and are a complete answer to anyone who ever doubted his ability to write accessibly and for the general reader. For the professional historian the chapter is notable, first for its argument for the postponement of Dionysius' tyrannical ambitions until a point later than that usually assumed, and secondly, for its treatment of the sources of Diodorus' Sicilian narrative for the period, a notoriously tricky question.

By the beginning of the 1990s, when volume v of the *Cambridge Ancient History* appeared, David Lewis was a towering name in classical Greek history locally, nationally, and internationally, especially after the death of Tony Andrewes in June 1990 removed the most obviously distinguished British practitioner of the previous generation. When at just this time Robin Osborne, whose Cambridge thesis Lewis had examined and whom Lewis helped to bring to Oxford, had the inspired idea of a combined celebration to honour Lewis' sixty-fifth birthday and the 2,500th anniversary of democracy as inaugurated by Clisthenes, the response from ex-pupils and colleagues was heartening

---

[59] First published in 1974 and still included in the 1992 impression of the 15th ed., at vol. 9, pp. 290 *et seq.*

and massive. The conference was held in July 1993 in Christ Church
and became a book, in fact both a Festschrift and a volume of conference proceedings rolled into one. The conference, called 'The History and Archaeology of Athenian Democracy', was internationally
attended: seventy-five scholars, and twenty-five contributors—not for-
getting David Lewis's wife, his four daughters, and his brother Philip,
all of whom attended the dinner which was held on the evening of the
penultimate day and at which Lewis himself spoke memorably and
wittily in reply to the toast to his health. During the four days of the
conference Lewis himself attended all the papers (a packed and punishing schedule) and commented in his acute but benign way after most of
them. By the end he seemed pleased, if exhausted.

The early 1990s also saw the culmination, in book form, of
another side of his life. This was *The Jews of Oxford* (1992), a history
of the Jewish community in Oxford written to commemorate the
foundation of the Congregation in 1842. We saw earlier that as an
undergraduate he was active in (indeed President of) the university
Jewish Society, and in mature life he served the community tirelessly,
eventually holding office as Secretary (1969–75) then President
(1977–9) of the Congregation. The greatest achievement of this
period was the financing and construction in the early 1970s, during
Lewis's secretaryship, of the new synagogue building in Nelson Street
in the suburb known as Jericho. Lewis was also a trustee of the
company formed in 1974 to hold the building, the Oxford Synagogue
and Jewish Centre Limited. All this is set out in the latter part of the
1992 book, with modest reticence about the author's own role, and a
sprinkling of crisp humour. (Of the first and very famous Danish
architect, Lewis comments 'in the spring of 1971, he was dismissed
and died, unfortunately in that order'.) The book is an absorbing read
throughout, showing on every page that modern social history lost
(but perhaps we should say it finally gained) a superb practitioner in
Lewis; but for the outsider the most interesting part is surely the
account (chapter 7) of the impact of the Second World War and of
the evacuation of Jews to Oxford from London and further away, with
the tensions thereby caused.

*The Jews of Oxford* was Lewis's only sustained piece of writing
about the modern world since his army education days; but the interest
in Jewish history is manifest throughout his career (he chose, after all
the title of Professor of *Ancient* History, rather than just Greek history,
and by 'ancient' he surely had in mind Jewish as well as Persian). His

bibliography is littered with reviews of Judaica,[60] including some of the most important works of the period such as the various volumes of Schurer-Vermes-Millar, *History of the Jewish People in the Time of Jesus Christ*. Lewis's most significant contribution in this area, apart from his improvements to the *Cambridge Ancient History* material, is the appendix on the Jewish inscriptions of Egypt at the end of Tcherikower, Fuks, and Stern, *Corpus Papyrorum Judaicarum*. Again, one may note the willingness to let his efforts be absorbed into a book which carried the names of other scholars on its spine; those efforts remain, however, a distinctive and important contribution to the whole work.

During the month after the 1993 conference in his honour, Lewis fell ill after a family holiday in Cornwall and told his friends that he had kidney trouble which would mean shedding some of his organisational load (editorial work on *CAH* vi$^2$; the direction of graduate studies in ancient history, a task he had taken up only recently). By September he knew that he had terminal cancer of the bone-marrow. His courage and calm in the ten months left to him were matched only by those of Barbara, who made sure he was at home as much as was possible, despite the need for regular hospital visits for blood transfusions, tests, and chemotherapy. Even the dialysis was done at home for a long period, in the room which had been planned as the study for his retirement. Miraculously, he continued to work, first on annotating his *Selected Papers* for Cambridge University Press, and then on Persian material (though he also managed to catalogue some of his father's collections of children's books). The most astonishing achievement of this period was the very successful course of lectures he gave in the spring term of 1994 (see p. 570, above). But he also took very seriously his role as an elector to the Lincoln Chair of Classical Archaeology and visited the Ashmolean Library to read work by candidates. This all took some organisation on his part and on Barbara's: the dialysis had to be performed every few hours so he could not be far from base (they did, however, manage a family visit to London). It was beneficial that he had for many years kept up to date with computer technology;[61] he was, for instance, using e-mail before most of us knew what that expression meant. This enabled him simply

---

[60] Not just reviews: see 'The First Greek Jew', *Journal of Semitic Studies*, ii (1957), 264 *et seq.*

[61] See the preface to *IG* 1$^3$, fascicle 2. Early in the history of serious computer use in Oxford, he was active in promoting computer facilities for arts subjects both in his college and in the university.

to bring his machine home from Christ Church and work from there. Although with characteristic detachment, and need to understand, he made himself an expert on the disease which was destroying him, he often got bored with thinking about it all and naturally expected amusement and information from visitors. I recall going into the garden as late as June of 1994 and (after the shortest possible social preliminaries) being interrogated about what I thought of Harold Mattingly's new argument for a late date for the Coinage Decree, just published in *Klio*. He pretended to be incredulous and shocked that I did not know about it; I think he was really rather pleased to be, where he always had been, a jump ahead. Incidentally, those who assume that a scholarly position once taken up can and should never be abandoned may like to know that he was intrigued and attracted by the new argument for the late dating, though it went against much that he had written.[62] Similarly, his view about the radical down-dating, by techniques of laser enhancement, of the Athenian alliance with Egesta in Sicily (Meiggs and Lewis, no. 37) was not hostile but open-minded: it did after all involve the application of new technology, and this as we have seen is something which never ceased to excite and fascinate him. What he felt about *that* particular breakthrough by Mortimer Chambers and his collaborators was that good scientific method demanded the wider application of the technique, on less controversial readings.[63]

When liver complications set in (June 1994) he went downhill very fast and died on 12 July. He was buried two days later in the Jewish section of the Wolvercote cemetery, and in November of that year a memorial service was held in the synagogue he had done so much to bring into existence. A David Lewis Memorial Lecture, endowed by private subscriptions topping up an initial gift from his brother Philip, is to be held annually in Oxford.

David Lewis's gifts were those of kindness and of illumination, of charity and clarity; I am tempted to add, Lewis-fashion, 'in that order', but I am not really sure which is the right order. His published work is voluminous and stands at the highest possible level of scholarly

---

[62] But note already 'The Athenian Coinage Decree' in I. Carradice (ed.), *Coinage and Administration in the Athenian and Persian Empires* (Oxford, 1987), pp. 53–71 at p. 53: 'I detect a suggestion that they [the organisers] hope for some degree of confrontation and that Lewis in 1986 is expected to hold the same views as Lewis in 1969. I shall say at once that I have no confidence that I know the truth about the problems . . . '.

[63] See *CR*, xliii (1993), 461. On the personal side, Mortimer Chambers recalls that when he sent Lewis an offprint of the relevant article, he received in return a postcard with the one word: 'Brooding'.

achievement; in a specialised and technical age he was a supremely accomplished specialist and technician, with a matchless eye for detail; but he never forgot the unity of the ancient world and wandered cheerfully across the borders of the constituent disciplines of his subject;[64] and his own historical reading, *outside* what on the most hospitable definition could have been called his subject, was wide and more than just a relaxation. On the contrary he put it to occasional but lively and illuminating use (witness the last few pages of *Sparta and Persia* where we are suddenly in the 1920s and the world of Curzon and the Treaty of Lausanne). Finally, the Greeks Lewis studied were real people whose ways of thinking could be illuminated by reference to our own, even when the issues involved were complex and arcane.[65] All this amounts to a distinctive and supremely able and variously talented academic personality.

But his real legacy to his many pupils and admirers is a peculiarly rich and generous scholarly method. He could see combinations, between old evidence and new, faster than anyone; his immediate second thought was to share his first thought. Particular examples of this will long continue to abound in the scholarly literature and in the published and unpublished work of his pupils. (Who but David Lewis could have dared to suggest that the Kallimachos, with no ethnic or other identifying feature, who features in a third-century Athenian list of donors, might be the famous poet?[66]) But even when all Lewis's own ideas, floated so prodigally, have got into print, the method, and the example, and the memory of the kindness and generosity, will survive. He died far too young; but we have vast amounts to be grateful for.

SIMON HORNBLOWER
*Oriel College, Oxford*

---

[64] I hope enough evidence of this has already been given; but for a choice final example see the suggestion at *Sparta and Persia*, p. 21 about the significance of the Aristophanic name Paphlagon. A year later (*CR*, xxxiii (1983), 175, reviewing A. Sommerstein's edition of the *Knights*, which missed this suggestion) Lewis ruefully remarked 'it serves me right for putting Aristophanica in a historical work'.

[65] See p. 196 of his 'The Athenian Rationes Centesimarum' in M. I. Finley (ed.), *Problèmes de la terre* (Paris, 1973) for an amusing parallel between some oddities of Athenian prices and what went on at Athenian furniture auctions in post-war England.

[66] This suggestion is to be found, with acknowledgment, in the D.Phil. thesis of one of Lewis's last graduate pupils, Graham Oliver, a study of the politics and grain supply of Hellenistic Athens. The inscription is *Supplementum Epigraphicum Graecum*, xxxii (1982), 118, col. 1, l. 70. Curiously, the review by Alan Griffiths of Alan Cameron's *Callimachus and his Critics* (1995), in the *Times Literary Supplement*, 12 April 1996, quotes Cameron as saying, that 'maybe the [Athenian] inscription honouring the poet with proxeny and citizenship . . . will turn up'.

*Note.* Sources, in addition to those specifically cited: a memoir by Lewis himself about his early years, compiled for the Academy; letters from and/or conversations with, the following: Mrs Barbara Lewis (who also supplied correspondence from various phases of her husband's life); John Boardman; Peter Brunt; Mortimer Chambers; Anna Morpurgo Davies; Pauline Hire; Michael Jameson; Richard Jenkyns; Oswyn Murray; Hilary O'Shea; Toni Raubitschek; Peter Rhodes; Richard Rutherford; and Homer Thompson. A draft of this memoir was commented on and improved by Richard Rutherford, Peter Rhodes, and Barbara Lewis, to all of whom I am grateful. For other sorts of help I am indebted to Jasper Griffin. The photograph was kindly made available by Richard Rutherford, Christ Church, Oxford.

KARL LEYSER                    *Deborah Elliott*

*Proceedings of the British Academy*, **94**, 599–624

# Karl Joseph Leyser
# 1920–1992

KARL JOSEPH LEYSER was born in Düsseldorf on 24 October 1920. His
father was a manufacturer of belts and braces, inheriting a family
business, while his mother, a young woman of stunning beauty whose
maiden name was Hayum, came from a Cologne family which owned a
factory producing gloves and stockings. After the terrible German
inflation of the 1920s, the Leysers settled down in a roomy, old-
fashioned house in one of the quieter parts of Düsseldorf. They were
Jewish, and when the Nazi regime came, every obstacle was placed in
the way of Otto Leyser. Scrupulously careful as he was to obey the new
regulations governing his exports to Holland and Belgium where his
markets mainly lay, he none the less fell victim to an employee's
denunciation and had to escape to Holland with his wife, Emmy, in
1937. It was in this year that Karl and his sister came to England, since
the continuance of their education would have been virtually impossible
in Düsseldorf. Indeed, the family was declared stateless by a decree of
1937 and its property in Germany was sequestered. Between 1937 and
1939 Karl's father built up a new factory in Holland, and his parents
lived in a small house at Edam. But ruin once again followed the German
occupation of Holland, and the couple lived in hiding and in the gravest
danger for the last two-and-a-half years of the war. Two weeks after the
German surrender in 1945, a certain Lieutenant (later Captain) Charles
Lyser of the Black Watch (one assumes that the newspapers which
reported this dropped the *e* on account of anti-German feeling at the
time) drove his jeep into Edam, and had the joy of finding his parents

© The British Academy 1997.

once again. He had been standing in the main square of Edam, wondering what to do and where to go, when a man who recognised his likeness to his parents approached him. 'My father', he said to the journalists, 'is 67 years of age, and my mother is more than 50. Now they are safely housed in their own home. The quisling who occupied it is in jail.' For a third time his father began to build up his business, but the toll of the war on his health had been too great, and a few months later he succumbed to an attack of angina and died. His mother settled in England in 1950, having been helped financially by her son from the time he became a Fellow of Magdalen, and she lived to be high in her nineties.

Karl's education in 1937 continued at St Paul's School, to which he was channelled by voluntary agencies for refugees, with various of his father's relatives, not least among them the distinguished medieval historian Wilhelm Levison, helping with the fees. There survives a charming Christmas letter of 1946 from Levison to Karl, beginning 'Lieber Karl—denn so sage ich, wie in alten Zeiten, auch zu dem Captain' ('Dear Karl—for so I address you as formerly, albeit now Captain':—an allusion to Karl's rank in the Army). There is a story that because Karl would have exceeded the then quota of non-Anglicans at St Paul's, he was at first smuggled by the charismatic Philip Whitting into his history class. In any event, Whitting was an inspiration from the start. Karl would later say that the most lasting and exhilarating trait of Whitting's teaching for himself was his use of incident, an anecdote or a saying, to illuminate 'as if by a flash' a whole historical landscape. He taught with verve and, 'each essay was an event; he went through them with the writers individually, taking if anything more pains than would College tutors'. The galaxy of open awards won by Pauline historians, Karl's own among them, told their own tale. 'But more important because more lasting', Karl added, 'was the exhilaration, the shared enjoyment of the work which sweetened and tempered its competitiveness'. None the less, like all clever boys, Karl was interested in his marks. They had just had a history essay returned to them, he wrote to his mother on 4 March 1938, and his was by far the best.

Philip Whitting, in his turn, was very impressed by Karl from the start. His report for the autumn term of 1937 refers to his deep thought about, and (for his age) great knowledge of history, his excellent preparation and his exceptional general knowledge. His knowledge was commented on by other reports that term. It is important, for the method of using a single event or anecdote to illuminate a whole historical landscape, a method which Karl would use to fine effect in his lecturing and writing, only works if one knows enough to find an apposite instance in one's repertoire. His tutor, A. N. G. Richards, wrote, 'he has clearly been well taught in the past and, for his age, can draw on a surprisingly wide range of illustration and example from history and literature'. He added that his chief temptation was discursiveness and indulgence in abstractions not based on any reality, but that he was rapidly introducing order and precision into his work, which now began to show the virtues and not the vices of a philosophical mind. Another of his teachers wrote, 'he must learn something of Gallic concision of style and purge himself of Teutonic turgidity and the habit of using long windy phrases where one or two short words will do'. This, however, showed less discernment as a criticism. What Karl achieved was not to change the quintessential Leyser into a Gallican scholastic (thank goodness!), but to bring clarity and control to his long rolling sentences which became such wonderful vehicles of Leyserian expression.

In the evenings Karl was sitting at home in Rugby Mansions (London W14) writing to his mother (in German of course), more than bearing out what these reports said. 'Goethe will do me good here', says one letter, 'for if one seeks a kind of delight and recreation after all the dry work, nothing is better than such a book for the spirit to turn to'. A month later (February 1938) he is alone listening to music while he writes. He likes Beethoven's Seventh Symphony best. 'I have no better friend when alone than such music, and more and more my knowledge of such works is broadening'. No apology is needed to expatiate on Karl's boyhood and youth, if one wishes to say something meaningful about his historical scholarship, for to an unusual degree in our time, his own personality and human experience were invested in his study of history. His school reports at this time indicate how fast his English was improving, and in later life he would come to think of himself as British even to the point of resentment at being taken for a foreigner. In his St Paul's days, however, he was willing to poke fun at the English with the best of the foreigners, showing early his gift for irony. 'Spring approaches', he writes in March 1938, 'and even the stiff English are becoming excited, and a sort of high spirits forces itself on one's attention'. Again, a week or so later 'the weather is already wonderfully fine and the sun continues to shine daily. The oldest Londoners do not know what is wrong and how it comes about'. Then, with a reference to his sporting activities, and also with just a hint of homesickness, he adds that if the St Paul's boys row under the bridges, the people stand and stare down, 'just as I used often to do if I went across the Rhine bridge'.

Over the Christmas holiday of 1937–8 Karl stayed with the Lloyds at Great Dixter in Sussex, the first of many stays, and became very friendly with the youngest son of the family, Christopher Lloyd, who would later become famous as a garden writer. It was Karl's earliest experience of English upper class life. The Lloyds took boys from refugee organisations for holidays, but Karl was the one who most became a part of the family. 'The days pass quickly', he wrote to his mother, 'with reading, various nice games, conversation, music, and miles-long walks' (*meilenweiten Spaziergängen*). He went with Mrs Lloyd and Christopher to London to see *The School for Scandal*, 'a comedy full of biting attacks on the loving concern of eighteenth-century widows and maidens to ruin the character and reputation of their fellow creatures'. He would be truly sorry, he continued, to leave a house so full of history from every period. After Karl's death, Christopher Lloyd wrote of their respect and affection for each other as teenagers, and of how he and his sister used to tease Karl, who took it all good-humouredly to the point of guying himself. 'As an urban man' (and for all his later contacts with the British and Irish upper classes this represents an important perception), 'he pretended to no communion with the country. When a friend asked him if he could identify a common daisy, he said he supposed it was a sort of cow flower. And when he had been for a walk by himself while staying here (in Great Dixter), he described some sheep he met as letting out an ironical shout'.

In 1939 he entered Magdalen College, Oxford, as a demy (or scholar), but after a year in residence and a brief spell of internment he joined the Army. From the war years we have a correspondence between Karl and Bruce McFarlane, the celebrated history tutor of Magdalen, remarkable alike for its volume, intensity, and high level of thought and feeling. It begins when the news of Karl's internment as an enemy alien reached McFarlane in July 1940. The idea of the nineteen-year-old Karl amongst so many elderly and distinguished-looking Germans may be one to savour now, but at the time internment came as a blow, and when it would end could not be predicted. His letter to McFarlane has real pathos: 'I ardently hope that one day I may again take my place among the students of Magdalen College. Will I be able to resume gown and all when the time comes?' And then, about the academics in the internment camp, 'we are sincerely attached to this country and all hope to be its citizens in a not too remote future'.

McFarlane's response was immediate and his letter of 11 July 1940 deserves to be quoted at length:

> Your letter with its sad but not unexpected news, arrived only this morning. I have seen Histed and I will pick out some books for him to send you this afternoon. I don't know that I shall choose well, so please write and give me a list of what you would most like and I will arrange for them to be sent to you. Also please let me know if there is anything else that you would like sent or done for you. You don't smoke, perhaps fortunately, but I should like to send you fruit or chocolate if I knew that you would care for it. I know that you are reluctant to make what you may think is a nuisance of yourself, but I hope that you will make every use of me possible, relying on my friendship *absolutely*. I want you to feel no doubt at all that you have in me someone who will stand by you and care for your welfare as a parent or a brother would. I hope that you will never forget that. And never forget to let me know what you want so that I may do my best to do it.

This imaginative and unstinting kindness which persisted throughout the war and thereafter was surely the bedrock of McFarlane's subsequent influence, and of their friendship. The same could be said for many of McFarlane's other pupils. Karl summed it up in a brilliant phrase when, less than a year before his own death, he spoke at a dinner to commemorate the twenty-fifth anniversary of McFarlane's death, and referred to McFarlane's friendship and concern and how they were a function of his 'resourceful shyness'. 'He was the past master of friendship', Karl concluded, 'and that has brought us together to-night.'

In his memoir of McFarlane (1976) Karl wrote of McFarlane's correspondence with his pupils and friends as a war service:

> He corresponded with them, writing hundreds of letters and so kept open their lines of communication with interests and aspirations then in abeyance. Parcels of books were dispatched to various theatres of war and home stations and the arrival of his letters was something to be looked forward to in Nissen huts, slit trenches, and gun-pits. He wrote with enjoyment and ease about people, his reading, his work, music, and the wartime College. He did not just want to entertain but to share.

The kindness and friendship of McFarlane's letters, however, imposed pressures on Karl. He is found frequently apologising for his own letters, highly wrought as they were. 'Yes, my letters were flat, and reading stopped early at OCTU'; 'how pleasant your musings as against mine'; or 'this is a skittish letter without the usual ponderous approach to writing'. McFarlane's letters imposed a strain of elevated response, and some of the gloom or anger at his situations which Karl's replies from time to time show may have been partly occasioned by the effort

to whack up a degree of 'sensitivity'. Having been posted to the middle
of nowhere in Midlothian (while still in the Pioneers before he joined
the Black Watch), and having in a letter of March 1941 exercised his
gift for characterisation which would constantly reappear in his historical writing by describing his new sergeant-major as 'a mountain of
debauch, shaky on his legs which cannot carry such a hulk', he ends
pathetically, 'Bruce, don't get angry and impatient with me, I am
having bad luck again'. Moreover it was well to beware before making
an apparently light request to McFarlane for a favour. Even Karl may
have been surprised when in reply to his asking for suggested reading
on the social and economic history of the Industrial Revolution in
August 1945, McFarlane sent a seven-page handwritten bibliography
of seventy-five items, all arranged in alphabetical order, followed by a
surely superfluous protestation that he could not 'possibly' spend a
whole morning in Bodley finding out the publishers. Quite often, on
the other hand, the emotional initiative shifted to Karl in these letters,
for McFarlane himself was not without his neurotic anxieties and self-
doubt. In a letter probably of 1943 to 1944, Karl wrote warning
McFarlane against his going into war work, saying emphatically that
it would be catastrophic. Then, apropos of some paper of which
McFarlane doubted that Sir Maurice Powicke, at that time Regius
Professor in Oxford, would approve, he added with the warm-heartedness
that his family and friends constantly experienced, 'Do you really
think I would 'deny thee' even unconsciously if Powicke disapproved
of your paper? You sound harassed, intimidated and distraught with
sorrows.' From such letters as this, he could easily pass to teasing his
formidable correspondent with impunity. 'I see you lying in your green
deckchair on the lawn, being nice to Juan [a cat], but sphinxish to all
and sundry else'. Again, not so teasingly, but with a *franchise* gained
over the years of correspondence, he wrote on 30 June 1944 about one
of McFarlane's sudden illnesses, 'is it accident or does it link up with
your ever mysterious personality?'

Karl transferred from the Pioneer Corps to the Black Watch at Perth
in 1943, and was commissioned in that regiment in June 1944, thereafter seeing active service with the 7th Battalion in North West Europe,
where he remained until the end of October 1945. He was mentioned in
despatches and became a captain, continuing in the Territorial Army
until 1963 where he rose to the rank of major. It was a source of great
pride to him for the rest of his life that he had been an officer of the
Black Watch and had fought for his country (he became a naturalised

British citizen in 1946) during the war. He threw himself into it. Once selected as officer material he had first to 'gain experience with British personnel'. 'I wish my new companions would spit less and wash more regularly', he wrote to McFarlane in June 1943. But from this opening there followed a letter both sympathetic and observant. 'The insolence of bosses in civil life, the ruthlessness of N.C.O.s in the army have not given them a sense of unbearable rankling. They do not even form a class or a community, but have remained sensitively individualists.' He goes on to describe how a scraggy-looking man came up to him, pressing pencil and paper into his hands. 'I wrote a letter for him. It goes without saying that only a very personal and important business could have called for a letter at all. How upset he was being helpless and thus forced to let a stranger peer into his affairs.' He had perceptive remarks to make also of his fellow officers-to-be. One, for instance, seemed worried about sex, 'at least so one might guess from the embarrassingly foolish jokes he made from time to time amidst the sound obscenities of normal people'. Once commissioned he wrote about his colonel, of whom he approved, 'I hope, though I cannot be sure, to win his good opinion. It matters a great deal. I have no social fluency to settle down here; only the strictest courtesy, good behaviour and the required degree of efficiency can be my aims.' On the seventh page of his letter he excused himself for writing so briefly! 'In the dead of night I'll have to turn out the guard. In the morning again there is a reveillé to attend to, breakfasts to inspect etc.' On active service in the war Karl liberated the village on the borders of Germany and Holland where lived the eight-year-old Arnold Angenendt, who would become a distinguished German medievalist. The two men only came to realise this fact late in Karl's life; it was a source of pride to both liberator and liberated.

All this is not irrelevant to the fact that when Karl's work on the Ottonian period began to gather momentum in the 1960s, his first two publications were two fundamental articles on the military build-up of the Saxon rulers. In the first, on the Battle of the Lechfeld (955), he showed how once the new-style heavily armed Saxon knights mounted on powerful war-horses could corner the Hungarians on their fast but light horses, they could deny the latter the advantages of their speed and crush them. The Battle of the Lechfeld was the decisive defeat of these dangerous external enemies, and was of vital importance in establishing the rule of Otto I over his kingdom. In the second article, on Henry I and the foundations of the Saxon Empire, he broadened the basis of demonstration to show how this military build-up had been achieved by training, fortifications and exploitation of resources. His war experience was not of course directly brought to bear in this work; only in his later writings did he actually cite his experience of combat, and then for comparatively incidental purposes like the observed effect of drunkenness in reducing fighting skills. But it helped to shape his historical interest. I once heard the philosopher, Anthony Flew, say that war experience had obviously imparted to the teaching of some Oxford dons immediately after it, not in particulars but in a general way, a noticeable grip and direction. So it was with Karl in these writings, and in two much later articles on Early Medieval and crusading warfare.

In his correspondence with McFarlane, Karl gave as good value as he got, in his descriptions of events and people in his life, in comments on the books he had read, and particularly in his accounts of theatre visits. One of these, Richard III at Hamburg in early July 1945, is so brilliant and characteristic that it deserves to be quoted at length:

> Laurence Olivier made a bland and convincing villain; that is to say, he succeeded in convincing the hearer and spectator of the necessity of his actions. Richard was obsessed with a hatred of all his associates because he appeared even to himself as an outcast and a monster . . . .. The scenes at the court of the dying King Edward were superb; the vicious enmities and bitter rooted venom of the family factions banished any feeling of sentimentality or pity for Richard's victims . . . .. Olivier may have run amok with one or two scenes, but then some of it seems almost impossible to act . . . .. Ralph Richardson made the best of Richmond—he has only one impressive line, 'the bloody dog is dead.' His personal combat with Richard was exciting. One did not know the issue, so hard did they hack at one another. Even there Olivier shone; for he died like the beast Richard was, kicking and slashing until the last flicker of life had left him. I was much impressed also in that scene where the younger of the two princes insults his uncle for his hunched back. Emilyn Williams and Donald Wolfit both pulled a terrible aside grimace and the assembled entourage raised their hands in virtuous horror. Here, there was a sudden complete silence, startling and awful, just for a moment, before conventional courtesies and glossings over and the sinister acceptance of the insult follow.

McFarlane, whose praise was rarely hyperbolic, replied, 'I haven't seen Olivier's Richard III. You make it sound interesting . . . . You ought I think to be a dramatic critic if you tire of history'. Karl never tired of history, but he poured quite a lot of his dramatic genius into his historical writing. 'The vicious enmities and bitter rooted venom' of the Ottonian family factions are dramatised with a will in *Rule and Conflict*. The insult of Ekkehard of Meissen barging uninvited into a dinner of Otto III's sisters Adelheid, abbess of Quedlingburg, and Sophia, soon to be abbess of Gandersheim, and helping himself to the food, is described with all the zest and horror of the above letter. And the suspicion and fear in which Henry I of England lived (whom C. Warren Hollister depicted as adept in the cultivation of *amicitia*), and the horrendous last journey of his body from Normandy to Reading Abbey, would make an apt commentary on 'the dog is dead'.

Karl, who returned to Magdalen at the beginning of 1946, was one of a remarkable trio of Magdalen medievalists who all got Firsts in 1947. The other two were Roger Highfield and Eric Stone. He then began to research on the political and financial background to the Good Parliament of 1376. This was the scheme outlined by McFarlane in a letter of January 1948 to J. G. (later Sir Goronwy) Edwards, where he called Karl the best pupil that he had ever had. Historian of Germany as Karl became, he never talked down the strong element of English history existing in the Oxford syllabus during the whole of his career; in 1962 he was a signatory to a fly-sheet circulated in the History Faculty which deprecated a proposal to reduce the amount of English history. So why did he shift his main interest to German history? This shift had already occurred by 1950 when he wrote to say that if appointed to a University Lectureship (he had been elected a Tutorial Fellow of Magdalen College in 1948), he would continue to lecture on the Salian and Hohenstaufen periods of German History. The Ottonians do not yet get a look in. He expressed the hope that he would research Anglo-Imperial relations in the Norman period; a fine article appeared on that subject, his first major publication, exactly ten years later. He also suggested that the career of the Empress Mathilda before 1126 would be a fruitful subject of investigation; he published an even better article on that subject, with a most moving intuition of the life and personality of Mathilda, forty-one years later. The slow pace of Karl's publications until his last years is often commented upon, but the truly remarkable feature of his record is how much of it represented the realisation of very long-term aims.

He himself gave a disarmingly simple answer to our question in a speech of 1984, the year he became Chichele Professor of Medieval History:

> Let no one think [he said,] that some inner drive, some deep-seated prompting, led me all along to the medieval Empire in the early and high Middle Ages. Not at all! The period I read for in Schools was late medieval European, beginning with the Council of Konstanz [*sic*, on paper and

perhaps significantly so]. Nor was there a road to Damascus, a sudden revelation that here—e.g. in tenth-century Saxony—lay my goal. No. I was simply told [by McFarlane]: 'do that' because no one else in Oxford looked after it in a much read period of General History in the syllabus, 919–1273. 'You've got German. You can read the stuff.'

The truth would appear to be more complex than this rhetorically effective reconstruction allows. While Karl undoubtedly stressed his Britishness and was angered by those who insisted on treating him as a foreigner, asking what more they wanted than that he had fought for his country in the war, he never allowed his German identity to be submerged. He was a superb English stylist who knew to a nicety how to achieve the desired and often highly dramatic effect in his writing; yet this writing is studded with germanisms, not least in the word order, in the Germanically placed 'evens' and 'alreadys', or in such an opening of a sentence as, 'Thirteen years old was also Hathui' . . . . It happened similarly in his speech, to the point of being catching. A colleague on the History Faculty Board told me how tickled he had been to hear Karl once say that the medievalists needed more *Spielraum*. The reason for it was that Karl, like so many German Jews, could never deny his German culture. Besides he was far too shrewd an historian to overlook the advantage that the entrée to two cultures gave him. McFarlane had already prevented this German identity from going under, and that in a most significant way, before he 'told' Karl to study German history. The reader will have noticed that in the Press reports of the discovery of his parents in 1945 not only was Karl's surname spelt Lyser to make it look less German, but his forename was also given in the English form of Charles, and so he signed his letters to McFarlane at the same period. Dropped into a letter of McFarlane dated 27 May 1945, however, is the single sentence paragraph, 'Do you want me to call you Charles?' And on 10 June 1945 he began his letter 'Dear Karl, I can't call you anything else; Karl is a better name than Charles, I think. Do you mind?' That must surely be the main reason why Karl never became Charles, though he perhaps tipped the balance slightly back again when his eldest child, Conrad, was called Charles Conrad Leyser. I remember Karl taking part in a historical 'Brains Trust' at the Merton 1066 Society in the autumn of 1957 when I was a graduate. Someone raised the question whether A. J. P. Taylor had been right to argue that there was a constantly recurring demonic trait in German history. Karl repudiated such nonsense with passion.

During the 1950s Karl established a reputation as one of the most exciting tutors in Oxford. We shall return to his teaching. I was never tutored by him, but none the less had a glimpse of what he was like in that role through being vivaed by him in the finals of 1957—on Rousseau! It was an unforgettable experience, both on account of his stimulating intellectual insight and of his immaculate courtesy. He also cut a dash as Dean (the disciplinary authority), within Magdalen at this time. Many undergraduates long remembered their interviews with him, interviews which often passed far beyond the misdemeanours which had occasioned them. One man, of whom there had been something about the light bulbs in the cloisters and a golf-club, asked by the Dean what he was reading and replying French and Russian, was told that he was studying one language which every educated person ought to know in any case, and one which no educated person needed to know. Another, who had sought to set his misdeeds in the philosophical context of the general weakness of the human condition, was told, 'the trouble with you, Hodgson, is not determinism but too much free will'.

This was not a good decade, however, for the advance of his scholarship. Part of the reason for that was undoubtedly that his teaching was based on very extensive reading, and not just in medieval history. Part of the reason was perhaps that he became something of a socialite. Reading through his correspondence with his upper class friends, some of them his former pupils, one notices phrases like, 'it was a nice treat; they were excellent grouse'; or in a letter from a lady friend beginning, 'Darling Karl', 'I had one week among the Scottish nobility which I loathed'; or from a male friend, 'I must come to Oxford for a Bullingdon dance or some such, next term: if you hear of it in good time and go yourself, can you let me know'. Affairs of the heart were also involved in all this, as is shown by the pathetic words, 'letters over which I spent hours and sometimes days failed to please you . . .' (Karl often laboured long over preliminary drafts of his never brief letters). Moreover, his highly effective method of being Dean required the maximum input of socialising and emotional energy. An undergraduate of the time described his method as 'going to everybody's party and staying the longest'. He added in a vignette worth quoting, 'if you waited to hear the end of his tortuous sentences he had wonderfully perceptive things to say about life (especially life under the Ottonian emperors)'. One letter of the 1950s sent to Karl by Richard Lumley, now Earl of Scarbrough, who described himself to Henrietta after Karl's death as 'one of his idlest and most undistinguished pupils', is also worth quoting for its charm and contemporary flavour. 'The terrible news has just been broken to me that I attacked you in a low and base manner at Folly Bridge. I am sorry. This is the fourth letter of apology I have had to write as a result of that night. Please send me all doctors' and tailors' bills.' McFarlane warned Karl about the direction his life was taking although he was far from suggesting that marriage would be the remedy. Once again, his own influence had itself not been absent. 'Dear Karl', went one of his letters during the war, 'I do so want to see you expand into an aristocrat'. In the 1950s his vision was being realised with a vengeance.

Although the decade issued in very few publications, however, it was in one respect (among others) of vital importance to his later scholarship. That scholarship was concentrated, albeit by no means exclusively, on the early medieval German aristocracy. His participation in British (and Irish) aristocratic life may not have had any specific lessons in it which he could apply to the Ottonian aristocracy, but it surely gave him (an urban Jew himself) that abiding sense of how aristocracies worked not so much on formal rules as through social nuances, reputation, symbols, gestures, and unspoken assumptions or understandings, a sense which would become a vital part of his intuitive approach to Ottonian society. One of the unfulfilled schemes of his later life was to write an article about aristocracy based on Mozart's Don Giovanni. I could never discover, however, that it would propound any theory, *spekulativer Mensch* as he was, rather than that it would describe the opera's many social nuances. His favourite piece in it was *O Statua Gentilissima*, in which Leporello, the valet, invites the stone statue of the Commendatore to dinner, but places the responsibility for the outrageous invitation squarely on the shoulders of Don Giovanni. *Il padron mio badate ben, non io*, he was fond of repeating.

The 1960s were altogether another matter from the 1950s. By 1960 Karl looked like a fine and influential tutor indeed, but one who would settle down to write the occasional statutory article in the Transactions of the Royal Historical Society, be a good college man, and enjoy the absorbing company of an ever-widening circle of friends. By 1970 he was recognised as one of the leading scholars in the world on the Ottonian Empire. True he had only as yet published three major articles on the subject, but they were all of the highest originality and importance. Moreover, much of the intense work which he did in the 1960s only fed through into print during the 1980s or even the early 1990s, as he himself later said. It is hard to resist the evidence for saying that this sea change was brought about by his marriage in 1962. In the autumn of 1960, when he had already begun to lecture on the Ottonians, Beryl Smalley of St Hilda's College urged one of her college pupils to attend his lectures. She found not only that they made sense as none of the books on the subject did, but also that they shed floods of light, and were gripping to listen to. Her name was Henrietta Bateman. Like her parents before her, Henrietta was highly educated, having been at Victoria College, Belfast, then a girls' school of good academic reputation, and at Cheltenham Ladies College. She could not draw Karl into an aristocratic social circle or even much of a family circle at all, for she had been orphaned at the age of eight. Nor had she much money; her education had been paid on a grandparental trust. She removed him, therefore, far from the anxieties which beset him whilst he tried to keep up with the fast-living sets, and she gave him security, as well as a family home which he had not known since the age of sixteen (and he was now forty-one). Among his aristocratic friends, however much one side of him gladly played up the image of the distinguished foreigner, the other side longed to be taken as one of themselves; but there are signs that they would persist in thinking of him as a foreigner; and small wonder when one considers his short stature, his dark and swarthy good looks, the naturally oily texture of his hair, and the strong German accent which remained amalgamated with the cultured army officer's diction. With Henrietta, lively and intelligent, possessed of an element of 'outsiderhood', Roman Catholic by conversion, and with socialist leanings, the troublesome issues of his class, his blood, and his Britishness or Germanness, at once fell flat on their face. Not least of all, to use Karl's phrase, she was a serious historical scholar herself, whose B.Litt. thesis on medieval hermits, produced in the days when the B.Litt. was still a reputable graduate degree, would have walked into a doctorate today. Karl once said to the present writer that he owed everything to Henrietta. This saying covered no doubt far more than can be known to anyone outside his family, but in so far as it pertained to his professional life, it did not mean that Henrietta had ever urged him to get on with his research or write the great book. It meant that she had released him to be a scholar, in fact to be himself.

Of the three major articles published by Karl on the Ottonians in the 1960s (there was also one on the polemics of the papal, or Gregorian, revolution) the first two have already been discussed. The third, on the early medieval German aristocracy, published in December 1968, was if anything the most important. It gave a wholly new face to the subject;

nobody had ever written about it like this before. Suddenly the bonds of constitutionalism and over-rigid anthropological modelling were broken and the reader found himself in the midst of a description of a social dynamic, which, despite its intricate detail, meant something in human terms, and not only to English scholars and students but also to the Germans. Its immediate acclaim was all the more remarkable as it is not easy to express its argument. Its nature is that of a cluster of cohering perceptions; its effect is polyphonic rather than monodic. Its theme is the disjunction between consciousness and being, between self-awareness, wishful thinking, idealisation, day-dreaming (to use words taken from the article itself) on the one hand, and harsh reality on the other, particularly the shifts and fragmentations of fortunes which destroyed the equilibrium of aristocratic kindreds. Highly effective use is made of the epic *Ruodlieb* to reconstruct the thought world of the aristocracy, an echo of the school reports which referred to his aptly applied knowledge of literature in writing about history. What Karl tried to do here can perhaps best be described in words he would later apply to McFarlane's Ford Lectures of 1953 on the late medieval English nobility. Having sung the praises of McFarlane's history for 'its deep sense of humanity, sometimes melancholy, often wry and sardonic, but always intuitive', he came to his 'fine sense of social nuances, the characterization of behaviour patterns, and the identification of attitudes and types without which the history of an aristocracy cannot be written'. The very success of the article with so many readers may actually have been due in part to the fact that its profound perceptions were not strait-jacketed into too precise a form of argumentation.

A decade later in 1979, this work on the aristocracy came to fruition in a book which is an undoubted masterpiece, *Rule and Conflict in an Early Medieval Society: Ottonian Saxony*, a study of the relations of the Ottonian rulers with their aristocracy. Written with density of ideas and factual detail, and in highly dramatic language, it was described by Patrick Wormald, reviewing it in the *English Historical Review*, as 'quite simply, the most original, penetrating and challenging study of this theme to appear in any language during recent times', and he added that the publisher (Arnold) was to be thanked and congratulated 'for winning the long race to get this author into print on such a scale'. The whole book read with total originality even to a considerable degree as from his earlier article. At first sight it looks like three discrete extended essays, entitled 'Otto I and his Saxon Enemies', 'The Women of the Saxon Aristocracy', and 'Sacral Kingship'. Amidst the richness of the first essay one can detect three major arguments. First, it was impossible for the Ottonians to follow the Carolingians in exercising a shared kingship, so that every one of the brothers could receive somewhere to be king of, because of the strength and deep roots of the families such as the Liutpoldings of Bavaria who held the duchies. Hence the Saxon ruling dynasty, the Liudolfings, became divided and feud-ridden as they struggled for the one kingship, even to the point of cousinly strife from reign to reign in succession disputes. Secondly, lesser men (but still aristocrats) needed to fuel conflicts within the ruling dynasty in order to channel their own grievances, and by taking sides, to establish in rebellion an alternative ruler in the one agreed kingship. Grievances arose through *co-hereditas*, by which kinsmen (and women) had a right to share in inheritances, which were partible, in quite unspecified proportions, leading to disappointed expectations and in-fighting between and within large groups of kindred. The king could never be seen to stand above such feuds, partly because as the only possible judge he was bound to add to the numbers of the disappointed, and partly because he was involved as a party himself by reason of the fact that so many of them involved his own kinsmen. Third (Karl himself would deeply disapprove of this sort of schematisation), many of the disappointed expectations which led other Saxons to side with royal rebels had to do with the distribution of the new frontier commands in the East, rich in Slav tributes. All this was written with the sharpest of eyes for resentments, possible only to someone who understood to a nicety how aristocracies worked in general, let alone this particular aristocracy, and who had no small sensitivity to the danger of losing face himself.

It follows from the fact that women were regarded as co-heirs in partible inheritances, that the Saxon women of the second essay are integral to the unified theme of the book, and that this essay is not only loosely connected to the first, as some have said. There are two extra ingredients here, which added to the seethings of Saxon men. First was the much greater life expectancy of women, if they once surmounted the period of child-bearing, in a warrior society, for they thereby became the residual legatees of much property at the expense of other relatives. Nuns, who were not excluded from their shares by reason of their religious life, did not even (in the normal way) have the health risks of child-bearing. Second was the fact that so much of the accumulated wealth of Saxon nunneries passed into the hands of kings or, by his arrangement, into the protection and ultimately the *proprietas* of bishops, and hence was siphoned off from the families to which it belonged, never to be a part of their inheritance pool again.

In the article of 1968 on the German aristocracy there was scarcely a word about sacral kingship, the subject of the majestic third essay of *Rule and Conflict*. That is the element which had come flooding in to Karl's treatment of king–noble relations by 1979. How is this connected to the first parts of the book? Only loosely as some have supposed? The answer is not at first sight entirely clear. Karl was a German romantic. If he was a Mozart in the felicity of his phrases, he was a Brahms in his structures. If Brahms kept to sonata form, he did not, as Mozart did, make it crystal clear at every point whereabouts in the structure he was, so that there can often be an abundance of rolling music before he even reaches the first subject. Several of Karl's articles are like this, and so is *Rule and Conflict*. In another way he was like Caspar David Friedrich. Many of Friedrich's landscapes were intended to make the viewer shiver, and it is always less likely that they would be represented under a clear sky than amid mists and storm clouds. Not for Karl, therefore, the neon-lighting of his purposes. In fact I can find only one sentence in *Rule and Conflict* which specifically addresses the issue of how the three essays are related. It is the first sentence of the preface, and it reads, 'The three studies presented here have a common theme'. Nevertheless, Karl would always have been perfectly happy to write articles, if they suited his purpose, rather than a book. The second sentence of the preface reads, 'They grew out of another book on the Saxon nobility as a ruling class which is not far from completion.' But although a long string of wonderful articles came out between 1979 and 1992, virtually nothing of this book was found after his death. Therefore we cannot possibly imagine that sacral kingship forms the third part of *Rule and Conflict* merely to fill out a book, or other than because he saw it as integral to the work as a whole. He had a purpose. What was it?

Karl thought that German scholars had treated sacrality too much as 'an inert body of ideas', whereas it needed to be seen as 'a diversified, growing, and changing phenomenon'. This had come out already in his review of Schramm's *Kaiser, Könige and Päpste*, published in 1975. His question was rather how sacrality acted in society, what were its functions, a question 'more often evaded than asked'. In apposition to his first question he put a second. 'What impression did the exalted and quasi-numenous image of the king make on those whose conduct it was meant to govern or at least to influence?' This question he had already raised at the International Historical Congress of 1965 in Vienna, fourteen years earlier, in a breath-taking intervention, where, rendered into two pages of print, many of the issues later considered in *Rule and Conflict* were dramatically and sharply outlined. His answer in 1965 was unequivocal. 'If the cult of sacred kingship created a distance between king and nobles', he said, 'it was a distance not of awe but of alienation'. Although in 1979 there is still much stress on how sacral kingship could never be a magic wand with which to bypass the murky world of conflict, his answer was not now so unequivocal. He no longer saw sacrality only as a source of alienation. He cited, for instance, the effect of six-year-old Otto III taking the field against the Liutizi Slavs in 986, partly to make the serving of the Polish Duke Miesko with the Saxon host possible. Indeed there would still now be mileage in considering the function of sacrality not with regard to the Saxons but to the emerging leaders of the Slav world.

One of the vital contributions made by Karl to the study of sacral kingship in *Rule and Conflict*, rather similar to that made by Janet Nelson in the case of the Carolingians, was to show that sacrality was nothing like the mere act of anointing from which all subsequent magic followed. It was a long and slow build-up of royal hagiography, acquiring relics, crown-wearings at great assemblies, and processions. In a brilliant passage on Henry II's sacrality he represents it as one long procession of solemn entries into cities, crown-wearings, and presidings at church dedications. During the 1970s two very important works of German scholarship impressed themselves on Karl's mind in this connection. One was Carl Richard Brühl's two volume work on the royal itinerary and the other was Josef Fleckenstein's book on the Ottonian chapel. It must be remembered that the Ottonians had no capital where major political events occurred and where a bureaucracy could be located. They travelled, and this not only for economic reasons, but because they could only rule by coming face to face with their subjects. Their rule was patrimonial, not bureaucratic. Their chapel travelled with them, with its chaplains, men often of high birth, intelligence, and religious devotion, who would walk into bishoprics, and with its sacred treasures, relics and books. All this Karl explained in his article on Ottonian Government, published in 1981, which could itself easily have made a fourth and integral part of *Rule and Conflict*. I once heard Karl say, in a paper to an undergraduate society in Oxford the text of which could nowhere be discovered after his death, that if one had the itinerary, the chapel, and the crown-wearings, one had the three main elements of Ottonian rule. Thus, in Karl's conception, the build-up of sacrality was inseparable from the itinerary, and the itinerary meant the face to face politics which was *the* mode of relationship between king and nobles.

There is another important advance on his Vienna intervention of 1965 in *Rule and Conflict*. In 1965 he made a point which would be repeated in 1979. 'How deeply the cult of kingship impressed the lay nobility is difficult to ascertain because its effect, like any negative effect, cannot be measured. How many rebellions did not happen because the *Vicarius Christi* was sacrosanct and unassailable is a question we cannot answer.' But by 1979 he had had an inspiration with regard to this point which it seems had not been vouchsafed to him so early as 1965. It was that even if sacral kingship could not prevent rebellions by reason of any awe it inspired, it could none the less make it easier for a failed rebel to submit without too much loss of face because he was submitting to a sacral person. In other words sacrality had a function of saving face among the nobility. He names some who 'lost less face' by giving themselves up as repentant sinners 'to God and the king' from whom they had strayed. 'Sacred kingship could not prevent risings but it could help to restore a measure of harmony afterwards and make reconciliation, even on very unfavourable terms, easier for the losers. Conversely it enabled an enraged king not to lose face in turn when he failed to or did not want to exact the full revenge which harsh custom, his own threats and reputation for terror demanded.' 'Loss of face' is a phrase which occurs several times in *Rule and Conflict*; it would remain with Karl as a significant motif in his later writings.

The insights gained by Karl from papers of two anthropologists, E. E. Evans-Pritchard and Max Gluckmann, which he used sparingly but with devastating relevance, were yet another reason for him to integrate his treatment of sacral kingship with that of relations between king and aristocracy. On the one hand it could not remove the reality of conflict and might even exacerbate the king's involvement in it. On the other hand, to quote Evans-Pritchard on the divine kingship of the Nilotic Shilluk, 'kingship actually embodied the contradiction between dogma and social facts'. The divine ruler, for this was a sacral kingship, while rebelled against when calamities struck or because of deep seated regional particularisms, stood for what unity could be achieved. Max Gluckmann, also writing of sacral kingships in Africa, perceived that what unified the people of structurally disunified kingdoms was the struggle for the agreed kingship. By analogy, and by a paradox, in

Ottonian society which had to be studied through the polarities of rule and conflict, sacral kingship, in one sense so at odds with the facts of conflict and the king's involvement in it, in another sense could be seen to have a function in favour of the ruler as the principle of unity.

What Karl did not argue, or argue directly, was that the religious ideas inherent in sacral kingship, and in the rich art and ceremonial which sprang from it, had in themselves a force to shape mundane reality. And in this he was surely wise, for the religious content of sacrality is here assumed while its sociological application is what is under discussion. However, the conclusion should not be drawn, as it sometimes is, that Karl was not interested in the history of religion. It was not in the forefront of his interests, but one can exaggerate his lack of interest in it. Both before and after *Rule and Conflict* his sense of the suffusion of the medieval social fabric with religion frequently comes to the surface. In writing on Byzantine-Western relations in the tenth century (1973) he had not overlooked the feature in Otto III's rule whereby according to Byzantine tradition highly placed laymen and even emperors had monks and ascetics as their spiritual counsellors and friends. Then in another article on the Hand of St James (1975) he had recognised that both Henry II of England and Frederick Barbarossa early in their reigns and vulnerable, hard-headed men as they were, attached vital importance to hanging on to or securing such a relic, and Karl dilated at length on the splendid marquee that Henry II had given Barbarossa in order to avoid handing over the relic. Prestige, of course; but as the article implicitly recognised, how could one derive prestige from relics which were not the object of religious devotion more widely? In the second of two highly original articles on Liudprand of Cremona (1985) he studied Liudprand's theology head-on in order to pose the question how it related to his historical writing. In connection with his masterly discussion of St Hugh of Lincoln, and the functions of a Holy Man in Angevin politics, delivered as a lecture in 1986, in a series of lectures to commemorate Hugh's becoming bishop of Lincoln in 1186 (published in 1987), one should bear in mind that he could assume the religious achievement which lay behind those functions, because this was brilliantly described by Henrietta Leyser earlier in the same series and volume. She and Karl had come into the series very much as a team.

We are fortunate to have *Rule and Conflict* at all. In 1977 Karl had a serious car accident from the after-effects of which he nearly died. It was this which, when he recovered, impelled him to work on the book, as he told many people, myself included, while he was writing it. Today, for purposes of Research Assessment Exercises it would be regarded as a starred piece of 'research'. But it does not really read like this. There is no suggestion of card indexes, labours of research assistants, or methodical accumulation of information about kins in his prosopography. Rather it reads like the spontaneous outpouring from a vast reservoir of knowledge by a scholar, who though doubtless checking his references, had a fabulously retentive memory. He may have had his method, and he was rigorous in his *Quellenkritik* and his use of sources only for purposes they would allow, but he never flaunted methodology. He knew the Ottonian aristocratic family connections inside out, but like Mozart's counterpoint in his mature works, his prosopography was allusive rather than formal. If his memoir of McFarlane may be taken as one of the best indicators of how he viewed his own work as an historian, he was inclined almost to scoff at McFarlane's accumulation of family histories, reconstruction of careers, and establishment of genealogies, in his work on the English aristocracy. 'McFarlane', he wrote, 'enjoyed this kind of drudgery to an almost dangerous degree.' His great admiration was reserved for McFarlane's 'intuitive' qualities. The peroration of Karl's own inaugural lecture as Chichele Professor was a plea for intuition, according to 'an Oxford tradition'. The tradition, of Wallace-Hadrill, Southern, and Powicke, was 'the intuitive practice of allowing imagination and literary sensibilities to open up direct lines of communication between the historian and his subjects, not least of all his medieval forbears'. Nowhere in *Rule and Conflict* does one see this 'intuitive practice' to more poignant effect than in the handling of charters, a kind of source which one might think the least susceptible to it, for instance where he writes to the demographic theme of male and female life expectancies. 'A mother took over the inheritance of the dying childless son', he says, 'with more right than his brother . . .' 'The widow Aeddila, who in 960 transferred four *curtes* to Otto I for the endowment of Hilwartshausen, had received them from the *hereditates* of her dying sons.'

The publication of *Rule and Conflict* opened the floodgates to a wonderful series of articles in the last thirteen years of Karl's life. Some have already been discussed or mentioned. Of the others I would single out five, although this is invidious since all are brilliant, and it is to some extent misguided since they form a corpus of work on the themes of self-awareness in historical writing, aristocratic dynamics, and (now coming more into the frame) state formation. Two of these five articles have the considerable achievement of working the West Frankish kingdom into the Ottonian picture, not by the conventional method of selection from the 'political narrative', but by profound prosopographical study. In particular, 'The Ottonians and Wessex', which first appeared in German in the prestigious Münster organ, *Frühmittelalterliche Studien* (1983), showed how Otto I's marriage to Edith of Wessex was part of a network of relationships which bound the various dynasties of East and West Francia together with that of Athelstan of Wessex, Edith's brother. This paper ends with a highly relevant vignette on pepper supplies in the Ottonian Empire. The paper on 'Ritual, Ceremony and Gesture: Ottonian Germany', takes us back to, and carries us forward from, that of 1968 on the German aristocracy. It is a vivid reconstruction of the symbolic language of aristocratic culture; it is in some measure, apropos of aristocratic mentality, the tenth-century counterpart to the role that the eleventh-century *Ruodlieb* plays in his earlier article. It also makes a point anticipated by Beryl Smalley in her *Study of the Bible in the Middle Ages* that tenth-century culture and expression was less based on writing than that of the Carolingians had been, and more on ritual. 'Frederick Barbarossa and the Hohenstaufen Polity' (1988) broke new ground in demonstrating how Barbarossa had built up, often by purchase with ready cash, dynastic Hohenstaufen lands as a fundamental resource of his rule. The supreme paper, however, of Karl's post-*Rule and Conflict* period must surely be his Raleigh Lecture of 1983, published in late 1984, 'The Crisis of Medieval Germany'. The crisis was that of the Saxon revolts of the 1070s against Henry IV, coincidental (but as he shows no more than coincidental) with the outbreak of the Investiture Contest; the latter was another crisis in itself, fired by 'the volcanic and brooding spirit of Gregory VII and the brazen heedlessness and yet also unquenchable sense of his own regality that dwelt in Henry IV'. Karl showed that the Saxon kings might grant to their nobles lands *in proprietatem* as well as making grants *in hereditatem*. The former in theory did not necessarily merge with the noble's *hereditas* but might remain part of the king's. These were what the south-western Salian successors to the Saxon kings made a concerted effort to recover, and with them the formerly rich resources of Saxon rule. No wonder that in Karl's presentation Henry III was such a hated figure to the Saxons, whereas in Tellenbach's view of things he had been a saintly exemplar of the imperial system. Karl pin-pointed here a radical shift in the Salian mode of rule from the Ottonian, a significant change of ideas. In his own words:

The Salians were not the Ottonians' sole heirs and it was *jure regni* that they had come by the lion's share of the Ottonian inheritance. What had been relationships of gift and mutual obligation between the Liudolfings and their Saxon followers became attributes of kingship as such, impersonal and enforceable rules, menacing staging-posts almost on the way to statehood or at least institutionalized and legally concrete dealings as against the face-to-face arrangements between princely givers and their military *comitatus*. The Saxon nobles could not fathom this development and it goes far to explain their deep-seated and lasting estrangement.

In April 1984 Karl became Chichele Professor of Medieval History. He had already been spoken of as one of the leading candidates for this chair in 1970 when Geoffrey Barraclough was surprisingly elected, to be succeeded in 1974 by Michael Wallace-Hadrill. Karl was thus Sir Richard Southern's successor at two removes. This worthy crowning of his career meant much to him, even though he would find that an Oxford professorship brought him more administrative work and less respect from within the university than he had anticipated. As he wittily said at his retirement dinner in 1988, referring to his thirty-six years as a college tutor at Magdalen and his last four as professor, 'I served thirty-six years before the mast, only to find in the last four that there was no quarterdeck.' But the Chichele Professor is first and foremost, by his scholarship, a flag-bearer of the medieval historians in the Oxford History Faculty, to the university as a whole and to the outside world. In this respect Karl did a first-rate job. He lectured and was present at high-powered conferences all over the world. Having been elected a Fellow of the British Academy in 1983, he became a Corresponding Member of the Directorate of the *Monumenta Germaniae Historica* in Munich, a Council Member of the Max-Planck Institute in Göttingen, a Corresponding Fellow of the Medieval Academy of America, and Distinguished Visiting Professor in Medieval Studies at Berkeley, California. I myself met him in Cornmarket Street around Christmas-time in 1983, on the very afternoon that he had heard of his election. He was not obviously walking to anywhere; indeed he was obviously not walking on Cornmarket Street but on air. He said to me—and it is one of the most engaging things that I have ever heard—'I'm it'. Lest anyone think that he would not otherwise have stopped in the street, I must add that one of the aspects of his hugely kind and generous personality was that he was one of the kindest and most generous stoppers-in-the-street (or elsewhere) for a chat that I have ever known, even when he was heavily laden with shopping. For his inaugural lecture, Karl took the title, *The Ascent of Latin Europe*, a luminous study of 'new forms of self-awareness' made through the chroniclers Adhémar of Chabannes, Rodulf Glaber, and Thietmar of Merseburg. Thietmar, the dramatic and masterful Saxon bishop historian of the early eleventh century, was a writer with whom Karl always felt a peculiar affinity. Indeed he and Widukind of Corvey probably had much to do with drawing Karl's interest towards the Ottonians. Now, in the lecture, an ironic smile played over his face and he drew himself up to his full five foot six as he said, 'The Ottonians liked good-looking bishops in the secular church—men of stature, literally, who stood out over the shoulders of the crowd as rulers should. Thietmar was small,' and so on. Was he not guying himself again? Karl continued, 'He had, however, an indefatigable memory, and an irresistible urge to record and write about himself, his kin, his contemporaries and the Ottonian *Reich* at large.' After the lecture he threw an enormous party in All Souls College, reminiscent of the feast given by Thietmar's family when he became a canon of Magdeburg.

For most of Karl's working life he was a college tutor at Magdalen, and evidently an inspired one. This is rather surprising at first sight, since his principal method of teaching was not one generally recommended by educationalists, namely the monologue. There were four main reasons why it worked. First, the monologues themselves were frequently inspired; secondly, they emanated from a person of great charisma; thirdly, he often referred appositely to points made by his pupils in their essays, showing that his talk was about them as well as about his own preoccupations; and fourthly, behind these tutorials lay his transparent personal kindness and concern towards his pupils. He would go to the ends of the earth to help an undergraduate or research student in trouble. One former pupil has asserted that Karl was the kindest man he ever knew. It is certain that many undergraduates did not know in the tutorials what Karl was talking about and had insufficient knowledge to get their bearings. But one does not need to understand a monologue to be inspired by it. A certain flavour of his tutorials may be had from two reminiscences of pupils. One is that of Sir Michael Wheeler-Booth, now Clerk of the Parliaments:

> To me he remains always as he was in a tutorial about Frederick Barbarossa, in which as was his wont he began to quote from chronicles in Latin—which I forget [it was Rahewin]—with a concluding passage beginning *talis vir*. He read it with his eyes gleaming and throwing himself into it with intense excitement as the achievements of the warrior emperor were described. After

the quotation there was a silence, and I said, 'Karl, I think you really are imagining yourself as Frederick Barbarossa'. He looked at me sharply and said something to the effect, 'perhaps I did, just a bit.'

The other reminiscence is from Tim Berner, now a successful solicitor in the City. In a private communication dated 24 December 1993, having said that Karl's method was to allow the pupil into the historical world he inhabited by showing him the particular parts that he happened to be exploring at the time, he continues:

> A precious memory (whether it is entirely accurate I cannot be sure) of how close he was getting to the world he described with such subtlety was an absorbing speculation towards the end of a tutorial, during which we lost all sense of time and place, about whether Henry IV, in flight in the Harz Mountains, had stumbled into Rudolf of Swabia (and his retinue) who realized of a sudden that he was looking on the face of the king and that rebellion might not be such a good idea after all.

The memory here is not quite accurate in that it was not Rudolf but the Saxon rebel Otto of Northeim who was in question. The whole matter forms a paragraph in *Rule and Conflict* where Karl describes the special gaze and glowing eyes of kings as an aspect of their sacrality. But the psychology of the memory is right, and, moreover, one sees from this how the magic spark, flashing to light in his tutorials, later illuminated whole landscapes in his published writings.

Karl's two very last pupils were undergraduates of my own college who went on a reading party to Penzance with Henrietta and himself in March 1992, only a month before his stroke. One of them wrote to Henrietta after his death, in a letter where Karl's kindness and teaching method are both highlighted:

> I must admit that at first the prospect of spending a week with such a renowned historian was somewhat daunting, but with the first pub lunch of the week this was soon dispelled, and the sessions with Karl will always remain in my memory . . . (especially) his wonderful blend of acute insight and anecdotal illustrations.

These two St Peter's undergraduates knew, after Karl's death, that they were the two luckiest people walking around Oxford.

Karl was deeply happy in his family life. Henrietta was the keel of this happiness, but Einhard would have commented, as he did of an even more famous Karl, on his great love for his children. He told me how proud he had been of the piece written by Conrad for transfer to D.Phil. status as an Oxford graduate student. Conrad is the only one who has followed him as a medieval historian, but at one time or another I heard him speak with great feeling and perceptiveness about the individual and very varied intellectual and social (and human) gifts of each of Ottoline, Crispin and Matilda as well. He was fond of saying in his later years, 'standing room only for the professor in his own house'. There was an irony in this, considering reports one heard that when he was comfortably sitting, one or other of his children would make sure that the TV was on the required channel, or whatever. In truth his saying was a proud boast about how the remarkable qualities of his wife and children made themselves felt to him.

After five weeks of lying in a coma following his stroke, Karl died on 27 May 1992. His funeral was an occasion of great sadness, sadness for his loss, and sadness because, having suffered no diminution of intellectual alertness and power before he was struck down, he therefore still had great scholarly achievements in him; but it was also an occasion of truly joyous celebration for a great and lovable man. Henrietta invited anyone to speak who wished. Sir Richard Southern rose, and with his fine bearing and euphonious voice said that Karl was one of the greatest historians of the century because of his covering and illuminating vast tracts of historical territory that had previously been unknown. He did not say that Karl was one of the greatest British historians or one of the greatest historians of Germany. There was no such qualification. He was simply one of the greatest.

He lies now in Islip churchyard. Beyond his grave one looks out towards miles of peaceful, rolling English countryside. On his gravestone are inscribed his name and dates in plain, elegant capitals, and at its foot the words *talis vir* (such a man!).

HENRY MAYR-HARTING
*Fellow of the Academy*

*Note*: All letters cited, except that from Mr Tim Berner to myself, come from the Karl Leyser archive, as do most of the citations from the texts of speeches, flysheets etc. I am very grateful to Henrietta Leyser for allowing me to use it and for much help generally. I am also indebted for advice to James Campbell and Gerald Harriss, and for permission to cite them by name as writers of letters to Tim Berner; Christopher Lloyd; Richard Lumley, Earl of Scarbrough; and Sir Michael Wheeler-Booth.

The following comprise Karl's publications (other than reviews): *Rule and Conflict in an Early Medieval Society: Ottonian Saxony* (Arnold, London, 1979); *Medieval Germany and Its Neighbours, 900–1250* (Hambledon Press, London,

1982); *Communications and Power in Medieval Europe*, 2 vols, *I The Carolingian and Ottonian Centuries, II The Gregorian Revolution and Beyond*, ed. Timothy Reuter (Hambledon Press, London, 1994), the latter with an admirable paper on 'Karl Leyser the Historian', pp. ix–xvi, by the editor. The last three volumes named above are all collections of articles. Also, 'Kenneth Bruce McFarlane, 1903–1966', *Proceedings of the British Academy*, 62 (1976), 485–506; and intervention on the ruling classes, *xiie Congrès International des Sciences Historiques* 1965, V *Actes*, ed. H.L. Mikoletzky (Vienna, 1965), pp. 165–6. Karl's reviews, many of them important, are listed in the bibliography to his Festschrift, *Warriors and Churchmen in the High Middle Ages: Essays presented to Karl Leyser*, ed. Timothy Reuter (Hambledon Press, London, 1992), which also contains a perceptive essay by Gerald Harriss on 'Karl Leyser as a Teacher'. Highly illuminating reviews should be noted, of *Rule and Conflict* by Patrick Wormald, *English Historical Review*, 96 (1981), 595–601, and of *Communications and Power* (2 vols.) by James Campbell, in *Bulletin of the German Historical Institute*, 17, no. 3 (1995), 41–8.

ALEC NOVE                    *Glasgow Evening Citizen*

*Proceedings of the British Academy,* **94**, 627–641

# Alec Nove
# 1915–1994

ALEC NOVE, for long Britain's most distinguished Sovietologist, was a political economist in a tradition which is now in danger of being squeezed out of university departments. He knew in intimate detail how the Soviet economy actually worked and he could communicate his knowledge in lectures (in several languages) and in his prolific writings with unique insight, clarity, and humour. He was also in his last years an especially perceptive critic of some of the policies pursued in the Russian transition to a post-Soviet economy. The pity is that the Russian Government did not make more use of his profoundly practical knowledge, based as it was not only on an exceptional understanding of the changing economic system and of the plight of real people in Russian society but also on his experience as a civil servant in the Board of Trade in early post-war Britain as this country gradually dismantled many of its wartime controls.

Alec Nove was also more than a political economist. He made significant contributions to the study of twentieth-century Russian economic history and to the political and sociological analysis of the Soviet Union. He was, furthermore, equally at home discussing Pushkin or the very latest works of Russian creative literature and, in pre-glasnost days, his reading of the major Soviet literary journals provided him with insights unavailable to those specialists who did not stray beyond *Pravda*, the Soviet statistical yearbooks, and specialised economic publications. In the years between the death of Stalin and the accession of Gorbachev, it was often possible to discover more of the

© The British Academy 1997.

truth about Soviet society in the form of 'fiction' than it was in the pages of *Pravda* ('Truth').

Alec Nove, whose original family name was Novakovsky, was born into a Russian Jewish family on 24 November 1915 in what was then Petrograd (later Leningrad) and is now restored to its original name of St Petersburg. His ancestors had lived for generations in the Ukraine where his paternal grandfather was a rabbi with a reputation for piety and scholarship and his maternal grandfather owned a windmill at the end of a railway line in Poltava province.

Alec's father was short but tough and, when conscripted into the Russian Army, gained a reputation as a weight-lifter and wrestler. He subsequently became politically active as a social democrat of the Menshevik variety, was arrested by the tsarist police and spent the years 1903–5 as a political prisoner. Following his release, he succeeded in attending the 1907 Congress in London of the Russian Social-Democratic Party and stayed long enough to earn his return fare while taking the opportunity to learn English. Once back in Russia he lived and worked illegally in St Petersburg, for Jews were not allowed to reside there unless they had a degree or were 'merchants of the first guild' (which meant, in effect, very rich).

Alec's mother, born in 1878, was a determined and energetic woman who, notwithstanding her father's strong disapproval, was committed to becoming a doctor. She gained admission to a women's medical faculty in St Petersburg and duly qualified as a physician in 1904. She wished to become an emancipated Russian and, once she had obtained her degree, she was able to live legally in the Russian capital. She had been practising as a doctor for some years in St Petersburg before she met her future husband in about 1912. Alec, her only child, was born when she was thirty-seven.

When Tsar Nicholas II abdicated in March 1917 Alec's mother informed him of this event and, as she later told him, he smiled. Since he was only one-and-a-half at the time, he had no memory of having made the desired political response. Alec's father held a junior post in the Provisional Government, but after the Bolsheviks seized power he was arrested by them. Upon his release, he worked for a time on the Bolshevik side in the civil war since, like many Mensheviks, he believed that the Whites were even worse. He stood for election to the Moscow soviet as a Menshevik and defeated his Bolshevik opponent, but the election was promptly annulled. In 1922 he was arrested again and exiled to Siberia but was given a choice between long-term exile and applying for an exit visa. He left the Soviet Union later that year and found a job in London with a Dutch firm trading with Russia. It took Alec's mother and her seven-year-old son another six months to get the necessary permission to leave Russia to join Jacob Novakovsky in Belsize Park.

When the family arrived in Britain they discovered that they had distant relatives living in Manchester who had arrived in Britain at the turn of the century. They had changed their name from Novakovsky to Nove and so the new immigrants followed suit. By 1924 Alec was a pupil at King Alfred School in North London. In due course he went on to the London School of Economics where he graduated in 1936 with an Upper Second in the B.Sc.(Econ.). He seems to have celebrated by paying a visit to Paris where he saw one of the great demonstrations of that period. On his return he undertook a number of research jobs but found no permanent employment. Shortly before the war he married Joan Rainford (who died in April 1995). There were two children of the union, David and Perry, but the marriage itself did not survive the war.

Early in 1939 Nove joined the Territorials and, when war came, served in the Royal Signals. He remained in the army until 1946, finishing as a major in Intelligence. He was among the last British soldiers to get back from France in June 1940 and felt enormously lucky to survive the war. He was always conscious that if he had remained in Russia he would either have ended, as the son of an anti-Communist, in the gulag or served in the Red Army in which the losses in the first two years of the conflict reached eight million. Moreover, all Jewish prisoners of war on the Russian front were killed on the spot by the Germans. Outside every town in occupied Russia and Ukraine—not just at Babyi Yar—there was a pit of machine-gunned men, women and children whom the Germans did not bother to transport to the death camps.

Even in the British Army, Alec Nove's luck held. Twice a ship on which he might have sailed was sunk: when half his unit was sent to Singapore he happened to be in the other half. His sense of just being a survivor deepened and haunted him all his life. Reflecting on this, in an autobiography even briefer than Hume's—just two pages—which he wrote for members of his family only a few years before his death, Nove observed:

> There but for the grace of God—but why should God have shown me grace? I was just lucky. Any children I may have had could have been killed too—

over a million children were massacred in those years, in Auschwitz, Treblinka, Majdanek, Belzec. A woman survivor of Auschwitz told me how she saw lorry-loads of weeping and praying naked children which stopped close to her hut—the gas-chambers were not yet ready to receive them. She said that she lost her faith in God that day, and who could blame her?

Having survived the war, Alec Nove had to decide on a career and in 1947 he joined the Civil Service, working at first in the Board of Trade on price control and export targets. From his experience in this department he learned much about what governments can and cannot do, which stood him in good stead later. Moreover, he continued to take a keen interest in the land of his birth, having—with the encouragement of his parents—steeped himself in Russian culture from his youth and being keenly interested in Russian history, literature, and the economic system. Even in his early years at the Board of Trade he was using his lunch-hour to pursue research on the Soviet Union and was soon submitting articles to the leading British quarterly journal in the field, *Soviet Studies*, and other publications.

Alec Nove married for a second time in 1951. His wife, Irene MacPherson, was a Scot from Glasgow, and when the Board of Trade agreed to allow Alec to spend two years in the Department of Soviet Studies at the University of Glasgow the offer was as acceptable to her as to him. Alec and Irene took charge of the two boys from the first marriage (David was later to become a tax inspector and Perry a detective inspector) and a third son—the only child of this happy, second marriage—Charles (in adulthood a BBC presenter) was born in 1960.

Nove's presence in the Department, even on a temporary basis (1952–4), transformed it while, at the same time, deepening his own interest in academic study. Nevertheless, he honoured his commitment to return to Whitehall, transferring in 1956 to the Economic Section of the Treasury and working for much of the next two years on Soviet affairs in conjunction with the Joint Intelligence Bureau of the Ministry of Defence. It was in 1958 that Nove became a full-time scholar, starting his university teaching career at the London School of Economics with the title of Reader in Russian Social and Economic Studies. Along with Leonard Schapiro, he provided the core of a formidable array of expertise on the Soviet Union at the LSE. In 1963, however, Nove was persuaded to apply for a new Chair and the directorship of the renamed Institute of Soviet and East European Studies at the University of Glasgow and was duly elected. Glasgow was to remain his home city and the University his academic base right up to the time of his death in May 1994. Although he formally retired from his teaching and administrative duties in 1982, the University's standing as an important centre of study of Russia and Eastern Europe continued to benefit from Nove's presence as an Honorary Senior Research Fellow.

The atmosphere of Glasgow suited him. He enjoyed talking with his colleagues and took an obvious pleasure in developing an argument and hitting on a piquant example to drive it home. He expressed himself with gusto and took pleasure in a wide variety of recreations which he listed as 'walking in the Scottish hills, travel, music, theatre, exotic dishes'. He was an opera-lover and an enthusiastic supporter of Scottish Opera who would also make the time to write articles for a friend to publish in Paris on the historical background to the great Russian operas such as *Boris Godunov* and *Yevgeny Onegin*. He had a keen interest in sport, including chess (which he played spiritedly) and most ball-games. He enjoyed watching football and did not confine his viewing to television but attended matches in Glasgow from time to time. He had learned to play cricket as a schoolboy in London and even when over the age of fifty he turned out occasionally for the Glasgow University Staff XI (as he had done more frequently for the LSE staff team), displaying an impressive agility in the field. His love of the countryside and hillwalking consolidated his affection for his adopted country, as was evident from the fact that this globetrotting academic returned year after year to the Western Isles, particularly the Isle of Coll, for his summer holidays.

Nove was, though, an inveterate traveller. He learned much from seeing places for himself and talking with people who lived in the Communist systems he was studying. Thus, he had a special interest in paying study visits to Russia and Eastern Europe, but he was also in great demand in the rest of the world as a visiting speaker and conference participant. He spent some time in the mid-1950s in the British Embassy in Moscow and in the early 1960s he travelled to Moscow by train with his wife and new baby. In 1962–3 he accepted an invitation from his friend, Roy Laird, to be the Distinguished Visiting Rose Morgan Professor at the University of Kansas for that academic year. Following his nominal retirement, he accepted a series of visiting professorships which took him, *inter alia*, to Columbia University, Berkeley, Paris, and Stockholm. His travels from the outset of his career as a full-time academic brought him often to the United States but also to Central and South America, to various parts of Europe, to China and Japan.

As a Russophile, he was, however, particularly pained by the denial to him over many years of a Soviet visa. At the beginning of the 1970s he was put on a KGB blacklist, along with a number of other British officials, academics and journalists, in retaliation for a large-scale expulsion of Soviet spies from Britain. When the International Political Science Association held its triennial conference in Moscow in 1979, and took a strong line with the Soviet authorities by insisting that unless everyone on the conference programme received a Soviet visa the event would be called off, Nove made sure he was on the programme. He took a lively part in the proceedings and had many useful conversations outside the conference halls. His belief that this visit would form a valuable precedent and ensure his freedom to return to Russia was, unfortunately, soon shattered. The senseless ban was restored, and it was not until the Gorbachev era, when so much altered in Russia, that Alec Nove was made welcome once more. So rapidly did things change then that Nove was not only invited to give lectures in Moscow on economic reform but also to write on that subject for *Kommunist*, the theoretical journal of the Communist Party which, in a sharp break with the past, was being turned into a forum for debate.

Indeed, Nove was attached to the British Embassy for six weeks in late 1989 as the first holder of a 'visiting fellowship' set up by the Ambassador, Sir Rodric Braithwaite, specifically to strengthen the Embassy's economic expertise. With sound judgement, he invited Alec Nove to be the first holder of this unusual post. Nove had extensive conversations with all the leading Russian economists from Leonid Abalkin to the young Yegor Gaidar and spent some time in Leningrad as well as Moscow. He was much impressed by the political changes, but remained gloomy about the economy, telling Braithwaite: 'Not only can't I see the light at the end of the tunnel. I can't even see the tunnel'. By the time he arrived in Moscow to take up this attachment to the British Embassy, Alec Nove was seventy-four, but as Rodric Braithwaite noted in his diary at the time, he was 'as splendid as ever'.

Nove's travels continued literally to the time of his death. It was after spending a short time back in his native St Petersburg and moving on to Sweden, where he received an honourary doctorate in Stockholm, that, along with his wife Irene, he took a holiday in Norway. On a day in which they had, in Irene's words, enjoyed an 'absolutely lovely sail on a Norwegian fjord', Alec had a massive heart attack that night and died in hospital the following day (15 May 1994). Characteristically, on the way to the hospital he had sat up in the ambulance and said: 'I'm perfectly all right, you know'.

Alec Nove was a prolific writer, but a scholar who did not write to fulfil the expectations of extraneous bodies but because he had something compelling to say. His urge to communicate his ideas and reflections was such that he could become quite agitated if deprived of either of his most basic tools—a pen and paper. One of us recalls an encounter on Lancaster station when he expressed great concern that he would not be able to buy writing paper until the train reached Carlisle. Luckily, it was possible to supply some sheets on the spot and doubtless a newspaper article or the outline of a more substantial chapter was completed before the train reached its destination. Alec Nove turned late in life to the computer, and his relationship with it was one of endless frustration. Not wholly accepting that computers did exactly what they were instructed to do, Alec would work himself into a frenzy, pounding his desk and on occasion shouting at the machine in exasperation.

As this suggests, Alec was not someone who hid his emotions. More often than not, however, it was a boyish enthusiasm he exuded as he hurried to share the knowledge of whatever latest article by a Russian writer or meeting with a Hungarian economist had impressed him. Even when he was expressing his irritation with the latest idiocy emanating from government, whether in London or Moscow, cheerfulness kept breaking out. He had a wonderful memory for the political jokes which were told in Russia and Eastern Europe during the Communist period and his highly effective use of them in lectures and conference speeches made these presentations as entertaining as they were instructive. He could give scintillating lectures on the basis of a minimum of notes (the back of an envelope often sufficing).

Alec Nove's first academic publication (in 1949) was on Soviet law and in the course of his career he went on to produce several hundred scholarly articles and contributions to symposia. Some of them he collected into books and they made up several of the eleven single-author books he published. In addition to these there were two co-authored volumes, and eight books of which he was editor and part-author. He had a remarkable ability to see what mattered and to make connections which others missed. So much of his output was of value that there is a certain arbitrariness in picking out his major works. There is no doubt, however, that simply in terms of explaining how the Soviet economy worked (and how much less efficient it was than Soviet propagandists claimed and Western politicians for a time feared), an important contribution was made by his first major book, *The Soviet Economy*, published originally in 1961. It went through three editions and was then radically rewritten as *The Soviet Economic System* (1977; 2nd edn., 1980; 3rd edn., 1986). His *Economic History of the USSR* (1969; 2nd edn., 1989; 3rd edn., 1992) also became a key text.

Nove was one of the first writers to show that behind the monolithic facade of the Soviet system bureaucratic battles were fought. He noted that the supposedly all-powerful State Planning Committee (*Gosplan*) was very reliant on information in the possession of the economic ministries, so that 'in practice the sheer volume of work and of decisions in *Gosplan* places very considerable powers in the hands of the ministries'. Nove, in *The Soviet Economic System*, used the term 'centralized pluralism' to encapsulate the tug-of-war which he saw as occurring between the ministries and *Gosplan* and the struggle for a greater share of resources among the various ministries. That was stretching the concept of pluralism too far, but it drew attention to an important aspect of Soviet political life which accounts from within the totalitarian paradigm tended to miss.

Nove's *Stalinism and After* (1975) was a work of political and social history which complemented his *Economic History of the USSR*. Even his most scholarly work was never especially heavily footnoted. He read widely, but his work is outstanding more for the quality of its insights than for the detail of its documentation. *Stalinism and After* was, even by Nove's standards, light on notes and it was written at high speed. In the preface Nove wrote: 'It is customary to express thanks . . . for the advice of colleagues, and I usually do so gratefully. This work, however, was largely written on a Hebridean island where I had no advice . . . '. Yet even that work, resting as it did on a lifetime of reflection on the subject, can still be read with enjoyment, notwithstanding its grim subject-matter, and for instruction, in spite of the vast amount of new information which has become available since it was written.

For all students of Russia and the Soviet Union the era which began when Gorbachev assumed the leadership of the Soviet Communist Party in March 1985 was one of mounting excitement. Not only were there momentous changes in the object of their study but a vast improvement in the quantity and quality of the sources on which that study could be based. In his book, *Glasnost' in Action: Cultural Renaissance in Russia* (1989) Alec Nove produced a substantial commentary on the fruits of the new openness for serious discussion of Stalin and Stalinism, religion and morality, social problems and the law, and the nature of the political and economic system. Writing the final pages of this book at the beginning of 1989, Nove observes:

> The essential point is that the open debate is now concerned with the very essence, the fundamentals, of the Soviet system—this for the first time in living memory. What kind of society did they have, and where are they now? Where are they going? One has a feeling that no one quite knows. Does this matter? After all, where are *we* going? In the Soviet Union it does matter, since the legitimacy of party rule rests upon its role of leading the people towards a goal.

While few people had been prepared to consider seriously the possibility that any Soviet leader would take the risk of embarking on radical reform until this actually happened (and some refused to acknowledge it even then), Alec Nove was one of the small minority who did not rule out in advance the coming to power of a reformer. Writing in the *Times Higher Education Supplement* in October 1980 Nove speculated as to whether 'a younger man, hiding his light under a bushel, might base his career on a far-reaching reform programme'.

In the year before his death Nove delivered the 1993 annual W. Averell Harriman Lecture at Columbia University, New York. He entitled it 'The Soviet Union in Retrospect: An Obituary Notice'. He argues that it was in the Brezhnev era that 'the party-state bureaucracy became a real ruling class', able to enjoy its privileges in secret and no longer threatened by arbitrary arrest. But growth rates declined and stagnation threatened. Nove goes on:

> So—enter Gorbachev and *perestroika*. He surely recognized the magnitude of the task. It is my conviction that history will treat his efforts more kindly than do his contemporaries. True, he did not know just how far his own reforming logic would take him. True as well, he wished to preserve the Soviet Union. But it was to have been a very different place. I wholeheartedly disagree with those who, like Richard Pipes, believed that Gorbachev had no greater ambition than to modernize and streamline the old system, that he was a younger Brezhnev, better dressed and with a more attractive wife. The advances in freedom of speech and of the press were astonishing indeed. He clearly wished to use *glasnost* to sweep away institutions and colleagues that stood in the way of change. His foreign-policy initiatives were far-reaching. But the skeptics obstinately refused to see that any fundamental change was in process, apparently in the belief that since this was impossible, any change that was actually occurring could not be fundamental because it was occurring. Even the withdrawal from Afghanistan and the willingness to allow Eastern Europe to go its own way did not

convince these inveterate skeptics, who now say that it was Reagan's speed
up in the arms race that 'won' the Cold War.

In that same lecture Nove attributes the failure to combine reforms with
the preservation of the Soviet Union to the incoherence of economic
reform under Gorbachev, to Gorbachev's inability 'to understand the
centrifugal force of *nationalism*' and to the dilemma of power whereby
the 'one effective political instrument was the Party acting through its
full-time functionaries' but as Gorbachev's reform programme became
more radical, the Party apparatus itself became a major obstacle to
change. Hence, Gorbachev 'sought to weaken and downgrade this
apparatus', but no alternative power structure emerged in time to halt
the process of political disintegration that got underway.

Alec Nove was so closely identified with Sovietology that his
contributions to economics were apt to be disregarded. He had begun,
though, in the 1960s to give thought to the principles by which industry
in public ownership should be guided. He developed his ideas in
*Efficiency Criteria for Nationalised Industries* (1973). He was alarmed
by the trend towards commercial principles of operation, i.e. the adoption of the same rules as would be followed by private industry in a
competitive situation. If nationalised industries were to model themselves on privately-owned undertakings, why were they nationalised in
the first place? Was there not a difference of purpose and did not all
businesses have to start from a clear view of their purposes? It can
hardly have surprised him that the upshot of adopting commercial
principles of pricing and profit-making should have been privatisation.

In reflecting on the criteria that ought to govern the behaviour of a
nationalised industry Nove was led to attack the over-simplifications of
current theory. It might seem that if public undertakings equated their
prices with marginal cost (as would happen under perfect competition),
their monopoly powers would be effectively curbed. Was it not enough
to follow this simple rule? Unfortunately, as Nove points out, the rule is
full of ambiguities and emerges from a conception of price determination that is a travesty of the actual competitive process. It assumes that
demand varies only in quantity and impinges on a homogeneous supply
that also varies in a single dimension. But in fact there are nearly
always differences in quality, customer service, punctuality, availability, and all that goes to goodwill, an important determinant of customer
choice and business behaviour but rarely mentioned in textbooks.

There is a further difficulty of applying the concept of marginal cost to a business situation. Nove was fond of citing transport to show how short-sighted could be decisions on transport facilities that were in keeping with current theory. How was a railway system to use the concept? Did it apply to a particular train service or to each particular journey? If a particular service made a loss in a system showing a profit was it to be instantly discontinued? If so, what of the impact on the use of other services? In any system there was likely to be a mixture of profitable and loss-making services; and, if all the loss-making services were abandoned might not the rest then become unprofitable too, even if hitherto the operation of the system as a whole had been in profit?

Much of the argument in *Efficiency Criteria for Nationalised Industries* revolves round the interaction of one economic activity with another so that a broad view has to be taken, not one which treats the system as a collection of fragments. The book is thus a critique of microeconomics to the extent that these linkages are neglected in most expositions of the subject. It is one of the merits of the book that it gives example after example of the links between apparently separate activities, providing the reader with a realistic picture of the complexity of business decisions. Nove insistently emphasised the limitations of market forces and the need to redirect them so as to take account of what the market ignored. It is no accident that many of his examples are drawn from railways, for Nove was a great supporter of public transport and never owned a car. He was fiercely critical of the practice of closing down 'uneconomic' branch railway lines.

Alec Nove was interested in theoretical problems of Socialism, although his own political beliefs were firmly in the social democratic (or democratic socialist) tradition. He was a Labour voter who spent much time rebutting the arguments of various schools of Marxists, on the one hand, and those of dogmatic free-marketeers, on the other. He was acutely conscious of the wide gap between the hopes of the prophets of Communism and the grim realities but conscious also of the weaknesses of capitalism. In *The Economics of Feasible Socialism* (1983, published in a revised edition as *The Economics of Feasible Socialism Revisited*, 1991) Nove set himself the task of working out a realistic prescription for the functioning of a socialist economy which would be free of the excesses and weaknesses of Communism and yet be 'feasible'. As he put it in his preface to that book: 'Brought up in a social-democratic environment, son of a Menshevik who was arrested by the Bolsheviks, I inherited a somewhat critical view of Soviet reality: if this really was socialism, I would prefer to be elsewhere. (Luckily, I *was* elsewhere!)'. Characteristically, he goes on:

> I feel increasingly ill-disposed towards those latter-day Marxists who airily ascribe all the world's evils to 'capitalism', dismiss the Soviet experience as irrelevant, and substitute for hard thinking an image of a post-revolutionary world in which there would be no economic problems at all (or where any problems that might arise would be handled smoothly by the 'associated producers' of a world commonwealth). I feel not too well-disposed either towards the Chicago school, whose belief in 'free enterprise' seems quite unaffected by the growth of giant bureaucratic corporations, and whose remedies for current ills seem to benefit the rich and ignore unemployment. And even Milton Friedman is preferable to the abstract model-builders whose works fill the pages of our professional journals, since he at least advocates action in the real world (even though I believe the action he advocates is wrong).

*The Economics of Feasible Socialism* is in part an exposition of the weaknesses of Marxist thinking and the highly unscientific socialism that Marx and his followers espoused. Marx provided no clear explanation of how the system was to work in the absence of a price mechanism and failed to recognise the inevitable centralisation and subsequent despotism implicit in a system unresponsive to price signals and relying purely on organisation and planning and hence on hierarchy. As a polemic against Utopian socialism Nove's book is highly effective. As a picture of a competitive, workable socialist system, it remains, however, much more sketchy. There is, for example, no mention of banks or any discussion of a capital market.

In most of his work, however, Nove is not concerned with elaborating a comprehensive alternative model to Communism, on the one hand, and the variety of capitalist economies to be found in the West, on the other. He is content to advocate improvement and reform. As he put it in the final chapter of *The Economics of Feasible Socialism Revisited*: ' "Permanent revolution" can be a disaster, as China's cultural revolution has shown. It disorganises, impoverishes, confuses. But permanent vigilance, *permanent reform*, will surely be a "must" '.

In a debate with Milton Friedman in 1984 Nove agreed with his antagonist on the weaknesses of Soviet-type planning, but made plain that he did not share Friedman's uncritical regard for market forces. Nove claimed that this rested on several unrealistic assumptions: that externalities were minor exceptions; that oligopoly was rare; that unemployment was due only to labour market imperfections; that economies of scale did not lead to the emergence of large corporations with extensive powers over prices; and that the distribution of property bore some recognisable relationship to present or even past economic merit. He suggested that their most serious disagreement related to those areas of human activity which should be wholly or partly excluded from the market. A market economy, he concluded, might be 'a necessary condition for human freedom, but it is certainly not a sufficient condition'.

Among the more notable of the many occasions on which each of the authors of this memoir encountered Alec Nove was when one of us took part in an all-day seminar at Chequers, convened by Margaret Thatcher early in her second term as Prime Minister. It was held on 8 September 1983 and Nove was one of eight academics who sat on one side of the table, while a formidable Government team sat on the other side. Margaret Thatcher was flanked by the Foreign Secretary, Sir Geoffrey Howe, and by her Minister of Defence at that time, Michael Heseltine. Others present included Malcolm Rifkind as Minister of State at the Foreign Office. Lady Thatcher, as she later became, devoted two-and-a-half pages of her memoirs to this seminar, while the late Sir Anthony Parsons, the Prime Minister's Foreign Policy adviser at the time, went so far as to say that it 'changed British foreign policy'. The academics present advocated a change of policy towards the Soviet Union from active avoidance of any contact with the 'evil empire' to a break with that aspect of President Reagan's policy and an attempt to seek dialogue and involvement in what was going on in Russia. Alec Nove was in a minority, though, on the scholars' side of the table in being so bold as to disagree explicitly with a statement by the Prime Minister (and only Heseltine, on the Government side, dared agree with *him*).

The invitation to Mikhail Gorbachev to visit Britain in December 1984 (three months before he became General Secretary of the Soviet Communist Party) had its origins in the September 1983 Chequers seminar. The evening before Gorbachev arrived in London, Alec Nove was one of four academics (as was one of the authors of this memorial essay) invited to 10 Downing Street to discuss Gorbachev, the Soviet Union, and Britain's relations with the Soviet Union with the Prime Minister and Foreign Secretary. It was a good meeting, in spite of the fact that none of the academics came into the category of 'one of us'—that is to say, the Thatcherite wing of the Conservative Party. Indeed, none of the four, it is safe to say, had voted Conservative in the previous General Election. The meeting over, the group had only just begun to descend the staircase at 10 Downing Street when Alec said loudly and clearly, 'I just wish she would consult us on domestic policy as well'. That, however, was hardly likely to happen. 'One of us' criteria were much more stringently applied in meetings on economic and social policy.

Surprisingly, Alec Nove never received any honour or mark of official recognition from British Government circles, although successive British Ambassadors to the Soviet Union greatly valued his advice. His fellow scholars were more generous in their appreciation of his enormous contribution to academic life. He was elected a Fellow of the British Academy in 1978, of the Royal Society of Edinburgh in 1982 and made an Honorary Fellow of the London School of Economics in the same year. He also received several honorary doctorates.

Nove had, of course, an independence of mind and intellectual honesty which made few concessions to fashion, whether the fashion of the New Left in its day or that of neoclassical economics in more recent years. He did not share the official Western optimism about the economic choices made by Russia in the post-Soviet period. In a paper written for *The Harriman Institute Forum* in the summer of 1992, Nove borrowed the title of Nikolai Bukharin's work of 1920, 'Economics of the Transition Period'. Bukharin, of course, was talking about a transition in quite another direction. Nove argued in this article that in 'Russia in particular, it is hard to see how one can rely on a market mechanism that has yet to be created, while decline accelerates and a new Time of Troubles looms ahead. To create the conditions for a market economy surely requires action, "interventionism", under conditions of dire emergency analogous to a wartime economy, with the real supply side in such disarray as to render impossible macroeconomic stabilization'.

In his (already-cited) Averell Harriman Lecture of 1993, he remained uncharacteristically gloomy, writing: 'The demoralized and confused Russian people ask yet again the eternal question, *kto vinovat?* (who is to blame?). What now? A new Time of Troubles, analogous to the anarchy that followed the death of Boris Godunov? Maybe. The only thing we can say for sure is that, unlike in 1611, Polish troops will *not* occupy the Kremlin. And then, in 1613, the first Romanov tsar imposed order. Who will do so tomorrow? And over what territory?' He ended his lecture by quoting the well-known lines of 'the national poet of my adopted country':

But Mousie, thou art no' thy lane
In proving foresight may be vain
The best-laid schemes o' mice an' men
Gang aft agley
And leave us nought but grief an' pain
For promised joy.
Still thou art blest, compared wi' me.
The present only toucheth thee.
But och, I backward cast my ee
On prospects drear,
An' forward, tho' I canna see,
I guess — an' fear.

ARCHIE BROWN
ALEC CAIRNCROSS
*Fellows of the Academy*

*Note.* A complete list of Alec Nove's books and an extensive and useful, albeit incomplete, list of his many articles, contributions to edited volumes, and book reviews are to be found in Ian D. Thatcher, 'Alec Nove: A Bibliographical Tribute', *Europe-Asia Studies* (formerly *Soviet Studies*), vol. 47, no. 8 (1995), 1383–1410.

KARL POPPER                    *Lotte Meitner-Graf*

*Proceedings of the British Academy*, **94**, 645–684

# Karl Raimund Popper
# 1902–1994

KARL POPPER was born in Vienna on 28 July 1902, and died in London on 17 September 1994.

## Vienna

He had two sisters: Dora, born in 1893, and Annie, born in 1898. Their father, Dr Simon Popper, had come to Vienna from Bohemia. In Vienna he took a law degree and afterwards became a partner in a law firm headed by the man who was to be the last liberal Mayor of Vienna. The firm's offices were on the first floor of a fine eighteenth-century building close by the cathedral. When Simon Popper took over as senior partner in 1896, a large adjoining apartment became the family residence. (Its present address is Bauernmkt 1; it was to become a Nazi headquarters.[1]) He was also a social reformer, writer, and scholar, with a fine library of some 10,000 books;[2] books were everywhere except the dining-room, where the grand piano reigned. Karl's mother, née Jenny Schiff, played the piano beautifully. Her whole family was musical, and two of her brothers had positions at the university. The Popper children were born into a cultured and wealthy home, and the family was well-connected. Konrad Lorenz was a childhood friend,[3] and the pianist Rudolf Serkin later became a lifelong friend.

© The British Academy 1997.
[1] KRP. (For sources and abbreviations see the Note on p. 684 below.)
[2] Melitta Mew.
[3] Karl Popper, *In Search of a Better World* (London 1992), p. 99.

Precisely on Popper's twelfth birthday Austria declared war on Serbia. At first the war did not have a too disturbing effect on the family, though all his cousins who were old enough became Army officers. His mother still took the family for summer holidays to the Alps. Rosa Graf, a sister of Freud's,[4] was a friend of the Popper family, and in the summer of 1916 she joined them in their mountain retreat. Her son visited them briefly on Army leave before going to the front. Soon afterwards news came that he had been killed, and the grief this caused deeply impressed Popper. Another family experience which he reported long afterwards concerned another family friend, Dr Karl Schmidt, a lawyer and now an Army officer, who was a regular visitor at the Poppers' home. On one occasion he told them over supper that he had been given the task of preparing the case for high treason against a certain Professor of Philosophy at the University of Vienna, now out of the country, called Tomas Masaryk. Masaryk was a traitor, he said, but also a wonderful man.[5]

By the time it ended the effects of the war were devastating. There came hunger-riots and inflation, and occasional shooting. The secure, comfortable world in which Popper had grown up was gone. At sixteen he left home and school, in a mood of private revolt. There followed a mixed-up, experimental period in which, while nominally enrolled at the University of Vienna, he tried being a manual worker, switched to being a cabinet-maker's apprentice, joined a workers' movement, became a Democratic Socialist and, briefly, a Communist. He earned a little money coaching American students. He and his friends walked in the mountains, read ravenously, and enjoyed music. Much of the Youth Movement's ethos, its belief in emancipation through education, its love of the open air and the mountains, its moral seriousness, became lifelong attitudes of his.[6] Its puritanism included a ban on all stimulants; in his childhood the sight of a drunken man falling under the wheels of a horse-drawn carriage had in any case given him a lifelong horror of alcohol.[7]

In 1919 he witnessed the shooting of some unarmed young

---

[4] His favourite sister, it seems (Ernest Jones, *Sigmund Freud: Life and Work* (London, 1953), vol. i, p. 11).

[5] This incident is touched on in *Unended Quest*, p. 15, and described at more length in a talk which Popper gave in Prague, in 1994, on receiving an honorary doctorate from Charles University.

[6] EHG.

[7] KRP.

Socialists outside a police station during a demonstration engineered by Communists. This turned him less against the police than against Marxism with its belief in revolutionary violence as a precondition for progress towards the dictatorship of the proletariat. As well as his break with Marxism, this year brought his first exposure to Einstein's revolutionary theory of gravitation which had recently passed Eddington's 'star-shift' tests. He attended a lecture by Einstein which left him in a whirl, but a fellow student took him through the theory.[8] He acted as an unpaid assistant to Alfred Adler, and worked with neglected children. Although, or perhaps because, he considered Schubert the last of the great composers, he attempted to get to know something about contemporary music by joining a society presided over by Schönberg. Later, in reaction against this, he entered the Department of Church Music in the Vienna Academy of Music. He was admitted on the basis of a fugue for organ he had written, and he continued to compose afterwards. (In 1992, at Bryan Magee's instigation, Gillian Weir played this fugue for him; sadly, he could no longer hear the higher notes.)

In 1925 he enrolled in the newly founded Pedagogic Institute. He was soon giving unofficial seminars to fellow students. He said that he learnt very little from the teachers there; but he now met two university professors, Karl Bühler and Heinrich Gomperz, who were important for his intellectual development. His investigations began to shift from the psychology to the logic of scientific inquiry. In 1928 he received his Ph.D., passing with the highest grade; his examiners were Bühler and Moritz Schlick. He now became a qualified schoolteacher. At this Institute he also met Josefine Henninger, or 'Hennie'; they married in 1930. It was the beginning of a remarkable partnership, each devoted to the other, which lasted until Hennie's death in 1985.

He was reading Kant intensively, and also works by contemporaries such as Rudolf Carnap, Kurt Gödel, Hans Hahn, Karl Menger, Hans Reichenbach, Richard von Mises, Friedrich Waismann, and Ludwig Wittgenstein. Gomperz introduced him to Victor Kraft, who was the first member of the Circle whom Popper had met and the author of a book on scientific method which he found valuable. He attended Carnap's seminar in about 1929, and an uncle introduced him to Herbert Feigl, who encouraged him to publish his ideas in a book. This launched

---

[8] 'I was fortunate in being introduced to these ideas by a brilliant young student of mathematics, Max Elstein, a friend who died in 1922 at the age of twenty-one' (*Unended Quest*, pp. 37–8).

him into the writing of *Die beiden Grundprobleme der Erkenntnistheorie* (published, in German, only in 1979). His typescript was much read and discussed by members of the Vienna Circle, including Neurath, Schlick, and Waismann, and he had intensive discussions with Carnap and Feigl in the Tyrol in the summer of 1932. Carnap presented some of Popper's unpublished ideas, with due acknowledgements, the following year, and Popper put out trailers for his book: a short note, 'A Criterion of the Empirical Character of Theoretical Systems', and another on the question of induction and the probability of hypotheses, published in *Erkenntnis* in 1933 and 1935.

The book's two basic problems were that of the demarcation of science from non-science and that of induction. He rather gave the impression that the first of these is a familiar problem which had been well recognised at least since Kant (in 1933 he referred to it as 'Kant's problem of the limits of scientific knowledge'), his contribution being to offer a new solution. Kant's demarcation problem, however, was different from his own. Of course inductivists, such as Bacon, Whewell and Mill, by laying down methods for science did thereby offer solutions to the demarcation problem; but that does not mean that they explicitly posed this problem. Once stated, it seems so obvious that one tends to assume that it must have been stated long ago, but I don't know of anyone who did explicitly state it before Popper. Anyway, the received view, as Popper read it, was that the empirical sciences are distinguished by their use of an inductive method; which brings us to his second basic problem. This goes back to Hume; he had pointed out that inductive inferences from observed to unobserved instances are logically invalid; but he also held that the belief-forming machinery with which humans, like other animals, are endowed by Nature works in an essentially inductive way. A logical puritanism that inhibited us from making such invalid inferences would be deadly. Fortunately, our robustly non-logical human nature excludes this.

Popper sought to solve his two basic problems at one blow with his falsificationist philosophy of science. What demarcates science from non-science (metaphysics, logic, mathematics, and pseudo-science) is not the verifiability but the falsifiability of its theories. The method of science also is not inductive; it does not start out from observations and generalise from them: it starts out from problems, which it attacks with bold conjectures. The latter are unverifiable and unjustifiable but, when well developed, have predictive implications which can be put to the test, the more severe the better. A test will be severe if made with sufficiently discriminating experimental apparatus on predictions which deviate (as Einstein's did from Newton's) to a small but detectable extent from unrefuted predictions of the previous theory, or if made on predictions which break new ground. On this view, scientific inferences are all deductive, either from conjectural premises to a falsifiable consequence or from a falsified consequence to the negation of the conjunction of the jointly responsible premises. The problem of induction therefore drops out. (Whether it drops out completely is a question which will come up again.)

A shorter version of this book was published as *Logik der Forschung* in 1934. This went on to tackle several large problems opened up by its falsificationist view of science. One concerned the nature and status of the statements in the empirical basis against which scientific hypotheses are tested. Another concerned simplicity, which fell nicely into place: simpler hypotheses are desirable, not because they are more likely to be true, but because they are easier to eliminate if false. The longest chapter, on probability, took off from a seemingly insuperable objection to the book's main view, namely that probabilistic hypotheses, which had come to play a vitally important role in science, are strictly unfalsifiable. It was followed by a chapter on quantum theory.

The book was brought to Einstein's attention through musical connections. Popper's friend Rudolf Serkin played with the Busch Chamber Orchestra and had recently married Adolf and Frieda Busch's daughter. Frieda knew Einstein, now in Princeton, through his violin-playing. In April 1935 she sent him a copy of *Logik der Forschung*, explaining that the author was a Jew living in Vienna and hence had no prospects: 'Have the great kindness to read the attached book. Your judgement, in case it is favorable to Popper, could perhaps help him to get somewhere!'[9] Not long afterwards the young secondary school teacher received a letter from Einstein which began: 'Your book pleased me very much in many respects.' He liked its rejection of the 'inductive method' in favour of falsifiability as the decisive feature of scientific theories; purged of certain mistakes the book 'will be really splendid'. He offered to help in getting it known. Popper replied

---

[9] I am indebted here to material made available to me by John Stachel from his work on the Einstein papers. Popper (*Knowledge and the Body-Mind Problem* (London, 1994), p. 116) later used the following incident in Adolf Busch's life to illustrate what he called the 'centipede effect': Busch was asked by another violinist how he played a certain passage. 'He said it was quite simple—and then found he could no longer play the passage'. Popper said it was a passage in Beethoven, but it seems that it was actually in Mendelssohn (EHG).

deferentially, but at some length, standing his ground where he thought he had been right. This elicited the reply from Einstein that appears in Appendix *xii of *The Logic of Scientific Discovery*.

As Frieda Busch's letter indicates, Popper had no hope of a university position in Austria at that time. Before the war, plenty of teachers at the University of Vienna had been Jews or of Jewish origin: now there was growing hostility towards them. Not that Popper regarded himself as Jewish. Both his parents were of Jewish descent, but had converted to Lutheranism, wanting to be assimilated. But that did not stop him from being seen as Jewish. Not only was becoming a university teacher out of the question, but remaining a schoolteacher was becoming difficult. He had been transferred to a school where most of the teachers were crypto–Nazis, and there, as he put it later, he was 'treated badly', while Hennie, who was teaching at another school and was not of Jewish origin, suffered for being married to a Jew.[10]

So anti-Semitism gave Popper one strong motive to emigrate, related to which was the deteriorating political situation. The city of Vienna had been under Socialist control since 1920, but there was a smouldering threat of civil war. In July 1927 he had been present when a large crowd of Social Democrats, protesting at an earlier shooting by rightists, were fired on by the police; nearly 100 people were killed. In 1934, not long after Hitler came to power in Germany, Social Democrats decided, under increasing provocation, to arm themselves. Popper had been against this: they would provoke violence from the right without knowing how to handle their new weapons properly.[11] (In Chapter 19 of *The Open Society* there is a discussion of Marxian ambiguity over violence, epitomised by Engels's *Take the first shot, gentlemen of the bourgeoisie!*) In February 1934 civil war broke out; after four days' fighting Dollfuss had won, and the Social Democrat party was declared illegal. (Dollfuss was murdered by Nazis a few months later.) Popper had been predicting a Nazi take-over for some time. (His prescience was attested by a friend from his youth, Frederick Dorian, who wrote to him from America in 1942 that they often recalled his remarkable predictions of the catastrophe.[12]) It was becoming urgent to find an opening abroad.

---

[10] Draft autobiography, Popper Collection (135, 10). This passage was subsequently deleted. I learnt of it through a reference (note 18) in Malachi Hacohen, 'Karl Popper in Exile', *Philosophy of the Social Sciences*, 26 (December 1996), 452–92.

[11] KRP.

[12] See above, n. 10, Hacohen, note 14.

*Logik der Forschung*, as well as being reviewed and discussed by Carnap, Hempel, Neurath (who called Popper the Vienna Circle's 'official opposition'), Reichenbach (whose review was harsh), and others, had been quite widely noticed in the English-speaking world. (A British publisher, Hodges, bought the rights in 1937 and the work of translating it into English was begun, but the results were judged unsatisfactory, and then the outbreak of war in 1939 put an end to it.[13]) At the International Congress of Scientific Philosophy in Paris in 1935, Susan Stebbing invited him to lecture at Bedford College, London. (She had invited Carnap the year before.) He received other invitations and spent altogether about nine months in England during 1935–6.

Popper decided to lecture not on his own ideas but on Alfred Tarski's semantic theory of truth. Tarski had been giving him tutorials on this in Vienna, and Popper was persuaded of its enormous importance. That truth is objective or 'absolute' was one of Popper's most enduring convictions, but attempts hitherto, by Wittgenstein and Schlick for instance, to elucidate the idea of a statement corresponding to a fact had failed. And now he learnt that Tarski had rehabilitated the correspondence theory of truth. One eye-opener for Popper was Tarsi's introduction of a metalanguage in which one can talk in the same breath about linguistic entities (words, sentences) in the object-language and about things outside the object-language, thereby enabling one to elucidate such semantic notions as a formula being *satisfied* by a certain state of affairs.

Popper also lectured at Imperial College on probability, and gave a talk to the Moral Science Club in Cambridge. (Braithwaite was involved in this; Popper hoped that Keynes would be there, but Braithwaite had to disappoint him.[14]) Altogether he met a lot of people. Ayer, whom he had known in Vienna, took him to the Aristotelian Society, where he had an encounter with Russell, and also introduced him to Berlin, Hampshire, Moore, and Ryle. He also met mathematicians and scientists, including Schroedinger. Two people whom he met in London were to be of crucial importance to him later: Ernst Gombrich, then a Research Fellow at the Warburg Institute, and F. A. ('Fritz') Hayek, a Professor of Economics at the London School of Economics. Both men were from Vienna, but Popper had not met

[13] Hacohen; and KRP to EHG, 21 May 1943.
[14] RB to KRP, 12 March 1936.

Hayek before and Gombrich only fleetingly (although his father had worked in Popper's father's law firm). Now Popper and Gombrich, both living in 'horrible bedsitters' in Paddington, were meeting frequently.[15] Popper had brought along an early version of 'The Poverty of Historicism' which he presented at Hayek's seminar at LSE; he also gave Hayek a copy of *Logik der Forschung*. He was introduced to Walter Adams, the then General Secretary of the Academic Assistance Council (or Society for the Protection of Science and Learning as it became).

Popper liked England. One thing that impressed him was milkbottles being left on London doorsteps; in Vienna they would have been stolen.[16] But the desperately needed job openings did not materialise. Then sometime in 1936 J. H. ('Socrates') Woodger drew his attention to an advertisement for a professorship and a lectureship in what was then the Department of Philosophy and Education at Canterbury University College, Christchurch, New Zealand. He applied for both posts. He gave Moore and Woodger as his referees, and submitted testimonials from Bühler, Carnap, Russell, and Tarski. In the meanwhile he went to the International Congress in Copenhagen in 1936 (where news came that Schlick had been killed).

After the Congress he stayed on for discussions with Niels Bohr at the latter's Institute. When he returned to Vienna he was faced with a choice. Felix Kaufmann, who admired him, had interceded on his behalf, and he was now offered academic hospitality in Cambridge, for one year at £150. Popper wrote to Kaufmann that he would never forget what he had done for him.[17] Shortly afterwards he was offered the lectureship at Christchurch. (The professorship went to an anthropologist called Ivan Sutherland, about whom more below.) He would have liked to go to Cambridge, but the New Zealand position was a permanent one, and with a starting salary of £400; moreover the Cambridge offer could be transferred to someone else. So he accepted the Christchurch offer and suggested that 'Fritz' Waismann be invited to Cambridge in his stead (which he was).

---

[15] Ernst Gombrich, '*The Open Society and Its Enemies*: Remembering Its Publication Fifty Years Ago', Lecture at the London School of Economics, 12 June 1995 (LSE Centre for the Philosophy of the Natural and Social Sciences), p. 2.
[16] KRP.
[17] See above, n. 10, Hacohen, notes 25–7.

## New Zealand

He arrived in Christchurch in March 1937, at the start of the academic year. Out of his first salary cheque he sent a subscription to the Society for the Protection of Science and Learning.[18] After the German annexation of Austria in March 1938 he set up a refugee organisation in New Zealand. (Among the people this helped was a Viennese photographer called Bata, who later took the photograph which appeared on the dust jacket of the Schilpp volume on Popper.[19])

New Zealand seemed light-years from continental Europe. His teaching duties were heavy; as the only philosopher, he had to do all the philosophy teaching in the department—logic, history of philosophy, ethics and politics, problems of philosophy, plus introductory courses. He also did courses for scientists under the auspices of the Royal Society of New Zealand, and WEA classes. If he was not entirely cut off when war came, this was largely due to the good offices of Carnap, Hempel, Oppenheim, and others in America who, among other things, subscribed on his behalf to the *Journal of Symbolic Logic*.[20] In his first year there he gave at a seminar what became a stunning little piece called 'What Is Dialectic?' (he was not yet banning *what-is* questions[21]). Against dialecticians who say that contradictions are welcome because they are fertile, it declared that they are fertile only so long as we strive to eliminate them.

He set about turning the talk he had given at Hayek's seminar into an article—and then something unplanned and rather extraordinary happened. A short section on essentialism which briefly mentioned Plato started growing; and it went on growing and growing until it became volume one of *The Open Society*. There are interesting differences between this volume and volume two, the critique of Marxism. He had been thinking critically about Marxism for many years; when he started to write about it with an intention to publish, in 1935, he was still writing in German. The Plato volume was written in English from the outset, and is altogether more lively and arresting. His shift to English as the language in which he lectured, wrote, and thought was a traumatic experience,[22] but it had a bracing effect. (A radio critic

[18] Brian McGuinness.
[19] Alan Musgrave.
[20] KRP to RC, 5 July 1943.
[21] Published in *Mind*, October 1940; reprinted as ch. 15 of *Conjectures and Refutations* (London, 1963).
[22] KRP.

remarked on the clarity of a talk on Newton which he gave on New Zealand radio: perhaps the speaker's unfamiliarity with the English language had restricted him to simple words?[23] The implied prediction that as Popper's mastery of the English vocabulary improved he would become increasingly obscure was not borne out.) He took to the new language astonishingly well. Margaret Dalziel was a great help,[24] and Fowler's *Modern English Usage* became a bible for him.

The completion of Popper's great book was a heroic achievement. It was written under most adverse conditions.[25] As well as language problems and his heavy teaching load, 'hopeless' library conditions,[26] and the near-impossibility of acquiring new books, he had himself to procure the paper on which that big book was written and rewritten again and again in his large, round handwriting, and typed and retyped by Hennie. His not being allowed departmental paper for research purposes brings us to what was perhaps the main adverse factor, the bitter hostility which developed between him and Sutherland, his Head of Department. (Sutherland was to commit suicide in 1952.[27]) It seems that things turned really nasty once New Zealand was at war with Germany. In 1940 Popper made an official complaint to the Rector, Dr Hight, to the effect that Sutherland had been spreading the allegation that he, Popper, was disloyal to the British cause (there was talk of his attending a party given by a refugee to celebrate the fall of Holland). Hight, who was highly supportive of Popper,[28] replied that he was convinced of Popper's absolute loyalty to the British cause.[29] According to Popper, Sutherland swore that he would drive him out of New Zealand. He also said that Sutherland denounced him to the police, who interrogated him.[30] However, it is not clear that Sutherland took the initiative here. Technically, Popper was now an 'enemy alien', and the police would have interviewed him as a matter of course.[31] Perhaps they routinely contacted his Head of Department, who welcomed the

---

[23] KRP.

[24] JAP to EHG, 29 July 1943.

[25] See Colin Simkin, *Popper's Views on Natural and Social Science* (E. J. Brill, 1993), Appendix One.

[26] KRP to FAH, 9 December 1943.

[27] Roger Sandall kindly sent me obituaries of Sutherland which appeared in the *Journal of the Polynesian Society*, 61 (1952), 120–9.

[28] Colin Simkin.

[29] Popper Collection (366, 5).

[30] Colin Simkin.

[31] Peter Munz.

chance to cast doubt on his loyalty. The police do not seem to have pursued any allegations he made. Matters did not improve with time. In 1944 Popper asked for an official investigation into his situation in the department, rendered intolerable by Sutherland. He also complained that the method of distributing the money for examiners had been revised in a way that deprived him of most of his share, although he was still doing all the examining in philosophy. There was now a new Rector, and it seems that nothing was done.

In March 1945 Popper wrote to Gombrich: 'This is the ninth year that I am doing *all* the teaching in philosophy, and I am the only member of the staff who has not got a salary rise in this time—or rather, there is no member who has not got at least four rises in this period'. He added: 'those of my friends who protested on my behalf against this treatment were told something like this: "We know that he is too good for this place. This we cannot help; and we shall not try to hold him if he wishes to go elsewhere".'[32] His salary did indeed remain fixed, at NZ £500, during his time in New Zealand. The advertisement for the lectureship, issued by the Universities Bureau in London in 1936, which gave the salary as £400 rising by two increments of £50 to £500, was ambiguous as between English and New Zealand pounds. He inquired about this at the time, but was obliged to sail before receiving an answer. It turned out that New Zealand pounds were meant; however, it was decided to set his salary at the equivalent of £400 sterling, namely NZ £500. So he started at the top of the Lecturer's scale. During 1940 it was decided to introduce a Senior Lecturer grade, with a minimum salary of £500 and a maximum of £650.[33] He was promoted as from January 1941, but put at the bottom of the scale, so his salary remained the same. Nor did he get any increment subsequently. The Poppers came to feel very poor. As well as a heavy mortgage, he had taken out an insurance policy to protect Hennie in the event of his death.[34] And there was the cost of the paper for the big book he was writing, to which would soon be added the cost of numerous cables about it, first to America and later to England.

With the Japanese drawing closer, Popper determined to finish it (its title was not yet decided), and worked at it day and night for days on end;[35] and he did 'finish' it (although no writing of his was ever safe

[32] KRP to EHG, 28 March 1945.
[33] W. J. Gardner, E. T. Beardsley, and T. E. Carter, *A History of the University of Canterbury, 1873–1973* (Christchurch, 1973), p. 292.
[34] Simkin, *Popper's Views*, p. 187n.
[35] JAP to EHG, 29 July 1943.

from subsequent revision) in October 1942. Now came the problem of
publication. If he submitted it himself to a publisher in England or
America and it was rejected, a year might go by before he got the
typescript back (assuming it was not lost *en route* through enemy
action). He needed someone in England or America to act for him.
The paper shortage being more severe in Britain, he decided to try in
America.

Some months later Hennie wrote: 'We soon had to realize that our
friends to whom we had sent the manuscript were letting us down
completely . . .. And now began an undescribably miserable time . . ..
We felt completely abandoned and cast out.'[36] And in *Unended Quest*
Popper wrote:

> . . . the reaction of those friends in the United States to whom I sent the
> manuscript was a terrible blow. They did not react at all for many months;
> and later, instead of submitting the manuscript to a publisher, they solicited
> an opinion from a famous authority, who decided that the book, because of
> its irreverence towards Aristotle (not Plato), was not fit to be submitted to a
> publisher (p. 119).

Those friends have until recently remained shrouded in anonymity and
ignominy. Their cover was first blown, so far as I know, by Hacohen.[37]
Popper had tried to get in touch with an old friend from Vienna, now in
New York, called Alfred Braunthal; and things might have gone better
if he had succeeded, but he had the wrong address and got no reply.
Then, all wound up and impatient, he did something rather daft. The
one person in America of whose address he was reasonably sure was a
Professor Dorian (mentioned earlier, who had recently congratulated
him for his prescience back in the 1920s about the impending catastrophe in Europe). Popper had doubts as to whether Dorian would be
interested; but instead of taking the obvious precaution of first writing
to ask whether he would accept this big undertaking, he sent him the
typescript, together with 'very full instructions', without prior warning.
Popper's fears turned out to have been justified; Dorian was not interested and did not read it,[38] but he did bring in another mutual friend
from their Vienna days, Fritz Hellin. Popper also doubted whether this
man would be sufficiently interested.[39] Then Popper at last got hold of

---

[36] JAP to EHG, 29 July 1943.
[37] See above, n. 10, Hacohen, notes 56, 57.
[38] KRP to AB, 21 May 1943. This and other correspondence is in Popper Collection (28,
1–8).
[39] KRP to AB, 21 May 1943.

Braunthal's correct address, and he too was enrolled. He did read it, and at last there came a ray of sunshine. He reported: 'So deeply was I moved by your writing, so excited was I and even thrilled that I devoured the entire book as it were in one gulp.'[40] He now collaborated with Hellin, who in August sent Popper a cable saying that the manuscript was with Friedrich, and adding, 'Be patient'. Carl J. Friedrich was Professor of Government at Harvard and author of *Constitutional Government and Democracy*. Although Popper wrote afterwards of their soliciting an opinion from an authority instead of submitting the manuscript to a publisher, Hellin and Braunthal would rightly have regarded him as someone who, if his response were positive, might persuade Harvard University Press to take it. They could not know that it would be negative. At about this time 'The Poverty of Historicism' was rejected by Moore for *Mind*. Popper and Hennie, already in a state of exhaustion, were now in despair.

In April 1943 Popper switched the search for a publisher to England. He wrote to Gombrich that he had finished a book provisionally entitled 'A Social Philosophy for Everyman', and asked him to take over the task of finding a publisher. Gombrich cabled his willingness, and Popper sent him copies of the typescript.

He also wrote to Hayek, one of the rather small number of teachers at LSE (which was now evacuated to Cambridge) who had not been absorbed into the war effort. He had met Popper only about four times, in 1935–6, but he had been greatly impressed both by Popper's talk at his seminar and by *Logik der Forschung*, and the two men had had some correspondence since 1940. He now formed the intention of getting Popper to LSE. Abraham Wolf, who had held a part-time Chair in Logic and Scientific Method at LSE (and a full-time one at UCL), had retired in 1941. Hayek's idea was that the part-time chair might be converted into a full-time readership, to be occupied by Popper, but he would have little hope unless he could persuade his colleagues on the Appointments Committee, especially Morris Ginsberg, Professor of Sociology, that Popper was taking an active interest in problems relating to the social sciences,[41] so he was delighted to learn of Popper's switch to social philosophy. On July 17 he received from Gombrich one of the typescripts of Popper's big book. He immediately began reading it and was 'profoundly impressed'.[42] In those days the chief members of the

---

[40] AB to KRP, 24 August 1943.
[41] FAH to EHG, 12 July 1943.
[42] FAH to EHG, 18 July 1943.

Appointments Committee at LSE were, beside Hayek, Carr-Saunders as Director, Ginsberg, Laski, and Tawney. Laski, who was reading the typescript as a publisher's reader for Nelson, was enthusiastic about it.[43] Carr-Saunders liked it.[44] (I will touch on Ginsberg's reactions later.) Hayek also showed it to Lionel Robbins, then seconded to the Economic Section of the War Cabinet, and he too was enthusiastic. In November 1943 Hayek was authorised by the Appointments Committee to write to Popper telling him that a University Readership in Logic and Scientific Method, tenable at LSE, would be advertised, and asking him if he would be a candidate. Popper replied that he would. He wrote to Gombrich: 'We are of course terribly excited, and shaken up in consequence of Hayek's airgraph'.[45]

Gombrich and Hayek tried to find a publisher, but without success at first. Cambridge University Press turned it down, and there were several more rebuffs. As well as Plato-reverence, there was, in those days of paper rationing, dismay at the book's size; and some admirers of the book, such as Robbins, felt that the critique of Marx was too long and heavy.[46] Hayek eventually turned to Routledge, who were publishing his own *The Road to Serfdom*. There Herbert Read read it and was enormously impressed. It was at last accepted.

Now came the business of getting it ready for printing. Gombrich has given a delightful description of his role in this onerous task.[47] He received as many as 95 aerogrammes (miniaturised airletters), containing instructions, often intricate, for amendments, especially to the Notes. Then there was the question of the title. As well as 'A Social Philosophy for Everyman' Popper toyed with 'Three False Prophets: Plato–Hegel–Marx' and 'A Critique of Political Philosophy'. This is perhaps the place to mention John Findlay, then Professor of Philosophy at Otago, since he had something to do with the eventual choice. He and Popper often visited each other during vacations; he found their discussions immensely profitable, but also immensely exhausting as Popper never knew when to stop. (It seems that Findlay sometimes broke off to take a nap. A female student once opened the door to Popper's room and then ran off terrified on seeing what appeared to be a corpse laid out on the floor.[48]) He found the Popper's house on the

[43]  FAH to EHG, 29 October 1943.
[44]  FAH to KRP, 27 December 1943.
[45]  KRP to EHG, 13 December 1943.
[46]  FAH to KRP, 29 January 1944.
[47]  See the lecture cited in n. 15, above.
[48]  Colin Simkin.

Cashmere Hills amazingly beautiful, with its views towards the Southern Alps. He said that he there persuaded Popper to drop the 'False Prophets' title.[49] Findlay's widow claimed that he won Popper over to 'The Open Society'.[50] Not that those three words settled the problem. The contract with Routledge had, 'The Open Society and its Antagonists'. Popper cabled, 'Consider Enemies Better'; whereupon the postmistress informed the police![51] He was able to persuade them that he did not consider Hitler & co. better than Churchill (whom he admired enormously) & co.

Back now to the LSE readership. The post had been advertised and a Board of Advisors set up. The decision would be taken in March–April 1945. There were nine applicants.[52] Apart from Popper the only one taken seriously was Casimir Lewy; it was agreed that the readership would either be filled by Popper or else not filled; in the latter case Lewy might be appointed a lecturer at LSE. It was by no means certain how things would go. Proofs of *The Open Society* were available to the Board. Ginsberg, whose support Hayek judged essential, was wavering. He had liked Chapter 14, on 'The Autonomy of Sociology'; but Hayek had now sent him 'The Poverty of Historicism' which he (Hayek) was in process of publishing in *Economica*, and it seems that Ginsberg became uneasy about the latter's implications for sociology;[53] he was also worried by what he saw as evidence of intellectual arrogance. The internal 'expert' (H. F. Hallett, the Spinoza scholar at King's College London) was opposed. In addition, Hayek, as Popper was dismayed to learn, would not be present when the decision was taken. (*The Road to Serfdom* had now been published in America by Chicago University Press, and they had arranged a lecture tour for him. He had timed it so that he would sail after the Board met, but the meeting was postponed and Hayek could not forgo his berth in a wartime convoy.[54]) Much would depend on the two external 'experts'. One was Sir David Ross, a

---

[49] J. N. Findlay, 'My Life: 1903–1973', in *Studies in the Philosophy of J. N. Findlay*, ed. Robert S. Cohen, Richard M. Martin, Merold Westphal (SUNY Press, 1985), p. 26. Findlay incorrectly wrote that Popper had had this house built. It was a single-storey wooden house.

[50] She had written this on the back of a copy of a photograph of Popper and Findlay in Dunedin in 1944, which I received thanks to R. S. Cohen.

[51] KRP.

[52] This paragraph is mainly based on LSE archives.

[53] FAH.

[54] FAH to KRP, 19 Mar 1945. For a hilarious account of what happened when he got to New York see *Hayek on Hayek: An Autobiographical Dialogue*, ed. Stephen Kresge and Leif Wenar (London, 1994), pp. 104–5.

distinguished Oxford moral philosopher and Aristotelian scholar, now in his late sixties; would his reaction to *The Open Society* be like Friedrich's?

In the event he came down strongly in favour of appointing Popper, as did the other external, L. J. Russell. When Hayek returned to LSE he was asked to tell Popper the decision. Popper and Hennie had gone to the mountains for a holiday, on doctor's orders. They went to a hotel at the foot of Mount Cook called The Hermitage, and they returned by bus. (Popper had briefly owned a car, but had long since given it up.) At its first stop the local postmistress came out with a cable for 'Karl Popper, c/o Bus from Hermitage';[55] it was from Hayek. This cable may have caused even more pleasure than the letter from Einstein. They sailed from Auckland at the end of November.

## Early Days at LSE

*The Open Society* was published in mid-November, and was already being talked about when they arrived in England in January 1946. Popper was a bright new star on the English philosophical scene, and he was much sought after. By early February he had been slotted into a symposium at the annual Joint Session, to be held in July. The other symposiasts were Ryle, who wrote a glowing review of *The Open Society*,[56] and Lewy. (Popper wanted Lewy to join him at LSE, but this fell through.[57] J. O. Wisdom joined him in 1948.) After this came an invitation to talk to the Cambridge Moral Science Club, in October.

Bertrand Russell, recently reinstalled in Trinity College, invited Popper to tea before the meeting, and I will first say a few words about their relationship. Among living thinkers Russell was, along with Tarski and Einstein, one of Popper's supreme heroes. Was this esteem reciprocated? When, quite a few years after this, Popper sent him a complimentary copy of *The Logic of Scientific Discovery* Russell wrote that he was very glad to get this translation of a book which he had read long ago, when it first appeared in German.[58] But the rather perfunctory testimonial he wrote for Popper in 1936 did not mention *Logik der Forschung*, and the pages of his complimentary copy of it remained

---

[55] KRP to FAH, 3 June 1945.
[56] *Mind*, 56 (April 1947), 167–72.
[57] CL to KRP, 15 July 1946; 4 October 1946.
[58] BR to KRP, 22 January 1959.

virtually uncut.[59] It seems that the complimentary copy of *The Open Society* which Popper had recently sent him might likewise have remained unread; for when Popper asked him to recommend it to the American publishers of *A History of Western Philosophy*, then in the American best-seller list, Russell asked to be lent a copy, explaining that he wanted first to 'reread' it, and having no house at present, his books were inaccessible.[60] When another copy came he did read it—and he was bowled over. He recommended it strongly to his publisher, and wrote Popper a testimonial calling it a work of first-class importance. In the annual National Book League lecture, on 'Philosophy and Politics', which Russell gave in October 1946, he said that the case against Plato has been 'brilliantly advocated' by Popper.[61]

There are varying accounts of this famous meeting of the Moral Science Club, and many of them contain identifiable mistakes. Even the minutes (which say that the meeting 'was charged to an unusual degree with a spirit of controversy') get the date wrong, giving 26 instead of 25 October 1946. Popper's own account, in *Unended Quest*, gets his title wrong, putting 'Are there Philosophical Problems?' which might have been better than the actual title as it appears in the printed programme and in the minutes, namely 'Methods in Philosophy'. (Three weeks later Wittgenstein gave a talk on 'what the method of philosophy is' which, according to the minutes, was a reply to Popper's talk.[62]) Although Popper's account mentions Russell's presence, it does not mention what Russell called out to Wittgenstein, on which most other accounts agree, though Munz's account has Russell calling out words which were surely spoken by Popper.[63] An American philosopher, Hiriam McLendon, who was studying under Russell at the time, subsequently wrote an account of this meeting as part of a planned biography of Russell (it does not seem to have been published).[64] It is interesting, and includes comments made by Russell the next day; but it has

---

[59] I. Grattan-Guinness, 'Russell and Karl Popper: Their Personal Contacts', **russell**: the Journal of the Bertrand Russell Archives, (summer 1992), p. 8, n. 8.

[60] BR to KRP, 22 July 1946.

[61] *Philosophy and Politics* (Cambridge, 1947), p. 11.

[62] See Brian McGuinness and G. H. von Wright (eds.), *Ludwig Wittgenstein: Cambridge Letters* (Oxford, 1995), p. 324.

[63] Peter Munz, *Our Knowledge of the Growth of Knowledge: Popper or Wittgenstein?* (London, 1985), pp. 1–2.

[64] It is in Popper Collection (36, 12).

Wittgenstein eventually subsiding where all other accounts have him storming out.

I will reconstruct what happened from the various sources as best I can. The meeting was in Braithwaite's room in King's College. Wittgenstein, who chaired the meeting, sat on one side of an open fire and Popper on the other. Russell was in a high-backed rocking-chair. Others present included Elizabeth Anscombe, Richard Braithwaite, C. D. Broad, A. C. Ewing, Peter Geach, Norman Malcolm, Margaret Masterman, Stephen Toulmin, and John Wisdom (A. J. T. D., not J. O.). There were also various students. The secretary's invitation to Popper had said that 'short papers, or a few opening remarks stating some philosophical puzzle, tend as a rule to produce better discussions than long and elaborate papers'. The minutes say that Popper began by expressing astonishment at the Secretary's letter of invitation (a footnote explains that this is the Club's form of invitation). Wittgenstein seems to have mistaken Popper's opening remarks for a complaint against the Secretary, and sprang to his defence. But Popper was taking the wording of the invitation as expressing the Wittgensteinian thesis that there are no genuine philosophical problems, only puzzles; and he set out to counter this thesis by bringing forward some real problems. One concerned induction. Wittgenstein dismissed this as a merely logical problem. Another concerned the question of actual (as distinct from merely potential) infinities. (One of the two theses in Kant's first antinomy says that the world must have had a beginning in time, otherwise an actual or completed infinity of time will have elapsed. Popper rebutted this many years later.[65]) Wittgenstein dismissed this as a mathematical problem. As his last example, Popper gave the question of the validity of moral rules. Wittgenstein, who had hold of the poker and was waving it about a good deal, demanded an example of a moral rule, to which Popper replied: 'Not to threaten visiting lecturers with pokers'. There was laughter, and Wittgenstein stormed out, angrily declaring as he went that Popper was confusing the issues; whereupon Russell called out, 'Wittgenstein, you're the one who's causing the confusion'.

The next day Russell told McLendon that he had never seen a guest so rudely treated, adding that Popper had more learning and erudition than all of them; and he afterwards wrote to Popper: 'I was much shocked by the failure of good manners on the side of Cambridge. . ..

---

[65] 'On the Possibility of an Infinite Past: a Reply to Whitrow', *The British Journal for the Philosophy of Science*, 29 (March 1978), pp. 47–8.

I was entirely on your side throughout, but I did not take a larger part in the debate because you were so fully competent to fight your own battle'.[66] In January 1947 Popper gave Russell's *A History of Western Philosophy* an encomium on Austrian radio: a great book and what makes it great is the man who has written it.[67]

*The Open Society* made a strong impression on some English politicians on the moderate left, such as Anthony Crosland, and on the moderate right, such as Edward Boyle. By the later 1950s, however, the book's ideas had rather lost their urgency in the West just because they had so largely won out. Hardly anyone believed any more in historical inevitability, let alone the inevitability of Communism, or in Utopian planning. But the book had still a tremendous potential appeal for intellectuals under Communist regimes. There would later be various samizdat translations of *The Open Society* and of *The Poverty of Historicism*.

Let me reproduce here a personal recollection from those days. A fellow student at LSE had told me it was worth going to Dr Popper's lectures 'to hear the great man thinking aloud'. I went, and I was riveted. He had no notes or other paraphernalia. Ideas seemed to flow from him. They were put forward, not as propositions for the audience to consider, but as hard-won truths; his combination of seriousness, lucidity, and conviction had an almost hypnotic persuasiveness. The seriousness was lightened by touches of humour and happy improvisations. On one occasion he was discussing whether 'All men are mortal' is a falsifiable hypothesis: suppose a man has survived various attempts to kill him; eventually an atom-bomb is exploded beneath him, but he descends smilingly to earth, brushing off the dust . . .. This much Popper had, I believe, prepared beforehand: but then came a pause, a sudden smile, a new thought: 'We ask him how he does it and he answers: "Oh, it's easy; I'm immortal".' His audience, which had been small to begin with, grew to fill a large lecture theatre. He said later that LSE in those days was a marvellous institution.

His published work, during the later 1940s, was mainly on logic, more specifically on the theory of natural deduction. This brought him into contact with, among others, Paul Bernays, E. W. Beth, and L. E. J. Brouwer. The latter became a notable friend during Popper's early years at LSE (there is a letter from him, headed 'Waiting-room of Liverpool Street station, December 10th 1947', which begins: 'My dear

[66] BR to KRP, 18 November 1946.
[67] **russell**: the Journal of the Bertrand Russell Archives, (summer 1992), pp. 19–21.

Popper, your duality construction and your new definition of intuition-istic negation have delighted me'.)

Quite soon after he came to LSE the question of a professorship began to exercise him. He was in his middle forties, he had become a world figure, and he needed the money (in those days a London professor's salary was nearly twice a reader's). But proposals to create a chair for him had run into the difficulty that no special subject of philosophy was taught there; his logic and scientific method courses were only for optional subjects. Should he turn elsewhere? Various possibilities were in the air; some would have meant leaving England. In 1948 Victor Kraft approached him about taking up a chair, presumably Schlick's old chair, in the University of Vienna. When Carnap had asked him a few years earlier, shortly after the German surrender, whether he would consider going back to Vienna if offered a position there, Popper had answered, 'No, never!',[68] and he did not waver now. (Sixteen members of his family had died as victims of Nazism,[69] though not any of his immediate family; his father had died in 1932; Dora committed suicide in the same year; his mother died soon after the *Anschluss* from natural causes; and Annie got away to Switzerland.) At the time of his retirement in 1969 he was still deterred from the prospect of a professorship in Austria by concern about anti-Semitism there.[70] After Hennie's death in Vienna in 1985, he did take on a post there, as director of a new branch of the Boltzmann Institute, but only for a few months.

Another possibility was that he would fill the chair at Cambridge from which Wittgenstein resigned as from the end of 1947. Braithwaite seems to have been one of several people in Cambridge who wanted him to apply; he kept Popper posted about developments.[71] He seems to have been an admirer since Popper's talk to the Moral Science Club in 1936; it was he, as a syndic of Cambridge University Press, who in 1943 had encouraged Hayek to submit *The Open Society* to them.[72] He was not a devotee of Wittgenstein (who had heard him snore in his lectures),[73] and was on Popper's side at the 'poker' meeting,[74]

---

[68] RC to KRP, 30 May 1945, KRP to RC, 23 June 1945.

[69] As he reported in a subsequently deleted passage in a draft of his autobiography, Popper Collection (135, 1). Again, I learnt of this through a reference (note 33) in Hacohen, above n. 10.

[70] KRP to FAH, 24 October 1969.

[71] RB to KRP, 13 October 1947; 5 December 1947.

[72] FAH to EHG, 18 July 1943.

[73] Quoted in Ray Monk, *Ludwig Wittgenstein* (London, 1990), p. 476.

[74] RB.

complimenting Popper afterwards for being 'the only man who had managed to interrupt Wittgenstein in the way in which Wittgenstein interrupted everyone else.'

Findlay also encouraged him,[75] and Popper seriously considered applying, but he eventually decided not to. Why? He must have learnt some discouraging information; Peter Medawar was an admirer who had quickly became a good friend; and he reports Popper asking him to say 'with the utmost frankness whether there was anything about his manner or behaviour or reputation that stood in the way of his receiving the advancement he sought'.[76] It seems that Medawar told him of certain people who had been hurt by his tactlessness.[77] Popper himself had a nice story about himself and C. D. Broad, now the senior professor at Cambridge. Broad was interested in paranormal phenomena, and around this time Popper attended a meeting, with Broad present, at which a speaker claimed that it would be an ostrich policy to ignore the mounting evidence for such phenomena. In the discussion Popper rose to 'say a word in favour of the ostrich'. Afterwards he suggested that this may have spoilt his chances.[78] (Georg von Wright got the chair, which is what Wittgenstein wanted.[79])

Another possibility was that Popper would go back to New Zealand, to Otago where Jack Eccles wanted him to succeed Findlay. Matters came to a head with a cable from Dunedin which Popper received on 28 October 1948, offering him the chair and asking for a quick reply. Things moved quickly. Popper turned to Hayek who turned to Robbins, who took command. He drafted a letter for Popper to write to Carr-Saunders saying that he must decide soon and that he was tempted.[80] Popper sent the letter on a Friday. The following Tuesday he got an encouraging reply, and at the scheduled meeting of the Appointments Committee the next day it was agreed to ask the university to confer on him the title of Professor of Logic and Scientific Method.[81] His admiring lecture audience gave him a big round of applause on 15 February 1949, after seeing his professorship announced in *The Times*.

This was an exhilarating time for him. He had now accepted an

---

[75] JF to KRP, 22 November 1947.
[76] Peter Medawar, *Memoir of a Thinking Radish* (Oxford, 1986), pp. 113–14.
[77] KRP to PBM, 26 October 1948.
[78] EHG.
[79] Monk, *Ludwig Wittgenstein*, p. 507.
[80] KRP to JCE, 7 November 1948.
[81] LSE archives.

invitation from Harvard University to give the William James Lectures in 1950 (John Dewey and Bertrand Russell were among previous lecturers). He was paid 'Hollywood rates', as he put it (ten lectures at $600 per lecture). His title was, 'The Study of Nature and of Society'. It was his first visit to America. He found it 'a marvellous country'[82] and was full of enthusiasm for things American.[83] For instance, he said that while Negroes were admittedly a depressed class, they were the least depressed depressed class in the world. He found some of the work of Harvard graduate students 'really outstanding'[84] (perhaps he had Tom Kuhn in mind). He visited other Ivy League universities. He gave the Woodward Lecture at Yale (I have described my experience of this occasion elsewhere[85]), and at Princeton he gave a seminar talk on indeterminism with both Einstein and Bohr in the audience! It seems that Bohr rather took over the discussion, and then went on and on; six hours after the meeting started the room contained just him at the blackboard with Einstein and Popper as his audience. 'He's mad', Einstein whispered.[86] In *Unended Quest* Popper described how he met Einstein three times, at the latter's request, and tried to argue him out of determinism. A good many years later, when Bartley was editing the *Postscript*, Popper drew his attention to evidence suggesting that his (Popper's) arguments may have had some influence on Einstein.[87]

Popper published a long, two-part argument for indeterminism in the first volume of the newly launched *British Journal for the Philosophy of Science*. This was the journal of the Philosophy of Science Group (later, the British Society for the Philosophy of Science), recently founded by Herbert Dingle. Popper was much involved with this, and became chairman of the group in 1951, succeeding his old friend Woodger.[88] In his chairman's address, which later became chapter 2 of *Conjectures and Refutations*, he resumed his stand against

---

[82] KRP to FAH, 29 April 1952.

[83] See the 1950 preface to the second edition of *The Open Society*.

[84] KRP to FAH, 29 April 1952.

[85] In 'Karl Popper: A Memoir', *American Scholar*, 66 (spring 1997), pp. 208–9.

[86] KRP.

[87] See: WWB to KRP, 12 June, 1979; *The Born-Einstein Letters*, ed. Max Born, trans. Irene Born (London, 1971), p. 221; Karl R. Popper, *The Open Universe*, ed. W. W. Bartley III (London, 1982), p. 2, n. 2.

[88] Popper claimed that his 1935 lectures at Bedford College had aroused Woodger's interest in Tarksi's work, which Woodger was now translating (*Unended Quest*, p. 108).

Wittgenstein (who had died the year before) on the reality of philosophical problems.

The money from the William James Lectures allowed the Poppers, on their return to England, to acquire what was to become a beautiful home, 'Fallowfield' in Penn, near High Wycombe. As Popper told Hayek, it had 'a really marvellous garden'. The centre of the living-room was soon occupied by an old Bechstein piano (traded in many years later for a new Steinway). They had also bought an adjoining plot, with the result that they were completely secluded. It helped to satisfy his love of nature and his desire for quietness. When Wolfgang Yourgrau first saw the garden he remarked jokingly that he could understand now why Popper's philosophy exuded such a sense of peace and calm! In New Zealand they had had a wireless and a gramophone,[89] but in Fallowfield the only things that made a noise, human voices apart, were the telephone, the piano, and the typewriter on which Hennie worked, usually in an upstairs room.

The house-hunting process left them exhausted, however, and at first the house filled him with dismay: 'we have ruined ourselves financially for a house which will cost many hundreds before it is really inhabitable. . . . [W]e have not slept properly for weeks because of mice and rats, and we have no proper heating arrangements, no proper hot water—nothing'.[90] He fell into a depression. Hennie became chronically ill and none of the doctors he got for her seemed any good. He confided to Hayek:[91] 'All this has somehow broken . . . me I feel a complete wreck . . . At the L.S.E. I have no friends . . . I have become highly dissatisfied with my teaching . . . Failure, failure wherever I look'. When I got back to LSE in 1950 after a year away I found his lecture audience diminished; the B.Sc. (Econ.) degree had been restructured and the student ethos seemed to favour accounting over philosophy. In early April 1952 he got a bad fright out at Fallowfield on finding Hennie collapsed and unconscious; she had suddenly fainted (and broken her cheek-bone in falling). He continued to be upset by the fact that Hayek had now left LSE for Chicago (with a childhood sweetheart as his new wife). In September 1952 he told Hayek that Hennie was much better (she had stopped seeing doctors; in those days a doctor's standard charge for a single visit was five guineas and, as she put it later, she

[89] JAP to EHG, 29 July 1943.
[90] KRP to FAH (undated, probably early November 1950).
[91] KRP to FAH, 23 September 1951.

became tired of being a five-guinea pig); but he still felt low: 'I try to like the School, but it has not been the same since you left, and I still feel a stranger there'.[92]

The charismatic glow in which he arrived in England had faded. When in 1951 Findlay, his old friend and admirer from New Zealand days, arrived at King's College London, across the Strand from LSE, he found Popper much changed: surrounded by a court of admirers, his conduct of his seminar magisterial, and his views of people moralistic and prejudiced.[93] Michael Polanyi was gravely offended by the treatment that Popper, as chairman, meted out to him when he read a paper (on 'The Stability of Beliefs', 6 March 1952) to the Philosophy of Science Group. David Armstrong, then an assistant lecturer at Birkbeck College, recalled that he 'went a few times to Karl Popper's seminar, but was repelled by the discipleship and the authoritarian atmosphere'.[94] Popper was considered by the Australian National University for a chair in Social Philosophy; they turned for advice to John Passmore, who had attended his seminar in 1948, and taken up the chair at Otago which Popper had declined. He was reported as saying that 'Popper lacked academic manners: one had to put up with being interrupted, misunderstood, prevented from getting a word in, and so on. Passmore thought this defect was compensated by the quality of what he had to say, but others thought him insufferable.'[95]

Popper was aware that something was wrong. I mentioned earlier his question to Medawar. Medawar consulted Ryle who told him that Popper had a reputation for being intolerant and overbearing.[96] Here is an entry from my diary for May 1951 (I was now an assistant lecturer at LSE): 'Popper drew me into his room and told me he was very dissatisfied with his relations with staff and students—only his relation with me seemed good. I told him that he bullied and awed people'.[97] People tended to find his critical intensity unnerving and sometimes invasive. He was not a good listener and had no knack for

---

[92] KRP to FAH, 10 September 1952.

[93] Ibid., p. 40.

[94] David Armstrong, 'Self-Profile' in *Profiles*, vol. 4, ed. Radu J. Bogdan (Dordrecht, 1984), p. 13.

[95] S. G. Foster and Marjorie M. Varghese, *The Making of the Australian National University* (London, 1996), p. 105.

[96] Medawar, *Memoir*, pp. 113–14.

[97] In confirmation of this diary entry I may perhaps mention that in the letter to Hayek (10 September 1952) where he said that he still felt a stranger at LSE, he called me 'the only bright spot'.

humorous, easy-going, gossipy, academic give-and-take, tending either to dominate the conversation or to withdraw. He could deflate an ego with a flashing look of contempt; and he did not endear himself to those he accused of plagiarism.

Another negative factor with respect to LSE was his fading interest in problems to do with the social sciences. This never sank to zero: when *The Poverty of Historicism* came out as a book in 1957 he added a striking new preface and the dedication: 'In memory of the countless men and women . . . who fell victims to the fascist and communist belief in Inexorable Laws of Historical Destiny'. In 1963 he gave an interesting lecture in Harvard on the role of the rationality principle in economics and the social sciences—though it was twenty years before this was published in English.[98] The centre of gravity of his thinking, however, was swinging back to his pre-war concerns, centred on physics. He was especially concerned with quantum physics and the need for a thoroughly objective interpretation of it. (The third volume of the *Postscript* is given over to this.)

Then there was his attitude to tobacco smoke. In those days LSE had a no-smoking rule for lectures, but other public places tended to be smoky. In his earlier days at LSE, Popper occasionally attended the Academic Board. (When uncertain how to vote he would, he once told me, watch the then Professor of Public Administration and then vote the other way.) He had also joined in conversations in the Senior Common Room, but he stopped going to such public places as a result of his increasing allergy; this was well publicised, making him the moving centre of a smoke-free zone and causing nervous stubbing-out movements in those who strayed into it. He reduced the time he spent in the school to little more than was needed for his lecture and weekly seminar. The pattern began to be established that to have a serious conversation with him required a visit to Fallowfield. As time passed, the number of his LSE colleagues who had seen him in the flesh shrank to a handful. What Hacohen calls 'his legendary seclusion in his house outside London' had begun. Visitors to Fallowfield were usually drawn into whatever problem was absorbing him, but he occasionally disconcerted them by unburdening his bitterness about some alleged plagiarism or the misdeeds of an ungrateful pupil.

He was, however, a beacon for quite a few gifted young people in

---

[98] In David Miller (ed.), *A Pocket Popper* (London, 1983). The whole paper has since been published in Karl R. Popper, *The Myth of the Framework* (London, 1994).

the 1950s. Paul Feyerabend had met him at the Austrian College in Alpbach in 1948; they took a shine to each other and in 1952 Feyerabend came to LSE to work under him on problems relating to quantum mechanics.[99] Czeslaw Lejewski and 'Bashi' Sabra were also there at that time. Joseph Agassi came soon afterwards, followed by Bill Bartley and Jerzy Giedymin. Ian Jarvie moved over from Anthropology. Popper also had a good many 'corresponding' pupils who, without enrolling at LSE, kept in close touch; for example, Hans Albert generally stayed in Germany, where he battled with the Frankfurt School, though often meeting up with Popper in Alpbach.

In about 1955 Popper had begun work on an English edition of *Logik der Forschung*, to be entitled *The Logic of Scientific Discovery*. It would have many additions, some to be incorporated in the same volume as starred footnotes or appendices; others would go into a separate *Postscript*. One of the new appendices contained papers written recently during a campaign against Carnap over the nature of confirmation, or *corroboration* as Popper later preferred to call it. (Around this time Popper was also writing for the Schilpp volume on Carnap a contribution which he believed to be annihilating.) His main negative thesis was that corroboration is not probabilification. A corroboration appraisal, for example that theory T is well corroborated, or that theory $T_2$ is better corroborated than theory $T_1$, is a historical report on how well the theories in question have stood up to tests so far. The degree of corroboration gained when a theory passes a test varies with the severity of the test. Let '$p(e, h \& b)$' denote the probability of a predicted experimental outcome $e$ given theory $h$ and relevant background knowledge $b$, and '$p(e, b)$' its probability given background knowledge alone. The severity of a test varies with the difference between $p(e, h \& b)$ and $p(e, b)$. The former will normally be 1; the nearer the latter approaches 0, or the more surprising the prediction would have been if the theory had not been advanced, the more severe is the test.

The above contrast between probability and corroboration was one of several factors which had given Popper an abiding interest in the probability calculus. The long chapter on probability in his *Logik der Forschung* had contained an anticipation of modern chaos theory: namely, a way of generating from a mathematical formula, a perfectly determinate sequence of 0s and 1s which, however, would be 'random',

---

[99] Paul Feyerabend, *Killing Time* (Chicago, 1995), p. 71.

in the sense of gambler-proof, up to the first n places (after that it would start repeating itself). His first publication in English, in 1938, had presented an axiom set for the probability calculus. This was superseded by an improved version in Appendix *iv of *The Logic of Scientific Discovery*. One problem that faced him was the following. Let $e$ be a logical consequence of the universal hypothesis $h$. Then we want to say that $p(e, h) = 1$. But $p(e, h) = \dfrac{p(e) \times p(h, e)}{p(h))}$ ; and Popper insisted that for any universal hypothesis $h$ we have $p(h, e) = p(h) = 0$; hence $p(e, h) = \dfrac{0}{0}$.

Another important contrast is between the probability of statements and the probability of events. Popper's understanding of the latter underwent an important change, in connection with his indeterminism. In *Logik der Forschung* he had adopted a frequency interpretation; he now shifted to a propensity interpretation. Take the statement that the probability of outcome $A$ under experimental set-up $B$ is one-half. The frequency interpretation reads this as saying that, if $B$ were endlessly repeated, the proportion of $A$s in the sequence of outcomes would tend, in the limit, to one-half. That is consistent with each outcome being causally determined. The propensity interpretation reads it as saying that, even if set-up $B$ were activated only once, or never, it always endows outcome $A$ and outcome non-$A$ with the same weight; thus the outcome is never causally determined.

The propensity interpretation is objectivist in the sense that it postulates weightings 'out there' answering to numerical concepts in our theories. That is in line with Popper's metaphysical realism. The latter also manifested itself in his views, which he first presented in a series of one-page letters to *Nature* during 1956–8, about the 'arrow of time'. His fundamental conviction was that time has its unique direction independent of whatever processes occur in it; hence it is not tied to the direction of entropy-increase. Suppose that a system (which might be the universe) undergoes certain processes between $t_1$ and $t_2$, at which time these processes are perfectly reversed. Then the system goes back to the state it was in at $t_1$ but time goes forward to $t_3$. He also claimed that there are classical processes, not involving entropy, which are in fact irreversible (though we can easily imagine them being reversed); for instance, an explosion that sends out an expanding circle of disturbance towards infinity.

Popper spent 1956–7 at the Stanford Center for Advanced Studies.

He was a disappointing visitor because he was working furiously trying to finish the *Postscript*, and they saw little of him. He had the galleys with him when he conducted a seminar in Alpbach in 1958, but Bartley, who had recently arrived from Harvard to study under him, persuaded him that it needed a lot of revising, and he duly embarked on this. Then he began to have worrying eye trouble (he feared he was going blind). He gave the Annual Philosophical Lecture for the British Academy, in January 1960 (it was entitled 'On the Sources of Knowledge and Ignorance' and became the Introduction to *Conjectures and Refutations*), and a few days afterwards he left for Vienna for operations on both eyes for detached retinas. The operations were successful, but he could not bring himself to resume correcting and proof-reading the *Postscript*, which was set aside. (It was eventually published, in three volumes under Bartley's editorship, only in 1982–3.)

Popper was happier now at LSE. His department, though small, had acquired a considerable reputation. It is perhaps significant that Russell in 1960 recommended a philosophically interested sixth-former to go to LSE, where the philosophy 'has the merit of being vigorous', rather than to Cambridge.[100] Oxford philosophers' attitudes to Popper varied. He was largely ignored by J. L. Austin and new-wave Ordinary Language philosophers, whom Popper likened to people who are always compulsively cleaning their spectacles instead of looking through them at the world, but Hampshire, Hare, Kneale, Quinton, Robinson, and Ryle admired him, and he was coming to be accepted as part of the British philosophical establishment. True, his actual presence was not in great demand, at least in Britain; he tended to be the big man who was *not* invited, but his writings were much sought after, contributions being invited to such prestigious anthologies as *Contemporary British Philosophy* (1956) and *British Philosophy in the Mid-Century* (1957). In 1958 he was elected a Fellow of the British Academy. This was a busy year for him. At the International Congress of Philosophy in Venice that year he presented a beautiful little historical piece on the significance of Leibniz's criticisms of Descartes for the developments in physics from atomism to the Faraday-Maxwell field theories.[101] He also gave the presidential address to the Aristotelian Society (with Sir David Ross in the chair): entitled 'Back to the Pre-Socratics', it drew a

---

[100] Grattan-Guinness, 'Russell and Karl Popper', p. 8.
[101] 'Philosophy and Physics', reprinted in *Quantum Theory and the Schism in Physics* (ed. W. W. Bartley III, London, 1982), pp. 165–73, and in *The Myth of the Framework*, ch. 5.

distinction between a *school*, such as that of Pythagoras, which makes it its task to preserve a doctrine, and a *critical tradition*, such as that inaugurated by Thales, based on a new relation between master and pupil, with the master tolerating, even encouraging, pupils' criticisms.

He had a powerful friend and supporter in Robbins, who became something of a father-figure for the Philosophy Department. (There had been a temporary coolness between them when Hayek left LSE for Chicago; Robbins felt bitter about this, but Popper remained loyal to the man who had 'saved his life' by rescuing him from New Zealand.) Robbins used to say that at that time there were two people of genius at LSE (the other was Bill Phillips of 'Phillips machine' and 'Phillips curve' fame). Robbins was one of the very few people to whom Popper was deferential. Perhaps I may reproduce here an amusing illustration of this. As Chairman of the Trustees of the Covent Garden Opera House, Robbins regularly invited friends to join his party in the royal box. In due course he invited Popper, adding that unfortunately a dinner-jacket is essential. Although Popper had, as we will see, good reason to decline this particular invitation, it was to him like a royal command. Julius Kraft once remarked to me, with a touch of exaggeration, that in the Popper household 'cooking an egg causes a great deal of excitement.' Well, acquiring suitable evening wear caused even greater excitement. Urgent appeals went out in all directions for advice and assistance. On the day in question, I drove the Poppers to the Gombrichs', where he changed. Eventually the bow-tie was fixed and everything seemed in place, but he had a last adjustment to make: he had brought a supply of cotton wool with which to stuff his ears, the opera being by Richard Strauss whose music he could not abide!

## Lakatos

Popper inspired in many of those who came to know him well an enduring affection, love, or devotion. Among those whose names have already come up one thinks of Jack Eccles, Herbert Feigl, Ernst Gombrich, 'Fritz' Hayek, Bryan Magee, Peter Medawar, Peter Munz, and Lionel Robbins. Others in this category include Donald Campbell, Ralf Dahrendorf, David Miller, Alan Musgrave, and Colin Simkin. But there was also a category of broken friendships, which came to include quite a few of his pupils: Joseph Agassi, Bill Bartley, Paul Feyerabend,

Imre Lakatos and, eventually, myself. (In Bartley's case friendship was restored, but that was exceptional.) Obituarists who avert their gaze from this area, as some do, leave out something emotionally important in Popper's life. There is no doubt which case carried the highest emotional charge; anyone who knew him at all well in his later years will have heard angry denunciations of Lakatos. Since his case is well documented, and has probably aroused more interest than the others, I will concentrate on it. Telling this substory uninterruptedly will mean running on ahead of the main story.

His case exemplifies what was said earlier both about Popper being a beacon for younger people, and about the interest of his critique of Marxism for intellectuals under Communist regimes. Lakatos had been an enthusiastic party man under the Communist regime in Hungary after the war. While still in his twenties he had risen to an important position in the Ministry of Education. And then, in 1950, after returning from a year at Moscow University, disaster struck. He was caught up in the Rajk Purge and imprisoned. (He claimed, and I can believe it, that the strain of interrogation had proved too much—for one of his interrogators!) He was released in 1953, and gained asylum in the Hungarian Academy of Science, were he had the run of the library. He still believed that Marxism was grounded on a scientific theory of history; and now he learnt that a certain Karl Popper had exposed this as a sham.[102] After the Uprising in late 1956, he got to Vienna, were he found his way to the university and introduced himself to Victor Kraft (who had filled the chair which Popper declined). He learnt that there was a possibility of a Rockefeller Fellowship, and said that he would like to study under Popper. Kraft advised against: Popper was a difficult man.[103] Then was there anyone in England with similar ideas? Yes, there was Braithwaite. So Lakatos went to Cambridge, where he embarked on a Ph.D., but he retained his desire to join Popper. Some three years later he delighted Popper and his seminar with his dramatised case-study of the 'Descartes-Euler conjecture', and he joined Popper's department in 1960.

It was not to be expected that coexistence with this colourful, irreverent man with his sharp wit and inexhaustible energy would be smooth and uneventful. There were flare-ups and occasional rows, often over typing assistance; Hennie was still doing a lot of typing for Popper,

[102] IL.
[103] IL.

but her burden had been reduced by secretarial assistance in the department, and Popper was fiercely jealous of this. However, there was an underlying amity. Lakatos's humour brought out an unsuspected playfulness in Popper. Lakatos had a habit of sending out jokey postcards; he once got one back from Popper, in Alpbach; its picture had been touched up. 'It's good', Lakatos commented, 'but what work he puts into being funny.' Here is Popper, in 1962, writing to Lakatos a few months after some flare-up:

> Dear Imre, It is very embarrassing that I have to tell you such a thing, but as, I suppose, you will prefer to hear from me direct rather from another source, I better tell you quite frankly and openly to your face that . . . (I hope you are thoroughly frightened by this time) . . . I am about to receive an honourary degree of Doctor of Laws from the University of Chicago.[104]

(The President awarded it to him in hospital; he had had some cardiac trouble.) And here is Popper, in 1965, telling Lakatos of another honour: 'The postman brought a letter "On Her Majesty's Service". Hennie thought "Income Tax". When she opened it she got a terrible shock. . . . [S]he got me first to bed, and only then showed it to me'.[105] (It was from Downing Street, sounding him about a knighthood.) Popper was enchanted by Lakatos's paper 'Proofs and Refutations'. He told Lakatos that it was 'a flawless piece of art, and the greatest advent [*sic*] in the philosophy of mathematics since the great logical discoveries around 1930–32'.[106] Lakatos spent 1964–5 in La Jolla, and the letters which Popper received from him then were, he said, 'a real delight, and a real tonic'.[107] Popper was worried that he might not come back: 'I am sad that you are away, simply because I am much happier with you here. I hope you will come back (the sooner the better); it would be a very great loss for me personally (to say nothing about the department) if you don't.' This letter contains 'a clear declaration of love'.[108] In America Lakatos was planning a colloquium, to be held at Bedford College, London, in July 1965. Popper had at first been lukewarm about the proposal, but in the event he supported it whole-heartedly.

In the late 1960s Lakatos turned increasingly from the philosophy of mathematics, where his ideas could be seen as an extension into new terrain of Popper's conjectures-and-refutations view of human

---

[104] KRP to IL, 12 December 1962.
[105] KRP to IL, 10 January 1965.
[106] KRP to IL, 11 August 1964.
[107] KRP to IL and WWB, 11 October 1964.
[108] KRP to IL, 15 December 1964.

knowledge, to the methodology of the empirical sciences, where his ideas were increasingly in competition with Popper's. When he sent Popper a piece of his work, he now tended to scribble on it the advice not to read it, and Popper tended to follow this advice. The start of their big rupture can be dated rather precisely. Back in 1963 Popper had received a major philosophical honour: he would be the hero of a volume in the Library of Living Philosophers, edited by Paul A. Schilpp; but it took several years for the list of contributors to be finalised. Lakatos had originally been asked to write on Popper and mathematics, but Popper suggested that he take the opportunity to bring together his scattered criticisms and present them in an orderly form. Lakatos agreed. In the meanwhile, during 1968–9, with student revolutions going on at LSE and other places, Popper was working on his intellectual autobiography for the volume (later published separately as *Unended Quest*). He was due to retire from LSE in September 1969. Regarding the pension he would get as grossly inadequate, he had arranged to spend the autumn of 1969 teaching at Brandeis University to make some money. Until he had finished the autobiography he was not allowed to turn to the critical contributions to the Schilpp volume, and he was still working on it when he arrived at Brandeis. He finally sent off this first draft on 7 October.

He was now at liberty to turn to the mountain of critical contributions which awaited him (they would occupy nearly 800 printed pages in what would become a monster volume). The task of replying was all the more daunting because he had a genuine aversion to reading about himself. He had not read Lakatos's contribution when the latter came over from Boston to give a lecture at Brandeis on 9 October. There had been some tension between them during the previous year (the student troubles at LSE did not help), but after this meeting Popper wrote him a friendly letter beginning, 'My dear Imre, It was very nice to have seen you here'.[109] Then, on 30 October, he wrote him a furious letter, sparked by a hurried look at Lakatos's long contribution, not to the Schilpp-volume, but to an anthology on Kuhn.[110] There was worse in store in Lakatos's essay for the Schilpp volume. Entitled 'Popper on Demarcation and Induction', this raised difficulties with Popper's 'solutions' of his two basic problems. As to demarcation: Popper had

---

[109] KRP to IL; the date, 28 October 1969, is in Lakatos's hand.
[110] *Criticism and the Growth of Knowledge*, ed. Imre Lakatos and Alan Musgrave (Cambridge, 1970).

rhetorically asked in connection with Freudian pseudo-science what evidence 'would refute to the satisfaction of the analyst not merely a particular analytic diagnosis but psycho-analysis itself?'[111] Lakatos agreed that Freudians had been nonplussed by this challenge; but what if we direct a similar challenge to Newtonian scientists; what evidence would refute not merely a particular application of it but Newtonian theory itself? As to induction: Lakatos did not of course claim that the method of science is inductive; he accepted that Popper had radically transformed our view of the way in which scientists, especially great scientists, typically proceed, but he did claim that without some inductive assumption Popper's philosophy could provide no bridge from a scientific theory's theoretical acceptability ('accept-ability$_2$') to its pragmatic reliability ('acceptability$_3$').

I would have preferred to pass over what comes next. In January 1970, back from Brandeis and now retired, Popper paid a visit to his old seminar, now presided over by Lakatos and myself. He told a friend that he had come back to an icy house, and found the LSE 'similarly icy'.[112] His subject was induction. Lakatos's criticisms of Popper on induction were well known to most members of the seminar, and we were curious to know what he would say in reply. Lakatos had told him beforehand that he would have to slip away ten minutes before the two-hour seminar was due to end, at 4 o'clock. Popper went on talking, with no mention of Lakatos or his criticisms, until 3.50. It was not a happy occasion. Younger members of the department tended to take Lakatos's side in the worsening conflict between the two men. After this one occasion he stayed permanently away from his old seminar.

In his written reply in the Schilpp volume, he declared that if Lakatos's criticism on demarcation were true, 'then my philosophy of science would not only be completely mistaken, but would turn out to be completely uninteresting'. The idea that what drives a good critical tradition is pupils criticising the master was overtaken, as Popper grew older, by a tendency to see those criticisms which he was unable to rebut quickly and effectively as threatening to deprive him of his achievements—'all that work wasted!' as he once bitterly put it to me. Popper never explicitly addressed Lakatos's criticism on induction. His *Objective Knowledge* (Oxford, 1972) opens with the words, 'I think I have solved a major philosophical problem: the problem of induction'.

---

[111] *Conjectures and Refutations* (London, 1963), p. 38n.
[112] KRP to CS, 22 January 1970.

A reference to Lakatos was expunged (though not from the index) and thereafter he never again referred to Lakatos in print. Lakatos died, quite suddenly, on 2 February 1974, before the Schilpp volume was eventually published, but Popper's bitterness towards him continued unabated.

## The 1960s

I now resume the main story, which had reached 1960. In that year Popper introduced a striking new idea at the first International Congress for Logic, Methodology, and Philosophy of Science, in Stanford, the idea of *verisimilitude*. He developed it further when he gave the Sherman Lectures, in November 1961 at University College London (with a flattering number of Nobel Laureates and Fellows of the Royal Society in the audience). Let theory $T_2$ be an advance on its falsified predecessor $T_1$, and suppose that, as typically happens, $T_2$ subsequently gets falsified in its turn. We might want to say that, though false, $T_2$ is closer to the truth than $T_1$. What could that mean? He gave an original and deceptively simple and persuasive answer (published in chapter 10 of *Conjectures and Refutations*, 1963): $T_2$ has more verisimilitude than $T_1$ if: (i) $T_2$'s truth content (those of its logical consequences that are true) includes $T_1$'s, (ii) $T_2$'s falsity content (those of its logical consequences that are false) is included in $T_1$'s; and (iii) at least one of these inclusions is strict. He considered this a major achievement. It tended to mitigate what many saw as the pessimism of his earlier philosophy of science. Suppose we have a historical sequence of scientific theories, $T_1$, $T_2$, $T_3$, in which $T_2$ gained a corroboration from a test which falsified $T_1$, and $T_3$ gained a corroboration from a test which falsified $T_2$. In 1934 Popper could have drawn no conclusions from this pattern of corroboration as to the truth of the latest theory, but he now claimed that corroboration is an *indicator* of verisimilitude.[113] Some saw this as a welcome, others as an unwelcome, shift away from his original, austerely non-inductive position. During a visit by Popper to New Zealand in 1973 Pavel Tichy showed him, in a seminar at Otago University, that his definition of verisimilitude breaks down. (This was also shown independently by David Miller.) Popper took this criticism calmly.

---

[113] *Objective Knowledge* (Oxford, 1972), p. 103, his italics.

Further striking new ideas were presented in 1965 in a lecture at Washington University entitled 'Of Clouds and Clocks'. This countered the thesis of classical atomism that seemingly 'cloudy' structures are really made up of clock-like bits with the contrary thesis that seemingly clock-like structures are really statistical aggregates of 'cloudy' bits. It also introduced the idea of a *plastic* (as opposed to *iron*) control. He had not paid much heed to Darwinism hitherto; there are no significant references to it in *The Open Society* and *Conjectures and Refutations*, and in *The Poverty of Historicism* he had endorsed a dismissal of the clash between Darwinism and Christianity as 'a storm in a Victorian tea-cup', but in this lecture he apologised for doing that, and declared the Darwinian theory of evolution very important. However, it was not easy for him, from his falsificationist standpoint, to account for the importance of this theory, which he declared 'almost tautological'.[114]

In the Herbert Spencer Lecture which he had given in 1961, but which was not published until 1972, he put forward a hypothesis which he undervalued and indeed actually forgot.[115] I call it the Spearhead Model of evolutionary development.[116] It argues from the assumption that an organism's control system and its motor system are sharply distinguishable, each with its own genetic basis, to the conclusion that in evolutionary developments control systems lead the way with motor systems following in their train; for control capacity may exceed motor power whereas the converse would be disadvantageous (he actually said 'lethal').

## Retirement

His retirement was long and unflagging. One of his oldest concerns was the mind-body problem, perhaps the most difficult of all philosophical problems. He brought to it ideas from various domains, including his old teacher Bühler's ideas about the expressive, signalling and descriptive levels of language. (He was always seized by the importance of language; one of his complaints about linguistic philosophers was that they had no philosophy of language.) He also brought in ideas from biology. At heart he was a Cartesian interactionist. (He once gave a talk,

[114] See *Unended Quest*, § 37.
[115] KRP to JW, 7 October 1969.
[116] In 'Popper and Darwinism' in Anthony O'Hear (ed.), *Karl Popper: Philosophy and Problems* (Cambridge, 1996), pp. 191–206.

at Oxford I think, contrasting his ideas with Ryle's in *The Concept of Mind*. His auditors repeatedly asked where Ryle had ever denied it. Finally, he declared that he believed in the ghost in the machine; they admitted that Ryle had denied that.) But his position on the mind-body problem became complicated by his increasing preoccupation with a World 3 of objective ideas existing independently of their origin in World 2 (subjective mind). The classic problem of relations between World 2 and World 1, or between minds and bodies, tended to get nudged aside by this other problem of the relation between World 2 and World 3. He presented his ideas on these issues in lectures at Emory University in 1969 (later edited by Mark Notturno and published with the title *Knowledge and the Body-Mind Problem: In Defence of Inter-action* (London, 1994). His concern to establish the reality of World 3 sometimes made it sound almost Hegelian, with scientific theories in it exerting, via World 2, an influence upon World 1. But he answered 'I don't think so' when asked whether World 3 ever *initiates* anything.[117] These ideas were developed in *The Self and its Brain* (New York and Berlin, 1977), half of which was written by him and the other half by Eccles.

In 1983 he published, in collaboration with David Miller, a two-page letter in *Nature* which aroused wide interest. Let *h* and *e* say respectively, 'All swans are white' and 'All observed swans are white'; since $p(h, e) > p(h)$, it looks as though inductive support and probabilistic support work together. However, Popper and Miller pointed out that *h* can be factorised into two conjuncts: (i) *e* and (ii) $h \leftarrow e$ (*h* if *e*), where (ii) represents that part of the content of *h* which goes beyond *e*; and *e* actually *lowers* the probability of (ii) (and raises the probability of (i) to 1, of course).

Popper went through a harrowing time during Hennie's long terminal illness. After her death, in 1985, he sold Fallowfield and moved to Kenley, where he worked on indefatigably, now assisted by Melitta Mew. He was in the news in August 1988. It seems that the Soviet delegation, which had undertaken to provide simultaneous translations of talks from and into Russian at the World Congress of Philosophy at Brighton, preferred to go on a sightseeing tour on the day the author of *The Open Society* was to give an address. An expanded version of this address went into *A World of Propensities* (Bristol, 1990). He published a collection of essays and addresses in 1992 and another in 1994.

---

[117] *Knowledge and the Body-Mind Problem*, p. 44.

A walk from this new house took him past a glider club; he was fascinated by the takings off and landings, and persuaded someone there to take him up. After that he would have liked to take lessons. This did not happen, but he did go up a second time at the suggestion of a German television company.[118] He was now comfortably off and could indulge his love of antiquarian books; perhaps he was also driven by memories of his father's lost library. He acquired first editions of Galileo's *Two Dialogues*, Hobbes's *Leviathan*, Gilbert's *De Magnete*, Hume's *Treatise*, Kant's three *Critiques*, and several of Kepler's works. With Newton's *Principia* and *Opticks* he had to be content with second and third editions.

There were many honours and awards, including: Sonning Prize 1973; Companion of Honour 1982; de Tocqueville Prize 1984; Catalunya Prize 1989; Kyoto Prize and Goethe Medal 1992; Otto Hahn Peace Medal 1993. His work has been translated into some forty languages, including some unusual ones, such as Mongolian. In his old age he was much sought out by world leaders and elder statesmen, including the then German President (Richard von Weizsäcker), the Emperor of Japan, the Dalai Lama, Helmut Schmidt (who visited him several times), Helmut Kohl (who publicly saluted him as a champion of the open society), Mario Soares, and most recently Václav Havel. A man who delivered a new garden seat was told that it was a pity its predecessor was no longer usable; many famous bottoms had sat on it.[119]

I will conclude with some scattered observations. The sheer amount of work he got through, sometimes working right through the night, is extraordinary. This was despite intermittent poor health. True, some of this may have been due to overwork and he was a bit of a hypochondriac; but frightening attacks of tachycardia began in his mid-fifties and he had frequent bouts of pneumonia. Yet he travelled a lot, especially in his later years. He also kept up an enormous correspondence (Hennie was heavily involved in this, not only typing much of it, but complying with his demand to preserve everything.) He had virtually no relaxations, apart from music, and some reading of such authors as Jane Austen, Anthony Trollope, and Hugh Lofting. *The Times*, which used to be delivered at Fallowfield mainly for Hennie's benefit, was stopped in about 1960. Apart from Alpbach, which usually made a happy break

[118] Melitta Mew.
[119] Robin Watkins.

for him though he hardly relaxed while there, I remember him taking off only two days (they both happened to be in March 1965), once to be knighted and once to visit Whipsnade Zoo. His enthusiasm for routine lecturing waned after about 1950. He preferred answering off-the-cuff, and questions from the audience were increasingly encouraged. The kind of teaching he enjoyed most was a tutorial with just one gifted pupil; for instance, Elie Zahar benefited in this way—as a doctoral student at LSE he was allowed the use of Popper's room, and when Popper came in to eat his sandwiches he might explain how, say, Ernst Mach constituted minds and bodies out of the units of his neutral monism. He could be over-confident of his own opinions. When he was in his late eighties someone who became a colleague in 1948, and whose appearance had changed considerably since, said to him, 'I'm John Wisdom'; 'No you're not' came the reply![120] He was physically small, with an expressive face. He could not dissemble his feelings; when he was happy they shone out and when he was angry they blazed out. He read with intense concentration, his eyes seeming to suck the meaning from the page.

He enriched the English language with some striking labels, or 'right-to-left definitions' to use one of them, for important ideas; for instance, 'the bucket theory of the mind', 'horizon of expectations',[121] 'moral futurism', 'the theory of manifest truth', and of course 'the open society'. He had a partiality for lowbrow English expressions like 'not my cup of tea' and 'I may pop off any time'. He took us aback at a conference on his philosophy at LSE in 1980 by announcing, after a talk in which Grünbaum had presented counter-examples to his thesis that Freud's psychoanalytical hypotheses are untestable, 'I may have to eat humble pie'.[122] He had a good line in self-deprecation; for instance, when answering Hilary Putnam in the Schilpp volume, he compared this 'leader of the younger generation of logicians' with himself, 'a tottering old metaphysician'.

As well as being a philosopher of unusual depth and clarity, the sheer range of his intellectual interests was astonishing. Among the more philosophically off-beat subjects on which he made interesting contributions are the rise of polyphonic music, and the very first

---

[120] Hans Reiss.

[121] David Miller tells me that Husserl had this expression.

[122] See the 1980 addition on p. 169 to his *Realism and the Aim of Science* (London, 1982); the acknowledgement to Bartley should have been to Grünbaum.

publishing of books (which he took to be Homer's *Iliad* and *Odyssey* in Athens around 550 BC; he suggested that 'printing' them, i.e. having them handwritten on papyrus by slaves, may have been less of a problem than marketing them).[123]

A remark in the Preface to *The Open Society*, 'Great men may make great mistakes', might have been a motto for much of his work; giant-slaying was a persisting motif. One thinks not only of individuals such as Plato, Hegel, Marx, and Freud, and perhaps Wittgenstein and Carnap, but also of various '-isms': he claimed to have slain logical positivism single-handed;[124] and there was essentialism, historicism, holism, probabilism, verificationism. But he also contributed importantly to our appreciation of various pre-Socratic thinkers, especially Anaximander, Heraclitus, Parmenides, and Democritus, and wrote generously and illuminatingly about various individuals; for instance, Kant, Schopenhauer, Boltzmann, and Tarski.

Natural scientists generally take a low view of philosophy of science, but some distinguished ones have been enthusiastic about Popper's ideas in this area. We saw Einstein taking them seriously in 1935 and again in 1950. Popper inspired a lifelong admiration in Eccles (already an FRS when he attended Popper's lectures on scientific method at the University of Otago in 1945),[125] and in Medawar;[126] both men found his conjectures-and-refutations view of science liberating. Popper's interest in problems to do with evolution and biology led to friendships with Ernst Mayr, and Alister Hardy and a renewal of his early friendship with Konrad Lorenz. Popper first met Erwin Schroedinger in 1936; after the war they often met in Alpbach. This was one of several friendships resulting from Popper's lifelong concern with quantum physics; others included Alfred Landé, David Bohm, Jean-Pierre Vigier, and John Bell. Herman Bondi was another admirer and friend. Nobel Laureates who admired him included Percy Bridgman (they met in Harvard in 1950), Dennis Gabor, and Jacques Monod (who introduced his philosophy of science to the French-speaking world with his preface to a translation of *The Logic of Scientific Discovery*; his brother Philippe translated *The Open Society*). It is fitting that Popper was one

---

[123] See *In Search of a Better World* (London, 1992), ch. 7.
[124] See *Unended Quest*, § 17.
[125] See Eccles's contribution to the Schilpp volume on Popper.
[126] See Medawar, *Memoir*.

of the small group who have been Fellows of the British Academy and of the Royal Society.

JOHN WATKINS

*The London School of Economics*

*Note.* I have drawn freely on Popper's autobiography, *Unended Quest* (Fontana, 1976), usually without footnote references. Another main source has been the microfilm copies, prepared by the Hoover Institution and made available to the British Library of Political and Economic Science, of papers in the Sir Karl Popper Collection in the Hoover Institution Archives, Stanford, California; letters are identified by author, recipient, and date, other papers by box and folder numbers. A reference consisting just of one person's name or initials will indicate a personal communication, oral or written.

I use the following abbreviations:
WWB = Bill Bartley; RB = Richard Braithwaite; AB = Alfred Braunthal; RC = Rudolf Carnap; JCE = John Eccles; HF = Herbert Feigl; JF = John Findlay; EHG = Ernst Gombrich; FAH = Fritz Hayek; IL = Imre Lakatos; CL = Casimir Lewy; PBM = Peter Medawar; JAP = Hennie Popper; KRP = Karl Popper; BR = Bertrand Russell; JW = John Watkins.

FREDERIC RABY

*Proceedings of the British Academy*, **94**, 687–704

# Frederic James Edward Raby
# 1888–1966

AT THE TIME OF HIS DEATH, on 30 October 1966, Frederic Raby had achieved an international reputation for his scholarship in the field of medieval Latin literature. This reputation was based principally on two massive works—*Christian-Latin Poetry* (1927) and *Secular Latin Poetry* (1934)—which together chart the immense field of medieval Latin poetry from its beginnings in the Christian-Latin poetry of late antiquity to the Latin hymns of the fourteenth century. Since the time of their publication these works have in effect defined the field of medieval Latin poetry for students in the English-speaking world.

Frederic Raby was born in Ely on 11 December 1888, the eldest son of Edward Raby, to a family that was comfortably well-off (Edward's father ran a successful grocery business in Ely). Frederic himself was one of five children, which included two elder sisters, Edith (b. 1886) and Winifred (b. 1887), a younger brother Frank (b. 1890), and a younger sister, Dorothy (b. 1894). In 1900 Edward and his young family moved from Ely to Hoole, on the outskirts of Chester, where Edward joined his brother-in-law in running a local bookstore known as Hukes' Library (an operation subsequently taken over by Mowbrays). As might be expected in these circumstances, the Raby family was of a very bookish orientation, as the children's surviving notebooks from the period charmingly illustrate. Frederic's father Edward had been a King's Scholar at Ely during the 1870s and was an excellent classicist. He helped young Frederic with Latin and Greek, but also introduced him to the pleasures of architecture, teaching him in particular how to

© The British Academy 1997.

recognise various periods of medieval architecture. Among Frederic's earliest recollections were memories of Alan of Walsingham's Lady Chapel at Ely; later, when the family had moved to Hoole, he frequently walked to the nearby church at Plemstall, which he sketched and photographed in a thorough manner (throughout his life he remained a very competent draughtsman).

In due course Frederic went to the King's School, Chester, for his secondary education. He worked (as he later put it) without enthusiasm, but won a number of prizes 'in very easy competition', including the sixth-form prize in scripture in 1906 (which consisted in a copy of the two-volume work by Alfred Edersheim, *The Life and Times of Jesus the Messiah* (1883)). The King's School was not at that time strong in classics, though there was one master with whom he worked through the *Annals* of Tacitus; in lieu of doing Greek at school he opted for German. Such classical training as he had he derived from his father, with whom he read Vergil, Horace, and Juvenal, as well as Plato and Thucydides. For the most part, however, he was left on his own, and was free to pursue his own intellectual enthusiasms. He later recalled that his principal guides to classical literature were (Sir John Pentland) Mahaffy's *History of Classical Greek Literature* (1880) and (C.T.) Crutwell's *History of Roman Literature* (1877), both of which he found unsatisfactory in that they did not adequately situate the literature in a historical context: a defect which he was later to attempt to rectify in his own literary histories. Even as a schoolboy Frederic Raby's range of reading was vast, and was finely balanced between ancient, medieval, and modern authors. He attempted to translate part of the *Odyssey* in the style of William Morris; his interest in Browning led him to Aeschylus; from his reading of Matthew Arnold (of whom he was later to say: 'I cannot overestimate what I owe to him as my ideal and my guide') he was fired with enthusiasm for Heine and Goethe; and from Rossetti's *Early Italian Poets* he derived his lifelong love of Dante. The unfocused nature of his literary interests apparently suggested to his teachers at the King's School that he would be unlikely to win a scholarship in classics, so he concentrated his attention on ancient and medieval history, where his guide was James Bryce's *Holy Roman Empire* (1863), which led him in turn to the twelfth century—to St Bernard, to Abelard and Heloise, and to his earliest experience of medieval Latin verse in the form of the *Hora novissima* of Bernard of Morlaix. His later intellectual orientation was thus in some sense already formed when he was a schoolboy: even at this stage he was already wondering when

Migne's *Patrologia Latina* would be accessible to him. In any event, he went to Cambridge in 1906 to sit the scholarship examinations, armed, as he later said, 'with an odd mixture of ignorance and out-of-the-way scraps of knowledge'. By chance he was able to recognise all the quotations on the general knowledge paper, and the Greek unseen turned out to be a passage of Thucydides which he knew intimately. Accordingly, he won an Open History Exhibition (then worth £60) to Trinity College, Cambridge, where he went in October 1907.

Frederic was one of a class of some 200 Trinity freshmen that year (which included *inter alios* Jawaharlal Nehru). The Master at the time was Henry Montague Butler, who created a deep impression on the young Raby through his recollection of early nineteenth-century worthies such as Lord Macaulay. This was the Trinity of G. E. Moore, Bertrand Russell, Henry Jackson, Hastings Rashdall, J. E. McTaggart, and A.W. Verrall. Raby's tutor was the mathematician, W. W. Rouse Ball, and his Director of Studies was Reginald Vere Laurence, to whom he later confessed to owing a good deal, though Laurence evidently directed Raby to a very small extent. In many ways Laurence was the spiritual opposite of Frederic Raby, especially in his pursuit of fine food and drink (so much so that he has been referred to as 'the bibulous historian R. V. Laurence'),[1] but Raby greatly admired the decoration of his Trinity rooms and the donnish life-style which Laurence represented. Above all, he enjoyed the 'spacious, bright Athenian air of that great college'.

In the early years of this century, the specified syllabus of the history tripos extended from classical antiquity to the present, and embraced economic as well as political history. Raby's chosen Special Subject was 'The Reign of Augustus', for which his principal superviser was J. C. Stobart of Trinity; but he also heard university lectures on the later Roman empire by T. R. Glover and Samuel Dill, on the barbarian invasions by J. B. Bury (who 'was not an inspiring lecturer'), on medieval history by H. M. Gwatkin, and on the history of political thought by G. Lowes Dickinson. He was grateful to all these teachers for training in the use of sources, and for inculcating the habit of reading foreign books and monographs. He later wrote that 'I made notes of everything I read, and I read and re-read my notes with care. In this way, I organised, I suppose, what success I had in examinations.'

---

[1] See T. E. B. Howarth, *Cambridge Between the Two Wars* (London, 1978), pp. 28 and 81–2.

Raby took a double First in history at Cambridge (Part I, 1909; Part II, 1910). In spite of this impressive result, and for reasons now irrecoverable, he was not offered a fellowship. He briefly entertained hopes of a position in the University Library, but these came to nothing. Instead, it was suggested that he should remain in Cambridge for a fourth year and then take examinations for the Higher Division of the Civil Service. During the academic year 1910–11 he was resident in Cambridge, studying philosophy (ancient and modern) and political economy, for which he followed the lectures of John Maynard Keynes. He took the Civil Service exams successfully in August 1911, and was appointed to HM Office of Works at an annual salary of £150.

Frederic Raby spent his working career at the Office of Works, until he retired from the Civil Service in 1948 at the age of sixty. He was employed successively in the Policy, Establishments and Finance Divisions of the Office, where one of his responsibilities, together with Statues and Brompton Cemetery, Royal Parks and Palaces, was Ancient Monuments. In particular, he was responsible for devising and establishing, in the reconstruction period of the early 1920s, an essentially simple (but in detail necessarily complicated) system of internal financial control which served the Office during the years of recession and expansion. It was the impression of those who worked with him that he ran Ancient Monuments policy almost on his own, at a time when (for example) the Roman Wall was being menaced by gravel operations, and large numbers of ancient monuments had to be taken into guardianship if they were to be kept from ruin. Late in life Raby recalled with particular pleasure his involvement in safeguarding the ruins of Furness Abbey, which the Cavendish family had placed in Office of Works guardianship in 1923, and in whose transformation into an outstandingly beautiful national monument Raby himself was actively concerned. His work brought him in contact with many eminent archaeologists, some of whom became his close friends, such as Cyril Fox, Alexander Keiller, and Mortimer Wheeler; through them, he developed an interest in prehistoric archaeology, and it was a pleasurable aspect of his job that he was obliged to visit sites such as Avebury during Keiller's excavations there. Although he was not trained as an archaeologist, he acquired some expertise in this field, and (for example) personally directed excavations beneath the high altar of the priory church at Thetford, where the Tudor chapel of Henry Fitzroy, the Duke of Richmond (Henry VIII's natural son), was identified. He wrote guidebooks not only to Thetford Priory, but also to nearby monuments such as Castle Acre Priory and Framlingham Castle. As a result of these interests he was elected a Fellow of the Society of Antiquaries in 1923 (among those who sponsored him was the great architectural historian and Chief Inspector of Ancient Monuments, Sir Charles Peers); Raby's ballot-paper specified that he was 'a student of mediaeval archaeology, particularly early ecclesiastical and monastic history'. After election, Raby regularly attended the Society's meetings, and subsequently became one of its Vice-Presidents (1940–6). Following his death in 1966, Raby was commemorated by the then President of the Society of Antiquaries, Francis Wormald, as having been 'the administrator who looked after the affairs of the division concerned with Ancient Monuments' and who was 'a staunch and good friend to archaeologists and to this Society'. His work on behalf of the Office of Works was recognised as early as 1927, when he was promoted to Assistant Secretary, and subsequently in 1934, when he was made Companion of the Bath. The award of the CB shows how highly his work was esteemed at that time (the CB is more characteristically awarded to Under-Secretaries). But he never rose above the grade of Assistant Secretary; and the reason must be that his intellectual interests, and ambitions, by then lay elsewhere.

With his appointment in the Office of Works, Raby moved to London, where he lived at first in the Pasmore Edwards Settlement in Tavistock Place; here he had a spacious bed-sitting-room large enough to house his growing library. It was here that he met Albert Mansbridge, founder of the Workers' Educational Association, who became a life-long friend (he was later a neighbour when Frederic and his family were living in Welwyn Garden City, and was treated as a sort of honorary grandfather by the Raby children). In 1914 Raby moved to the University Hall of Residence in Carlyle Square, Chelsea, where he stayed until he married. With the outbreak of war he enrolled at once in the Royal Navy, but as a result of his poor eyesight he was almost immediately discharged; he subsequently did searchlight duty and volunteer work with a boys' club in London's East End (his younger brother, Frank, was killed at the Somme in 1916). It was also during the war that Frederic married his wife, Joyce, and set up home in Battersea. The story of how he met his future wife is characteristic of the man, and bears repeating. While he was still up at Cambridge he spent a period of study leave with a friend at the seaside resort of Hunstanton (Norfolk); there the two young men were spied walking on the beach by a group of schoolgirls, then also at Hunstanton on vacation. One of the girls,

Frederic's future wife Joyce Mason, wolf-whistled at the boys. Frederic was subsequently able to establish that the girls in question were from Huntingdon Grammar School; whereupon he went to the school in Huntingdon and waited at the gate until the girls were leaving; having identified the girl in question, he chased her to her home. The meeting thus having been effected, the two in due course became properly acquainted, and eventually married (at Huntingdon) in 1917. Joyce Raby was a high-spirited woman who, until family responsibilities intervened, was briefly a schoolteacher with strong interests in amateur dramatics and English literature. During the early years of their marriage, when they were living in Battersea, the young couple undertook a strenuous campaign of reading together, which took them pleasurably through the novels of Henry James and the works of a number of French writers, including Ernest Renan, Anatole France and Charles Péguy. For a number of years they lived in Battersea, where their son John was born in 1924; the following year, the family moved to Welwyn Garden City, where their daughter Jane was subsequently born in 1931. There were no further children.

As soon as he was established in London, Frederic had begun laying plans for a large-scale monograph on a medieval subject, namely a history of Frederick Barbarossa. Work on this project involved him in close and methodical reading of twelfth-century Latin sources, published for the most part in the 'Monumenta Germaniae Historica'. In this undertaking he was greatly assisted by the resources of the London Library, from which he was able to borrow books (an inestimable benefit for scholars who are denied access to a well-stocked university library) and which took the initiative of acquiring many periodicals and obscure publications in medieval Latin for Raby's own use.[2] How he found the time and energy for such a project is unclear: it cannot have been easy to carry out research of the highest standard while holding a full-time (and intellectually demanding) position at the Office of Works. In later life he used to say that most of his reading had been done on daily train journeys between Welwyn Garden City and his

---

[2] Cf. the remarks in his preface to *Secular Latin Poetry*: 'It is difficult to give a just estimate of the extent to which the London Library helped me during the years when this book was being written. Through the constant kindness of the Librarian and other officers of the Library my access to its resources was made easy, and many of the books were specially procured at my request. Most of the texts and many important periodicals relating to Medieval Latin literature are available there, and in this great institution the scholar who has but little leisure finds exactly what he needs' (I, viii).

office at Storey's Gate (SW1); but there is an abiding suspicion, given the enormous amount of reading he was able to achieve, that the flexible timetables of the ministry also contributed to his scholarship. In any event, the book on Barbarossa never came to fruition, because it was overtaken by (what was to become) an even larger project. While visiting the Union in Cambridge, Raby had come across a copy of Archbishop (R.C.) Trench's *Sacred Latin Poetry* (1849), and had conceived the notion of producing a similar but updated study on the whole range of Christian-Latin poetry, one which (as he later said) 'would make a contribution to the history of medieval civilization and would not be a bare literary history like Manitius'; he was adamant that he should remain a historian and not simply a medieval Latin philologist. Accordingly, he 'plunged into large-scale production with all the courage of ignorance and of inexperience'. As he had done as an undergraduate, he kept careful notes on the full extent of his vast programme of reading, and reread and reassembled these notes. Eventually the project grew and the notes coalesced: but, as he was later to record, he could not by then 'recall the stages by which what was intended to be a brief essay written for my own instruction and without thought of publication, became a volume of some 450 pages'.

When the work was complete, Raby sent his manuscript to the Clarendon Press, where it was received enthusiastically by Kenneth Sisam. However, Sisam realised that there were aspects of the work which could be improved by fuller awareness of recent scholarly publication, and he therefore asked the great patristic and liturgical scholar, Dom André Wilmart (1876–1941),[3] who at that point (1925) was at Farnborough, to comment on it. In due course Wilmart got in touch with Raby, and thus was initiated one of the closest friendships of Raby's life. Wilmart had been domiciled in London between 1917–19, and then at Farnborough from 1919 until he was called in 1928 to the Vatican Library; he spent every summer (August and September) between 1921 and 1934 at the British Museum. While he was still in England, he and Raby saw a good deal of each other, and Raby's children remember that Wilmart was one of the very few scholars who were ever invited to dine at the Raby home. Wilmart had an encyclopaedic knowledge of medieval Latin literature, but it was above

---

[3] See J. Bignami-Odier, L. Brou, and A. Vernet, *Bibliographie sommaire des travaux du père André Wilmart*, Sussidi eruditi 5 (Rome, 1953), pp. 7–10 and 14–18 (Wilmart's own account of his life and writings).

all his interest in liturgical and devotional texts, particularly hymns, which was to inform Raby's book and to determine the future direction of his scholarly interests. In order to accommodate Wilmart's suggestions, Raby spent a period of leave in Cambridge, staying at his old college and working assiduously through recent periodical literature in French, German, and Italian in the University Library.

The revised work—a monograph of nearly 500 pages in length—was entitled *A History of Christian-Latin Poetry from the Beginnings to the Close of the Middle Ages*, and was published by the Clarendon Press in 1927. The title fairly indicates the scope of the work: in it Raby attempted to define the emergence and development of a distinctively Christian idiom in Latin poetry, both popular and learned, from the earliest Christian hymns (fourth century) to the Franciscan verse of the thirteenth and early fourteenth centuries. Within this scope, he was concerned to illustrate new and characteristically medieval forms, and to show why these forms cannot be judged adequately by the canons of Classical Latin taste. Accordingly, although the book follows a chronological structure, the reader's attention is drawn to innovations in form, rhythm, and rhyme, especially in typical medieval Latin genres such as hymns, sequences and rhymed offices. Within this framework, Raby is able to highlight the most important individual voices: Ambrose and Prudentius in the earliest period, the Victorines in the twelfth century, then John Pecham, Bonaventure, Thomas Aquinas, and Jacopone da Todi in the thirteenth. The breadth of reference and detailed comparison is underpinned throughout by an awareness of the work of continental scholars, principally Max Manitius, Wilhelm Meyer, and Karl Strecker, and is illustrated by copious quotation. In short, the book provides a compendium—and in some sense an anthology—of what may be regarded as the most distinctive aspects of medieval Latin poetry, together with bibliographical orientation in the most pertinent European scholarship on the subject.

The book was warmly received by reviewers, particularly by Max Manitius and Karl Strecker in Germany. Through its publication, Raby was instantly established as an authority on medieval Latin literature, and thereby came into contact with the international community of medievalists, many of whom were to become close friends, notably Sir Stephen Gaselee, Claude Jenkins, A. G. Little, Rose Graham, Charles Johnson, Helen Waddell, G. G. Coulton, Karl Young, and A. Hamilton Thompson. His contacts with this wider world of medieval scholarship were inevitably to deflect his interest away from his duties at the Office of Works.

In his (very positive) review of *Christian-Latin Poetry*, Karl Strecker had pointed out that the emphasis of Raby's book on *Christian* poetry was in some sense misrepresentative, in that it ignored the vast body of medieval Latin secular verse. In light of the warm reception of *Christian-Latin Poetry*, the Clarendon Press invited Raby to undertake a complementary volume devoted specifically to secular Latin verse. Seven years later Raby published his *A History of Secular Latin Poetry in the Middle Ages*, an even longer study which consisted of some 800 pages, printed in two volumes by the Clarendon Press in 1934. In this work Raby attempted to trace the influence of classical rhetoric in verse composition, and to identify those features of medieval Latin poetry which were unprecedented in classical antiquity, particularly those which can be regarded as reflexes of vernacular verse. Once again the scope is vast: he begins by tracing the effects of rhetorical training as reflected in Roman literature, especially the flamboyant style known as 'Asiatic', and then following this tradition in the Latin poets of late antiquity (including Ausonius, Claudian, Sidonius Apollinaris, Dracontius, and many others). The core of the book is devoted to analysis of how medieval Latin poets, from the Carolingian period onwards, and culminating in the epic poets of the twelfth century such as Alan of Lille and John of Hauville, applied the rhetorical devices of classical literature in their verse. In the course of his exposition, Raby treats various innovative medieval genres which grew out of this rhetorical tradition, including the characteristic form taken by satirical verse of the twelfth century, and by the so-called Latin *comoediae*; but his principal focus is on the new forms of lyric verse which originated in the eleventh and twelfth centuries, perhaps as reflexes of vernacular verse, and were best typified in collections such as the 'Cambridge Songs' and the poetry of Walter of Châtillon. In *Secular Latin Poetry*, as in its predecessor, Raby illustrated his discussion with copious quotation, and provided valuable bibliographical orientation from his own extensive knowledge of secondary scholarship in European languages other than English. The two works—*Christian-Latin Poetry* and *Secular Latin Poetry*—are complementary (though inevitably there is some amount of overlap); together they provide an elegant introduction to what is best and most original in medieval Latin poetry, both in Christian poetry and in poetry derived from classical and vernacular traditions.

Once he had completed *Secular Latin Poetry*, Raby was free to turn his hand to other enterprises. Through his contact with Rose Graham he was invited to contribute the article on Bede to the *Dictionnaire d'histoire et de géographie ecclésiastiques*, and he also contributed an important survey of Anglo-Latin literature to the *Cambridge Bibliography of English Literature*. But through his friendship with Dom Wilmart, as well as from his reading of poets such as Charles Péguy, he began to reflect deeply on the role of the Church in the modern world. He had been brought up as a Methodist, but during his time at Cambridge had become an atheist, and so remained for many years (his son John, for example, born in 1924, was on principle not baptised). However, during the 1930s he came under the influence of the Christian philosopher Baron Friedrich von Hügel (1852–1925), who was a spiritual mentor of Dom Wilmart, and was the chief spokesman of the 'Modernist' movement in the Roman church. 'The Baron', as he was known, had lived in Kensington, and exerted considerable influence in cultured circles in England. He was widely read in medieval theology, and it was his aim to make the 'old church' intellectually inhabitable for modern-day Christians—to interpret the pristine faith in terms of the philosophy and science of later, and the latest, times. Raby never met 'The Baron' (he thought he had once seen him sitting in the reading room of the London Library), but he immersed himself in his writings, and contributed a chapter on 'Baron von Hügel' to a work entitled *Great Christians*, edited by R. S. Forman (1933). He also edited, in 1933, a collection of essays under the title *The New Learning, a Contribution to a General View of the World* (the preface of which was written by his old friend Albert Mansbridge). His own essay for the volume, on 'History', is deeply indebted to von Hügel, and reflects his own abiding interest in the relevance of medieval culture and literature to the modern Christian life. At the same time he was examining the principles of his own faith (his reflections are set out at length in an unpublished book, composed in 1932–3, on *The Christian Life in the Modern World*). The result of these reflections, prompted by his reading of von Hügel, was that he turned at this time to the Church of England, and remained a devout Christian for the rest of his life.

Another of Raby's scholarly enterprises came to fruition during the 1930s. One of the most valuable and enduring aspects of his *Christian-Latin Poetry* is its treatment of English devotional lyrics of the thirteenth and fourteenth centuries. Inspired once again by André Wilmart, who was a pioneer in the study of devotional literature of this period,

Raby started to work on the poetry of John of Howden (d. *c*.1275), sometime chaplain to Queen Eleanor, the mother of Edward I. John was the author of a sizeable corpus of Latin verse, including lengthy poems such as the *Philomena*, *Canticum amoris*, *Cythara*, and *Viola*, which at the time of *Christian-Latin Poetry* (1927) had not been published. In his first two books, Raby had relied entirely on published materials, and had seldom referred to unprinted sources; but he had an abiding interest in manuscript sources, as is clear from a comment he made in *The New Learning* concerning the study of the Middle Ages: 'it offers a field of research for those who love the finer pleasures of scholarship, and delight in the use of unprinted sources'. He therefore undertook to edit the poems of John of Howden (excepting the *Philomena*, which had been printed in Germany in 1930) from their manuscript sources. The resulting edition, *Poems of John of Hoveden*, was published by the Surtees Society in 1939. The work clearly reveals Raby's gift for editing medieval Latin verse, and it is a pity that he did not devote further scholarly effort to this end.

It is nevertheless astonishing that Raby was able to accomplish as much as he did—two works of literary history totalling some 1,300 pages and a major edition of a hitherto unknown medieval Latin poet—while in the full-time employment of the Office of Works. Only occasionally could the two facets of his intellectual activity have come together, but on one memorable occasion in the late 1930s they did so, in circumstances that deserve to be recorded. In the winter of 1937–8, the Director of the Warburg Institute, Dr Fritz Saxl, was attempting to negotiate the removal of the Warburg Library from its premises in Thames House on the Embankment, to more spacious accommodation in the Imperial Institute building of the University of London. However, the proposed removal involved structural alteration, which in turn required the permission of HM Office of Works. Saxl wrote a number of letters concerning the urgency of the move to Frederic Raby at the Office of Works, who was responsible for approving the expenditure in question. Negotiations of this sort inevitably involved delay. Since the learned members of the Warburg Institute were well aware of Raby's reputation as a medieval Latinist, however, they asked the young Ernst Gombrich (now Sir Ernst) to express the urgency of the case to Raby in medieval Latin verse, in the hope of expediting matters. Gombrich composed the following verses and sent them, under Saxl's name and on the Institute's behalf, to Raby:

Stella desperantium, miserorum lumen
  Rerum primum mobile, nobis quasi numen
Audias propitie supplicantem sonum
  De profundis clamitat studii patronum
Otium molestum est, et periculosum
  Menses sine linea vexant studiosum.
Statum hunc chaoticum noli prolongare
  Animam et domum nos fac aedificare
Libros nostros libera turri de seclusa
  Quibus mus nunc fruitur gaudeat et Musa,
O, duc nos ad gratiae sempiternum fontem
  Unde tibi lauri frons coronabit frontem.
      qui in Bibliotheca Warburgiana
      studiis se dedere ardent.

Raby replied immediately to Saxl, in the same verse-form:

Doctor disertissime, rector venerande,
  Omnibus amabilis semper et amande,
Congemiscens audio verba deprecantum
  Imo corde vocibus tactus eiulantum.
Set nunc tibi nuncio gaudium suave,
  Te et tuos liberans studiosos a ve.
Eant Libri Libere. Deus sit tutamen
  Libris et legentibus in eternum. Amen.

Raby's poem, dated 26 January 1938, was accompanied by a more prosaic note in English, authorising the works: 'Dear Dr Saxl, The attached reply, unworthy to be compared with your own composition, which has been much admired here, needs a gloss to the effect that the Office of Works are writing at once to London University, authorising the alterations, subject to a few precautions being taken in the carrying out of the work. I wish you all success in your new quarters.'[4]

During the Second World War, the Office of Works was temporarily removed to Rhyl in North Wales, from where its much-reduced operations were directed by Raby himself. By now the family had moved from Welwyn Garden City to Harpenden, and Raby was unavoidably separated from them. Tragically, in 1942, his wife Joyce died unexpectedly under anaesthetic during a minor operation on a nerve in her arm. Although the Raby children were now eighteen and eleven years old,

---

[4] The correspondence between Raby and Gombrich was privately printed by Gombrich at the Friends' Press (Fitzwilliam Museum, Cambridge) in 1984, under the title, *The Warburg Institute and H.M. Office of Works. E.H. Gombrich in memory of Frederic Raby*. As Gombrich commented, 'The whole stands as a nostalgic tribute to a vanishing tradition of the Civil Service, and as a memorial to a most humane and lovable scholar.'

respectively, the death of his wife undoubtedly put him under great personal strain, one result of which was that a year or so later he was given sabbatical leave from the Office of Works on medical grounds (defined at the time as a 'tired heart'). He took this leave at St Deiniol's Library (founded by Gladstone) in Hawarden, not far from Rhyl and very near to Chester where he had been raised as a boy. The Librarian (and later Warden, 1948–56) of St Deiniol's Library at that time was Dr A. R. (Alec) Vidler, who was a close friend of Raby's, and shared with him an enthusiasm for the Spanish mystics, an enthusiasm which they were both able to pursue when Vidler returned to Cambridge as Dean of King's College in 1956. Vidler was also the editor of the journal *Theology*, and at his invitation Raby contributed articles on Frédéric Ozanam and John Neville Figgis. During the war Hawarden was home to a number of refugees from Nazi Germany, including Hans Ehrenberg (Professor of Philosophy at Heidelberg) and Georg Misch (Professor of Philosophy at Göttingen), author of the massive *Geschichte der Auto-biographie*. Raby was able to draw Misch's attention to several examples of medieval Latin autobiography, including Guigo the Elder (d. 1137), prior of the Grande Chartreuse, whose works had been edited by André Wilmart (though Misch does not acknowledge the debt). One gets the impression that Hawarden at this time was functioning as a sort of institute of advanced studies.

Shortly after the end of the war Raby retired from the Civil Service (on 11 December 1948, at the age of sixty); but he continued his involvement in the activities for which his Civil Service career had prepared him: he was a Trustee and Governor of Dr Johnson's House (Gough Square), and served from 1949 to 1956 on the Cathedrals Advisory Committee (now the Cathedrals Fabric Commission for England), where he was involved *inter alia* in post-war restoration work at Exeter Cathedral and in plans for the redecoration of Audley Chantry at Salisbury Cathedral. By the time of his retirement from the Civil Service, however, his interests lay in resuming the scholarly career at Cambridge which thirty-six years' employment at the Office of Works could be seen as having interrupted.

By the time war broke out in 1939, Raby had achieved an international reputation in the field of medieval Latin literature, and a number of honours consequent upon that reputation followed. He was elected a Fellow of the British Academy in 1941, and an Honorary Fellow of Jesus College, Cambridge, in the same year. In 1942 he was elected Corresponding Fellow of the Mediaeval Academy of America, the same

year in which he received the degree Litt.D. from the University of
Cambridge. (He was subsequently to be awarded an honorary D.Litt.
from the University of Oxford in 1959.) Of all these honours, the one
which was to determine the course of his remaining life was the election
to Jesus College, Cambridge. Within Jesus College the principal architect of Raby's election was Frederick—or Freddy, as he was invariably
known—Brittain (1893–1969) who was, like Raby, a keen student of
medieval Latin literature.[5] Like Raby, Brittain was interested in the
forms of medieval Latin lyrics and their reflexes in vernacular literatures, an interest which was articulated in *The Medieval Latin and
Romance Lyric to AD 1300* (1937). Since 1930 Medieval Latin had
been recognised in Cambridge as a specified subject under the aegis
of the Faculty of Modern Languages, and Brittain had been largely
involved in teaching it; accordingly, when in 1946 the first university
lectureship in the subject was established at Cambridge, Brittain was
appointed to the post. Brittain had met Raby through a mutual friend
(Edward Wynn, Bishop of Ely 1941–56), and had realised at once both
what an asset Raby would be to the incipient programme of medieval
Latin studies in Cambridge, and how much Raby himself aspired to
return to academic life. Accordingly, when Raby retired from the Civil
Service in 1948, given that his wife had died six years earlier, he was
able to move to Cambridge and into residence at Jesus. He was given a
house at the end of Park Terrace, overlooking Parker's Piece—'in just
such surroundings', he wrote in his diary, 'as I had imagined for myself
in my dreams of the future when I was an undergraduate'. Since he was
at that time sixty years old, and since the normal age of retirement in
Cambridge was then sixty-seven, it was possible for his Honorary
Fellowship to be held in abeyance, in order to enable him to take up
an ordinary Fellowship for seven years (1948–55). During those seven
years Raby supervised Jesus undergraduates in history (who included,
curiously enough, his own son John), though he never had occasion to
deliver a lecture to the University. He was a kindly superviser whose
manner rose to nothing more than mild sarcasm even when treating
cases of flagrant plagiarism in his undergraduates' supervision essays.
In general he pitched himself fully into the college life from which he

---

[5] On Raby's career at Jesus, see Frederick Brittain, *It's a Don's Life* (London, 1972), pp.
216–18, as well as the obituary of Raby (also by Brittain) in the *Jesus College Report 1967*,
pp. 51–3 (which reproduces an excellent drawing of Raby done in 1965 by William E.
Narraway; the same drawing is reproduced, less well, in *It's a Don's Life*, pl. VI).

had long felt himself an exile. During the years in which he was a teaching fellow, he occupied rooms on the same staircase as Freddy Brittain. The two became inseparable companions (Frederic acted as best man when, late in life, Freddy married Muriel Cunnington in 1959); they lunched and dined together every day during term-time, both meals being preceded by a single glass of sherry in Freddy's rooms. Frederic took snuff once a day in the Combination Room following dinner. On occasions when he presided at high table, his conversation was memorable for its intellectual range and for the nature of his quotation, embracing St Augustine, Dante, George Herbert, Dr Johnson, and P. G. Wodehouse, and many more. He was active in college societies, including the Roosters (an informal Jesus dining club, of which Freddy Brittain was a lifelong champion) as well as university societies, including the John Mason Neale Society, which he attended unfailingly, but to which he was never persuaded to deliver a paper, in spite of his incomparable knowledge of medieval Latin hymns.

Whereas during his time with the Civil Service, the pursuit of two careers had demanded rigorous self-discipline, with the result that Raby had managed to publish an enormous amount, the period of his fellow-ship at Jesus College saw less scholarly publication, perhaps because self-discipline was no longer such an urgent necessity. He revised his *Christian-Latin Poetry*, taking the opportunity to incorporate discussion of John of Howden and to update the bibliography, for a second edition which was printed in 1953; a similarly updated second edition of *Secular Latin Poetry* appeared in 1957. During these years he also produced *The Oxford Book of Medieval Latin Verse*, which was published in 1959; but although this is a convenient anthology (including some amount of annotation) which goes far beyond the scope of its predecessor (edited by Sir Stephen Gaselee in 1925), it cannot be said to break new ground, and many of the pieces included in *The Oxford Book* had already been 'anthologised' (in some sense) by their treatment, with extensive quotation, in *Christian-Latin Poetry* and *Secular Latin Poetry*. With the exception of a brief article published posthumously in 1968, *The Oxford Book of Medieval Latin Verse* was Raby's last publication. He died peacefully in his sleep on 30 October 1966.

Frederic Raby was a modest and kindly man, a gentleman in the older sense of the word, a model of courtesy who radiated friendship, and was an enchanting companion, both for the genial warmth of his personality as well as for the astonishing breadth of his learning. (It was said among the Fellows of Jesus that, in his time, there was no more learned scholar in either Oxford or Cambridge, and the present-day Fellows of Jesus who knew Raby still express wonderment at his knowledge of arcane aspects of their own disciplines.) He never said an ill-word of another scholar's work. His pleasures in life were modest: he derived great pleasure and enlightenment from a number of trips to France and Italy; he enjoyed playing cricket and walking in the country-side, and (during his time at Jesus) the companionship of other scholars and a daily pinch of snuff (he was a non-smoker). He attended college chapel regularly and took Communion every Sunday during term. His abiding interest in the church is reflected in his membership of the Central Council for the Care of Churches, the Ely Diocesan Advisory Committee, the Additional Curates Society and the Alcuin Club. He is said to have had a wonderful way with children, whom he treated as his equals and contemporaries, even in his late seventies.

Frederic Raby's scholarly reputation needs to be understood in the context of medieval Latin studies in Britain in the early twentieth century.[6] At that time the study of medieval Latin verse was the province of amateurs and dilettantes, epitomised by works such as John Addington Symonds's *Wine, Women and Song: Medieval Latin Students' Songs*, Helen Waddell's *The Wandering Scholars*, and Gase-lee's aforementioned *Oxford Book of Medieval Latin Verse*. Raby's two great works transformed the perception of the field in the English-speaking world, and put the study of medieval Latin poetry on a professional level by revealing both the extent and nature of the poetry itself, as well as the world of modern European scholarship which is necessary for its elucidation. It could be said that Raby's work makes accessible to English-speaking scholars the riches of Max Manitius's immense *Geschichte der lateinischen Literatur* (published in three massive volumes in Munich between 1911 and 1931), a work to which Raby was happy to acknowledge his indebtedness. Raby's work is of more limited scope than that of Manitius, since it treats only poetry, and it lacks the abundant reference to manuscript sources which makes Manitius's work indispensable even today. Raby's work has other limitations as well: his opinions were sometimes based on acquaintance with no more than the first few pages of a work, and in such cases his

---

[6] See M. Lapidge, 'Medieval Latin Philology in the British Isles', in *La filologia medievale e umanistica greca e latina nel secolo XX*, Testi e studi bizantino-neoellenici 7 (Rome, 1993), pp. 153–88, with discussion of Raby's work at p. 172.

judgement is often wrong. No scholar, however, not even Raby, could manage to read every line of medieval Latin verse. What is remarkable is how very often his control is precise and his judgement sound. It is likely that today, some sixty years after their first publication, his two great works have a smaller audience than they once had: there are fewer and fewer students who can read a long quotation in Latin (to say nothing of Greek) without the aid of a translation, and his literary judgements, though the expression of an urbane and cultured scholar, will inevitably seem somewhat old-fashioned. However, the immense range of his learning and the modesty of its presentation can still serve as a model for younger scholars, and there can be no doubt that the present healthy state of medieval Latin studies in Britain and North America owes a great deal to the work of Frederic Raby.

MICHAEL LAPIDGE

*Fellow of the Academy*

*Note.* Frederic Raby died three years before I took up permanent residence in this country, and I unfortunately never had the opportunity of meeting him. I have therefore been obliged to rely on the memories of others. My greatest debt is to John Raby, who generously made available to me his father's papers, and helped me with many aspects of his earlier career. The papers include two volumes of Frederic's unpublished memoirs, which he entitled 'APOMNHMONEYMATA', the first (written in 1944–5) pertaining to his early schooling in Chester and Cambridge, as well as to his years with the Office of Works, and the second (written 1957, updated in 1964–5) concerning his time at Jesus College, Cambridge, but consisting largely of anecdotes pertaining to distinguished persons whom he had known. His unpublished writings also include the manuscript of a book entitled 'The Christian Life in the Modern World', written in 1932–3. Without access to these unpublished works it would have been impossible to compile the present memoir. I am also extremely grateful to John Raby, and to his sister, Mrs Jane Caven (née Raby) for commenting on an earlier draft of this memoir. I had the honour of being invited to dine in Jesus College with those Fellows of the college who knew Raby personally, and I am most grateful to them all for sharing their memories with me: Dr Ilya Gershevitch, Dr M. J. Waring, Mr E. F. Mills (Archivist of Jesus College), Dr L. E. R. Picken, and Mrs Muriel Brittain (widow of Freddy Brittain). I have drawn on a memoir of Frederic Raby's career in the Office of Works written in 1967 by Sir Edward Muir, now in the possession of the Academy, and supplemented by a letter (dated 20 January 1981) by Dr A. J. Taylor, formerly Chief Inspector of Ancient Monuments, who at an early stage of his career worked under Raby's supervision at the Office of Works. Dr Taylor was also kind enough to comment on an earlier draft of this present memoir, and I am much indebted to him for help in clarifying the account of Raby's Civil Service career. Professor Christopher Brooke shared with me his unrivalled knowledge of the University of Cambridge, and helped me to eliminate many inaccuracies and infelicities from an earlier draft of this memoir. I am also very grateful to A. R. D Wickson, Headmaster of the King's School, Chester, for answering my queries about Raby's school career; to Jonathan Smith, Archivist of Trinity College, Cambridge, for help with Raby's career at Trinity; and to Adrian James (Assistant Librarian, Society of Antiquaries of London) for supplying useful information on Raby's membership of the Society of Antiquaries. Dr Richard Gem (Secretary, Cathedrals Fabric Commission) and Miss Judith Scott kindly supplied me with information on Raby's work for the Cathedrals Advisory Committee. Dr Rosalind Love helped by looking through the minutes of the John Mason Neale Society for me. Professor Geoffrey Martin, formerly Keeper of Public Records, made enquiries on my behalf concerning Raby's time with the Office of Works, and provided helpful exegesis on the hierarchies of Civil Service employment. Two friends, Peter Dronke and J. B. Trapp, helped with information of various kinds. I am obliged to say, finally, that in many conversations with people who knew Frederic Raby personally, I have encountered only warmth and affection, and have not heard a harsh or critical word spoken about him.

Frederic Raby's unpublished papers are to be deposited in the archives of Jesus College, Cambridge, where they will be accessible to scholars in the future. His two volumes of memoirs are to be published as: F. J. E. Raby, APOMNHMO-NEYMATA: *Recollections of a Medieval Latinist*, ed. M. Lapidge (Biblioteca di 'Medioevo Latino', Florence).

*Editorial note.* The Academy is grateful to Professor Lapidge for volunteering in 1996 to prepare this obituary, after it had lain dormant for many years.

AUSTIN ROBINSON                    *Ramsey & Muspratt*

*Proceedings of the British Academy,* **94**, 707–731

# Edward Austin Gossage Robinson
# 1897–1993

I

AUSTIN ROBINSON was born on 20 November 1897 at Toft in Cambridgeshire, the eldest child of 'an impecunious clergyman', Albert Robinson,
who read mathematics as a scholar of Christ's College, Cambridge and
became a wrangler. He was ordained at the age of twenty-four, and
spent the next eight years as a curate. Austin's mother, Edith Side-
botham, was the daughter of a clergyman who was the vicar at Bourne
near Farnham in Surrey for thirty-three years. As Alec Cairncross
(1993: 4) has told us, it was a very happy marriage. The Robinsons
had four children: three boys and a girl. The children had a happy
childhood, even though their father was a remote and distant figure
so that their mother did the lioness's share of their upbringing. The
upbringing itself fostered self-reliance, fun and games as well as
providing an introduction to a sense of duty and the practical application of Christian principles.

Scholarships were necessary for Austin's education and he duly
obtained them, first to Marlborough and then to Christ's (he came top
of the St John's/Christ's group of Cambridge Colleges). Classics was
Austin's subject. He was 'rigorously drilled' in its grammar by an
eccentric schoolmaster, A. C. B. Brown. This allowed him to jump all
the necessary hurdles but it dimmed his enthusiasm, so that his heart was
never completely captured. It did ensure that Austin wrote in a distinctively agreeable style in his books, articles, reviews, and letters—he was

© The British Academy 1997.

a prolific writer of letters which were noted for their lucid elegance as well as for their substance.

Austin obtained his scholarship to Christ's in late 1916. Before taking it up, he joined the Royal Naval Air Service to train as a test pilot of seaplanes, an occupation which he loved. His 'most military' activity was to chase but never catch a Zeppelin (Cairncross 1993:11). The war itself was a deeply significant and traumatic event in his life. In his autobiographical essay (Austin Robinson 1992: 204) he wrote: 'In the modern world, deeply concerned with the dreadful threat of a nuclear war, it is too often forgotten how terrible was the mortality of that pre-nuclear conflict. Of the twenty senior boys in the "house" into which I had gone . . . in 1912, thirteen were dead before I got to Cambridge in the summer of 1919'. He came up to Cambridge 'a very different person'. Though never a pacifist in 'the technical sense', like hundreds of others who had seen war at first hand, 'almost all of [his] generation of Cambridge undergraduates', he was determined to try to make a world in which war was never again used to settle its problems. 'Naive we may have been, but we were nonetheless sincere' (Austin Robinson 1992: 204).

Austin spent his first fifteen months at Cambridge reading classics—his college 'was unsympathetic to [his] view that [he] should use a classical scholarship to be taught the more professional aspects of designing aeroplanes' (Austin Robinson 1992: 204). He duly obtained a First. He then went with relief to economics. A major influence on this decision was hearing Maynard Keynes give a lecture in the course of lectures which became *The Economic Consequences of the Peace* (1919). C. R. Fay, who then taught economics at Christ's, persuaded the college to allow Austin to make the switch and he lent Austin the Marshalls' *Economics of Industry* and Tawney's *Acquisitive Society* to start him off. Austin read them, Taussig's *Principles* and Marshall's *Principles* during the day in the summer of 1921, while working each evening as 'poor-man's lawyer' in the dockyards of Liverpool, getting 'a remarkable education regarding the life and problems of the poor' (Austin Robinson 1992: 205). Austin found Fay an enthusiastic supervisor who was sublimely uncomprehending of the economic theory to be found in Marshall (much as Fay worshipped Marshall himself). This led to furious arguments in supervisions, forcing Austin to make explicit and coherent theoretical arguments in order to drive out misunderstandings and incoherence. When Fay left Christ's for Canada, Austin went to Dennis Robertson and Gerald Shove. Though he felt he was well instructed by powerful minds, his supervisions never again had the same magic.[1]

Austin graduated with a First in 1922 (the same year as Maurice Dobb who also obtained a First). He began to research in economics at Corpus Christi, which was then renowned for its unique brand of High Church, high Toryism. Having to argue with intelligent colleagues who took very different views on economic and social matters was of inestimable value to Austin, especially after he became a Fellow in 1923 and had to teach as well as to argue and understand. To understand for Austin was to act, he was always a 'hands on' political economist. By 1925 he had moved from lecturing on Money, Credit and Prices, with which he was never happy, to what was and remained his favourite subject, Industry (Cairncross 1993: 17–18).

## II

In 1922 Joan Maurice came up to Girton to read economics, having read history at St Paul's Girls School. She 'graduated' in 1925; she and Austin, whose pupil she had been, married in 1926 (thus releasing Austin from being the one unmarried Fellow resident in Corpus Christi).[2] Soon after they married, the Robinsons went to India where Austin was to tutor the young Maharajah of Gwalior, then aged about ten. Cairncross tells a graphic tale of Austin's experiences there, how he combined an increasing knowledge of British India and the Princely States with involvement in the complex intrigues of the court, and especially in clashes with the strong-willed and all but impossible mother of his pupil. As far as Austin's future career was concerned, not only did the visit in a general way kindle his love for the sub-continent and its peoples but it also introduced him to the problems of economic development in a very practical way. He contributed a first-class piece of applied political economy to *The British Crown and the Indian States* (1928). He drew on inadequate statistics and showed judgement and imagination in estimating fiscal flows to and from the Princely States to British India.

---

[1] Shove, who later became renowned as a teacher (see Kahn 1987), was shy and ill at ease with returned servicemen because he felt they despised people who had been conscientious objectors during the war. Austin and Shove became firm friends as colleagues in the 1930s.

[2] The Maurices were a formidable and numerous clan whom Austin found 'a trifle frightening' (Cairncross 1993: 19).

The Robinsons were in India for nearly two years.[3] Austin returned to Cambridge to start afresh his long academic career there; it was only seriously interrupted by his distinguished service in Whitehall during the Second World War. He became a University Lecturer in 1929 and a Fellow of Sidney Sussex in 1931. (Joan became a University Assistant Lecturer in 1934.) Austin had known Keynes since his undergraduate days—he had quickly been admitted to Keynes's political economy club where, early on, he read a paper which made a big impression.[4] In 1934 Keynes invited him to become assistant editor of the *Economic Journal* with the consequence that Austin was eventually to write more reviews probably than any other economist before or since. The appointment also marks the start of his long association with the Royal Economic Society (RES) itself, editor for thirty-six years, secretary for twenty-five years (from which post he retired in 1970), and sixty years service in all to the society.[5]

## III

Dennis Robertson asked Austin to write the book on *Monopoly* for the respected 'Cambridge Economic Handbooks' series. Austin ended up writing two books (1931, 1941) as he cleared the ground for *Monopoly* by writing on *The Structure of Competitive Industry*, a project which became a book in its own right. Its *Economic Journal* reviewer, Philip Sargant Florence (to whose lectureship Austin had been appointed when Sargant Florence went to the Chair at Birmingham), rightly praised it as the potential classic it was to become—'a most original contribution . . . lively style . . . obvious . . . fund of industrial experience to back it [up]—' (Sargant Florence 1932: 66). He was as complimentary about *Monopoly* when nearly a decade later he was again the *Economic Journal* reviewer (perhaps as review editor, Austin wanted to see how Sargant Florence reacted second time around?). Sargant Florence gave the first book both high praise and stringent criticism. The praise was

---

[3] Joan returned before Austin and may have helped to draft parts of the report in the United Kingdom (Tahir 1990: 21).

[4] It was applauded: 'a most unusual tribute' (Cairncross 1993: 15).

[5] In a letter (22 November 1988) to Aubrey Silberston, who was then secretary of the RES, Austin set out his future agenda for both the society and journal. He wanted the society to speak for the profession as he felt it had in Keynes's day and the journal to be the 'journal of the profession as a whole'.

for the excellent structure of the argument which gave outstanding unity
to the book. Austin looked at the optimum size of firms from a number
of points of view—techniques, management, product(s), marketing, for
example—then brought all these aspects together, reconciled in the size
of a real firm. The criticism related to a fuzziness of definition, that in
much of his argument, it was not clear whether Austin was referring to
plants' 'scale of operations' or to firms' 'scale of organisation'. Nevertheless, Austin's work essentially established in an excellent way in
Cambridge what we now call industrial organisation. He blended
together a judicious mix of theory, facts, and policy—always his
approach to economic issues—thus deserving 'the gratitude of all
who wish to bring description closer to theoretical economics' (Sargant
Florence 1932: 69). His reviewer had one main criticism of the second
volume, that Austin confused the difficulties of creating a monopoly
and circumventing competition with those of controlling an established
monopoly. Despite this, Sargant Florence felt the author managed 'to
pack in most of the real world of monopoly while arguing all the time
patiently from first principles' (Sargant Florence 1941: 483).

Austin's Christianity and his interest in development came together
when in the 1930s he took part in two major studies of African
problems, the first of which required him to visit what is now Zambia.
The Archbishop of York asked Pigou in 1932 to suggest someone to
join a commission of enquiry under the auspices of the International
Missionary Council, to spend six months in Africa analysing the impact
of copper mining on indigenous society. Cairncross (1993: 51) says
Austin's chapters in *Modern Industry and the African* 'constitute one of
the first attempts by an economist to arrive at a view of what makes for
successful economic development in a backward country'. There, he
used the new ideas that were emerging in Cambridge as Keynes
moved from *A Treatise on Money* (1930) to *The General Theory*
(1936), spurred on by the criticisms and suggestions of the 'circus',
of which Austin was a key member.[6] They gave him the rudiments of a
national accounting framework in which to think about structures and
imbalances as between rural and urban sectors, overseas trade and

[6] The 'circus' was a group of young economists—Austin and Joan Robinson, Piero Sraffa,
Richard Kahn, and James Meade—who met to discuss the *Treatise on Money*. Their
deliberations were usually reported to Keynes by Kahn who then conveyed Keynes's
reaction to the 'circus' members, see Austin Robinson (1985) and Richard Kahn (1985)
for their recollections.

development, and the impact of government expenditure and taxation on economic systems.

Austin was also always interested in individuals as such (and their groupings); so, as he thought about rural underemployment and poverty, he was keen to use the potential skills and aspirations of people *where they were,* rather than advocate large migrations or the creation of huge urban concentrations. In his letters he wrote much about the characteristics of the Africans with whom he came into contact, using as his *numeraire* the various groupings of Indians he had known and/or observed in the 1920s. He wrote reflecting first impressions: 'In India where servants are perfect we say "This is evidently a servile race. They can't rule themselves". In South Africa we say "These people can't even lay a table. How can they run a country?"' (Cairncross 1993: 55). For him, economic development had to build on the characteristics of the people as they were, or would become, and he was what we would call now very much a 'horses for courses' person. He was always suspicious of all-purpose general theories and their accompanying models which were thought to be applicable regardless of time or place. In fact he said of the Cambridge developments of those years associated with Keynes and his colleagues:

> It was . . . a great step forward in economic thought when Keynes insisted that we should have . . . a theory that was valid not only with full (or near-full) employment, but also with unemployment—and that we should know quite clearly which of the propositions of economics were universally valid, and which were valid only in conditions in which it might be true that an increase of one activity was possible *only* at the expense of another activity (Austin Robinson 1947: 44; emphasis in original).

His other work on Africa in the 1930s did not require him to go there but it was nevertheless a major contribution, two long chapters, 157 pages in all, in Lord Hailey's *African Survey* (1938). Austin spent the vacations of the three years 1934–7 working in Chatham House on the chapters. The *Survey* itself was set up in response to an appeal by General Smuts in 1929—he called for a survey of Africa's affairs as a whole, reviewing developments in each country and to what extent they were affected by and gained from modern knowledge. Austin drew on the work of S. F. Frankel on capital investment in Africa and Charlotte Leubuscher on African foreign trade for the external aspects (chapter 19), and on Hailey's own 'immensely conscientious' notes for the internal aspects (chapter 20). The quality of Austin's chapters was such as to give the 'chapters a place amongst the classics of economic literature' (Noel Hall, quoted by Cairncross 1993: 73).

Austin increasingly assimilated the new lessons Keynes was developing, so much so that he was to review *The General Theory* (1936) for *The Economist* (29 February 1936), the only ever signed review in that journal (and then it was initials only, E.A.G.R.). Evidently the paper gave Austin's review a title of which he disapproved (it was misleadingly—because far too narrow—called 'Mr Keynes on Money') and also may have altered the emphasis and balance by editorial cuts. When Austin complained to Keynes of this, Keynes said it served him right for publishing in the yellow press. The review was perceptive and accurate, as to the essential nature of the new theory. It could be read with profit today by modern students to allow them both to get the essence of the theory and of how the advanced world still works. Austin's classical training was in evidence. In commenting on Keynes's polemical passages, Austin wrote: 'Like Horace's schoolmaster, Mr Keynes whips his pupils into agreement, where modest reasonableness, many will feel [not Austin, though], would better have achieved this end' (Austin Robinson 1936: 472).

What is illuminating, considering the muddled debates that were to occur, was that Austin had a clearer view of the meaning of the equality of saving and investment and the roles which it played in the analysis than perhaps even the author himself. He refers also to Keynes's masterly and clear style in previous writings and deplores its comparative absence in *The General Theory*: 'Many will sigh for the earlier Keynes who possessed in unusual bounty the gift of translating theoretical ideas into realities and conveying them in words of one syllable' (Austin Robinson 1936: 472). Austin himself uses plain language to good effect both to describe the existence of the underemployment rest state and the process by which it may (or may not) be reached in the economy as a whole. His keen sense of industrial organisation is evident when he explains that the non-profitable levels of output as a whole away from the rest state mean that the positions are not sustainable, even in the short term.


## IV


Austin spent the war years in Whitehall, working in two different sections. He went first to the Offices of the War Cabinet, subsequently joining the Economic Section when it, and what became the Central Statistical Office, were set up. Austin came to Whitehall much impressed by Keynes's talk to the undergraduate Marshall Society in Cambridge on the issues contained in Keynes's booklet, *How to Pay for the War* (1940). It also convinced him of the fundamental need for reliable estimates of national income and expenditure on a continuing basis. These were to be provided by Austin recruiting James Meade 'to get the logic right' and Richard Stone for 'his remarkable familiarity with British economic statistics' (Cairncross 1993: 79). Cairncross tells us that Austin 'always regarded [getting] the annual national income accounts on a consistent basis as his chief contribution to the war' (Cairncross 1993: 79). In February 1942 Austin became the Economic Advisor and Head of the Programmes Division in the Ministry of Production. The lessons he learnt in these two sections he regarded as the most important elements in his long apprenticeship as an economist (Austin Robinson 1992: 219).

His wartime tasks and experiences reaffirmed his belief that macro-economic analysis without simultaneous attention to the micro-economic details of firms and industries, supplies of specific types of labour and capital goods, and of infrastructure, is seriously flawed. As someone who had absorbed Marshall very deeply, Austin always connected together the long-term development implications of short-term changes and vice versa.

After the war in Europe ended, Austin went to Germany as a member of a small committee on how Germany should be treated in the post-war era. Austin kept a diary which was 'remarkably lucid, coherent and perceptive [conveying] a remarkable picture of the contrasts between town and country, occupiers and occupied, movement on the roads and inertia elsewhere, devastation and disorder on the grand scale but some things still working normally and in good order' (Cairncross 1993: 91). In a letter to Keynes of 16 June 1945 Austin wrote: 'Fact, cold hard fact, is almost certainly different [but he] preferred [his] stories, and as the theologians say when pressed too hard, the story may convey the picture without being literally true' (Austin Robinson 1986a: preface, no page number.) Austin went on to Russia where he emphasised perceptively 'the complete ascendancy of defence over opulence in the mind of the Communist government—an ascendancy that continued throughout the postwar years in a measure unequalled anywhere else' (Cairncross 1993: 94).

Austin drew on his wartime experiences twenty years later when in his Marshall Lectures of 1965, *Economic Planning in the United Kingdom: Some Lessons* (published in 1967), he set out what is still a blueprint for policy-making in a free society which is nevertheless determined to employ all its citizens and direct its overall development in the long term as well as in the short term. He returned to the same themes in his review article (Austin Robinson, 1986b) of Alec Cairncross's account of the transformation from war to peace (Cairncross 1985). As well as playing a key role in manpower planning during the war, Austin was also involved in the determination of the import needs and export possibilities of the United Kingdom in the post-war period. Though he applauded his general approach, Cairncross thought he was too pessimistic about the possible outcomes in his detailed estimates of what was possible and needed.

Austin was never persuaded on this and as late as 1986 pointed out that the original estimates, made in 1943, were made on the assumption that the war against Japan after Germany was defeated would be a long, drawn-out affair, eighteen months to two years or more. Dropping the atomic bombs in 1945 drastically shortened the relevant time period and brought forward the beginning of the transition. Austin argued that they had identified the main problems: the balance of payments where exports were no more than twenty-eight per cent of their 1938 volume. There were shortages of steel, timber, coal and energy generally, and also of certain labour skills. Cairncross summed up: '. . . when the risks are high, as they were in 1947, it is not the outcome that is the best measure of a man's judgement but how the risks seemed to good judges at the time, and there were few who foresaw a future materially more fortunate than [Austin] did' (Cairncross 1993: 108).

Austin returned to university life after the war, feeling that he was not 'tough enough to carry on indefinitely under the pressure [he] had worked during the [war] years' (Austin Robinson 1992: 218). (He certainly fooled us all!) His reputation was such that Whitehall and the Government would not let him go completely. Twice for extended periods he was called back at Stafford Cripp's insistence. He spent a year in London helping to draft the *Economic Survey for 1948* and the *Economic Survey for 1948–52*, six months in Paris with the Office of the European Economic Community (OEEC) ensuring that the Marshall Plan could go through. He chaired 'the committee that drafted the collective report to Congress, showing that we collectively had plans that would make us viable' (Austin Robinson 1992: 219). With that task done, his 'long apprenticeship' ended, he was on 'the threshold of a subsequent forty years as an academic' (ibid.). Nevertheless, he kept his links with Government and Government service for many decades afterwards; he served on selection boards for the Civil Service and through the National Institute of Economic and Social Research (NIESR) and development agencies, he influenced advice given and personnel chosen. His scholarly contributions were recognised by his election as a Fellow of the British Academy in 1955.

V

Increasingly in the post-war period, Austin was drawn towards the problems of developing countries. He was an indefatigable founder of and worker for the International Economic Association (IEA), of which he was Treasurer (1950–9), President (1954–62) and General Editor (1950–80). Austin edited or co-edited twelve volumes of its conferences, world and small. The bulk of them were concerned with development issues. To them all Austin made lucid, carefully considered contributions.[7]

Cairncross (1993) cites the IEA volumes either edited by Austin or to which he contributed chapters in his bibliography of Austin's writings. A selection of the titles alone indicate the breadth of Austin's interests and knowledge: *The Economic Consequences of the Size of Nations* (1960), 'Foreign trade in a developing economy', a chapter by Austin in Kenneth Berrill (ed.), *Economic Development with Special Reference to East Asia* (1964); *Problems in Economic Development* (1965); *The Economics of Education* (edited with John Vaizey, 1966); 'The desirable level of agriculture in advanced industrial economies', a chapter in Ugo Papi and Charles Nunn (eds.), *Economic Problems of Agriculture in Industrial Societies* (1969); *Backward Areas in Advanced Countries* (1969); *Economic Growth in South Asia* (edited with Michael Kidron, 1970); *The Economic Development of Bangladesh* (edited with Keith Griffin) (1974); *Appropriate Techniques for Third World Development* (1979).[8]

---

[7] Ken Arrow and Tony Atkinson (July 1994) have written that Austin thought that the small conferences generated the most valuable discussions but in order to guard against exclusiveness he urged the need for regional conferences. 'As General Editor, he wielded his pencil forcefully'—the pay off was the academic quality of the conference volumes.

[8] I should also mention that Austin was at the 1975 S'Agaro Conference on the Microeconomic Foundations of Macroeconomics which I chaired. I expected we would jointly edit the volume of the same title (1977), but after I sent Austin a draft of the introduction he generously suggested that I do it alone.

His commentaries were always clearly expressed, he combined optimism tempered with caution, and he tried to delineate clearly the boundaries within which academic economists could speak with (relative) authority and outside of which they were trespassing without good reason. Thus in the 1960 volume (which arose from a conference held in 1957—as with the effects of changes in the quantity of money, the publication of IEA volumes is subject to uncertain and variable lags), he wrote that it was 'not for us, as a group of academic economists, to reach political conclusions, and we made no attempt to do so' (xxi). The subject of this particular conference—the relation of size to economic prosperity—had, its editor wrote, received very little discussion in the 180 years since the publication of *The Wealth of Nations*. Typically, Austin started by getting definitions straight and asking why the concept of a nation was relevant for economic analysis. He found the answer in the discontinuities which the boundary of a nation provides—some natural, some institutional, for example tariffs, limits on the movement of labour. In our day (Austin's then), the nation had renewed itself because it had become the unit for Government action and economic activity. (Are we now leaving this era?)

Austin pointed out that the definition of size differed according to the purpose in hand. At the conference they examined the USA (a rich country), Switzerland, Belgium, and Sweden (which were exceptions to the size rule). Austin noted that Switzerland achieved necessary economies of scale by relying on export markets, while Belgium achieved high living standards by concentrating on the unfashionable factors of industrial efficiency and hard work (both dear to Austin's heart). He pointed out that with few exceptions technical economies are exhausted by firms of quite moderate size. He also formed the impression that most of the major industrial economies of scale could be achieved by a relatively high income per capita country with a population of fifty million. Foreign trade could provide an escape (from size) but a precarious one and the economic arguments for further integration of nations, so as to create wider markets, were not overwhelmingly conclusive—the political arguments were, of course, another matter, a topical conclusion in 1996. Size was obviously useful for defence but not exclusively for anything else.

Austin's chapter on foreign trade in developing countries in Kenneth Berrill's 1964 IEA volume started with a list of intellectual debts: Ragnar Nurkse, Harry Johnson, Berrill himself, David Bensusan-Butt, Hla Myint, and Phyllis Deane. He first identified two impacts of international trade on the development process. The first was positive: by aiding specialisation and accumulation in those activities in which productivity is highest, the process of development may be accelerated. The second, which was negative, arose because often the propensity to import runs ahead of the power to export, so imposing constraints associated with threatening balance of payments difficulties. If higher rates of interest are used, for example, to protect foreign exchange reserves they may lead to an uneasy equilibrium characterised by under-loading of the economy and a slow rate of development. Though the ratio of exports to imports reflects in the very long term the size of country concentration and range of endowments, the exports to income ratio is the ultimate constraint, a point which Austin illustrates by reference to the historical experience of the United Kingdom and Japan. A typical Austin emphasis is that the better use of resources may often have been more important than a slightly higher rate of accumulation.

He lists five channels of causation whereby a rise in the exports to income ratio may contribute to the acceleration of growth: by a transfer of resources from low to high productivity areas; by ridding any industry of dependence solely on home markets (but if this is achieved by foreigners' investing and producing the benefits to the home country may be minimal); by the spread of higher industrial efficiency first introduced through international trade; by what we now call the demon-stration effect, knowledge of new products or products not previously known in the country leading to increased desires to produce them and for increased incomes to purchase them. The most important aspect for Austin though is that a high level of trade and possible imports provides a means of escape from both major and minor errors of planning and production. He illustrated these principles by looking at the experiences of India and Pakistan. An important emphasis that emerged was that he was sceptical of the potential of price changes, for example devalua-tions, as opposed to the power of income and quantity changes.

In his opening address to the Second World IEA Congress in Vienna in September 1962, the subject of which was the problems of economic development, Austin said that the topic was chosen deliber-ately, adding: 'Just as in the 1930s almost all schools of economists were concerned with problems of economic fluctuations . . . today [they were] mostly concerned with attempting to understand the causes of economic growth' (Austin Robinson 1965: xv). Austin expressed the wish that these developments would help to eliminate poverty which does so much damage to human happiness and that they would help to close rather than to widen the gap between the poor and the rich nations. He referred to the profound difficulties associated with defining and measuring the stock of capital goods in a world of continually changing prices and technologies, adding that even more insoluble problems arise when we try to define and measure stocks of scientific and engineering knowledge or of freedom of opportunity—all variables which complement one another in the development process.

He criticised Rostow's (then) attempts to generalise historical experiences of rapid growth in more advanced economies and to apply this directly in policies for 'backward countries'. For Austin (as for Marshall) change is continuous, not abrupt, that is to say, in general there is no 'take-off'. Nevertheless, to increase the speed of development attention must be paid as much to creating the right institutions and economic framework as to potential supplies of capital. Especially vital is education to allow developing countries to absorb knowledge and skills. Reflecting the influence of Keynes and his followers, Austin referred to the need to understand the causes of fluctuations in the prices of primary products and to devise schemes to reduce them. Austin returned to the role of foreign trade in development, to export-led growth and balance of payments constraints. He stressed the need to model interrelationships between countries, taking explicit note of the sizes of price and especially of income elasticities of exports and imports. He urged that, in order for small emerging countries to escape from the penalties of smallness, markets be opened to both their traditional and newly emerging exports, even manufactures—still a tract for our times.

The quantity and quality of the population of nations was always a foremost concern of Austin's. He gave explicit voice to it in the volume on *The Economics of Education* (1966) which he edited with John Vaizey, a pioneer of the subject in the United Kingdom. In the introduction, Austin itemised the conceptual difficulties and the deficiencies of the available statistics. He was also careful to show that education was gravely misconceived if viewed solely (or even at all) as a consumption good. In these days of consumer sovereignty in all things, it is refreshing to be reminded that investment and production are vital aspects of economic and social life as well, and that while a balance must be struck, neglect of any is detrimental to human welfare. Austin has wise things to say about taking into account the future effects on activity of the stocks of educated persons as well as analysing the current flows; and that in our statistics, we neglect the collection of data on the educational attainments of immigrants and emigrants at our peril.

In 1969 Austin edited a volume on backward areas in advanced countries. All advanced countries have such areas; one reason why they persist is because individual entrepreneurs cannot be expected to take into account all the factors which from a national point of view are relevant for the location of industries. Austin was (and remained) an unrepentant interventionist. He argued that with the possible exception of the USA, people were not indifferent to where they live or have lived. It followed that the principles of international trade rather than the analysis of a single country were appropriate for considering backward areas and what may be done about them.

*Appropriate Technologies for Third World Development* (1979) was a topic especially suited to Austin's humanitarianism and 'nuts and bolts' philosophy. All his working life he emphasised that development on the spot using already established communities was most to be preferred. Promoting the appropriate technologies for such a process had been hampered by artificially cheap capital facilities, tax holidays, and similar measures. He also stressed that there are appropriate products as well as methods of production, very much a close-to-the-ground view which reflected his frustrated engineer side—as did his emphasis on the crucial role which the ability to provide adequate maintenance of machines plays in the process of development.

Other volumes which he edited relate to developing countries such as Sri Lanka and Bangladesh, on which we comment below. Austin also wrote many reports on development themes. His biographer, Alec Cairncross, has singled out for special praise a report for the United Nations Development Programme, which Austin wrote in the mid-1970s at the request of I. G. Patel (who had been his pupil in the 1940s). Cairncross regards it as the single best and most impressive account of the principles of development to come from Austin's pen. We discuss now its main features, features already present in embryo in his 1920s work in India and 1930s work in Africa.[9]

His focus was on 'the massive underemployment and unemployment in many developing countries'. Austin asks why they are so persistent and he sets out six constraints on a policy of increasing

---

[9] This section is based on the 1996 Kingsley Martin Memorial Lecture (Harcourt, forthcoming). The page references (150–2) are to Alec Cairncross's discussion of the report (Cairncross 1993).

demand to draw these workers into employment and allow incomes to rise.

The usually dominant constraint is the failure of domestic food production to match expanding incomes, so that import demand rises. Unless exports match this, expansion is constrained by balance of payments problems. Austin's orders of magnitude for a typical developing country with population growth of two-and-a-half per cent a year and a target growth rate of seven per cent a year is that the constraint will bite if agricultural output does not grow by five per cent a year. Top priority must therefore be given to overcoming this constraint by creating the necessary agricultural surplus.

Austin also stressed that the 'weakness in the exchange mechanism between town and country was sometimes the main constraint'. Undernourished farm workers consumed the additional food so that the demands of the urban population, swollen by an inflow from rural areas, went into imports: hence the need for effective organisation for buying, financing, transporting, and distributing the agricultural surplus needed in the city. As befits an economist of the same university as Malthus, Austin also recognised the need to limit the import content of consumer goods, not least 'luxury' goods.

The fourth limitation was inadequate accumulation due to low saving rates, inefficient methods of finance and also the high import content of investment.

The fifth and sixth constraints are associated with the limitations of skills available—administrative as well as productive, especially in industry where education systems may not be geared to produce them. Austin thought it may be necessary to create ' "small-scale low-capital-intensive occupations" with "very large numbers of small craftsmen, traders, entrepreneurs starting successful small business" ' (151) in order to bypass the problem.

Strangely, Austin does not mention cultural factors which could be an important part of the explanation of differences between countries, for example acceptance of discipline in the industrial sector: strange, because, as we have seen, his letters from India and Africa are full of details on just these characteristics of the local populations.

Austin then discussed the dual economy aspect of development— the contrast between modern sectors and traditional sectors, and the choice this raises of whether to go for rapid development through faster growth and lower capital inputs per jobs, or a gradual transition and the consequent need to 'revitalise and reinvigorate the traditional economy'. He had advocated the latter advance in the 1930s.

Finally, he recognised fully the problems associated with rapid population growth which in some cases meant absorbing 'as much as three quarters of all national investment . . . in merely standing still' (152).

We may illustrate Austin's approach, in particular, his well developed sense of relevant orders of magnitude in the simple macro development models which he carried in his head, by briefly examining the arguments of his Kingsley Martin Memorial Lecture, 'The economic development of Malthusia' (Austin Robinson 1974), which was given in Cambridge on 6 March 1974. There, he used Bangladesh as his example. He started by stating the question which was asked '[o]ne hundred and seventy five years ago [by] a shy young Fellow of Jesus'. The question is 'whether economic development was possible, or whether it would be frustrated by the growth of population' (Austin Robinson 1974: 521). To say that 'Malthus has been discredited by subsequent history' is, says Austin, 'a very dangerous half truth', for while the advanced countries have broken through the Malthusian barrier into cumulative growth, the rest of the world has not; it 'continues to live under conditions of near stagnation, little above the subsistence level, in very much the conditions that Malthus envisaged' (Austin Robinson 1974: 521).

Austin worked out two scenarios for the next twenty years in Bangladesh according to whether it continued with Malthusian-type birth and death rates, or with European-type through which it had broken out of the Malthusian trap. He relates these statistical exercises to the actual plans then being proposed in Bangladesh. His sense of the interrelationships of the broad aspects of the economy is beautifully done. He shows that in the most favourable scenario, a considerable proportion of the problems of unemployment, underemployment and poverty would be overcome by the end of the period; while with the other scenario, Malthus's worst fears would have been realised and an opportunity available now (1974) would have been lost for ever. It is pleasing to report in 1996 that Austin's 'waking hopes' (Austin Robinson 1974: 532) are nearer to being achieved than his worst fears realised (see, for example, Reddaway (1996)).

## VI

In the Faculty of Economics and Politics itself, Austin not only taught but also played a major role in its administration. The building which now bears his name (it was so christened at the party in honour of his ninetieth birthday) is very much the outcome of his enthusiasm and persistence. Austin was appointed to a Chair in 1950. As well as lecturing and supervising, Austin had long spells as Secretary of the Faculty Board and also as its Chairman. The clashes between the Keynesians and the Robertsonians were fierce and unyielding in the post-war years. Austin did his best to bring peace and maintain cohesion. James Meade, who came to Cambridge in the late 1950s and who was witness to some of the toughest debates, thought that Austin tried hard to be fair and obtain principled compromises, even if often in practice they favoured one side more than the other. In any event, Austin was faced with a virtually impossible task in a faculty where consensus is defined as agreeing with whoever is speaking.

In September 1965 Austin retired from his Chair (he was succeeded by Joan). He was to have nearly thirty years more of extremely active life. He was physically frail towards the end—he was knocked off his bicycle by a motorist about ten years before he died and injured his back. It continued to trouble him despite the efforts of a renowned osteopath who ministers, usually most effectively, to the underworld of the back sufferers of Cambridge, including the present writer. Nevertheless, some of his best papers were written in his eighties and early nineties. The editors of the *Cambridge Journal of Economics* often used him as a reliable, critical, but fair-minded referee. In a book published in 1984, *Economics in Disarray*, Austin's contribution, a comment on Peter Wiles on the full-cost principle, stands out for its clarity and deep economic intuition. It reflects his knowledge of firms, his exchanges in the 1950s with the full-cost theorists of Oxford, and his experiences from his years as a Syndic of the Cambridge University Press. And, of course, he wrote his superb autobiographical essay. 'My apprenticeship as an economist' for Szenberg's 1992 volume on *Eminent Economists*, which, together with his obituary of Keynes in the March 1947 *Economic Journal*, most typically reflect Austin's great strengths as an economist, perceptive human being, and elegant stylist.

## VII

Austin was elected to a Fellowship in Sidney Sussex in 1931. From then on the college was a central focus of his life, especially after Joan died in 1983 and Austin moved from the house in Grange Road to a flat opposite the college itself. Roger Andrew, a former Bursar of Sidney who was close to Austin, writes: '[Austin's] enthusiasm for the College and his concern for it [are] known only to those within its framework. The ideal for College life is the City State of Plato in which like minds administer and further the affairs of the establishment. Austin filled this position admirably . . . . His philosophy was to guide and to bring those other members by persuasion to a similar belief'. His daughter, Barbara Jeffrey, writes that 'he also felt it was important to college life that people should be able to get on well with one another'.

In his address at the Memorial Service for Austin in November 1993, Alan Hughes, Austin's colleague and an economics Fellow of Sidney, spoke of Austin's role as an active mender of the investments committee responsible for the management of the stock-market portfolio set up in the 1960s, of his many gifts of, for example, silver plate and carpets for public rooms and of the 'exceptionally generous bequest to Sidney to further education and research'. He described Austin in retirement 'as a familiar figure in college, especially in the continuation of his life-long association with the chapel. His interest in sport . . . meant that any other fellow with a similar interest in following [horse racing, and rugby] on TV would often find an agreeable companion in Austin', not least because of the wine he provided to offset the bitter reaction to an Oxford try on 'a gloomy mid-winter Tuesday'.

## VIII

Austin had a long life, worked extraordinarily hard, and was associated with a breath-taking number of institutions in academia, Government, and internationally. Of all these institutions he was, in his own words, a willing 'slave'. As with many of his generation, he found delegation difficult and this caused clashes and misunderstandings, sometimes leaving Austin feeling hurt and unappreciated by other officers of the organisations for which he worked so hard and, overall, served so well.

I wrote to a selection of people from these and other institutions who knew Austin, asking for their impressions and evaluations. What emerged is the respect and affection in which he was held in so many spheres: respect for his outstanding abilities, affection for him as a person even though his stature and personality were such that I do not think my correspondents felt they were able to get really close to him, much as they may have wished to.

I start with Gavin Reid (14 September 1993) who came to know Austin when at Darwin on a sabbatical in 1987–8. Reid 'was impressed with his willingness to extend courtesy to an academic transient', and he thought that Austin set 'very high standards' which nevertheless were achievable by 'mere mortals'.

Robin Matthews (6 March 1994) worked closely with Austin in the 1940s, 1950s and 1960s in the Faculty and also on the *Economic Journal* when Matthews was review editor. He singled out Austin's contributions to economics, emphasising the *range* of topics to which he made original contributions. Though Austin did not keep up to date with the literature, he 'had a knack of identifying what was important'. Matthews identified four fields: firm and industry, development economics, 'practical macro' from the viewpoint of the economic advisor (all predictable), and the economics of R and D; not so predictable, but just as impressive. Matthews concluded that Austin was a most serious and optimistic economist who 'believed that economics was capable of doing good'.

Frank Hahn's views (6 June 1994) are, as ever, complementary to those of Matthews.

> Austin was a born 'mandarin' . . . impatient of theory which abstracted from the 'real world'. His aim was to improve the world whether it was the small world of Cambridge, the Indian subcontinent or the Royal Economic Society. His memoranda . . . were perfect instances of what such writings should be: lucid, precise, and brief.

Referring to Austin's many years as Secretary of the RES, Hahn highlights Austin's role 'as the moving force getting Keynes' writings collected and edited', a judgement which is echoed by several other economists who knew the background story to the Keynes papers. Hahn concluded:

> Austin was socially a cut above many of his more recent colleagues. He had enormous self-confidence, and spoke in upper-class Cambridge English. He was also apt to favour those he knew—especially in Cambridge—when it came to jobs and honours. This was not really a sign of the 'old school tie' syndrome. He simply took it for granted that the best minds, and indeed the morally most reliable minds, were to be found in Cambridge. After that he

would allow some merit to Oxford and London, but not much beyond that. This was a failing, but one found it hard to blame him for being faithful to beliefs formed when England and its Universities were very different from what they are now.

Hahn's conclusion is, I believe, accurate, revealing of both writer and subject, stating things which ought to be stated but which could only be done by someone with Hahn's insight and self-confidence.

Austin was long associated with the NIESR. Two former Directors, Bryan Hopkin and David Worswick, sent me recollections of Austin's role there and much else besides. Bryan was a pupil of Austin's at Cambridge in the 1930s, David was an Oxford graduate. Their appraisals naturally differ, at least on the surface but not on fundamentals if read carefully between the lines, especially Worswick's. Worswick tells an amusing tale of how, at Robert Hall's prompting, he concocted a seventy-and-over rule to rid the Executive Committee of Austin and one other 'old man' (which soon took off Hall himself). To their credit, 'both departed gracefully . . . without enquiring too closely into the origin of the rule'. Worswick then described his personal experiences of working with Austin when Worswick was President of the RES and in the IEA, when he often remembered that rule. He could not condone Austin treating the edition of the Keynes papers and the IEA as 'personal fiefdoms'. His reason told that it would have been better if Austin had brought in more and younger people to take over some of his responsibilities. Yet, Worswick concluded, Austin 'was so good at what he did . . . that [he was] not so sure!'

Hopkin (5 June 1994) reported on Austin's massive contributions during Hopkin's time as Director (1952–7). Austin 'took a detailed interest in all the work . . . going on, [gave] wise and informed counsel . . .' and personal support to Hopkin. Austin was the ideal person to fill such a role because he knew and was respected by so many people, he criticised work incisively but gently, and was well behaved even in the most difficult circumstances.

I turn now to American evaluations, starting with Paul Samuelson's (7 July 1994), and then Bob Solow's (17 June 1994). When President of the IEA, Samuelson 'was most content to have [Austin] run me and all in sight'. He thought that, as an economist, Austin was original and lucid, that he had good judgement which was not affected by dislike or personality. He considered it remarkable that he 'never heard [Austin] utter a sour criticism of any in the Cambridge menagerie'. Solow praised Austin's role in the IEA, highlighting the length of the conferences under Austin's guidance, which enabled serious discussion of papers, and that Austin's force of character made sure that authors wrote the papers that the conference needed. Solow liked Austin, not least for his plain speaking, which contrasted with '[a] lot of Cambridge conversation [which struck Solow] as a move in a game (whose rules and objectives [he did not] know)'. I wish to emphasise the importance of the views of Samuelson and Solow—both liked Austin 'a lot'—because another distinguished American economist felt that Austin did not like Americans and that he was, in a thoughtless English way, anti-Semitic—as well as being imperious and overbearing on occasions.

In the body of the essay I tried to give due weight to Austin's contributions to development economics. One person who knew of these at first hand is Esra Bennathan. In a letter of 18 July 1992 to Alec Cairncross (which they kindly let me see), Bennathan mentions that after being interviewed by Austin for the Civil Service in 1961 he discovered that an 'admired colleague' at Birmingham regarded 'Austin with the utmost suspicion, a dangerous figure of the Establishment, a duplicitous nature hiding behind an ascetic and saintly face'. Bennathan's long experience of Austin was 'totally different'. His lengthy letter is concerned not only with Austin's crucial gifts as an economist but also with his practical Christianity, especially in helping academics in what became Bangladesh both to escape persecution and to build up their libraries and laboratories.

Bennathan summed up his idea of Austin's 'private and instinctive' approach to development issues: '[Austin] work[ed] through and for people . . . . [He] . . . measur[ed] his effectiveness by his effect upon them, their actions and their progress . . . [Austin] nurtur[ed], encourag[ed] and sponsored those he [thought] promising, without expecting too much'. Bennathan found this totally impressive and sympathetic.

Finally, Bennathan quotes the oral tradition that Keynes regarded Austin as 'his brightest student'. [Bennathan] had 'never heard a clearer explanation of Ramsey's social utility function, and the asymptote to Bliss, than that given by Austin in the Diamond Hotel, Poona, surrounded . . . by very actively loving American couples relaxing from meditative exertions in Rashneeshi's Ashram just round the corner'.

I. G. Patel (5 July 1955) knew Austin as a supervisor (1946–9) and then 'in many capacities'—visits to India (sometimes as a family guest), IEA conferences, consultant to UNDP, Council of the RES. His first impression of him was 'of a very generous and rather shy and self-effacing person'; his final summing up: 'Generous, self-effacing and deeply committed'.

Hans Singer (4 October 1994) also paid tribute to Austin's generosity and first-rate intelligence. Austin was the secretary of 'a small committee at Cambridge' set up in the early 1930s to help two German refugee students of whom Singer was one. Though not Singer's Ph.D. supervisor, Austin gave him 'invariably helpful' advice on some problems in his dissertation. Austin's 'empirical approach and clear language were a great help to a new arrival, bewildered . . . by the incomprehensible lectures and papers by Wittgenstein and Piero Sraffa [as well as] by the intricacies of liquidity preference'. Always 'young Singer' to Austin, 'up to shortly before his death people . . . from Cambridge [carried] greetings from [Austin] to "young Singer"'.

Perhaps Susan Howson (3 October 1994) may be allowed a last word: 'I have a great admiration, as well as love, for Austin, who always struck me as one of the most sane members of our profession'.


# IX


To the end of his life, Austin remained mentally rigorous and alert. During the alarm a few years ago about the impact on health of certain French cheeses, Austin was asked at lunch in Sidney Sussex by a Fellow in his late eighties whether they should eat them. Austin said: 'It is only dangerous for pregnant women and old people—and we do not belong to either category'. Austin had a fine sense of humour which was often combined with sharp, even wicked end lines about his contemporaries, delivered with a twinkle. He enjoyed gossip and barbed, but not malicious comments in private, for he was, first and foremost a kindly man, who nevertheless was realistic about, and comforted by the fact that foibles as well as achievements characterise the human condition.

Though Austin is on record as saying that the optimum length of time to see a grandchild is half an hour, both he and Joan were proud and fond of their five grandchildren and had, especially after the arrival of grandchildren, excellent rapport with their daughters and their respective husbands, who in turn appreciated the love and support they could depend upon. In May 1993, Austin had a bad fall and was taken to Addenbrookes Hospital in Cambridge. He died peacefully on the morning of 1 June, having heard some of his favourite Bible readings and prayers the night before.

Austin Robinson was the role model *par excellence* for the aspiring applied political economist. At his Memorial Service in Sidney Sussex Chapel on 20 November 1993, one of the readings was the parable of the talents. Some thought this a peculiar choice; but a close friend who knew Austin intimately thought it peculiarly appropriate because Austin could not abide those who did not use their talents to the full. For Austin economics was a 'hands on' subject—the sole object of theory was for it to be applied to explanation and then to policy proposals: 'no economist is more dangerous than the pure theorist without practical experience and instinctive understanding of the real world that he is attempting to analyze, seeking precision in a world of imprecision, in a world he does not understand' (Austin Robinson 1992: 221). His Christian upbringing, in which works were emphasised even more than faith, and his wartime experiences led him to a life of service to his discipline and to humanity, and especially to those least able to help themselves, victims of both oppression and the malfunctionings of social systems.

G. C. HARCOURT
*Jesus College, Cambridge*

*Note.* I especially thank, but in no way implicate, Marjorie Chibnall, Phyllis Deane, Alan Hughes, and Barbara Jeffrey for their comments on a draft of the memoir. In writing it I have drawn extensively on Alec Cairncross's 1993 biography of Austin and on Austin's 1992 autobiographical essay in Szenberg (1992). Finally I am most grateful to the economists who responded so willingly to my request for their recollections of Austin and their evaluations of his contributions.

# References

Berrill, Kenneth (ed.) (1964), *Economic Development with Special Reference to East Asia* (London: Macmillan).

Cairncross, Alec (1985), *Years of Recovery: British Economic Policy 1945–51* (London: Methuen).

— (1993), *Austin Robinson. The Life of an Economic Advisor* (Houndmills, Hants: Macmillan; New York: St Martin's Press).

Davis, J. Merle (ed.) (1933), *Modern Industry and the African* (London: Macmillan; new edn., London: Frank Cass, 1967).

Hailey, Lord (ed.) (1938), *African Survey* (Oxford: Oxford University Press; reprinted 1945).

Harcourt, G. C. (ed.) (1977), *The Microeconomic Foundations of Macroeconomics* (London: Macmillan).

— (ed.) (1985), *Keynes and his Contemporaries* (London: Macmillan).

— (forthcoming), 'Two Views on Development: Austin and Joan Robinson', *Cambridge Journal of Economics*.

Kahn, Richard (1985), 'The Cambridge "Circus" (1)' in Harcourt (1985), 42–51.

— (1987), 'Shove, Gerald Frank (1888–1947)' in John Eatwell, Murray Milgate, and Peter Newman (eds.) (1987), *The New Palgrave. A Dictionary of Economics*, 4 (London: Macmillan), 327–8.

Keynes, J. M. (1919), *The Economic Consequences of the Peace* (London: Macmillan) *C.W.*, Vol. II, 1971.

— (1936), *The General Theory of Employment, Interest and Money* (London: Macmillan) *C.W.*, Vol. VII, 1973.

— (1940), *How to Pay for the War. A Radical Plan for the Chancellor of the Exchequer* (London: Macmillan) *C.W.*, Vol. XXII, 1978, 40–155.

Reddaway, Brian (1996), 'The Bangladesh Economy in a World Perspective' in Abu Abdullah and Azizur Rahman Khan (eds.), *State, Market and Development: Essays in Honour of Rahman Sobhan* (Dhaka: University Press), 289–304.

Robinson, E. A. G. and others (none explicitly named) (1928), *The British Crown and the Indian States* (London: P.S. King).

— (1931), *The Structure of Competitive Industry*, Cambridge: (Cambridge University Press; rev. edn. 1953).

— (1936), 'Mr Keynes on Money', *The Economist*, 24 February, 471–2.

— (1941), *Monopoly* (Cambridge: Cambridge University Press; reprinted 1956).

— (1947), 'John Maynard Keynes 1883–1946', *Economic Journal*, LVII, 1–68.

— (1960), 'The Size of the Nation and the Cost of Administration' in E.A.G. Robinson (ed.), *The Economic Consequences of the Size of Nations* (London: Macmillan), xiii–xxii.

— (1964), 'Foreign Trade: Foreign Trade in a Developing Country', in Berrill (1964), 212–32.

— (ed.) (1965), *Problems in Economic Development* (London: Macmillan).

— (1967), *Economic Planning in the United Kingdom: Some Lessons* (Cambridge: Cambridge University Press).

— (1969), 'The Desirable Level of Agriculture in Advanced Industrial Economies' in Ugo Papi and Charles Nunn (eds.), *Economic Problems of Agriculture in Industrial Societies* (London: Macmillan), 26–50.

— (mid-1970s), *Future Tasks for UNDP: Report to the Administrator of the United Nations Development Program*.

— (1974), 'The Economic Development of Malthusia', *Modern Asian Studies*, 8, 521–34.

— (ed.) (1979), *Appropriate Technologies for Third World Development* (London: Macmillan).

— and J.E. Vaizey (eds.) (1966), *The Economics of Education* (London: Macmillan).

— and Michael Kidron (eds.) (1970), *Economic Development in South Asia* (London: Macmillan).

Robinson, Austin (1984), 'Comment', in Wiles and Routh (1984), 222–32.

— (1985), 'The Cambridge "Circus" (2)', in Harcourt (1985), 52–7.

— (1986a), *First Sight of Postwar Germany May-June 1945*, private circulation (printed by Brian Allen, The Cantelupe Press, Great Abington, Cambridge).

— (1986b), 'The Economic Problems of the Transition from War to Peace: 1945–49', *Cambridge Journal of Economics*, 10, 165–85.

— (1992), 'My Apprenticeship as an Economist' in Szenberg (1992), 203–21.

Sargant Florence, P. (1932), 'Review of *The Structure of Competitive Industry* (1931)', *Economic Journal*, XLII, 66–70.

— (1941), 'Review of *Monopoly*', *Economic Journal*, LI, 481–3.

Szenberg, Michael (ed.) (1992), *Eminent Economists. Their Life Philosophies* (Cambridge: Cambridge University Press).

Tahir, Pervez (1990), 'Some Aspects of Development and Underdevelopment: Critical Perspectives on Joan Robinson' (Cambridge: unpublished Ph.D. dissertation).

Wiles, Peter and Guy Routh (eds.) (1984), *Economics in Disarray* (Oxford: Basil Blackwell).

JAMES SUTHERLAND            *James Russell & Sons*

*Proceedings of the British Academy*, **94**, 735–750

# James Runcieman Sutherland
# 1900–1996

JAMES SUTHERLAND was born on 26 April 1900 in Aberdeen. His father, a stockbroker, emigrated to South Africa soon after his son's birth, and Sutherland, together with his two elder sisters, Margaret and Nellie, were therefore brought up by their mother. Perhaps because of this he was particularly close to his maternal grandfather, John Runcieman, and to his Uncle Frank, his mother's brother. His grandfather had a farm at Auchmill, some fifty miles north of Aberdeen, and Sutherland spent his summer holidays there throughout his childhood. The Runcieman family had been farmers and gardeners since at least the mid-eighteenth century, a fact that Sutherland recalled with pleasure and that must have helped to determine his own lifelong interest in gardening. His adoption of the name Runcieman (he was christened simply James) marks the importance of his mother's family in his upbringing. On his father's side, his grandfather had been a minister of the United Free Church of Scotland and there was some expectation in the family that Sutherland might follow the same calling. His father's sister, Aunt Allie, was remembered with affection. She regularly took her nephew and his sisters to performances at His Majesty's Theatre in Aberdeen and it was there that he first encountered Shakespeare in a production of *Macbeth* by F. R. Benson's company and *The Taming of the Shrew*, with Martin Harvey as Petruchio. Aunt Allie later moved to London where Sutherland visited her at the age of twenty, his first journey outside Scotland.

Just before his tenth birthday he was deeply affected by the death from appendicitis of his younger sister, Nellie, whom he remembered to

© The British Academy 1997.

the end of his life as 'vivacious, pretty and intelligent'. From the age of
seven he was educated at Aberdeen Grammar School. In the Upper
School he was particularly influenced by the classics master, George
Middleton, who had narrowly missed appointment to a chair at the
University of Aberdeen, and under his guidance Sutherland won the
Smith Gold Metal, awarded annually for translation from English to
Latin. In English he was taught by William Murison, author of a
substantial book on *English Composition*, whom he remembered for
his 'insistent exposure of pomposity', for mining 'a deep vein in the
Scottish character that leads to an instinctive tendency to plain speaking'. At his first attempt at the Higher School Certificate Examination
he did well in Latin and Greek but failed in mathematics and, as he
liked to recall with a wry bemusement, in English. He passed in both,
however, in the following year.

In 1917 he entered the University of Aberdeen and in his first year
took Latin, Greek, English and zoology. He had intended to read for an
Honours degree in classics but he found the Latin course 'dull and
disappointing'. He was surfeited by a diet of Tertullian's *Apologia* in
the first term and the Greek course was insufficiently challenging
compared with what he had already achieved at school. He was, however, encouraged to specialise in English by the lectures of Professor A.
A. Jack whom he greatly admired and whose influence he often warmly
acknowledged in later life. His sister Margaret, who had graduated in
English, was by this time Professor Jack's research assistant. Jack, who
had given the Clark Lectures at Cambridge in 1914, succeeded H. J. C.
Grierson in the Aberdeen Chair in 1915. He ranged in his own published work from Chaucer and Shakespeare to Thackeray and the
Brontës and he commanded the respect and admiration of his students.
Eric Linklater, a contemporary of Sutherland both at school and university and a close friend, described Jack as possessing 'a heart in love
with . . . Shakespeare's panegyric tongue . . . and a learned delight in
his compact imagination', together with 'the innocence, the capacity for
pure amazement, that is the key to Wordsworth'.[1] Sutherland commented that Jack 'was remarkably sensitive to linguistic impressions of all
kinds . . . and he made us feel that we were all his intellectual equals,
and that we could be trusted to respond to the verbal nuances and nicer
distinctions he habitually offered for our consideration'. These qualities

[1]  Eric Linklater, *The Man on My Back: An Autobiography* (London, 1941), p. 76.

clearly had a major influence on the direction of Sutherland's academic development.

He graduated with a first class degree in 1921, having made no definite decision about a career. The early family ambition that he should enter the ministry had been quietly abandoned and he now considered journalism. Much of his spare time at university had been taken up with student journalism, first as a contributor to the thriving college magazine *Alma Mater* and then as editor. *Alma Mater* appeared eleven times a year, contained news and acted as a record of university affairs but also had a substantial literary section. Sutherland contributed poetry, satirical verse drama, a mock-Pepysian diary on the tribulations of university life, and pseudonymous letters, sometimes on both sides of a question. All this, together with the practical experience of dealing with contributors, printers, and, on occasion, outraged readers, no doubt encouraged his later interest in the minutiae of Restoration and eighteenth-century journalism but it bore no immediate fruit. He was offered a few months' trial with the *Aberdeen Free Press*, but the terms were poor and he turned it down. He now somewhat reluctantly applied for admission to a teachers' training course, and gained some urgent practical experience by taking over a further education class in English literature, but almost immediately he experienced one of those turns of fortune that determine the pattern of a life. One of his lecturers at Aberdeen had taught for a time in Canada and had been asked at short notice if he could suggest someone to fill a vacant instructorship in English at the University of Saskatchewan in Saskatoon at what must have seemed the princely salary of $2,000 a year. Sutherland left almost immediately on a boat from Glasgow to Montreal, a ten-day passage, followed by a seventy-two hour train journey to Saskatoon.

At Saskatoon he taught freshman English, a junior set-text class beginning with Chaucer, and a senior course on English Romantic poets. Saskatoon was a new city. It had been founded in 1882 and became the site of the University of Saskatchewan as recently as 1906, but it was a vigorous community and Sutherland recollected his two years there with pleasure. On his return to Britain for the summer vacation in 1922 he made the first of many visits to the United States, taking in Minneapolis, Chicago, and New York.

In 1923 Sutherland entered Merton College, Oxford, to work under David Nichol Smith for the B.Litt. This move, encouraged by Professor Jack, and supported by the award of the Murray Scholarship from Aberdeen, was a decisive one, for Nichol Smith can be seen as a focal

point of many factors which were important to the development of
Sutherland's critical practice and to his conception of English as a
university discipline. Many of these influences centred, in fact, on
Scottish universities. Nichol Smith was himself a Scot, born in Edinburgh in 1875, and he had read English at Edinburgh under David
Masson, a former Professor of English at University College London,
one of the great founders of English as a university subject which he
perceived as necessitating both linguistic and literary study, together
with an awareness of the need for history as a complementary discipline. In 1895, the year of Nichol Smith's graduation, Masson retired
and was succeeded by George Saintsbury who employed Nichol Smith
briefly as a research assistant. Later, he became an assistant to Walter
Raleigh who had succeeded A. C. Bradley in the Glasgow English Chair
in 1900, and when Raleigh was appointed to the first English Chair at
Oxford in 1904, Nichol Smith, after a period as Professor of English at
Newcastle, followed him to become Goldsmiths' Reader in 1908. His
interests were predominantly, though not exclusively, in the eighteenth
century, especially in relation to Augustan responses to Shakespeare,
and he was a distinguished editor and annotator of eighteenth-century
texts. The combination of scholarship and criticism that is suggested by
this descent was one which Sutherland, always aware of a kind of
apostolic succession in the teaching profession, was in turn to make
his own. His own warm and sympathetic assessment of Nichol Smith
was expressed in the obituary he wrote for *Proceedings of the British
Academy*, 1962.

His first intention had been to work on the Shakespearian editor
Edward Capell, but he was guided by his supervisor towards Nicholas
Rowe and began research which took him to the core of eighteenth-
century literary London since Rowe, editor, translator, poet, and dra-
matist, was a friend of Congreve, Addison, Steele, Swift, and Pope. He
began seeking information about Rowe in the files of Queen Anne
newspapers, thus initiating what was to prove a lifelong research
interest in Restoration and eighteenth-century journalism. Lecture
courses he attended included Nichol Smith on 'Early Eighteenth-
Century Literature' and Percy Simpson on 'Textual Criticism'.

Sutherland gained the Chancellor's English Essay Prize in 1925 for
an essay on 'Form in Literature' and he continued to write verse,
publishing in *Outlook*, *Cherwell*, and *Isis*. In 1926 some of this work,
together with poems from *Alma Mater*, was collected and published by
Blackwell in a volume entitled *Leucocholy*. Many of the poems are

melancholy or ironic reflections on the limitations of life as a student but, while they express common enough frustrations and anxieties of youth, they also point to a real concern to probe the relationship between literature and life, a concern that may have derived from A. A. Jack who, Linklater says, always insisted that a proper reading of literature 'required some small apprenticeship in living'.[2] It may also reflect the fact that many of his close friends were ex-servicemen (Sutherland had been medically graded C3 in 1918 and was not called up), and an awareness of events in an unsettled post-war Europe. On a visit to Italy in 1924, for example, he witnessed a blackshirt demonstration in Rome. He always recognised, as he said later, 'that there are more important things in life than even great literature, and . . . the critic who is not aware of this is not to be trusted'.[3]

In the summer of 1925 Sutherland accepted a one-term vacancy in University College Southampton and in the autumn he was appointed to a lectureship in the University of Glasgow where he stayed for five years. The Regius Professor was William Macneile Dixon, who had followed Raleigh in the chair, and amongst colleagues were Peter Alexander, who himself became Regius Professor in 1935, and Bernard Wright, who later held the chair at Southampton. The department was large, with 700 ordinary students, divided into three groups for lectures. Sutherland, apart from tutorials and classes with honours students, was assigned a course on European thought and culture from the Middle Ages to the Renaissance and, as he later said, with a characteristic touch of amused self-deprecation: 'Most of what I imparted to my students must have been new to . . . them, for it was certainly new to me.' In Glasgow he completed his thesis on Rowe which was accepted for the B.Litt. in 1927. An offshoot of this work was the handsome edition of *Three Plays* by Nicholas Rowe published by Eric Partridge's Scholartis Press in 1929, and an article, 'Shakespeare's Imitators in the Eighteenth Century', in *Modern Language Review* (1933). He also broadened his range beyond the eighteenth century with an edition of Dekker's *Shoemaker's Holiday* (1931). Moreover, in 1930, he published *Jasper Weeple*, a Utopian fable (he later called it 'a poor man's *Gulliver's Travels*') in which Jasper visits the idyllic society of Midanglia, finding there a satiric contrast to contemporary England. The usual targets—education, the law, marriage— are attacked with some verve, but overall the story

[2] See above, n. 1.
[3] James R. Sutherland, *The English Critic* (London, 1952), p. 14.

lacks narrative drive and the writing is too literary and even toned. Sutherland later recognised its weaknesses but for some years he nurtured the ambition to succeed in fiction, completing two further, though unpublished, novels.

At this time Sutherland was something of a sportsman. He enjoyed tennis which he had first played on a court on his grandfather's farm and he had played rugby football at stand-off half for his school and university in Aberdeen. At Oxford he had taken up hockey, and now in Glasgow he played regularly for the university team. He was also a keen walker and modest golfer.

He left Glasgow in 1930 when he was appointed by C. J. Sisson to a Senior Lectureship at University College London and he was to remain within the University of London for the rest of his career, becoming Professor of English at Birkbeck College from 1936–44; Professor of English Language and Literature at Queen Mary College from 1944–51; and Lord Northcliffe Professor of Modern English Literature, University College London, from 1951–67.

In 1931 he married Helen Dircks, daughter of Will H. Dircks, an editor and critic. She was herself the author of two volumes of imagist verse, *Finding* (1918) and *Passenger* (1920) and later developed an independent and successful career as an advertising copy-writer. The young couple are remembered from the early days of their marriage as elegant ballroom dancers. Dancing had long been one of Sutherland's accomplishments and he once wrote that 'the slow fox-trot . . . is enshrined on my memory as one of the notable cultural achievements of the 1920's'. The marriage was to be a long and happy one. They lived at first in London, but soon moved to Long Wittenham, south of Oxford, to a house with a garden sloping to the River Windrush. They stayed there for twenty years, moving then to nearby Sutton Courtenay, to a house with a substantially larger garden. In Oxfordshire, Sutherland was able to pursue a love of gardening which continued into his eighties, and in the Windrush he could indulge an enthusiasm for fishing which had begun when he was a boy and which took him to holidays not only in Scotland but in Ireland and Norway.

In publishing his first critical book *The Medium of Poetry* (1933) in the 'Hogarth Lectures in Literature' series, issued by Virginia and Leonard Woolf, Sutherland joined a distinguished list. Previous contributors to the series had included H. J. C. Grierson, Edwin Muir, Allardyce Nicoll, and G. D. H. Cole. Here he develops ideas which had taken earlier shape in his submission for the Chancellor's English

Essay Prize and he acknowledges the influence of A. A. Jack 'who started several of the hares that I have chased in the following pages'. He examines 'how far the medium of poetry influences the mind of the poet', distinguishing broadly between poets who 'translate' experience into verse, and for whom fidelity to the experience itself is paramount, with others who are responsive to suggestions arising from the metre, rhyme scheme and form of the medium itself. The most penetrating parts of the discussion are attempts to catch the poet in mid-thought by the analysis of early drafts, a method particularly effective in the chapter on 'Rhyme'.

*The Medium of Poetry* was a gathering together of threads from earlier work. In London, Sutherland now had for the first time the opportunity to use the resources of the British Museum, the Public Record Office, and the Victoria and Albert Museum to pursue the kind of archival research that he found increasingly absorbing. He at first began to prepare an edition of the plays of Susannah Centlivre, a friend of Nicholas Rowe, for the Scholartis Press but this had to be abandoned when the press ran into financial difficulties. Some of the research was, however, published in a later article, 'The Progress of Error: Mrs Centlivre and the Biographers' (*Review of English Studies* (1942)). This shows Sutherland at his best, using minute knowledge of the period to support urbane but extremely sharp reflections on the inventions and inaccuracies which accumulate in biographical tradition. Work at the Public Record Office on lawsuits on the equity side of Chancery eventually marked out two major lines of research: on Defoe and Pope. His first article on Defoe, 'Some Early Troubles of Daniel Defoe' (*Review of English Studies* (1933)) showed a characteristic eye for detail and pertinacity in pursuing a complex trail of evidence. It threw light on Defoe's early commercial activities by examining nine different lawsuits in which Defoe was accused of malpractice or failure to honour agreements and obligations. 'A Note on the Last Years of Defoe' (*Modern Language Notes* (1934)) adduced further material from Chancery records to show how Defoe was pursued by litigation to the very end of his life. For some scholars minutiae of this kind would have had an essentially antiquarian interest but Sutherland saw beyond the events themselves to the picture of a man more than usually engaged with the life of his time. Defoe appealed to him precisely because he was not simply a literary figure but a man who, when he published *Robinson Crusoe* at the age of fifty-nine, 'invented' the novel almost as a sideline to a life of multifarious activity. It is his indomitability, his 'refusal to take a knock-out', his ability to ride the fluctuations of political life, which appeals.

The major biography *Defoe* (1937), a beautifully lucid account of the complexities of Defoe's life, was a seminal work that fostered much critical interest in Defoe although, as Sutherland remarked a little sadly in the second edition of his work (1950), the interest was much stronger in America than in Britain, an ironic state of affairs given that Sutherland shows himself constantly aware of the Englishness of Defoe's make-up which he saw with the objectivity of a Scot. Sutherland helped to redress this imbalance in his later *Defoe: A Critical Study* (1971), a rounded view of Defoe's wide-ranging achievement which remains the best single account of Defoe as journalist, pamphleteer, and poet, as well as writer of fiction. Sutherland had an unrivalled skill in demonstrating how Defoe negotiated the 'twilight world between fact and fiction'. His analysis of Defoe's 'confident audacity' in the use of his sources for *Memoirs of a Cavalier* or *History of the Pyrates* remains exciting, as do his comments on the little regarded 'sentimental' aspects of *Col. Jack*.

A second major line of research developed in parallel with the work on Defoe. In 1932 John Butt, another pupil of Nichol Smith, became (at the age of twenty-eight) general editor of the projected Twickenham Edition of Pope's poetry. He assembled a strong team which included several scholars at that time still in their early thirties whose subsequent work would transform our view of the eighteenth century: Geoffrey Tillotson, Maynard Mack, and F. W. Bateson, and also James Sutherland who undertook *The Dunciad*. The problems to be faced in producing a satisfactory edition of *The Dunciad* were formidable. The poem exists in two substantially different versions, involving a change of hero and expansion from three to four books; in both versions it contains an elaborate satirical commentary that threatens to submerge the text; it was subjected to devious stratagems of obfuscation and concealment at its first appearance and continuously amended through some thirty editions published in Pope's lifetime. Moreover, it is full of obscure topical allusions that demand careful annotation. To present such a complex of textual and explanatory material in a manageable form was itself a challenge. Sutherland's solution enabled the material to appear in a single volume and his arrangement has proved its practicality over time. He gives the two main versions of the poem itself complete in the 1729 and 1743 Quarto texts but reduces the otherwise unmanageable weight of the apparatus by cross-referencing in cases where the 1729 commentary was unchanged in later editions. His collations and explanatory notes achieve an impressive level of clarity and detail and are supported by a Biographical Appendix, an extremely useful guide to Grub Street. Comparison with the earlier standard edition by Elwin and Courthope demonstrates an astonishing advance. In a review, Louis Bredvold rightly praised the editor's 'dexterity and lucidity . . . in presenting so intricate a subject'.[4] It has become an essential tool for eighteenth-century scholars and seems unlikely to be superseded.

An offshoot of Sutherland's major work on Defoe and Pope was the interesting and perhaps undervalued book *Background for Queen Anne* (1939). 'What separates us from the past more than anything else', Sutherland says, 'is that we always see it as we see a landscape from the top of a hill', absorbing the main features but missing the detail. What we need to see to form an accurate impression of the past 'is more triviality and less importance'. *Background for Queen Anne* gives a close-up of some figures who were newsworthy, even notorious, in their day and who still attract by their 'persistent vitality', even though they have now merged into the background. Their names were once on everyone's lips and they appeal to what Sutherland unapologetically calls 'a crude and probably inartistic concern for things that actually happened'. Amongst the group was Richard Burridge, a notorious blasphemer who became a household word, a bugbear to frighten children, and John Lacy, a miracle worker and prophet who caused an immense sensation by making a claim that he would resurrect a certain Dr Thomas Emes from the dead. The material for these brief lives derives largely from newspapers and pamphlets and each chapter is introduced by a miscellaneous collage of news items which gives a lively sense of the quotidian scene.

A different sort of literary context was the subject of Sutherland's first post-war book, *A Preface to Eighteenth-Century Poetry* (1948). In his Warton Lecture on 'Wordsworth and Pope', delivered at the British Academy in 1944, he had argued that Wordsworth's literary criticism, with its 'evangelical, even . . . messianic note' had 'done a good deal of harm to literary criticism by calling upon us to make a choice where no choice was necessary', to respond to Wordsworth's 'egotistical sublime' at the expense of other kinds of poetry. *A Preface to Eighteenth-Century Poetry* attempts to clear away the prejudices created by Wordsworthian tradition, extended and reinforced as it had been by

---

[4] For Bredvold's review of *The Dunciad*, see *Modern Language Notes*, 60 (1945), 501–2.

Matthew Arnold, and to invite readers to approach Augustan poetry on its own terms. At his back Sutherland was aware, too, of the immense popularity of the Metaphysicals. Reread today, *A Preface* can at times seem a little over-apologetic, but this is a sign of how well it did its work and how much the strengths of Augustan literature are now taken for granted. When I was an undergraduate in the late 1940s and early 1950s the period was still deeply unfashionable amongst students and the newly published *A Preface* presented an unexpected challenge. By using his breadth of reading in critical and periodical literature to establish the assumptions and attitudes of the age, however, Sutherland helped to recreate a taste that has led in the last forty years to a major re-evaluation of the period.

The tone of *A Preface*, however, already seemed remarkably civilised. The general tendency of literary criticism in the twentieth century had been to become both more systematic and more dogmatic, with a consequent narrowing of focus that Sutherland deplored. In an inaugural lecture, *The English Critic*, delivered at University College London in 1952, he firmly stated his own position at a time when he saw a present danger that criticism was no longer content to be, in Pope's phrase, 'the Muse's handmaid' but aspired to become an independent activity. He found the English critical tradition exemplified in qualities characteristic of the work of four critics. The 'urbanity', 'sedate cheerfulness and lively discursiveness' of Dryden's unpedantic essays. The independence and openness of Johnson's writing, with its interest in literary biography and conviction that literature is important in proportion as it deals with life. The personal immediacy and capacity to communicate enjoyment that springs from Hazlitt's determination to 'feel what is good and give reasons for the faith that is in me'. Finally, perhaps to the audience most surprisingly, the 'controlled impressionism' of Saintsbury, his development of a connoisseurship in books analogous to the evolution of a mature taste in wine. Coleridge was excluded because his undoubted greatness was too individual to form part of a tradition and Arnold because he 'cared too much' and tried to give literature a greater significance than it could properly sustain.

All this was boldy challenging at a time when much excitement was being generated by the moral earnestness of F. R. Leavis, the intensive analyses of Cleanth Brooks's *The Well-Wrought Urn* (1947), and the systematic theorising of Wellek and Warren's *Theory of Literature* (1949). The argument of *The English Critic* was recapitulated and endorsed in a leading article in the *Times Literary Supplement*, which acted as a red rag to the critical bulls, and it laid Sutherland open to charges of dilletantism. He knew that he was being unfashionable but he did not waver in his belief that criticism should be a humane and social activity, addressed to and meeting the needs not only of academics but of men and women who lived in the world, and he was able to put his case because his own research record was unassailable. He was greatly in demand as a supervisor, especially by students from the United States where he was well known. *A Preface* was based in part on a course given at Harvard in 1947 during the first of many post-war visits to American universities. Between 1947 and 1970 he held visiting pro-fessorships at Harvard, Indiana, UCLA, Pittsburgh, and New York and he was Clark Library Fellow, also at UCLA.

His years as Northcliffe Professor were happy ones. The School of English within the University of London was strong and flourishing and he was at home among such colleagues at other colleges as Geoffrey Tillotson (Birkbeck), Geoffrey Bullough (King's), Una Ellis Fermor and later Kathleen Tillotson (Bedford), Harold Jenkins (Westfield), and Gladys Willcock and later George Kane (Royal Holloway). The tradi-tion of University College itself as a secular and unexclusive institution devoted to the broadening of higher education was congenial to his temperament and to his own Scottish inheritance. The terms of the Northcliffe Chair gave him powers as Head of Department, but Hugh Smith, his colleague as Quain Professor, was a very willing participator in the burdens of administration. He also felt a close rapport with a number of younger colleagues who shared his own research interests, notably Basil Greenslade and Charles Peake whose help is acknowl-edged in various volumes.

In public he could appear a reserved man, with a somewhat formal, unfailingly courteous manner, given emphasis by the precise intona-tions of his Aberdeen upbringing. All who knew him well, however, remember him as a man of deep and generous feeling. He enjoyed conversation and was a memorable raconteur, and he had a wide circle of friends whom he and Helen entertained both at Sutton Courtenay and in their London clubs.

One particular enterprise in which he took pleasure had the aim of fostering academic co-operation in a social setting. Nowadays it is widely understood by literary critics that each generation 'constructs' its own sense of the past in response to changing cultural and social pressures, and the recognition of this truth was anticipated when in 1954 Sutherland joined with a group of colleagues in establishing the

Crabtree Foundation to honour the work of Joseph Crabtree, a sadly
neglected poet whose life of exactly one hundred years (1754–1854)
spanned the transition from the Classical to the post-Romantic period.
Sutherland's first annual Oration, *Homage to Crabtree*, surveyed the
scanty existing scholarship and laid down many important guidelines
for the future. The success of this scholarly venture, in which the
*Memoirs of Martinus Scriblerus* have always exerted an important
influence, and which has remained closely associated with University
College London, will be marked in 1997 by the publication of *The
Crabtree Orations, 1954–1994*.

In the later part of his career Sutherland received many honours. He
became a Fellow of the British Academy in 1953 and was awarded
honorary doctorates at the universities of Aberdeen (1955), Edinburgh
(1968), and Liège (1974). He was invited to give several important
lecture series, including the Walter Scott Lectures at the University of
Edinburgh (1952), the Alexander Lectures in Toronto (*On English
Prose*, published 1957), the Clark Lectures in Cambridge (*English
Satire*, published 1958), and the W. P. Ker Memorial Lecture in
Glasgow (1962). The Clark Lectures in particular will continue to
give a good impression of his qualities as a lecturer to those who never
heard him. On the podium he was an impressive figure, spare and
elegant and incisive in manner. He was always—whether addressing
first-year undergraduates or a distinguished general audience—meticulously prepared, informative, lucid, mindful of the occasion, and possessing, as he said of Hazlitt, 'the secret of communicating his
enjoyment' and stimulating his listeners. He used anecdote and imagery
to excellent effect: it was characteristic of Swift, he said, in *English
Satire* 'to proceed by a sort of jujitsu method, by which the victim of
satire was thrown by his own weight'. He discriminated ('*Jonathan
Wild* is a brilliant and sustained performance . . . but no one ever
wished it longer'). He had a connoisseur's sensitivity to the writer's
tone of voice, especially with Dryden and Pope, and he analysed
linguistic effects with a subtle precision that gives far more solidity
to his observations than the ease of manner might at first suggest. It
could be argued that he sometimes tried to cover too much ground—
both *On English Prose* and *English Satire* survey so broad a chronological span that they are inevitably uneven—but the reader finds, even
now, an impressive combination of perspective and close-up views.

His distinction as a speaker led to appointment as Public Orator of
the University of London from 1957–62. The main function, at the

annual Foundation Day ceremony, was to present honorary graduands for the award of a degree *honoris causa*, a rhetorical exercise in which the desire to 'enliven morality with wit' places the speaker on something of a tightrope in an atmosphere of formal academic ceremonial. Amongst the many graduands he presented were Princess Margaret, Earl Mountbatten of Burma, Sir Kenneth Clark and, closest to the Orator's own interests, Professor John Dover Wilson.

Following his retirement in 1967 he continued to be extremely active, first completing his contribution to *The Oxford History of English Literature*, a series planned before the war, with F. P. Wilson and Bonamy Dobrée as general editors. The first volume to be completed, Douglas Bush's *The Early Seventeenth Century*, appeared in 1945 and the last some forty-four years later. Inevitably, it was difficult to maintain an overall sense of direction and common purpose to the series and to a large extent each volume had to establish its own terms of reference. Sutherland had undertaken the volume *English Literature in the Later Seventeenth Century* with Hugh Macdonald, but following Macdonald's death in 1958 he became solely responsible for the work which appeared in 1969. What above all gives unity to his discussion of the period is his interest in the new Restoration relationship between authors and readers arising from the development of a well-organised, London-based, literary community. The socialising of literary experience is seen as the central fact of Restoration theatre, but it is important also in essays (Dryden's 'lively discursiveness'), philosophy (Locke's *Essay on Human Understanding* grew out of discussion between 'five or six friends meeting at my Chamber') and historical writing. Another distinguishing mark of Sutherland's volume is the degree of attention given to many minor writers 'who are being neglected' although 'their writing still has life and individuality'. Quite often one can see that these figures mirror Sutherland's own attitudes, especially in the case of Gilbert Burnet, a Scot with strong antiquarian interests, an aptitude for scholarly research, and a fondness for gossip and anecdote. Amongst the major figures Dryden and Bunyan are central, and the long section on Bunyan is particularly sympathetic and acute. When the volume was published there were inevitably some who decried the nature of the *Oxford History* itself as gossipy and anecdotal, lacking the rigour of modern methodologies, but Sutherland's volume was well received for its 'humanity, judgment and humour'.

Next came Lucy Hutchinson's *Memoirs of the Life of Colonel*

*Hutchinson* (1973), edited from a recently rediscovered manuscript and replacing an edition by C. H. Firth (1885).

The final book, *The Restoration Newspaper and its Development*, is a fitting conclusion to Sutherland's long-standing interest in journalism and it is written with characteristic verve, an undimmed eye for the texture of social life, and a continuing pleasure in 'things that actually happened'. It is a descriptive rather than an analytical account of its subject, but it is an absorbing study. The overall emphasis is biographical. Sutherland never forgets that the newspapers he discusses— often, though not always, extremely fugitive titles—were produced by men and women who were throughout the period subject to legal and political pressure, whose sources of information were uncertain and variable (foreign news might dry up completely if storms hindered shipping), and who entirely lacked the machinery of modern news-gathering. One of the finest chapters, 'The newspaper men and women', brings together much important information about people who com-bined proprietorial, editorial, and journalistic functions and, as in the studies of Defoe, Sutherland communicates his admiration for the indomitability and practical expertise of these little known figures. This section of the book will, like the Biographical Appendix to the Twickenham *Dunciad*, continue to be an important reference tool, while other chapters give a vivid account of the content of Restoration news-papers and show the speed with which journalism developed an empha-sis on lurid crime, executions, and topical trivia.

Helen died in 1975, and in 1977 Sutherland married Eve Betts, widow of Ernest Betts, the critic and historian of film, a marriage which brought renewed happiness to his final years. He became close to Eve's children and grandchildren, and he was able to enjoy a kind of family life that he had not previously experienced. In 1988 they moved from Sutton Courtenay to Murray Court in Oxford, called, to Sutherland's pleasure, after Sir James Murray, the first editor of the *Oxford English Dictionary*. The accolade of the knighthood conferred in 1992 was a culminating and greatly appreciated honour. He remained alert and active to the end of his life (a final article, on Swift, appeared in 1993), though sadly affected by a stroke in 1992. He died on 24 February 1996.

In a Viewpoint article in the *Times Literary Supplement* in 1974 Sutherland reflects on his own career and on some of the accidents that shaped it, and concludes that an essential fact for him was the strong and untutored pleasure in literature that developed when he was young and that provided the motor for his activities. Without this primary enthusiasm and the opportunity to read with 'avidity and uncritical delight', criticism will be barren. 'Unless', he writes, 'a young man has gone through a period of running wild in literature, as the young Keats ran wild in *The Faerie Queene . . .* I doubt if he will ever become the sort of literary critic to whom I would want to pay much attention'. Rather similarly, in his Queen Mary College inaugural, *English in the Universities* (1945), he said that what he looked for in selecting students was an instinctive response 'to words and rhythm, to the cadence of English speech, English prose, English verse, to the sound-value of the words themselves and in combination, and the complete fusion of words and meaning'. Sutherland himself retained this kind of responsiveness throughout his life (he could always quote prodigiously from memory) and the pure enjoyment of literature is evident in everything he wrote, as is his belief that literature is not at bottom arcane or the preserve of scholars but a freely available good.

It is appropriate that he should be known to a very wide range of readers through his editorship of *The Oxford Book of English Talk* (1953) and *The Oxford Book of Literary Anecdotes* (1975), both highly successful volumes. Neither could have been compiled without a lifetime of eclectic reading and a refusal to set rigid bounds between canonical and non-canonical writing. *English Talk* draws heavily on law reports, a 'rich source of idiomatic material' which brings us as close as we can now get to the 'spontaneous feelings and sentiments of whores and vagabonds, thieves and pickpockets'; *Literary Anecdotes* includes some stories only loosely connected to literature but which, Sutherland says, 'I believe most readers would wish to see included and which, in any case, I could not bring myself to omit'. There is a generosity and inclusiveness here that is entirely typical. His greatest achievements are to be found, I believe, in *The Dunciad* and the life of *Defoe* but both the edition and the biography depend on an approach to literature that was consistent from first to last in his work, and that links him to the tradition that he defined so well in *The English Critic*.

JOHN CHALKER

*Queen Mary and Westfield College, London*

*Note.* In preparing this essay I have been greatly indebted to Dr Christopher Betts, Sir James's stepson, and his wife Ann, to whom I am most grateful. Dr Betts not only provided much information drawn from personal knowledge but also made available the typescript of extensive, though incomplete, memoirs written by Sir James in his eighties. The memoirs have been my most important source of information concerning his upbringing, education, and early teaching experience but they do not extend beyond the 1930s. I have also benefited from discussions with Lord Quirk, Professor George Kane, and Professor Harold Jenkins, and from correspondence with Professor Norman Jeffares. Mr Bryant Bennet kindly made available a copy of *Homage to Crabtree*. I have been guided also by personal knowledge gained during my years as a student at Queen Mary College from 1949–54 and as a member of staff in the English Department of University College from 1958–74.

CHRISTOPHER THORNE

*Proceedings of the British Academy*, **94**, 753–767

# Christopher Guy Thorne
# 1934–1992

CHRISTOPHER THORNE CAME LATE TO ACADEMIC LIFE, and to the scholarship which was to bring him election to the British Academy in 1982 and to an international reputation. Prior to his appointment, in 1968, as Lecturer in International Relations, at the University of Sussex (with successive promotions to Reader and Professor of International Relations) he had worked as history master successively at St Paul's and Charterhouse schools and for the Further Education Service of the BBC. Nor did he immediately launch into the field of exploration that he was to make his own, the application of ideas drawn from the social sciences to the history of international relations, especially of international relations during the Second World War. His first work, *The Approach of War, 1938–1939*, was a conventional exercise in diplomatic history, based in the main on the published British, German, American and Italian diplomatic documents covering the two years before the outbreak of the Second World War. Very largely written and conceived before his entry into university life, it owed a good deal to the example of Sir Lewis Namier's masterly reconstructions of British and French policy on the basis of the 'coloured books' published at the beginning of the Second World War. By contrast with earlier and more sensational work based on the same source by two disciples of A. J. P. Taylor and the iconoclastic *Origins of the Second World War* of the master himself, Thorne's work embodied much of the re-evaluation of British and French policy in the years of appeasement, which had been in progress in Britain since the late 1950s. *The Approach of War* reflected his work

© The British Academy 1997.

as a teacher and educator; it provided a thorough and succinct summary of all the printed sources; it was to prove a godsend to university teachers faced with an increasing demand from their students for historical courses covering the origins of the Second World War. But even Thorne's measured evaluation of British policies was to give way half-way through the book to what he later admitted to be a loss of temper with Neville Chamberlain; the latter part of the book was devoted to a hostile and all-too-familiar critique of British foreign policy, based on the premise that even after the issue of the British guarantee to Poland at the end of March 1939 it reflected Chamberlain's concept of appeasement and was inspired by his guidance — a view which now would command less support than it did when Thorne wrote. The influence of Namier and the Churchillian critique of appeasement was still too strong and too persistent for any one of Thorne's generation to challenge it head on. Moreover, the task of re-evaluating the contemporary debate over British policy towards Nazi Germany in general, and the Czechoslovak crisis of 1938 and the Munich agreement in particular, poses basic problems of the role of moral judgement in the writing of history which are still far from proper understanding, let alone agreed solutions, even among historians. Christopher Thorne retained until his death the strongest of moral disapprobation of the policies adopted by the British government of the day and the arguments advanced then and subsequently to justify them.

By the time his book had appeared, however, the basis of his work, like that of most of his contemporaries, had been revolutionised by the reform of the Public Records Act in 1967 to permit the release of public records on the opening of the thirty-first, as opposed to the fifty-first, year since their creation. This was to set in motion the wholesale release of private and public papers from all but the intelligence services of government on a scale then only exceeded by practice in the United States. The result of this was that it became possible for historians to look beyond the concepts of governments and nations hitherto employed in the analysis and exposition of foreign policy into the formal and informal relationships and hierarchies, factions and rivalries which actually existed within those small groups constitutionally responsible for the conception and conduct of a nation's foreign policy and between their members and the societies they served and within which they lived and acted. It also became possible to discuss the role in the overall conduct of foreign policy, not merely of ambassadors and foreign ministers, but of the military, of senior members of the bureaucracy and the directorates in the fields of finance, banking and overseas trade, and to distinguish between the formal structures of power and authority and the actual relationships between the persons who occupied those structures.

Thorne was himself to benefit from the spread of this opening of the archives from the practice of the United States and Britain to Britain's western neighbours (in particular from the opening of the Dutch archives), as he was from the accessibility of the Japanese archives captured in 1945 by the British and American occupying forces and used in the Tokyo war crimes trials of 1947–8. Without this sea-change in the release of archives and the consequent encouragement of those who had retired from public or political service in Britain to follow the example of their American contemporaries in preserving their papers and releasing them to university, regional or national archives for public access, the kind of changes that a few pioneers in Italy, France and Britain were already proposing should be introduced into the practice of international history, so far as the history of the origins and course of the Second World War were concerned, would have been difficult, if not impossible, for another two decades.

Even while his first book was going through its proof stages, Thorne was coming to echo the dissatisfaction with traditional diplomatic history which had already inspired these pioneers. Characteristically, however, Thorne found his own way to these conclusions without any real interaction with his forerunners, of whom Professor W. N. Medlicott of the London School of Economics was then the leading practitioner and advocate of such a widening in Britain. He was, however, to become a great friend of those members of the Department of International History at the LSE whose work impinged upon his own. The dedication of his second work, *The Limits of Foreign Policy; The West, the League and the Far Eastern Crisis of 1931–1933* (London, 1972) to the French historian, Pierre Renouvin, and to Captain Stephen Roskill RN, the official historian of Britain's war effort at sea was in part misleading. Like his fellow innovators at London and Cambridge he had read Renouvin's basic text, *Introduction aux Relations Internationales*, published by Renouvin and his successor, J. B. Duroselle, in the 1950s, on which those European historians of international relations, grouped in the Paris-Geneva axis of the journal *Relations Internationales*, founded their work; he was also familiar with Renouvin's work on the history of the Far East in the twentieth century. And he had profited from the revival of war studies under Sir Michael Howard at King's College,

London, a field represented in Cambridge by Captain Stephen Roskill RN, the moving spirit in the establishment and operation of the Archives Centre of the Library of Churchill College, Cambridge, at which so many public servants from the British military and civil services were to deposit their papers. This collection, together with the additional collections of private political manuscripts at the University Library of Cambridge, the Bodleian, the Liddell Hart Library of King's College, London, the Library of Birmingham University, and a multitude of smaller collections around the country, when taken with the unhindered access to papers from the Cabinet Office, Prime Minister's private office, Foreign Office, Treasury, and Chiefs of Staff papers resulting from the two Public Records Acts of 1958 and 1967, now made it possible for historians to envisage a model of the policy-making process in which the accumulation of information, the formulation of policy proposals at all levels of responsibility, from the lowliest to the highest, and the roles of individuals, factions, groups, Ministers and their advisers, could be identified and followed, if necessary, day by day or even hour by hour. Moreover, with similar, if not even richer, access to the records of the other major powers, especially those of the United States, it was now possible to chart the interactions, the perceptions and misperceptions, the understandings and misunderstandings, the conceptions and misconceptions, which governed the whole process of relations between the powers, to a degree profoundly more sophisticated than that entertained by most theorists of international relations.

Thorne was to pay his obligatory respects to those theorists (such as the French political sociologist and news commentator, Raymond Aron) whose writings came within the limits of the analysis now possible for historians of international relations using the archives of all the powers whose relations they were studying. But his real originality was shown by passages in the preface to *The Limits of Foreign Policy*. Here he revealed that since his arrival at Sussex he had been expected to teach and master the field of 'foreign policy analysis', favoured by Departments of International Relations throughout the United States and Britain. On his own he had come to the same dissatisfaction that made other historians of international relations in Britain dismiss this as a mishmash of *idées reçues* which ignored the dynamic and interactive nature of relations between states. Equally he had become dissatisfied with traditional diplomatic history.

In common with many who have been trained as historians, [he wrote,] I have to admit to a deep scepticism regarding the search which is being conducted by some political scientists for general theories and predictive formulae that can be applied to international relations . . . the designing of theoretical patterns at a quasi-theological level can degenerate into a self-indulgent and fruitless pastime, however attractive the notion of discovering all-embracing explanations and solutions for international conflict, say, in an age when such a phenomenon threatens to destroy mankind itself . . . the theoretical structures that have been erected around a particular subject such as foreign-policy decision-making . . . tend to be unduly static, for example, to allow insufficiently for the on-going nature of foreign policy, where the conscious major decision is the exception rather than the rule, and to have nothing to offer when it comes to weighing the relative significance of any one factor on a specific occasion . . ..

The more traditional discipline of narrative diplomatic history, even when practised by a master of that craft, is surely also open to question . . .. Many such studies — and I do not except my own — have often adopted a brusque approach . . . where causality is concerned, and in this context have failed to make use of work being done in neighboring areas of study such as social psychology . . . that approach to international history which treats states as so many billiard balls, each one a discrete unit with its own and ready made set of aims and interests, bears little relation to the world of international politics as it now exists — or perhaps ever existed . . .. The infinitely complex nature of foreign policy formulation . . . is still frequently simplified to the point of falsification, either by isolating a single aspect of that policy from all other issues that were having to be faced by officials at the time, or by ignoring the interplay between international factors and those arising within domestic politics . . ..

Thorne certainly saw his work as contributing to the development of the theoretical study of international relations. Indeed, he added to the bibliographical section of his second book a separate entry listing those works that had influenced him. He devoted a substantial part of the work to the examination of the interactions between the official policy-makers and various unofficial pressure groups, individuals and newspapers in the various countries involved both in the events in Manchuria and China which were the focus of his study and in the states members of the League of Nations where those events were examined, pronounced upon, and eventually and unsuccessfully acted upon.

In his analysis of his own work, it must be said that Thorne displayed a surprising ignorance of how the discipline of international history had developed in the 1930s, especially in the United States in the ever-more-sophisticated analysis of the 'war guilt' issue and the influence of public opinion, pressure groups, and the press and other opinion-forming agencies upon public policy in France, Germany and Britain, in the decades before 1914. Indeed it is tempting to see much of his criticism of the state of 'diplomatic history' as a reaction to the rejection by some noted Oxbridge historians of the work of most, if not all, of their American colleagues and the diversion of the work of those radical German *émigré* critics of the official German line on 'war guilt', the Pan-German League, the Navy League, the steel cartels, and the Liberal-National and German Nationalist parties in the Reichstag to suit their general rejection of all things German as inherently, if not genetically, perverse. But the move he made with *The Limits of Foreign Policy* into international relations in the Far East, where the principal actors were Japan, China, Britain and the United States, with smaller parts played by the Netherlands and France, together with the emergence of a separate sense of national interest and identity in Australia, was to lead him into a field which he was to make his own, the role of what, for want of a better word (and the only word available is miserably imprecise and inadequate), has come to be called 'cultural' differences between the various politico-social systems and organisations which represent the various states and powers on the decision-making processes, the mutual perceptions and misperceptions of one another, and the consequent misjudgements and misunderstandings which were to pave the way to the ignominious if not foredoomed defeats, first of the colonial empires and then of their Japanese challengers.

In this move he could draw on the assistance of schools of historians in both Japan and the United States which had already plunged well beyond the exercise of nationalist historiography which marked the majority of work by those American diplomatic historians whose belief in American exceptionalism had confined their study to the history of American foreign relations, based entirely on American archives. Indeed, attempts to make sense of the conduct of foreign policy-making in Japan in the inter-war period which did not take account of the peculiar lack of any overall central control of the Japanese political system, and the quasi-feudal rivalries between different factions in the Japanese army, the High Command of the Japanese Navy, the Foreign Ministry, the Treasury, the officials of the Court and the *genro*, the elder statesmen, who had been for so long the inspiration towards modernism, had by the end of the 1960s been largely abandoned by historians of the Pacific War in both countries, as simplistic in the extreme. Thorne was to stay within this area for the rest of his tragically short career. It is characteristic of his bent for examining all the labels with their accompanying presuppositions employed by his fellow historians that he should devote the beginning of the preface of his fourth book, *The Issue of War, States, Societies and the Far Eastern Conflict of 1941– 1945* (London, 1985), to defending his preference for calling his field that of the 'Far Eastern' war against charges that it embodied a 'Eurocentrist' approach. For his American critics, of course, Japan and the western Pacific represent the Far West not the Far East, whether approached by sea or by that most modern of historical workhorses, the economy class of a jumbo jet.

His greatest work, seen from the point of view of the historian alone, was to be his third. Entitled *Allies of a Kind; the United States, Britain and the War Against Japan, 1941–1945* (London, 1978), it concentrated on the separate war in the Pacific and the Far East of the Western allies against Japan, and the at times highly strained relations between the various groups of British and United States policy-makers, in Delhi, Sydney, Singapore and Hawaii, not to mention their superiors in Washington and London. The picture he drew had very little to do with that of militant pan-Anglo-Saxonism so assiduously cultivated by Winston Churchill's memoirs and was impossible to reconcile with Harold Macmillan's mythological invocation of Greeks and Romans in his memoirs, in support of his picture of Anglo-American 'interdependence'; instead he depicted British imperialism at its often most insufferable sense of cultural superiority vying with a simpleminded American belief in the claims of any would-be Asian political figure who professed to speak in the name of the 'people' of his particular geographical area, as it might be a Soekarno for Indonesia or a Ho Chi Minh for Indo-China, even where the existence as a single political entity of that geographically-defined area had been entirely created by the European colonial overlord. No history of Anglo-American relations in the Roosevelt-Churchill era could ever be the same after Thorne's examination of the issues involved in the Far Eastern war. His most striking argument, that Roosevelt and his strategic advisors committed American power to the support of Britain's imminently evanescent empire in Malaya and Singapore for fear of the effect of a Japanese attack in South-East Asia on Britain's ability to withstand and contain Hitler's empire in Europe, has still not taken hold of the dominant schools of historiography in either the United States or Britain. Perhaps it conflicts too deeply with the image of Pearl Harbour, and the determination of the US Navy to fight the war against Japan without British participation to be acceptable in the United States; while, in Britain, the fall of Singapore, the experience of the Japanese contempt for British military power displayed on the bodies of those who surrendered to them, and the whole complex set of attitudes involved in the dismissal of General Slim's victorious army of 1945 as 'the forgotten army', not to mention that latest development in the school of historical study of the British empire that is obsessed with 'declinology' as the inevitable *até* following the hubris of imperialism, has stood in the way of a similar recognition outside the small number of specialists in Far Eastern international history.

In writing *Allies of a Kind* and his subsequent studies, *Racial Aspects of the Far Eastern War of 1941–45* (London, 1982), (a reworking of his Raleigh lecture of 1980), *The Issue of War* (already mentioned), the collection of essays published as *Border Crossings: Studies in International History* (Oxford and New York, 1988), and *American Political Culture and the Asian Frontier, 1943–1973*, Thorne drew on records in Japan, Australia, the Netherlands, India, the United States and Britain. Of these, *The Issue of War* was in a sense the most ambitious of his works, representing an attempt on his own to write that full history of the war in the Far East which he had originally envisaged as a work of collaboration.

It is a work which is difficult to evaluate today on the terms in which it was conceived. Thorne wrote, as he admitted in the preface, under the influence of 'the times through which I myself have lived (which have helped direct my attention towards such themes as race relations and the position of women in society)', and he could well have added, of a conception of the public image of the war in the Far East, which had been formed by the immediate experience of that war and the very strong racial and anti-Oriental images fostered by Allied propaganda on the record of Japanese feelings of racial superiority as expressed in the treatment both of Allied war prisoners and civilian internees in the lands they overran in the opening year twelve months after the Japanese attack on Pearl Harbour. While it would be untrue to say that the general public in Britain has accepted his more balanced and historic view of the Far-Eastern War, it has won such general acceptance among historians that on rereading it, one is often surprised to realise how far what is now generally accepted required such hard labour on his part to establish.

The need to counter this hostile, not to say diabolised image of Imperial Japan, led him to an examination in depth of the conflict of cultures embodied in the practices of the war in the Far East and its antecedents. His own attitudes, impeccably liberal on such subjects as Indian and Indonesian nationalism, induced him to place the events of 1942–5 in a setting of the contacts, conflicts and interactions of the various forms of Asian politico-social 'culture', with the European and American 'imperial' powers. His approach and arguments owed a great deal to those Anglo-Saxon and European sociologists whose dissatisfaction with or 'alienation' from their own cultures had persuaded them to find benefits and advantages in the various and diverse societies of Eastern and South-Eastern Asia. And he sometimes seemed to make no distinction between those for whom their explorations of Eastern societies were a means of drawing parallels with their own to the disadvantage of the cultures which had borne them, and the more disinterested, objective enquiries of their colleagues. (In addition, like most of his contemporaries, he accepted unquestioningly the dominant Nehruist school of Indian historiography and neglected the vast resources of loyalty to the Raj and support for the King-Emperor in India, without which the conduct of the war against Japan from the Indian base would have been impossible.) The small and unhappy group of Indian National Army collaborators with the Japanese engaged his attention far more than the 'loyalist' (or as contemporary American observers called them, the 'mercenary') forces of the British-led Indian army. And where Indonesia was concerned he seems to have accepted the claims of the Javanese social climbers who were eventually successful in exploiting the power vacuum left by the Japanese surrender and resisting the attempt on the part of the Dutch to re-establish their empire in the East Indies, to represent an Indonesian national spirit rather further than the subsequent history of that unhappy and enormous archipelago of races, political cultures, religions and islands would justify.

In this he betrayed his own lack of confidence in exploring what the social sciences could offer historians in the way of tools and concepts with which to tackle the problems of intercultural relations on the scale with which he was concerned. The prefaces in which he explained his approach and the methodology which he had adopted were redolent of apology designed to disarm those whose claims to expertise he was, or so he seemed to think, invading — as though an amateur violinist was apologising to a Heifetz for tackling some peculiarly difficult passage in a violin concerto which Heifetz had made his own. In crossing the 'lines of demarcation that separate the various human disciplines' he felt it necessary, or so he wrote, to 'acknowledge my position as a tyro'. This was both unnecessary and unworthy of his abilities and historical imagination and the range and scale of the problems, especially of those of change over time on a national and extra-national basis, with which his task had engaged him. For it is impossible for an international historian tackling the problems of the twentieth century to avoid becoming in the process a historian of 'global' or world history without exercising the most rigid and ultimately distorting of controls over the concepts he encounters and the questions which the material poses of itself. Thorne was incapable of such self-mutilation. Neither the range of his vision nor the generosity of his personality allowed of such a possibility.

In explaining the scope of *The Issue of War* as covering the impact of that conflict not only on the societies of Eastern and South-Eastern Asia but also on those of Britain, the Netherlands, France and the United States he argued, first, that those Western societies had been involved for many years in a 'network of relationships' with the peoples of the area; and, secondly, that these Western societies had despatched substantial forces to fight in that part of the world and had given every sign of regarding the outcome of the fighting there as of 'considerable importance in relation to their own, post-war, futures'. Such a perspective was very different from that of his Anglo-Saxon contemporaries who wrote of the Vietnamese or Indonesian 'national struggle against colonialism' in terms reminiscent of nineteenth-century liberal historians of Italian unification. Thorne's vision and historical 'reach' was too large for such anachronistic stenosis.

The third reason he gave was that he wished to take the opportunity to 'abrogate the boundaries between Western and non-Western history', a phrase he borrowed from the title of a book by the American historian, Eric Wolf, *Europe and the People without History* (Berkeley, 1982). It is significant of the generational change since that of Arnold Toynbee, that Thorne should neither mention his name nor his *Study of History*, nor even the practice of the annual *Surveys of International Affairs* with which Toynbee had launched his occupancy of the Chair of International Relations at Chatham House from 1925–58, and should find it necessary to defend what would now seem to be an inevitable part of the work which he, Thorne, had set himself. But the comment is more one on the discontinuities in British historiography and the isolation of the International Relations school of writers in Britain from the traditions of international history than on Thorne's own enormously extensive and tireless range of contemporary reading, or on the sterling work he put in reviewing Chatham House's own archives and advising on their preservation, or in drawing on their war-time material in his analyses of British attitudes and concepts.

As has already been noted he found himself dependent on the state of development of concepts in those social sciences which seemed to be interested in the same kind of problems which he was encountering. One can perhaps trace the influence of his colleagues at Sussex, especially the sociologist of Japan, Ronald Dore, in the comparative absence from his reading lists of works by social anthropologists (Margaret Mead, the American, is the only name he mentions). Work by social psychologists, interested as they are in investigative and experimental work among small groups, which necessarily excludes the important, the very busy, and the formally and informally structured groups of political, diplomatic and military, policy-makers with which historians such as Thorne are concerned, he found, as others have, to be 'to an equal degree, awakening and disappointing' of one's appetite — as Charles Lamb wrote of the Wednesday luncheon menu at his primary school.

As with most of Thorne's work, the detail and complexity of his exposition does not lend itself easily to summary. To say, for example, that he refused to categorise Imperial war-time Japan as Fascist or totalitarian, is more a comment on the facile drawing of ideological and contemporary classifications by Allied, in particular, American analysts and propagandists, and the length of time it takes historiography to purge itself of such misconceptions once they have entered the literature, than to recognise quite how far Thorne was opposing himself to facile attempts to reduce the Second World War to one between democracy and Fascism, or between European imperialism and the emergent (and therefore presumably incapable of imperialism) non-European Third World.

Thorne himself was never quite clear on the question of how to handle such misconceptions. At one moment he seems to argue that such statements are not in accordance with observable historical 'reality' — which, if that kind of approach is accepted, is obvious — and that therefore those who use them are, wittingly or unwittingly, inventing categories for their own purposes into which the historical realities can only be fitted by distortion or mutilation. At other times he

seems to take the equally acceptable historical view that such statements do, in practice, have a historical validity as evidence, not insofar
as they can be shown to correspond with objective phenomenological
evidence, but insofar as important and influential sections of the policy-
makers, the opinion-leaders and the opinion they generated, held such
statements to be 'true' or valid, and allowed their actions, decisions and
anticipations to be governed by such analyses. But he does not always
make the distinction between these two levels of argument clear — an
indication, perhaps, that he took less account of the difference between
perceptions of reality and objective 'reality' itself than his successors
would make, always provided that they acknowledged the existence of
an objective reality apart from, yet observable by, the percipient. He
was never publicly severe with those with whom he disagreed, displaying in this, as in the help he so unceasingly gave to fellow
historians of every nationality, the generosity of nature which was
one of his most endearing characteristics.

*Border Crossings* was a less integrated work than its three great
predecessors. It is in fact a collection of essays, conference papers, and
contributions to collective works, generated during the latter years of
his career. The title reflects his own concern with the increasingly cross-
disciplinary nature of his work (in parenthesis he seems as obsessed
with what in trade union terms used to be called 'demarcation disputes'
as any British trade unionist of the 1950s). It also reveals the increasing
Americanisation of his work, in the sense that his arguments are
increasingly directed to American audiences, in terms which reflect
American values and historiographical developments. Accused once,
jokingly, by a British friend at a conference in the United States, of
'going native', he reacted with a degree of protest that revealed his
sensitivity to such a taunt. But the demand for his presence at such
conferences, and the sheer number of American historians of ability
who shared his interests and friendship in some sense made the increasing casting of his views in terms and in a vocabulary with which they
were familiar, inevitable. It is hardly surprising that his reputation stood
so high among historians in the United States.

His reputation stood no less high in Japan. He acknowledged freely
his debt to Professor Chihiro Hosoya, the leader of those Japanese
historians of the Second World War who were pursuing a history which
should be neither a nationalist nor a Marxist distortion of the record. His
own approach, neither demonising nor minimising the influence of
Japanese military feudalism and nationalism in the processes which

led to the Japanese decision for war and empire in East Asia, fitted closely with the social and political analysis employed by Hosoya and his allies. His acceptance of the Japanese motivation as a drive for modernisation rather than westernisation of their political culture and the perils surrounding such a process, paid the Japanese the compliment of taking their leaders' actions and justifications of their actions at their own value, while in no way denying those aspects of Japanese behaviour towards other Asian cultures and peoples as towards their European victims which were to redound most heavily to Japan's detriment during and after the war.

Scholarship of the scale Thorne practised does not come either easily or cheaply either in financial or personal terms. He was generously treated by the University of Sussex in terms of leave and by British, American, Dutch and Japanese foundations in terms of financial support. But there is no disguising that the sheer volume of the records he came to master, their extreme geographical distribution and the stresses of cheap air travel that his research imposed made enormous demands on his health and physical stamina. Moreover he set himself a relentlessly punishing schedule. At least one distinguished historian of the war in the Far East was forced to withdraw from a proposed joint enterprise by his unwillingness or inability to keep up with the schedule Thorne set him. Thorne was physicaly strong, a big bull of a man, a player of rugby in his younger days, a trained baritone with the physique professional singing demands. But the pace at which he worked and the scale of his travels were paid for with severe and, to his friends and family, regular and alarming breakdowns in health. These were aggravated by the heating system at his Sussex home, which was discovered after several years to have been discharging noxious gases into the air he and his wife breathed. His increasingly senior position in the University of Sussex also exposed him to the ever-increasing administrative, managerial and policy-making demands imposed on the universities by forces external to the university system. His early death can be counted, at least in part, as just one of the unnecessary losses of excellence imposed by those who are unable to recognise something they find themselves unable to quantify.

At Thorne's death in April 1992, there were those of his contemporaries who muttered *sotto voce* that he had very largely come to the end of what he had to say, or even that he was beginning to repeat himself. It is true that he showed little interest in the two directions into which so many of his contemporaries, let alone his younger colleagues, in the study of international history were developing their interests, the respective roles of propaganda and intelligence in policy-making and the conduct of foreign relations; although he had written to some point on the subject of Japanese and western propaganda in the Far East. Nor did he share their interests in the post-war history of East-West relations which the advance of the opening of British records into the post-war era made possible. His isolation from his British colleagues (he once said that he was happy not to be part of a Department of History of International Relations) weakened his connections with British political perceptions and preoccupations. And as already noted, his contacts with social scientists were serendipitous rather than structured. His closest and deepest friendships were with American historians of American radicalism such as Professor Lloyd C. Gardner of the University of Rutgers, a man whose originality of judgement and perception could more readily be appreciated as part of the American historiographical tradition.

The change in emphasis in his later years showed itself in what appeared to be a much greater willngness to rely on and cite the work of American social scientists, work which he was not in a position either to check or to evaluate. He whose major works had rested on a complete and overwhelming preoccupation with the primary sources was producing papers and articles which revealed that his gargantuan appetite for reading had in no way diminished but whose nourishment was designed for appetites and tastes other than those which he had developed himself. This is, of course, the dilemma which all synoptic historians face; that in attempting to absorb and bring together the work of others in a variety of what seem to be relevant fields, they may only be synthesising the current states of knowledge and perceptions of those fields rather than the finished outcome of schools of original research unbiased by any current political or social, overt or hidden agendas. Thorne's admirers, among whom the author of this memoir counts himself, maintained that this stage of his thinking would soon have given way to his inimitable ability to read into his new field of study, patterns and concepts not hitherto seen by others. But, alas, we were never to see our hopes realised.

Christopher Thorne's literary and historical remains constitute a most remarkable contribution, perhaps the crucial contribution, to the restructuring of the historiography of the Second World War and its antecedents in the Far East in the last three decades. But to leave his work with that judgement would be to do Christopher Thorne an injustice. His work called attention to and concentrated on the impossibility of depicting, let alone analysing, the development and conduct of relations, including wars, between the political units into which the world is divided, if there is no recognition of the very different sets of beliefs, values, social relationships, traditions, hierarchies, divinities even, obtaining among the peoples of the units involved. In writing about this, Thorne suffered, as we all do, from the cultural inadequacies, the presuppositions, the redolent cultural essences, the overtones and undertones embedded in the language which is all that we have in which to record our perceptions and communicate them to others. He suffered too, from the absence of theoretical and analytical training from the standard historical degrees in Britain, and the fear of departure from the certainties of established historical method which governed the majority of his colleagues and forestalled any perceptive dialogue between him and those of his contemporaries who were also feeling their way towards newer and deeper analyses of the tasks set them by the new richness of evidence available to historians working in the mid-twentieth century. But despite these inhibitions peculiar to his own development (and there are no practitioners of his discipline of whom similar inhibiting factors cannot be adduced), the work he produced is still as new and as fresh and as profoundly stimulating as if it were newly-minted. Only we can no longer rely on those sudden encounters at the Public Record Office or outside the British Library, in the wings of some American conference or airport waiting-room, to elucidate what we in our purblindness could not at first comprehend. He was a man of many friendships, unusual insights and colossal energies. He did not father a school; and one cannot but feel that his work stands more on its own than as part of a larger British body of thought. Not that he could not work with others. He worked closely with the British Committee for the History of the Second World War and contributed regularly to their bilateral conferences. He did his country great credit internationally. It is perhaps an indication of the sense of loss his contemporaries still feel that one is left at the end with a feeling of dissatisfaction. He should not have died so young; and he has at the moment no replacement.

D. CAMERON WATT
*Fellow of the Academy*